1,000,000 Books
are available to read at

Forgotten Books

---

www.ForgottenBooks.com

Read online
Download PDF
Purchase in print

ISBN 978-1-334-10375-9
PIBN 10600960

This book is a reproduction of an important historical work. Forgotten Books uses state-of-the-art technology to digitally reconstruct the work, preserving the original format whilst repairing imperfections present in the aged copy. In rare cases, an imperfection in the original, such as a blemish or missing page, may be replicated in our edition. We do, however, repair the vast majority of imperfections successfully; any imperfections that remain are intentionally left to preserve the state of such historical works.

Forgotten Books is a registered trademark of FB &c Ltd.
Copyright © 2018 FB &c Ltd.
FB &c Ltd, Dalton House, 60 Windsor Avenue, London, SW19 2RR.
Company number 08720141. Registered in England and Wales.

For support please visit www.forgottenbooks.com

1 MONTH OF FREE READING

at

www.ForgottenBooks.com

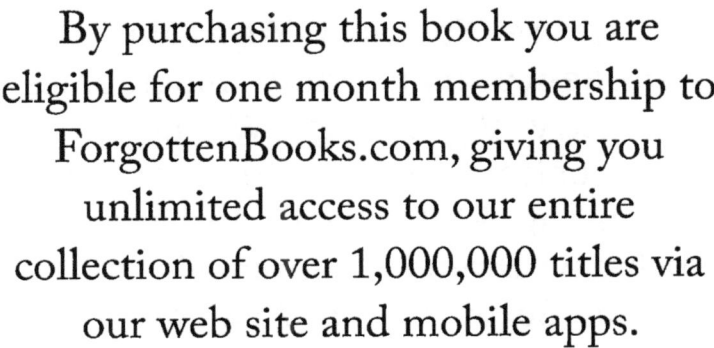

By purchasing this book you are eligible for one month membership to ForgottenBooks.com, giving you unlimited access to our entire collection of over 1,000,000 titles via our web site and mobile apps.

To claim your free month visit: www.forgottenbooks.com/free600960

* Offer is valid for 45 days from date of purchase. Terms and conditions apply.

English
Français
Deutsche
Italiano
Español
Português

www.forgottenbooks.com

Mythology Photography **Fiction**
Fishing Christianity **Art** Cooking
Essays Buddhism Freemasonry
Medicine **Biology** Music **Ancient Egypt** Evolution Carpentry Physics
Dance Geology **Mathematics** Fitness
Shakespeare **Folklore** Yoga Marketing
Confidence Immortality Biographies
Poetry **Psychology** Witchcraft
Electronics Chemistry History **Law**
Accounting **Philosophy** Anthropology
Alchemy Drama Quantum Mechanics
Atheism Sexual Health **Ancient History**
Entrepreneurship Languages Sport
Paleontology Needlework Islam
Metaphysics Investment Archaeology
Parenting Statistics Criminology
Motivational

THE BIBLIOGRAPHER'S MANUAL

OF

ENGLISH LITERATURE

CONTAINING

AN ACCOUNT OF RARE, CURIOUS, AND USEFUL BOOKS, PUBLISHED IN OR RELATING TO GREAT BRITAIN AND IRELAND, FROM THE INVENTION OF PRINTING; WITH BIBLIOGRAPHICAL AND CRITICAL NOTICES, COLLATIONS OF THE RARER ARTICLES, AND THE PRICES AT WHICH THEY HAVE BEEN SOLD IN THE PRESENT CENTURY

BY

WILLIAM THOMAS LOWNDES.

NEW EDITION, REVISED, CORRECTED AND ENLARGED.

VOL. I.

LONDON:
HENRY G. BOHN, YORK STREET, COVENT GARDEN.
1857.

J. Billing, Printer and Stereotyper, Guildford, Surrey.

NOTICE.

LOWNDES' BIBLIOGRAPHER'S MANUAL having become an extremely scarce and expensive work, selling at auction for upwards of seven pounds, with a prospect of its increasing in price, the present Publisher thought he should render an acceptable service to the Book-collector, and especially to Booksellers, by reissuing it in a cheap and popular form. With this view he purchased the copyright from the late Mr. Pickering's executors, intending to confine himself to a verbatim reprint, with the exception only of such corrections and additions as had already been made in his own business copy, or might chance to be communicated by friends. But, on examining the first few proofs, he unexpectedly found so much to correct and complete, that he felt it necessary to change his plans, and bestow considerably more care upon the editing than he originally contemplated. Accordingly every sheet has been read over at least four times, once by himself, the others by his assistants; notwithstanding which, he has reason to fear that many errors and omissions will remain.

It has not been attempted to make the book perfect, but merely to amend and improve it, by supplying manifest deficiencies, and completing the accounts of such works as were in progress when Lowndes wrote. Some of the additions are marked by brackets; but this plan having, in many instances, been found inconvenient, by far the greater number are without any indication; such, for instance, as the articles 'Bible,' 'Blake (Wm.),' and 'Breviaries,' which have been entirely rewritten.

New editions of old or standard works are frequently, though not invariably, mentioned; but *entirely new works*, first published since the time of Lowndes, are intentionally excluded, being reserved for a Supplementary Volume of Modern Literature; on this principle Macaulay's History of England will be omitted, while new editions of Hume, and the elder historians, will be duly noticed.

Who have hitherto assisted, or may hereafter assist, either continuously or occasionally, must remain to be stated at the conclusion of the work; in the mean time, the communication of any corrections or additions will be thankfully received by

HENRY G. BOHN.

York Street, Covent Garden,
Nov. 28, 1857.

THE
Bibliographer's Manual.

B.—*See* ANTRO-BUS, Benj.

A. F.—A Letter sent by F. A. touching the Proceedings in a private Quarell and Vnkindnesse, between Arthur Hall and Melchisedech Mallerie, Gentlemen, to his very Friend L. B. being in Italy. With an admonition by the Father of F. A. to him, being a Burgesse of the Parliament, for his better Behaviour therein. (London, by Henry Bynneman, 1579-80.) 4to.

Black letter, 16 sheets (128 pages). For this publication, which was adjudged a false and seditious libel by the House of Commons, Hall was imprisoned six months, fined 500 marks and expelled the house. It presents a curious view of the habits and manners of the young men of family and fashion in the reign of Elizabeth. It is reprinted in the *Miscellanea Antiqua Anglicana*.

A. H.—Partheneia Sacra, or the mysterious Garden of the Sacred Parthenis. Paris, by John Cousturier, 1633. 8vo.

Written by an English Catholic. The engravings are neat, and the poetry above mediocrity. Bindley, Pt. ii. No. I., 2414, 1*l*. 11s. 6d. Lloyd, 1*l*. 12s. White Knights, 8068, mor. 2*l*. 14s. Fonthill Library, 3146, 3*l*. 9s. Towneley, 1*l*. 18s.

A. H.—Scourge of Venus. *See* VENUS.

A. J.—*See* ALLEN, J.
— *See* ANDREWS, John.
— *See* ASKE, Ja.

A. P.—Eubulus; or, a Dialogue wherein a rugged Romish Ryme (inscrybed Catholicke Questions to the Protestant) is confuted, and the Questions thereof answered by P. A. Aberdene by Edward Raban, 1627. 4to.

Attributed to Patrick Forbes, Bishop of Aberdeen. Inglis, No. 548, 1*l*. 11s. 6d.

A. R.—*See* ALLOT, Robert.
— *See* ARMIN, Robert.
— *See* AYLET, Robert.

A. T.—The Massacre of Money, by T. A. London, 1602. 4to.

In verse, probably written by Thomas Acheley. Roxburghe, 3342. Heber, p. 4. 112. 2*l*.

A. T.—History of the Azores, or Western Islands. Lond. 1813. 4to.

With maps and other engravings. Dedicated to the Earl of Moira, by T. A., Captain of Light Dragoons, 7s. A miserable compilation.

A. W.— A speciall remedie against the furious force of lawless love; and also a description of the same with other delightfull devices of daintie delights to passe away idle time with pleasure and profit, newly compiled in English verse by W. A. Imprinted at London by Richd. Jones, 1579. 4to. *Black letter*.

A. W.—*See* AUBRELL, Wm.

ABAUZIT, Firmin. — Reflections on the Eucharist, on Idolatry, on the Mysteries of Religion, with Paraphrases and Explanations of sundry parts of Scripture, &c. &c.; translated from the French, by E. Harwood, D.D. Lond. 1770. 8vo. 4s.

The author of this work, by profession an Arian, was the correspondent and friend of Sir Isaac Newton. Another edition, entitled 'Miscellanies,' appeared in 1774, 8vo. Abauzit likewise wrote an Essay on the Apocalypse, which was ably answered by Dr. Twells.

ABBADIE, James. Vindication of the Truth of the Christian Religion, translated from the French, by H. Lussan. London, 1694-8. 8vo. 2 vols. 8s.

An excellent work. Several other treatises of this learned Protestant Divine have been translated into English.

Abbaye of the Holy Ghost. See ALCOCK, John, Bishop of Ely.

Abbot of evyll profytes. The Copy of the Commaundement generall by the. London by me Peter Treverys. 4to.

Black letter. Four leaves.

ABBOT, —. Jesus præfigured, or a Poeme of the holy Name of Jesus. Permissu Superiorum, 1623. 4to.

Nassau, 136. 16s.

— Charles, D.D. Flora Bedfordiensis—arranged according to the System of Linnæus, with occasional Remarks. Bedford, 1798. 8vo. pp. 370, with six plates, 5s.

— George, (successively Bishop of Lichfield and London, afterwards Archbishop of Canterbury.) Quæstiones sex, totidem Prælectionibus in Schola Theologica Oxoniæ, pro Forma habitis, discussæ et disceptatæ Anno 1597. Oxoniæ, 1598. 4to. pp. 224, and an index, 7s. 6d.

Reprinted at Frankfort, 1616, 4to. by Abr. Scultetus.

— Exposition upon the Prophet Jonah. Lond. by Richard Field, 1600. 4to. 5s.

Dedicated 'To Thomas Baron of Buckhurst, Lord Treasurer,' 638 pages, Reprinted in 1613. Abbot was one of the prelates appointed by James I. to translate part of the New Testament into English.

— Treatise of the perpetual Visibility and Succession of the true Church in all Ages. Lond. 1624. 4to.

With Abbot's arms impaled with those belonging to the see of Canterbury. Published anonymously.

— Briefe Description of the whole World. Lond. 1634. 12mo.

With a frontispiece, containing the author's portrait, by W. Marshall, 5s. Nassau, pt. i. No. 1, 10s. Of this work, which, according to Ant. à Wood, was commonly called 'A bot's Geography,' there have been many editions, viz. 1599, 1600, 1608, 1608, 1613, 1617 (the ninth), 1620, 1624, 1634, 1635, 1638, 1642, 1656, 1664.

ABBOT.—The Life of Dr. George Abbot, Lord Archbishop of Canterbury. To which are added the Lives of his two Brothers, Dr. Robert Abbot, Lord Bishop of Salisbury; and Sir Morris Abbot, Knt. Lord Mayor of the City of London. Guildford, 1797. 8vo. with four plates.

In this will be found an account of the hospital at Guildford, founded by this Archbishop, with copies of the charter and statutes. Heath, 1589, 9s. 6d. Nassau, Pt. i. 2, 10s.

— John. The natural History of the rarer Lepidopterous Insects of Georgia.—Edited by Sir J. E. Smith, M.D. London, 1797. folio. 2 vols. pp. 208, with 104 coloured plates.

A sumptuous work. Edwards, No. 742, morocco, 18l. 10s. Saunders in 1818, morocco, 14l. (Some copies are very indifferently coloured, and not worth half these prices.)

—, Robert, Bishop of Salisbury. A Mirror of Popish Subtilties. Lond. by Tho. Creede, 1594. 4to. pp. 226, besides dedication, &c. 7s. 6d.

This learned prelate, who was considered one of the first polemical divines of the age, likewise published several other controversial treatises which are held in some estimation.

ABBOTSFORD CLUB BOOKS. See *Appendix*.

A, B, C, The, with the Paternoster, Aue, Crede, and ten Commaundementes in Englysshe, newly translated and set forth at the Kynges most gracyous Commaundement. London, by R. Lant. 8vo.

Black letter. Printed on one side, to be folded so that the blank leaves may be pasted together, and form one leaf of two, or four small leaves of the whole sheet. Several other editions are noticed in Ames' Typographical Antiquities.

A, B, C, The Surfeit to. London, 1656. 12mo.

ABDALLA.—Arrivall and Entertainements of the Embassador Alkaid Yaurar Ben Abdalla, with his Associate Mr. Robert Blake, from Muley Mohammed Sheque, Emperor of Morocco, &c. London, 1637. 4to.

With a portrait of the ambassador by Glover. Sotheby's, in Dec. 1822, 2*l*. 11s. Gordonstoun, 129, 4*l*. 18s.

ABDIAS. *See* OBADIAH.

ABDOLLATIPH. Abdollatiphi Historiæ Ægypti Compendium, Arabice et Latine. Oxon. 8vo.

In the British Museum. 'Hic Liber inter rarissimos numerandus est, a Thoma Hyde edi cæptus est, sed morte erepto, nunquam perfectus desinit Pagina 96.' Bibl. Askev. No. 802, 3*l*. 3s.

— Abdollatiphi Historiæ Ægypti Compendium, Arabice et Latine. Partim ipse vertit, partim a Pocockio Versum edendum curavit, Notisque illustravit, J. White. Oxon. 1800. 4to. 1*l*. 1s.

An edition of the Arabic only, 10s. 6d. A translation of this valuable work will be found in vol. xv. of Pinkerton's Collection of Voyages and Travels, and in Part ii. of White's Ægyptiaca.

— Abdollatiphi Bagdadensis Vita, Auctore Ibn Abi Osaiba, e Codd. MSS. Bodleianis descripsit et Latine vertit Johannes Mousley. Oxon. 1808. 4to. pp. viii. and 78, 6s.

This volume should accompany the Compendium.

Abdulkurreem. The Memoirs of Khojek Abdulkurreem, who accompanied Nadir Shah, on his Return from Hindostan to Persia; &c. translated from the original Persian, by Francis Gladwin, Esq. Calcutta, 1788. 8vo. pp. 219, 5s.

ABEL, Clarke. Narrative of a Journey in the Interior of China, and of a Voyage to and from that Country, in the Years 1816 and 1817. London, 1818. 4to. with maps and other engravings.

Abel held an official appointment in Lord Amherst's Embassy. Drury, 127, 1*l*. 15s.

Abel and Kilvert, 1641. *See* Wine.

ABELARD, Peter.—Petri Abælardi et Heloissæ Epistolæ, a prioris editionis erroribus purgatæ, et cum Cod. MS. collatæ, curâ Ricardi Rawlinson. Lond. 1718. 8vo. pp. viii. and 279, besides the title and dedication to Dr. Mead.

The best edition of Abelard's letters. Bishop of Ely, 41, 7s. 6d. LARGE PAPER. Drury, No. 1, russia, 1*l*. 2s. Williams, No. 1, morocco, 1*l*. 14s.

— Letters written by Abelard and Eloisa, with a succinct Account of their Lives and Misfortunes, by John Hughes, Esq. To which are subjoined seven Poems by various Authors. London, 1808. 8vo. With 7 plates, 5s.

Another translation of these letters will be found in the Rev. Jos. Berington's Lives of these unfortunate Lovers.

ABENDANA, Isaac. Discourses of the ecclesiastical and civil Polity of the Jews. London 1709, 8vo. 3s. 6d.

A sensible and judicious selection from the works of Abendana.

ABERCROMBY, David. Academia Scientiarium, or the Academy of Sciences, with the Names of those famous Authors that have written on every particular Science in English and Latin. Lond. 1687. 8vo. 5s.

This writer likewise published a Discourse on Wit. London, 1685. 12mo. 3s. Protestancy to be embraced. London, 1682, 8vo. 5s.

— Patrick, M.D. The martial Atchievements of the Scots Nation. Edinb. 1711-15. fol. 2 vols. 1*l*. 15s. to 2*l*. 2s.

The first volume abounds in the marvellous, but the second is valuable on account of its accurate information respecting the British history in the 14th and 15th Centuries. Roxburghe, 8771, 5l. 7s. 6d. An edition was publishd 1762, 8vo. 4 vols. Abercromby likewise published two tracts, in answer to Defoe's History of the Union.

ABERDEEN, George, Earl of. An Inquiry into the Principles of Beauty in Grecian Architecture. London, 1822. post 8vo. pp. 217. Published at 7s. (Also prefixed to the 'Ionian Antiquities,' vol. 2.)

Drury, No. 2, 11s.

Aberdeen, An Account of the Antiquity of, with the Price of Grain and Cattle from 1435 to 1591. Edinb. 12mo.

Inglis, No. 1, 18s.

Abergavenny, Barony of. *See* BIRD, W.

ABERNETHY, John, Bishop of Caithness. A christian and heavenly Treatise, containing Physicke for the Soule; newly corrected and enlarged by the Author. Lond. 1622. 4to.

With a portrait of the author. Reprinted 1630. The edition 1622, Gordonstoun, 30, 6s.

— John, M.A. Discourses concerning the Being and natural Perfections of God, 2 vols. Sermons on various Subjects, 4 vols. and scarce and valuable Tracts and Sermons, 1 vol. Lond. 1740-51. 8vo. 7 vols. 1l. 11s. 6d.

The works of this eminent presbyterian divine are held in considerable estimation, particularly his discourses on the Divine Attributes.

— John. Surgical Works and Physiological Lectures, London, 1826, etc. 8vo. 4 vols. 2l. 2s.

— Thomas. Abjuration of Poperie, by Thomas Abernethie: sometime Jesuite, but now penitent Sinner, &c. A Warning to come out of Babylon, in a Sermon preached by Master Andrew Ramsay at the Receiving of Mr. Thomas Abernethie into the Societie of the truely reformed Church of Scotland. Edinb. 1638. 4to.

Two Tracts, 10s. 6d.

Aberwick.—A true Report of a straunge and monsterous Child, born at Aberwick, in the Parish of Eglingham, in the County of Northumberland, this fifth of January, 1580. Lond. for Tho. Gosson. 8vo.

Black letter. One sheet, with a wood cut of the child in the title-page, by 'Raphe Cooke, Paynter in Barwick upon Tweed.' This monstrous child, the offspring of Eli. nor Urine, was of the male sex, and shaped like two children from the shoulders upwards: one ear of each head was shaped like that of a horse, the other like a hog's.

ABINGDON, or Habington, Thomas. The Antiquities of the Cathedral Church of Worcester: to which are added the Antiquities of the Cathedral Churches of Chichester and Lichfield. London, 1717 or 1737, 8vo.

Worcester, pp. xxxv. 240, and Index, 8 pp. with title-page, also preface and errata, 2 pp.: Lichfield, pp. xlviii. and 62, ending with the catch-word 'An.' Roxburghe, 8601, 16s. 6d. Heath, 4698, 16s. 6d. Dent, Pt. i. 2, 1l.

ABRABANEL, Isaac. Proëmium Commentariorum in Leviticum, ex Heb. in Lat. cum Notis per L. C. de Veil. Lond. 1683. folio.

The works of this writer are held in considerable estimation by Rabbinical writers.

ABRENETHÆUS, Adam. Ecloga regalis de Matrimonio Caroli Regis et Henriettæ Mariæ. Lutet. 1625, 4to.

In the British Museum.

Abridgment (A general) of Cases in Equity. Lond. 1793, 1769. fol. 2 vols.

Vol. i. 5th edition, pp. 417, 1793. Vol. 2, 2nd edition, 1769. The best edition of an esteemed work. Sotheby's in 1821, 2l. 12s. 6d.

Abstract (An) of certain Acts of Parliament of certaine of her Majesties Iniunctions, &c.

Without Place, about 1584. 4to.

Black letter. pp. 266, besides a short Epistle to the Christian Reader, 10s. 6d.

— A Counter-poyson modestly

written for the Time to make Answere to the Abstract. (London, by R. Waldegrave, 1584.) 4to.
Black letter. pp. 195, with two epistles prefixed, 6s.

— An Answer to An Abstract of certeine Acts of Parliament, &c. Lond. by H. Denham, 1584. 4to.
Black letter, pp. 350, besides the preface, 6s. By Archb. Whitgift.

ABUDACNUS, seu Barbatus, Joseph. Historia Jacobitarum, seu Coptorum in Ægypto, Lybia, Nubia, Æthiopia tota, et Parte-Cypri Insulæ habitantium. Edita per Tho. Mareschallum. Ox. 1675. 4to. 6s.
A translation by Sir Edward Sadleir was published 1692 & 3. 4to. 5s.

ABU ISMAEL. *See* Tograi.

ABULFAZEL. *See* Ayeen Akbery.

ABULFEDA, Ismael. Chorasmiæ et Mawaralnahræ, hoc est Regionum extra Fluvium Oxum Descriptio, ex Tabulis Abulfedæ, Arab. et Lat. a J. Gravio. Lond. 1650. 4to. 64 pp. 5s.
Also in the Geograph. Min. edited by Hudson.

— De Vita et Rebus gestis Mohamedis Arabicum primus edidit, Latine vertit, Præfatione et Notis illustravit Joan. Gagnier. Oxon. 1723. folio.
A curious and important work. Heath, 2667, 1l. In Rivington and Cochran's Catalogue, No. 735, was a copy corrected throughout for a new edition by Simon Ockley. Gagnier began to publish the 'Takweem al Boldam,' but died when the 72nd page was printed off.

ABUL-PHARAJIUS, Greg. Excerptum de Rebus gestis Richardi Angliæ Regis in Palæstina: Syriac. et Lat. a Paulo Jac. Bruns. Oxon. 1780. 4to. 3s. 6d.

— Specimen Historiæ Arabum, sive Gregorii Abulfarajii de Origine et Moribus Arabum succincta Narratio, in Linguam Latinam conversa; Opera et Studio Edv. Pocockii. Oxon. 1650. 4to. 9s.
Arabic Text, 30 pp. Notes, date 1648, pp. 390. Golius in the preface to his Lexicon Arabicum calls this book 'opus præclarum,' and the author 'doctissimus.'

— Specimen Historiæ Arabum, accessit Historia veterum Arabum ex Abu'l Feda; Curâ Ant. Is. Silvestre de Sacy. Edidit Josephus White. Oxonii, 1806. 4to. With a portrait of the author by W. N. Gardiner, 1l. 1s.

— Historia Dynastiarum Orientalium, Arabice edita et Latine versa ab Edv. Pocockio. Oxon. 1663. 4to. 2 vols. 18s.
Vol. 1. Arabice, pp. 565, with two titles, and a dedication to Gilbert, Bishop of London, together four leaves. Vol. 2, Latin, B to K k k, in fours, with title; dedication to Charles II. and Preface to the Reader, 6 leaves. A curious and very interesting work. Of volume 2 some copies have a new title-page, 'Historia Orientalis,' 1672, with an addition of 'Præfatio ad Lectorem,' 5 pages.

ABU TALEB KHAN, Mirza. Travels in Asia, Africa, and Europe, in the years 1799-1802, translated from the Persian by Charles Stewart. London, 1810. 8vo. 2 vols. pp. 738, 16s.
This work, according to the Quarterly Review, is 'not only a curious, but a very agreeable present to the western world.' Reprinted 1814. 12mo. 3 vols. The original was published at Calcutta in 1812, in royal 8vo. 1l. 5s.

ACA, Anthony of. The Historie, Life, and Miracles of the blessed Virgin, Sister Joane of the Crosse. St. Omers, 1625. 12mo.
A notice of this absurd production will be found in Beloe's Anecdotes, iii. 110-11.

Academie.—Choix des Memoires de l'Academie des Inscriptions et Belles-Lettres. London, 1777. 4to. 3 tom. 12s.
A tolerable selection. Bishop of Ely, 670. 1l. 5s.

Academy of Compliments, enriched with many witty Poems, and pleasant Songs, excellent Similitudes, Comparisons, Fancies, Devices, and delightful Fictions. London, 1655, 12mo. 10s. to 15s.
An edit. 1670, Stanley, No. 678, 16s. 1713. White Knights, No. 6, morocco, 30s. 1680. Ireland, in 1801. No. 54, 13s. 6d.

Academy of Compliments, (A new) with an exact collection of the

newest and choisest Songs a la Mode, both amorous and jovial. London, 1669. 12mo. With frontispiece, 10s. to 15s.
Frequently reprinted. Edition 1671, Nassau, Pt. 1. 6, 14s. 1681. Stanley, 679, 1l. 1s.

Academy of Compliments, or whole Art of Courtship, being the rarest and most exact way of wooing a Maid or Widow, by the way of Dialogue or complimental Expressions. London, 12mo.
An abridgment of the 'Jardin d'Amour.' White Knights, No. 7, 5s.

Academy of Pleasure, furnished with all kinds of complimental Letters, Discourses, and Dialogues, with a variety of new Songs, Sonnets, and witty Inventions. London, 1656. 12mo.
A rare work, with engraved title, by Vaughan, containing portraits of Drayton, Quarles, Wither, and Jonson, and a portrait of the author? in the dress of a book chapman. Nassau, Pt. 1. 3. russia, 8l. 18s. 6d. Townley, 1665, 2l. 5s.

Accedence (Latin). Printed in Caxon's Hous by W. de Word' at Westmynstre. 4to. (No date, but before 1497.)
Contains A viij. B vi. Dr. Dibdin says W. de Worde printed an edition of 'The Long Accydence' in 1513, 4to.

ACCUM, Frederic. System of theoretical and practical Chemistry. London, 1803. 8vo. 2 vols. 10s.
Of this edition there were a few copies printed on paper manufactured from straw. Accum published many other treatises on Chemistry, Mineralogy, &c., mostly compilations from other works.

ACERBI, Joseph. Travels through Sweden, Finland, and Lapland, to the North Cape, in the years 1798 and 1799. London, 1802. 4to. 2 vols. with 17 engravings, 1l. 5s.; copies with the plates of natural history coloured, 1l. 15s.
This work has been attacked by Rihs, a Swede, for misrepresenting the Swedes, and for having borrowed largely without acknowledgment from Leemius; and also by his fellow-traveller, Skioldebrand, for having appropriated his views and designs. Drury, 129. russia, 1l. 14s. Fonthill, 427, 2l. Earl of Kerry, 177, 8l.

ACHARYA, Bhascara. Lilawati: or, a Treatise on Arithmetic and Geometry, translated from the Sanscrit by John Taylor, M.D. Bombay, 1816. 4to.

ACHELYE. See ATCHELYE.

ACHERLEY, Roger. The Britannic Constitution, or the fundamental Form of Government in Britain, demonstrating the original Contract entered into by King and People. London, 1727 or 1741. fol. 10s. 6d.—L. P. 18s.
This writer likewise published, "The Free Parliament," 1731, 8vo. 3s. 6d., and in 1780 appeared: 'Reasons for Uniformity in the State, being a Supplement to the Britannic Constitution,' 8vo.

ACHESONE, James. The Militarie Garden, or Instructions for all young Souldiers. Edinb. 1629. 4to. with a folding plan.
Gordonstoun, 72, 13s. Inglis, 97, 17s.

ACHILLES TATIUS. The History of Clitophon and Leucippe, from the Greek, by W. B. [urton]. Lond. by Tho. Creede, 1597. 4to.
A translation mentioned by Ant. à Wood, and also by Warton, but unknown to Ames or Herbert.

—— The loves of Clitophon and Leucippe, Englished by A. H. [Anthony Hodges]. Oxford, 1638. small 8vo. with a frontispiece.
According to Ant. à Wood, 'There were two impressions of this translation made in that year (1638), and in one of them are commendatory copies of verses made by several poets of the university.' Bindley, Pt. 1. 25, 1l. 8s. An abridged translation was published in 1720, 12mo. 2s. 6d.

ACKERMANN. See Repository of Arts. Oxford. Microcosm. Westminster, &c.

ACLAND, Hugh Dyke. A brief Sketch of the History and present Situation of the Vaudois. London, 1825. 8vo. *Plates by Finden.*
An interesting article on the History of the Vaudois, with a notice of this work, will be found in the Quarterly Review, xxxiii. 184-176.

Acme and Septimus, 4to. 9s.
Thirty-six copies printed. *See Boswell,* 3062.

Acolastus, the Comedy of, 1540. See FULLONIUS, Gul., and Nicholson (S.).

ACONTIUS, James. Stratagematum Satanæ Libri viii. Oxon. 1631. 12mo.
Dedicated to Queen Elizabeth, with a frontispiece, 6s. A very popular work, which has been translated into many European languages. The original was first printed at Basle, 1565; reprinted 4to. London, 1648; 12mo. Oxford, 1650. The translation appeared in 1648—'Acontius's Satan's Stratagems, or the Devil's Cabinet Council Discovered,' 4to. Sir M. M. Sykes, Pt. i. 102. 11s. Reprinted 1651.

ACOSTA. The remarkable Life of Uriel Acosta; to which is added Mr. Limborch's Defence of Christianity, in answer to Acosta's Objections. London, 1740. 8vo.
This tract was translated and edited by John Whiston, the bookseller. It was revised by Dr. Roper.

—— Joseph d'. The History of the East and West Indies, translated from the Spanish, by E. G. [probably Edward Grimstone]. London, 1604. 4to.
This work, which is quoted by Doctor Robertson as standard authority, has also been translated into French, Flemish, Italian, and German, Gordonstoun, 130, 19s. 6d. Horne Tooke, No. 1, 1l. 1s. North, Pt. iii. 574. morocco, 3l. 7s.

Acta Apostolorum, Græco-Latina, Litteris majusculis, a Codice Laudiano, Characteribus uncialibus exarato, descripsit ediditque T. HEARNIUS qui et Symbolum Apostolorum ex eodem Codice subjunxit. Oxon. 1715. royal 8vo.
Of this work (which is usually adjoined to the series of HEARNE'S WORKS) only 120 copies were printed, all upon royal paper. Duke of Grafton, No. 15, 7l. 16s. Brockett, 1469, 8l. Bishop Randolph, No. 65. 8l. 2s. 6d. King and Lochée's in 1810, 10l. 10s. Heath, 4270, 13l. 2s. Gough, 1662, 20l.

Acta Apostolorum, variorum Notis tum Dictionem tum Materiam illustrantibus, suas adjecit Hastings Robinson, A.M. Cantab. 1825. 8vo. 9s. 6d.

Acta Regia. *Vide* RAPIN de Thoyras.

Actuum Apostolorum et Epistolarum tam Catholicarum quam Pauli Versio Syriaca Philoxeniana, ex Cod. MSS. Ridleii, nunc primum edita cum Interpret. et Annotat. Jos. White. Oxon. 1799. 4to.
This work generally accompanies White's edition of the Syriac Evangelists.

Actes of the Apostles (The) translated into Englishe Metre by Christofer Tye, Doctor in Musyke, &c. wyth Notes to eche Chapter to synge and also to play upon the Lute, &c. 1553. London, by Nycolas Hyll and Wyllyam Seres. 8vo.
Black letter. Contains N 4, in eights. This version contains the first 14 chapters only; there are variations in the colophon. Noticed by Warton in the xlvii. section of his History of Poetry. Gough, 18, russia, 3l. 3s., but now worth considerably more. Bindley, 8l. 15s.

Acts of the Apostles.—The Actions of the Apostles; translated from the original Greek. By the Rev. John Willis. Lond. 1789. 8vo. pp. 295. 3s.
This translation is in little estimation.

ACTON, Thomas Herman. Reports of Cases argued and determined before the Commissioners of Appeals in Prize Causes; also, an Appeal to the King in Council, concerning the Judgments in June 1809. Lond. 1809-11. royal 8vo. vol. 1 and vol. 2, pt. 1. (all printed) 1l. 1s.

Actor (The), a Treatise on the Art of Playing, interspersed with theatrical Anecdotes, &c. London, 1750-5. 12mo. 2 vols. 4s. to 6s.
A very sensible performance, written by Aaron Hill.

Actors' Remonstrance, (The) or Complaint, for the silencing of their Profession and Banishment from their severall Playhouses. London, 1643. 4to.
A satirical tract, containing some curious and amusing particulars of the means resorted to by players to procure subsistence on the suppression of the theatres in 1642. One hundred copies were reprinted in 1822, 8vo. 2s. 6d. from the copy in the British Museum.

Actors (The Tragical) or the Mar-

tyrdome of the late King Charles. Printed for Sir Arthur, 1660. 4to.
Rhodes, 408, 11s.

Actors. Refutation of the Apology to Actors. 4to. 1615.
Bindley, 1l. 1s.

ACWORTH, Geor. LL.D. De visibili Rom' anarchia contra Nich. Sanderi Monarchiam προλεγομένον Libri duo. Lond. apud Joh. Dayum, 1573. 4to. pp. 215, besides tables of contents for the two books.
Reprinted in 1622, 4to. This writer assisted Archb. Parker in his Antiquitates Britannicæ.

Adagia in Latine and English, contayning fyve hundreth Proverbes. Aberdeen, 1622. 12mo.
A copy is in the British Museum.

ADAIR, James. The History of the American Indians, particularly those Nations adjoining to the Missisippi, East and West Florida, Georgia, South and North Carolina, and Virginia. London, 1775. 4to. 15s.
In this very curious work, the author, who was a resident in North America above forty years, endeavours to trace the Indians to a Hebrew origin.

— R. A Sketch of the Character of the late Duke of Devonshire. London, 1811. 4to.
A privately printed tract, with a portrait of the Duke, 1l. 1s. 50 copies.

ADAM, Alex. LL.D. Roman Antiquities, or an Account of the Manners and Customs of the Romans. London, 1822. 8vo. 6s.
A very useful and much esteemed work, generally recommended in preference to Dr. Kennett on the same subject. This eminent scholar, who was rector of the High School of Edinburgh, likewise published several other elementary books, particularly a Latin Dictionary, which is highly esteemed, and has been frequently reprinted.

— Robert. The Religious World displayed. To which is subjoined a view of Deism and Atheism. Edinb. 1809. 8vo. 3 vols. 18s.

A new edititon appeared in London, 1823, 8vo. 2 vols.; and an Abridgment in 1824, 12mo.

— Robert. Ruins of the Palace of the Emperor Dioclesian at Spalatro in Dalmatia. London, 1763 or 4. Atlas fol. with 71 plates.
A splendid work. Roxburghe, 9062, russia, 3l. 13s. 6d. Nassau, Pt. ii. 1655, russia, 3l. 13s. 6d. Gough, 213, 4l. 4s. Baker, 265, 4l. 10s. Dent, Pt. i, 138, russia. 4l. 18s. Willet, 109, 5l. 15s. 6d. Marq. of Townshend, 189, 6l. 6s.

— Robert and James. Works in Architecture. London, 1773-1822. imperial folio. 3 vols. with 105 plates, 7l. 7s.
A highly valuable work, containing plans, elevations, sections, and details of the principal buildings erected in Great Britain during the reign of King George III., with designs for interior and exterior decoration, (some copies have the ceilings coloured.) Fonthill, 3218, (vols. 1 and 2.) 10l.

— Thomas, of Wintringham. The Works. London, 1822. 8vo. 3 vols. Published at 1l. 7s.
The works of this author are not critical but doctrinal. His private thoughts on Religion have been frequently printed.

Adamites.—A Nest of Serpents discovered, or a Knot of old Heretiques revived, called the Adamites. —The Adamites Sermon.—A new Sect of Religion called the Adamites. London, 1641. 4to.
Three Tracts, each with a wood cut. King and Lochee, in March, 1810, 1l. 5s.

ADAMO, Anthony de. An Anatomi as well of the Mass as of the Mass Boke. 1556. With a Sermon of the Sacrament. 1556. 8vo.
Black letter. In all 264 leaves, and two of the faults. Maunsell mentions an edition of the date of 1555. Bright, 45, 2l. 12s.

ADAMS, Frauncis. Writing Tables, with a Kalendar for XXIIII. Years, with sundry necessarye Rules. 1594. Oblong 16mo. 2l. 2s.
In this work is the following sentence, ' Printing was found out at Mentz 1459, and first brought to London by William Caxton, mercer.'

— George. Essays on the

Microscope. The second Edition, with considerable Additions and Improvements, by Frederick Kanmacher, F.L.S. Lond. 1798. 4to. with 32 folio plates.

An esteemed work. Earl of Kerry, 18l, 1l. 15s. The former edition 1787, 4to. Willet, 65, 1l. 11s. 6d.

— Lectures on natural and experimental Philosophy, with Additions by Wm. Jones. London, 1799. 8vo. 5 vols.

The former edition appeared in 1794. Willet, 2, 1l. 19s. Earl of Kerry, 17, 2l. 2s. This writer, who was instrument maker to his Majesty, published some other useful works, several of which have been reprinted, with Additions by W. Jones.

— J., LL.D. Reports of cases in the Ecclesiastical Courts. London, 1826. 8vo. 2 vols. 2l. 10s.

— Rev. James. The Pronunciation of the English Language vindicated from imputed Anomaly and Caprice; in two Parts, with an Appendix. Edinb. 1799. 8vo. pp. 164, 5s.

This work, according to Park, contains 'many ingenious remarks on languages and dialects, though the style of the writer is characterized by much whimsical eccentricity.' A former work, entitled Euphonologia Linguæ Anglicanæ, appeared in 1794, 8vo. 5s.

— John. Index Villaris; or, an exact Register, alphabetically digested, of all the Cities, &c., in England and Wales. The third Edition. London, 1700. folio, with a map, 12s.

'His large map,' says Bishop Nicolson, 'with the contractions of it afterwards, must be acknowledged to be done with good pains, judgment, and exactness.' The former editions, 1680 and 1690, 5s. each. LARGE PAPER. Edwards (Edition 1680) 62, morocco, 1l. 1s. Heath (Edition 1700) 4530, 1l. 11s. 6d.

— John. The renowned City of London; surveyed and illustrated in a Latine Poem—translated into English by W. F., of Gray's Inn. London, 1677? 4to.

Fourteen leaves. This poem, unnoticed by Gough in his Anecdotes, is reprinted in the tenth volume of the Harleian Miscellany.

— John, LL.D. History of the principal Republics in the World. A new Edition. London, 1794. 8vo. 3 vols. 15s.

The former edition of this work, entitled 'A Defence of the Constitution of the United States of America, appeared in 8vo. 3 vols. 1787-8. Adams likewise published 'An Essay on Canon and Feudal Law,' 1782, 8vo. (5s.) and took an active part in modelling the constitution of the United States, of which he was vice-president under Washington.

— Rev. John. View of Universal History, from the Creation to the present Time. London, 1795. 8vo. 3 vols. 12s. to 15s.

This writer published many other useful works, well calculated for the improvement and entertainment of youth.

— Captain John. Sketches taken during two Voyages to Africa, between the years 1786 and 1800; including Observations on the Country between Cape Palmas and the River Congo, &c. &c. &c. London, 1823. 8vo. pp. 265. Published at 7s. 6d.

A valuable little work.

— John Quincy. Letters on Silesia, written during a Tour through that Country in the Years 1800, 1801. London, 1804. 8vo. pp. 400, with a map, 7s.

A work containing some interesting information, especially on the manufactures of Silesia. This writer has likewise published a curious and interesting work on our ancient weights and measures, printed at Washington, 1821.

— Joseph, M.D. Memoirs of the Life and Doctrines of the late John Hunter. London, 1816. 8vo. 9s.

This able physician has likewise published some valuable works, particularly 'Observations on Morbid Poisons.' London, 1807, 4to. 1l. 1s.

— Robert. Expeditionis Hispanorum in Angliam vera Descriptio, anno 1588. Roberto Adamo, Authore. 1589. 4to.

Accompanied with eleven maps. 'Angustinus Ryther sculpsit.' The Queen's arms are on the last map. These maps will also be found in 'A Discourse concerning the Spanish Fleet in 1588, by Petricio

Ubaldino,' 1589. Copies of both works are in the British Museum.

Adams Robert. The Narrative of Robert Adams, a Sailor, who was wrecked in the year 1810, on the Western Coast of Africa, was detained three years in Slavery by the Arabs of the Great Desert, and resided several months of that period in the City of Tombuctoo; with a Map, Notes, and an Appendix. London, 1816. 4to. 10s. 6d.
A curious, marvellous, but authentic narrative. The Notes by Mr. Dupuis, the British Vice-Consul at Mogadore, will, says the Quarterly Review, be read with interest, and may be consulted with advantage. Drury, 180, 12s. Fonthill Library, 3689, 1l. 10s.

— T. History of the ancient Town of Shaftesbury, from the Founder, Alfred the Great. Sherborne, (1809) 12mo.
Contains pp. 221, (B—Ee 5.) with title, a list of subscribers, pp. 5, and portrait of Alfred the Great, by T. J. Woodman.

— Thomas. Commentary upon the second Epistle of Saint Peter. London, 1633. folio. 10s to 15s.

— Workes, viz. The White Devil, the Fatal Banket, the Sinner's Passing Bell, &c. London, 1629. folio. 10s. to 15s.

— William, M.A. Complete History of the Civil Wars in Scotland, 1644-6. Second Edition, with considerable Additions. Edinb. 1724. 9s.
The first edition, with a new title-page.

— William, D.D. An Essay on Mr. Hume's Essay on Miracles. London, 1752. 8vo. 2s 6d
An admirable answer to Hume, reprinted 1754. This able writer likewise published several volumes of Sermons, &c.

— William. Vitruvius Scoticus, a Collection of Plans, Elevations, and Sections of Public Buildings, &c. &c. in Scotland. Edinburgh, (1750) folio, with 160 plates by Cooper. 63s.
Fonthill, 1921, 6l.

— Sir William. A practical Inquiry into the Causes of the frequent Failure of the Operations of Depression, and of the extraction of the Cataract, as usually performed, &c. London, 1817. 8vo. 16s.
A valuable accession to the chirurgical library. This celebrated oculist has likewise published several other works on the same subject.

— See BODRUGAN (Nicholas).

ADAMSON, Henry. The Muses Threnodie, or Mirthful Mournings on the Death of Mr. Gall, with a Description of Perth, and an Account of Gowrie's Conspiracy. Edinburgh, 1638. 4to.
Lloyd, 205, 6l. 8s. 6d. This work was reprinted at Perth, 1774, 8vo. 2 vols. with Notes, by James Cant, 9s. to 12s.

— John. The Muses' Welcome to King James VI. at his return to Scotland, anno 1617. Edinb. 1618. folio.
With portrait. A copy is in the British Museum. All the speeches are reprinted in Nichols' Progresses of King James. Dowdeswell, 618, 2l. 5s. Nassau, Pt. i. 200, 2l. 14s. Bindley, Pt. ii. 1055, 6l. 2s. 6d. Sotheby's, in April, 1822, 5l. 5s. Constable, 262, 7l.

— The Traveller's Joy; to which is added, The Ark, a Poem. 1623. 12mo.
Perry, 1l. 3s.

— Dioptra Gloriæ Divinæ; seu, Enarratio Psalmi xix, et in eundem Meditationes. Edinb. 1637. 4to.
This writer likewise published 'Methodus Religionis Christianæ.' Edinb. 1637, 8vo.

— John. Memoirs of the Life and Writings of Luis de Camoens. Lond. 1820. crown 8vo. 2 vols. with a portrait of Ignez de Castro, 1l. 4s.
An elegant, amusing, and elaborate performance, for which the author was elected an honorary member of the Royal Academy of Portugal. Large paper, 1l. 16s.

— Patrick, Archbishop of Saint Andrews, The Recantation of, also his Answere and Refutation of the Buke falslie called the King's Declaration. 1598. 8vo.

ADAMSON, Poemata sacra, et alia, Opera, Studio T. Voluseni. Londini, 1619. 4to.
Roxburghe, 2753, 7s. 6d. Gordonstoun, 34, 10s. 6d. Bindley, pt. i. 526, 12s.
This writer, who was one of the commissioners for settling the constitution of the Church of Scotland, likewise published 'De Sacro Pastoris Munere Tractatus,' Lond. 1619, 8vo. 'Refutatio Libelli de Regimine Ecclesiæ Scoticanæ,' Lond. 1620, 8vo. and Sermons, 1623, 8vo.

— Catechismus, Edin. 1581. See Catechismus.

— Vita et Palinodia, 1620. See MELVIN, A.

ADANSON, Michael. Voyage to Senegal, the Isle of Goree, and the River Gambia. Translated from the French. London, 1759. 8vo. 6s.
An interesting work, chiefly relating to Conchology, reprinted in vol. xvi. of Pinkerton's Collection of Voyages and Travels. Fonthill Library, 2851, 16s.

ADDINGTON, Stephen, D.D. A Dissertation on the religious knowledge of the ancient Jews and Patriarchs; to which is added, a Specimen of a Greek and English Concordance. Lond. 1757. 4to. 3s. 6d.
This work, written by a dissenting minister of considerable learning, contains, according to Orme, some sensible reasoning and biblical illustration. He likewise published 'The Life of St. Paul,' 1784, 8s. 6d., and several other works.

— Sir William. An Abridgement of Penal Statutes. The fourth edition, with Additions. By Sir William Addington. To which is added a Continuation of the Statutes to the 51st. Geo. III. London, 1812. 4to. 2l. 2s.
The former editions of this work appeared 1775. 1786. 1795.

ADDISON, Joseph. The Works. edited by Tickell. Lond. 1721, 4to. 4 vols. with portrait and plates.
Roxburghe, 6958, 2l. 4s. Marquis of Townshend, 127, 3l. Large paper. Willet, 68, 4l.

— The Works. Birmingham, Baskerville, 1761. 4to. 4 vols. with portrait and plates, by Grignion after Hayman.
A beautiful and esteemed edition. Copies of this, as well as the other works, printed by Baskerville, are seldom found free from stains. Roxburghe, 6960, 5l. 15s. 6d. Willett, 69, 6l. 12s. 6d. Heath, 1666, 6l. 15s. Drury, 131, 7l. Marquis of Townshend, 129, morocco, 8l. 8s. Baker, 141, with plates, proofs and etchings, 9l. 5s. Williams, 105, morocco, by Derome, 14l. 14s.

ADDISON, Joseph. The Works. Lond. 1804. 8vo. 6 vols.
Large paper. Sotheby's in 1820, 2l. 8s. Earl of Kerry, 626, russia, 4l. 4s.

— Works, with Notes by Bishop Hurd. Lond. 1811. 8vo. 6 vols. portrait, 3l. 12s. Large paper, 5l. 8s. (Republished entire, with large Additions, in Bohn's British Classics.)
Dr. Johnson observed of Addison, 'Whoever wishes to attain an English style, familiar but not coarse, and elegant but not ostentatious, must give his days and nights to the volumes of Addison.'

— The Miscellaneous Works in Verse and Prose, and Remarks on several parts of Italy, &c. in 1701, 1702, 1703, with Life by Tickell. London, 1765. 8vo. 4 vols. with portrait.
Grave, No. 2, 2l. 10s. Roscoe, 1407, 3l. 11s. Frequently reprinted in 12mo.

— Evidences of the Christian Religion, with Notes, by G. Seigneux de Correvon, translated by Purdy. London, 1807. 8vo. 7s.
This valuable posthumous treatise, much esteemed both at home and abroad, has been frequently reprinted, and is inserted by Bishop Watson in his Collection of Theological Tracts.

— Dialogues upon the Usefulness of Ancient Medals, especially in relation to the Latin and Greek Poets. London, 1726. 12mo. 3s.

Addisoniana. Lond. 1804. 12mo. 2 vols. 10s. 6d.
A collection of anecdotes and facts connected with the life, times, and contemporaries of this celebrated writer, (by Sir Richard Phillips.)

Addison, Lancelot, D.D. West Barbary; a short Narrative of the Revolutions of Morocco and Fez, with their Customs, Oxf. 1671. 8vo. 5s.
Reprinted in vol. xv. of Pinkerton's Collection of Voyages and Travels. This

learned divine, the father of Joseph Addison, likewise published a life of Mahomet, an account of the Jews, &c., which are held in some estimation.

ADDISON [Mr. a pseudonyme]. Collection of interesting Anecdotes, Memoirs, Allegories, Essays and poetical Fragments, tending to amuse the Fancy and inculcate Morality. 1794-97. 8vo. 16 vols. (Rarely found complete.)

— Addition to the Sea Journall; or Navigation of the Hollanders into Java, with a Vocabulary of Words used at St. Laurence. Imprinted by Wolfe, 1598. 4to.
Black letter, with cuts. Jadis, 267, 3l. 19s.

— Addresses.—The genuine rejected Addresses, presented to the Committee of Management for Drury Lane Theatre; preceded by that written by Lord Byron, and adopted by the Committee. London, 1812. 8vo. 4s.

— Rejected Addresses; or the New Theatrum Poetarum. Lond. 1812. 12mo. 5s.
A jeu d'esprit, by Horace and James Smith, comprising a number of parodies on living poets, executed with great humour, discrimination, and good taste. It has been frequently reprinted.

ADDY, William. Stenographia, or the Art of Short Writing, completed in a far more compendious method than any yet extant. London, 1695. 8vo. with portrait, by J. Sturt, 5s.
More remarkable for the accuracy and elegance of its graphical execution, than for any considerable improvement in the art.

ADLERFELD, Gustavus. Military Memoirs of Charles XII. King of Sweden. London, 1740. 8vo. 3 vols. with plans of the battles and sieges, 12s.
Written with great fidelity, by the gentleman of the bedchamber to Charles XII.

Admiralty.—Laws, Ordinances, and Institutions of the Admiralty of Great Britain, Civil and Military. London, 1746, or 1767. 8vo. 2 vols. 12s.

ADMIRALTY. Statutes relating to the Admiralty, Navy, and Ships of War, &c. Lond. 1768, 4to. 10s.
The edition of 1742 or 1755, 5s.

Admonition, A faithful, of a certain true Pastor or Prophete, sent into the Germanes at such time as certain great Princes went about to bryng Alienes into Germany, and to restore the Papacy, the Kingdom of Antichrist, Now translated into English, with a Preface of M. Philip Melancthon. Greenwich, 1554, 4to.
At the end of this curious treatise, is 'A Praier to be said of all true Christians against the Pope, and al the Enemies of Christ and hys Gospel,' which is reprinted in Morgan's Phœnix Britannicus, p. 95. Dr. Dibdin, in his edition of Ames, mentions a copy of this treatise, printed by R. Kele.

Admonition (Ane) to the Antichristian Ministers of the Kirk of Scotland, (a poem). 12mo. 1581.
Perry, 2l. 13s. 6d.

Admonition to the Bishoppes of Winchester, London, and others, &c. Roane by Michael Wood, 1553. 16mo. 15 pp.
Black letter. This treatise begins on the back of the title-page.

Admonition to the Parliament. See CARTWRIGHT, T^{h}oms^s.

Admonition to the People of England. See COOPER, Thomas, Bishop of Lincoln.

ADOLPHUS, John. The British Cabinet; containing Portraits of illustrious personages, engraved from Original Pictures; with Biographical Memoirs, by John Adolphus. London, 1799-1800, 4to.
In little estimation. Lloyd, 206' 1l. 5s. Bindley, pt. i. 117, 1l. 8s. Bishop of Ely, 163, 1l. 10s. LARGE PAPER, in folio; Roxburghe, 8591, 3l. 18s.

— The History of England, from the Accession of K. George III. to 1783. Fourth Edition. London, 1817. 8vo. 3 vols, 1l. 1s.
The former editions appeared in 1802, 1805. This work is intended as a continuation of Hume and Smollett.

— John. The Political State of the British Empire. London, 1818. 8vo. 4 vols. 18s.

This author, a barrister of considerable professional reputation, likewise published Biographical Memoirs of the French Revolution, 1799, 8vo. 2 vols. 9s., and a History of France, 1790—1802, 1803, 8vo. 2 vols. 9s.

Adventurer, The, a periodical paper, commencing Nov. 7, 1752, to March 9, 1754, folio.

One hundred and forty Nos. in 2 vols. 10s. 6d. Duke of Grafton, 409, 2l. 4s. This periodical was conducted by Dr. John Hawkesworth, with the assistance of Drs. Richard Bathurst, Sam. Johnson, and Jos. Warton, reprinted 1754, &c. 12mo. 4 vols., and 8vo. 3 vols., and inserted in the various editions of the Essayists. An elegant edition was published by Sharpe, 1806, 12s.

Advocates, Catalogue of the Library of the Faculty of. *See* Scotland.

ADY, Thomas. A Candle in the Dark, or a Treatise concerning the Nature of Witches and Witchcraft. London, 1656, 4to.

An excellent article on Witchcraft will be found in the Retrospective Review, vol. v. 87—136.

ADYE, Stephen Payne. A Treatise on Courts Martial; also an Essay on Military Punishments and Rewards. Eighth Edition. London, 1810. 12mo. 5s.

The former editions of this treatise appeared 1769, 1785, 1801, 1805.

ÆGIDIUS Columna. Tractatus solennis Fratris Egidij de Ordine Fratrum Augustinensium de Peccato Originali. Oxoniæ, MCCCCLXXIX. 4to.

A copy is in the Bodleian Library.

ÆLFRED. *See* ALFRED.

ÆLFRIC, successively Bishop of Wilton and Archbishop of Canterbury. A Saxon Treatise concerning the Old and New Testaments now first published in print with English of our Times, by William L'isle of Wilburgham. London, 1623. 4to. 10s. 6d.

Contains A—V 3, with title and prefatory matter 30 leaves. Nassau, pt. i. 149, 15s.

In this work will be found a very learned Epistle, by W. L'isle, and reprints of (1) 'A Testimony of Antiquity, touching the Sacrament,' with a Preface by Josselin. (2) The Words of Elfric, written to Wulfsine, Bishop of Scyrburne, &c. (3) 'The Lord's Prayer, the Creed, and Ten Commandments, in the Saxon and English Tongue.' These articles were previously printed by John Day.

ÆLFRIC Society. *See* Appendix.

ÆLIANUS, Claudius. De Natura Animalium Libri xvii. Gr. et Lat. curante Abr. Gronovio. Londini 1744. 4to.

2 vols.—vol. i. pp. 608. Vol. ii. pp. 605 —1128. An excellent and ample edition. Gossett, 244, 1l. 11s. 6d. Willett, 72, 1l. 15s. Large paper, Drury, 133, morocco, 3l. 4s. Dent, pt. i. 116, (with the Varia Historia, Lug. Bat. 1731, 2 vols.) in morocco, 11l. In the Classical Journal, No. 28, are J. Stackhousii Emendationes in Ælianum.

ÆLIANUS, Claudius. A Registre of Hystories in English, by Abr. Fleming. London, for Thomas Woodcock, 1576. 4to.

Black letter, pp. 176, with a dedication to Dr. Goodman, and commendatory verses. Sir M. M. Sykes, 109, 1l. 6s.

— Various Histories, translated by T. Stanley. London, 1665. 8vo. 5s.

This translation is by the son of the learned editor of Æschylus, and was reprinted 1670, 1677.

— Tactics, or the Art of Embattelling an Army, translated by John Bingham. London, 1616-31. folio, 2 vols. 1l. 1s.

ÆLREDI, Opera, opera et studio, R. J. Gibboni, additi anonymi rithmi de laude Virginitatis, 4to. Duaci 1631. 1l. 11s. 6d.

ÆNEAS Sylvius. *See* PICCOLOMINI.

ÆNIGMAS. Thesaurus Ænigmaticus, or a Collection of the most ingenious and diverting Ænigmas or Riddles. Lond. 1725. 8vo. 4 parts in 1 vol.

White Knights, Pt. i. 15, 9s.

ÆRODIUS, or Ayrault, Peter. A Discourse for Parents' Honour and Authoritie. Translated by John

Budden, LL.D. London, 1614. 12mo. 5s.
Occasioned by the author's son, having been seduced by the Jesuits.

ÆSCHACIUS, Major. Rationis et Adpetitus Pugna : hoc est, de Amore Edvardi iij Regis Angliæ. 1592. 18mo. 1*l*. 10s.
An edition Hafn. 1612, 4to., of which a copy is in the British Museum. Bindley, pt. ii. 743, 1*l*. 6s.

ÆSCHINES. Æschinis Oratio in Ctesiphontem ; et Demosthenis Oratio pro Corona, Gr. et Lat. cum Notis P. Foulkes et T. Freind. Oxon. 1695. 8vo.
Best edition, with portraits of the orators, 5s. to 7s. LARGE PAPER. Dent, pt. i. 13, morocco, 1*l*. 6s. Steevens, 194, 1*l*. 10s. Williams, 11, morocco, 1*l*. 11s. Reprinted 1715, 1726, 1782. Of the edition 1715 there are copies on large paper. Williams, 12, morocco, 1*l*. 13s.

— Ibid. Græce, cum Delectu Annotationum. Oxon. 1801. 8vo. Large paper, 10s. 6d.
Reprinted, Oxon, 1807, 1814, and 1820, 8vo., of which editions there are likewise copies on large paper, 3s.

— The Orations of Æschines against Ctesiphon and Demosthenes de Corona. Translated and illustrated with Notes by Andrew Portal. Oxford, 1755, 8vo. 5s.
A correct and almost verbal translation, reprinted 1814, 12mo. Dr. Thomas Leland likewise published an excellent translation, with very learned and useful notes.

— See DEMOSTHENES.

ÆSCHYLUS. Tragœdiæ, cum Scholiis Græcis, Fragmentis, Versione et Comment. T. Stanleii. Londini, 1663 or 1664, folio.
An edition of pre-eminent excellence. Some copies want the dedicatory epistle, and the privilege. Dent, pt. i. 139, mor. 4*l*. 2s. Steevens, 451, 4*l*. 5s. Duke of Grafton, 652, russia, 4*l*. 10s. Williams, 113, (erroneously described as L. P.,) morocco, 5*l*. Drury, 177, morocco, 5*l*. 10s. Roxburghe, 3555, 6*l*. Sir M. M. Sykes, pt. i. 138, morocco, 7*l*. 7s. Heath, 3514, russia, 9*l*. 9s. Fonthill, 3355, 11*l*. 11s. (There is no *Large Paper*, although so announced in Williams's Cat.)

— Tragœdiæ, Græce, cum variis Lectionibus. Glasg. 1746. 4to.
A most correct edition of Stanley's Text, elegantly printed. Drury, 137, 9s. FINE PAPER. Heath, 3516, 15s.

— Ibid. Gr. Cum Versione Latina et Lectionibus variantibus. Glasguæ, 1746, small 8vo. 2 vols. 16s. 6d. Fine paper, 15s.
A neat edition, though not so correct as the 4to. edition of the same date.

— Ibid. Gr. cum Versione Latina. Glasguæ, 1794, veneunt Londini, 1806. 8vo. 2 vols. 10s. 6d.
Printed from a copy of Pauw's edition (Hag. Com. 1745), corrected by the celebrated Porson; without the Professor's consent or knowledge. LARGE PAPER. Williams, 20, morocco, 4*l*. 8s.

— Ibid. Græce, cum Emendationibus et novis Lectionibus. Glasguæ, Foulis, 1795. folio, published at 4*l*. 4s.
A handsome edition, printed from the text of Stanley, corrected by Professor Porson. 52 copies were printed on small, and 11 or 12 on large paper. Flaxman's designs are frequently inserted. Large paper. Sir M. M. Sykes, Pt. i. 137, with Flaxman's plates, in morocco, 14*l*. 10s. Dent, Pt. i. 140, mor., by Roger Payne, 6*l*. 6s.

— Ibid. Græce, recens. C. G. Schütz. Oxon. 1806. 8vo. 2 vols. 10s. 6d. large paper, 16s.
Reprinted 1810 and 1815, of which there are likewise copies on large paper. In 1819, Stanle 's Latin version appeared, 8vo. 6s.

— Ibid. Græce, ex Editione C. G. Schütz. Oxon. 1809. 32mo.
A neat little edition, 3s. 6d.

— Tragœdiæ quæ supersunt deperditarum Fabularum Fragmenta et Scholia Græca, ex editione Thomæ Stanleii, cum Versione Latina. Accedunt variæ Lectiones et Notæ VV. DD. Criticæ et Philologicæ, quibus suas passim intertexuit Samuel Butler. Cantab. 1809-15. 8vo. 8 vols. or 4to. 4 vols.
Combe, 14, 4*l*. 19s. LARGE PAPER, in 4to. 4 vols. Drury, 138, russia, 6*l*. 15s. Shortly after the publication of the first volume of this edition, the following appeared :
A Letter to C. J. Blomfield, containing Remarks on the Edinburgh Review of the Cambridge Æschylus. By Samuel Butler, Bishop of St. Asaph, Camb. 1810, 8vo.
A Letter to the Rev. S. Butler, from the Rev. J. H. Monk, Greek Professor in the

University of Cambridge, with Mr. Butler's Reply. Camb. 1810, 8vo.

— Tragœdiæ, Græce ex recensione C. G. Schutzii, cum Scholiis Græcis et Notis. Londini, 1823. 8vo. 3 vols.

A neat edition, published at 2l. 2s. An edition Gr. et Lat. ex Edit. Schutz. Lond. 1823, small 8vo. 2 vols, 14s., and another Græce, cum Notis Wellauer, 8vo. 2 vols. Cantab. 1827, 16s.

— Novæ Editionis Tragœdiarum Æschyli Specimen, curante Antonio Askew. 1746. 4to.

A pamphlet of very rare occurrence.

— Prometheus vinctus, cum Stanleiana Versione, Scholiis α, β, (et γ ineditis) amplissimisque Variorum Notis; quibus suas adjecit, necnon Scholia de Metro, Anglicanum Interpretationem T. Morell. Londini, 1773. 4to. 5s.

— Prometheus Vinctus, ad Fidem MSS. emendavit, Notas et Glossarium adjecit C. J. Blomfield. Editio quarta. Cantab. 1825. 8vo. 6s.

The former editions of this admirably edited play appeared in 1810, 1812, 1817. Bp. Blomfield likewise edited the following:
Choëphoræ. Cantab. 1824.
Septem contra Thebas. Ib. 1812, 1817, 1824.
Persæ. Ib 1814, 1818.
Agamemnon. Ib. 1818, 1822.

— Eumenides, Gr. recensuit Geo. Burgess. Lond. 1822. 8vo.

Drury, 33, russia, 6s. 6d. Burgess likewise published the Supplices, 1821, 3s. 6d.

— The Tragedies, translated by R. Potter, with Notes. London, 1777-8. 4to. 9s.

The second edition, corrected, with Notes, London, 1779, 8vo. 2 vols. 10s. 6d. A correct, elegant, and most beautiful version, reprinted in 1 vol. 8vo. Oxford, 1808. London, 1809, 1812.

— Translated into English Prose. Oxford, 1822. 8vo. Published at 12s.

In 1824, two translations of the Agamemnon appeared, one by John Symons, the other by Hugh Stuart Boyd.

ÆSOPUS. Æsopicarum Fabularum Delectus, Gr. et Lat. item Fabulæ Hebraicæ, et Arabicæ selectæ, ex recensione A. Alsop. Oxonii. 1698. 8vo. 4s. to 5s.

Warton says this is a valuable and esteemed edition, not sufficiently known. In the preface, Alsop took the side of Boyle against Bentley. LARGE PAPER. Dent, pt. 1. mor. 16s. Drury, 39, mor. 19s. Williams, 22, morocco, 1l. 9s. White Knights, pt. 1. 19, mor. by Roger Payne, 1l. 13s. Stanley, 437, mor. by Roger Payne, 2l. 18s.

— Fabularum Æsopicarum Collectio quotquot Græce reperiuntur. Accedit interpretatio Latina. Oxon. 1718. 8vo.

The text of this edition, edited by John Hudson, under the name of Marianus, is said to be incorrect, but the notes are valuable, 4s. to 6s. LARGE PAPER. White Knights, pt. 1. 20, morocco, 1l. 18s. Williams, 23, morocco, 2l. 5s. Stanley, 438, morocco, by Roger Payne, 3l. 13s. 6d.

— Fabulæ metrice, cum Commento. London, ap. W. de Worde, 1503.

"It may be questioned," says Dr. Dibdin, "whether a perfect copy of this book be in existence." An imperfect one is in the British Museum.

— Æsopi et Vita ex maximo Planude desumpta et Fabellæ iucundissimæ, Lond. apud W. de Worde, 1535, 8vo.

Contains m 4 in eights, besides the life and index, This is considered a great curiosity, being printed in Italic.

— Æsopi Fabulæ. Londini, apud Tho. Marsh. 1580.

From this edition, W. Bulloker made his translation.

— Æsopi Fabulæ, Versibus descriptæ, per Humf. Roydonum. Londini, H. Jackson, 1596. 8vo.

An edition not noticed by Ames, Herbert, or Dr. Dibdin. Inglis, No. 6, morocco, 4l.

— Æsopi Fabulæ. Glasg. 1754.

Dent, Pt. i. 19, mor. 8s.

— The subtyl Historyes and Fables of Esope. Translated in to Englysshe, by William Caxton, &c. Emprynted by me William Caxton at Westmynstre, M.CCCC.LXXXIIII, folio.

Black letter, with wood cuts. The Fables of Æsop end on the reverse of fol cv; at fol. cvi begin those of 'Avian,' and conclude at fol. cxx; and on the reverse of the same leaf begin those of 'Alfonce.' Those of 'Poge the Florentyn,' begin at fol. cxxxviii, and end at fol. cxlii, where Caxton takes leave of his work, 'Now then I will finish, &c.' The volume contains 142 leaves, as far as sign. s 6 in octaves. A copious account of this edition will be found in Dr. Dibdin's edition of Ames, 1.

208-20. A perfect copy is in the library of K. George III.

ÆSOP. The Fables of Esope. Enprented by me Richard Pynson, folio.
Black letter, containing sign. G in Octaves. Printed from Caxton's edition, with the omission of Æsop's life. An imperfect copy of an edition printed by Laurence Andrewe was formerly in the possession of Mr. Herbert. Rodd, 49, (wanting title, sheets A B and Eiiij,) but extending to sig. 8v, on the reverse of which is Colophon, with Pynson's device underneath. 11*l*. 15*s*.

— The Fables of Esope in Englishe with all his Lyfe and Fortune, 8vo.
Black letter, pp. clxi. A copy, wanting the imprint and part of the title, is in the possession of F. Douce, Esq.

— The morall Fables of Æsop the Phrygian, compyled into eloquent and ornamental Meter, by Robert Henrison, Schoolemaster of Dumfermling. Edinburgh, 8vo.
Black letter. Of this edition, only one copy is at present known. Constable, 412, 19*l*. 10*s*.

— The Fables of Æsope in Englishe, with all his Life and Fortune; —whereunto is added, the Fables of Auian, and also the Fables of Poge the Florentyne, very pleasaunte to read. London, by Henry Wykes for John Waley, 8vo.
Black letter. Containing 134 leaves and a table. Perry, Part i. 109, 1*l*. 13*s*. White Knights, 24, 4*l*. 4*s*.

— Æsop's Fables, in true Ortography, with grammar Notz. Herunto ar also coioned the shorte Sentencez of the wyz Cato, imprynted with lyke form and order: both of which Authorz are translated out of Latin intoo English, by William Bulloker. London, by Edmund Bollifant, 1585. 8vo.
Black letter. The Fables on 319 pages and a table; the Cato 31 pages. Sotheby's in July, 1821, 10*l*. 10*s*.

— The Fabulist metamorphosed and mythologyzed, or the Fables of Esop translated out of Latine into English Verse, by R. A. Gentleman. London, 1634, 8vo.
Lloyd, 18, 5*l*. 5*s*.

— Æsop's Fables, with the Fables of Phædrus moralized. Published by H. P. Lond. 1646. 12mo.

— The Fables of Esop in English, whereunto are added, the Fables of Avian and of Poge the Florentine. Lond. 1647, 8vo. 12*s*.
Black letter. Caxton's translation, though not a faithful reprint.

— Fables with their morals in verse, front. and woodcuts. Camb. 1650.
Southgate, 1818, 4*l*.

— The Phrygian Fabulist, or the Fables of Æsop extracted from the Latine copie, and moralized by Leon. Willan. Lond., 1650, 8vo.
Bindley, Pt. iii. 2197, 8*l*. 13*s*. 6*d*.

— Fables paraphrased in verse, by John Ogilby. Lond. 1651, 4to.
With cuts by Hollar. First edition. Nassau, Pt. i. 152, mor. 1*l*. 7*s*. Bindley, Pt. iii. 972, 1*l*. 15*s*. Inglis, No. 99, 1*l*. 19*s*.

— The Fables of Esop in English; with all his Life and Fortune; whereunto are added the Fables of Avian, &c. London, 1658. 12mo.

— The Fables paraphras'd in verse, adorned with sculpture, and illustrated with annotations, by John Ogilby. Lond. 1665, folio.
The plates mostly by Hollar. A translation still in estimation. Fonthill, 2476, 3*l*. 10*s*. White Knights, Pt. i. 185, morocco, 4*l*. 14*s*. 6*d*. Republished folio, 1668. Bindley, Pt. ii. 1714, 1*l*. 11*s*.

— Æsop's Fables, with his Life in English, French, and Latin. The English by Tho. Philipott; the French and Latin by Rob. Codrington. London, 1666, folio.
With 112 sculptures, by F. Barlow. The greater part of the impression of this edition was burnt in the fire of London. Bindley, Pt. i. 166, 2*l*. 9*s*. LARGE PAPER, 10*l*. 10*s*.

— Æsop explained in English and Latin verse. Lond. 1672, 8vo.
Nassau, Pt. i. 15, 16*s*.

— The Fables paraphrased in verse, adorned with sculptures, and illustrated with annotations, by John Ogilby. Lond. 1672-3. 8vo. 2 vols.

Nassau, Part i. 14, 16s.—Vol. 2, entitled Æsopics, 1678. Lloyd, 20, 7s. Perry, Pt. ii. 917, 8s. 6d.

— Æsop explained in English and Latin verse, with a collection of English Proverbs and Sayings. London, 1682. 12mo. 10s. to 12s.

— Æsop's Fables, with his Life in English, French, and Latin, newly translated, illustrated with one hundred and twelve sculptures, and thirty-one new figures, representing his life, by Francis Barlow. London, 1687. folio.

Nassau, Part i. 202, 2l. 12s. 6d. W. Knight's Lib. Part i. 186, 3l. 3s. Grave, 156, morocco, 4l. 14s. 6d.

LARGE PAPER. Sotheby's in 1825, 4l. 4s. Fonthill 3349, 8l. Stanley, 439, russia. 8l. 8s. Reprinted 1703, in folio, 2l. 2s. This work is much admired for the accurate delineation of the animals, and for the freedom with which the subjects are etched. The verses under the sculptures in the life are by Mrs. Aphra Behn; plate 17 (which is indecent) is frequently wanting.

— Three centuries of Æsopian Fables in English prose, done from Æsop, Phædrus, Camerarius, and others, by Philip Ayres, Esq. London, 1689. 8vo. 3s. 6d.

Reprinted 1702.

— Fables of Æsop and other eminent Mythologists, with Morals and Reflections by Sir Roger L'Estrange. London, 1692-4. folio. 2 vols. 9s.

This version was reprinted in folio, vol. i. 1694, and n. d. vol. ii. 1699 and 1704, also frequently in 8vo. 2 vols., viz. 1703, 8, 14, 15, 24, 38.

— Æsop's Fables, with the Moral Reflections of Mons. Baudoin, translated from the French, with the Life of Æsop, by John Toland. London, 1704. 8vo. 5s.

— Truth in Fiction, or Morality in Masquerade; a collection of Fables from Æsop and others, done into English verse, by Edmund Arwaker. Lond. 1708, 8vo. pp. 350, 4s.

Bibl. Anglo.-Poet. No. 6, 10s. 6d.

— Fables of Æsop and others. Translated into English, with an Application to each Fable, by Samuel Croxall, D.D. London, 1722. 8vo. 3s. 6d.

Often reprinted. The celebrated novelist, Samuel Richardson, likewise published an edition of Æsop's Fables, with Reflections.

— Fables, in English and Latin interlineary, by John Locke. London, 1723. 8vo. second edition, with sculptures, 1l. 1s.

This book, by the celebrated Locke, is little known, and is not included in the editions of his works.

— Select Fables of Æsop and other Fabulists, by Dodsley, printed by Baskerville, Birmingham, 1764. small 8vo. plates.

This is considered the best translation of Æsop. The first edition appeared in 1761, and of late years it has been frequently reprinted. Gosset, 1857 (date 1761), 17s. 6d. Bindley, Pt. iii. 1562 (date 1761), 15s. Baker, 646 (date 1764), with proof plates and original drawings, 4l. 14s. 6d.

— Fables, with Life. London, Stockdale, 1793. Royal 8vo. 2 vols. with 112 engravings.

White Knights, Part i. 25, morocco, 1l. 19s.

— Fables. Lond. 1797. 12mo.

A beautiful edition, published by Heptinstall, with copper-plate engravings to each fable, reprinted by Whittingham and others with the same plates. Bindley, Pt. i. 18, 12s.

— The Fables of Æsop and others, with Designs on Wood by Thomas Bewick. Newcastle, 1818, 8vo. 1l. 1s. Royal, 1l. 5s. Imperial. 1l. 11s. 6d.

Of this work there is a second edition, printed 1823, both in demy and royal, but not in imperial 8vo.

Of Æsop there have been several other translations, viz., one by H. Steers. 1804, 8vo. 3s. 6d. Another by Jefferys Taylor, of Opgar, 1821, 12mo. 4s.

— Some Observations on the Fables of Æsop, as commented upon by Sir Roger L'Estrange. By a Divine of the Church of Scotland (James Gordon, Bishop of Aberdeen.) Edin. 1700. 8vo. 5s.

— Æsop in Select Fables, viz. a Tunbridge, at Bathe, at Epsom, at

Whitehalle, from Tunbridge, at Amsterdam. London, 1698. 8vo.
Lloyd, No. 19, 14s.

ÆSOP. — Æsop's Fables burlesqued. London, 8vo. with a frontispiece.
Dent, Pt. i. 20, 10s.

Africa. Western Africa; being a Description of the Manners, Customs, Dresses, and Character of its Inhabitants. London, 1821. 12mo. 4 vols. with 47 engravings, 1l. 1s.

— Proceedings of the Association for promoting the Discovery of the interior parts of Africa. London, 1790-1803. 4to. 2 vols. with maps.
Printed for the use of the members of the association. Roxburghe, 7331, 2l. 15s. An edition was afterwards published in 8vo. 2 vols. 10s. 6d.

— Reports (18) of the Directors of the African Institution. London, 1807-1824. 8vo.

AGAPETUS. The Preceptes teachyng a Prynce of a noble Estate his Duetie, translated into Englysshe by Thomas Paynell. London, by Tho. Berthelet. 16mo.
Black letter. Reprinted in 1563, with Lud. Vives' Introduction to Wisdom, by Ri. Morisine.

AGAS or Aggas, Radolph. Preparative to Platting of Landes and Tenements, for Surueigh. London, by Tho. Scarlet, 1596. 4to.
Black letter. On 20 pages. This celebrated surveyor published the first map of London in 1560, republished in 1618, and in 1737.

AGATHARCHIDIS et MEMNONIS Historicorum, quæ supersunt omnia, e Græco iam recens in Latinum traducta, per Rich. Brettum. Oxoniæ, ex Officinâ typographicâ Josephi Barnes, 1597. 16mo. 10s.
Pp. 140, besides dedication to 'D. Thomæ Egertone'. It is also contained in the Geographi Minores, edited by Hudson.

Agathocles.—The Sicilian Tyrant, or the Life of Agathocles. London, 1678. 8vo. with portrait of Agathocles (i. e. O. Cromwell) inscribed 'Tyrannus,' 5s.

This work, intended as a parallel to O. Cromwell, was written by Richard Perrinchief. Nassau, Pt. ii. 479, 5s. 1661. An edition was published in 1661. Lloyd, 1162. LARGE PAPER, 10s. 6d. A poem on the subject was published 1683, by Thos. Hoy, M.D.

Age.—The cheating Age found out, 4to.
A collection of wood-cuts, with verses. Bindley, pt. i. 2192, 16s.

Ages.—The Four Ages of England; or, the Iron Age, with other select Poems: written in the Year 1648. London, 1675. 8vo. pp. 94.
Bibl. Anglo.-Poet, No. 715, 12s. Perry, pt. i. 1614, 4s.

— Ages of Sinn, or Sinnes Birth and Growth, with the Stepps and Degrees of Sin, from Thought to final Impenitence. London, circa 1656. 4to.
Nine engravings with English verses underneath each of them, published by T. Jenner. Bindley, pt. i. 154, 5l. 15s. 6d. Perry, 5l. 10s.

Aggeus. See Haggai.

AGLIONBY, William. Painting illustrated in three Dialogues; with the Lives of the most eminent Painters from Cimaibue to Raphael and Michael Angelo. Lond. 1685. 4to.
This gentleman likewise published another work 'On Painting.' London,1719.4to.

AGNESI, Donna Maria Gaetana. Analytical Institutions, translated into English by the Rev. John Colson. London, 1802. 4to. 2 vols. 2l. 2s.
An excellent translation of a very useful work, published at the expense of Baron Maseres, under the care of the Rev. John Hellins.

Agnew.—Sketch of a genealogical and historical Account of the Family of Vaux, Vans, or De Vallibus; now represented in Scotland by Vans Agnew, of Barnbarrow, &c. in the County of Wigton, Scotland. Pembroke, 1800. 4to. pp. 36.
Privately printed. A copy is in the Royal Institution.

Agriculture. Communications to the Board of Agriculture, on Subjects relative to the Husbandry and Internal Improvement of the Country. London, 1797-1811. 4to. 7 vols. *plates.*

Agriculture.—The Substance of a Lecture on the Advantages which have resulted from the Establishment of the Board of Agriculture. By the Secretary of the Board (Arthur Young). Lond. 1809. 8vo. 3s. 6d.

—— Review and complete Abstract of the Reports of the Board of Agriculture from the several Departments of England, by Wm. Marshall. London, 1817. 8vo. 5 vols. 1*l*. 1s.

These reviews were published separately, viz., the Northern Department, 1808; the Western, 1810; the Eastern, 1812; the Midland, 1815, and the Southern and Peninsular, 1817.

Agricultural Surveys of Great Britain and Ireland.

ENGLAND.

Bedfordshire, by Thos. Stone, 4to. 1794
—— by Thos. Batchelor, 8vo. 1808 or 1813
Berkshire, by W. Pearce, 4to. 1794
—— by Wm. Mavor, LL.D., 8vo. 1809 or 1813
Buckinghamshire, by Wm. James and Jacob Malcolm, 4to. 1794
—— by the Rev. St. John Priest, 8vo. 1810 or 1813
Cambridgeshire, by C. Vancouver, 4to. 1794
—— by the Rev. W. Gooch, 8vo. 1811 or 1813
Cheshire, by Thomas Wedge, with an Appendix, 4to. 1794
—— H. Holland, 8vo. 1808 or 1813
Cornwall, by Robert Fraser, 4to. 1794
—— by G. B. Worgan, 8vo. 1811
Cumberland, by J. Bailey and G. Culley, 4to. 1794
Cumberland. *See* Northumberland.
Derbyshire, by Tho. Brown, 4to. 1794
—— J. Farey, 8vo. 3 vols. 1811, 13, 17
Devonshire, by Robert Fraser, 4to. 1794
—— C. Vancouver, 8vo. 1808 or 1813
Dorsetshire, by John Claridge, 4to. 1793
—— W. Stevenson, 8vo. 1815
Durham, by Jos. Granger, 4to. 1794
—— John Bailey, 8vo. 1810 or 1813
Essex, by Messrs. Griggs, 4to. 1794
—— C. Vancouver, 4to. 1795
—— A. Young, 8vo. 2 vols. 1807
Gloucester, by Geo. Turner, 4to. 1724
—— Tho. Rudge, 8vo. 1807 or 1813
Hampshire, by A. and W. Driver; to which is added, the Isle of Wight, by the Rev. Mr. Warner, 4to. 1794

Agricultural Surveys:
Hampshire, including the Isle of Wight, by C. Vancouver, 8vo. 1810 or 1813
Herefordshire, by John Clark, 4to. 1794
—— Duncumb, A. M., 8vo. 1805
Hertfordshire, by D. Walker, 4to. 1795
—— A. Young, 8vo. 1804
Huntingdonshire, by Thomas Stone, 4to. 1793
—— Geo. Maxwell, 4to. 1793
—— R. Parkinson, 8vo. 1811 or 1813
Kent, by John Boys, 4to.
Brentford, 1794, 8vo. 1796 or 1805
Lancashire, by John Holt, 4to. 1794
—— from the Communications of Mr. John Holt, &c. 8vo. 1795
—— by Dr. Dickson, revised by Stevenson, 8vo. 1806
Leicestershire, by John Monk, 4to. 1794
Leicestershire, by Wm. Pitt, and Rutlandshire, by R. Parkinson, 8vo. 1809 or 1813
Lincolnshire, by Tho. Stone, 4to. 1794
—— A. Young, 8vo. 1799
Second Edition, 18—
—— A Review of Young's Survey, by Tho. Stone. Second Edition, 8vo. 1800
Man, Isle of, by Basil Quayle, 4to. 1794
Not published for sale.
Middlesex, by Tho. Baird, 4to. 1793
—— Peter Foot, 4to. 1794
—— J. Middleton, 8vo. 1798, 1807
Monmouthshire, by John Fox, 4to.
Brentford, 1794
Monmouthshire, by C. Hassall, 8vo. 1812
Norfolk, by N. Kent, 4to. 1793, 8vo. 1794
—— by A. Young, 8vo. 1804
Northamptonshire, by J. Donaldson, 4to. Edinb. 1794
—— by W. Pitt, 8vo. 1809
Northumberland, by J. Bailey and G. Culley, 4to. 1794
Northumberland and Cumberland, by J. Bailey and G. Culley; and Westmoreland, by A. Pringle. The Third Edition, 8vo. 1805
Nottinghamshire, by Rob. Lowe, 4to. 1794, 8vo. 1798
Oxfordshire, by R. Davis, 4to. 1794
—— by A. Young, 8vo. 1809 or 1813
Rutlandshire, by J. Crutchley, 4to. 1794
—— by Rich. Parkinson. *See* Leicestershire.
Shropshire, by J. Bishton, 4to. Brent 1794
—— Jos. Plymley, 8vo. 1803
Somersetshire, by John Billingsley, 4to. 1794, 8vo. Bath, 1798
Staffordshire, by W. Pitt, 4to. 1796 8vo. 1794
Suffolk, by A. Young, 4to. 1794. 8vo. 1798. 1804.
Surrey, by W. James and J. Malcolm, 4to. 1794
—— Stevenson, 8vo. 1809

Agricultural Surveys:
Sussex, by A. Young, 4to. 1793, 8vo. 1808
Warwickshire, by J. Wedge, 4to. 1794
—— by A. Murray, 8vo. 1815
Westmoreland, by A. Pringle, 4to.
Edinb. 1794
—— See Northumberland.
Wiltshire, by Tho. Davis, 4to. 1794
8vo. 1811 or 1813
Worcestershire, by W. T. Pomeroy, 4to. 1794
—— W. Pitt, 8vo. 1813
Yorkshire, East Riding, by I. Leatham, 4to. 1794
—— by H. E. Strickland, 8vo. York, 1812
Yorkshire, North Riding, by John Tuke, 4to. 1794, 8vo. 1800
—— West Riding, by Messrs. Rennie, Brun, and Shirreff, 4to. 1794
—— by R. Brown, 8vo. Edinb. 1799

WALES.
Wales, by Walter Davies, 8vo. 3 vols. 1810-15
—— (North), by George Kay, 4to.
Edinb. 1794
Brecknockshire, by John Clark, 4to. 1794
Caermarthenshire, by C. Hassall, 4to. 1794
Cardiganshire, from the Communications of Tho. Lloyd, Esq., and the Rev. Mr. Turner, 4to. 1794
Glamorganshire, by John Fox, 4to. 1796
Pembrokeshire, by C. Hassal, 4to. 1794
Radnorshire, by John Clark, 4to. 1794

SCOTLAND.
Northern Counties and Islands, by Sir John Sinclair, Bart. 4to. 1794
Central Highlands of Scotland, by Marshall, 4to. 1794
Aberdeenshire, by James Anderson, LL.D. 4to. Edinb. 1794
Aberdeenshire, by Geo. Skene Keith, 8vo. Aberdeen, 1811
Angus, or Forfarshire, by the Rev. Roger, 4to. Edinb. 1794
—— by the Rev. J. Headrick, 8vo. 1831
Argyleshire, by James Robson, 4to. 1794
—— by John Smith, D.D. 8vo. 1805, 1812
—— and Western part of Invernesshire, by James Robson, 4to. 1794
Ayrshire, by Col. Fullarton, Edinb. 1793
—— W. Aiton, 8vo. Glas. 1811
Banffshire, by Souter, 8vo.
—— by James Donaldson, 4to.
Edinb. 1794
Berwickshire, by Alex. Lowe, 4to. 1794
—— by Rob. Kerr, 8vo.
1806 or 1809, or 1813
Bute, by W. Aiton, 8vo. Glas. 1816
Caithness, by J. Henderson, 8vo. 1812
Clackmannanshire, by J. F. Erskine, 4to.
Edinb. 1795
Clydesdale, by John Naismith, 4to.
1794. 8vo. 1798. 1806

Agricultural Surveys:
Dumbartonshire, by the Rev. David Ure, 4to. 1794
—— by the Rev. A. White and Duncan Macfarlane, D.D. 8vo. Glas. 1811
Dumfriesshire, by Bryce Johnston, D.D., an Appendix, 4to. 1794
—— by Dr. Singer, 8vo. Edinb. 1812
Elgin, or Moray, by James Donaldson, 4to. 1794
Fifeshire, by R. Beatson, 4to. 1794
—— by J. Thomson, D.D. 8vo. Edinb. 1800
Galloway, by J. Webster, 4to. Edinb. 1794
—— by the Rev. S. Smith, 8vo. 1813
Hebridæ, or Hebrides, by Rob. Heron, 4to. Edinb. 1794
Hebrides, by James Macdonald, 8vo. 1811
—— by Walker, 8vo. 2 vols.
Inverness, by James Robertson, D. D. 8vo. 1808
Kincardineshire, by T. Donaldson, 4to. 1794
—— by J. Robertson, D.D. 8vo. 1810
Kinrosshire, by the Rev. D. Ure, 4to. 1794
Lothian (East), by G. B. Hepburn, 4to. 1794
—— (East), by R. Somerville, 8vo. 1805
—— (Mid-), by George Robertson, 4to.
Edinb. 1793, 8vo. Edinb. 1795
—— (Mid-), by Rob. Bald, 8vo. 1812
—— (West), by James Trotter, 4to.
Edinb. 1794, with an Appendix, 8vo. 1812
—— (Mid-), Abridged Report, 4to. 1795
Nairn, &c., by James Donaldson, 4to. 1794
—— and Moray, by the Rev. W. Leslie, 8vo. 1811
Peebles, by the Rev. Charles Finlater, 8vo. Edinb. 1802, 1814
Perth, Banff, Northampton, and Mearns, or Kincardine, by James Donaldson, 4to. 1794
Perth, by James Robertson, D.D. 8vo.
Perth, 1799
Perthshire (Southern Districts of), by James Robertson, D.D. 4to. 1794
Perthshire, Carse of Gowrie in, by James Donaldson, 4to. 1794
Renfrewshire, by John Wilson.
—— by Alex. Martin, 4to. 1794
Ross and Cromarty, by Sir George Stuart Mackenzie, 8vo. 1813
Roxburghe and Selkirk, by Robert Donglas, D.D. 8vo. Edinb. 1798, 1802
Roxburghshire, by the Rev. D. Ure, 4to. 1794
Stirlingshire, by R. Belsches, 4to.
—— by Graham, 8vo.
Sutherland, by J. Henderson, 8vo. 1815
Selkirk, by Thomas Johnston, 4to. 1794
Tweeddale, by Thomas Johnston, 4to. 1794
Orkney Islands, by John Shirreff, 8vo.
Edinb. 1814

Agricultural Surveys:
IRELAND.
Antrim, by the Rev. John Dubourdien. 8vo. 2 vols. Dublin, 1812
Armagh, by Sir Charles Coote, Bart. 8vo. ibid. 1804
Cavan, by Sir Charles Coote, Bart. 8vo. ibid. 1802
Cork, by the Rev. Horatio Townsend, 8vo. ibid. 1810
Clare, by Hely Dutton, 8vo. ibid. 1808
Donegal, by James M'Pharlan, M.D. 8vo. ibid. 1802
Down, by the Rev. John Dubourdieu, 8vo. ibid. 1802
Dublin, by Lieutenant Joseph Archer, 8vo. ibid. 1802
— Observations on Archer's Statistical Survey, by Hely Dutton, 8vo. ibid. 1802
Galloway, by the Rev. Sam. Smith, 8vo. London, 1810
Kilkenny, by Wm. Tighe, 8vo. Dublin, 1802
King's and Queen's Counties, by Sir Charles Coote, 8vo. 2 vols. ibid. 1801
Kildare, by Tho. Jas. Rawson, 8vo. ibid, 1807
Leitrim, Mayo, and Sligo, by James M'Pharlan, M.D. 8vo. 3 vols. ibid. 1802
Londonderry, by the Rev. Geo. Vaughan Sampson, 8vo. ibid. 1802
Meath, by Robert Thompson, 8vo. ibid. 1802
Monaghan, by Sir Charles Coote, Bart. 8vo. ibid. 1801
Tyrone, by John M'Evoy, 8vo. ibid. 1802
Wexford, by Robert Frazer, 8vo. ib. 1801
Wicklow, by Robert Fraser, 8vo. ib. 1801

AGRIPPA, Henry Cornelius. Of the Vanitie and Uncertaintie of Artes and Sciences, englished by Ja.(mes) Sa.(nford), Gent. Lond. by Henry Wykes, 1569. 4to. 9s.
Black Letter. Reprinted 1575. An excellent article on this work will be found in the Retrospective Review, vol. xiv., 181-206.
— The Vanity of Arts and Sciences. London, 1676. or 1684. 8vo. with portrait, 5s.
— Three Books of Occult Philosophy, translated by J. F(reake). Lond. 1651. 4to. with portrait.
Fonthill, 407, 10s. Sotheby's in April, 1822, 1l. 4s. Roxburghe, (4 books, 1651-65) 12s. 6d. Inglis, No. 102, (4 bks., 1651-65) 13s.
— Fourth Book of Occult Philosophy, translated by Robert Turner. London, 1665. 4to. 5s.
This book is spurious. Another version appeared in 1786, 8vo. 4s.

AGRIPPA.—Treatise of Nobility, and the Excellency of Woman-kind, translated by David Clapham. London, 1542. 8vo.
Black Letter. Composed in compliment to Margaret of Austria.
— The Praise of Matrimony, translated by David Clapham. London, by Tho. Berthelet, 1545. 8vo.
Black Letter. Bright, 1845, fine, 3l. 4s. Bindley, date 1540.
— The Glory of Women, translated by Edward Fleetwood. London, 1652. 4to.
— Female Pre-eminence, translated from the Latin, by Henry Care. London, 1670.
With a fulsome dedication to Queen Catherine.

Ahmad Bin Abubeker, Bin Wahshih. See HAMMER (Jos.)

AICKIN. Siege of Londonderry in verse. Dublin, 1699. 8vo.
Nassau, pt. i. 19, 11s.

AIKIN, Arthur. — Journal of a Tour through North Wales and Part of Shropshire; with observations in Mineralogy and other branches of Natural History. London, 1797 or 1798. 8vo. pp. 231. 4s.
An admirable specimen of a mineralogical and geological tour. Fonthill, 2148, 9s.
— Arthur and C. R. Dictionary of Chemistry and Mineralogy. Lond. 1807. 4to. 2 vols. with an Appendix, 1814. 4to. 5l. 15s. 6d.
An invaluable condensation of Chemical and Mineralogical science, the most comprehensive in the English language.
— Edmund. Designs for Villas, and other Rural Buildings. Lond. 1808. 4to. With 31 plates, 18s.
— Essay on the Doric Order of Architecture. London, 1810. imperial folio, 15s.
— Plans, Elevation, Section, and View of the Cathedral Church of St. Paul, London; engraved by J. Le Keux from Drawings by James Elmes, architect; with an historical and descriptive account by Edmund Aikin, architect. London, 1813. Elephant 4to.

Five plates, with an Essay of 18 pages, (B—F.) also title and preface of 2 pages, signed J. B. (John Britton.) Some copies were printed in Atlas 4to. This publication originally appeared in the first volume of 'The Fine Arts of the English School.'

— John, M. D. Essays on Song Writing, with a collection of such English songs as are most eminent for poetical merit. To which are added some original pieces. London, 1772. 8vo. 3s. 6d.

A much esteemed and elegant collection, reprinted at Warrington, 1774, and Dublin, 1777.

— New edition, with additions and corrections, and a supplement by R. H. Evans. London, 1810. crown 8vo. pp. 380. 9s.

The best edition.

— Vocal poetry, or a select Collection of English Songs. To which is prefixed, an Essay on Song Writing. Lond. 1810. post 8vo. pp. 304. 9s.

This edition, as well as that of R. H. Evans, is considerably enlarged. Dr. Aikin likewise published 'An Essay on Application of Natural History to Poetry,' 1777, small 8vo. 2s. 6d.; and 'Letters on a Course of English Poetry,' 1804, 12mo. 3s.

— Letters from a Father to his Son, on various Topics relative to Literature and the Conduct of Life. London, 1793-1800. 8vo. 2 vols. 9s.

— Description of the Country from thirty to forty miles round Manchester. London, 1795. 4to.

Contains pp. xvi. 624, with list of subscribers, and 73 plates, 2l. 2s. LARGE PAPER. 3l. 13s. 6d.

The large map is frequently wanting. Willett, 74, russia, 2l. 5s. Edwards, 647, russia, 2l. 10s. Beckford, 1817. No. 144, russia, 2l. 15s.

— Lives of John Selden, and Archbp. Usher, with Notices of the principal English Men of Letters with whom they were connected. London, 1811, 8vo. 6s.

— Annals of the reign of King George III. from its commencement in 1760 to his death in 1820. Third edition. London, 1825, 8vo. 2 vols. 1l.

An abridgement in 12mo. 4s. 6d.

— England Delineated. London, 1818, 8vo. 14s.

The former editions of this useful work, chiefly designed for the use of young persons, appeared in 1788, 1795, 1803.

— and others. General Biography; or Lives of the most eminent persons, arranged according to alphabetical order. London, 1799-1815, 4to. 10 vols.

'A worthless compilation,' according to Gifford. Sir M. M. Sykes, pt. 1. 122, 3l. 10s. Hollis, 172, 12l.

— Lucy. Memoirs of the Court of Queen Elizabeth. Lond. 1818, 8vo. 2 vols. with portrait of the Queen, 1l. 5s.

Reprinted 1823.

— Memoirs of the Court of King James the First. London, 1822, 8vo. 2 vols. 1l. 4s. Reprinted 1826.

Vol. I. pp. 444, with portrait. Vol. II. pp. 408, 1l. 4s. An admirable historical work, 'nearly,' says the Edinb. Review, 'as entertaining as a novel, and far more instructive than most histories.'

— Life of Joseph Addison, 2 vols. small 8vo. London, 1843. 10s. 6d.

Severely reviewed by Macaulay in the *Edinburgh Review*, July, 1843.

— Memoirs of John Aikin, M.D., with a selection of his miscellaneous Pieces, biographical, moral, and critical. London, 1824, 8vo. 2 vols. 1l. 4s.

AILMER, John, LL.D. Musæ Sacræ: seu Jonas, Jeremiæ Threni, et Daniel, Græco redditi Carmine. Oxoniæ, 1652, 12mo. 5s.

According to Ant. à Wood, Ailmer was 'accounted an excellent Grecian, and a good Greek and Latin poet, as appears by this book, which he composed when a young man.'

AILMER. See AYLMER.

AINSLIE, John. Treatise on Land Surveying. Edinb. 1812, 4to. with plates, 18s.

AINSWORTH, Henry. Annotations on the five books of Moses, the Psalms, and the Song of Solomon. Lond. 1639, folio, 1l. 1s. to 1l. 7s.

Best edition of a laborious and useful work, containing a literal translation of all the books mentioned, as well as annotations on them. The substance is given in the Latin Synopsis of Poole.

— Two Treatises. The first of the Communion of Saints; the second, entitled an Arrow against Idolatry. To this edition is prefixed some Account of the Life and Writings of the Author. Edinburgh, 1792. 8vo. pp. 344. 3s. 6d.

The other writings of this eminent Nonconformist Divine of the sect called Brownists, who died 1622, are in some estimation.

— Robert. Dictionary of the Latin Tongue. London, 1752. folio, 2 vols. 3l. 3s.

The first edition of this work was published 1736, 4to. Reprinted with additions by Patrick, 1746, 4to. 2 vols. 25s. LARGE PAPER, 35s. 1751, 4to. 28s. 1761, 4to. A very correct edition, 1l. 11s. 6d. By Thomas Morell, 1773. 1778. 1783. 1796. 1808. 1l. 11s. 6d. to 2l. 2s. each. The edition, 1752, in folio. Willett, 112, 4l. 4s. (This folio edition, which is considered the best, was reprinted without *abridgment*, but with considerable additions by the Rev. B. W. Beatson and Wm. Ellis, in one vol. imperial 8vo. Lond. 1840, and since, 16s.)

— Another Edition, revised by Dr. Carey. London, 1816. 4to. 2l. 15s.

Reprinted 1823. There have been abridgements of this work by Young, Thomas, Morell, and Jamieson.

— Wm. Marrow of the Bible in Verse. London, 1652. 12mo. 7s.

Nassau, pt. i. 25, 17s.

Air Bank.—An Account of the Fall of the Air Bank. 1778. 4to.

Roxb. 9352, 1l. 3s.

AIRAY, Henry. Lectures upon the whole Epistle of St. Paul to the Philippians. London, 1618. 4to.

The work of a rigid Calvinist.

Aires and Dialogues, Select, composed by John Wilson, C. Coleman, H. and W. Lawes, &c. London, 1653. folio, 2l. 2s.

A valuable and esteemed collection. Reprinted 1659. 1669. Bindley, pt. iii. 1250, date 1669, 3l. 5s.

AITON, William. Hortus Kewensis; or a Catalogue of the Plants cultivated in the Royal Botanic Garden at Kew. London, 1789. 8vo. 3 vols. 10s. 6d.

A most curious, instructive, and excellent botanical work, which for scientific arrangement and execution has never been surpassed.

— Hortus Kewensis. New edition, enlarged by his Son, W. T. Aiton. London, 1810-1811. 8vo. 5 vols. 3l. 3s.

An Epitome of this edition was published 1814, 8vo. 12s. Some copies were printed with references to where the plants are figured, 16s.

Ajax his Speech to the Grecian Knabbs; from Ovid's Metam. Lib. xiii. Consedere duces, et vulgi stante corona, &c., attempted in broad Buchans, by R(obert) F(orbes), Gent. To which is added a Journal to Portsmouth, and a Shop-Bill, in the same Dialect; with a Key. Edinb. 1765, 12mo. 5s.

To this edition the Polemo Middinia is subjoined. An edition, Edinb. 1754. Roxburghe, 3461, 9s.

Akbar, or Akber. *See* Ayeen Akbery.

Akbur of Betlis. Fragments, containing Reflections on the Laws, Manners, Customs, and Religions, of certain Asiatic, Afric, and European Nations. London, 1784-5. 8vo. 3 vols.

AKENSIDE, Mark. Poems. London, 1772, 4to. With portrait, ætat. 35. Profile by E. Fisher, 12s. Copies on fine writing-paper, 18s.

An elegant edition. Akenside's Poems are inserted in Anderson, Chalmers, and every subsequent Collection of British Poets. Heath, 1764, 1l. 3s. On fine writing paper, Hollis, 173, 1l. 11s. 6d. Roscoe, 1419, 1l. 17s.

— Works. New Brunswick, New Jersey, 1808, 12mo. 2 vols. 7s. 6d.

This edition contains some pieces never before printed. In 1796 was published his Pleasures of Imagination, with a critical Essay, by Mrs. Barbauld, 12mo. with plates after Stothard, 5s.

Akerby, George. Life of Mr. James Spiller, the late Comedian. London, 1729. 8vo. *portrait*.

ALABASTER, William. Roxana Tragœdia & Plagiarii Unguibus vindicta, aucta et recognita ab Authore. Londini. 1632. 12mo. with front. by

Gaywood, containing an interior view of the theatre.

Praised by Dr. Johnson as a composition equal to the Latin Poetry of Milton. Boswell, 31, 5s. 6d. Inglis, No. 9, 6s. Reed, 8469, 8s. Nassau, pt. i. 26, morocco, 1l. A surreptitious edition was published the same year.

—— Lexicon Pentaglotton, Hebraicum, Chaldaicum, Syriacum, Talmudico—Rabbinicum et Arabicum. Londini, 1637. folio, 6s.

This writer likewise published several other works, and is styled by Ant. à Wood, 'the rarest poet and Grecian that any one age or nation produced.' He attended as chaplain on Robert, Earl of Essex, in the Cadiz voyage, where he changed his religion, and wrote 'Seven Motives' for what he had done, answered by John Racster, 1598, and by Roger Fenton, 1599.

ALAN, William, Cardinal. *See* ALLEN.

ALANE or ALANUS. *See* HALES.

Alarum for London; or, the Siege of Antwerp; with the ventrous Actes and valorous Deeds of the lame Soldier. Acted by the Lord Chamberlain's servants. London, 1602. 4to.

The plot is taken from 'The tragical History of the City of Antwerp.' Rhodes, 5, 1l. 19s. Inglis' Old Plays, 133, 4l. 10s.

Alazono-Mastix; or, the Character of a Cockney: in a Satyricall Poem. Dedicated (as a New-Year's-Gift) to the Apprentices of London. By Junius Anonymus, a London Apprentice. Lond. 1651. 4to. pp. 16.

An account of this curious satirical poem will be found in the Retrosp. Review, viii. 328-35.

Alban, St.—De inclyti et gloriosi Protomartyris Anglie Albani quem in Germania et Gallia Albinum vocant, Conversione, Passione, Translatione, ex Miraculorum Choruscatione. (Coloniæ, 1502.) 4to. black letter, 3l. 3s.

This very rare life of the English Saint and protomartyr, St. Alban, is dedicated to K. Henry viii. by the Abbot and Monks of the Monastery of St. Pantaleon, in Cologne.

—— *See* ALBON.

Albans, St. Some Account of the Church of St. Alban, Illustrative of the Plans, Elevation, and Sections of that Building. London, 1813. atlas folio.

Published by the Society of Antiquaries. North, pt. i. 137, 1l. 17s.

ALBEMARLE, Duke of. *See* MONK.

ALBERIUS Trencurianus, Claudius. A Demonstrative Oration of the Resurrection of the Deade. London, by Hugh Singleton, 8vo.

Black Letter. 15 leaves. Dedicated to the 'Draper's Societie,' by W. M. the translator.

ALBERONI, Julius, Cardinal. The political Testament; exhibiting a general View of the Politics and Interests of the several Courts of Europe. Translated from the Italian. London, 1753. 8vo. 5s.

A compilation of no authority, written by Maubert de Gouvest. A life of the Cardinal by G. Moore, appeared in 1808, 8vo., likewise a publication entitled 'Cardinal Alberoni's Scheme for reducing the Turkish Empire to the Obedience of Christian Princes,' without date.

ALBERTI, Leon Battista. Della Architettura, della Pittura, della Statua, &c. in Italian and English, by James Leoni. Lond. 1739. folio. 3 vols. with plates, 1l. 11s. 6d.

Fonthill, 877, 2l. 1s. An edition, London, 1726, 3 vols.

ALBERTUS MAGNUS. Liber Aggregationis seu Liber Secretorum Alberti Magni de Virtutibus Herbarum, Lapidum et Animalium quorundam. In Civit. London. per Wilh. de Mechlinia. 4to.

Black Letter. A. to D. in eights, E. six, and four without catch words or pagination. A 1, is blank. The most elegant specimen of Machlinia's press, according to Dr. Dibdin. A copy is in Earl Spenser's Library. White Knights, pt. i. 134, morocco, 7l. 10s.

—— The Booke of Secretes, ——, of the Vertues of Herbes, Stones, and certaine Beastes. Also a Booke of the same author of the maruaylous thinges of the world, and of certain effectes caused of certayne Beastes. London, by Wm. Copland. 16mo. 10s. 6d.

Black Letter. A. to L. 4. in eights. The last leaf blank. An edition of Albertus'

Secrets was published 1637, 12mo. in black letter, 5s.

ALBERTUS MAGNUS. De Secretis Mulierum: or the Mysteries of Human Generation fully revealed, faithfully rendered into English, with explanatory Notes, and approved of by the late John Quincy, M.D. London, 1725. 8vo. 5s.

A publication by Edmund Curll.

ALBERTUS, Sigandus. Liber Modorum Significandi Alberti. Apud Villam Sancti Albani, 1480. 4to.

Black letter. 46 leaves. a. b. c. d. e. in eights, and f. in sixes. The text begins on the recto of a. 1. A copy is in the Royal Library at Paris. Dr. Dibdin notices two other editions of this work, one without date, the other 1515, both printed by W. de Worde.

ALBIIS, Th. de. *i. e.* Thomas WHITE.

ALBIN, Eleazar. Natural History of English Insects. London, 1720. 4to. With 100 plates coloured, 1*l*. 11s. 6d.

Sotheby's in 1826, russia, 1*l*. 18s. Willett, 79, date 1724 5*l*. 10s.

— Natural History of English Insects, with Notes and Observations by W. Derham. London, 1749. 4to. 100 coloured plates, with a page of the text to each, 2*l*. 2s.

— Insectorum Angliæ Naturalis Historia, cum Annotat. Gul Derham. Lond. 1731. 4to. with 100 coloured plates.

— Natural History of Birds. London. 1731-4-8, 4to. 3 vols. 2*l*. 12s. 6d.

Vol. i. pp. 96, and 101 coloured plates. Vol. ii. pp. 92, and 104 coloured plates. Vol. iii. pp. 95, and 101 coloured plates. Willett, 81, 8*l*. 18s. 6d. A French translation, with Derham's Notes, &c., was published, a la Haye. 1750, 4to. 3 vols.

— Natural History of Spiders and other curious Insects. Lond. 1736. 4to. 1*l*. 1s.

pp. 76, with 53 coloured plates, and a portrait of Albin on horseback, by J. Scotin. The principal parts of this well-known work are inserted in the 'Aranei of Thomas Martyn,' 1793, 4to. Willett, 80, 3*l*. 7s. M. of Townshend, No. 138. Birds, Insects, and Spiders, 1736-49, 4to. 5 vols. 16*l*. 16s.

— Natural History of English Song-Birds; a new edition, corrected, with several Improvements under the article of Canary Birds. London, 1779. 8vo. With plates, plain, 3s. coloured, 7s.

The former editions, London, 1737, 1747, 1759, and Edinb. 1776.

— History of Esculent Fish, with North's Essay on Fish and Fish Ponds. Lond. 1794. 4to. pp. 80, with 18 coloured plates, 16s.

In little estimation.

— John. A History of the Isle of Wight, from the earliest times of authentic information to the present period. Newport, 1795, 8vo. With a sheet map. 8s.

Fonthill, 2140, 1*l*. 12s.

ALBINE, called De Seres, John de. A notable Discourse, discussing who are the right ministers of the Catholike Church: with an Offer made by a Catholike to a learned Protestant, wherein shall appere the difference betwixte the open knowen Church of the Catholikes, from the hid unknowen Congregation of the Protestantes. Duaci per Johannem Bellerum, 1575, 16mo.

The work, the running title of which is ' A notable Discourse against Heresies,' is introduced by a preface, and consists of 98 leaves, numbered. The ' Offer' C. in eights, the last leaf blank. This work, written against Calvin and his Disciples, was answered by Thomas Spark and Robert Crowley.

ALBINOVANUS, C. Pedo. The Elegies, with an English version, by J. Plumtre, D.D. Kidderminster, 1807. 12mo. pp. 127, 4s. FINE PAPER, 5s. 6d.

The original will also be found in Maittaire's Corpus Poetarum Latinorum.

ALBINUS, Bernard Siegfred. Anatomical Tables of the Skeleton and Muscles of the Human Body. London, 1749-50. impl. folio. 29 Nos. in 1 vol. 3*l*. 3s.

A complete anatomical description of the human skeleton and muscles, very accurately engraved. The following should accompany this much-esteemed work. 1. Three whole-length anatomical tables, representing a man, and a woman, 5s. 2. A compleat system of the blood vessels on four sheets, with tables of explanation on seven sheets, 7s. 6d. 3. A complete system of the nerves, on four sheets, with tables of explanation, 7s. 6d. Willett, 114, (complete) 6l.

— Another Edition, 1777. folio. with explanations in 4to. 2l. 2s.

Albion's Queene. The famous Historie of. London, 1601. 4to.

Black letter. Of this romance, (of which only one copy is known, wanting sheet A.) Queen Katherine is the heroine.

Albon and Amphabel.—The glorious Lyfe and Passion of Seint Albon, Prothomartyr of Englande, and also the Lyfe and Passion of Saint Amphabel, translated out of Frenche and Laten in to Englishe, by John Lydgate, Monke of Bury. Saynt Albon, 1534. 4to.

The whole contains y, in fours. In seven line stanzas, four on a page. A copy of this extremely rare work is in the British Museum.

Alborow.—The Life of the holy and blessed Virgin, Sainte Alborow. (Richard Pynson) 4to.

From Maunsell's Catal. p. 67, col. 2.

ALBUCASIS. De Chirurgia, Arab. et Lat. cura Johannis Channing. Oxon. 1778. 4to. 2 vols. 1l. 5s. LARGE PAPER, 1l. 16s.

A valuable work. In Dr. Freind's History of Physic is a very elaborate analysis of Albucasis's works and practice.

Alcantara's (P.) Golden treatise of Mental prayer, by Giles Willoughby. 12mo. port. and front. Bruxelles, 1632, 10s. 6d.

ALCÆUS.

The purest text of this poet will be found in the Museum Criticum, vol. 1, pp. 421-44, edited by Bishop Blomfield.

ALCEDO, Don Ant. de. Geographical and Historical Dictionary of America and the West Indies, with large additions and Compilations, by G. A. Thompson. London, 1812-15. 4to. 5 vols.

Thompson's edition for its additions, &c. is infinitely more valuable than the original. Sir M. Sykes, pt. i. 125, 5l. 5s. Duke of York, 235, 5l. 5s.

Alchemy.—Marrow of Alchemy, a Poem. London, 1654. 4to.

Nassau, pt. i. 2197, 19s. Sir P. Thompson, 463, 17s. 6d.

ALCIATUS, Andrew. Emblemata. *See* WILLET, Andrew.

To this work, first published Paris, 1565, subsequent writers, particularly George Wither, have been greatly indebted.

ALCIDALIS and ZELIDA, History of, a Tale of the fourteenth century. Lond. 1789. 8vo.

Some copies have a fictitious title, purporting to have been printed at Strawberryhill, MDCCLXXXIX., and have produced considerable prices, viz. Sotheby's in June, 1827, 1l. 6s. Brockett, 2947, 1l. 13s. Goldsmid, 373, 2l. 5s.

Alcilia: Philoparthens loving Folly. 12mo. R. Hawkins, 1613.

Bright, 45, (two leaves wanting) 3l. 10s.

— Philoparthens louing Folly. With the Love of Amos and Laura, by S. P. [Samuel Page.] Lond. for Richard Hawkins, 1619. 12mo.

The poem of Amos and Laura is dedicated to the celebrated Izaak Walton.

— Whereunto is added Pigmalion's image, with the loves of Amos and Laura, and also Epigrammes by Sir J. H. [Harrington] R. Hawkins, 1628, 4to.

Lloyd, 208, 10l. Freeling, 10l. 5s. Chalmers, 10l. Jolly, 43, 12l. 5s.

ALCINOUS, in Platonicam Philosophiam Introductio, Gr. et Lat. (ediderunt Jo. Langbænius et Jo. Fellus.) Oxon. 1667. 8vo. 2s. 6d.

An excellent edition. A translation of the introduction to the Platonic Philosophy will be found in Stanley's History of Philosophy.

ALCIPHRON's Epistles, in which are described the domestic Manners, the Courtesans, and Parasites of Greece, (translated from the Greek by the Rev. Mr. Monro and the Rev. Wm. Beloe.) London, 1791. 8vo. 4s.

This work is in general (says Dr. A. Clarke) well done; and is accompanied by very useful notes.

ALCOCK, John. Successively Bishop of Rochester, Worcester, and Eli, Spousage of a Virgin to Christ. 4to. 1486.

— Gallicantus et Cōfratres suos curatos in Sinodo apud Bernwell, xxv. die mensis Septembris, 1498. (Lond. per R. Pynson) folio.

The work consisting of 26 leaves, (A—D vi. in eights,) is divided into xvi chapters. A copy is in the library of Earl Spencer.

— Sermo Johis Alcok, Epi Elien. Enprinted at Westmestre bi Wynkin the Worde. 4to.

Black letter, extends to d viij. In this sermon the Bishop directs his hearers to obtain full knowledge of all proclamations as registered in the Court of Chancery. Two short extracts from this work to confirm the elucidation of the well-known line in Hamlet—

'Unhouseld, disappointed, unanel'd,' will be found in the British Bibliographer, ii. 532-3.

— Mons Perfectionis, otherwyce called in Englyssh, the Hylle of Perfection. Emprynted by Rycharde Pynson, in the xiii yere of K. Henry the vii. (1497.) 4to.

Black letter, e iij. An exhortation to the Carthusians, recommending prayer, obedience, and the solitude of the cell. Willett, 1629, (with the Abbaye of the Holy Ghost,) 9l. 19s. 6d. Dr. Dibdin, in his much improved edition of Ames, notices three editions, one by Pynson, 1497, and two by W. de Worde, 1497 and 1501.

— The Abbaye of the Holy Ghost. Westmestre, by W. de Worde, 4to.

Black letter, 18 leaves printed in double columns. Willett, 1629. (with Mons Perfectionis,) 9l. 19s. 6d. Maunsell mentions an edition of the date of 1531.

ALCORAN. *See* MAHOMET.

Alcoran of the Franciscans. *See* FRANCIS, St.

ALDINI, John. An Account of the late Improvements in Galvanism, &c. London, 1803. 4to. with plates, 9s.

In 1819 was published another work by this author, entitled 'General Views on the Application of Galvanism to Medical Purposes.' 6s.

ALDRICH, Henry, D.D. Artis Logicæ Compendium. Oxon. 1691. large 8vo. Six sheets. With Aristotle's portrait in the title page, 3s.

Reprinted, with variations and additions, 1696, 1704, 1750, and still used as a text book at Oxford. A translation, with Questions, appeared in 1825, 12mo. 3s. 6d.

— The Elements of Civil Architecture, translated by the Rev. Philip Smyth. Lond. 1789, royal 8vo. with 55 plates, and a portrait of Aldrich, after Kneller, 12s. to 15s.

According to the Rev. J. C. Eustace, 'a very clear and concise treatise on the general principles, proportions, and terms of this art, and may be recommended as a good work of the kind for the use of beginners.' A third edition was published at Oxford, in 1821. Unpublished editions of the Elem. Archit. and Instit. Geom. at Bindley's Sale, pt. i. No. 204, brought 1l. 1s.

ALDUS. *Vide* MANUTIUS, Aldus.

Alector, the Cock, 1590. *See* ANEAU, Bart.

ALEMAN, Mateo. The Life of Guzman d'Alfarache; or, the Spanish Rogue: to which is added the celebrated Tragi-Comedy, Celestina. Done into English from the new French Version, and compar'd with the original (Spanish). By several Hands. Lond. 1708. 8vo. 2 vols. With sculptures, by Gaspar Bouttats.

Roxburghe, 6347, 1l. 10s. Of this very popular Novel, or Romance, there have been several translations, in folio, 1623, 1630, 1634, 1656, 10s. to 15s. each. In the Retrospective Review, vol. v. 189—205, is an excellent notice of this work, which contains a fund of acute and comprehensive observations on almost every rank in society, from the most abject to the most elevated. An edition 'epitomiz'd into English, by A. S. Gent,' appeared in 1655. 8vo.

ALEMAND, Louis Augustine. Histoire Monastique d'Irlande. Paris, 1690. 12mo. 5s.

This work was afterwards enlarged by Captain Stevens, and published under the title of Monasticon Hibernicum. *See* ARCHDALL.

ALEN. *See* ALLEN.

ALES, or ALESIUS. *See* HALES.

ALEXANDER de Alexandria, in iii Libros Aristotelis de Anima. Impressum per me Theodoric Rood de Colonia in alma Vniu'sitate Oxon. M.CCCC.LXXXI. Small folio.

Printed in double columns. G 6 and Y 8 are blank leaves. A copy wanting the title page is in the British Museum.

— de Villa Dei. Textus Alexandri cum Sententiis Constructionibus. Lond. Rich. Pynson, 1505. 4to.

Black letter, 50 leaves. Reprinted 1518, 4to. This work was for some centuries the most favourite manual of grammar used in schools. Dr. Dibdin mentions an edition of 1503, printed by W. de Worde, but questions its existence; and in the Bibl. Llwyd. No. 452, was a copy printed by Pynson, 1516, which produced 1l. 11s.

Alexander, Aphrodisiensis ad Imperatores de Fato et de eo quod nostræ Potestatis est. Ammonius Hermeæ in Libri Aristotelis de Interpretatione Sectionem secundam, Gr. et Lat. Londini, 1658, small 8vo. 3s. 6d. to 5s.

ALEXANDER, James Edward. Travels from India to England, 1825-6. London, 1827. 4to. with maps and plates, published at 1l. 11s. 6d.

'A performance,' says the Quarterly Review, 'obviously very juvenile, but containing many lively and interesting descriptions, more particularly of scenes in Burmah and Asia Minor.'

— John. Paraphrase upon the Fifteenth Chapter of the First Epistle to the Corinthians, with critical Notes and Observations, and a Preliminary Dissertation. A Commentary, with critical Remarks upon the sixth, seventh, and part of the eighth Chapters of the Romans. To which is added a Sermon on Ecclesiastes ix. 10, composed by the Author the day preceding his Death. Lond. 1766. 4to. 5s.

The work of an Unitarian, containing a few good critical remarks. Hollis, 174, 12s. 6d.

— Will. *See* STERLINE, Earl of.

— William. Medulla Historiæ Scotiæ, being a History of the Lives and Reigns of the Kings of Scotland, from Fergus I. to Charles II. Lond. 1685. 12mo. 5s.

— A short Survey of the Lineal Descent of the Sovereign Princes in Europe. Edinb. 1704. 8vo.

Constable, No. 13, 7s.

— William, M.D. The History of Women, from the earliest Antiquity to the present Time. London, 1779. 4to. 2 vols. 12s.

Reprinted 1782, 8vo. 2 vols. Heath, 1420, 12s. 6d.

— William. Sketches from Nature, made in China. London, 1797. royal 8vo.

This ingenious artist was draftsman to Earl Macartney during his embassy to China, and afterwards in the print department of the British Museum. *See* COMBE, Taylor, and Costume of China.

— Observations on the construction and Fitting up of Meeting Houses, &c. for Public Worship. Lond. 1820. 4to. with plans, &c. 9s.

· Alexander, a Romance. *See* No. 46 Bannatyne Club.

Inserted by Weber in his Collection of Metrical Romances, vol. i. In the Library of the Hon. W. Maule of Panmure is a translation (probably unique) of this romance into Scotish verse, printed by Alexander Arbuthnot.

Alexander and the King of Egypt. A mock Play, as it is acted by the Mummers every Christmas. Newcastle, 1788. 4to.

Rhodes, No. 7, 11s.

ALEXIS of Piedmont. The Secrets, in Four Parts, translated by William Warde. London, by H. Bynneman, 1568. 4to.

Black letter. This work, which has been translated and published in every European language, is by Haller attributed to Hieronymo Rosello. Inglis, 106, 15s. Reprinted 1595, 10s. 6d. and 1615, 7s. 6d. The following is a list of the separate editions of the four parts. Part i. 1559, 1562, 1563, 1569, 1580. Part ii. 1563, n. d., 1567, 1580. Part. iii. 1566, 1578. Part iv. (translated by Rich. Ambrose) 1569, 1578.

ALEYN, Charles. The Battailes of Crescey and Poictiers. London, 1633. 8vo. pp. 138.

Second edition. White Knights, pt. i. 55, 1l. Lloyd, 23*, 1l. 4s. Nassau, pt. i. 27, 1l. 11s. 6d. Garrick, No. 12, (with the Historie of Henrie the Seventh) 2l. 5s. Bibl. Anglo-Poet. No. 555. The former edition appeared in 1631.

— The Historie of Henrie, of that name the Seventh King of England. With that famed Bataile upon Redmore, near Bosworth. London, 1638. 8vo.

Contains pp. 160. (A, 2 leaves, B—K, in eights, and L, 6 leaves) with portrait of the King, by Marshall. Strettell, 10, 17s. Sir M. M. Sykes, pt. i. 39, 17s. pt. ii. 1, 1*l.* 1s. Lloyd, 24, 18s. Jadis, 95, 18s. Bibl. Anglo-Poet. No. 10, morocco, 1*l.* 16s. Nassau, pt. i. 28, 2*l.* 2s. Dowdeswell, 3, 2*l.* 12s. 6d. Aleyn likewise published the History of Euryalus and Lucretia, translated from the Latin epistles of Æneas Sylvius.

ALEYN, John. Select Cases in B. R. 22, 23, and 24 K. Charles I. with the Names of the learned Counsel who argued the same. London, 1681 or 1688. folio. 8s.

Alfagus and Archelaus. A notable history of two faithful lovers, named Alfagus and Archelaus, wherein is declared the true figures of Amitie and Freyndshyp. Imp. by Colwell, 1574. 4to.

Black letter, Roxburghe, 10*l.* 10s. Sotheby, May, 1856, 80*l.*

ALFIERI, Vittorio. Quindici Tragedie, dedicate all' Autore medesimo ed aggunteri sue Memorie letterarie, con la Merope di Maffei, e l'Aristodemo di Monti; dall' Editore il Dott. Antonio Montucci. Edinborgo, 1805-6. 12mo. 3 vols. 1*l.* 1s.

A very neat and correct edition. Zotti published an edition of 'Tragedie scelte.' 12mo. 2 vols. 10s.

— The Tragedies, translated by Charles Lloyd. London, 1815. 12mo. 3 vols. 10s. 6d.

An excellent translation.

— Vita di Vittorio Alfieri. Londra, 1806. 8vo. 2 vols. 10s.

An English translation of this poet's Life appeared in 1810. 8vo. 2 vols. 10s.

ALFORDUS (M.) Britannia illustrata sive Lucii, Helenæ Constantini, Patria et Fides. 4to. Antv. 1641.

Horner, 1854, 3*l.* 5s.

ALFORDUS, M. *Vide* GRIFFITH, Michael.

ALFRED the Great. The Will of King Alfred, with Notes by Thos. Astle. Oxford, 1787. 4to. 5s.

This work was superintended by Sir H. Croft, and contains the illustrations of Mr. Manning. Dr. Johnson observed, that the notes are 'very judicious and accurate, but, they are too few.' Roscoe, 461, 6s. 6d.

This illustrious monarch likewise was translator of Bede's Ecclesiastical History, Boethius' Consolation of Philosophy, and a Portion of the historian Orosius. For the Lives of him, *see* ASSER, Menevensis; BICKNELL, Alex.; SPELMAN, Sir John; POWELL, Robert.

ALGAROTTI, Francis. Sir Isaac Newton's Philosophy, explained for the Use of the Ladies; in six Dialogues of Light and Colours. From the Italian, by Eliz. Carter. London, 1739. 12mo. 2 vols. 6s.

Reprinted 1742. Several other pieces of Algarotti's have been translated into English, viz. Letters containing the State of the Persian Empire, 1769. 12mo. 2 vols. 5s. Essays on Painting and on the Opera, 1764. 1767. 12mo. 2 vols. 5s. &c.

Algiers Voyage, in a Journall, or briefe Reportary of all Occurrents hapning in the Fleet of Ships sent out by the Kinge his most excellent Majestie, as well against the Pirates of Algiers as others. London, 1621. 4to.

North, pt. iii. 597, 19s. Gordonstoun, 128, 1*l.* 5s.

Algorisme. *See* Arithmetic.

ALHACEN. The History of Tamerlane the Great, by his Favourite Alhacen, a learned Arabian. Translated into English, with Notes, by L. Vane. London, 1753. 8vo. 4s.

Reprinted 1783, 12mo. 2s. 6d.

ALI BEY. Travels of Ali Bey in Morocco, Tripoli, Cyprus, Egypt, Arabia, Syria, and Turkey, between the years 1803 and 1807, written by himself. London, 1816. 4to. 2 vols. with plates.

This traveller, whose original name was Domingo Badia y Leblich, was a native of Spain. He, under his assumed character, procured access to many places, to which Christians were not permitted to go; from this cause his travels are instructive and curious, but they certainly disappointed the expectations of the public. Drury, 147, russia, 3*l.* 5s.

ALI Ebn Abi Talebi. Sententiæ, Arab. et Lat. e Codd. MSS. descripsit, Latine vertit, et Annotationibus illustravit Cornelius van Waenen. Oxonii, 1806. 4to. pp. xvi. and 428, 1*l.*

A correct and valuable edition.

ALI. Sentences of Ali, Son-in-Law of Mahomet, translated from an Arabick MS. in the Bodleian, by Simon Ockley. London, 1717 or 1718. 8vo. 3s. 6d.
Likewise to be found in Ockley's History of the Saracens, third edition.

Alien Priories. *See* GOUGH, Richard.

Alimony, Lady, or the Alimony Lady, an excellent pleasant new Comedy. London, 1659. 4to.
Attributed by Ant. à Wood to Thomas Lodge and Robert Greene. Rhodes, 225, 14s. Reed, 7485, 1l. 2s.

Ali Pacha of Janina, Vizier of Epirus, The Life of, including a compendious History of modern Greece. London, 1823. 8vo. with portrait and plates, 10s. 6d.

Alsiaunder, Kyng. *See* Alexander, a Romance.

ALISON, Archibald. Essays on the Nature and Principles of Taste. Fourth Edition. Edinb. 1816. 8vo. 2 vols. 16s.
An excellent and highly pleasing work, first published 1790, 4to. 1 vol. 10s. 6d.

— Sermons, chiefly on particular occasions. Edinb. 1814-15. 8vo. 2 vols. 16s.
Frequently reprinted. According to Dr. Dibdin, the beautiful and refined fancy and melodious style of this writer render his works deserving of a conspicuous place in every well-chosen library.

— Richard. An Houres Recreation in Musicke, apt for Instruments and Voyces. Lon. 1606. 4to.
Bibl. Anglo-Poet. No. 116.

Alithinologia, 1664-1667. *Vide* LYNCH, John.

ALLAN, George, of Darlington. Collections relating to Sherburn Hospital, in Durham. Printed in the year 1771. 4to.
Fifty copies printed without signatures or paging, consisting of 156 leaves, and 4 plates. Bindley, pt. i. 1640, 2l. 9s. Dent, pt. ii. 1037. 1l. 15s. 8l.t. M. M. Sykes, pt. i. 1003. 3l.

— Collectanea Dunelmensia. Tracts relating to the County of Durham, 4to.
Bindley, pt. i. 1641. 5l. 7s. 6d. Leigh and Sotheby's in Nov. 1800. 5l. 15s. 6d. Sotheby's in Dec. 18²²2. 5l. 15l. 6d.' Allan in March, 1822, no. 623. 19l. A tract, entitled 'Address and Queries relative to a History of Durham.' Darlington, 1774. Brocket, 217, 1l. 6s.

— Catalogue of Books and Tracts, printed at the private press of G. Allan, Esq. Newcastle, 1818. 8vo. 7s.
One hundred copies printed. At the sale of the library of Mr. Brockett (Cat. No. 231) a collection of the tracts printed at the Darlington private press, were sold for 52l. 10s.

— Robert. Dictionary of the ancient Language of Scotland. Edinb. 1804. 4to. No. 1, 3s.

— A Treatise on the Operation of Lithotomy. Edinb. 1808. folio. with plates, 1l. 1s.
This eminent surgeon likewise published an esteemed work, entitled 'A System of pathological and operative Surgery,founded on Anatomy,' 8vo. vol. i. 1819, 12s. 6d. vol. ii. 1822, 12s. 6d, vol. iii. pt. i. 1824. 8s. 6d.

ALLASON, Thomas. Picturesque Views of the celebrated Antiquities of Pola in Istria. London, 1819. folio.
This work was printed in super-royal folio, pp. 67, with 10 plates and 4 vignettes, engraved by the Cookes, H. Moses and C. Armstrong, 2l. 2s. imperial folio, corresponding in size,with Stuart's Athens, with proof plates on French paper, 3l. The same with plates on India paper, proofs, 3l. 10s.

ALLDAY, John. A complainte of the poor husbandmen. Imp. T. Hackett.
Black letter (Ritson Bib. Poet).

ALDRIDGE, W. T. Goldsmith's Repository: containing a concise elementary Treatise on the Art of assaying Metals, &c. London, 1789. 8vo. pp. 382. 9s.
A useful work.

ALLEINE, Joseph. Alarm to unconverted Sinners and other Works. Edinb. 1752. 12mo. 2 vols. 10s. 6d.
The writings of this non-conformist Divine are in some estimation, particularly his Alarm to unconverted Sinners, which has been often reprinted. His life was

ALL ALL 31

published by Rich. Baxter, 1672 and 1677, 8vo., and also by George Newton, 1673, 8vo. See Dr. Bliss's Wood's Athen, Oxon. iii. 819-22.

— Richard. Works, in four Parts. London, 1671. 8vo.

The writings of this zealous non-conformist (of which the above only forms a part) are much admired by those of Calvinistic sentiments, particularly his Vindiciæ Pietatis, 1664-6, 3 pts. A list of his writings will be found in Bliss's edition of Wood's Athenæ Oxon. iv. 13-15.

ALLEN, Benjamin. Natural History of the Chalybeate and Purging Waters of England, with their Essays and Uses. Lond. 1699. 8vo.

Dent, pt. i. 29, morocco, 15s. 6d. Allen also published the Natural History of the Mineral Waters of Great Britain, 1711. 8vo. Dent, pt. i. 30. mor. 12s.

— Edmond. Catechisme, that is to say a Christen Instruccion of the principall Pointes of Christes religion. London, 1551. 8vo. Black letter.

White Knights, pt. i. 53: morocco, 1l. 4s. A former edition, according to Dr. Dibdin, appeared in 1548.

— J. The younger Brother, his Apologie, or a Father's free Power disputed, for the Disposition of his Lands, &c. Oxf. 1624. 4to.

A notice of this work will be found in Oldys' British Librarian, 210—212. Gordonstoun, 39, 13s. Reed, 6517, 16s.

— John. Royal Spiritual Magazine, or Christian's Grand Treasure. Lond. 1761. 8vo. 3 vols. with plates, 15s.

Reprinted 1809. 8vo. 3 vols.

— Spiritual Exposition of the Bible, or the Christian's Gospel Treasure. Lond. 1765. fol. 2 vols. 2l. 2s.

Reprinted lately in 8vo. 4 vols. 2l. 10s. FINE PAPER, 3l. 3s.

— Modern Judaism, or a brief account of the Opinions, Traditions, Rites, and Ceremonies of the Jews in modern Times. London, 1816. 8vo. 10s. 6d.

The best work on modern Judaism in our language.

— Robert. The oderifferous garden of charitie, the most heavenlyest and holyest beatitude or blessing of God unto man, &c. London, 1603. 8vo.

Collation, 242 pages, besides Epistle dedicatory 8 pages, a general inscription 2 pages, and Errata 1 leaf.

— Thomas. Chain of Scripture Chronology, from the Creation to the Death of Christ, in seven Periods. London, 1659. 4to. 5s.

The most esteemed of this celebrated Non-conformist's works, with a frontispiece by Hollar, reprinted 1668.

— Thomas. History and Antiquities of the Parish and Palace of Lambeth. London, 1824-7. 8vo. 1l. 16s. 4to. 3l. 12s.

Mr. Allen has since published a History of London, 5 vols. 8vo. Yorkshire, 6 vols. 8vo. Lincolnshire, 2 vols. 4to. and other Topographical works.

ALLEN (or Alan), William, styled Cardinal of England. Defense and Declaration of the Catholike Churches Doctrine touching Purgatory, and Prayers for the Soules departed. Antwerp, by John Latius, 1565. 8vo. 10s.

Containing O o 7 in eights: This, according to Warton, 'was the basis of Alleyn's polemical reputation. It abounds, though, more in rhetoric than argument, and contains much ingenious declamation and sophistry.'

— Treatise made in Defence of the lauful Power and Authoritie of Priesthood to remitte Sinnes: of the Peoples Duetie for Confession of their Sinnes to Gods Ministers: and of the Churches Meaning concerning Indulgences, commonly called Pope's Pardôs. Lovanii, apud Joannem Foulerum, 1567. 16mo.

Contains pp. 412, with an index, besides an address and preface. Answered by Dr. Will. Fulke of Cambridge.

— Apologie and true Declaration of the Institution and Endeuours of the two English Colleges, the one in Rome, the other now resident in Rhemes. Mons in Henault, 1581. 8vo. 10s. 6d.

Contains 122 leaves. The running title of this book (which, according to Bolton in his Hypercritica, is 'a princely, grave, and flourishing piece of natural and exquisite

English') is 'An Apology for the English Seminaries.'

— An Admonition to the Nobility and People of England and Ireland concerninge the present Wares made for the Execution of his Holines Sentence, by the high and mightie King Catholike of Spain. By the Cardinal of Englande, 1588. 8vo.

Contains 60 pages, including the title. This work, together with A Declaration of the Sentence of Pope Sixtus the 5th, were printed at Antwerp, in order to be dispersed in England, when the Spaniard should arrive there. For a further notice of this work, *see* Nicolas's edition of Davison's Poetical Rhapsody, i. lxxiv. and Lingard's England, 8vo. viii. 585—9.

— Cardinal Alan. Justification pour le Catholique Chevalier, le Sieur Guillaume Stanley sur la rendition de la ville de Deventer. Paris, 1588.

Bright, 45. 4*l*. 4s.

— Gul. Ad persecutores Anglos pro Catholicis domi focisque persecutionem sufferentibus, contra fulsum libellum inscriptum Justitia Britannia, vera responsio 8vo. sine loco aut anno.

An answer to Cecil, Lord Burleigh's Execution of Justice in England, (at Doway in 1584.) Thorpe, 1838, mor. 2*l*. 2s. Sotheby, 1824, 1*l*. 10s.

— styled Cardinal of England. A Defence of English Catholiques against a slanderous Libel, intituled, The Execution of Justice in England. (Ingolst. about 1584) 8vo. 7s.

Contains 218 pages, besides preface, contents, and 'the faultes' corrected. This book, published anonymously, but confidently attributed to Cardinal Allen by Ant. à Wood, was answered by Dr. Tho. Bilson in 'The true Difference between Christian subiection and vnchristian Rebellion.' Oxf. 1585. The running title of Allen's treatise is 'An Answere to the Libel of English Justice.'

— *See* Titus. Col. Silas.

— D. D. Works, with a Preface by Bp. Williams, and a Sermon at the Funeral of Allen, by Bp. Kidder. Lond. 1707. Folio, 10s. 6d.

ALLESTREE, Richard, D. D. XL Sermons preached before the King, and on solemn occasions. Oxford, 1684. folio, with portrait by D. Loggan, 10s. 6d.

Best edition, with a life of Allestree published by Bishop Fell. To Bishop Fell and Dr. Allestree have been attributed the works written by the author of the Whole Duty of Man.

ALLEY, Rev. Jerome. Vindiciæ Christianæ; a comparative Estimate of the Genius and Temper of the Greek, the Roman, the Hindu, the Mahometan, and the Christian Religions. Lond. 1826. 8vo. 16s.

— William, Bishop of Exeter. ΠΤΩΧΟΜΥΣΕΙΟΝ, the poore Man's Librarie. London, by John Day, 1565. folio, 2 tomes.

Black letter. This work consists of lectures (7 and 5) upon the first epistle of St. Peter, with 'Miscellanea,' that is, many curious anecdotes and explanations of persons, places, &c., which, says Dr. Dibdin, manifest the author's extensive reading. Tome 1, fol. 292, the prefixes consist of some Latin verses of four pages, and an epistle dedicatory to 'Lorde Russel, Earle of Bedforde.' Tome 2, without any title-page, contains fol. 140, after which, tables for both tomes, on fourteen leaves more.

— Another edition, faithfully corrected and amended. London, by John Daye, 1571. folio. in 2 tomes. 1*l*. 11s. 6d.

Black letter. Tome 1 ends on folio 217, having the same prefixes as the edition of 1565. Tome 2 contains 110 leaves, with a title, and two indexes at the end.

ALLIBOND, John, D. D. Rustica Academiæ Oxoniensis nuper reformatæ Descriptio, in Visitatione Fanatica Octobris sexto, &c. A.D. 1648, cum Comitius ibidem anno sequente: et aliis Notatu cum Indignis. Folio.

A Latin poem of exquisite humour, twice printed in 1648; reprinted 1705, fol., and again with an Hudibrastic translation, by Edward Ward, in the fifth volume of the Somers collection of Tracts. A very curious copy with a complete key in MS. is to be found in Wood's study, No. 423.

ALLISON, Thomas. Voyage from

Archangel in Russia, in the year 1697, with an Account of the Ship and Company wintering near the North Cape, in the latitude of 71. London, 1699. 8vo. 5s.
Reprinted in the first volume of Pinkerton's Collection of Voyages and Travels.

ALLIX, Peter, D.D. Reflexions upon the Books of the Holy Scripture to establish the Truth of the Christian Religion. London, 1688. 8vo. 2 vols. 7s.
Reprinted in one volume, London, 1809, and Oxford, 1822, and also in vol. 1 of Bishop Watson's Collection of Theological Tracts, who states this work has been always held in great repute for the plainness and erudition with which it is written.

— Remarks upon the History of the Churches of Piedmont. London, 1690, 4to. 7s.
Reprinted Oxford, 1821, 8vo. 7s.

— Remarks upon the History of the Albigenses. London, 1692. 4to. 7s.
Reprinted Oxford, 1821, 8vo. 6s. 6d.

— Judgment of the Ancient Jewish Church against the Unitarians. London, 1699. 8vo. 10s.
A curious and interesting work, published anonymously. Gossett, 71, 1l. 1s. Reprinted Oxford, 1821, 8vo. 7s. 6d.

— Diatriba de Anno et Mense Natali Jesu Christi. London, 1710. 8vo. 3s. 6d.
An erudite work, in which Allix endeavours to shew that the Messiah was born not in winter, but in the spring. Reprinted 1722, 12mo.
A catalogue of the elaborate writings of this learned divine of the Church of England will be found in Watt's Bibliotheca Britannica.

ALLOT, Robert. England's Parnassus, or the choicest Flowers of our modern Poets, with their poeticall Comparisons, &c. whereunto are annexed other various Discourses both pleasaunt and profitable. London. N. L. C. B. and Th. Hayes. 1600. Small 8vo.
Of this work, reprinted by Park in the Heliconia, Warton observes, that the method is judicious, the extracts copious, and made with a degree of taste. The volume consists of title, dedication to Syr Thomas Mounson, Knt. to the reader, and errata six leaves: work B—Kk (510 pp.) afterwards a leaf, frequently wanting, containing 10 lines, commencing 'Fame's windy trump,' &c. (It is believed that this leaf belongs to another book.) Lloyd, 429, 2l. White Knights, pt. i. 61, mor. 2l. 12s. 6d. Sir M. M. Sykes, 41, mor. 2l. 16s. Strettell, 11, russia, 3l. 3s. Boswell, 898, 3l. 7s. Inglis, 14, 3l. 15s. Bindley, pt. i. 2108, 4l. 16s. Bibl. Anglo-Poet. 1, 20l. Roxburghe, 3171, 21l. Col. Stanley, 13l. 13s. Brand, 1l. 13s. Perry, 1l. 16s. North, 4l.

ALLWOOD, Rev. Philip. Literary Antiquities of Greece. Also, Remarks on some Observations in the British Critic. London, 1799, 1801. 4to. 15s.

— Twelve Lectures on the Prophecies relating to the Christian Church, being the ninth portion of those founded by Bishop Warburton, with a supplement. London, 1815, 1819. 8vo. 3 vols. 18s.

Almanac, a spiritual, wherein every Christen man and woman, may se what they ought daily to do, or leave undone, &c., &c. Impr. by R. Kele, n.d. 10s. 6d.

Almanac, The Owles, prognosticating, 4to. 1618. See Owls.

ALMON, John. Biographical, Literary, and Political Anecdotes of several of the most eminent persons of the present age, with an Appendix. London, 1797. 8vo. 3 vols.
This work, though partial, is interesting, as containing many curious particulars of the political characters and contests of the day. Reed, 3496, 12s. Sotheby's in 1827, 1l. 4s. An edition, 1790, 8vo.

Almond for a Parrat. See MARTIN MARPRELATE.

Alphabetum Latino Anglicum; Institutio compendiaria totius Grammaticæ quam—Rex noster hoc nomine evulgari iussit, &c. Londini, (in offic. T. Berthelet.) 4to. 1542.
The first part has 41 leaves, the last 40 leaves. Dr. Dibdin in his edition of Ames, mentions a copy on vellum, curiously illuminated.

Alphabetic Writing. Conjectural Observations on the Origin and

VOL. I. D

Progress of Alphabetic Writing. London, 1772. 8vo. 3s.
Written by the Rev. Charles Davy.

ALSOP, Antony. Odarum Libri duo. Londini, 1752. 4to. 5s.
These odes have been much admired, as breathing at once the ease and festivity of Horace, at the same time preserving his remarkable felicity of diction, without servility.

— George. The character of the Province of Maryland. London, 1666. 12mo.
A rare work, with a map and a portrait of Alsop, Æt. 28, six English verses. Lloyd, 27, 2l. 1s. Sotheby's in December, 1822, 2l. 2s. Another work entitled 'An Orthodox Plea,' 1669, with a portrait by W. Sherwin, 9s.

— Vincent. Anti Sozzo: an Answer to W. Sherlock's Discourse on Christ. London, 1675. 8vo. 7s.
A witty book, written by a celebrated non-conformist divine, who likewise published several other works which are held in some estimation.

ALSTEDIUS, John Henry. The beloved City, or the Saints' Reign on Earth, a thousand Years. London, 1643. 4to.
In this work Alstedius asserts, that the faithful shall reign with Jesus Christ 1000 years; after which will be the general resurrection, and the last judgment.

— Templum Musicum, or the Musical Synopsis. Translated from the Latin by John Birchensha. London, 1664. 8vo. with frontispiece by Chantry, 5s.

ALSTON, Charles, M.D. Lectures on the Materia Medica; also Directions for the Study, and an Appendix on the method of Prescribing. London, 1770. 4to. 2 vols. 12s.
In little estimation. This writer likewise published several other medical and botanical works.

ALTHAM, Roger, D.D. Sermons on several occasions. London, 1732. 8vo. 2 vols. 6s.
Williams, 35, 1l. 6s.

ALTIERI, Ferdin. Italian and English Dictionary, corrected and improved by Evangelist Palermo. Lond., 1750 or 1751. 4to. 2 vols. 15s.
Best edition. The former one of 1726, Willett, 82, 2l. 7s.

ALUREDUS Beverlacensis. *Vide* Hearne, Thomas.

ALVARUS, Eman. De Syllabarum Quantitate, Ars Metrica, et Lusus Poetices. London, 1730. 8vo. 6s.
A valuable grammatical treatise. LARGE PAPER. Dent, part i. 32, russia, 16s. Williams, 37, russia, 1l. 19s.

ALVES, Robert. Sketches of the History of Literature. Edinb. 1794, 8vo. pp. 298, 3s. 6d.

ALYNTON, Robert. Libellus Sophistarum. London, per W. de Worde, 1525. 4to.
Dr. Dibdin in his edition of Ames, notices five editions of this work; three by W. de Worde, and two by Pynson.

Amadis of Gaul.—The Treasurie of Amadis of Fraunce, translated from the French. Imprinted by Hen. Bynneman, 4to. Black letter.
Not mentioned by Herbert. North, pt. iii. 736, 1l. 7s. Inglis, 110, 1l. 19s. Goldsmid, 266, 5l.

— The History of Amadis de Gaule (Four Books) written in French by the Lord of Essars, Nicholas de Herberay. Translated by Anthony Munday. Lond. 1619. folio.
In this translation, says Dr. Southey, every trait of manners, which were foreign to Herberay, or obsolete in his time, are omitted, and all the foolish anachronisms and abominable obscenities of the Frenchmen are retained. Parts iii. and iv. have separate title pages of the date of 1618. Steevens, 1153. 2l. 8s. Hibbert, 5l. 12s. 6d. Bennett, 7l.

— The Fifth Book of the History of Amadis de Gaule, by J. J(ohnson). London, 1664. 4to. 10s. 6d.
Black letter.

— The Sixth Book of the History of Amadis de Gaule, translated by Francis Kirkman. London, 1652. 4to. 10s. 6d.

— The History of Amadis of Greece, together with the Enterprises of his Cozen Lucencio. London, 1694. small 4to. 15s.
Black letter, pp. 220. A translation from the seventh book of the Amadis de Gaul,

Nassau, pt. i. 157, russia, 19s. Roxburghe, 6363, 1*l.* 6s. Goldsmid, No. 407, date 1693, 1*l.* 11s. 6d.

— Amadis of Gaul, by Vasco Lobeira, from the Spanish Version of Garciordonez de Montalvo, by Robert Southey. London, 1803, 12mo. 4 vols. 1*l.* 16s.

An esteemed translation.

— A Poem in Three Books; freely translated from the first Part of the French Version of Nicholas de Herberay, Sieur des Essars; with Notes: by William Stewart Rose, Esq. London, 1803. crown 8vo. pp. 220. 6s.

Drury, 56, 8s. 6d.

Ambassador (The) his Behaviour, Charge, Privileges and Familie. London, 1603. 12mo. 5s.

Dedicated to Wm. Earle of Pembroke. Another work on this subject, entitled 'The perfect Ambassador,' was published 1651, by Francis Thynne.

AMBLER, Charles. Reports of Cases argued and determined in the High Court of Chancery, with some few in other Courts. London, 1790, folio, pp. 783, 1*l.* 5s. to 1*l.* 10s.

This volume consists of cases in Lord Hardwicke's time, with a few later determinations in the Court of Chancery, and fills up the time between Lord Hardwicke and Lord Thurlow. An Edition, Dublin, 1790, 8vo. 12s.

Amboyna. A true Relation of the Proceedings against the English at Amboyna, in the East Indies, by the Netherlandish Governour and Council there. Lond. 1624, 4to. with front. 12s.

Frequently reprinted. In the British Museum are many tracts relative to this cruel massacre, and in the second volume of the Oxford Collection of Voyages and Travels, six tracts relative to the affair will be found. North, pt. iii. 579. Three Tracts, 2*l.*.

AMBROSE, Isaac. The whole Works. London, 1701. folio, with portrait, 1*l.*

The works of this noted presbyterian teacher are much esteemed by the Calvinists, particularly his 'Looking unto Jesus,' first published, London, 1658, 4to. and frequently since reprinted both in 4to. and 8vo. Editions of the works were published 1674. 1682. 1689. 1769. in folio. Glasgow, 1796. 8vo. 4 vols. Manchester, 1799. 8vo. 2 vols.

AMBROSE, Saint, Bishop of Milan. St. Ambrose of Oppression; translated by John Oswen. Worcester, by John Oswen, 1550. 16mo.

Mentioned by Maunsell, p. 2.

— A devout Praier, expedient for those that prepare themselves to say Masse, &c. translated by Tho. Paynell. London, by John Cawood, 1555. 16mo.

Black letter.

— Two books of the Vocation and Callyng of all Nations; newly translated by Henry Becher. Lond. R. Watkins, 1561. 8vo.

Black letter, contains T 4 in eights. Sotheby, June 1856. 1*l.*

— Christian Offices Cristal Glass, in three Books, translated into English, by R. Humphrey. London, 1637, 4to.

Humphrey likewise translated two letters concerning the restoring the altars to the victorious senate, written by St. Ambrose, 1637, 4to.

AMBROSS, Miss. The Life and Memoirs of the late Miss Ann Catley the celebrated actress; with Biographical Sketches of Sir Francis Blake Delaval, and the Hon. Isabella Pawlet, Daughter of the Earl of Thanet. London, 1790. 8vo. pp. 56. with portrait, 5s.

Amera Singha. *See* COLEBROOKE.

America.—Voyages and Discoveries in South America, the first up the River of Amazons to Quito, in Peru, and back again to Brazil, by Christopher D'Acuna. The second up the River of Plata, and thence by Land to the Mines of Potozi, by M. Acarete. The third from Cayenne into Guiana, in Search of the Lake of Parima, by M. Grillet and Bechamel. Done into English from the originals. London, 1698. 8vo. with maps.

D 2

Heath, 2749, 5s. Nassau, pt. ii. 865, 7s. Roxburghe, 7358, 14s.

America. An Account of the European Settlements in America. In Six Parts. London, 1758. 8vo. 2 vols. 10s. 6d.

This excellent work, frequently reprinted, has been confidently attributed to the celebrated Edmund Burke, but he never acknowledged himself the author.

— Travels through the Interior Parts of America. In a Series of Letters. By an Officer (Thomas Anburey). London, 1789, or 1791. 8vo. 2 vols.

Dent, pt. 47, 1l. Drury, 57, 1l. 3s. Fonthill, 2779, 1l. 14s.

— Summary View of America, containing a Description of the Face of the Country, and of several of the principal Cities: and Remarks on the social, moral and political Character of the People. By an Englishman. London, 1824. 8vo. pp. 503. published at 10s. 6d.

A valuable work, written in a luminous and candid manner.

— Bibliothecæ Americanæ Primordia. *See* KENNET, Bishop of Peterborough.

— Bibliotheca Americana; or, a Chronological Catalogue of Books, &c. &c. upon the Subject of North and South America, with an Introductory Discourse on the present State of Literature in those Countries. Lond. 1789. 4to. pp. 271.

Bindley, pt. i. 926, 4s. 6d. Fonthill, 850, 9s.

— Laws of the United States of America, past at the first Session of the first Congress; continued by the Acts of Congress to 1801. Philadelphia, 1796-1801. 8vo. 5 vols. 2l. 2s.

American Atlas, or Guide to the History of North and South America, and the West Indies. Philadelphia, by Carey and Lea. Small Atlas folio, 5l.

Consisting of 58 charts, coloured.

American Philosophical Society. Transactions of the Society held at Philadelphia, 5 vols. 1789-1802. New Series, Vol. i. 1804. Philadelphia. 4to. 6 vols.

For Transactions of various other Societies, *see* Philadelphia. Boston.

American Preacher.—Discourses selected from the American Preacher. Edinb. 1796. 8vo. 2 vols.

Williams, 591, 1l. 11s. 6d.

American Traveller, by an old and experienced Trader. London, 1769. 4to. 5s.

A valuable work by Alexander Cluni, published, it is said, under the auspices and at the command of Lord Chatham.

AMERIE, Robert. Chester's Triumph in Honor of her Prince, as it was performed upon St. George's Day, 1610, in the foresaid Citie. London, 1610. 4to.

Dent, pt. i. 965, 7l. 10s. Rhodes, 462, 8l. 12s.

AMES, Joseph. Catalogue of English Heads, or an Account of about 2000 Prints, describing what is peculiar to each, &c. Lond. 1748, 8vo.

The Fothergill Collection. The first attempt at giving a list of portraits, since followed up by Granger, Noble, Bromley, Walpole,&c. Dent. pt. i. 85, 5s. 6d. Bindley pt. i. 76. 8s. Dowdeswell, 6, 8s. Strettell, 5 10s. 6d.

— Typographical Antiquities; being an Historical Account of Printing in England, &c. Lond. 1749. 4to.

Contains pp. 589, besides dedication, preface, list of subscribers 5 leaves, and index, 13 leaves. Bindley, pt. i. 121, 13s. 6d. Willett, 77, 1l. 11s. 6d. Ames likewise published a 'Catalogue of English Printers from 1471 to 1600,' 4to. 2 leaves.

— A new Edition, considerably augmented by William Herbert. London, 1785, 8, 90. 4to. 3 vols.

Of this edition 500 copies were printed on small, and 50 on large paper. SMALL PAPER.—Bp. of Ely, 156, 2l. 8s. Bindley, pt. i. 122, 2l. 12s. 6d. Willett, 78, 4l. 8s. LARGE PAPER.—Edwards, 22, 3l. 6s. Dent, pt. i. 124, russia, 3l. 7s. Towneley, pt. ii. 1061, russia, 4l. 17s. Roxburghe, 6580, 6l. 10s.

— A new Edition greatly enlarged, with copious Notes, by T. F.

Dibdin, D.D. London, 1810, 12, 16, 19. 4to. vols. 1, 2, 3, 4.
An invaluable work, which it is much to be regretted has not been completed, for want of sufficient encouragement. Sir M. M. Sykes, 877, 3 vols. 5*l.* 5*s.* Bindley, pt. ii. 388, 3 vols. 5*l.* 12s. 6d. Brockett, 103, 4 vols. 7*l.* 17s. 6*d.*. LARGE PAPER, only 66 copies printed, with additional portraits. White Knights, pt. i. 142, 2 vols. 13*l.* 13s. Towneley, pt. i. 505, 2 vols. 31*l.* 10s. Beckford, 1817. No. 186, 3 vols. 26*l.* 5s. Perry, pt. i. 1485, 4 vols. 22*l.* 11s. 6d. Dowdeswell, 311, 4 vols. 23*l.* 10s. Strettell, 617,4 vols. with duplicate proof impressions, 34*l.* 13s.

— William, D.D. Fresh Suit against Roman Ceremonies in God's Worship; or a Triplication to Dr. Burgess's Rejoinder for Dr. Morton. London, 1633. 4to. with a portrait by W. Marshall, 6s.

— Exposition of both the Epistles of the Apostle Peter, illustrated by Doctrines out of every Text. London, 1641. 4to. 6s.
This work was originally published in Latin at Amsterdam, in 1625-6-30. Mosheim acknowledges, that 'the productions of Ames are not void of merit, considering the times in which they were written.'

— Puritanismus Anglicanus. London, 1641. 4to.
This work, containing the chief doctrines of the Puritans, was originally published in Latin at Francfort, 1610. 8vo.
A copious list of the casuistical and controversial writings of this eminent puritan divine, who was born in 1576, and died in 1633, will be found in Watt's Bibliotheca Britannica.

AMHERST'S, Lord, Embassy to China. *See* ABEL, Clarke.
ELLIS, Henry.
HALL, Basil.
M'LEOD, John.

Amilec; or, the Seeds of Mankind, translated from the French. London, 1753. 12mo. 4s.
An ingenious philosophico-satirical romance, shewing the analogy between the propagation of animals, and that of vegetables.

AMMIANUS. *Vide* MARCELLINUS.
AMNER, John. Sacred Hymns of three, four, five, and six Parts, for Voices and Viols. London, 1615. 4to.

— Richard. Essay towards the Interpretation of the Prophecies of Daniel, with occasional Remarks upon some of the most celebrated Commentaries on them. London, 1776. 8vo. 5s.
An ingenious though unconvincing work, written by an Unitarian. The author likewise published 'An Account of the positive Institutions of Christianity.' 1774. 8vo. 2s. 6d. and 'Considerations on a future State,' &c. 1797. 8vo. 5s.

AMORY, Thomas. Memoirs of several Ladies of Great Britain. London, 1769. 12mo. 2 vols. 10s.
Hollis, 828, 12s. 6d. The former edition of this work appeared in 1755. 8vo. with two letters to the reviewers. An excellent notice of this Unitarian romance will be found in the Retrosp. Review, vi. 100—13.

— Life of John Buncle, Esq. London, 1825. 8vo. 3 vols.
The former editions of this amusing and singular work, which is a sort of sketch of his own life, appeared in 1756-66. 2 vols. 8vo. and 12mo. 4 vols. Edition, 1766, Hollis, 768, 2 vols. 17s.

AMOS, William. Minutes in Agriculture and Planting, illustrated with dried Specimens of natural Grasses. Boston and London, 1810. royal 4to. 6s.
This author likewise published, 'The Theory and Principles of the Drill Husbandry.' London, 1794. 4to. 7s. 6d. and 'Minutes of Agriculture and Planting.' London, 1804, 7s. 6d.

AMOS and LAURA, by S. P. *See* PAGE, S., and ALCILIA.

Amours of English Gallantry, in several Poems. London, 1675. 8vo.
Perry, pt. i. 131, 1*l.* 11s. Bindley, pt. i. 58, 4*l.* 18s.

Amours of Messalina, late Queen of England, (Mary of Este, Queen of James II.) London, 1689. 12mo.
Perry, pt. i. 44, 8s. 6d. Editions in French appeared in 12mo. in Cologne, 1689, and Ville-Francbe, 1691.

AMSINCK, Paul. Tunbridge Wells and its Neighbourhood, illustrated by a Series of Etchings and Historical Descriptions. By Paul Amsinck, Esq. The Etchings executed by Letitia Byrne. Lond. 1810. royal 4to. 1*l.* 5s. LARGE PAPER, 1*l.* 15s.
Contains pp. 183 (B— to 3 A—2.) with

title, advertisement 1 page, list of subscribers 3 pages, list of plates 2 pages, and 31 plates.

Amurath. — Most rare and straunge Discourses of Amurathe the Turkish Emperor that now is, of the Warres between him and the Persians, and also of the Tartars and Muscovites. London, for Hackett, 4to.
Not noticed by Ames, Herbert, or Dr. Dibdin. Nassau, pt. ii. 188, 2*l*. 2s.

Amygdala Britannica, 1647. *See* WITHER, George.

AMYRALDUS, Moses. Discourse concerning divine Dreams mention'd in Scripture, translated from the French, by James Lowde. London, 1676. 8vo. 5s.
A curious work by an eminent French Protestant Divine. A translation of his 'Treatise concerning Religions' appeared in 1660. 12mo. 4s.

Anabaptists anatomized and silenced in a Public Dispute. London, 1654. 8vo. with front. by Cross.
Nassau, pt. i. 34, 15s. In the British Museum Catalogue are many tracts, &c. relating to the Anabaptists.

ANACREON. Odæ, Gr. et Lat. cum Notis et variis Accessionibus, Opera et Studio Josuæ Barnes. Cantab. 1705. 12mo. with three portraits, viz. of Anacreon, the Duke of Marlborough, and Barnes, 6s.
Reprinted Cantab. 1721, and Lond. 1734. The edition of 1721 is preferred, that of 1734 is incorrect. Edition 1705. Gosset, 101, 10s. Heath, 3453, 16s. 6d. Bindley, pt. i. 208, 16s. 6d. Williams, 40, morocco, 1*l*. 11s. Edition 1721. White Knights, 105, 9s. Dent, pt. i. 39, morocco, 19s.

— Carmina Gr. et Lat. Mendis purgavit, Notasque cum nova Interpretatione litterali adjecit Will. Baxter. Londini, 1710. 12mo.
An excellent edition according to Harwood. Gosset, 102, 7s. 6d. Dent, pt. i. 38, mor. 11s. 6d. A former edition appeared in 1695. Dent, pt. i. 37, 8s.

— Carmina, Gr. et Lat. cum Notis et Indice (edente Mich. Maittaire). Lond. 1725. 4to. 15s.
One hundred copies printed. Bindley, pt. i. 522, russia, 1*l*. Duke of Grafton, 439, 1*l*. 10s.

— Carmina, Gr. cum Novis Versionibus, Scholiis, et Notis (edente Mich. Maittaire). Lond. 1740. 4to.
One hundred copies printed on common, and six copies on fine writing paper, 5*l*. 5s. This edition contains the notes of Buthillerius, which are not in that of 1725. Drury, 2800, russia, 19s. Willett, 83, 1*l*. 2s. Bp. of Ely, 170, 1*l*. 6s.

— Carmina Gr. cum Notis perpetuis. Accedunt ejusdem ut perhibentur Fragmenta et Poetriæ Sapphus, quæ supersunt. Lond. 1742. 12mo. 5s.
An elegant edition edited by Trapp. Heath, 3453, 11s. Roscoe, 840, 17s.

— Carmina, cum Sapphonis et Alcæi Fragmentis, Græce. Glasg. 1751. 32mo.
An elegant little edition. Dent, pt. i. 40, mor. 9s. 6d. Drury, 72, mor. 5s. Some copies were printed upon silk. A neat edition of Anacreon and Sappho, Gr. et Lat. was published at Glasgow, 1744. 12mo. 4s.

— Carmina, Græce. Glasg. 1757. 12mo. 5s. 6d.
This edition, says Dr. Harwood, does credit to the University of Glasgow, both in regard to splendour and correctness. A neat and correct edition of Anacreon, Gr. et Lat. by Gail, Dublin, 1801, 8vo. 6s.; also another containing Anacreon, Sappho, and Alcæus, Gr. et Lat. Glasg. 1801. small 8vo. 3s. 6d.

— Odaria, ad Textus Barnesiani Fidem emendata. Accedunt Variæ Lectiones curâ Edwardi Forster. Londini, 1802. small 8vo.
An elegant edition, ornamented with vignettes. Bindley, pt. i. 221, 5s. LARGE PAPER. Brockett, 29, 10s. 6d. White Knights, 109, mor. 15s. Drury, 78, mor. 1*l*. 2s. A few copies were printed on vellum, 5*l*. 5s. to 10*l*. 10s.

— Anacreontica, Græce; recensuit Notisque criticis instruxit Fred. Henr. Bothe. Oxonii, 1809. 8vo. 5s. LARGE PAPER, 8s.
Printed for N. Bliss, who likewise published an edition, Oxon. 1812. 24mo. 3s.

— Anacreon. Bion. Moschus. Kisses, by Secundus. Cvpido crucificied by Ausonius. Venvs Vigils, incerto Authore. Excitations. Sylvia's Park. by Theophile. Acanthus

ANA   ANA   39

Complaint, by Tristan. Oronta, by Preti. Echo, by Marino. Love's Embassy, by Boscan. The Solitvde, by Gongora. A Platonick Discourse upon Love, written in Italian by John Picus Mirandula in Explication of a Sonnet, by Hieronimo Benivieni. Printed in the year 1651. 8vo.
An elegant and much-esteemed version by the learned Thomas Stanley, of which a reprint, consisting of 150 copies, appeared in 1815.

— Anacreon done into English out of the original Greek, (by T. Wood, A. Cowley, Oldham, and Francis Willis.) Oxon, 1683. 8vo. 3s. to 5s.
Another translation of Anacreon and Sappho, by Sewell, 1713, 12mo. 2s. 6d.

— translated into English Verse; with Notes explanatory and poetical. To which are added, the Odes, &c. of Sappho. By John Addison. London, 1735. 12mo.
A good translation, with the Greek Text, and useful notes. White Knights, 110, 6s. Fonthill, 3548, 8s.

— Anacreon, Sappho, Bion, Moschus, and Musæus, translated by a Gentleman of Cambridge, (Francis Fawkes, M.A.) London, 1760. 12mo.
An esteemed translation, reprinted 1789, 12mo. and inserted in Anderson and Chalmers' Collections of the Poets. Dent., pt. i. 45, 5s. 6d. Fonthill, 3549, 9s.

— Anacreon and Sappho, with Pieces from ancient Authors, &c. (by E. B. Greene.) London, 1768. 12mo.
In little estimation. Garrick, 56, 7s. 6d. and 57, 7s. A literal translation of Anacreon, was also published by the Rev. D. H. Urquhart, 1787. 12mo. 2s. 6d.

— Odes, translated into English Verse, with Notes by Thomas Moore. London, 1800. 4to. pp. 280, with three plates, 15s.
An elegant, spirited, and highly poetical version, frequently reprinted in 12mo. The edition 1802, 12mo. 2 vols. on LARGE PAPER, Dent, pt. i. 46, mor. 1l. 2s.

— The Odes translated into English Measure, by Lord Thurlow. Lond. 1823. 8vo. 5s.
Of Anacreon there have been other translations, viz. by the Rev. Hercules Younge, 1802, 12mo.; by Thomas Girdlestone, M.D., 1803, crown 8vo. 3s. 6d.; by the Rev. Thomas Gilpin, 1807, 12mo. 3s.; by T. Orger, L.L.D. 1825, 12mo. 3s. 6d.

Analecta Græca Majora et Minora. *Vide* DALZEL, A.

Analogia Honorum. *See* LOGAN, J.

Analytical Review from the Commencement in 1788 to 1798 inclusive; also vol i. of a New Series, for 1799. London, 8vo. 29 vols.
Dr. Geddes was a principal contributor to this periodical. Hollis, 28, 29, 3l. 1s.

ANASTASII Sinaitæ Anagogicarum Contemplationum in Hexameron, Lib. xii. hactenus desideratus; cui præmissa est Expostulatio Pet. Allix de S. Chrysostomi Epistolam ad Cæsarium Monachum adversus Apollinarii Hæresin. Londini, 1682. 4to. 5s.
Published by the celebrated French critic And. Dacier.

Anas. Selections from the French Anas: containing Remarks of eminent Scholars on Men and Books; together with Anecdotes and Apophthegms of illustrious Persons. London, 1797. 12mo. 2 vols. 7s.
Reprinted by Sir R. Phillips in 3 vols. 1805.

Anastasius. *See* HOPE.

Anatomie of a Woman's Tongue, divided into five Parts; Medicine, a Poison, a Serpent, Fire, and Thunder. London, 1638. 4to.
A scarce poetical tract.

Anatomie of the World, with its Frailtie and Decay, a Poem. Lond. 1621. 8vo. Two Parts.
Perry, pt. i. 132, 1l. 8s.

Anatomy of a Hande in the Manner of a Dyall, necessary for all People. Imprented at Holy Well, by Wyllyam Follingham for Richarde Bankes. 1544. 12mo.
Black letter.

ANAYA, A. Essay on Spanish Literature, followed by a History of the Spanish Drama, and Specimens of the Writers of the different Ages. London, 1818. 12mo. 5s.

ANDERSON, Adam. Deduction of the Origin of Commerce from the earliest Accounts. Carefully revised, corrected and continued to the present Time. London, 1801. 4to. 4 vols.

A justly celebrated and valuable work, replete with useful information, though in some measure superseded by David Macpherson's Annals of Commerce. The first edition appeared 1764. folio. 2 vols. 15s. Heath, 1408, 1*l*. 15s. Another edition, 1789, 4to. 4 vols.

— Æneas. Narrative of the British Embassy to China, in 1792, 1793, and 1794. Lond. 1795. 4to. 12s.

This narrative of Earl Macartney's Embassy is of little value in comparison with that of Sir G. L. Staunton, Bart. Fonthill, 3086, 2*l*. An abridgment (in 8vo.) also appeared in 1795.

— Journal of the Forces which sailed from the Downs in April, 1800, on a secret Expedition under the command of Lieut. Gen. Pigot, till their arrival in Minorca, and continued through all the subsequent transactions of the Army to the surrender of Alexandria: with a particular account of Malta. Lond. 1802. 4to. with engravings, 10s. to 15s.

Fonthill, 3106, 2*l*. 4s.

— Sir Edmund. Reports in the Common Pleas, chiefly in the reign of Q. Elizabeth, in French. London, 1664, 5. folio. 2 parts, with portrait by W. Faithorne, 10s. LARGE PAPER, 15s.

Sotheby's in 1824. 1*l*. Among the MS. Harl. 4817, are ' Les Reportes de Seignior Edm. Anderson, senr. chiefe Justice de Common Banc.'

— Henry. The Court Convert, or a sincere Sorrow for Sin, faithfully traversed, expressing the Dignity of a true Penitent. Printed for the Author, 18mo. 5s.

Contains pp. 9 to 32, with a title and epistle dedicatory. Some copies of this poem have the name of Audley as the author.

— James. Ane godly Treatis, calit the first and second Cumming of Christ, with the Tone of the Winternycht. 1595. Edinburgh, be Robert Smyth. 16mo.

A poem in seven-line stanzas consisting of 16 leaves. Another edition was printed at Edinburgh by Andro Hart.

— Essay showing that the Crown and Kingdom of Scotland is imperial and independent. Edinburgh, 1705. 8vo. 5s.

For this work, written to confute the mistakes of Drake, and misrepresentations of Atwood, the parliament of Scotland ordered the author a reward, and thanks to be delivered to him by the Lord Chancellor.

— Collections relating to the History of Mary Queen of Scotland: with an explanatory Index of the obsolete words, and a Preface. Edinb. 1727-8. 4to. 4 vols. 2*l*. 2s.

LARGE PAPER, 3*l*. 3s.

— Royal Genealogies, or the genealogical Tables of Emperors, Kings, and Princes, from Adam to these Times. Lond. 1732. folio.

The most useful and valuable work of the kind, and probably the most difficult and laborious one ever undertaken by author or printer. Sir M. M. Sykes, pt. i. 146, LARGE PAPER, russia, 6*l*. 5s. Some copies bear the date of 1736, with new addenda and corrigenda after the preface. Bindley, pt. i. 159, 3*l*. 3s. Nassau, pt. i. 203, 2*l*. 8s.

— Selectus Diplomatum et Numismatum Scotiæ Thesaurus, auxit et locupletavit Thomas Ruddimanus. Edinb. 1739. folio. 8*l*. 8s.

A highly valuable and useful work, with plates engraved by Sturt. Dent, pt. i. 146, 6*l*. 6s. Towneley, pt. i. 72, 6*l*. 15s. Nassau, pt. i. 204, 7*l*. 12s. 6d. Sir M. M. Sykes. pt. i. 145, 7*l*. 17s. 6d. Brockett, 268, 10*l*. 10s. It is said some copies were printed upon fine paper. The introduction by Ruddiman was afterwards inadequately translated and published with notes. Edinb. 1773. 12mo. 2s. 6d. Brockett, 2853, 9s.

— A Genealogical History of the House of Yvery: in its different Branches of Yvery, Luvel, Perceval and Gournay. London, 1742. royal 8vo. 2 vols.

This work, written principally by the Rt. Hon. John Percival, first Earl of Egmont, was privately printed.

Collation.—Vol. I. Title, pp. i—xii, 1—30, xiii—xxxvii. (misprint xxix.) title to book 1, pp. 1.—457 (misprint 455).

N.B. In some copies p. xxxvii. has been cancelled, and by additional matter extended to p. xli.

Detached Genealogical Tables.
Auberie de Bellomonte.
XII Tables of the eldest Branch of the House of Yvery, on seven leaves.
Table to Book III.
Descent from the Barons of Kary.
Table to Book IV.
Table the first of the fifth book (at the back) the quarterings of Sir Richard de Perceval, first of that name.
Table the second of the fifth book.

PLATES.
'Orate pro Anima Ryc. Perceval.'
The Manor of Weston-in-Gordano.
Tomb of 'Rycharde Percyvale—M.CCCC lxxxiii.'

Vol. II. Title, ' To the Reader,' 2 leaves, title to book vi. pp. 1—583. Pages 446 and 447 are missing, and between pp. 452-3, are duplicate pages 453 to 460.
Detached Genealogical Tables.
Table to the sixth book.
Sydenham, Cave, Tilly, Kitsford, Peckstone and Redmere.
House of De la More.
Earls of Flanders, &c.
The thirty-two Quarterings of the Children of John, Lord Visc. Perceval, and the Lady Catharine Cecil his wife.
Table to Book 7.

PLATES.
The Mannor of Sydenham.
Loghart Castle, near Mallo^w in Ireland.
Castle of Liscarrol, in the County of Cork.
The Castle of Kanturk.
Map of Part of the Estate of the Right Hon. John Percival, Earl of Egmont.
Monument.
Mount Pleasant, near Tunbridge Wells.
Beverston Castle.

PORTRAITS engraved by Faber.
Rich. Perceval Esq. died 1620.
Alice, Wife to Rich. Perceval Esq. living 1599.
The Right Hon. Sir Philip Parceval Kt. died 1647.
Catharine, Wife to Sir Philip Perceval Kt died 2 Jan. 1681-2.
George Perceval Esq. ob. 25 March 1675.
The Rt. Hon. S^r In^o. Perceval Bart. ob. 1665.
Catharine, Wife to S^r. Iohn Perceval Bart. died 17 Aug. 1679.
Robert Perceval Esq. dyed 5 of June, 1677.

Sir Philip Pareeval Bart. dyed 11th of Sepr. 1680.
Sir In^o. Perceval Bart. died 1686.
Catharine, Wife to S^r. In^o. Perceval Bar^t. died 2^d of Feb^{ry}. 1691-2.
The Honble. Philip Perceval Esq. born 13th of Novr. 1686.
The Right Honble. Iohn Perceval Earl of Egmont born July 12, 1683.
The Rt. Honble. Catharine, Wife to John Perceval Earl of Egmont, born 1689.
Sir Philip Parker K^{nt}. knighted by Q. Elizth. 1578.
Catherine, Wife to Sir Philip Parker Knt.
The Right Hon. John L^d. Visc^t. Perceval born 24 of Feb. 1710-11.
Catharine, Wife to John L^d. Visc^t. Perceval marr^d. 15.Feb. 1736-7.

The Right Hon. Sir Philip Perceval K^{nt}. died 1647. Engraved by W. H. Toms, 1788.

There are four portraits of THE RAWDONS, which were engraved for an intended History of that family—the portraits are sometimes inserted in the House of Yvery, but form no part of the work.

Fonthill, 2210, 14l. 14s. M. of Townshend, 33, russia, 20l. Brockett, 33, morocco, 23l. White Knights, pt. i. 113, morocco, 14l. Bindley, pt. l. 34, 15l. Evans in March, 1814, 18l. 18s. Duke of Grafton, 906, 16l. 5s. 6d. Nassau, pt. i. 37. mor. 22l. Dent, pt. i. 48, russia. 21l. 10s. Maddison, 29l. Baker, No. 13, (with the arms emblazoned, ruled with red lines, and bound in morocco) 31l. 10s. Gough, No. 64 (without portraits) 4l. 10s.

ANDERSON, James, LL.D. An Account of the present State of the Hebrides and Western Coasts of Scotland. Edinb. 1785. 8vo. with a map, 5s.

Written expressly to point out means of improvement.

— The Bee, or Literary Weekly Intelligencer. London, 1790-4. Small 8vo. 18 vols. with portraits.

Complete sets of this valuable periodical work, in which Dr. Anderson received material assistance from men of taste and learning, are of rare occurrence. It was printed on three papers, coarse, common, and fine. Constable, No. 17, 1l. 10s.

— Essays relating to Agriculture and Rural Affairs. Fifth Edition, with Additions and Corrections. London, 1800. 8vo. 3 vols. 10s. 6d.

The first edition appeared 1775. 8vo. 1 vol. anonymously.

— Recreations in Agriculture

and Natural History, Arts and Miscellaneous Literature. London, 1799-1802. 8vo. 6 vols. 1*l.* 10s. ROYAL PAPER, 2*l.* 2s.

A copious list of this eminent Agricultural writer's works, will be found in Watt's Bibliotheca Britannica.

ANDERSON, James, M.D. Letters to Sir Joseph Banks, Bart. on the Cochineal Insects discovered at Madras. Madras, 1788-9-90. 4to. with plates, 10s. 6d.

This writer likewise published 'An Account of the Importation of American Cochineal Insects into Hindostan.' Madras, 1795.

— John, M.A. Defence of the Church, Government, Faith, Worship and Spirit of the Presbyterians. Glasg. 1714. 4to.

— John. Observations on Roman Antiquities discovered between the Forth and Clyde. Edinb.1804.4to. Roxburgh^ee, 8777, 5s. 6d.

— Account of a Mission to the East Coast of Sumatra in 1823, under the Direction of the Government of Prince of Wales's Island. London, 1826. 8vo. with maps and plates, 16s.

A critique on this work appeared in the Quarterly Review, xxxiv. 99—110.

— Patrick, M.D. The Colde Spring of Kinghorne Craig, his admirable and new tryed Properties, so far foorth as yet are found true by Experience. Edinb. 1618. 4to.

With wood-cut view of the 'Colde Spring,' on back of title. Gordonstoun, 60, 1*l.* 11s. 6d. Another work of rare occurrence by this author is entitled 'Grana Angelica.' Edinb. 1635. 12mo.

— R. Rudiments of Tamul Grammar; combining with the Rules of Kodun Tamul, or the ordinary Dialect, an Introduction to Shen Tamul, or the elegant Dialect of the Language. Lond. 1821. 4to. 18s.

— Walter, D.D. History of France during the Reigns of Francis I. and Charles IX. To which is prefixed, a Review of the general History of the Monarchy, from its Origin to that Period. London, 1769. 4to. 2 vols. 10s. 6d.

— History of France, from the Commencement of the Reign of Henry III. to the general Peace of Munster. London, 1775-82. 4to. 5 vols. 1*l.* 11s. 6d.

This writer's French histories are in no estimation.

— Philosophy of Ancient Greece Investigated; with Remarks on the delineated Systems of their Founders; and some Account of their Lives and Characters, and those of their most eminent Disciples. Edinburgh, 1791. 4to. pp. 585. 15s.

A work of much learning, written with a view to supply the deficiencies of Stanley's History of Philosophy.

— W. A pittilesse mother that most unnaturally murthered two of her own children at Acton, upon Holy Thursday 1616. Black letter, 4to. n.d.

Jolley, 1843, 2*l.* 18s.

— William. London Commercial Dictionary and General Sea-Port Gazetteer; with the Duties of Customs and Excise brought down to the present time. A new edition. London, 1826. 8vo. 1*l.* 1s.

A useful work.

ANDRADA, Jacintho Freire of. Life of Don John de Castro, Viceroy of India, wherein are seen the Portuguese Voyage in the East Indies, their Discoveries and Conquests there, &c. translated by Sir Peter Wyche, Knt. London, 1664. folio, with a head by Faithorne and cuts.

The work from which this is translated is esteemed one of the best written books in the Portuguese language. Roxburghe, 9217, 7s. M. of Townshend, 196, 11s.

ANDREAS, Anthony. Anthonii Andreæ super duodecim Libros Metaphysicæ Quæstiones, per Thomam Penketh. Per me Johannem Lettou, 1480. folio.

Supposed to be the first book printed in the City of London. Dr. Dibdin states, that a copy of this work, wanting two leaves at the beginning, is in the library of Magdalen College, Oxford. Several other editions were published abroad in the 15th Century.

— Bartimeus. Certaine Sermons upon the fifth Chapiter of the Songs of Solomon. London, 1583. 16mo.

Black letter. 140 leaves, paged from Introduction. Dedicated to Lorde Henrie Earl of Huntington, Lorde Hastings, &c. White Knights, 115, mor. 1*l*. 1s. An edition, 1595. Inglis, 19, 10s.

ANDREWE, Laurence. The wonderful Shape and Nature of Man, Beastes, Serpentes, Fowles, Fishes, and Monsters, translated out of diuers Authors, by Laur. Andrew, of Calis, and printed at Antuerpe, with Pictures, by Joh. Doesborow (1510), folio.

Black letter. Laurence Andrewe likewise published 'The Valuation of Golde and Siluer,' and a translation of 'The Boke of Distyllacion, by Jherom Brunswyke.'

— Thomas. The Unmasking of a feminine Machiavell. Lond. 1604. 4to.

Contains 22 leaves. Dedicated to M. D. Langworth, Archdeacon of Wells. A poetical tract of little merit, containing a description of the Battle at Newport, in Flanders, 22nd June, 1600. Inglis, Old Plays, 4to. No. 2, 3*l*. Nassau, pt. 1. 164, 6*l*. 6s. Bright, fine, 5*l*. 15s. 6d.

ANDREWS, George. Dictionary of the Slang and Cant Languages. London. 12mo. 5s.

ANDREWS, Saint, Archbishop of. *See* Hamilton, John, D.D.

— Capt. Journey from Buenos Ayres, through the Provinces of Cordova, Tucuman, and Salta, to Potosi, thence by the Deserts of Caranja to Arica, and subsequently to Santiago de Chili and Coquimbo. Lond. 1827. post 8vo. 2 vols. pp. 665.

A clear and sensible work, containing much valuable information.

— George. Reports of Cases in the Court of King's Bench, in the 11 and 12 years of King George III. with additional Notes and References, &c. by G. W. Vernon. London, 1792. 8vo. 10s. 6d.

Best edition. The former edition 1754, in folio, 7s. 6d.

— H. C. Botanist's Repository for new and rare Plants, containing *coloured* Figures of such Plants as have not hitherto appeared in any similar Publication, with Descriptions in English and Latin. Lond. 1797—1815. 4to. 10 vols. 664 plates.

Edwards, 730, 6 vols. 15*l*. 15s. White Knights, pt. 1. 156, 8 vols. 20*l*. 9s. 6d. Roscoe, 1767, 9 vols. 30*l*. 19s. 6d. Sir M. M. Sykes, pt. 1. 255, 10 vols. morocco, 39*l*. 7s. 6d.

ANDREWS, H. C. Coloured Engravings of Heaths, the Drawings taken from living Plants only, with the appropriate specific character, full Description, &c. Lond. 1802-9. folio, 4 vols. with 288 coloured plates.

The fourth volume, published like the others in numbers, not having been completed till about 1830, is often wanting.

Beckford, 1817, No. 198, 3 vols. only, 15*l*. 4s. 6d. White Knights, No. 191, dedication copy, 3 vols., morocco, 21*l*. 10s. 6d. Roscoe, No. 1768, 3 vols. 26*l*. 5s.

— Heathery, or a Monograph of the Genus Erica, with the Descriptions in Latin and English. London, 1804-12, 6 vols. royal 8vo. 300 coloured plates, pub. at 13*l*. 10s.

Mr. Andrews likewise published a work on Roses, 2 vols. 1805-28, 129 coloured plates, at 13*l*., and another on Geraniums, 2 vols. 4to. 1805, 124 coloured plates, at 9*l*. 9s.

— James Pettit. Anecdotes, &c. ancient and modern, with observations. London, 1789-90. 8vo. 6s.

Contains pp. 470. Addenda, pp. 106, with a front. representing a man distilling from an alembic. This amusing and humorous collection has been several times reprinted.

— History of Great Britain (from the Landing of Julius Cæsar to the Accession of Edward VI.) connected with the Chronology of Europe, with Notes, &c. London, 1794-5. 4to. 2 vols. with Vignette title.

Contains pp. 477 and 366. The notes to this valuable historical work contain a great variety of curious and amusing particulars. Sir M. M. Sykes, pt. 1. 254, 1*l*. 15s. Heath, 4374, 2*l*. 2s. Fonthill, 651, 2*l*. 13s.

— John. Anatomie of Basenesse; or the foure Quarters of a Knaue. Flatterie, Ingratitude, Enuie, Detraction. Lond. 1615. 4to.

Five sheets, dedicated to Sir Robert Sydney, by J. A. Besides this poetical tract (a copy of which is in the Bodleian) this 'painful preacher of God's work' published other things on religious subjects, a list of which will be found in Dr. Bliss's edition of Wood's Athen. Oxon. ii. 493-5.

ANDREWS, Plans of the most capital Cities of Europe, and some remarkable Cities in the other three parts of the world; with a description of their most remarkable Buildings, &c. &c. London, 1792. 4to. with 42 folding coloured plans, 15s.

This map-seller and engraver also published An Historical Atlas of England, 1797, in folio, 12s.

— John, L.L.D. History of the War with America, France, Spain and Holland, 1775—83. London, 1786. 8vo. 4 vols. 12s.

A judicious compilation. Andrews likewise published 'The History of the Revolutions of Denmark,' 1774. 8vo. 2 vols. 10s. 6d.

— Lancelot, successively Bishop of Ely, Chichester, and Winchester. Opuscula quædam posthuma. Londini, 1629. 4to. 10s. 6d.

— Præces Privatæ, Gr. et Lat. Oxon, 1828. 18mo. (Ed. P. Hall, *Pickering*, 1839, 1848, &c.)

This manual of devotions, formed of sentences from the sacred scriptures, and the writings of the fathers, was compiled by this learned prelate for his own private use. It was found after his decease 'worn in pieces by his fingers and wet with his tears.' The first edition was printed at Oxford, 1674, 18mo. with a portrait by D. Loggan, 15s. A translation by N. Drake appeared 1675, 18mo. 3s., and another by George Stanhope, D.D. 1730, 8vo. 4s., which latter has been frequently reprinted. (A new translation by P. Hall, *Pickering*, 1839.)

— XCVI Sermons, published by his Majesties Special Commandment. Lond. 1631. folio, with portrait, 1l. 1s.

Reprinted 1635. 1641. 1661. Some of this eminent divine's sermons were published in 1589, without his consent.

— Patern of Catechistical Doctrine, or Exposition of the Ten Commandments. London, 1642. folio, with portrait, 9s.

Reprinted 1650. 1675. each with a portrait.

— Collection of Posthumous and Orphan Lectures delivered at St-Paul's and St. Giles's. Lond. 1657. fol. with a portrait by Vaughan, 15s.

The most popular of all his productions. A former edition 1649. folio. 12s.

— Seventeen Sermons modernised by the Rev. Charles Daubeny, Archdeacon of Sarum. London, 1821. 8vo. 10s. 6d.

This learned and eminent divine published several other works, chiefly controversial, particularly Tortura Torti, 1609, 4to. and Responsio ad Apologiam Card. Bellarmini, 1610, 4to. both of which are considered unanswerable.

—W. Eusebius. Review of Fox's Book of Martyrs, 3 vols. 8vo. 1826.

Androboros, a Biographical Farce in three acts, viz. the Senate, the Consistory, and the Apotheosis, printed at Moropolis (i. e. Μωρος πολις) since August. (1709.) 4to.

A copy of this whimsical piece, by Coxeter, attributed to Governor Hunter, is in the Kemble Collection of Plays.

Andromeda Liberata. 1614. *See* CHAPMAN, George.

ANDRONICUS, a Tragedy. Impieties long Successe, or Heaven's late Revenge. London, 1661. 8vo.

A copy is in the British Museum.

ANDRONICUS RHODIUS. Ethicorum Nicomacheorum Paraphrasis, Gr. cum Interpretatione Dan. Heinsii. Cantab. 1679. 8vo. 3s. 6d.

The variorum Edition, not equal to that of Leyden, 1617, 8vo. Copies of the Cambridge edition of 1679, on FINE PAPER, are very rare.

— Editio altera. Subjungitur Andronici Libellus περι παθον (edente Th. Gaisford). Oxon. 1809. 8vo. 8s.

A valuable critical edition.

— Paraphrase on the Nicomachean Ethics of Aristotle, translated by William Bridgman. London, 1807. 4to. 18s.

In this translation Bridgman was greatly assisted by Thomas Taylor, the translator of Plato, Aristotle, &c.

ANEAU, Bart. ΑΛΕΚΤΟΡ. The Cock. Containing the first Part of the most excellent and mytheologicall Historie of the valorous Squire Alector; Sonne to the renowned Prince Macrobius Franc-Gal; and to the Peerelesse Princesse Priscaraxe, Queene of High Tartary. London, 1590. 4to.

Black letter. A copy in Longman and Co.'s Catalogue for 1816, No. 5482, (supposed unique) was marked 15*l.* 15s.

Anecdotes of Polite Literature. London, 1764. 12mo. 5 vols.

An amusing and judicious selection, very neatly printed. Steevens, 944, 16s. 6d. Hollis, 30, 1*l.* 2s.

Angel.— The Life of the Rev. Fa. Angel, of Joyeuse, Capuchin Preacher. Douay, 1623. 8vo. with three portraits.

A copy is in the British Museum. Nassau, pt. 1. 1967, russia, 1*l.* 10s. Lloyd, 112, 1*l.* 19s. Inglis, 872, 2*l.* 15s. Brand, 3*l.* 3s.

ANGEL, John. History of Ireland. Dublin, 1781. 12mo. 2 vols. 5s.

ANGELL, Christ. Christ. Angell a Grecian, who tasted of many Stripes and Torments inflicted by the Turkes, his Account of the Cruelties he endured; also his Epistle in commendation of England, particularly Oxford and Cambridge, where he resided for some years. Oxford, 1617. 4to. with wood cuts.

In Greek and English. Marq. of Townshend, 145, 1*l.* 6s. Inglis, 112, 1*l.* 11s. Nassau, pt. 1. 166, 2*l.* Sotheby's, 1818, 4*l.* 4s.

— Encomion of the famous Kingdom of Great Britain, and the two flourishing sister Universities, Cambrige and Oxford. Camb. 1619. 4to.

A copy is in the Bodleian Library.

— Enchiridion de Institutis Græcorum Gr. et Lat. Cantab. 1619. 4to. 15s.

A Latin copy of this work 'learnedly noted' by George Fhelavius, according to Ant. à Wood, appeared at Francof. 1655. 8vo. entitled Status et Ritus Ecclesiæ Græcæ. Copies of both editions are in the British Museum. Angell likewise published 'De Antichristo,' 1624, 4to.

— John. Stenography, or Short Hand improved. London, 1758. 8vo. 4s.

The preface or dedication to this system, which is complex and difficult, was written by Dr. Samuel Johnson.

ANGELO, Dominico. L'Ecole des Armes. Londres, 1763. oblong folio.

Roxburghe, 1718, 7s. 6d. Duke of York, 273, 1*l.* 11s.

— Michael. A Selection of Twelve Heads from the Last Judgment of Michael Angelo, by R. Duppa, F.S.A. London, 1801. imperial folio.

Of this work, very few copies were printed; the copper plates have been destroyed. It was published at 4*l.* 4s.

ANGELONI, Battista. Letters on the English Nation, translated from the original Italian. London, 1755 or 6. 8vo. 2 vols. 3s. 6d.

A libellous work, written by Dr. Shebbeare, under the feigned name of a Jesuit. Willett, 23, 6s.

ANGELUS, *Anglice* ANGEL or ANGELL.

ANGELUS a S. Francisco. Certamen Seraphicum Provinciæ Angliæ pro Sancta Dei Ecclesia, Opera et Labore Angeli a S. Francisco. Duaci, 1649. 4to. with portraits, 3*l.* 3s.

Written by N. Mason. A copy is in the British Museum. Sotheby's in 1816, 17*l.* 17s. Evans in 1817, 9*l.* 9s. Gardner, 1854, 2*l.* 4s. Sotheby's, 1856, 3*l.* 15s.

— Apologia pro Scoto-Anglo. Duaci. 1656. 12mo.

A copy is in the British Museum.

Angler.—The Angler: a Poem in six Cantos: by Piscator. (by T. P. Lathey.) London, 1819. 12mo. pp. 234. 6s.

Copies on THICK PAPER (20 printed) 10s. On VELLUM (unique) Sotheby's in 1823, 4*l.* 12s.

(Republished with a new title, 1820.)

— The experienced Angler, 1662. See VENABLES, Robert.

— The Gentleman Angler. London, 1726. 8vo. 5s.

Reprinted 1736, n. d. and in 1786, as a novel publication.

— The North Country Angler; or, the Art of Angling as practised in the Northern Counties of England. Leeds, 1800. 8vo.

The first edition of this treatise was published London, 1786. 8vo.

Angler.—The Universal Angler, or that Art improved in all its Parts, especially in Fly-fishing. London, 1766. 8vo.

— The Angler's Magazine, by a Lover of that healthful and innocent Diversion, (by Geo. Smith). London, 1754. 12mo. 3s.
<small>Haworth, 791, 10s. 6d.</small>

— The Angler's Manual: or, concise Lessons of Experience. Liverpool, 1808. oblong 8vo. with Etchings by Howitt.
<small>Some copies were printed in 4to.</small>

— The Angler's Vade Mecum. London, 1681. 12mo. 5s.
<small>Reprinted 1689, 1700.</small>

— The Anglers, eight Dialogues in Verse, with Notes. London, 1758. 12mo. 3s. 6d.
<small>A well-written little work, (ironical—ascribed to Dr. Scott), consisting of 56 pp. with an address to the reader. Haworth, 787, 9s.</small>

— *See* ANGLING.

ANGLESEY, Arthur Annesley, Earl of. Memoirs, intermixed with moral, political, and historical Observations, by way of Discourse, in a Letter (to Sir Peter Pett): to which is prefixed, a Letter written by his Lordship during his Retirement from Court. London, 1693. 8vo. 5s.
<small>Published by Sir Pet. Pett, Knight. An answer to this work by Sir Peter Thompson, Bart. will be found appended to 'The Earl of Anglesey's State of the Government and Kingdom,' &c. London, 1694. 4to. 4s.</small>

— Privileges of the House of Lords and Commons. London, 1702. 8vo. pp. 172.
<small>Heath, 4409, 8s. 6d. An account of this nobleman, with a list of his writings, will be found in Dr. Bliss' Edition of Wood's Athen. Oxon. iv. 181-7, 579.</small>

Anglesey.—The History of the Island of Anglesey, with the Memoirs and genealogical account of Owen Glendour. London, 1775. 4to. 5s.
<small>Intended as a supplement to Rowland's Mona Antiqua Restaurata.</small>

Angleterre. — Les Chroniques. *Voyez* BOUCHARD, Allain.

Angleterre, Discourse des Troubles nouvellement advenuz du Royaume d'Angleterre au Moys d' Octobre, 1569; avec une Declaration, faicte par le Comte de Northumberland, et autres grand Seigneurs d'Angleterre. Lyon, 1570. 8vo.

— Annales des Choses memorables d'Angleterre sous Henry Paris, 1647. 4to.
<small>Towneley, pt. i. 313, in morocco, 1l. 18s.</small>

— Description des Guerres d' Angleterre et de France. Amst. VIII. 1668. 4to.
<small>Bindley, pt. ii. 785, 13s. 6d.</small>

— Histoire des Evenemens tragiques d'Angleterre, et des derniers Troubles d'Ecosse, contenant une Relation des Conspirations contre les Rois Charles II. et Jacques II. Cologne, 1686. 12mo.
<small>Constable, 424, 5s. Towneley, pt. ii. 443, with portraits, 18s.</small>

— Histoire d'Angleterre, representée par Figures par F. A. David, accompagnées d'un Precis historique (par le Tourneur et autres). Paris, 1784-1800. 4to. 3 vols. 2l. 2s.
<small>In very little estimation. Some copies are printed on vellum paper.</small>

— De la Constitution de l'Angleterre et des Changemens qu'elle a éprouvés dans son Esprit que dans ses Formes, depuis son Origine jusqu' à nos Jours: avec quelques Remarques sur l'ancienne Constitution de France. Par un Anglois, (M. Frisell). Seconde Edition. Paris, 1820. 8vo. 99 pp.
<small>A valuable little work.</small>

Anglia.—De Persecutione Anglicans Epistola, 1582. *Vide* PARSONS, Robert.

— Descriptiones quædam illius inhumanæ et multiplicis Persecutionis quam in Anglia propter fidem sustinent Catholicæ Christiani. folio.
<small>Six pages, with prints. In a sale at Sotheby's in 1824, the following, 'De Persecutione Anglicana Libellus, 6 plates, Romæ, 1582,' was sold for 2l. 15s.</small>

— Relatio felicis Agonis, quem pro Religione Catholica gloriose subierunt aliquot e Societate Jesu Sacerdotum in ultima Angliæ Persecutione. Pragæ, 1683. 4to. with portraits, 2l. 2s.

— Regni Angliæ sub Elizabetha Religio et Gubernatio Ecclesiastica. Lond. 1729. 4to. 5s.

Angling.—A Catalogue of books on Angling, with some brief notices of several of their authors. London, 1811. 8vo. pp. 21.

By Sir Henry Ellis, originally printed in the British Bibliographer, of which fifty copies were taken off separately. Sotheby's in June, 1827. 13s. (Reprinted with additions by Mr. Pickering, and again by Mr. Russell Smith, 1s. 6d.)

— The Art of Angling. 1653. 4to. See BARKER, Thomas.

— New and excellent Experiments and Secrets in the art of Angling. London, 1675. 12mo. with frontispiece and cuts, 6s.

Sotheby's in 1823, 1l. 1s. Reprinted 1677 and 1684.

— The true Art of Angling. Lond. for Ustonson, 1770. 12mo.

Haworth, 782, 12s.

— An Essay on the right of Angling in the River Thames, and in all the other navigable rivers. Reading, n. d. 8vo.

(Reprinted, 1787.) Haworth, 777, 14s.

— See ANGLER.

Anglorum, Metamorphoses, or Reflections upon the late changes of Government in England. 1660. 8vo.

Lloyd, 858, 4s.

— Metamorphosis, sive Mutationes variæ Regum, Regni, Rerumque Angliæ. Anno. 1653. 12mo. 5s.

Principally taken from Clement Walker's History of Independency, by M. Z. Boxhornius.

— Speculum, or the Worthies of England in Church and State, alphabetically digested into the several Shires and Counties therein contained, &c. Lond. 1684. 8vo. pp. 974. 6s.

An abridgment of Fuller's Worthies of England, with a continuation. The preface is signed G. S. Nassau, pt. 1. 39, 10s. Bp. of Ely, 25, 14s. 6d. Gough, 66, 1l. 1s.

ANGUS, W. Seats of the Nobility and Gentry in Great Britain and Wales, in a collection of select Views engraved by W. Angus, from Pictures and Drawings by the most eminent Masters, with Descriptions of each View. Lond. 1787-1810. oblong 4to. 63 plates.

Prints, 2l. 2s. Proofs, 5l. 5s.

In little estimation except the impressions be good. Bindley, pt. 1. 126, 3l. 15s. Fonthill, 1311, 5l. 5s. Graves, 97 (Proofs) 5l. 12s. 6d. The copper-plates of this work were lately in existence, and many copies have been struck off under the old date.

Annalia Dvbrensia: Vpon the yeerely Celebration of Mr. Robert Dover's Olympick Games vpon Cotwold Hills. London, 1636. 4to.

Contains pp. 72, A—K 2, with a frontispiece, in the lower part of which is Captain Dover on horseback. (Very rare.) In Dr. Bliss's edition of Ant. à Wood's Athenæ Oxonienses, iv. 222-3, will be found an account of this curious work,—ORIG. EDIT. Bibl. Anglo-Poet. 891, 7l. 7s. Bindley, pt. 1. 152, 12l. 12s. Saunders in 1818, 13l. 2s. 6d. Thorpe, 10l. 10s. Midgley, 8l. 8s. REPRINT. Boswell, 918, 2l. 10s. Nassau, pt. 1. 168, russia, 2l. 11s. Towneley, pt. 1. 302, 3l. 13s. 6d.

Annals of the Fine Arts, (Edited by Jas. Elmes and B. R. Haydon). Lond. 1816-20. 8vo. 17 Nos. in 5 vols. with plates, 1l. 11s. 6d.

— See FINE ARTS.

ANNE BULLEN, Queen of K. Henry VIII. Epistre contenant le Proces criminel faict a l'Encontre de la Royne Anne Boullant d'Angleterre, en Vers par Carles Aulmosnier du Daulphin. Lyon, 1545. 12mo.

Sir M. M. Sykes, pt. 1. 243, 1l. 10s. In Nichols' Progresses of Q. Elizabeth, will be found the Ceremonial of Marriage and Verses and Ditties made at her Coronation. In the Household Book of Henry VIII. are many curious facts relating to Anne Boleyn.

ANNE, Queen of King James I. Academiæ Oxoniensis Funebria sacra Annæ Reginæ. Oxon. 1619. 4to. 6s.

Another 'Lachrymæ Cantabrigienses.' Cantab. 1619, 4to. 6s.

— Fifth Child of K. Charles I. ΣΨΝΩΔΙΑ, sive Musarum Cantab. Concentus et Congratulatio ad Regem Carolum de quinta Sobole

clarissima Principe, sibi nuper felicissimè nata. Cantab. 1637. 4to.
Bindley, pt. iii. 581, 5s.

ANNE, Queen of Great Britain. The Life of Queen Anne. London, 1721. 8vo. 2 vols. 5s. *See* BOYER, A.

ANNESON, Jas. *i.e.* MAXWELL, Jas.

ANNET, Peter. The Free Enquirer. London, 1762. folio.
For this deistical publication the author was pilloried, and imprisoned. Annet was probably author of the following, for the most part published without his name:
Judging for ourselves; or, Free-thinking the great Duty of Religion, 1739, 1794.
The History of Joseph considered, by Mencius Philalethes. 1744.
The Conception of Jesus considered, 1744.
The Resurrection of Jesus considered, in Answer to the Tryal of the Witnesses. 1744. 1st Edition, n. d. 2d. spurious. 3d. with great amendments, 1744.
The Resurrection reconsidered, 1744.
The Resurrection of Jesus demonstrated to have no Proof.
(The History of Man after God's own heart. *Replied to by Dr. Chandler.*)
The Resurrection Defenders stript of all Defence, 1745.
The Sequel of the Resurrection of Jesus considered, (1745).
Observations on the Life of St. Paul.
The History and Character of Paul examined.
A Letter to Gilbert West, Esq. and to the Author of the Observations on St. Paul's Conversion, 1748.
Supernaturals examined.
Social Bliss considered, 1749.
A Collection of the Tracts of a certain free Enquirer, noted by his sufferings for his opinions, 1766.
Lectures, 1768, with a portrait of Annet, by Darling.
Short Hand. Three Editions.

ANNILO, Orosius. Dissertatio de Bello Dano-Anglico, 4to. 6s.

Annual Biography and Obituary from 1817 to 1837, inclusive, 8vo. 21 vols. 5*l.* 5s.
Published at 15s. each.

Annual Register, from its commencement in 1758 to 1790 inclusive, 32 vols. Continuation published by Otridge, Baldwin, and others, 1791-1827 inclusive, 37 vols., and Index from 1758 to 1819, 1 vol. London, 8vo. 70 vols. (Since continued to 1856, and still proceeding.)
Roxburghe, 7454, (1758—1801) 16*l.* 16s.
Earl of Kerry, 23. (1758—1817) 29*l.* 8s. Fonthill, 1139. (1758—1819) 24*l.* Duke of York, 111, (1758—1823) 21*l.* Drury, 89, (1758—1825) 41*l.* 10s.
This valuable publication originated with Robert Dodsley, at the suggestion of Edmund Burke, who was for some years editor and principal contributor.
Some time after the year 1791, the copyright and stock from 1758 to 1790, were purchased by Otridge and other booksellers. After which period Messrs. Rivingtons, who had for a short time previously (during the illness of Mr. Dodsley) been agents for the work, published a rival continuation, which lasted from 1791 to 1812, and again from 1820 to 1824, when the two merged by arrangement into one.
Some sets of the work have been made up by substituting Rivington's continuation, with fictitious titles. How to distinguish the substitution may be ascertained by referring to the preface of the General Index published by Baldwin & Co. in. 1826, 8vo. price 1*l.* 4s.
A general index, 1758—80, was published by Dodsley, in 1783; another, 1781—90, by the Rivingtons, in 1799; (and a third, superseding the previous ones, from the commencement to 1819, in 1826. And, as this complete Index is only applicable to the original, or Dodsley series, the volumes published by Rivingtons are generally rejected.)

Annual Register. A Continuation, 1791—1800, 11 vols. 1801—1812, 12 vols. 1820—4, 5 vols. Published by Messrs. Rivingtons. London, 8vo.
This continuation, though not generally adopted, for the reason stated above, has the character of being carefully compiled.

— The New Annual Register from its commencement in 1780, to 1825, inclusive. Lond., 8vo. 46 vols.
Andrew Kippis, D.D. was many years editor of this Annual, (and Dr. Gregory and Alex. Chalmers were large contributors). Drury, 90, (1780—1825, 46 vols.) 7*l.* Sotheby's in 1827, (1780—1806, 27 vols.) 3*l.*

Annual Register. The Edinburgh Annual Register, from the commencement in 1803 to 1827. Edinb. 8vo.
Sir Walter Scott was the ostensible editor of this work. Drury, No. 1285, (1808—23, 22 vols.) 5*l.*

Annual Review, from the commencement in 1802, to its finish in 1808, by Arthur Aikin. London. royal 8vo. 7 vols. 1*l.* 1s.

An excellent periodical, which met with but little encouragement.

Annus Mirabilis. Lond. 1660, &c. 4to.

An annual publication, much censured by Ant. à Wood.

Anonymiana. *See* PEGGE, Samuel.

ANQUETIL, Louis Peter. Summary of Universal History; exhibiting the Rise, Decline, and Revolutions of the different Nations of the World, from the Creation to the present Time. Translated from the French. London, 1800. 8vo. 9 vols. 2*l.* 10s.

Said to be an abridgment of the English Universal History. Earl of Kerry, 22, bound in vellum, 4*l.* 5s. A translation of Anquetil's Memoirs of the Court of France during the reign of Louis XIV., and the Regency of the Duke of Orleans, was published 1791, 8vo. 2 vols. 10s. 6d.

ANSON, George, Lord. A Voyage round the World, 1740—4, compiled from Papers, and other Materials of the Right Hon. George, Lord Anson, by Richard Walter, M.A. (Benj. Robins,) London, 1748. 4to. with 42 plates.

In Davis' Olio, pp. 1—4, is an article as to who was the compiler of this voyage. Heath, 2806, 1*l.* 18s. Willett, 88, 2*l.* 2s. LARGE PAPER. Gough, 183, 2*l.* 4s. Nassau, pt. i. 169, 2*l.* 5s. Baker, 145, with a drawing of Lord Anson, by Wale, 3*l.* 8s. Roxburghe, 7160, 3*l.* 10s. Marq. of Townshend, 146, 8*l.* 16s. Reprinted 1749, 4to. 1748, 8vo. 1767, 4to. 1776, 4to. Also in Callander's Voyages, vol. iii., in Harris, and other collections.

— A Supplement to Lord Anson's Voyage round the World, containing a Discovery and Description of the Island of Frivola. By the Abbé COYER. To which is prefixed an introductory Preface by the Translator. Lond. 1752. 8vo. 2s. 6d.

A satirical romance on the French nation.

ANSPACH, Lewis Amedeus. Summary of the Laws of Commerce and Navigation, adapted to the Island of Newfoundland. Lond. 1809. 8vo.

This author likewise published a History of the Island of Newfoundland, London, 1819, 8vo. pp. 512, with two maps.

VOL. I.

— Lady Craven, Margravine of. The Sleep-walker. Strawberry-Hill. 1771. 8vo.

A translation from the French of Pont de Vile, of which only 75 copies were printed. Sir M. M. Sykes, pt. iii. 891, 1*l.* 4s. Strettell, 1609, mor. 1*l.* 5s. Roxburghe, 4374, 1*l.* 10s. Brockett, 2950, 2*l.* Utterson, 1852, 2*l.* 3s. Lady Craven likewise published 'The Miniature Picture,' 1781, 8vo. Roxburghe, 4373, 7s. 6d., Nourjad, Hammersmith, 1806, 5s., and others.

— Journey through the Crimea to Constantinople. In a Series of Letters from the Right Hon. Elizabeth, Lady Craven, to the Margrave of Brandebourg Anspach and Bareith. Lond. 1789. 4to. pp. 332, 15s.

Fonthill. 361, 1*l.* 8s.

— Pleasant Passetime for Christmas Evenings, or the Predictions of Cosmopolitus Occultarius, &c. London, 1795. 12mo.

Privately printed. A copy on vellum at the sale of the Mac-Carthy library brought 63 fr.

— Letters from Lady Craven to the Margrave of Anspach, during her Travels through France, Germany, Russia, &c. in 1785 and 1787. Second Edition, including a variety of Letters not before published. London, 1814. 4to.

— Memoirs of the Margravine of Anspach, written by herself. London, 1826. 8vo. 2 vols. with portraits, 28s.

ANSTEY, Christopher. Poetical Works, with some Account of his Life and Writings, by his Son. London, 1808. 4to. with plates.

Nassau, pt. i. 170, 1*l.* 14s. The writings of this celebrated person have been much admired, particularly the New Bath Guide, which has gone through many editions. His 'Election Ball,' 1776, 4to. had cuts after the manner of Hogarth. C. Anstey, in 1774, published a poem in 4to. entitled 'The Priest dissected,' which he afterwards suppressed.

ANSTIS, John, Garter King of Arms. Curia Militaris, or a Treatise of the Court of Chivalry. London, 1702. 8vo. 4s.

This curious Tract (never published)

contains only the introduction, and contents of the treatise, pages xli.

ANSTIS, John. Letters to a Peer concerning the Honour of Earl Marshall. Lond. 1706. 8vo. pp. 52, 5s.

An enlarged and amended edition. The original was published in 1708, 8vo. pp. 35.

— The Register of the most noble Order of the Garter, usually called the Black Book; with Notes and an Introduction. London, 1724. folio. 2 vols.

Vol. i. pp. 470. Editor's Appendix, &c. pp. 72, besides a preface, &c. pp. 34, and an allegorical frontispiece by J. Sympson. Vol. ii. pp. 500, with an introduction, 59 pages. Dent. pt. i. 150, morocco, 2l. 12s. 6d. Marq. of Townshend, 198, 3l. 13s. 6d. LARGE PAPER. Nassau, pt. i. 205, russ. 3l. 3s. Sir M. M. Sykes, pt. i. 147, mor. 3l. 5s. Heath, 1618, russia, 3l. 17s. Willett, 127, russia, 7l. 7s. Fonthill, 2427, 10l.

— Observations introductory to an historical Essay upon the Knighthood of the Bath. London, 1725. 4to.

Contains pp. 88. At the end 'A Collection of Authorities referred to in the Introduction.' Bindley, pt. i. 135, 7s.

This work contains all which could be collected on the Order of the Bath, from the earliest period to the time when its learned author wrote, and exhibits proofs of great industry and research. An account of the changes which took place in the Order in 1815, with observations on the subject, will be found in the Retrospective Review, N. S. vol. i.

ANSTRUTHER, Alexander. Reports of Cases in the Court of Exchequer, from Easter Term 32 Geo. III. to Trinity Term, 37 Geo. III. London, 1817. royal 8vo. 3 vols. 2l. 5s.

The former edition 1796-7. royal 8vo. 3 vols. 15s.

Answere, An, to a Papystycall Exhortacyon to avoyde false Doctryne, under that Colour to mayntayne the same. Without place or date. 8vo.

Black letter. In verse, the Exhortation and Answer being printed alternately: the first in six line stanzas, the latter in Skeltonical doggrel.

Answere, An, to the proclamation of the Rebels in the north. Imp. by Seres, 1569.

Black letter, 8vo. in verse. Bib. Ang. Poet. 20l.

Answere, An, to a Romish rime lately printed, wherein are contayned Catholick questions to the Protestants. 1602. 4to.

Bindley, 708, 2l. 12s. 6d. Longman, 1819, date, 1608, 2l. 12s. 6d.

Antar. See HAMILTON, Terrick.

Antenor. Travels in Greece. See LANTIER, E. F.

ANTES, John. Observations on the Manners and Customs of the Egyptians. London, 1800. 4to. with a map.

Fonthill, 432, 8s. Reprinted Dublin, 1801. 12mo.

Anthologia. 1655. See FULLER, Thomas, D.D.

ANTHING, Fred. History of the Campaigns of Count Alex. Suworow Rymnikski, translated from the German. London, 1799. 8vo. 2 vols. 8s.

Anthologia, seu selecta quædam Poemata Italorum qui Latine scripserunt. Lond. 1684. 12mo. 5s.

Published by Bp. Atterbury, with an elegant preface.

Anthologia Hibernica. See Ireland.

Anthologiæ Græcæ a Constantino Cephala conditæ Libri tres: edidit J. J. Reiske. Oxon. 1766. 8vo. 5s.

Published with an elegant Latin preface, by Tho. Warton, editor of Theocritus. LARGE PAPER. Heath, 3355, 10s. Dent, pt. i. 54, 1l.

Anthology. A Selection of Greek Epigrams from Brunck's Anthology, with an English translation. Oxon. 1791. 12mo. 2s. 6d

— Translations chiefly from the Greek Anthology, with Tales and miscellaneous Poems, by Bland and Merivale. Lond. 1806. 8vo. 7s.

A volume of considerable merit, in which will be found a beautiful translation of some noble lines from the Medea of Euripides, and a Greek epigram by Dr. Johnson. Drury, 472, mor. 10s.

— Collections from the Greek Anthology, and from the pastoral, elegiac and dramatic Poets of

Greece, by the Rev. R. Bland and others Lond 1813. 8vo. pp. 525. 12s.
(Republished with omissions and additions in 1833, 8vo.)
A valuable poetic version. LARGE PAPER. Drury, 913, russia, 1l. 9s.
— The English. *See* RITSON, Joseph.

Anthony.—The Lyfe of Saynte Anthonye. Impr. by Julyan Notary (1520) 4to.
Black letter.

Anthony, King of Portugal.—The Explanation of the Right and Tytle of Anthonie the First, King of Portugall, concerning his Warres for the Recouerie of his Kingdome. Leyden, in the Printing House of Christopher Plantyn. 1585. 4to.
Contains pp. 54, and 'A Pedigree or Table of Genealogie,' &c. Bindley, pt. ii. 1206, 5s. Lloyd, 509, 16s. Sir P. Thompson, 232, 1l. 11s. 6d.

ANTHONY, Francis, M.D. Medicinæ Chymicæ et veri potabilis Auri Assertio, ex Lucubrationibus Fra. Anthonii Londinensis in Medicina Doctoris. Cantab. 1610. 4to. 5s.
This defence is divided into seven chapters, the last enumerates the several distempers which his aurem potabile cures; among which is the plague itself.

— Apologia Veritatis illuscescentis pro Auro Potabili, &c. Lond. 1616. 4to. 5s.
The Apology and Defence were likewise published in English, 1616. 4to. In answer to this noted empiric, Dr. Gwinne published 'Aurum non Aurum.' Lond. 1611. 4to. and Dr. Cotta 'The Anti-Apology.' Oxford, 1623. 4to.

— John. Lucas Redivivus, or the Gospel Physician, prescribing (by Way of Meditation) Divine Physic, &c. London, 1656. 4to. with portrait by T. Cross.
This writer was the son of the noted empiric, and likewise published 'The Comfort of the Soul,' 1654. 4to.

Antichrist. — Downfal of Antichristes Mas. 1546.
A poem of thirty octave stanzas, in which, says Warton, the nameless satirist is unjustly severe on the distresses of that class of mechanics who get their living by writing and ornamenting service-books for the old papistic worship.

— A short description of Antichrist with a Warning. (About 1548) 8vo.
Black letter. White Knights, 123, mor. 1l 15s.

Antidote against Melancholy, made up in Pills, compounded of witty Ballads, jovial Songs, and merry Catches. London and Westminster, 1661. 4to. with a plate.
Lloyd, 216, 2l. 12s. 6d. Jolley, 1843, mor. n. d. 6l. 6s.

— A collection of merry Songs, with Music. 1749. 12mo.
Nassau, pt. i. 46, 10s. Dent, pt. i. 60, 12s. Boswell, 72, 12s. Sotheby's in 1825, 1l. 7s.

Antidotharius, The. Imprynted by me, R. Wyer, 16mo.
Black letter. Contains sign. E in fours, half sheets. 'It seems to have been,' says Herbert, 'from these little cheap physical treatises, which perhaps sold for an halfpenny, or at most for a penny, that the old women were furnished with their nostrums.' There were several editions by Wyer, differing here and there in the spelling of a few words. Two will be found in the British Museum. Inglis, No. 23, 1l.

Anti-Dvello, or a Treatise in which is discussed the Lawfulness and Vnlawfulness of single Combats: together with the Forme of severall Dvells performed in this Kingdom upon sundry Occasions. London, 1632. 4to. pp. 63, with plate of Guiye of Warwick.
Reed, 3304, 1l. 13s.

— *See* SELDEN.

ANTI-SPANIARD, 1590. 4to.
Black letter. Reed, 3305, 14s. 6d.

Antigua.—Collect. of Exotics from the Island of Antigua. By a Lady. Lond. 1800. fol. 2l. 2s. coloured.

— Laws of Antigua, consisting of the Acts of the Leeward Islands, from Nov. 1690 to April, 1798; and the Acts of Antigua, from April, 1668, to May, 1804; with analytical Tables of the Acts, and an Index. 1805—18. 4to. 3 vols. 7l. 7s.

Anti-Jacobin. — The Anti-Jacobin, or Weekly Examiner, from Nov.

E 2

20, 1797, to July 9, 1798. London, 4to. 36 Nos. with a Prospectus.
All that was published in 4to.

Anti-Jacobin, or Weekly Examiner. Lond. 1799. 8vo. 2 vols.
Said to have been edited by Wm. Gifford, Esq. Roxburghe, 7008, 9s. Drury, 101, 1l. 1s.

Anti-jacobin Review and Magazine, or Monthly Political and Literary Censor, from the Commencement in 1798, to the Conclusion in 1821. 8vo.
Gifford, Frere, and Canning, were contributors to this periodical. In the early volumes are caricatures by Gillray. Heath, 4491, 30 vols. 7l. 17s. 6d. Duke of York, 115, 61 vol. 1799—1821, 4l. 4s.

— The Poetry of the Anti-Jacobin [by Gifford, Canning, Frere, Ellis]. London, 1801. 4to. 15s.
Frequently reprinted in 12mo.

ANTIOCHENUS, Joan. *Vide* MALALA.

Antipus. — The Comparison betwene the Antipus and the Antigraphe, or Answere thereunto, with Apology or Defense of the same Antipus and Reprehence of the Antigraphe. (Lond. by John Daye) 4to. n. d:
Black letter, six leaves. In doggrel metre. Roxburghe, 3290, mor. 6l. 6s.

Antiquarian Repertory: a Miscellany intended to preserve and illustrate several valuable remains of old Times. Lond. 1775-84. 4to. 4 vols. with plates.
This valuable work was compiled by, or under the direction of, Francis Grose, Thomas Astle, and other eminent antiquaries. Dent, pt. i. 279, russia, 3l. 4s. Bindley, pt. i. 109, 3l. 8s. Towneley, pt. ii. 105, russia, 4l. 14s. 6d. Reed, 3302, 5l. Fonthill, 1865, 6l. 5s.

— A new edition, with many valuable additions. Lond. 1807-9. 4to. 4 vols.
Published and edited by Jeffery the bookseller. The very able preface to this edition was written by Edmund Lodge, Esq. (The fourth vol. contains the 'Northumberland Household book,' edited by Bp. Percy.) Dent, pt. i. 280, russia, 5l. 2s. 6d. Bindley, pt. i. 110, 3l. 8s. LARGE PAPER, Dent, pt. i. 281, bds. 7l. 7s. Nassau, pt. i. 173, 9l. Fonthill, 1155, 9l. Brockett, 238, russia, 13l. 12s. 6d.

Antiquarian and Topographical Cabinet, and Itinerary. *See* STORER and GREIG.

Antiquaries of London.—Archæologia, or Miscellaneous Tracts relating to Antiquity. London, 1770 —1856. 4to. 36 vols. Index to vols. 1—15. 1809. 4to. and Index to vols. 16—30. 1844. 4to.
The fourth and eighth volumes are of rare occurrence. Steevens, 1737, 12 vols. 12l. Edwards, 70, 12 vols. 17l. 6s. 6d. Roxburghe, 8573, 13 vols. in russia, 39l. Towneley, pt. ii. 104, 14 vols. 22l. Reed, 1768, 15 vols. with Ordinances and Liber Quotid. 22l. 10s. Willett, 95, 16 vols. with Liber Quotid. Ordinances, and Index, 30l. Baker, 148, 16 vols. with Index, 21l. 10s. Dent, pt. i. 290, 16 vols. Index and Liber Quotid. 29l. Duke of York, 255, 17 vols. and Index, 21l. 10s. 6d. Bindley, pt. i 106, 18 vols. and Index, 32l. 10s. Nassau, pt. i. 181, 19 vols. Index, Ordinances, and Liber Quotid. russia, 35l. Combe, 139, 19 vols. and Index, 21l. Drury, 388, 20 vols. pt. i. of vol. 21, Ordinances and Lib. Quotid. 33l. 12s.

— Queries proposed to gentlemen in the several parts of Great Britain. Lond. 1754. 8vo. 3s.

— Three Chronological Tables of the Members. By Sir John Fenn. London, 1784. 4to.

— Liber Quotidianus Contrarotulatoris Garderobae, Anno Regni Regis Edwardi I. vicesimo octavo, A.D. 1299 and 1300. 1787. 4to. 12s.
This volume, (edited by John Topham), says Mr. Nicolas, ' abounds in highly interesting information, illustrative of the history, manners, expenses, army, navy, provisions, costume, &c. of the 13th century, and as an adjunct to historical and antiquarian inquiries, it cannot be too highly estimated. Few MSS. have been so well edited; but amidst much ground for praise, it is to be regretted that it does not contain an index, an omission which considerably lessens its utility.'

— Collection of Ordinances and Regulations for the Government of the Royal Household, made in divers Reigns, from Edward III. to William and Mary, and also Receipts in Antient Cookery, 1790. 4to. 12s.
'This collection contains many curious illustrations of the manners of our ancestors, and especially of the royal house-

holds, prices of provisions, &c., and may be deemed one of the few text books for antiquarian inquiries.'

— List of the Members of the Society of Antiquaries from 1717 to 1796; 1798. 4to.
By Richard Gough.

— Copy of the Royal Charter and Statutes, and of Orders and Regulations established by the Council of the Society. London, 1800. 4to.

The charter, &c. of this society were likewise printed in 8vo. 1752, 1759, 1764, 1790.

Five Dissertations, viz: Webb (P. C.) on Domesday Book and Danegeld. Webb (P. C.) and Dr. Pettingall, two Dissertations on the Heraclean Table. Pettingall (Dr.) on the Tascia, 4to. 7s.

Magni Rotuli Scaccarii Normanniæ sub Regibus Angliæ: the Norman Rolls of the times of Henry II. and Richard I. Ed. by Thos. Stapleton, 1840-44. 2 vols. 8vo. 15s.

— A Catalogue of the printed Books and MSS. in the Library of the Society. London, 1816. 4to.

The society have likewise published the following Prints, viz.:—

Le Champ de Drap d'Or. The interview of Henry VIII. and Francis I. between Guines and Ardres in June 1520. From the original Picture in Windsor Castle. With an historical Description by Sir Joseph Ayloffe, Bt. 4to. pp. 45, 1771. folio. 2l. 2s.

Encampment of the English Forces near Portsmouth, MDXLV. from a coeval Painting at Cowdray in Sussex. With an historical Description, by Sir Joseph Ayloffe, Bart. 4to. pp. 20, 1778. folio. 1l. 5s.

The embarkation of K. Henry VIII. at Dover, May XXXI. MDXX. From the original Picture in Windsor Castle. With a Description by John Topham, Esq., 4to. pp. 42, with two etchings, 1781. folio. 1l. 11s. 6d.

The procession of K. Edward VI. Feb. XIX. MDXLVII. previous to his Coronation. Engraved from a coeval Painting at Cowdray, in Sussex, by James Basire. With an Account, in 4to. pp. 20, 1787. folio. 1l. 11s. 6d.

The Departure of K. Henry VIII. from Calais, July XXV. MDXLIV. The Encampment of K. Henry VIII. at Marquison, July MDXLIV. The Siege of Boulogne by K. Henry VIII. MDXLIV. Three Prints from coeval Paintings at Cowdray, in Sussex. With a Description. 4to. pp. 32. 1788. folio. 2l. 2s.

A set of the above prints with the Cathedrals of Exeter, Bath, and Durham, and St. Stephen's Chapel, in 1 vol. Roxburghe, 8608, 21l. 10s. 6d.

Prints engraved by George Vertue, viz.: Plan of London and Westminster, as it was near the Beginning of the Reign of Q. Elizabeth, by R. Agas. 1748. Eight plates, 10s.

Views of the Chappel of St. Thomas on London Bridge. 1747-8. Two plates, 4s.

An exact Surveigh of the Streets, Lanes, and Churches comprehended within the Ruins of the City of London, by John Leake. 1723. Two plates, 3s.

Two Views of St. Martin's Church in the Fields, with the Plan. Three plates, 2s. 6d.

The tesselated Pavement at Stunsfield, in Oxfordshire. One plate, 1s.

Views of Mr. Lethiullier's Mummy. 1724. Two plates, 1s.

Nine historical Prints representing Kings, Queens, Princes, &c. of the Tudor family, with a Description of 21 pp. Republished by the Society, 1766. 2l. 7s.

Portraits of K. Charles I. and his Queen. One plate, 5s.

Plan and elevation of the Petty Canons' Houses at Windsor. 1s.

Lincoln's Inn Chapel, with the Ambulatory, 1751. 2s. 6d.

A Survey and Ground Plot of the Royal Palace at Whitehall, 1747, 2s.

The Market Cross at Chichester, 1749. 2s.

The View of the Charity Children in the Strand upon the VII of July, MDCCXIII, 1715. Two sheets 7s. 6d.

Portrait of Sir John Hawkwood (Joannes Acutus Eques Britannicus) 1771. 1s. 6d.

Views of the Ruins of Stanton Harcourt, in Oxfordshire, drawn and etched by Earl Harcourt. Four plates, 1l. 1s.

For other Publications by this Society, see

CONYBEARE, J. J.
CÆDMON, —
FOLKES, Martin.
Vetusta Monumenta.
ROY, William.
Bath,
Westminster,
Exeter,   } Cathedrals,
Durham,   } &c.
Gloucester,
Albans, St.

The last six articles in one volume. Drury, 200, 8l. 18s. 6d. Strettell, 1045, russia, 11l. 5s. Dent, pt. i. 509, 12l. 12s.

Antiquities.—Essay on the Study of Antiquities. *See* BURGESS, Thomas, Bishop of St. Davids.

— Miscellaneous Antiquities. *See* WALPOLE, Horace, Earl of Orford.

Anti-Theatre from Feb. 15, 1719-20, to April 4, 1720. London, 15 numbers complete.

[Reprinted by Nichols in 1791, 8vo.]
Written in opposition to the popular paper of Sir Richard Steele, entitled The Theatre.

ANTON, Robert. Philosophers' Satyrs. London, 1616. 4to. 15s.

These dull satires are entitled from the seven planets. Some copies bear the date of 1617, and the title of 'Vices Anatomie.' Bindley, pt. i. 156, 1*l.* 1s. Constable, 188, morocco, 8*l.* 3s.

Antonie (The tragedie of), done into English by the Countesse of Pembroke, 18mo. 1599; a copy in Edin. Collection.

ANTONINUS, Marcus Aurelius. De Seipso, seu Vita sua, Libri XII. Gr. et Lat. cum Annotationibus M. Casauboni. Lond. 1643. 8vo. 5s.

A neat and accurate edition.

— De Seipso, studio, operaque Thomæ Gatakeri. Cantab. 1652. 4to. 6s.

A valuable edition. Copies on large paper are rare. An elegant little edition was printed Oxon. 1680. 12mo. 3s.

— Editio altera, aucta et idoneis Script. veterum Testimoniis firmata, a Geo. Stanhope. Lond. 1697, 4to. 5s.

A good edition. Copies on large paper are very rare. Askew, 2*l.* 2s.

— Recogniti et Notis illustrati, a Nic. Ibbetson. Oxon. 1704. 8vo. 3s. 6d.

An excellent edition, according to Dr. Harwood, with some epistles at the end, attributed to Antoninus. LARGE PAPER. Sotheby's in 1824, 1*l.* 1s. Drury, 102, morocco, by Roger Payne, 1*l.* 9s. Dent, pt. i. 62, morocco, by Roger Payne, 1*l.* 16s. Williams, 48, 49, morocco, 1*l.* 6s. and 1*l.* 19s.

— cum Comment. Th. Gatakeri, necnon M. Antonini Vita, a Geo. Stanhope. Londini, 1707. 4to. 6s.

A Reprint of the edition of 1697. The Glasgow editions of 1744 and 1751. 3s., or on FINE PAPER, 4s. The edition 1744, on FINE PAPER, Williams, 50, morocco, 15s.

ANTONINUS. The golden Boke of Marcus Aurelius, Emperour and Oratour, translated out of Frenche into Englishe by John Bourchier Knyghte Lorde Barners. London in the House of Tho. Berthelet (1534) 16mo. 1*l.* 1s.

Black letter. Contains Oo vij, in eights. The first impression of this popular work. Reprinted 1536, 1537, 1542, 1546, 1553, 1554, 1556, 1557, 1559, 1566, 1576, 1586, 1587, in 4to. and 16mo.

— Meditations, translated with Notes by Meric Casaubon, D.D. Fifth edition, with the Life of Antoninus translated from the French of Dacier, by W. King. London, 1692. 8vo. 5s.

Reprinted 1694 and 1702. The editions of 1634, 1635, 1664, and 1673, are of the same value. There is a copy of the edition of 1634 in the British Museum, with the MS. notes and additions of the editor.

— Conversations with himself, his Life by M. Dacier, and the Mythological Picture of Cebes the Theban, translated by Jeremy Collier. London, 1701. 8vo. 5s.

An inelegant translation, abounding with vulgar and ludicrous expressions, reprinted 1708, 1726.

— Commentaries, translated by James Thompson. London, 1747. 8vo.

Edwards, 222, 4s.

— Meditations newly translated out of the Greek, with Notes and a Life of the Author by Jas. Thomson. Glasgow, 1749, 12mo. 2 vols. 5s.

'Correct in the main, but deficient in point of elegance.'—*Monthly Rev.*

An edition 1764, 4th. Edit. Reed, 1665, 10s. 6d. Williams, 51, morocco, 15s.

— Meditations. A new translation by R. Graves, M. A. Bath, 1792. 8vo. 5s.

The best English version of Antoninus, rendered particularly valuable by the judicious notes of the translator.

ANTONINUS PIUS. Antonini Iter Britanniarum, Commentariis illustratum Thomæ Gale. Opus posthumum, revisit, auxit, edidit R. G(ale). Accessit Anonymi Rave-

nantis Britanniæ Chorographica. Londini, 1709. 4to. 5s.
A good edition. Heath, 4520, 9s. 6d. Saunders in 1818, 71, 14s. Another edition will be found in Leland's Itinerary, vol. iii. 1711.

— Iter Britanniarum, with a new Comment, by the Rev. Thomas Reynolds, A.M. Cambridge, 1799. 4to. with two maps.
Dent, pt. i. 263, 10s. 6d. Towneley, pt. ii. 109, 10s. 6d. LARGE PAPER, 1l. 11s. 6d. For Commentaries
See BURTON, and GIBSON.

Antonio and Mellida (The history of), 1602. 4to.
Bindley, 3l. 3s.

ANTONIOTTO, Giorgio. L'Arte Armonica: or, a Treatise on the Composition of Music, in three books; with an Introduction on the History and Progress of Music, from its beginning to this time, translated into English. London, 1760. folio. 2 vols. 12s.
A tolerable translation of a very elaborate and skilful performance.

ANTROBUS, Benjamin. Buds and Blossoms of Piety, with some Fruit of the Spirit of Love. London, 1691. 8vo.
Nassau, pt. i. 360, 3s. Bibl. Anglo-Poet 897, 1l. 5s.

Antwerp. — Antwerp's Unytie. An Accord or Peace in Religion and Government, concluded by his Highness, &c. London, 1579. 8vo.
Black letter. A copy is in the British Museum.

— Newes from Antwerp, 10 Aug. 1580. Translated partly out of French and partly out of Lattin. London, 4to.
Black letter. E 2 in fours. Herbert mentions another work relating to this city, printed 1576, entitled 'The Spoile of Antwarpe.'

— Entertainment of Frauncis the Frenche Kings Brother at Antwerp. London, 1582. 16mo.
Black letter.

— Historie of the Citie of Antwerpe since the Departure of Phillip King of Spain out of Netherland, ill 1586. Lond. 1586. 4to.

Black letter. 27 leaves. Lloyd, 749, 17s. Hollis, 658, 16s. Bindley, pt. ii. 1882, 1l. 7s.

Ape-Gentle-woman, or the Character of an Exchange Wench. 1675. 4to.
Strettell, 173, 10s. White Knights, pt i. 162, 2l.

Aphthonii Sophistæ Præexercitamenta Fabula, interprete viro doctissimo [Gentiano Herveto] dedicat. ad Jacobum Bernardum Londiniensi. S. P. Lond. R. Pynson, 1521. 12mo.

APICIUS Cælius. *Vide* CÆLIUS.

Apocalypse. *See* St. John.

Apocrypha.—The Volume of the Bokes called Apocripha. London, by John Day and Wylliam Seres. (1549) 16mo.
Black letter. A.—Yy. iii. A full page contains 33 lines. Copies are in the British Museum and Lambeth Libraries. Inglis, 26 (sheet B. wanting) 15s.

— With critical Observations by Charles Wilson. Edinb. 1801. 8vo. 3s. 6d.
In the British Museum is an Essay concerning the Books commonly called Apocrypha. London, 1740. 8vo.

— *See* BIBLE.

APOLLINARIUS. — Interpretatio Psalmorum Versibus Heroicis: Ex Bibliotheca Regia. Londini, 1590. 16mo. 4s.
Contains pp. 202, and errata. Elegantly printed in pica Greek.

Apollo.—The British Apollo; or curious Amusements for the Ingenious. London, 1708—10. folio. 3 vols. 1l. 1s. [And a few numbers of a fourth vol.]
An abridgment of this curious periodical work, 'containing 2000 Answers to Questions in most Arts and Sciences,' was published 1726 and 1740, 12mo. 3 vols. Edition, 1740, Gosset, 883. 16s. 6d. Roxburghe, 6708, 12s. Nassau, pt. i. 330. 15s.

— Apollo Christian or Helicon Reformed. London, 1617. 8vo.
Six Poems, dedicated to Algernon Lord Percie. Sir M. M. Sykes, pt. i. mor. 20l.

— Apollo shroving, 1627. *See* HAWKINS, William.

— Apollo's Cabinet, or the Muse's

Delight. A Collection of English and Italian Songs, Cantatas and Duets, with the Music. Liverpool, 1756.
Nassau, pt. 1. 52, 1*l.*

Apollo.—Apollo's Feast, pleasant Intrigues, Old Tales, Witty Poems, &c. London, 1703. 8vo.
Perry, date 1718, 1*l.* 18s. Bindley, pt. 1. 24, 1*l.* 1s.

APOLLODORUS. — Ἀπολλοδώρου τοῦ Ἀθηναίου Γραμματικοῦ, Βιβλιοθήκης, ἢ περὶ Θεῶν Βιβλίον ά. In usum scholæ Westmonasteriensis. Londini, 1686. 8vo.
Edited by Thomas Knipe, chief master of Westminster School.

APOLLONII, Guil. Consideratio quarundam Controversiarum, ad Regimem Eclesiæ spectantum quæ in Angliæ Regno hodie agitantur; ex Mandato et Jussu Classis Walacbrianæ conscripta. Lond. 1644. 8vo.
An English translation was published 1645, and in 1647, appeared 'The supreme Power of Christian States vindicated against Gulielmus Apollonii.' 4to.

APOLLONIUS PERGÆUS.—de Sectione Rationis Libri ii. ex Arabico MS. Latine versi. Accedunt de Sectione Spatii Libri ii. restitui: præmittuntur Pappi Lemmata et Præfatio ad Septimum Collectionis Mathematicæ Græcæ, Opera et Studio Edm. Halley. Oxon. 1706. 8vo. 5s.
An edition of the Conics, Lat. will be found in Barrow's edition of Archimedes.

— Conicorum Libri octo et Sereni Antissensis de Sectione Cylindri et Coni Libri duo, Gr. et Lat. edente Edm. Halley. Oxon. 1710. folio. 1*l.* 1s.
A very correct and elegant edition.
LARGE PAPER. Roxburghe, 1449, 30s. Heath, 1305, russia, 4*l.* 4s.

— Locorum planorum Libri duo, restituti a Rob. Simson, M.D. Glasguæ, 1749. 4to. 7s. 6d.
A valuable edition.

— Inclinationum Libri duo Restituebat S. Horsley. Oxon. 1790. 4to. 18s.
A valuable edition, edited by Bishop Horsley.

— The Two Books concerning Tangencies, &c. by John Lawson, B.D. second edition, with two supplements, &c. Lond. 1771. 4to. 6s.
In this work Lawson has proved himself a faithful translator, and an able geometrician. The former edition was published at Cambridge, 1764, 4to. 'A Restitution of the Geometrical Treatise of Apollonius Pergæus on Inclinations,' by Reuben Burrow, 1779. 4to. 2s. 6d.

APOLLONIUS Rhodius. Argonauticorum Libri IV. Gr. edidit, nova fere Interpretatione illustravit, &c. Joan. Shaw. Oxonii. 1777. 4to. 2 vols.
An edition more beautiful than correct. Heath, 3483, russia, 1*l.* 12s. Drury, 390, russia, 1*l.* 11s. 6d. Sir M. M. Sykes, pt. 1. 268, russia, 2*l.*

— Ibid. Gr. et Lat. edidit, &c. Joan. Shaw. Oxon. 1779. 8vo. 2 vols. 10s.
LARGE PAPER. Dent, pt. 1. 68, morocco, 18s. Williams, 56, morocco, 1*l.* 15s.

—Argonautics, in four Books, by Francis Fawkes. The whole revised, corrected and completed by his coadjutor and editor, (the Rev. H. Meen) who has annexed a translation of Coluthus' Greek Poem on the Rape of Helen, with Notes. London, 1780. 8vo. 5s.
An easy, fluent and perspicuous translation, according to the Monthly Review. An excellent translation of 'The Loves of Medea and Jason,' was published by the Rev. J. Ekins, 1771. 4to. 1772. 12mo. 2s. 6d.

—Argonautic Expedition, translated into English Verse. (By Edward Burnaby Greene.) London, 1780. 8vo. 2 vols. 5s.
Inferior to Fawkes's translation.

— Argonautics, translated into English Verse, with Notes critical, historical, and explanatory: and Dissertations by W. Preston, Esq. Dublin, 1803. 12mo. 3 vols. 12mo. 12s.
(Reprinted by *Sharpe* in his edition of the Poets, 4 vols. 18mo. *frontispieces*, 10s.)
This version, according to Dr. Nathan Drake, is greatly superior to those of his predecessors, accompanied by interesting notes and observations.

Apollonius of Tyre. Kynge Appolyn of Thyre, translated by Rob. Copland. London, by W. de Worde, 1510. 4to.

Black letter. This romance forms the 153d chapter of an edition of the Gesta Romanorum, printed in 1488, and is considered by Mr. Douce as the probable original of the play of Pericles. Roxburghe, 6353, 110*l.*

Apollonius, Lucina and Tharsia. The Patterne of Paineful Adventures, containing the most excellent, pleasant, and variable Historie of Prince Appollonius, the Lady Lucina his wife, and Tharsia his Daughter, translated by T. Twine. London, 1607. 4to.

Black letter. Steevens, 1195, 2*l.* 2s. Utterson, 1852. An edition printed by Valentine Simmes, n. d. 7*l.* 7s.

Apology, Royal, with a Parallel of Doleman, Bradshaw, Sidney, &c. London, 1684. 4to.

Nassau, pt. ii. 983, 2*l.* 5s.

Apologia sanctæ sedis Apostolicæ quodmodum procedendi circa Regimen Catholicorum Angliæ, tempore persecutionis. 8vo. 1631.

Thorpe, 1838. mor. 1*l.* 11s. 6d.

Apophthegms, Witty, delivered at several times and upon several occasions, by King James I. the Marquis of Worcester, Francis Lord Bacon, and Sir Thomas More. London, 1658. 12mo.

With a frontispiece by Marshall, containing their portraits. Lloyd, 1253, 14s. White Knights, 4500, morocco, 15s. Nassau, pt. ii. 1274, 1*l.* An edition 1671. Perry, pt. i. 2812, 12s.

Apostles Creed, the History of the. *See* KING, Sir Peter.

Apostolical Epistles. A new literal Translation, from the original Greek, of all the Apostolical Epistles; with a Commentary and Notes, philological, critical, explanatory and practical. To which is added a History of the Life of the Apostle Paul. By Jas. Macknight, D.D. Edinburgh, 1795. 4to. 4 vols. 8*l.* 8s. Without the Greek Text, 3 vols.

According to Mr. Orme, 'This is one of the most useful, and of the most dangerous books on the New Testament, which has thrown considerable light on the Epistles, and, at the same time, has propagated most pernicious views of their leading doctrines.' Gosset, 3419. 3 vols. 5*l.* 5s.

— Another Edition. Lond. 1816. 8vo. 6 vols. Without the Greek Text, 4 vols.

Drury, 2518, 6 vols. 2*l.* 10s.

— Fathers. *See* WAKE, Archb. of Canterbury.

Apparel.—Advertisements, partly for due Order in the publick Administration of the Holy Sacrament, and partly for the Apparel of all Persons Ecclesiastical, &c. Lond. 1564.

Reprinted in Sparrow's Collection of Articles, &c. Dr. Dibdin in his edition of Ames, notices a broadside on the subject of Apparel, printed by Jugge and Cawood, entitled 'A Decree of the Priuye Counsell at Westminster. Anno 1559.' Besides which, the following tracts, printed in black letter, have appeared.

A brief Discourse against the outwarde Apparell and ministring Garmentes of the Popishe Church, 1566. 16mo. 15s. Contains C. in eights. The introduction is in verse. Reprinted 1578. Horner, 1854. mor. 16s.

A briefe examination for the Tyme, of a certain Declaration lately put in print in the Name and Defence of certain Ministers in London, refusing to weare the Apparell prescribed. London, [1566], 4to. The examination contains * * * * * * 2, in fours; the letters annexed, D. in fours. Bindley, pt. ii. 1210, 9s. 6d. Inglis, 117, 1*l.* 3s. Constable, 238, 1*l.* 6s.

An Answere for the Tyme to the Examination put in Print, without the Authours Name, pretending to mayntayne the Apparell prescribed. 1566. 16mo. 15s. Contains 153 pages, and a folding table after p. 18; also, an additional paragraph to come in at p. 23, after these words, 'to render our reasones.' The 16 first pages are not numbered. Sotheby, June 1856, 1*l.* 1s.

To my louynge Brethren, that is troublyd about the Popishe Apparrell, two short comfortable Epistles. [1566.] 16mo. 15s. Contains C, in fours. On the first leaf of Herbert's copy was in MS. 'Gylbyes Epistell.' Horner, 1854. morocco, 1*l.* 8s.

An Answere to a Question, that was mouyd, whi the godly Men wold not weare a Surples. [1566.] 16mo. 15s Contains C. in fours.

Judgement of M. Henry Bullinger, declaring it lawfull for the Ministers of the Church to weare the Apparell prescribed by the Laws. London, 1566. 16mo. 15s.

Apparitions. An Essay on. *See* MORETON, Andrew, and DEFOE.

About 1640—60, many tracts were published concerning Apparitions, which have sometimes produced considerable sums, viz. 15s. to 20s. at auctions. Several of them may be seen in the British Museum.

APPERT. Art of preserving all kinds of Animal and Vegetable Substances for several years, translated from the French. London, 1811. 12mo. 5s.

Published by order of the French Minister of the Interior, on the report of the Board of Arts and Manufactures.

APPIAN. The avncient Historie and exquisite Chronicle of the Romane Warres, with a continuation. London, 1578. 4to.

Black letter. Contains pp. 445, then a table in double columns, on four leaves. According to Herbert there were two editions of Appian, 1578. Bindley, pt. i. 146, 10s. Horne Tooke, 19, 1l. 1s.

— History in Two Books. Translated into English by J. D. (John Davies). London, 1679. folio. 5s.

Other editions were published, London, 1696, 1703, in folio. The work is dedicated to the Earl of Ossory.

Appius and Virginia. *See* P—— (R.)

APPREECE, J. *See* RHESE, John.

Apprius. The History of King Apprius, (*i. e.* Priapus). London, 1728. 8vo.

One of Curll's publications. Perry, pt. i. 20gd, 7s.

APSLEY, Sir Allen, Knt. Order and Disorder; or the World made and undone. Being Meditations upon the Creation and the Fall, as it is recorded in the beginning of Genesis. London, 1679.

A poem in five cantos.

APTHORP, East, D.D. Letters on the Prevalence of Christianity before its civil establishment: with observations on a late (Gibbon's) History of the Decline of the Roman Empire. London, 1778. 8vo. 5s.

'The author has enriched his work with many learned remarks, and especially with a catalogue of civil and ecclesiastical historians, which the reader will find to be very useful.'—Bishop Watson.

— Discourses on Prophecy; read in the Chapel of Lincoln's-Inn, at the Lecture founded by Wm. Warburton, late Lord Bishop of Gloucester. Lond. 1786. 8vo. 2 vols. 10s.

A most excellent and highly esteemed work.

APULEIUS, Lucius. The xi Bookes of the Golden Asse, translated out of Latine into English, by Will. Adlington. Lond. 1566. 4to.

Black letter. Dedicated 'To Thomas Earl of Sussex. (from) Vniuersity. Coll. Oxon. 18 Septemb. 1566.' Reprinted, 1571, 4to. 1582, 8vo. 1596, 4to. 1600, 4to. 1639, 4to. That of 1582 is the most rare. Edition, 1596, Forster, 113, mor. 2l. 3s. Nassau, pt. i. 176, 5l. 7s. 6d. Edition, 1596, White Knights, 165, russia, 2l. 18s. Edition, 1639, Bindley, pt. i. 145, 1l. 8s. White Knights, 166, morocco, 2l. 11s. Edit. 1582. Triphook, 6l. 6s.

— Metamorphosis, or Golden Ass, and Philosophical Works, translated by Thomas Taylor. London, 1822. 8vo. 15s. LARGE PAPER, 1l. 10s.

An esteemed version by the translator of Plato and Aristotle. Some copies of the small, and all the large paper copies, have suppressed passages, generally placed at the end of the volume.

Bishop Warburton supposed that this work was intended, not only as a satire upon the vices of the times, but as a laboured attempt to recommend the mysteries of the Pagan Religion, in opposition to Christianity, to which he represents him as an inveterate enemy. This opinion, however, has been contested by Dr. Lardner.

— Metamorphoses and other works. *See Bohn's Classical Library.*

— Fable of Cupid and Psyche: to which are added a poetical Paraphrase on the Speech of Diotima, in the Banquet of Plato, &c. &c., with an Introduction, in which the meaning of the Fable is unfolded, [by Thomas Taylor.] London, 1795. 8vo. 4s.

A translation of the Loves of Cupid and Psyche, by Lockman, will be found in Fontaine's Loves of Cupid and Psyche, 1744, 8vo.

— Cupid and Psyche, translated by Hudson Gurney, Esq. Lond. 1799. 8vo. 5s., 4to. 7s. 6d.
An excellent poetical translation of the most beautiful story which antiquity has left us. Third edition, 1801. Goldsmid, 15l, 8s. An edition, 1844. (*Reprinted in Bohn's ed.*)

— The new Metamorphosis: being the Golden Ass, alter'd and improved to the modern time and manners. Written in Italian by Carlo Monte Socio, and translated from the Vatican MS. London, 1708, 9, 8vo. 2 vols.
Roxburghe, 6574, 12s. 6d. Fonthill, 490, 15s. Bindley, pt. iii. 835, 18s. 6d. Nassau, pt. i. 53, 1l. Reprinted 1821, 8vo. 2 vols. with a fraudulent view of passing it off as a translation of Apuleius.

— Another Edition. Lond. 1724. 12mo. 2 vols. with plates by Hogarth.
Ireland, 1801, No. 77, 1l. 1s. Baker, 19, 2l. 6s.

AQUEPONTANUS, Joannes. *Anglice*, BRIDGWATER, John.

AQUINO, Charles de. Sacra Exequialia in Funere Jacobi II. Regis. Romæ, 1702. folio. 15s.
Printed at the charge of Cardinal Barberini. Gough, 2034, 1l. 2s.

ARA, Jehan. *See* OUSELEY, Sir Wm.

Arabian Nights' Entertainments, translated from the French. London, 1724. 12mo. 6 vols.
Bindley, pt. i. 10, 18s. 6d. This old translation is not only incorrect, but coarse and vulgar in its diction. It has, however, been frequently reprinted in 12mo. 4 vols. A valuable edition was published in 1798, by Richard Gough, considerably enlarged from the Paris edition, with notes of illustration, and a preface, in which the supplementary tales published by Dom Chavis are proved to be a palpable forgery.

— Translated by the Rev. Edward Forster. Lond. 1802. 8vo. 5 vols. with plates after Smirke's designs.
A very elegant translation. Demy 8vo. Duke of York, 125, 2l. 11s. Saunders' in 1818, 3l. Royal 8vo. with proof plates, Nassau, pt. i. 54, russia, 3l. 9s. Sotheby's in 1824, morocco, 4l. 9s. Quarto, with proofs before the letters, Sir M. M. Sykes, pt. i. 271, bds. 5l. 12s. 6d. Sotheby's in May, 1828, 7l. 17s. 6d. Drury, 533, morocco, 12l. 15s. Two copies were printed with proof plates on satin. Brockett, 243, morocco, 18l. 7s. 6d. An edition of Forster's translation has been published in 12mo. 4 vols., and on LARGE PAPER, in 8vo.

— Translated by William Beaumont. Lond. 1811. royal 12mo. 4 vols. 1l.
A most entertaining volume in elucidation of these oriental fictions, was published by the Rev. Richard Hole, 1797. 8vo. 5s.

— To which is added, a Selection of new Tales, now first translated from the Arabic Originals; also an Introduction and Notes, by Jonathan Scott, LL.D. Lond. 1811. royal 18mo. with frontispieces, 6 vols.
This edition was carefully revised and occasionally corrected from the Arabic. The introduction and notes are valuable, as illustrative of the religion, manners, and customs of the Mahommedans. Post octavo, with plates by Smirke. Sotheby's in May 1823, 2l. 5s. Demy octavo, with plates. Earl of Kerry, 625, 4l. 8s. The original has been printed at Calcutta, edited by Mc. Naghten, 4 vols. royal 8vo. 1839-42. 6l.

— With plates after the Designs of Rich. Westall. London, 1819. 12mo. 4 vols. 1l. 8s.
An elegant edition. In 1814 was published the Adventures of Hunchback, with prints by Daniell, from drawings by Smirke. Imperial 4to. North, pt. i. 35, (proofs on INDIA PAPER) 5l. 12s. 6d.
[There have been many new editions of the Arabian Nights since this period, including LANE'S TRANSLATION, which must be reserved for an appendix.]

— New Arabian Nights' Entertainments; selected from the original Oriental MS. by Jos. Von Hammer, and now first translated into English by the Rev. G. Lambe. Lond. 1826. fcp. 8vo. 3 vols. 18s.

Arabian Tales, translated from the original Arabic into French; and from the French into English, by Robert Heron. Edinburgh, 1792. 12mo. 4 vols. 10s.
Sir M. M. Sykes, pt. i. 74, 12s. Fonthill, 1962, 13s.

Arabic and Persian Tales. *See* SCOTT, Jonathan, LL.D.

ARAGO, J. Narrative of a Voyage round the World, by Captain Freycinet during the Years 1817, 18, 19, and 20, on a scientific expedition

undertaken by order of the French Government. Lond. 1822. 4to. map and plates.
A frivolous and worthless narrative, full of ridiculous blunders. Quarterly Review. Duke of York, 253, 19s. Brockett, 1292, 1l. 11s. 6d.

ARATUS. Phænomena et Diosemeia, cum Theonis Scholiis et Eratosthenis Catasterismis, etc. Græce. Accesserunt Annotationes in Eratosthenem et Hymnos Dionysii. (Curante Jo. Fell.) Oxon. 1672. 8vo. 5s.
An excellent critical edition. Gossett, 158, morocco, 11s. Williams, 64, mor. 18s. Dent, pt. i. 74, morocco, by Roger Payne, 1l. 15s. Dr. Bliss observes, 'In the copy of Aratus, in Mr. Dodwell's study, there is a printed letter prefixed to the notes upon the hymns, from Dr. Bernard to Mr. Dodwell, which I never saw in any other copy.'

— Diosemeia, notis et collatione scriptorum illustravit Tho. Forster. Lond. 1815. 8vo.
Translations from Aratus will be found in Jabez Hughes' Miscellanies, 1737, 8vo.

ARBUTHNOT, Alexander. Orationes de Origine et Dignitate Juris. Edinb. 1572. 4to.
The author of this learned and elegant performance published Buchanan's History of Scotland. A life of him will be found in Irving's Scottish Poets, vol. ii.

— Archib. Life and Adventures of Simon Fraser, Lord Lovat. London, 1746. 12mo. with portrait by W. Hogarth, 6s.

— Life and Adventures of Miss Jenny Cameron. London, 1746. 12mo. 4s.
Brockett, 44, 11s. Reprinted Boston, 1750, 8vo.

— John, M.D. Tables of ancient Coins, Weights and Measures, explained and exemplify'd in several Dissertations. London, 1727. 4to. 10s. 6d.
A standard work of great learning and value, though not wholly free from inaccuracies. Heath, 1435, 1l. 2s. Drury, 336, (with Langwith's Observations, 1747) 1l. 6s. Stanley, 77, russia, 1l. 18s.
In 'Literæ de Re Nummariâ," 1729, 8vo. written by —— Smith, will be found Remarks on these Tables. In the year 1747, were published Observations on them by the Rev. Benj. Langworth, D.D. 4to. 5s. Gosset, 3187, 10s. 6d.

— Tables. To which is added an Appendix, containing Observations by Benj. Langwith, D.D. London, 1754. 4to.
Best edition. Brockett, 244, 1l. 1s. Dent, pt. i. 288, 1l. 5s. pt. ii. 1074, 17s. Sir P. Thompson, 95, 1l. 11s. 6d. Willett, 93, 2l. These valuable Tables were translated into Latin by Daniel Koenig, and published at Utrecht 1756.

— The Miscellaneous Works. Glasgow, 1750, or 1751. 8vo. 2 vols.
These volumes were pronounced by the Doctor's son not to be the works of his father, but a gross imposition on the public. Willett, 35, 10s. 6d. Dent, pt. i. 75, 16s. Reprinted 1770, 12mo. 2 vols. 10s. 6d. In the Retrospective Review, viii. 285—304, will be found an account of the life and writings of Dr. Arbuthnot.

ARCANDAM. Booke to find the fatall Destiny, Constellation, Complexion, and naturall Inclination of euery Man and Childe by his Birth. With an Addition of Phisiognomy, tourned out of French into our vulgar Tongue by William Warde. Lond. 1578. 4to. 10s. 6d.
Black letter, with wood cuts, contains C 4, in eights. Reprinted 1592, 1617, 1652, and 1674. Edition 1617, North, pt. i. 75, 1l. 10s. Edition 1652, Roxburghe, (Supplem. No. 648) 5s. White Knights, 4366, 5s.

ARCEUS, Franciscus, M.D. Method of curing Woundes with other Precepts of the same Arte, translated into English by John Read, Chirurgeon. Whereunto is added the exact Cure of the Carbuncle, translated out of Johānes Ardern: &c. Imprinted by Thomas East, 1588. 4to. 10s. 6d.
Black letter. In this work will be found 'A Complaint of the Abuse of the noble Arte of Chirurgerie,' by John Read, in metre.

ARCHÆOLOGIA. See Antiquaries of London.

Archæologia Æliana, Tracts published by the Society of Antiquaries at Newcastle. Newcastle, 1816—27. 4to. vol. i. in 2 pts. 1l. 10s.; vol. ii. in 3 pts.; vol. iii. in 2 pts.; vol. iv. in 2 pts.; each part at 15s.

Archæological Association Journal, vol. 1--12. 1844--1856, *and continued quarterly*. *See* Appendix.

Archæological Institute of Great Britain. *See* Appendix.

Archaica, containing a Reprint of scarce old English Prose Tracts, with Prefaces critical and biographical, by Sir E. Brydges, Bart. London, 1815. 4to. 2 vols.

This work was published with the Heliconia by Mr. Park, (forming together 5 vols.) of which 200 copies only were printed.

Contents:—Greene's Philomela—Greene's Arcadia—Southwell's Triumphs over Death—Breton's Characters and his Good and the Bad—Nash's Christ's Tears over Jerusalem—Harvey's Four Letters and Sonnets, touching Robert Greene—Harvey's Pierce's Supererogation—New Letter of Notable Contents—Brathwayte's Essays upon the Five Senses.

Stre^{tt}ell, 171, 2*l*. 2s. Nassau, pt. i. 179, 2*l*. 4s. Saunders' in 1818, 2*l*. 12s. 6d.

Archbishops. — The Forme and Maner of makyng and consecratyng of Archebishoppes, Bishoppes, Priestes and Deacons, M.D.XLIX. Rich. Grafton excud. 1549. 4to.

Black letter. Contains K, in fours. Marq. of Townshend, 156, 3s. 6d. Bindley, pt. ii. 1023, 1*l*. 10s. [Reprinted in the works of Francis Mason.]

— A short Treatise of Arch-Bishops Lords Spiritual. Printed in the year 1641. 4to.

Reprinted in the 6th number of Morgan's Phœnix Britannicus.

ARCHDALE, John. A new Description of the fertile and pleasant Province of Carolina. London, 1707. 4to.

North, pt. iii. 599, 8s.

ARCHDALL, Mervyn, A.M. Monasticon Hibernicum: or, an History of the Abbies, Priories, and other Religious Houses in Ireland. Dublin, 1786. 4to.

A valuable and esteemed work, containing pp. 820, besides title, dedication, list of subscribers, and introduction, xv. pp. an index and errata, 4 leaves; also a map of Ireland, 1786, and 18 plates of costume. Dent, pt. i. 289, russia, 1*l*. 18s. Fonthill, 1819, 1*l*. 16s. Marq. of Townshend, 155, 1*l*. 17s. Nassau, pt. i. 180, 2*l*. 5s.

ARCHDEKIN, Richard. Of Miracles, and the new Miracles done by the Relicks of St. Francis Xavier, in the Jesuits' College at Mechlin. Louvanii, 1667. 8vo.

— Vitæ et Miraculorum Sancti Patricii, Hiberniæ Apostoli Epitome: cum brevi Notitia Hiberniæ, et Prophetia S. Malachiæ, &c. Lovan. 1671. 8vo.

ARCHEE, or ARCHY. *See* ARMSTRONG, Archibald.

ARCHENHOLZ, M. d'. Picture of England, translated from the French. London, 1790. 12mo. 2 vols. 4s.

A wretched translation. Archenholz published the following work relating to Great Britain—' Annalen der Brittischen Geschichte.' Tubingen, 1789-98. 8vo. 20 vols.

ARCHER, Rev. James. Sermons for every Sunday in the Year. 1st and 2d Series. London, 1817, 22. 8vo. 4 vols. 2*l*. 2s.

These excellent Roman Catholic Sermons have passed through several editions.

— John, M.D. Every Man his own Doctor: to which is added, an Herbal. London, 1673. 8vo. with portrait.

White Knights, pt. i. 219, 10s. The former edition appeared in 1671. In Beloe's Anecdotes, i. 199-200, is a list of inventions by this celebrated physician.

Archers. Aim for. 12mo. 1638. with Plan of Finsburie, and port.

Brand, 2*l*. 4s.

Archery.—Art of Archerie. London, 1634. 8vo. with a frontispiece.

Nassau, pt. i. 63, 8s. Bindley, pt. i. 72, 14s. North, russia, 2*l*. 2s.

— Poems in English and Latin on the Archers and Royal-Company of Archers, by several Hands. Edinb. 1726. 12mo. 5s.

— *See* Hansard's Book of.

ARCHIMEDES. Quæ supersunt omnia, cum Eutochii Commentariis (Græce). Ex recensione Josephi Torelli, cum nova Versione Latina. Accedunt Lectiones variantes ex Codd. Mediceo et Parisiensibus. Oxon. 1792. folio.

The most complete and magnificent edition of this author's works. Willett, 134, 1*l*. 15*s*. LARGE PAPER. Dent, pt. i. 154, morocco. Drury, 382, russia, 2*l*. 19*s*.

ARCHIMEDES. Arenarius, et Dimensio Circuli : Eutocii Ascalonitæ in hanc Comment. Gr. cum Versione et Notis Joh. Wallis. Oxonii. 1676. 12mo. 3*s*.

A former edition appeared 1666.

— Opera, Apollonii Pergæi Conicorum Libri IV. Theodosii Sphærica, methodo nova illustrata per Is. Barrow. London, 1675. 4to. 6*s*.

A neat edition, highly praised by Montucla.

— Arenarius, translated from the Greek, with Notes and illustrations (by G. Anderson). To which is added, the Dissertation of Christopher Clavius on the same Subject, from the Latin. Lond. 1784. 8vo. 3*s*.

A masterly translation, with curious and pertinent notes and illustrations. Portions of the Theorems of Archimedes will be found in Whiston and Barrow's versions of Euclid.

Architecture.—The Grecian Orders of Architecture delineated and explained from the Antiquities of Athens, also Parallels of the Orders of Palladio, Scammozzi and Vignola, to which are added Remarks concerning public and private Edifices ; with Designs. London, 1768. folio. 1*l*. 5*s*.

— Rudiments of ancient Architecture, with a Dictionary of Terms. The second Edition, much enlarged. London, 1794, royal 8vo. with 11 plates, and a portrait of James Stuart on the title page, 6*s*.

A very useful work, reprinted 1804, 1810. The first edition appeared in 1789.

— Essays on Gothic Architecture, by the Rev. T. Warton, Rev. J. Bentham, Captain Grose, and the Rev. J. Milner, with a Letter to the Publisher. The second Edition, to which is added a List of the Cathedrals of England, with their Dimensions. London, 1802. 8vo. with twelve plates, 10*s*. 6*d*.

A valuable and esteemed work, reprinted

1808, 10*s*. 6*d*. The first edition appeared in 1798, 6*s*. Sir M. M. Sykes, pt. iii. 1068, 14*s*. Fonthill, 1068, 17*s*.

ARCHYTAS, &c. Political Fragments of Archytas, Charondas, Zaleucus, and other ancient Pythagoreans, and Ethical Fragments of Hierocles, translated from the Greek, by Thomas Taylor. Lond. 1822. 8vo. 6*s*.

Fragments of Archytas will be found in Gale's Opuscula Mythologica, &c. Cantab. 1670. Amst. 1688.

Ardai Viraf Nameh, or the Revelations of Ardai Viraf; translated from the Persian and Guzeratee Versions, by J. A. Pope. London, 1816. 8vo. 5*s*.

Arden of Feversham.—The lamentable and true Tragedie of M. Arden of Feversham in Kent. Printed for Edward White, 1592. 4to.

This black letter play, from which Lillo has not unfrequently copied whole lines, was reprinted 1599, 4to., 1633, 4to., and lastly 1770, 8vo., with a ridiculous preface imputing it to Shakespeare, 3*s*. 6*d*. LARGE PAPER, 6*s*. Edition 1599, Forster, 1144, 3*l*. Edition 1633, Rhodes, 1*l*. Sotheby's in Nov. 1826, 1*l*. 7*s*. Roxburghe, 4049, 1*l*. 7*s*. Forster, 1127, 1*l*. 14*s*. Bindley, pt. i. 157, 2*l*. 2*s*. Jolley, 1849, (2 leaves MS.) 1*l*. 13*s*.

ARETÆUS of Cappadocia. Ætiologica, Semeiotica et Therapeutica, Gr. et Lat. ex Recensione et cum Notis Joannis Wigan. Oxonii. 1723. folio. 10*s*. 6*d*. LARGE PAPER, 1*l*. 1*s*.

Of this beautiful and correct edition 300 copies were printed.

— Aretæus : consisting of eight Books on the Causes, Symptoms and Cure of acute and chronic Diseases, translated from the original Greek, by John Moffat, M.D. London, 1785. 8vo. 5*s*.

A translation, according to the Monthly Reviewers, generally correct, and which gives pretty nearly the sense of the original. [A new translation by Reynolds, 8vo. 1837.]

ARETINUS, Leonard. *Vide* ARISTOTELES. PHALARIS.

— The Historie of Leonard Aretine, concerning the Warres betwene the Imperialls and the Gothes for the possession of Italy, translated by Arthur Goldyng. London, 1563. 16mo.

Black letter. 180 leaves, besides an epistle and preface. Sotheby's in 1825, 2*l*. 8s. White Knights, 227, morocco, 3*l*. 4s.

- ARETIUS, Benedictus. A short History of Valentinus Gentilis, the Tritheist, translated into English (with a Preface by Dr. South). London, 1696. 8vo. 3s.

Gosset,

— Jacob. Primula Veris, seu Panegyrica ad excell. Principem Palatinum. In Regis Jacobi Inaugurationem Carmen. In Nuptias illustr. Principis Frederici et Elizabethæ Meletemata. Lond. 1613. 4to.

A copy is in the British Museum.

ARFEVILLE, Nicolay d'. La Navigation du Roy d'Escosse Jacques cinquiesme du Nom, autour de son Royaume, et Isles Hebrides et Orchades, soubz la Conduite d'Alexandre Lyndsay, excellent Pilot Escossois. Paris, 1583. 4to. with a map.

A copy is in the British Museum. [An English translation of it is contained in *Miscellanæ Scotica*.]

ARGALL, John. Introductio ad Artem Dialecticam. Lond. 1605. 8vo.

A 'very facete and pleasant' book, according to Ant à Wood.

— Rich. The Bride's Ornament; poetical Essays upon a divine Subject. London, 1621. 4to.

This poet, who was patronised by Bishop King, published a version of Solomon's Song. *See* Solomon. Bindley, with the Song of Songs, 533, 5*l*. 7s. 6d. Perry, 3*l*. 12s.

— Funeral Elegy, consecrated to the Memory of his ever honoured Lord John King, late B. of London. &c. 1621.

These two poems were issued with the Song of Songs in 1621.

ARGALL; in the British Museum Catalogue Leigh's Accedens of Armory is erroneously attributed to Richard Argall.

ARGENSOLA (Barth. Leon. de). The Discovery and Conquest of the Molucco and Philippine Islands; translated from the Spanish. [by Capt. Jno. Stevens.] London, 1708. 4to. with 4 plates.

Dent, pt. i. 291, 7s. 6d. Nassau, pt. i. 183, 8s. Towneley, pt. ii. 115, 10s. 6d.

Argumentum Anti-Normanicum: a seasonable Treatise, wherein is proved that William the Conqueror did not get the imperial Crown of England by the sword, but by the election and consent of the people. London, 1689. 8vo. 5s.

This publication, occasioned by a work of William Pettyt's, entitled 'Antient Rights of the Commons of England,' 1680, was answered by Dr. Brady in his Introduction to Old English History. It is by some attributed to Atwood, and by others to Cooke or Johnson.

ARGYLE, Archibald Campbell, Marquis of. Instructions to a Son, and Maxims of State. London, 1661. 12mo. with scarce portrait.

Lloyd, 34, 19s. Roxburghe, Supplement, 541, 1*l*. 3s. Bindley, pt. i. 51, 1*l*. 4s. Stanley, No. 18, russia, by Roger Payne, 2*l*. 12s. 6d. Glasgow, 1743, (*spurious*) 4s. 6d.

The author was beheaded in 1661, and his son in 1685.

— The Charge of High Treason against the Marquess of Argyle and his Complices, Jan. 23, 1661. London, 1661. 4to.

In the Roxburghe Library was a copy of the above, with the Marquis's answer, &c. Seven Tracts, no. 1080, 1*l*. 11s. 6d. A similar collection is in the British Museum.

— Duke of. Catalogus Librorum, A.C.D.A. (Archib. Campbell Ducis Argatheliæ.) Glasguæ, 1758. 4to.

Privately printed. Reed, 184, 7s. 6d. Brockett, 747, 11s. Dibdin, 2, 11s.

ARIOSTO, Lodovico. Orlando Furioso. Birmingham, 1773. 8vo. and 4to. 4 vols. with plates by Bartolozzi and others.

The last production of Baskerville's press. Brunet in his Manuel du Libraire mentions, that the plates in the 4to. are not so good as those in the 8vo. edition, and likewise that some sheets in the first volume seem to have been reprinted. OCTAVO, Willett, 41, 6*l*. Strettell, 41, morocco, 5*l*. Baker, 153, morocco, (with the addition of several proofs.) 12*l*. 15s. QUARTO, Drury, 339, morocco, 10*l*. 10s. Fonthill, 2418, morocco, 10*l*. 5s. Dent, pt.

1. 292, morocco, 12*l*. Stanley, 268, morocco, 21*l*. Heath, 2042, morocco, 22*l*. 1s.

ARIOSTO, Lodovico. Orlando Furioso, with an explanation of equivocal words, and poetical figures, and an elucidation of all the passages concerning history and fable. By Agostino Isola. Camb. 1789. 8vo. 4 vols.

A very correct edition of the original. Steevens, 598, 17s.

— Orlando Furioso, con note, castigato da Leonardo Nardini, ad uso degli Studiosi della Lingua Italiana. Londra, 1801. 12mo. 4 tom. 14s.

A neat edition. Drury, 220, 1*l*. 10s. Other editions by Romualdo Zotti, London, 1814. 12mo. 4 vols. 16s.; by Boschini, 1815, 18mo. 6 vols. 8s.

— Orlando Furioso in English Heroical Verse, by (Sir) John Harington. London, by Richard Field, 1591. Folio, pp. 450, 1*l*. 5s.

The title containing port. of Sir John H. engraved by W. Rogers. First edition. According to the Quarterly Review, a translation of considerable merit, written in sterling English; on the contrary by Ellis termed an inaccurate and feeble version. Bibl. Anglo-Poet, 316, 3*l*. 3s. Jadis, 204, 1*l*. 16s. Christie, May 5, 1839. LARGE PAPER, old calf, gilt, ruled with red lines. 4 leaves, inlaid, 10*l*. 5s.

— Orlando Furioso, now secondly imprinted. London, 1607. folio, pp. 450.

Garrick, 267, 1*l*. 1s. Bibl. Anglo-Poet. 317, 2*l*. 12s. 6d.

— Orlando Furioso, now thirdly revised and amended, with the addition of the author's (*i. e.* Harington's) Epigrams, (4 Books.) London, 1634. folio, pp. 496.

The title page is engraved, and has Harington's portrait at the bottom, by Cockson. Towneley, pt. ii. 155, 2*l*. Nassau, pt. i. 206, 2*l*. 1s. Bindley, pt. i. 167, 2*l*. 5s. Roxburghe, 2973, 2*l*. 16s. Sir M. M. Sykes, pt. i. 312, mor. 3*l*. 3s. Bibl. Anglo-Poet. No. 318, 3*l*. 13s. 6d. Heath, 2043, mor. 3*l*. 13s. 6d.

— Orlando Furioso in Italian and English, by Temple Henry Croker. London, 1755. 4to. 2 vols. 1*l*. 5s.

In some copies of this edition (which is in no estimation,) the name of Temple Henry Croker is given, in others *(erroneously)* that of William Huggins appears as the translator. It is said that many copies were destroyed by fire.

— Orlando Furioso, translated, with notes, by John Hoole. London, 1783. 8vo. 5 vols. with port. of Hoole.

According to the Quarterly Review, Hoole is the most contemptible of translators, and grossly ignorant of the Italian language. Reprinted 1799, 8vo. 5 vols. (some on large paper). 1807, royal 18mo. 5 vols. &c. and inserted in Chalmers' Collection of Poets. Edition 1783. Heath, 2044, 1*l*. 10s. Williams, 66, 1*l*. 7s. Edition 1799. LARGE PAPER, Nassau, pt. i. 57, 1*l*. 18s. Fonthill, 1816, with proof plates, 4*l*. 10s. A first volume of this translation was published, with vignettes, after Mortimer, 1773. 8vo. Garrick, 32, 9s.

— The Orlando reduced to twenty-four books, the narrative connected, and the stories disposed in a regular series, by John Hoole. London, 1791. 8vo. 2 vols.

In little estimation. Reed, 6585, 7s. Edwards, 154, morocco, 1*l*. 7s.

— Orlando Furioso, translated into English verse by William Stewart Rose. London, 1825—31. 8 vols. post 8vo. published at 3*l*. 16s.

A spirited and faithful translation, says T. Moore. A translation in English prose, with notes, by Christopher Johnson, 8vo. vol. 1, has just appeared. (*Discontinued.*)

— An Abregement of Roland Furious, translait out of Ariost; together with some Rhapsodies of the author's youthful Braine: and last, ane Schersing out of true Felicete, composit in Scottesh Meiter be Stewart of Baldyneis.

For an account of this MS. in Advocates' Library, *see* the Restituta, vol. i. pp. 313—17.

— Le Satire ed altre Rime, Lib. ii. con le Annotazioni di Paolo Rolli. Londra, 1716. 8vo. 3s.

LARGE PAPER, D. of Grafton, 628, 5s.

— Satyres, in English, by Gervis Markham. London, 1608. 4to. pp. 108.

This version is claimed by Robert Tofte in a note (p. 6) of his translation of Bened. Varchi's Blazon of Jealousie. Perry, pt. iv. 396, 13s. Bindley, pt. i. 341, 16s. Gor-

donstown, 100, 2l. 10s. Sotheby's in May, 1823, 2l. 12s. 6d. Perry, 3l.
— Seven planets gouerning Italie, with a new addition of three most excellent Elegies, written by the same Lodovico Ariosto. Lond. 1611. 4to.
The edition of 1608 with a new title-page, and the addition of the three elegies with a separate pagination.
— Satires, (five translated by the Rev. — H—rt—n, the second and last by the editor, the Rev. T. H. Croker.) London, 1759. 8vo. 3s. 6d.
— Two Tales, the one in Dispraise of men, the other in Disgrace of Women; with certain other Italian Stanzas and Proverbs. By R.(obert) T.(ofte) Gentleman. London, 1597. 4to.
Farmer, 11s. 6d.
— Comedie, Scholastica, dei Suppositi, e la Lena. Londra, 1737-9. 12mo. 3 vols. 7s. 6d.
A translation of the *Suppositi* by Geo. Gascoyne appeared in 1586, and is reprinted in the third volume of Hawkins's Origin of the Drama. See GASCOYNE.

ARISTÆNETUS. Love Epistles, translated from the Greek into English Metre, (by Richard Brinsley Sheridan and N. B. Halhed.) Lond. 1771. 8vo. 5s.
A much esteemed version. A former version, entitled 'Letters of Love and Gallantry,' 1750, 8vo. 4s. and translations, or rather imitations, of some of the epistles will be found in Tom Brown's Works.

ARISTARCHUS. De Magnitudinibus et Distantiis Solis et Lunæ liber. Pappi Alex. Fragmentum e secundo Libro Collectionis Mathematicæ. Gr. et Lat. Notis Joh. Wallis. Oxon. 1668, 8vo. 4s.
Also inserted in the Opera Mathematica of Wallis. Oxon. 1699, in folio.
— or the Principles of Composition. London, 1791. 8vo. pp. 432, 10s. 6d. (Reprinted. Lond. 1822.)
This work, written by the ingenious and learned Dr. Withers, was originally published in numbers. At the end, are Remarks on Dr. Johnson's Dictionary, with proposals for a new English Dictionary.

ARISTEAS. Historia LXXII. Interpretum, Gr. et Lat. Accessere

Veterum Testimonia de eorum Versione. Oxonii, 1692. 8vo. 4s.
A spurious work. LARGE PAPER. Drury, 221, 1l. Williams, 70, morocco, 1l. 10s. Reprinted by Archdeacon Hody, with a confutation in 'De Bibliorum Textibus originalibus,' Oxon. 1705, folio.
— History of the Septuagint written by Aristeas 1900 years since. Newly done into English by J. Donne. The second edition revised and very much corrected from the original. London, 1685, 8vo. 5s.
The first edition of this translation was published in 1633, 12mo. 3s. LARGE PAPER, 6s.
— History of the seventy-two Interpreters: to which is added, the History of the Angels, and their Gallantry with the daughters of Men, written by Enoch, the Patriarch. Published in Greek, by Dr. Grabe, made English by Ed. Lewis, of C.C.C. Oxford. London, 1715. 12mo. 4s.
Another translation of Aristeas will be found in Wm. Whiston's Authentic Records, pt. ii. 8vo. 1727. The celebrated poet Thomas Moore is said to have been greatly indebted to Enoch's History in his poem entitled the Loves of the Angels.

ARISTIDES, Ælius. Opera omnia, Gr. et Lat. cum Notis et Emendationibus Gul. Canteri, &c. Adjunctis insuper Veterum Scholiis, et Prolegomenis Sopatri Apameensis. Ex Recensione Sam. Jebb. Oxonii, 1722-30. 4to. 2 vols.
'Editio longe præstantissima,' Gosset, 294, 3l. 5s. LARGE PAPER. Drury, 340, 6l. 16s. 6d. Dent, pt. i. 293, morocco, 3l. 2s. 6d. Sir M. M. Sykes, pt. i. 276, morocco, 8l. 15s. Willett, 97, 9l. Heath, 3603, russia, 10l. 15s.

ARISTOPHANES. — Comœdiæ, Græce, ex optimis Exempl. emendatæ; cum Latina Versione, variis Lectionibus, Notis et Emendationibus: accedunt deperditarum Comœdiarum Fragmenta, et Index Verborum, Nominum propriorum, &c. a Rich. Fr. Phil. Brunck. Oxonii. 1810. 8vo. 4 vols. 18s.
A reprint of the edition Argentor. 1781-3. 8vo. 4 vols. with the notes at the

foot of the text. Royal octavo, 1*l*. 7s. Quarto, published at 10*l*. 10s. Drury, 844, russia, 2*l* 14s.

ARISTOPHANES.—Comœdiæ, Gr. ex Edit. R. F. P. Brunck. Oxon. 1814. 32mo. 3 vols.

A neat edition. Drury, 231, mor. 18s.

— Comœdiæ, &c. Gr. et Lat. variis Lectionibus, &c. cum R. F. P. Brunck. Lond. 1823. 8vo. 8 vols. published at 2*l*. 2s.

An edition, without Notes, small 8vo. 3 vols. 1*l*. 11s. 6d.

— Comœdiæ cum Scholiis et Varietate Lectionis, recensuit Imm. Bekkerus. Accedunt Versio Latina, deperditarum Fragmenta, Index locupletissimus, Notæque Reisigii, Beckii, Dindorfii, Schutzii, Bentleii, Dobreii, Porsoni, Elmsleii, Hermanni, Fischeri, Hemsterhusii, &c. &c. Lond. 1828, 8vo. 5 vols. 3*l*. 15s.

A highly valuable edition. LARGE PAPER, 5*l*. 15s. 6d. The 'Annotationes,' 3 vols. may be had separately, 2*l*. 5s. Several of the plays, viz. Aves, Nubes, Plutus, and Ranæ, were also published separately.

— Plutus et Nubes, Gr. et Lat. cum notis Joh. Lengii. London, 1732. 8vo.

In this beautiful and correct edition 'in usum studiosæ juventutis,' the Scholia are placed beneath the text: it also contains two useful indexes, and a life of Aristophanes by Frischlinus. Heath, 3574, 6s. 6d. The former edition appeared in 1695, 2s. 6d. An edition of the Plutus, by Dobree, is annexed to 'R. Porsoni Notæ in Aristophanem.' Cant. 1820, 8vo.

— Nubes, Græce, ex Editione Kusteri. Glasg. 1744, 12mo.

Williams, 73, 11s. Another edition, 1755. 3s.

— Equites, Græce. Oxon. 1593. 4to.

— Acharnenses, Gr. cum Annotationibus (P. Elmsley.) Oxonii. 1809. 8vo.

This edition was suppressed by its learned editor.

— Comedies, (5) translated by T. Mitchell, A.M. Lond. 1820-22. 8vo. vols. i. and ii.

A highly valuable and classical version.

— Four Comedies translated into English, (viz. the Clouds, by R. Cumberland; Plutus by H. Fielding and Wm. Young; the Frogs by C. Dunster, and the Birds by —). Lond. 1812. 8vo. 7s.

— The Clouds, now first entirely translated into English, with the principal Scholia, and Notes critical and explanatory, by James White. London, 1759. 12mo. 3s. 6d.

An admirable version done in a species of easy blank verse, with learned and judicious notes. Roxburghe, 4376, 2s. 6d. Reed, 8011, 2*l*. 3s. A translation of the Clouds, will be found in Stanley's History of Philosophy.

— A pleasant Comedie entituled Hey for Honesty, down with Knavery. Translated out of Aristophanes his Plutus, by Thomas Randolph; augmented and published by F. J. Lond. 1651. 4to. 4s.

In this play the celebrated architect Sir Christopher Wren performed the character of Nænias. Rhodes, 1932, 5s. 6d. Roxburghe, 5687, 4s.

— The World's Idol; or Plutus the God of Wealth, from the Greek, by H. H. B. together with his Notes and a short Discourse upon it. London, 1659, 4to.

Roxburghe, 4378, 8s. Rhodes, 447, 16s. There is a translation of the Plutus, by E. F. J. Carrington, Esq. 8vo. 1826, and of the Birds, by the Rev. H. F. Cary, 8vo. 1824, 5s. likewise a literal translation with notes of Plutus and the Frogs. Oxford, 1822, 8vo. 8s.

ARISTOTELES. De Vitiis et Virtutibus, cum Georgii Gemisti Plethonis Libello de Virtutibus, Gr. et Lat. ex Recensione Edv. Falconer. Oxon. 1752. 8vo. 3s. 6d.

— Aristotelis Ethicorum Nicomacheorum Libri X. Gr. et Lat. cum Notis Gul. Wilkinson. Oxon. 1716. 8vo.

A highly valuable and esteemed edition. Roxburghe, 1909, 5s. 6d. Williams, 76, morocco, 1*l*. 12s. LARGE PAPER. Heath, 4269, 1*l*. 5s. Drury, 249, morocco, by Roger Payne, 1*l*. 6s. Dent, pt. i. 89, mor. 1*l*. 15s. D. of Grafton, 141, morocco, 2*l*. 8s. Williams, 77, mor. 2*l*. 9s. Reprinted Oxon. 1808, 1809, 1818, of which editions there are copies on large paper. (Small paper, 8s. large paper, 14s.)

— Aristotelis Ethicorum Textus

per Leonardū Aretinū lucidissime tranalatus, correctissimeq; impressus Oxoniis. M.CCCC.LXXIX. 4to.
The second production of the Oxford Press, contains A—Y 6, in eights. A 1 blank. A copy is in the Bodleian, All Souls, and Pembroke Libraries, Oxford, and also in Lord Spencer's Collection.

— Ethicorum ad Nicomachum Libri decem per Quæstiones expositi, per Sam. Heilandum. Ex Officina Henr. Bynneman. 1581. 4to.
A copy is in the British Museum.

— Politica et Œconomica, ex Edit. Sylburgii, cum Versione Lambini et Synopsi Analytica Duvallii. Oxon. 1810. 8vo. 2 tom.
A neat and correct edition, Drury, 254, russia, 1l. 1s.

— De Rhetorica seu Arte Dicendi Libri tres, Græcolat. (edidit Theod. Goulston). London, 1619, 4to. 5s.
Contains 239 pp. with title, dedication to Prince Charles, preface, &c. 3 leaves, also table, index of authors, and errata, 3 leaves. Copies on LARGE PAPER are extremely rare. Goulston's, according to Dr. Dibdin, was the most popular of the versions of Aristotle's Rhetoric in our country during the 17th century. Reprinted Lond. 1696, 4to. and Camb. 1728, 8vo.

— Ibid. Gr. et Lat. cum Notis Variorum (Cura Gul. Battie.) Cant. 1728. 8vo. 5s.
A very excellent edition.

— Ibid. Gr. cum variis Lectionibus et Notis (edente W. Holwell). Oxon. 1759. 8vo. 12s.
A very correct and beautiful edition, printed without accents. Heath, 3627, 1l. 1s. LARGE PAPER. Dent, pt. i. 88, morocco, 1. 7s. Williams, 80 mor. 1l. 8s. Sir M. M. Sykes, pt. i. 87, morocco, 1l. 15s. Drury, 250, morocco, 2l. 3s.

— De Rhetorica Libri iii. ad Fidem MSS. recogniti, cum Versione Latina. Oxon. 1805. 8vo. 6s.
A very useful as well as elegant edition 'in usum juventutis academicæ.' Reprinted in 1809 and 1820.

— Animadversiones Variorum in Arist. de Rhetorica Libros iii. Oxon. 1820. 8vo. 11s.
Williams, 81, morocco, 1l. 1s.

— De Mundo Liber, Græce, cum Versione Latina Gul. Budæi. Glasg. 1745. 12mo. 3s.

— De Poetica Liber, Latine conversus et analytica Methodo illustratus, a Theod. Goulston. Lond. 1623. 4to. 5s.
Goulston is styled by Ant. a Wood, 'an excellent Latinist and a noted Græcian.' Goulston's edition was reprinted Cant. 1696. 8vo. with additional notes, 2s. 6d.; and at Glasg. 1745. 8vo. 4s.

— Ibid. Gr. et Lat. cum Notis. Oxonii, 1760. 8vo. 4s.
A very good edition 'J. Chelsume Dono amicim. Editoris, J. P.' MS. note. LARGE PAPER. Sir M. M. Sykes, pt. i. 86, mor. 18s. Dent, mor. 2l. Williams, 66, mor. 19s.

— Ibid. ex Versione Theod. Goulstoni. Lectionis Varietatem, Verborum, Indicem, et Observationes suas adjunxit T. Winstanley, A.M. Oxon. 1780. 8vo. 6s.
This excellent edition, says Dr. Harwood, will ever be a monument of the editor's learning and industry; but it is more calculated for the critic than the student. LARGE PAPER. Heath, 4362, 10s. Drury, 244, morocco, 18s. Dent, pt. i. 86, morocco, 1l. 5s. Williams, 79, morocco, 1l. 10s.

— Ibid. Textu Gulstoniano; cum Prælectione, Versione et Notis Editoris, Gul. Cooke. Accedit Elegia Grayiana, Græce. Cantab. 1785. 8vo. 3s. 6d.
A respectable edition. LARGE PAPER. Dent, pt. i. 87, morocco, 1l. 11s. 6d. Drury, 245, morocco, 2l. 15s.

— Ibid. Græce et Latine. Lectionem constituit, Versionem refinxit, Animadversionibus illustravit Thomas Tyrwhitt. Oxon. 1794. 4to.
A very elegant and accurate edition. Steevens, 171, 1l. 8s. Drury, 346, mor. 1l. 9s. Dent. pt. i. 296, morocco, 1l. 10s. Roscoe, 148, morocco, 1l. 14s. Sir M. M. Sykes, pt. i. 282, russia, 1l. 15s. LARGE PAPER, in folio, 30 copies printed, which were reserved by the delegates of the University press as presents to eminent persons. Bp. Randolph, 181, morocco, 37l. 16s.

— Ibid. Gr. a Tho. Tyrwhitt, curante T. Burgess. Oxon. 1794. 8vo. 4s. FINE PAPER, 5s.
Reprinted Oxon. 1806 and 1817, of which editions there are copies on LARGE PAPER.

— Pepli Fragmentum, pluribus auctum Epitaphiis, partim nuper editis, partim nunc primum e Codice Harleiano (Curante T. Burgess.) Dunelmiæ, 1798. 8vo.

ARISTOTELES. Logica, seu Introductio in totam Aristotelis Philosophiam ab Armenico Idiomate in Latinum versa; Adjicitur Oratio Dominica quâ a Christo prolata aperti erant Coeli. Luc. 3. 21, e Syriaco versa. Dublin. 1657. 12mo.

— Excerpta ex Aristotelis Organo: de Simplicibus Terminis, de Propositione, et de Syllogismo. Accedunt Pselli de quinque Vocibus Liber, et Simplicii in Categorias Prolegomena. Oxon. 1802, 8vo. 4s.

ARISTOTLE. Works, translated and illustrated with copious Elucidations, by Thomas Taylor. London, 1806-12. 4to. 10 vols.

Of this valuable translation, the only complete one extant in the English language, fifty copies only were printed, at the expense of William Meredith, Esq. The volumes (of some of which a few extra copies were printed, of all excepting the two marked with an asterisk) appeared as follows:

*The Physics (pp. xix. and 575) 1806.
The Organon (pp. 844) 1807.
*The Treatises on the Heavens, on Generation, and Corruption, and on Meteors (pp. viii. and 1608, with a plate of mathematical figures) 1807.
The Treatises on the Soul, on Sense and Sensibles, &c. (pp. xlv. and 520, with a plate of mathematical figures) 1808.
The History of Animals and Treatise on Physiognomy (pp. xxii. and 487) 1809.
The Treatises on the Parts, and progressive Motion of Animals, Problems; and his Treatise on indivisible lines (pp. vii. 607. viii. and 62) 1810.
The Rhetoric, Poetic, and Nicomachean Ethics (pp. xxviii. and 604) 1811.
The Great and Eudemian Ethics, the Politics and Economics (pp. viii. and 535) 1811.
The Metaphysics, &c. (*second edition*) (pp. xxix. and 686) 1812. (A first edition was published in 1801, and contains an elaborate *Introduction*, and an Essay on *Nullities*, not republished in the second.)
A Dissertation on the Philosophy of Aristotle, by Thomas Taylor (pp. xxviii. and 577) 1812.

Copies are in the Bodleian Library and London Institution. Watson Taylor, 36l. 15s. North, pt. 1. 280, 30l. 9s.

— Ethiques, now newly translated into English, from the Italian by John Wylkinson. London, Rich. Grafton, 1547. 16mo.

Black letter. Contains L 3 in eights, half sheets, with a preface, dedicated to Edward, Earl of Derby. Sotheby, 1856, 1l. 9s.

— Politiques, translated out of Greeke into French, with Expositions, by Loys Le Roy, called Regius, translated out of French into English. London, 1597. folio. 7s.

Contains 393 pages and a table. Dedicated to 'Sir Robert Sidney Knight,' by I. D. 'To the courteous Reader.' 'To Henrie King of Fraunce and Poleland, the third of that name,' by Loys Le Roy. 'Interpres ad Lectorem,' in ten Latin hexameters. The genuine work, according to Warton. Again 1598. Roxburghe, 1220, 3s.

— Ethics and Politics, comprising his practical Philosophy, translated from the Greek. Illustrated by Introductions and Notes, the critical History of his Life, and a new Analysis of his speculative Works, by John Gillies, LL.D. &c. London, 1797. 4to. 2 vols. 15s.

A translation executed with strict fidelity and great classical taste. Reprinted 1804, 1813. 8vo. 2 vols. each. Edition 1804. Earl of Kerry, 13, 1l. 4s.; and 1813. Drury, 255, 25s. Thomas Taylor published an answer to Dr. Gillies' Supplement to his Analysis of Aristotle's Works, 1804, 8vo. 3s. 6d.

— New Translation of the Nicomachean Ethics of Aristotle, by a Member of the University. Oxford, 1818. 8vo. 8s.

— Treatise on Government, translated from the Greek, by William Ellis, M.A. London, 1776. 4to. 15s.

A faithful and perspicuous version. Reprinted 4to. London, 1778.

— Rhetorick, made English by the Translators of the Art of Thinking. London, 1686. 8vo. 3s.

Reprinted 1693, 8vo. and Oxford, 1816, 12mo.

— Rhetoric, translated with Notes, by D. M. Crimmin. London, 1812. 8vo. 8s.

— Rhetoric, translated, with an Introduction and Appendix, by John

Gillies, LL.D. 12s. Lond. 1823. 8vo. 12s.
An excellent translation.

Aristotle's Rhetoric, literally translated from the Greek; with Notes, by a Graduate of the University. To which is added, an Analysis of Aristotle's Rhetoric, by Thomas Hobbes, of Malmsbury. Oxford, 1823. 8vo. 12s.

— Rhetoric, Poetic and Nicomachean Ethics, translated by Thomas Taylor. London, 1818. 8vo. 2 vols. 12s.
Drury, 253, 20s.

— Metaphysics, translated with copious Notes, &c. by Thomas Taylor. London, 1801, 4to. 1l. 1s.
This edition contains some valuable matter by the translator, not reprinted in the ninth volume of his complete translation of Aristotle's works.

— Art of Poetry, translated from the original Greek, with Dacier's Notes. London, 1705, 8vo. 2s. 6d.
A translation of Dacier's French version, reprinted 1709 and 1714.

— Poetics, translated from the Greek into English. London, 1775. 8vo. 2s. 6d.
'So very literal,' says Mr. Pye, 'as to be absolutely unintelligible to any person not acquainted with the original.'

— Treatise on Poetry, translated with Notes on the Translation and on the Original; and two Dissertations on poetical and musical Imitations, by Thomas Twining, M.A. Oxford, 1789. 4to. 1l. 1s.
Contains pp. 567. Of this translation all the literary journals have spoken in terms of very high and justly-merited praise. Drury, 347, 1l. A Second Edition, improved by D. Twining, M.A. Lond. 1812. 8vo. 2 vols. Drury, 248, 11s.

— Poetics, translated from the Greek, with Notes by Henry James Pye, Esq. London, 1792. 4to.
An edition far superior to that of 1788. 4to. According to the Monthly Reviewers, 'Mr. P. has executed the difficult and laborious task with elegance, force, and precision.' Roscoe, 150, 1l. 1s.

— The Secret of Secrets of Aristatyle, with the Governale of Princes and euery Maner of Estate, with Rules of Helth for Body and Soul, newly translated out of French, by Robert Copland. London, printed by Robert Copland, 1528. 4to.
Black letter. A to I, in fours. A forgery, according to Warton, consecrated with the name of Aristotle. Weber says it was composed in verse by Pierre de Vernon in the 12th century.

— De Cursione Lunæ. The Course and Disposition of the Dayes of the Moone in Laten and in Englishe, whiche be good and whiche be badde, after the Influences of the Moone. Drawen out of a Boke of Aristoteles de Astronomiis, &c. (London, by Richard Fakes.) 16mo.
Black letter. A kind of astrological fortune telling treatise, in which the author descants on each particular day, in old English verse.

— The Nature and Dysposycion of the vij Dayes in the Weke, and sheweth what the Thondre in euery Month in the Yere, chaunsynge, doth protende and sygnyfye. With the Course and Dysposycion, of the Dayes of the Moone whiche ben good, and whiche ben bad, after the Influences of the Moone. Drawen out of a Laten Booke of Aristotiles Astronimis. Imprinted by me Robert Wyer. 16mo.
Black letter. Contains B in eights.

— The Problems of Aristotle with other Philosophers and Physitions; wherein are obtained divers Questions, with their Answers, touching the Estate of Mans Bodie. Lond. 1595. 16mo. 10s. 6d.
Black letter. After the problems of Aristotle, are those of Marcus Antonius Zimaras Sanctipetrinas, 97 in number. Then those of Alexander Aphrodisevs, 142 in number. The work was frequently reprinted in the 17th century.
Many other works have been published, to which the name of Aristotle has been falsely affixed, but they are of no value or estimation.

ARITHMEUS, Valens. Mausolea Regum, Reginarum, Dynastarum, Nobilium, sumptuosissima, artificiosissima, magnificentissima, Londini

Anglorum, in Occidentali Urbis Angulo structa, h. e. eorundem Inscriptiones omnes in Lucem redactæ. Cura Valentis Arithmæi, Professoris Academici. Literis et Sumptibus Joannis Eichorn. Francof. Marchion. 1618. 12mo.
A copy is in the British Museum.

Arithmetic.—An Introduction for to lerne to reken with the Pen and with the Counters, after the true Cast of Arismetyke or Awgrym in hole Numbers, and also in broken; newly corrected and certayne Rules and Ensamples added thereunto, in 1536. Imprented 1537. 8vo.
Black letter. Contains 8. v. and three blank leaves: Numbers to the end. This work was reprinted 1539, 1546, 1574, 1581, and 1595.

ARLINGTON, Earl of. Letters to Sir William Temple, Bart. 1665-70. to Sir Rich. Fanshaw, the Earl of Sandwich, the Earl of Sunderland, and Sir Wm. Godolphin, during their respective Embassies in Spain, 1664-74: as also to Sir Robert Southwell in Portugal. London, 1701. 8vo. 2 vols. 10s. 6d.
Contain pp. 454 and 480. These letters afford an insight into the secret and obscure management of affairs during the above interesting period. Willett, 42, 1l. 10s. Roxburghe, 8489, 9s.

Armada (Spanish). See Spanish.

ARMIN, Robert. Discourse of Elizabeth Caldwell, who, with some other Complices, attempted to poison her Husband. Lond. 1604. 4to.
One of the original actors in Shakespeare's Plays.

— Nest of Ninnies, simply of themselves, without Compounds. London, 1608. 4to.
Black letter. (Reprinted by the Shakespeare Society. See Appendix).

— History of the Two Maids of More Clacke. London, 1609. 4to. See Maids.
The title contains a portrait of the author in his stage dress. Rhodes, 468, MS. title 1l 5s. Reed, 7690, 2l. 10s. Sotheby's in Nov. 1826. 2l. 12s. Inglis' Old Plays, 9, 3l. 3s. Sotheby's in 1823. 7l. 17s. 6d. Jolley, 1843, 2l. 10s. Halliwell, May, 1856, 5l. 12s. 6d.

— The valiant Welchman; or, the Chronicle History of the Life and valiant Deeds of Caradoc the Great, King of Cambria, now called Wales. Lond. 1615. 4to.
Reprinted 1663. 4to. Edition, 1615. Rhodes, 468, 18s. Inglis' Old Plays, 1615. No. 10, 2l 7s. Date 1663, with front* Roxburghe, 4355, 6s. 6d. Rhodes, 471, 12s. Reed, 8451, 1l. 2s. Sotheby's in Feb. 1824-1l. 7s. Brand, 1l. 16s.

— Italian Taylor and his Boy. London, 1609. 4to.
Extends to H 2. Inglis, 122, 6l. Sotheby's in 1823, 7l. King and Lochée's in March 1810, 10l. 10s. Gordonstoun, 101, 12l. 12s. Reprinted in fac-simile, 1811, 4to. 5s.

Arminian Heresie, 1628. See R.J.

Arminian Nunnery; or, a briefe Description and Relation of a late erected monasticall Place, called the Arminian Nunnery, at Little Gidding, in Huntingdonshire. Printed by Thomas Underhill, 1641. 4to.
Contains pp. 10, with a view of the nunnery and the whole-length figure of a nun, as a vignette, in the title page. Gough, 41⁶, 1l. 3s. King and Lochée's in March 1810, 1l. 2s. Nassau, pt 1. 186, 2l. 2s. Reprinted by Hearne in the first volume of Peter Langtoft's Chronicle.

ARMINIUS, James, D. D. The Works, translated from the Latin. To which are prefixed, the Life of the Author, Extracts from his Letters, &c. By James Nichols. London, 1825. 3 vols. 8vo. with port. 2l. 8s.
An excellent translation, 'with important matter in the prolegomena and notes.'

— The Life and Death of James Arminius and Simon Episcopius. Now published in the English Tongue. London, 1672. 12mo. 5s.

Arms borne by Families of Great Britain and Ireland. (The principal historical and allusive) with their respective Authorities, collected by an Authority, with a Representation of the Arms on copper-plates. London, 1803. 4to.
Contains pp. viii. and 552. This useless, and in many places nonsensical, compilation is usually attributed to Col. De la Motte. The major part of the impression was destroyed in the fire at Nichols' Print-

ing Office. Sir M. M. Sykes, 1498, 1l. 7s. Roxburghe, 8675, 1l. 1s.

ARMSTRONG, Archibald. Archy's Dream, sometime Jester to his Majestie but exiled the Court by Canterburies Malice. With a Relation for whom an odd Chaire stood void in Hell. 1641. 4to.

One Sheet. The frontispiece represents Archbishop Laud in bed with a cloven foot at the bed side, a great sword in the window, and Archy standing by. White Knights, pt. i. 171, 4l. 4s. Brand, 1l. 13s.

— Archee's Banquet of Jests, or change of cheare. 8vo. Portrait of Archee.

Brand, date 1639, fac simile port. 4l. 10s.

— Archee's Banquet of Jests, new and old. Lond. 1657. 12mo. with a portrait of Archee whole length, and four verses, by T. Cecill.

North, 4l. 7s. Gardner 1854, mor. 10l. Inglis, 30, morocco, 5l. 15s. 6d. 1665, with port. Sotheby's in May 1823, mor. 1l. 1s. R°dd' 1821, date 1636, 7l. 7s. in 1824 4l. 14s. 6d.

— Jests found in his Closet after his decease. London, 1660, with portrait engraved by Gaywood, inscribed 'This is no Muckle John nor Sommers William.'

In Ireland's Catalogue 1801, No. 482, was 'Life of Archee, Jester to James and Charles the First, with portrait by Cecill.' 4to. 7s.

— John, Col. History of the Navigation of the Port of King's Lyn and of Cambridge, and the rest of the trading Towns in those Parts; and of the navigable Rivers that have their Course through the Bedford Level. London, 1725. folio.

Contains pp. 148, besides preface, errata, and list of subscribers' names, eight pages, also seven maps and plates. In 1766, the old title, preface and contents were cancelled, and new ones printed, and after the table of contents is an addition of 'An Abstract, consisting of two pages.

— John. History of the Island of Minorca. Second Edition. London, 1756. 8vo.

Contains pp. 264, with five plates. Dent, pt. i. 91, 5s. 6d. Towneley, pt. i. 269, 7s. Fonthill, 2696, 14s. The first edition appeared in 1752.

— John, M.D. Miscellanies. London, 1770. 12mo. 2 vols.

Nassau, pt. i. 60, 7s. In 1744 was published The Art of preserving Health. By John Armstrong, M.D. A new edition, with a critical Essay on the Poem, by J. Aikin, M.D. 1795, 5s. [He published the 'Œconomy of Love' in 1736, which edition was considered obscene, and suppressed. It was modified in 1768 and all subsequent editions.]

— R. A., A.M. Gaelic Dictionary, in two Parts; 1. Gaelic and English; 2. English and Gaelic. Lond. 1825. 4to. Pub. 3l. 13s. 6d.

Armstrong. — The pleasant History of Jonny Armstrong, 4to. 8s.

ARNALD, Richard. Critical Commentary upon the Apocrypha. Lond. 1744, 8, 52. Folio, 3 Parts, 2l. 2s.

This judicious and valuable work usually accompanies the commentaries of Patrick, Lowth, and Whitby, and is the scarcest volume of the set. It has been reprinted 1806, 1809, 1822, 4to. 1l. 1s. each. Edition 1744, Gough 2729, with MS. notes by Jer. Markland, 7l. 7s.

Arnalte and Lucenda, entitled the evil entreated lover or the melancholy knight, translated into English verse by Lawrence. 4to. 1639.

Reed, 2650, 2l. 5s. Bindley, 16l. 16s.

Arnalte and Lucenda. See HOLLYBAND, Claudius; Lawrence (Leonord).

ARNAUD, Henri. History of the glorious Return of the Vaudois to their valleys in 1689. Translated from the original by Hugh Dyke Acland, Esq. with sketches of the country, engraved by Finden. London, 1826. 8vo. 1l. 10s.

ARNDTIUS, Johannes. De vero Christianismo Libri IV. cum Judiciis ejus de Theologia Polemica, Lat. ex Versione A. W. Boemi. Lond. 1708. 8vo. 2 vols.

The most esteemed work of all those written by this celebrated Protestant divine. Roxburghe, 401, 7s. 6d. It has been translated into English 1712-44, 8vo. 2 vols. and again, by W. Jacques, 1815, 8vo. 2 vols. 9s. each. An edition of the translation by W. H. Boehm. Lond. 1720. 8vo. 3 vols. Williams, 82, 1l. 19s.

Arno Miscellany: a Collection of fugitive pieces by a Society called the Oziosi. Florence, 1784. 8vo. 7s. 6d.

Privately printed.

ARNOLD, John. An Account kept during thirteen months in the Royal Observatory at Greenwich, of the going of a pocket Chronometer. A Letter from Mr. Christian Meyer, Astronomer to the Elector Palatine. On the Longitude, in a Letter to the Commissioners of that Board. An Answer to an anonymous letter on the Longitude. Lond. 1780-2. 4to. Four Tracts, 10s. 6d.

— Richard. Chronicle. In this Booke is conteyned the Names of the Balyfs, Custos, Mayres, and Sherefs of yͤ Cite of London from the Tyme of Kynge Richard the first, called Cure de Lyon, which was crowned y iii day of Septēbre yͤ yere of our Lorde God xi°Lxxxix. Small folio. (Antwerp, John Doesbrowe, 1502).
First edition. Black letter. Fol. cxviii. with a 'Kalender' commencing on A ii. It is described in the Censura Litteraria, vi. 112—9. White Knights, 32l. Pickering 1854, russia, 15l. 10s.

— The Names of the Baylyfs, Custose, Mayers, and Sherefs of the Cyte of London, &c. (1521.) folio.
Black letter. A 4 leaves, A 1 blank. B 1—C 4, 12 leaves, then B 1—U 5, 120 leaves. A full description of this edition, (in which according to Hearne, the history comes much lower than the first,) will be found in Oldys' British Librarian, pp. 22—26.

— The Names of yͤ Baylifs, Custos, Maiers, and Sherefs of the Cyte of Londō, &c. folio.
Black letter. The signatures are irregular, A containing the table of contents, 4 leaves, the first of which is blank, then another sign. A with 8 leaves; B 4, on the first leaf of which begins the numbering of the leaves; C 8—E 8; F 6—Q 6; R 8; S 6; T 6; V 5, the last page of which is blank. A very full description of this edition will be found in Herbert's Ames iii. 1746-51. Copies of the various editions have been sold as under: Mason, 15l. 15s. Brand, 18l. 18s. Lansdowne, 7l. 17s. 6d. Sir P. Thompson, 147, 18l. Roxburghe, 8355, 22l. 1s. Nassau, pt. i. 207, 7l. Sir M. M. Sykes, 454, 12l. 12s. D'''r't, Pt. i. 159, mor. 5l. 5s.

— The Customs of London, otherwise called Arnold's Chronicle; containing among divers other matters the original of the celebrated Poem of the Nut-brown Maid. Reprinted from the first edition, with the Additions included in the second. Lond. 1811. 4to. pp. lii and 300, 1l. 1s.
A faithful reprint, with a judicious introduction, by Francis Douce, Esq. Warton observes of this work, that it is perhaps the most heterogeneous and multifarious miscellany that ever existed.

Arnold de Noua Villa. The Defence of Age and Recouery of Youth. Impr. by me Robert Wyer, 16mo.
Black letter. Contains B, in fours. Inglis 32, 1l. 10s.

— Thomas. M.D. Observations on the Nature, Kinds, Causes, and Prevention of Insanity. Lond. 1800. 8vo. 2 vols. 9s.
A very entertaining work, containing the opinions both of ancients and moderns upon this subject, illustrated by a variety of curious facts. A former edition appeared 1782-6. 8vo. 2 vols.

ARNOT, Hugo. Collection and Abridgement of celebrated criminal Trials in Scotland, from A.D. 1536 to 1784, with historical and critical remarks. Edinb. 1812. 8vo. 10s. 6d.
The former edition, 1785, 4to. Roxburghe, 1079, 11s. Bindley, pt. i. 118, 6s.

— History of Edinburgh, from the earliest accounts to the present time. To which is added an Appendix. Second Edition. Edinb. 1789. 4to. pp. 674, with large plan and 20 engravings.
Best edition of an useful and entertaining work. Roxburghe, 8785, 1l. 3s. The former edition appeared in 1779. Nassau, 188, 9s. Heath, 4725, 1l. 10s.

ARNWAY, John, D.D. Tablet, or Moderation of Charles the First, Martyr, with an Alarum to the subjects of England. Hague, 1650. small 8vo.
Of this edition, according to Ant à Wood, a few copies only were printed. It was reprinted at London, 1661, with port. of Charles I. 8vo. by the care of Will. Rider, who married the author's near kinswoman. The edition 1661. Dowdeswell, 18, 5s. 6d. Towneley, pt. i. 263, 10s. 6d.

Arraigning and indicting of Sir

John Barleycorn and J. Robins the author, 1575. 4to.

ARRIAN'S History of Alexander's Expedition, transl. from the Greek, with notes, historical, geographical, and critical, by John Rooke. To which is prefixed Le Clerc's Criticism upon Q. Curtius. Arrian's Indian History. His Account of the division of the Empire after Alexander's death. Raderus's Tales. A Catalogue of the Authors who have wrote his history. A Chronology of the whole, and a complete Index. Lond. 1729. 8vo. 2 vols. 12s. to 14s.
[Reprinted 2 vols. 8vo. 1814. 10s.]
A very useful and valuable work, faithfully and accurately executed. Edwards, 215, 5s. Gough, 132, 1l. 4s. Roxburghe, 7532, 1l. 8s. Constable, 28, mor. 2l. 2s. Reprinted 1814, 8vo. 2 vols. 12s.

— Voyage round the Euxine Sea, accompanied with a Geographical Dissertation and Map. To which are added three Discourses. By William Vincent, D.D. Lond. 1805. 4to.
The original will be found in Hudson's Geographiæ veteris Scriptores.
— See VINCENT.

ARROWSMITH, A. General Atlas, constructed from the latest authorities. Lond. 1827. royal 4to. with 53 maps, 1l. 16s. Coloured, 2l. 12s. 6d.
This celebrated hydrographer has published a variety of maps, highly valued for their accuracy.
[Since this period, the Arrowsmiths have published many Atlases. Their best is in large folio, of recent date, 67 coloured maps, 17l. 17s.]

— John, D.D. Armilla Catechetica: a Chain of Principles, or an orderly Concatenation of Theological Aphorisms and Exercitations, wherein the chief heads of Christian Religion are asserted and improved. Camb. 1659. 4to. 10s. 6d.
Williams, 111, morocco, 2l. 8s. Reprinted Edinb. 1822. 8vo. 8s. This work, and likewise the author's Tactica Sacra, 1657. 4to. and other publications, rank high among the Puritanical writings. Tactica Sacra, Williams, 110, 1l. 10s.

— John Pauncefort. The Art of instructing the Infant Deaf and Dumb. Lond. 8vo.
In this interesting little volume the plan of the celebrated Abbé De l'Epée is reprinted.

Arrowsmith and Herst. A true and exact relation of the death of two Catholics [Edmund Arrowsmith and Richard Herst] who suffered for their religion at the Summer Assizes, held at Lancaster in 1628. Republished with additions. Lond. 1737. 8vo. with their portraits, 5s.

ARSANES. Orations of Arsanes against Philip, the trecherous Kyng of Macedone : of the Embassadors of Venice against the prince that vnder a crafty league with Scanderbeg, layed snares for Christendome ; and of Scanderbeg, praying ayde of Christian Princes agaynst periurous murdering Mahumet, and agaynst the old false Christian Duke Mahumetes confederate. With a notable example of God's vengeance vppon a faithlesse Kyng, Quene, and her children. Lond. by John Daye. 16mo.
Black letter. Contains V 2, in fours, half sheets. 'A notable example,' &c. Then A in eights, including the title and a blank leaf prefixed. Day printed three editions without date. The work is by Tanner, (Bibl. Brit. 551,) ascribed to Thomas Norton. Nassau, pt. i. 2468, 1l. 6s. Sir M. M. Sykes, pt. ii. 577, 1l. 15s.

ARTEMI. Memoirs of the Life of Artemi, of Wagarschapat, near Mount Ararat, in Armenia, from the original Armenian. Written by himself. Lond. 1822. 8vo. pp. 374, 7s.

ARTEMIDORUS. Interpretation of Dreams, digested into five Books. The Tenth Edition, corrected by an original copy, with the Life of the Author, &c. Lond. 1690. 12mo.
A work formerly in considerable estimation, as will appear from the numerous editions published. An edition of the date of 1644, (by Barnard Alsop) is in the British Museum. An edition, 1669. Inglis, 87, 11s.

ARTHINGTON, Henry. Principall Points of Holy Profession, touching these three estates of Mankind. 1.

Their Creation. 2. Their Subversion. 3. Their Restoration, &c. Composed in Verse, by H. A. Printed by Tho. Pavyer, 1607. 4to.

Bright, 1845, cut, 2*l*. 3*s*.

An account of Arthington will be found in Weever's Funeral Monuments.

— The seduction of Arthington by Hackett. Printed by R. B. for T. Man, 4to. (n. d.) 1592.

Jolley, 1843, 1*l*. 19*s*.

ARTHUR, King of Great Britain. Assertio Arturij Regis Britanniæ, 1544 and 1554, 4to. with the translation by Rich. Robinson. 1582 or 1583. 4to. *See* LELAND, John.

— King of Great Britain. A Book of the noble Hystoryes of Kynge Arthur, and of certeyn of his Knyghtes, reduced into Englysshe by Syr Thomas Malory, Knyght, and by me William Caxton, deuyded into xxi. Bookes, chapytred and emprynted and fynyshed in th' abbey Westmestre, 1485. folio.

Black letter. The proheme commences on the recto of sign A ij, and terminates on the recto of sign iiij, and is succeeded by the table, which occupies the 14 subsequent leaves. The first chapter begins on the recto of sign a j; and the entire volume extends to three leaves after sign ee iij. in eights; the latter having but six leaves. A perfect copy of this edition is in the library at Osterley Park, belonging to the Earl of Jersey. Another (unfortunately defective) is in Earl Spencer's library. [From the Wygfair Collection, 4 *leaves wanting*, 320*l*.] *See* Ames by Dr. Dibdin, i. 241—55. Brit. Bibliogr. i. 49. Bibl. Spencer, iv. 403—9.

— The Booke of Kynge Arthur and of his noble Knyztes of the round Table. Westmestre, by Wynkyn de Worde, 1498, folio.

Black letter. The signatures run in three sets, exclusive of a table of eight leaves. First a to v, in eights and sixes, alternately; v has eight leaves. Next A, B, C, in sixes; D, eight; E, six; F, G, H, in eights, I to V, inclusively, in sixes; X, four, Y, five. As the third set, A, B, C, D, E, in sixes, E vj being blank. Of this edition, a reprint of Caxton's, only one copy is known, which is in the possession of Earl Spencer. In Dr. Dibdin's Edition of Ames, vol. i. 248—52, the variations in this edition from that of Caxton's are given; and a very copious description, with specimens of the wood cuts, will be found in the Bibl. Spencer. iv. 403-9.

— The Booke of Kynge Arthur, &c. Lond., by Wynkyn de Worde, 1529. folio.

Black letter, with cuts. A notice of Archdeacon Wrangham's copy, said to be unique, will be found in Cole's Bibliographical and Descriptive Tour, 1824, 1—9. Archd. Wrangham, 75. Table impft. 51*l*.

— The Story of Kynge Arthur, and also of his Knyghtes of the Rounde Table. London, by W. Copland, 1557, folio.

Black letter. Each of the 21 books has a wood-cut prefixed. The last leaf contains the device of the printer. Dent, pt. i. 162, morocco, 20*l*. 9*s*. Utterson, 252. Impft. 10*l*.

— King of Great Britain.—The Story of King Arthur; and also of his Knights of the Rounde Table. Lond., by Thomas East, folio.

Black letter. Oo 6, in eights. This edition differs in a few phrases (but not materially) from Caxton's. Dent, pt. i. 163, morocco, by Roger Payne, 13*l*. Roxburghe, 6356, 27*l*. 6*s*. Goldsmid, 1816, 156, 42*l*. Pickering, (Title fac-simile, and mended) mor. 13*l*. 10*s*.

— An edition, Lond. T. East. 4to. no date.

— The History of the renowned Prince Arthvr. As also all the noble Acts and heroicke Deeds of his valiant Knights of the Rovnd Table. Lond. Stansby, 1634. 4to.

Black letter, with three titles and three frontispieces. This edition is probably a reprint from East's edition, and is the last of any value in the estimation of collectors. Bindley, pt. i. 340, 2*l*. 3*s*. Lloyd, 224, 2*l*. 9*s*. Nassau, pt. i. 190, 8*l*. Dent, pt. i. 298, russia, 4*l*. Inglis, 123, 4*l*. 4*s*. Sir M. M. Sykes, pt. i. 287, morocco, 5*l*. 7*s*. 6*d*. White Knights, pt. i. 327, russia, 6*l*. 6*s*. Reed, 2655, 7*l*. 10*s*. Garrick, 221, 8*l*. North, pt. iii. 737, russia, 8*l*. 10*s*. Towneley, pt. i. 885, 12*l*. 5*s*. Roxburghe, 6357, russia, 12*l*. 12*s*. Stanley, 746, russia, 18*l*. Longman, 1814, 8*l*. 8*s*. Thorpe, 1820, 7*l*. 7*s*. Triphook, 1815, 9*l*. 9*s*. Gardner, 1854, morocco, 4*l*. 8*s*.

— The History of the renowned Prince Arthur, &c. Lond. 1816. 24mo. 3 vols. with frontispieces.

A correct reprint of the edition of 1634. (edited by Jos. Haslewood). Another edition was published, 24mo. 2 vols. about the same time.

—The Byrth, Lyfe and Actes of Kyng Arthur; of his noble Knyghtes of the rounde Table, &c. With an Introduction and Notes, by Rob. Southey. Lond. 1817. 4to. 2 vols. 2*l.* 2s.
[Reprinted from Caxton's edition of 1485.] LARGE PAPER. Midgeley, 586, 5*l.* 5s. This work, says Sir Walter Scott, 'contains a short abridgment of the most celebrated adventures of the Round Table; and being written in comparatively modern languages, gives the general reader an excellent idea of what romances of chivalry actually were.' The Life of King Arthur, by Joseph Ritson, was published 1825.

— The avncient Order, Societie, and Vnitie laudable of Prince Arthure, and his knightly Armory of the Round Table. With a threefold assertion friendly in Fauour and Furtherance of English Archery at this day. Translated and collected by R. R. (Richard Robinson.) Lond. by John Wolfe, 1583. 4to.
Black letter. Contains M, in fours, with wood cuts. A particular description of this book will be found in the British Bibliographer, i. 125—35, and in Moule's Bibl. Herald, art. xxx. pp. 26—30. Sir M. M. Sykes, pt. i. 289, mor. 6*l.* 6s.

— of Little Britain. The Hystory of Arthur of Lytell Brytayne, translated out of Frensshe in to Englishe, by the noble Johan Bourghcher, Knyght, Lorde Barners, newly imprinted. Lond. by Robert Redborne. folio.
Black letter. The text printed in double columns, commences on sign A, preceded by the title, prologue and table. In the whole clxxiiii leaves, numbered at the last folio lxix. Copious descriptions of this edition will be found in the Brit Bibl. iv. 228—33, and in Dr. Dibdin's Ames, iv. 190-2. Roxburghe, No. 6355, Very imperfect, (erroneously attributed to Copland) 6*l.* 10s. [An edition printed by Thos. East. *no date.* Small 4to. Black letter, with woodcuts. Ends Nn 7, page 279.]

— New Edition, edited by E. V. Utterson. Lond. 1814. 4to.
With a series of plates, in outline, from illuminated drawings. Drury, 357, 1*l.* 12s. With coloured plates. Sir M. M. Sykes, pt. i. 290, 4*l.* 1s. LARGE PAPER, (25 printed) with duplicates of the plates printed in colours, heightened with gold. 8*l.* 8s. Sotheby's in 1824, morocco, 7*l.* Brockett, 249, russia, 11*l.* 1s. 6d.

Arthur, Prince. An allegorical Romance; the Story from Spenser. Lond. 1779. 12mo. 2 vols. 5s.
Written by Alex. Bicknell.

— Uther Pendergon's son. *See* Hughes (Thomas).

ARTHUS, Gotardus. Dialogues in the English and Malaiane Languages, translated by Augustine Spalding. Lond. 1614, 4to.
A copy is in the British Museum.

Articles.—The Articles of our Fayth. The X Comaündementes. The vii Works of Mercy. The vii dedely Synnes. The vii pryncypall Vtues. And the vii Sacramentis of holy Chirche whiche euery Curate is bounde for to declare to his Paryshens iiii Tymes in the Yere. Impressum per me Richardum Pynson. n. d. 4to.
Black letter. 4 leaves. White Knights, pt. i. 329, morocco, 4*l.* 4s.

Articles to be enquired of in the Kynges Maiesties (Edward VI.) Visitacion. Rich. Grafton excud. (1547.) 4to.
Black letter. 6 leaves. According to Dr. Dibdin there were two editions printed this year by Grafton. The latter has head titles to the several parts. In Strype's Eccles. Memor. ii. p. 48, &c.

Articles to be enquired of in the Visitations to be had within the Diocese of Canterbury, in the second year of the reign of Edward the Sixth. Lond. by Richard Grafton, 1548. 4to.
Black letter. Contains 86 articles on eight leaves. Reprinted in Sparrow's Collection of Articles, &c.

Articles to be enquired of, in the Visitation of the Diocess of London, by Nicolas [Ridley] Bishop of London, in the fourth year of Edward the Sixth. Lond. by Reynold Wolfe, 1550. 4to.
Black letter. Reprinted in Sparrow's Collection of Articles, &c. Dr. Dibdin notices 'Articles of Visitation (Arch. Cranmer) in the Diocese of Norwich,' 1599, 4to.

Articles to be enquired of, in the generall Visitation of Edmonde [Bonner] Bisshope of London,

1554 in the Citie and Diocese of London. Londini in Ædibus Joannis Cawodi, 1554. 4to.

Black letter. E 3, in fours. Reflections on these articles were published by John Bale, and a translation, with many quaint and pertinent remarks in the margin, appeared under the following title, 'Nova Inquisitio Hæreticæ Pravitatis in Regno Angliæ, scripta populari Lingua Gentis, et impressa Lundini; conversa autem in Latinum Sermonem, ut omnes Pii intelligant, quam salutaris ipsa sit, et quantum optare debeant, similem fieri in aliis etiam Regnis Inquisitionem. Lipsiæ; 1555.'

Articles to be enquyred, in thordinary Visitacion of the Lorde Cardinall Pooles Grace Archebyshop of Caunterbury wythin hys Dioces of Cantorbury. In the yeare of our Lorde God. m.v.c.lvi. 4to.

Black letter. 4 leaves. According to Herbert only some of these articles are mentioned by Collier, more by Strype, though not in the same words. Together they will not make up the complete number of 21 touching the clergy, and 33 relating to the laity.

Articles to be enquired in the Visitation in the first Yere of the Raigne of Elizabeth, &c. Lond. by Richard Jugge and John Cawood, 1559. 4to.

Black letter. Contains B 8, in fours. Reprinted in Sparrow's Collection of Articles, &c.

In Herbert's and Dr. Dibdin's editions of Ames's Typog. Antiquities will be found many editions of Visitation articles from 1567 to 1600, likewise many of a much later period are in the British Museum.

Articles agreed upon by the Bishops and other learned and godly Men in the last Convocation at London in 1552. To root out the Discord of Opinions and establish the Agreement of true Religion. Published by the Kings Majesties Authority 1553. Lond. by John Day, 1553. 4to.

Reprinted in Sparrow's Collection of Articles, &c. and in Burnet's History of the Reformation. These 42 Articles published by the authority of K. Edward VI. were repealed by Q. Mary soon after her accession. Another edition, Rich. Grafton, excud. 1553, 4to. Black letter.

Articles of Religion. A Declaration of certain principal Articles of Religion, set out by the Order of both Archbishops, Metropolitans, and the rest of the Bishops, for the Unity of Doctrine to be taught and holden of all Persons, &c. Lond. by R. Jugge, 1561.

See Bishop Burnet's History of the Reformation, pt. ii. Records, p. 336.

Articles. A Brefe declaration of certain principall articles of religion, set out by order and aucthoritie as well of the Right Honbl. Sir Henry Sidney, General Deputie of Irelande, &c., as by the Archbyshops and Byshopes, and other of her Majesties Hygh Commissioners, for causes ecclesiastical in the same realme. Imp. by Humfrey Powel. Dublin. 20th Jan. 1566. 4to.

The only copy known is in Trinity College Library, Dublin.

Articles whereupon it was agreed by the Archbishoppes and Bishoppes in the Conuocation holden at London, 1562, for the Auoiding of the Diuersities of Opinions, and for the Stablishyng of Consent touching true Religion. Put forth by the Queenes Aucthoritie. Lond. by R. Jugge and J. Cawood, 1571. 4to.

Black letter. Contains D 2, in fours. Jugge printed other editions, with and without dates, and John Daye also printed an edition in 1571. 4to.

— Another edition. Lond. by Christ. Barker, 1579. 4to. 7s.

Black letter. From this edition all subsequent ones have been printed.

— Another edition. Reprinted by his Majesties Commandment, with his Royal Declaration prefixed thereunto. Lond. 1630, 4to.

This edition is reprinted in Sparrow's Collection of Articles, &c.

Articles.—The XXXIX Articles of the Church of England, illustrated by copious Extracts from the Liturgy, Homilies, &c. and confirmed by numerous Passages of Scripture, By the Rev. William Wilson, B.D. Lond. 1821. 8vo. 6s.

— The Religion of the Reforma-

tion as exhibited in the thirty-nine Articles of the Church of England. 1826. 12mo. 7s.
— of Religion agreed vpon in the Conuocation holden at Dvblin in 1615. Lond. 1628. 4to.
A copy is in the British Museum.
Articuli de quibus in Synodo Londinensi M.D.LII. ad tollendam Opinionum Dissentionem, et Consensum verae Religionis formandum inter Episcopos et alios eruditos Viros convenerat, Regia Authoritate in lucem editi. Londini, apud Reginaldum Wolfium, 1553, 4to.
Reprinted in Bishop Sparrow's Collection of Articles, &c.
— Ibid. Lond. apud Reg. Wolfium. 1563. 4to.
Printed also, according to Dr. Dibdin, in 8vo. the same year, with the first clause of the 20th article.
— Ibid. Lond. Jo. Day. 1571. 4to.
Consisting of 12 leaves. Reprinted in Sparrow's Collection of Articles, &c. There were several other editions printed about this time.
Articuli per Archiepiscopum, Episcopus, et reliquum Clerum Cantuariensis Prouinciæ, in Synodo inchoata Londini, 24 Nouemb. A.D. 1584, Regniq; serenissimæ Dom. Elizabethæ, 27mo stabiliti, et Regia Auctoritate confirmati. Lond. in ædibus C. B. (Chr. Barker, 1584.) 4to. 7s.
Reprinted in Bishop Sparrow's Collection of Articles, &c. Another edition was published by Abel Jeffes without date.
Articuli Christianæ Fidei quam Ecclesia profitetur Anglicana, Versu (quoad ejus fieri potuit) expressi facillimo, a Joanne Glanvillo. Oxon. 1613. 4to.
Consisting of six sheets.
Articuli ad Narrationes novas pertin. formati. Londini, apud Pynson (1525) 16mo. 10s. 6d.
Black letter. A commentary and some rules upon the count, declarations, &c. contained in the 'Novæ Narrationes.' Reprinted frequently prior to 1550.
ARTIS. Edmund Tyrrell. Antediluvian Phytology, illustrated by the Fossil Remains of Plants peculiar to Coal Formations. Lond. 1825. royal 4to. plates, published at 2l. 10s.
(Since incorporated in Mantell's Pictorial Atlas, 1850.]
Artist, The, a Series of Essays relative to Painting, Poetry, Sculpture, Architecture, the Drama, Discoveries of Seamen, &c. Lond. 1809-10. 4to. 2 vols. 15s.
Edited by Prince Hoare.
ARTOPÆUS, Peter. The Diuisyon of the Places of the Lawe and of the Gospell, gathered out of the hooly Scriptures, by Petrum Artopæum. Whereunto is added two Orations of Praying to God made by S. John Chrysostome, translated into English. Imprinted by me Gwalter Lynne. 16mo.
Black letter. Dr. Dibdin notices an edition of the year 1548, without the two orations of S. John Chrysostom.
Arts. The Handmaid to the Arts. Lond. 1764. 8vo. 2 vols. 15s.
A useful book (by Robert Dossie). The former edition of 1758. 8vo. 2 vols. 12s. Reprinted 'with considerable additions and improvements,' 1796. 12mo. 2 vols. 9s.
— Transactions of the Society instituted at London for the Encouragement of Arts, Manufactures, and Commerce. From the commencement in 1783, to the year 1827, inclusive. Lond. 8vo. 44 vols. with plates.
[Since continued to end of 1845, forming 55 vols. (including Indices). After which, a NEW SERIES, 1846 to 1848, 2 parts small 4to., 1l. 1s. Discontinued, and after a time replaced by JOURNAL' OF THE SOCIETY OF ARTS, and of the Institutions in Union, Nov. 26, 1852, to present time, *in Weekly Nos* at 3d. each.]
Willett, 2257, (vols. 1 to 27,) 11l. 11s. 1783—1809. Dent, pt. ii. 8¹¹, (42 vols.) 10l. Sotheby's in 1825, (1783—1823), 40 vols. 5l. 10s.
ARUNDELL, Rev. F. V. J. A Visit to the Seven Churches in Asia, with an Excursion into Pisidia. Lond. 1828. 8vo.
ARUNDEL and SURREY, Alathea Talbot, Countess of. Nature unbowelled; her choicest secrets digested into receipts, whereunto are annexed many rare and hitherto

unimparted inventions. Lond. 1665. 8vo. with portr. by Hollar, 12s.

ARUSIENS, Philip, Bishop of. *See* Pestilence.

ARVIEUX, Laurent, Chev. d'. Travels in Arabia the Desart; done into English by an eminent hand. Lond. 1718. 8vo. with plates
Willett, 47, 6s. 6d.

ARVIRAGUS and PHILICIA, as it was acted at the private house in Black fryers by his Majesty's servants, 12mo. 1639.
Nassau, 17s.

ARWAKER, Edmund. *See* HUGO.

Ascanius, or the young Adventurer; a true history (of the Pretender). Lond. 1746. 12mo. 5s.
Bindley, pt. i. 60, 8s. Dent, pt. i. 96, 1l. Reprinted 1769, &c.

Ascanius Moderne, ou l'illustre Avanturier. Edinbourg, 1763. 12mo. 2 pties. avec figures, 6s. to 10s.
A romantic account of the adventures of the Pretender.

Ascensius Declynsons, with the playne Expositor. Without place, printer's name, or date. 4to.
Black letter. Contains D, in sixes. Mr. Heber possessed a copy of this grammatical treatise, which Dr. Dibdin suspects was printed abroad. Heber, part 2, 357. 1l. 12s.

ASCHAM, Anthony. A little Herball of the Properties of Herbes, newly amended and corrected, wyth certayn additions. M.D.L. Lond. by John Kynge. 16mo.
Black letter. Contains K 7, in eights. White Knights, 252, 10s. 6d. Dr. Dibdin notices an addition of the date of 1550 printed by W. Powell. Powell's Edition, White Knights, 251, 19s.

— A lytel Treatyse of Astronomy. M.D.LII. By Anthony Askam. Lond. by Wylliam Powel. 16mo.
Black letter. Fol. xxi. with a table of nine pages. Maunsell, in his catalogue, pt. ii. p. 2, notices an edition of the date of 1550. Ascham likewise published several other astronomical tracts.

— Of the Confusions and Revolutions of Government. Second edition, with additions. Lond. 1649. 8vo. 5s.

Hollis, 43, 8s. 6d. The best edition, containing nine chapters more than in that of 1648. A censure of this work by Bishop Sanderson, appeared in 1649. 8vo. 3s. This republican was assassinated in Spain by six exiled royalists, in 1650, of which an account was published 1651. 4to. reprinted in the fourth volume of the Harleian Miscellany.

ASCHAM, Roger. English Works, with notes and observations, and the author's life. By James Bennet. Lond. (1761) 4to. 10s. 6d.
The life of Ascham, and the dedication to the Earl of Shaftesbury, were, according to Boswell, written by Dr. Sam. Johnson. Bindley, pt. i. 138, russia, 17s. Horne Tooke, 28, 17s. 6d. Dent, pt. i. 300, morocco, 2l. 4s.

— English Works. Lond. 1815, 8vo. 1l. 1s.
Bindley, pt. i. 13, 14s. Drury, 266, morocco, 1l. 13s.

— Apologia pro Cœna Dominica contra Missam et eius Prestigias: &c. Londini, ex Typog. H. Middletoni, 1577. 8vo.
Contains pp. 296, besides dedication to the Earl of Leicester, some hexameters, and an epistle to the reader. Boswell, 109, 7s. 6d. Reprinted 1587.

— Epistolarum Libri tres, &c. Huc accesserunt pauca quædam eiusdem R. A. Poemata. Item Oratio Ed. G (rant) de Vita et Obitu R. A. et eius Dictionis Elegantia. Londini in Officina H. Middletoni, 1578. 8vo. 10s. 6d.
Dedicated to Q. Elizabeth. Reprinted 1581, 1590.

— Ibid. edidit Elstob. Oxon. 1703. 8vo. with a frontispiece by M. Burghers, containing ten English portraits, and the author reading a letter to Q. Elizabeth.
The best edition of the letters, though without Ascham's poems. These letters are very valuable for style and matter, and are almost the only classical work of the kind written by an Englishman; though, according to Warton, the latinity of Ascham's prose has little elegance. Gossett, 198, 7s. 6d. Bindley, pt. i. 14. 7s. 6d. Williams, 8vo. mor. 1l. 7s. LARGE PAPER, Heath, 4254, 18s. 6d. Dent, pt. i. 97, mor. 2l. 2s. Williams, 88, mor. 2l. 16s.

— The Scholemaster. Lond. by John Daye, 1570. 4to. 18s.

Black letter. Contains 68 leaves, besides the dedication to Sir W. Cecil, Knt., and a preface by the author. Reprinted 1571, 1573, 1579, 1589.

— The Schoolmaster, with notes and additions by James Upton. Lond. 1711. 8vo.

Horne Tooke, 27, 8s. 6d. LARGE PAPER, Bindley, pt. i. 11, 9s. 6d. Williams, 89, morocco, 1l. 5s. An edition 1743. Gossett, 199, 12s. Bindley, pt. i. 12, 4s. 6d. 'A book,' says Dr. Campbell, 'that will be always useful, and everlastingly esteemed on account of the good sense, judicious observations, excellent characters of ancient authors, and many pleasant and profitable passages of English history, which are plentifully sprinkled therein.'

— A Report and Discourse of the affaires and state of Germany, and the Emperor Charles his Court, duryng certaine yeares (1550—2), while the said Roger was there. Lond. by John Daye. 1552. 4to. 8s.

Black letter. Contains 36 leaves. This account is stated by Dr. Campbell to be one of the most delicate pieces of history that ever was penned in our language, evincing its author to have been a man as capable of shining in the cabinet as in the closet. There are two other editions, one 1570, the other without date.

— Toxophilus, the Schole of Schootinge, conteyned in two Bookes. Londini, in Ædibus Ed. Whytchurch. 1545. 4to.

Black letter. Contains Y in fours, besides eight leaves of introductory matter. First edition, dedicated to K. Henry VIII. The rarest and most valuable, in a pecuniary point of view, of all Ascham's publications. An excellent article on Toxophilus will be found in the Retrosp. Review, iv. 76—87. Reprinted 1571 and 1589. Edition 1545, Perry, pt. i. 198, 1l. 13s. Haworth, 738, russia, 1l. 16s. Edition 1571, Gordonstoun, 73, 2l. 2s. Edition 1589, Steevens, 1505, 2l. 10s. Bindley, pt. i. 189, 1l. 1s. Sir M. M. Sykes, 293, 9s, Roxburghe, 1716, 2l. 2s.

— Toxophilus. To which is added, a Dedication and Preface by the Rev. John Walters. Wrexham, 1788. 12mo. 5s.

A nearly verbatim reprint of the first edition, with 'Extracts from Books subsequent to the date of Toxophilus.'

ASGILL, John. An Argument, proving, that according to the Covenant of eternal Life, revealed in the Scriptures, Man may be translated from hence into that eternal Life, without passing through Death. Dublin, 1698. 8vo. 7s. 6d.

For this remarkable treatise upon the possibility of avoiding death, Asgill was expelled from the parliaments of Ireland and England. He likewise published several other works, chiefly on political controversy, formerly in considerable repute.

ASH, John, LLD. A new and complete Dictionary of the English Language. To which is prefixed, a comprehensive Grammar. Lond. 1775, or 1795. 8vo. 2 vols. 18s.

This dictionary, though of no standard authority, is useful, as containing obsolete, provincial, and cant words and phrases, besides a multitude of technical terms. Edwards, 9, russia, 1l. 8s.

ASHE, Thomas. Fasciculus Florum; or a Handful of Flowers gathered out of Sir Edw. Coke. Lond. 1618. 12mo. 4s.

This compiler likewise published several tables to the Year Books, Lord Coke's and Dyer's Reports, &c.

— Capt. T. Travels in America, in the year 1806, for the purpose of exploring the rivers of Alleghanny, Monongahela, Ohio, and the Mississippi, and ascertaining the Produce and Condition of their Banks and Vicinity. Lond. 1808. 12mo. 3 vols. 9s.

According to the Quarterly Review, Ashe 'has spoiled a good book by engrafting incredible stories on authentic facts.'

— Commercial View and Geographical Sketch of the Brazils in South America, and of the Island of Madeira. Lond. 1812. 8vo. 5s.

Ashe travelled on the continent of America several years.

ASHLEY, Robert. Almansor the learned and victorious King that conquered Spain, his Life and Death. Lond. 1627. 4to. 9s.

A translation from a Spanish copy, printed at Saragoza 1608. Bindley, pt. i. 144, 10s. 6d. Nassau, pt. i. 134, 18s. Thorpe, 1838, 5s. 6d. Ashley also published an Account of Cochin China. See BARBI, Chr.

ASHMOLE, Elias. Fasciculus Chemicus: Chymical Collections expressing the Ingress, Progress, and Egress of the secret Hermetic Science out of the choicest and most famous Authors, by James Hasolle [*i. e.* Elias Ashmole.] Lond. 1654. 12mo. with a front. containing Ashmole's portrait, inscribed 'Mercuriophilus Anglicus.' 5s.

Prefixed are prolegomena, according to Ant. à Wood, 'farc'd with Rosy-crucian languages.'

— Theatrum Chemicum Britanicum, containing several poetical Pieces of our famous Philosophers who have written the Hermetique Mysteries in their own ancient Language. Lond. 1652. 4to.

Contains pp. 510, with plates printed on the letter-press, with the exception of one at p. 117, frequently wanting. Roscoe, 1437, 1*l.* 3s. Inglis, 128, mor. 1*l.* 8s. Nassau, pt. i. 195, russia, 1*l.* 10s. North, pt. iii. 761, mor. 1*l.* 13s. Gordonstoun, 61, 1*l.* 15s. Bindley, pt. i. 141, morocco, 2*l.* 12s. 6d. Bibl. Anglo-Poet 4, 3*l.* 10s.

This work gained Ashmole great reputation, and was the means of extending his acquaintance in the literary world. To some copies a portrait (a bust by Faithorne) is added. [*The portrait belongs to the next article.*]

— The Way to Bliss, in three Books. Lond. 1658. 4to. 4s. With Portrait by Faithorne.

An attempt to prove the possibility of such a thing as the philosopher's stone. According to Ant. à Wood. 'pen'd by an unknown author living in the reign of Qu. Elizabeth.'

— The Institution, Laws, and Ceremonies of the most noble Order of the Garter. Lond. 1672. folio.

Contains A to 4 U, in fours, with title and imprimatur, 2 leaves; Appendix, a to c c, two leaves each, c c 2, containing the errata [there are no printed pages 131-134, 137-149]: portrait of K. Charles II. by Sherwin, and 30 plates mostly engraved by Hollar, pp. 51, 86, 94, 131, 132, 134, 137, 139, 140, 142, 144, 146, 147, 202, 223, 224, 229, 234, 235, 247, 404, 515, 576, 593, 642, 708-9, 710-11, 712-13, 714-15, 716-17. A laborious and highly valuable work, drawn up with great perspicuity and care. A copious analysis will be found in Oldys. British Librarian, 119-26. Lloyd, 255, 4*l.* 12s. Marq. of Townshend, 205, 5*l.* 15s. 6d. Dowdeswell, 135, russia, 6*l.* Towneley, pt ii. 148, 6*l.* 5s. Heath, 1617, 7*l.* Willett, 144, 7*l.* 14s. 6d. Bindley, pt. i. 160, 5*l.* 18s. 6d. LARGE PAPER, Fonthill, 3677, 19*l.* Dent, pt. i 164, morocco. 21 *l,* Nassau, pt. i. 209, 24*l.* 3s. Sir M. M. Sykes, 319, mor. 25*l.* 14s. 6d. Edwards, 587, mor. 42*l.*

Some copies have a reprinted title of the date of 1693, with the catalogue of knights-companions continued to that time.

An abridgment, with a continuation of the list of the Knights, &c. was published London, 1715, 8vo. pp. 565, with a portrait of George Augustus Prince of Wales, to whom it is dedicated, and plates, 7s. 6d. LARGE PAPER, 12s. Willett, 48, 2*l.* 5s.

— Antiquities of Berkshire, with a large Appendix, &c. Lond. 1719 or 1723. 8vo. 3 vols.

Vol. i. pp. cxxviii. and 194, also a portrait of Ashmole, by M. Vdr. Gucht, and a sheet map, containing a view of Windsor Castle, by W. Hollar. Vol. ii. pp. 195—580, with Errata, 2 pages. Vol. iii. pp. 428, with two plates, pp. 210 and 331. This scarce work by no means supplies the place of an history for that county; as it contains little more than epitaphs and some pedigrees. White Knights, pt. i. 249, morocco, 5*l.* 2s. 6d. Heath, 4692, 5*l.* 5s. Towneley, pt. ii. 25, 6*l.* 6s. Sir P. Thompson, 20, 6*l.* 12s. 6d. Willett, 49, 11*l.* 11s. LARGE PAPER. Nassau, pt. i. 70, 10*l.* 5s. Dent, pt. i. 99. 21*l.*

— History and Antiquities of Berkshire. Reading, 1736. small folio.

Contains pp. 17—840, and index, 2 pages, besides the life, consisting of 8 pages, and a map, by H. Moll. Dent, pt. i. 165, 3*l.* 5s. Marq. of Townshend, 204, 3*l.* 16s. Nassau, pt. i. 10, russia, 5*l.* Sir M. M. Sykes, pt. i. 318, 6*l.* 8s. 6d.

— Memoirs of the Life of Elias Ashmole, Esq. drawn up by himself by way of Diary: with an Appendix of original Letters. Lond. 1717. small 8vo. 3s. 6d to 5s.

Reprinted 1774. *See* BURMAN, Charles.

ASHMORE, John. Certain selected Odes of Horace englished, and their arguments annexed; with Poems, ancient and modern, of divers subjects, translated. Whereunto are added, both in Latin and English, sundry new Epigrammes, Anagrammes, Epitaphes, &c. Lond. 1621. 4to.

Contains pp. 102. Nassau, pt. i. 196, mor. 1*l.* 10s. Bibl. Anglo-Poet. 890, 4*l.* 4s.

ASHWELL, John. The Letters whyche Johan Ashwell Priour of Newnham Abbey besydes Bedforde,

ASI   ASM   81

sente secretly to the Bishop of Lyncolne, M.D.XXVII. Where in the sayde Pryour accuseth George Joye, that Tyme beyng Felow of Peter College in Cambrydge, of fower Opinions: with the answere of the sayde George unto the same Opinyons. (At the end.) At Straszburge 10 Daye of June. ¶ Thys lytell Boke be delyuered to Johan Ashwel, Priour of Newnhā Abbey, besydes Bedford, with spede. 16mo.

Black letter. Contains D 4, in eights. Sotheby's in 1825. 2*l*. 4s. Horner, 1854. mor. 2*l*. Bright, 2*l*. A notice of this curious work will be found in the Retrosp. Review, N. S. vol. ii. 96—102.

Asia.—Dissertations and miscellaneous Pieces relating to the History and Antiquities, &c. of Asia. Lond. 1792-6. 8vo. 3 vols. 12s.

A selection of essays from the Asiatic Researches.

— Asiatic Annual Register from 1799 to 1810-11 inclusive. Lond. 8vo. vols. i. to xii.

Lawrence Dundas Campbell was editor till 1809. Fonthill, 2701, (12 vols.) 6*l*. 16s. 6d.

— Asiatic Journal and Monthly Register for British India and its Dependencies, from its Commencement in Jan. 1816 to the present Time. Lond. 8vo.

A number is published on the first of every month, 3s. 6d. each. [Discontinued May, 1845, up to which period the series forms 59 vols., 6*l*. 6s. to 8*l*. 8s.]

— Asiatic Miscellany, consisting of original Productions, Translations, Fugitive Pieces, &c. Calcutta, 1785-6. royal 12mo. 2 vols.

To this work Sir Wm. Jones was a large contributor. [All his contributions are incorporated in the Supplement to the *Quarto* edition of his works.] Fonthill, 1235, 1*l*. Another work entitled ' The New Asiatic Miscellany.' Calcutta, 1788. 8vo. 3 vols. and ' The New Asiatic Miscellany.' Calcutta, 1789. 4to. 1 vol.

— Asiatic Researches; or, Transactions of the Society instituted in Bengal, for enquiring into the History and Antiquities, the Arts, Science, and Literature of Asia. Calcutta and Serampore, 1788-1839,

VOL. I.

4to. [with Index to the first 18 vols.] 21 vols. with plates, 42*l*.

Sir M. M. Sykes, pt. i. 295, 11 vols. russia, 22*l*. 11s. 6d.

— Another Edition. Lond. 1799-1807, 12 vols. 4to. 6*l*. 6s. Reprinted in 1^2 vols. 8vo. 18^06. &c., 3*l*. 3s., —both discontinued.

Roxburghe, 8877, 6 vols. 4to. 8*l*. 13s. 6d.

— Transactions of the Royal Asiatic Society of Great Britain and Ireland. Lond. 1824-34. 4to. 3 vols. (or 9 parts), pub. 8*l*.

— Journal of the Asiatic Society of Bengal, 1832-56, 25 vols. 8vo. and still proceeding at the rate of 7 Nos. annually. (The early vols. are scarce.)

— Journal of the Royal Asiatic Society, 1834-56, 16 vols. 8vo. Lond. Parker. Pub. in parts, very ii_{regu}larly, mostly at 6s. each. Vols. 11, 14, & 15, are not yet completed. 9*l*. 2s.

Asinus Onustus. The Asse overladen. To his loving and deare Mistresse, Elizabeth the blessed Queene of England [1589.] 4to.

This book was reprinted in 1642, with this additional anecdote, ' This book was delivered to Queene Eliz : being at Nonesuch Jul. 27. Anno 1589.'

ASKE, James. Elizabetha Triumphans: conteyning the damned Practizes that the divelish Popes of Rome have used ever sithence her Highnesse (Q. Elizabeth) first coming to the Crowne, with a Declaration of the Manner, how her excellency was entertained by her Souldyers into her Campe Royall at Tilbery in Essex ; and of the Overthrow had against the Spanish Fleete. London, 1588. 4to.

Black letter. pp. 44, dedicated ' To Julius Cæsar, Doctor of the Civill Law.' A Poem in blank verse, reprinted in the second volume of Nichols' Progresses, &c. of Q. Elizabeth. Dent, pt. i. 301, 2*l*. 9s. Forster, 916, 2*l*. 12s. 6d. Inglis, 129, 7*l*. Gordonstoun, 103, 7*l*. 7s. Bindley, pt. iv. 337, 8*l*. 18s. 6d. Saunders in 1818, 13*l*. Bibl. Anglo-Poet. 2, 15*l*.

ASKEW, Anne. *See* BALE, John. CROWLEY, Robert.

ASMA, T. De Divortio Henrici

G

VIII. Regis Angliæ cum Catharina Arragonica Dissertatio. Lug. Bat. 1787. 4to. 7s.

Aspeden Church.—Survey of the present State of Aspeden Church, Herts, June 1793. Lond. 1796. 4to. 3s. 6d.
Contains pp. 13, with four plates.

ASPIN, J. Systematic Analysis of Universal History to the Death of Alexander. Lond. 1826. 4to. 2 vols,
Published in parts at 5s. each.

Assembly-man, The. *See* BIRKENHEAD, Sir John.

ASSER Menevensis. Annales Rerum gestarum Ælfredi Magni, recensuit Franc. Wise, A.M. Oxonii. 1722. 8vo.
Contains pp. xxx. and 181, besides title, and a port. of Alfred, by Vertue; to the reader, 4 pages; a second title and subscribers' names. At p. 137, is a specimen of Asser's Life of Ælfred, in the Saxon character. Roxburghe, 8532*, 7s. Towneley, pt. i. 162, 9s. LARGE PAPER. Heath, 4291, 19s. Nassau, pt. i. 72, 1l. 2s. Sir M. M. Sykes, pt. i. 1594, 1l. 3s. Dent, pt. i. 105, mor. 1l. 15s. Williams, 90, mor., 2l. 10s.
This life was first published by Archb. Parker, in the old Saxon character at the end of his edition of Thomas of Walsingham's History, Lond. 1574, folio; and it is likewise to be found in Camdeni Anglica, &c. Francof. 1603. folio.

Assisarum Liber. (Lond. apud Rich. Pynson) 16mo.
Black letter. Contains c.lliii. leaves. A table is prefixed. This book is without either title or colophon, but has Pynson's device on the last page.

Assisarum et Placitorum Coronæ (Liber.) (Lond. by John Rastel, 1516.) folio.
Black letter. Contains sign. 8 8, in the second alphabet; a and b, in the first alphabet have eight leaves each, all the rest sizes. Prefixed is a table, with an English prologue by John Rastel. This valuable work, according to Dr. Dibdin, is in the Norman or Law French, and contains the assizes and pleas of the crown for the whole reign of K. Edw. III. Bp. of Ely, 223, 8s.

Assize of Bread.—The Boke named the Assise of Bread, &c. Imprynted by me T. Colwell, in the House of Rob. Wyer. 4to.
Black letter. At the sale of Nassau's Library, pt. i. 197, this edition was sold for 1l. 10s. A great variety of editions are noticed in Herbert and Dr. Dibdin's editions of Ames, Gough's British Topography, and likewise in Clarke's Bibl. Legum. An edition in black letter, 1626, with wood cuts. Nassau, pt. i. 198, 16s.

Assises, the Great, holden in Parnassus. *See* WITHER, George.

A'STLE, Thomas. An Account of the Seals of the Kings, Royal Boroughs, and Magnates of Scotland. Printed in the year 1792. imper. fol.
Contains pp. 44, with 5 plates. Dedicated to the Earl of Leicester. This forms a portion of the third volume of the Vetusta Monumenta. Some copies were printed as a separate publication. Fonthill, 1918, 2l. 6s.

— Origin and Progress of Writing, as well hieroglyphic as elementary; *many plates*. Sec. ed. improved. Lond. 1803. 4to. [& large paper, fol.]
The completest work on the subject of writing extant in this or any other language. Inglis, 258, 1l. 17s. LARGE PAPER in royal folio. Baker, 267, 1l. 15s. Dent, pt. i. 166, 2l. 14s. Nassau, pt. i. 211, 2l. 9s. Sir M. M. Sykes, pt. i. 321, russia, 4l. 4s. The former edition 1784, 4to. Bindley, pt. i. 136, 17s. 6d. Willett, 101, 1l. 14s. Stanley, 75, 2l. 18s.

ASTLEY, Thomas. Collection of Voyages and Travels. *See* Voyages and Travels.

ASTON, Anthony, commonly called Tony. *See* CIBBER, Colley.

Astrea, or the grove of beatitudes, represented in emblems and by the art of memory. Cuts, 12mo. 1665. 10s. 6d.

Astrea's Tears. *See* BRATHWAITE, Richard.

Astronomy.—Memoirs of the Astronomical Society of London. Lond. 1822-57. 4to. 25 vols.

— Monthly Notices. Vols. 1—17, 8vo.

— The Dyfference of Astronomy, with the Gouernayle to kepe Mans Body in Helth, all the foure Seasons of the Yeare. Impr. by me Robert Wyer. 16mo.
Black letter. Contains E in fours. Dr. Dibdin notices two other works on this subject, printed without date by Wyer.

Asylum for fugitive Pieces in

Prose and Verse, not in any other Collection: with several Pieces never before published. Lond. 1785-9. 12mo. 4 vols. 7s. 6d.
Chiefly of a political nature, collected by John Almon, the publisher.

Atalantis, The new. *See* MANLEY, Mrs.

Atchievements.—The Martial Achievements of Great Britain and her Allies, from 1799 to 1815. Lond. Elephant 4to. 3l. 3s.
With fifty-one coloured plates. Duke of York, 2884, 3l. 5s. LARGE PAPER, Dent, pt. ii. 758, morocco, 10l. 10s.

— The Naval Atchievements of Great Britain and her Allies, from 1793 to 1817. Lond. Elephant 4to.
With coloured plates. [Uniform with the Martial Achievements, and of the same value.]

Athenæum, The, a Magazine of literary and miscellaneous Information from the commencement in 1807 to the finish in 1809. Lond. 8vo. 5 vols. 1l. 1s.
A valuable miscellany edited by John Aikin.

ATHANASIUS. Four Orations against the Greeks, and his Oration against the Gentiles. Translated from the Greek, by Mr. S. Parker; with a Confutation of Mr. Whiston's impious Doctrine. Oxford, 1712. 8vo. 2 vols.
In Whiston's Collection of ancient monuments, 8vo. 1713, are translations of Athanasius' Life of Anthony the Monk, and on the Incarnation of the World.

— Life and actions of St. Athanasius, together with the Rise, Growth, and Downfall of the Arian Heresie: collected from primitive Writers, by N. B. P. C. Lond. 1664. 8vo. 5s.

ATCHELEYS, Thomas. Most lamentable and tragical historie conteyning the tyrannie which a Spanish gentlewoman named Violenta executed upon her lover Didaco. J. Charlewood, for J. Butter, 1576. 12mo. (Ritson Bib. Poet.)

ATHENAGORAS, Opera, Gr. et Lat. cura Fell. Oxon. 1682. 18mo. 3s. 6d.
A good edition. LARGE PAPER. Williams, 91, morocco, 1l. 8s.

— Legatio pro Christianis et de Mortuorum Resurrectione, Gr. et Lat. cum Notis variorum, Studio Edw. Dechair. Oxon. 1706. 8vo. 5s.
According to Dr. Harwood, this is a very elaborate edition of Athenagoras, and does great honour to the learning and industry of the editor. LARGE PAPER. Heath, 4257, 8s. 6d. Williams, 92 mor. 1l. 19s.

— The Apologetics. 1. For the Christian Religion. 2. For the truth of the Resurrection. With two Fragments, one attributed to Josephus, and the other to Methodius, concerning the State of the Dead. With the original Greek printed in the Appendix. Done into English, with Notes and Dissertations by David Humphreys, B.D. Lond. 1714. 8vo. 6s.
In 1573 was published 'The Discourse of Athenagoras touching the Resurrection of the Dead, by Richard Porder.'

Athenian Gazette. *See* DUNTON, John.

Athenian Letters: or the Epistolary Correspondence of an Agent to the King of Persia residing at Athens during the Peloponnesian War. Lond. 1741-3. 8vo. 4 vols.
Of this edition twelve copies only were printed, at the expense of the authors, viz. the Hon. Mr. Yorke (late Earl of Hardwicke), the Hon. C. Yorke, Rev. Dr. Rooke, Rev. Dr. Green, Bishop of Lincoln, Daniel Wray, Esq., Rev. J. Heaton, H. Coventry, Esq., Rev. Mr. Lawry, Mrs. Kath. Talbot, Rev. Dr. Birch, and the Rev. Dr. Salter. One letter on the life, &c. of Hippocrates, was written by Dr. Heberden.

— A new edition. Lond. 1781. 4to.
One hundred copies printed for presents. Subsequent to this, the following pirated edition appeared in Dublin, under a London imprint.

— A new Edition. Lond. (Dublin) 1792. 8vo. 2 vols.
With a front. to vol. i. A very neat edition. Bindley, pt. i. 1, 17s. 6d. Another edition was published at Basil, 1800, in 3 vols. 8vo. 10s. 6d.

— A new Edition, to which is

prefixed a Geographical Index. Lond. 1798. 4to. 2 vols. with engravings, and a map of ancient Greece.

Brockett, 261, 4*l*. 4s. Strettell, 168, 2*l*. 6s. Bindley, pt. i. 3, 2*l*. 6s. LARGE PAPER, printed for presents. Earl of Kerry, 178, russia, 3*l*. 15s. Fonthill, 3892, boards, 2*l*. 2s.

An edition, 1810. Hollis, 182, 2*l*. 14s.

—— Mercury, }
—— Oracle, } See DUNTON, John.
—— Sport. }

Athens.—Ruins of Athens, with Remains and other valuable Antiquities in Greece. Lond. 1759. imperial folio.

Drury, 405, 2*l*.

Atherton, Bishop of Waterford. The Life and Death of John Atherton, Bishop of Waterford, who for 'nce t, b———y, and many other enormous crimes, after having lived a vicious life, dyed a shameful death ; and was, on the 5th of December last past, hanged on the Gallows Green at Dublin, and his man John Childe, being his Proctor, &c. 1641. 4to.

With wood-cut on back of title. Gordonstoun, 126, 1*l*. 3s. Nassau, pt. i. 2379, 1*l*. 13s. Sotheby's in Dec. 1822, 2*l*. 3s. For other works respecting this prelate, See BERNARD, D.D. Nicholas, and KING, D.D. John.

ATKINS, John. Relation of a Voyage to Guinea, Brazil, and the West Indies. Lond. 1737. 8vo. 3s. 6d.

This volume, which chiefly consists of the personal adventures of the author, will, however, afford some insight into the manners and habits of the people. Willett, 5*l*, 10s.

ATKINSON, James. Account of the State of Agriculture and Grazing in New South Wales. Lond. 1827. 8vo. 7s. or with a map, 14s.

'A useful little work.'

—— John. Compendium of the Ornithology of Great Britain, Lond. 1820. 8vo. Published at 8s.

—— John Augustus. *See* Costumes.

—— John Augustus and James Walker. A picturesque Representation of the Manners, &c. of the Russians, illustrated by 100 copperplates, beautifully coloured, with an explanation of each in English and French. Lond. 1803-5, or 1812. folio, 3 vols.

Dent, pt. i. 168, in 1 vol. russia, 3*l*. 11s. Nassau, pt. i. 212, 3*l*. 16s. D. of York, 1502, 5*l*. 5s.

—— William. Views of Picturesque Cottages, with Plans. Lond. 1805. 4to. 15s.

Duke of York, 479. 1*l*.

ATKYNS, John Tracy. Reports of Cases argued and determined in the High Court of Chancery, in the time of Lord Chancellor Hardwicke. The third edition revised and corrected, with Notes and References by F. W. Sanders. Lond. 1794. royal 8vo. 3 vols.

Best edition of a very valuable collection of reports. Sotheby's in 1821 and 1824. 5*l*. 15s. 6d. and 5*l*. 10s. The former editions 1765—8. folio, 3 vols. 1*l*. 1s. 1781-2. 8vo. 3 vols. 2*l*.

—— Richard. Original and Growth of Printing. Lond. 1644. 4to.

Contains 4 sheets, with front. by D. Loggan, containing portraits of King Charles I., Archb. Sheldon, the Earl of Clarendon and the Duke of Albemarle. The falsity of Atkyns' arguments in favour of Corsellis as the first printer in England, in opposition to Caxton, are ably exposed by Dr. Middleton. Sir P. Thompson, 103, 3*l*. 15s. Bindley, pt. i. 123, 3*l*. 15s. Horner, 1854, 5*l*. Gardner, 1854, 2*l*. 3s.

—— Sir Robert, Knt. The ancient and present State of Glocestershire. Lond. 1712, folio. [best edition.]

History 859 pages, and index 7 pages, besides title, preface, and advertisement 7 pages, and the author's epitaph. The work contains 74 plates (including a portrait of the author), the whole engraved by T. Kip, excepting the first ten.

Some copies of this work were destroyed by fire in the printing office of Bowyer's father, in White Friars. [And many of those in commerce are scorched or stained.] According to Bishop Nicolson, 'many of the materials were gathered by Dr. Robert Parsons, Chancellor of the diocese.' Beckford, 1817. 95, 13*l*. 2s. 6d. Marq. of Townshend, 206, 18*l*. 10s. Dent, pt. i. 169,

mor. 14*l.* 14s. Willett, 145, 15*l.* Nassau, pt. i. 213, russia, 15*l.* 15s. Sir M. M. Sykes, pt. i. 323*, russia, 16*l.*
— The second Edition. Lond. 1768. folio.
History 452 pages, and index 6 pages, besides title, preface, and advertisement, 6 pages, the author's epitaph and directions for placing the 73 plates, 2 pages. This edition has not the author's portrait. Republished by Wm. Herbert, the editor of Ames' Typographical Antiquities. Great part of this second edition was likewise destroyed by fire. M. of Townshend, 207, 2*l.* 15s. LARGE PAPER. Lloyd, 256, russia, 3*l.* 9s. Heath, 4693, russia, 4*l.* 14s. 6d, Bindley, pt. i. 158, 6*l.* 10s.
— Parliamentary and Political Tracts. Lond. 1734 or 1741, 8vo. 6s.
These tracts are valued as a treasure of legal knowledge. M. of Townshend, 2324, 7s. 6d. Heath, 4413, 18s. 6d. 'The true and ancient Jurisdiction of the House of Peers,' 1699, folio, 5s. and 'The Case of Sir Robert Atkyns,' are not included in this volume.

Atlas.—The English Atlas. Oxon. 1680, 1, 2, 3. royal folio, 4 vols. 1*l.* 5s.
Published by Moses Pitt, and highly commended by Ant. à Wood, in whose Athenæ Oxonienses an account of the various contributors will be found.

ATTERBURY, Francis, Bishop of Rochester. Sermons and Discourses complete. Lond. 1740. 8vo. 4 vols. with portrait, 1*l.* 4s.
Willett, 52 (4 vols. with portrait, 1730-4). 1*l.* 17s. Gosset, 260, date 1751, 1*l.* 5s. Reprinted in 1820. 8vo. in 2 vols. with portrait, 18s. Williams, 2 vols. 1743, 1*l.* 9s.

— Miscellaneous Works, with historical Notes, by John Nichols. Lond. 1789-98. 8vo. 5 vols. 2*l.* 10s.
This collection contains all Atterbury's correspondence and tracts, and a vast mass of curious and interesting ecclesiastical history.
An edition entitled 'The Epistolary Correspondence and Miscellanies,' 1783-96. 8vo. 5 vols. The 5th volume, which is the same in both editions, is very scarce, and often deficient in sets. His private correspondence was published by Sir D. Dalrymple, afterwards Lord Hailes, 1768. 4to. 2s.6d.

Atterburyana; being Miscellanies by the late Bishop of Rochester, &c. Lond. 1727. 8vo. 5s.
One of Curll's publications.

ATTERSOL, William, Commentarie on the Booke of Numbers. Lond. 1618. folio, 7s. 6d.
This writer likewise published a Commentary upon the Epistles of St. Paul to Philemon, 1618 and 1633, 7s. 6d., and other works.

ATWOOD, George. Treatise on the Rectilinear Motion and Rotation of Bodies, with a Description of original Experiments relative to the subject. Lond. 1784. royal 8vo. 1*l.* 1s.
A highly valuable work. This eminent mathematician likewise published 'An Analysis of a course of Lectures on the Principles of Natural Philosophy,' 1784. 8vo. 5s. and 'A Dissertation on the Construction and Properties of Arches,' with a Supplement, 1801-4, 4to. 18s.

— W. Superiority and direct Dominion of the imperial Crown of England over the Crown and Kingdom of Scotland, &c. Lond. 1704. 8vo. 5s.
This book, which was replied to by Anderson in 1705, was, by the Parliament of Scotland, ordered to be burnt by the hands of the common hangman.

AVALE, Lemeke. A Commemoration or Dirge of Bastarde Edmonde Boner, alias Sauage, vsurped Bisshoppe of London. Compiled by Lemeke Auale, 1569. Imprinted by P. O. 8vo.
Black letter, c vj in eights, twenty-two leaves. A most virulent piece of personal invective, written in the Skeltonic measure, in which the descent of Bonner is pretended to be traced from a juggler, a cutpurse, and a Tom o'Bedlam. Bindley, pt. i. 1857, 3*l.* 15s.

AUBEE.—Analysis of the Constitution of the East India Company, and of the Laws passed by Parliament for the Government of their Affairs. Lond. 1826. royal 8vo. 1*l.* 11s. 6d.
A valuable and useful publication.

AUBREY, John. Natural History and Antiquities of the County of Surrey. London, 1719. 8vo. 5 vols.
Vol. I. consisting of title, licence from Ogilby, account of the work, pp. xlviii. Evelyn's letter to Aubrey, 9 pages,' to the Reader,' 2 pages, title, the history 258 pp.

index 6 pages, with a portrait of the author, folding map of the county, and view of Richmond Palace. Vol. ii. pp. 307, with Index, p. i—viii. Vol. iii. pp. 368, with index, 8 pages. Vol. iv. pp. 279, and index 8 pages, with a west view of Albury, and a genealogy of the family of Evelyn. Vol. v. pp. 420. (pp. 417 to 420, not numbered), with 8 plates of marbles. Sotheby's in 1826, morocco, 7*l*. 12s. 6d. Sir P. Thompson, 21, 9*l*. 16s. 6d. LARGE PAPER. Dent pt. i. 103, russia, 19*l*. 5s. Willett, 54, 22*l*. 1s. Towneley, pt. ii. 26, russia, 26*l*. 5s. Nassau, pt. i. 77, 26*l*. 15s. 6d. Beckford, (1817), 125, mor. 29*l*. 8s. Payne and Foss, 1850, mor. ex. 16*l*. 15s.

— Miscellanies upon various Subjects. A new Edition with considerable improvements. To which is prefixed some Account of his Life. Lond. 1784. 8vo. 5s.

A very curious work, treating of Day-fatality, Omens, Dreams, Apparitions, &c. The former editions appeared 1696, 1714, 1721, 1728, 1731. The first edition contains an oval portrait, pasted as a vignette on the title-page.

AUBRY, M. Oxonii Dux poeticus, sive Latinis Versibus hexametris et pentametris Descriptio Oxonii, 1795. 8vo. pp. 64.

A poetical translation entitled 'The Beauties of Oxford,' by William Wills, A.M. Louth, n. d. pp. 78.

AUDLEY (Lord). The arraignment and conviction of, 1642, 4to. Rare port.

Towneley, 3*l*. 13s. 6d.

— Lady Eleanor. Strange and wonderfull Prophecies. Lond. 1649. 4to.

Bindley, pt. iv. 588, with six tracts by the same, 1*l*. 10s. Farmer, 1*l*. 3s.

AUDLEY.—The Way to be Rich, according to the practice of the great Audley, who begun with two hundred pounds, in the year 1605, and dyed worth four hundred thousand pounds this instant November, 1662. Lond. 1662. 4to. pp. 38.

This tract may justly be called the Miser's Magazine, being full of precepts and precedents in the great art and mystery of thriving. Roxburghe, 9269, 14s. Bindley, pt. ii. 2531, 2*l*. 6s.

AUDOENUS, Joannes. *See* OWEN.

AUELA, Don Lewes de. The Commentaries of Don Lewes de Auela and Suniga, of the great Wars in Germany by Charles the Fifth against John Frederike Duke of Saxon, and Philip the Lantgraue of Hesson, with other gret Princes and Cities of the Lutherans, translated out of Spanish into English, An. Do. 1555. Londini, in Ædibus Richardi Totteli. 16mo.

Black letter. Contains U 6, in eights. The dedication to 'Edwarde Earle of Darby,' is signed John Wilkinson.

AUERELL, William. A wonderfull and straunge Newes which happened in the Countye of Suffolke and Essex, the first of February, being Fryday, where it rayned Wheat, the space of vi or vii Miles Compas. London, for Edward White, 1583. 16mo.

Black letter. 14 leaves.

— A maruailous Combat of Contrarieties, malignantlie werking in the Members of Humaine Creatures, by W. A. Lond. by Th. Hacket, 1588. 4to.

Black letter. Dedicated 'to Maister George Bond, Lord Mayor of London.

— Four notable Histories, applyed to foure worthy Examples: as 1. A Diall for Daintie Darlings. 2. A Spectacle for negligent Parents. 3. A Glass for disobedient Sonnes. 4. And a Myrrour for virtuous Maydes. Whereunto is added a Dialogue expressing the Corruptions of this age. Written by W. A. Lond. for Tho. Hacket, 1590. 4to.

Black letter. An edition of the date of 1584, 4to. unknown to Ames, Herbert, or Dr. Dibdin. Inglis, No. 4331, 4*l*. 6s.

AUGUSTINE, or AUSTIN, St. De Hæresibus, cum Notis Welchman. Oxon. 1721. 8vo. 5s.

— The Rule of Saynt Augustyne, bothe in Latyn and Englysshe, with two Exposycyons. And also ye same Rule agayn onely in Englysshe without Latyn or Exposycyon (by

Rycharde Whytforde). Lond. by W. de Worde, 1525. 4to.
Black letter. Contains folios lxxxviij with title and last leaf containing the printer's device. Dr. Dibdin notices a reprint of this edition in 1527, also the Rule 'in Englysshe alone' (1525).

— The Myrrour of the Church, made by Saynt Austyn of Abyndon. Lond. by W. de Worde, 1521. 4to.
Black letter, 36 leaves, with 26 woodcuts. An edition, W. de Worde, 1527. 4to.
An edition, 'Sothwarke, by Peter Treueris,' Inglis, 132, 4l. 4s.
The following translations of portions of St. Augustine appeared in the sixteenth century.
Two Bokes, thone entitled of the Predestination of Saintes; thother of Perseuerance vnto thende; whervnto are annexed the Determinacions of two auncient generall Councelles, by John Scory, the late B. of Chichester (about 1548. 16mo).
A Woorke concernyng adulterous Mariages. Lond. 1550. 16mo.
S. Austine's twelve Steppes of Abuses, by Nich. Lesse. 1550. 16mo. Bindley. pt. i. 4s, 17s.
Twelve Sermons, by me Tho. Paynell, 1555, 16mo.
An Introduction to the Loue of God, by Edm. [Freke] Bishop of Rochester. Lond. 1564. 16mo.
Certaine select Prayers gathered out of S. Augustine's Meditations, also his Manuell. 1574, 1577, 1586, and no date. 16mo. An edition 1580, Nassau, pt. i. 79, 13s.
An Introduction to the Loue of God, by Edmund [Freke] Bishop of Norwich, turned into English Meter by Robt. Fletcher, 1581. Lond. 16mo.
S. Augustines Ladder to Paradice, by T. W. Lond. 1581. 16mo.
A pretiovs Booke of heavenlie Meditations, by Thomas Rogers, Lond. 1581. 24mo.
S. Avgvstines Manvel, by Tho. Rogers, 1581, 1586, 1591. 16mo. 7s. to 10s. 6d. each.
S. Augustines Praiers, by Tho. Rogers. Wherevnto is annexed S. Augustines Psalter, 1581, 1591. 16mo.
A Glasse of vaine Glory, by W. Prid. Doct. of the Lawes, with certaine Prayers added thereto, 1593, 1600. 12mo. 1585, Jolley, 1843, mor. 3l.

— St. Augustine of the Citie of God, with the Comments of Ludovicus Vives. Englished by J. Healey. Lond. 1620. folio. 18s.
Second and best edition: the former was published in 1610. 9s.

— S. Austin's Confessions, translated by Sir Tobie Matthew. Lond. 1624, 16mo.
A catholic translation sold, according to Ant. à Wood, for sixteen shillings a copy, though, as John Gee saith, it might have been afforded for 2s. 6d.

— S. Augustin's Confessions, translated by William Watts. Lond. 1631. 18mo. with a front. by Vaughan, 5s.

— The Life of S. Augustine. The first Part. Written by himself in the first ten Books of his Confessions. Lond. 1660. 8vo.

— St. Augustin's Confessions, with the Continuation of his Life to the End thereof, extracted out of Possidius, and the Father's own unquestion'd Works, by Abr. Woodhead. Lond. 1679. 8vo.

— Meditations, and Treatise of the Love of God, translated by Geo. Stanhope, D.D. Lond. 1701. 8vo. 4s.
Reprinted 1708, 1714, 1720, 1728, 1745; the edition 1708 on LARGE PAPER. Williams, 96, morocco, 2l. 12s.

— A goodly Narration how S. Augustine, the Apostle of England, raysed two dead Bodies at Longcomptō, Warwickshire, collected out of divers authors. Translated by John Lidgate, Monke of Bury. Printed at S. Austens at Canterburie (1525). 4to.
From Maunsell's Catalogue, p. 6.

— St. Augustin's Religion collected from his own Writings, by John Brierly or Brerely, (i. e. James Anderson of Lancashire). Lond. 1620. 8vo. 4s.
J. Brierly was a popish priest, and wrote his book to prove that St. Augustin held the Popish doctrine. This was answered in two other books with the same title; the first anonymously, 4to. Lond. 1624. 3s. the second by Wm. Crompton, 4to. Lond. 1625, and again by the same in a work entitled St. Augustin's Sums, 4to. Lond. 1625. 5s.

— The Kernell of the historical Part of S. Augustin's Confessions. Paris, 1638. 8vo.

Towneley, pt. i. 461, 1*l*. 11s. 6d. In the Bibl. Monast. Fleetwood, No. 416, is 'The Kernell of St. Augustin's Confessions,' 1536. 8vo.

AULUS GELLIUS. *Vide* GELLIUS, Aulus.

AUNGELL, John. The Agreement of the holy Fathers and Doctors of the Churche vpon the chiefest articles of the Christian Religion. Lond. by William Harforde(1555). 16mo.
Black letter. Contains P. 4, in eights. Dedicated to 'Q. Marye, wyfe to Phillip.'

AUNGERVILLE, Richard de. *Vide* BURY, Ric de.

AURELIANUS. *Vide* CÆLIUS Aurelianus.

AURELIO. The History of Aurelio and of Isabell, Daughter of the Kinge of Schotlande, nyewly translatede in foure languages, Frenche, Italien, Spanishe, and Inglishe. Impressa en Anuers, 1556. 12mo.
Written by Jean de Flores. It has been erroneously stated, that Shakspeare's Tempest was formed on this favourite romance, the scene of which is laid in Scotland. Nassau, pt. i. 1570, 1*l*. 1s. Gordonstoun, 925, 1*l*. 1s. An edition also in four languages. Bruxelles, 1608. Bindley, pt. ii. 926, 1*l*. 11s.

AURELIUS, Abrah. In Nuptias Frederici V. Comiti S. Palatini ad Rhenum, &c. et Elizabethæ Magni Brit. Regis Filiæ, Epithalamium. Lond. 1613. 4to. 5s.

— Marcus. *Vide* ANTONINUS, Marcus Aurelius.

— VICTOR, Sextus. The Lives of the illustrious Romans, translated by several young gentlemen educated by M. Macdowell. Lond. 1693. 8vo.
An edition of the original will be found with Justinus. Lond. 1586. 8vo.

AURELLIO,Gio Battista. Examine di varii Giudicii de i Politici, e della Dottrina e de i Fatti de i Protestanti veri e de i Cattolici Romani. Londra nella Stamperia di Gouanni Wolfio, 1587. 4to.

AUSTEN, or Austin, D. Aurelius. *See* AUGUSTINE, St.

AUSTIN, Gilbert, A.M. Chironomia, or a Treatise on Rhetorical Delivery; together with an Investigation of the Elements of Gesture, and a new Method of the Notation thereof. Lond. 1806. 4to. with plates, 1*l*. 1s.
Williams, 112, morocco, 3*l*. 3s.

— Samuel. Urania; or the heavenly Muse, in a Poem full of Meditations for the Comfort of all Souls at all Times. Lond. 1629. small 8vo. 10s. 6d.
Sotheby's in 1821, 1*l*. 10s.

— Naps upon Parnassus : a sleepy Muse nipt and pincht, though not awakened. Lond. 1658. 8vo.
Sir M. M. Sykes, 171, 1*l*. 1s. Nassau, pt. i. 83, 1*l*. 1s. Strettell, 971, 1*l*. 5s. Bindley, pt. i. 98, 3*l*. 5s. Pt. iii. 2193, 1*l*. 18s. Lloyd, 884, 2*l*. 12s. 6d. Perry, 1*l*. 13s.
Austin likewise wrote a Panegyric on K. Charles II. Lond. 1661. 8vo.

— William. Certaine devout, godly, and learned Meditations. Lond. 1635, folio, with port. and frontispiece by G. Glover. 10s. 6d.
This work gives us a favourable idea of the piety of the author.

— Atlas under Olympus, an heroick poem. Lond. 1664, 8vo.
Bindley, pt. i. 44, 1*l*. 1s. Lloyd, 41, 17s. Sir M. M, Sykes, pt. i. 170, 19s. Perry, 1*l*. 8s.

— The Anatomy of the Pestilence, a Poem, in three parts. Lond. 1666, 8vo. with a portrait.
Bindley, pt. i. 45, 6*l*. 16s. 6d.

— Steps of Abuse. Daie, 1550.
Bindley, 17s.

— Hæc Homo, wherein the excellency of the creation of Woman is described by way of an essay. Lond. 1637. 12mo.
Taken in some degree from Agrippa De Nobilitate et Præcellentia Fœminei Sexus. Prefixed are a portrait of Mary Griffith, with a watch, by G. Glover, also an engraved title by Glover, containing the author's portrait. Bindley, pt. i. 88, 14s Fonthill, 1516, 18s. Nassau, pt. i. 82, 1*l*. Towneley, pt. i. 266, 1*l*. 4s.

Autography, British. *See* THANE.

Automathes. The Case of. *See* KIRKBY, John.

AVAUX. The Negociations of Count d'Avaux, Ambassador from Lewis XIV. to the States-General of the United Provinces. Lond. 1754-5. 12mo. 4 vols. 10s. 6d.

Interesting as containing the secret history of the rise and motives of the Duke of Monmouth's rebellion, and the intrigues of the Court of France in favour of K. James II. against the Prince of Orange.

AVELLANEDA, A. F. de. *See* CERVANTES, M.

AVESBURY, Rob. de. *See* HEARNE, Thomas.

AVISON, Charles. Essay on Musical Expression. Lond. 1775. 12mo. 4s.

Best edition of an amusing and ingenious performance, written with a view of exalting Geminiani, Marcello, and Rameau, at the expense of Handel. The first edition was in 1753, shortly after appeared Remarks (by Hayes), to which Avison replied.

Ayeen Akbery; or the Institutes of the Emperor Akber. Translated from the original Persian (of Abul-Fazel), by Francis Gladwin. Calcutta, 1783—6. 4to. 3 vols. 2l. 2s.

The best edition. Willett, 226, russia, 2l. 10s. Sir M. M. Sykes, pt. i. 304, 2l. 3s. Fonthill, 3351, 9l. 9s. Reprinted London, 1800, 4to. 2 vols. 16s., 8vo. 2 vols. 10s. 6d. The edition in 1772, 4to. 1 vol. is of no value.

AYLET, Robert, LL.D. Susanna; or the Arraignment of the two Elders, in verse. Lond. 1622. 8vo.

Sir M. M. Sykes, 172, 1l. 10s.

— Peace, with her foure Garders: Thrift's Equipage: Susanna: Joseph, or Pharaoh's Favourite. Lond. 1622. 8vo.

Mentioned in the Restituta, iv. 39.

— A Wife not ready made but bespoken, by Dicus the Batchelor, and made up for him by his fellow shepheard Tityrus: in four pastorall Eclogues. The second edition, wherein are some things added, but nothing amended. Lond. 1653. 8vo. pp. 26.

A poetical pleading for and against marriage. Jolley, 1843, (2 leaves torn), 1l. 14s.

— Divine and Moral Speculations, in Metrical Numbers, upon various subjects. Lond. 1654. 8vo. with portrait by T. Cross.

Nassau, 84, 1l. 2s. Bindley, pt. i. 80 (with the Wife not ready made, 1653,) 2l. 7s.

— Devotions; viz. 1. a good woman's prayer. 2. The humble man's prayer, by R. A. D. L. Lond. 1655. 8vo.

Contains pp. 15, with a front. by Cross, representing a female figure at prayer. Each part of these devotional exercises is preceded by a short poem. Very rare.

AYLIFFE, John, LL.D. The antient and present State of the University of Oxford. Lond. 1714 or 23. 8vo. 2 vols.

Vol i. B—Mm, besides title, dedication, preface, and list of subscribers. Vol. ii. A—Y 4, and a—m 8, besides title. Ordered to be burnt by the common hangman. Bindley, pt. i. 6, 7s. 6d. Bp. of Ely, 22, 8s. Nassau, pt. i. 78, 8s.—LARGE PAPER, Heath, 4687, 1l. 1s. Dent, pt. i. 107, 1l. 11s. 6d. Williams, 104, morocco, 3l. 10s.

— Case of Dr. Ayliffe, at Oxford. Lond. 1716. 8vo. 5s.

Contains pp. i—xxvi. 27—98, and Appendix, pp. i—xiv. This tract is sometimes found with the author's History of Oxford.

— Parergon Juris Canonici Anglicani; or a Commentary by way of supplement to the Canons and Constitutions of the Church of England. Lond. 1726 or 1734. fol.

Brockett, 3565, 5s. Sotheby's in 1824, 10s. Ayliffe likewise published 'New Pandects of the Roman Civil Law.' Lond. 1734. folio, 8s.

AYLMER, John, Bishop of London. An Harborowe for faithfull and trewe subiectes against the late blowne Blaste, concerning the Gouernemēt of Wemen. Anno 1559. At Strasborowe, the 26 of Aprill. 4to.

1829, 4l. 10s. Roman letter. R 3, in fours, dedicated 'To Francis Erle of Bedford and the Lord Robert Duddeley.' According to Bishop Nicolson, 'an able answer to John Knox, published anonymously.' A life of Aylmer was published by Strype.

AYLOFFE, Sir Joseph, Bart. Calendars of the ancient Charters, &c. and of the Welch and Scottish Rolls, now remaining in the Tower of London, &c. &c. Lond. 1772 or 1774. 4to.
This work was begun by the Rev. P. Morant. Heath, 4392, 14s. 6d.

AYMON. The Hystory of the four Sonnes of Aymon. Emprynted the 8th day of May, 1504. folio.
Black letter. From the colophon to Copland's edition we are assured that an edition was printed by W. de Worde.

— The foure Sonnes of Aimon. Emprynted by W. Copland, 1554. folio.
Black letter, with wood cuts. Contains Clxxvii. folios. Of this highly interesting romance some copes are printed for Thomas Petyt, others for Robert Toye. Roxburghe, 6361, morocco, 55l. Brunet, in his 'Manuel du Libraire,' Paris, 1820, vol. iii. p. 175-6, notices several French editions of this romance.

AYRE, William. Memoirs of the Life and Writings of Alexander Pope. Lond. 1745. 8vo. 2 vols. with portraits.

AYRES, Philip. Emblems of Love, in four Languages. Dedicated to the Ladyes. Lond. 8vo.
Contains pp. 180. The plates engraved by Nicholls. White Knights, pt. i. 267, 6s. Bibl. Anglo-Poet. 9, 1l. 1s.—An edition of the date 1683, White Knights, pt. i. 268, 5s. Bindley, pt. i. 52, 9s. Sir M. M. Sykes, 174, 11s.

— Lyric Poems, made in Imitation of the Italians. Of which many are Translations from other Languages. Lond. 1687. 8vo.
Contains pp. 190, with frontispiece. Sir M. M. Sykes, 173, 2s. Reed, 6547, 8s. 6d. Bibl. Anglo-Poet. 8, 12s.

AYSCOUGH, Rev. Samuel. An Index to the remarkable Passages and Words made use of by Shakespeare, calculated to point out the different Meanings to which the words are applied. Lond. 1790. royal 8vo. 15s. to 20s.
A work of great labour, highly valuable and useful. Reprinted Dublin, 1791, and London, 1827, in demy 8vo. 15s., so as to range with the editions of Shakespeare.

— Catalogue of the MSS. preserved in the British Museum, hitherto undescribed. Lond. 1782. 4to. 2 vols.
An elaborate and highly useful catalogue. Bindley, pt. i. 120, 14s. Sir M. M. Sykes, pt. i. 306, 19s.—LARGE PAPER, Steevens, 84, 1l. 13s.

AYSCU, Edward. Historie, contayning the Warres, Treaties, Marriages, and other Occurrents between England and Scotland, from K. William the Conqueror vntill the happy Vnion. Lond. 1607. 4to. 15s.

AYTOUN, Sir Robert. Basia sive Strena Cal. Jan. Lond. 1605. 4to.
Several poetical pieces of Ayton's will be found in the Delitiæ Poetarum Scotorum. Amst. 1637.

Azores. A Report of the Truth of the Fight about the Isles of Açorees, this last Summer; betwixt the Revenge and an Armada of the King of Spaine. Printed for W. Ponsonbie, 1591. 4to.
Black letter, 14 leaves. This tract, said to be 'penned by the honorable Sir Walter Raleigh,' is reprinted in Hakluyt, vol. ii. A copy of the tract is in the British Museum.

B.

A. —— See BROME, Alexander.—Heinsius.

B. A. D.— Court of James the First, King of Great Britain and Ireland; with divers Rules, most pure Precepts, and selected Definitions, lively delineated. Lond. 1620. 4to. with port. of James, by Vaughan.
Dowdeswell, 257, 8s. 6d. Gordonstoun, 251, 1l. 5s.

B. C.—(BARKSDALE, Clement) Lusus Amatorius: sive Musæi Poema, &c. Cui aliæ (tres scilicet) accedunt Nugæ Poeticæ. Londini, 1694. 4to.
The first of these 'Nugæ Poeticæ' is

'Fragmentum Libri quinti Poematis verè divini quod Paradisus Amissa inscribitur.'
B. E.—*See* BOLTON, Edmund (and BENLOWES, E.)

B. G.—A newe Booke called the Shippe of Safeguarde. London, by W. Seres, 1569, 16mo.
Black letter. Extends to F ij in eights. An allegorical poem on the life of man, extending to 219 octave stanzas.

B. G.—Beware the Cat. London, by Edw. Allde. 1584. 8vo.
Black letter. F 4, in eights. Dedicated to John Young, Esq. by G. B. The subject of this curious book is the presumed power of conversation in birds, which is denied by some, and asserted by others. It is satirical of the Romish Church. Roxburghe, 6651, 1l. 5s. Loscombe, 1854 (title wanting), 5l.

B. G.—*See* Chess.

B. G. Knight.—*See* BUC, Sir George.

B. H.—*See* BLOUNT, Henry. BOLD, Henry. BURNELL, Henry.

B. I.—A brife and faythfull Declaration of the true Fayth of Christ, made by certeyne Men susspected of Heresye.—Per me J. B. 1547. 16mo.
Black letter. Contains B, in eights. Probably written by John Bale. Inglis, 223, 10s.

B. I.—Letter, sent by I. B. unto his very freende, R. C., wherein is conteined a large Discourse of the peopling and inhabiting the Countrie called the Ardes and other adjacent in the North of Ireland, and taken in hand by Sir Thomas Smith, one of the Queenes Maiesties Priuie Counsel, and Thomas Smith, Esquire, his Sonne. Lond. by Henry Binneman (1572), 16mo.
Black letter. 31 leaves, folded in'fours. Copious extracts from this interesting historical tract will be found in the Censura Liter. vii. 20—6, 236—44. A copy is in the British Museum. White Knights, 2397, 10l. Hanrott.

B. I.—*See* BRADFORD, John.

B. J.—Caveat against Fortune, with divers Histories approving the same. Lond. by A. Jeffes. 12mo.
Not mentioned by Herbert. Gordonstoun, 323. (1l. 11s. 6d.)

B. J.—The Drudge, a Piece of Gallantry. Lond. 1673. 8vo.
Lloyd, 43, 7s. 6d.

B. J.—[Bulteel, John.] London's Triumph. Robert Titchburn, Mayor. At the expense of the Skinners' Company. Lond. 1656. 4to. Very rare.

B. M. G.—*See* BUCHANAN, George.

B. N.—*See* BILLINGSLEY, Nicholas. BRETON, Nicholas.

B. N.—Discourse of Trade. Lond. 1690. 8vo.
Marq. of Townshend, 3153, 11s.

B. O.—Questions of profitable and pleasant Concernings, called by the Reporter the Display of vaine Life, together with a Panecea or suppling Plaister to cure if it were possible the principall Diseases wherewith this present Time is especially vexed. Lond. 1594. 4to.
Dedicated 'To Robert Earle of Essex, &c.—O. B. The Epistle to the Reader.' 34 leaves. Then 'The Argument,' 4 leaves more.

B. P.—Juvenilia sacra, or divine youthfull Meditations. Lond. 1664. 8vo.
Lloyd, 44, 4s.

B. R.—The difference betweene the auncient and later Phisicke. Lond. Robert Walley, 1585. 8vo.
Black letter. Sotheby, June 1856, 16s.

B. R.—The Plowmans Complaint of sundry wicked Liuers, and especially of the bad Bringing up of Children, written in verse by R. B. Lond. for Hughe Corne, 1580. 8vo.
From Maunsell's Catalogue, p. 81.

B. R.—Greens Funerals in xiv Sonnets. Lond. 1604. 4to.
R. B., says Ritson, is supposed to be Richard Barnfield.

B. R.—Adagia Scotica, or a Collection of Scotch Proverbs, &c. Collected by R. B. Very usefull and delightful. Lond. 1668. 12mo.

B. R.—*See* BARON, Robert.
BRATHWAIT, Rich.
BROME, Richard.
BURTON, R.

B. T.—Life and Death of the

merry Devil of Edmonton, with the pleasant Prancks of Smug the Smith, Sir John, and mine Host of the George, about the Stealing of Veneson, by T. B. [Thomas Boewer.] Lond. 1632. 4to.
Black letter, woodcut on title. Steevens, 833, 2l. 6s. This tract has been reprinted by Caulfield.
— *See* Merry.

B. T.—A newe dialogue betweene the Angel of God and the Shepherdes in the Felde, concerning the nativitie and birth of Jesus Christe, &c. 8vo. John Daye, n. d.
Heber, 6l. 6s.

B. T.—Love will find out the Way. A Comedy by T. B. Lond. 1661. 4to.
Shirley's Constant Maid with a new title. Roxburghe, 4398, 1l. 11s. 6d.

B. T.—*See* BASTARD, Thomas.

BAYLY, Thomas.

BREWER, Anthony.

B. V.—*See* BOURNE, Vincent.

B. W.—That which seemes best is worst, exprest in a paraphrastical Transcript of Juvenals tenth Satyre, together with the tragicall Narration of Virginias Death interserted. Lond. 1617. 8vo.
Perry, 3l. 4s. Lloyd, 699, 4l. 10s.

B. W.—*See* BAGWELL, William.

BABBAGE, Charles, M.A. Comparative View of the various Institutions for the Assurance of Lives. Lond. 1826, 8vo. 10s. 6d.
A book well calculated to convey important information on a subject in which numbers are interested.
Mr. Babbage has published a Table of Logarithms of the natural Numbers from 1 to 108000, 1827, royal 8vo. 12s., and a Ninth Bridgwater Treatise.

Babbler, The. Lond. 1767. 12mo. 2 vols.
These essays originally appeared in Owen's Weekly Chronicle. Gosset, 279, 4s. Fonthill, 1398, 16s.

Baber.—Memoirs of Zehir-eddin Muhammed Baber, Emperor of Hindustan, written by himself, in the Jaghatai Turki, and translated partly by the late John Leyden, Esq. M.D. partly by William Erskine, Esq. With notes and geographical and historical introduction; together with a map of the countries between the Oxus and Jaxartes, and a Memoir regarding its Construction, by Charles Waddington, Esq. Lond. 1826. 4to.
A very curious and admirably edited work, according to the Edinb. Review, xlvi. 39.

Babes in the Wood.—The cruel Uncle, or the hard-hearted Executor. Woodcut, black letter. 18mo. C. Crouch for F. Coles, 1670.
Sotheby, 1856, 3l. 17s. (uncut.)

BABINGTON, Benjamin. Adventures of the Gooroo Paramatan: a Tale in the Tamul language: accompanied by a Translation and Vocabulary, together with an Analysis of the first Story. Lond. 1822. 4to. pp. 248, 18s.

— Gervase, successively Bishop of Llandaff, Exeter, and Worcester. Works containing comfortable Notes upon the Five Books of Moses, &c. Lond. 1615. folio, with portrait by R. Elstracke.
Reprinted 1637, folio, 9s. Many of the works of this learned English prelate were published separately, 1583—1604.

— John. Pyrotechnia, a Treatise on Fire works. Lond. 1635. folio, with portrait, a small oval, by J. Droeshout, in the title, 10s. 6d.

BABRIAS. *Vide* TYRWHITT, Thos.

Babylon. — Inscriptions copied from Stones and Bricks, and other Antiquities, discovered among the Ruins of ancient Babylon. Lond. 1803. five sheets, 1l. 1s.

Baçan, Don Albaro de, Marquis of Santa Cruz. Discourse of that which happened in the Battell foughte betweene the two Navies of Spaine and Portugall, at the Islands of Azores, Anno Dom. 1582. Lond. 12mo.
A copy is in the British Museum.

— Relation of the expougnable Attempt and Conquest of the Ylands

of Teroera, and all the Ylands thereto adjoyning : don by Don Albaro de Baçan. Lond. (1583) 12mo.
A copy is in the British Museum.

Bacchus Bountie; describing the debonnaire dutie of his bountiful godhead by Philip Foulface of Aleford. Ryckham, 1594. 4to.
Bib. Ang. Poet, 6*l*. Brand, date 1593, 2*l*. 2s. [Reprinted in Harln. Miscellany.]

Bacchus and Venus, or a select Collection of Songs, &c. to which is added a Collection of Songs, in the Canting Dialect, with a Dictionary explaining all the burlesque and canting terms used by the several tribes of Gypsies, Beggars, &c. Lond. 1737. 12mo.
Inglis, 46, 13s. Sotheby's in 1824, 16s. Nassau, pt. i. 87, 1*l*. 18s.

Bachelor. *See* Batchelor.

BACHILER, Samuel. Discourse proving by many and forcible Reasons, what great Dangers will hang over our Heads of England and France, &c. Printed 1626. 4to.
Gordonstoun, 205, 12s.

BACKUS, Isaac. History of New England, with particular reference to the Baptists. Boston, New England, 1777. 8vo. 2 vols. 15s.

BACON, Francis, Baron of Verulam, Viscount St. Albans. Works. Lond. 1730. folio, 4 vols. with portrait by Vertue.
Published by John Blackbourne. Roxburghe, 6964, 2*l*. 15s. LARGE PAPER, printed on writing paper, 6*l*. 6s. A few copies of Mallet's life, and the additional pieces contained in the edition of 1740, were printed to complete this edition at 10s. 6d. the small, and 15s. the large paper.

— Works, with several additional Pieces; to which is prefixed a new Life of the Author, by David Mallet. Lond. 1740. folio, 4 vols.
A few copies printed on a superfine LARGE PAPER, Sotheby's in Dec. 1822, 6*l*. 5s. Mallet's life was published separately in 1740. 8vo. 4s.

— Works, with a Life of the Author, by Mallet. Lond. 1753. folio, 3 vols. with portrait by Vertue.

An edition more methodical, more elegant, and every way more complete, than any preceding. Roscoe, 719, 3*l*. 8s.— LARGE PAPER, Williams, 116, morocco, 11*l*. 0s. 6d.

BACON. Works. Lond. 1765. 4to. 5 vols. with portrait by Vertue.
This beautiful and accurate edition was corrected throughout by the Rev. John Gambold, and the Latin volumes revised by W. Bowyer. Brockett, 462, 8*l*. 8s. Nassau, pt. i. 367, russia, 10*l*. 15s. Heath, 1671, 13*l*. 13s. Williams, 213, morocco, 16*l*. 16s.

— Another Edition. Lond. 1778. 4to. 5 vols. with portrait.
A reprint of the edition of 1765. Dent, pt. i. 307, russia, 6*l*. 6s. H lli, 184 9*l*.

— Works. Lond. 1803. 8vo. 10 vols.
The first complete edition in 8vo.— LARGE PAPER. Saunders in 1818, russia, 9*l*. 9s. Drury, 306, russia, 10*l*. 10s. Reprinted 1819, 1826, 10 vols, of which edition there were likewise copies on large paper.

— Works. Edited by Basil Montagu, Esq. with a new Life, Lond. 1825-34. 17 vols. 8vo. 8*l*. 18s. 6d. or LARGE PAPER, 26*l*. 5s.
This edition has been carefully collated with the original editions and translations, and contains numerous letters, portraits, and fac-similes, which are not to be found in any other. LARGE PAPER, imperial 8vo. (60 copies printed) 1*l*. 11s. 6d. each volume.

— Philosophical Works methodized and made English from the Originals; with occasional Notes, by Peter Shaw, M.D. Lond. 1733. 4to. 3 vols.
This edition does not contain the whole of Lord Bacon's works. [The translator has extensively altered Lord Bacon's arrangement by way of improving it.]

— Works. A new Edition. Lond. 1815. 12mo. 12 vols. 3*l*. 3s.
A reprint of Dr. Shaw's edition.

— Essayes (10). Religious Meditations. Places of Perswasion and Disswasion. Lond. by John Windet, for Humfrey Hooper, 1597. 16mo.
A 4, B—G, in eights (A 1 and G 8 blank). First edition dedicated to Mr. Anthony Bacon. The Meditationes Sacræ are in Latin. Perry, pt. i. 560, 3*l*. 3s. Bindley, pt. i. 672, 3*l*. 6s. Jadis, 6, 5*l*. 19s. 6d.

BACON, Francis. Essaies. Religious Meditations. Places of Perswasion and Disswasion. Lond. by John Windet, for Humfrey Hooper, 1598. 24mo.

Second Edition, in which the Meditationes Sacræ are translated into English. A to E 4, in twelves. Bindley, pt. i. 673, 1l. 8s. Inglis, 47, morocco, 2l. 9s.

— Third Edition. Lond. for John Jaggard, 1606. 16mo.

This appears to be a pirated reprint of the second edition. A to G in eights. (A 1 and G 8 blank.) Nassau, pt. i. 88. 5s.

— Fourth Edition. Lond. by John Beale, 1612. small 8vo.

An enlarged edition, dedicated to his brother Sir John Constable, Knight, containing, according to the table of contents, 40 essays, but the two last are not printed in the work. A to Q, in eights. (A 1 and Q 8 blank.) Lloyd, 45, 11s. Reed, 1684, 1l. 2s. Jadis, 7, 1l.

— Fifth Edition. Lond. for John Jaggard, 1612. 16mo.

Contains A—O in eights. (G only sixes, and A 1 blank.) Another pirated edition, divided into two parts: the first a reprint of that of 1606: the second the additional Essays from the former edition of 1612, but the publisher was not aware that Bacon had enlarged some of the Essays in the former part. It, however, contains the Religious Meditations and Places of Perswasion and Disswasion, not to be found in the former one of 1612. Boswell, 128, 9s.

— Sixth Edition. Lond. for John Jaggard, 1613. 16mo.

This edition contains, according to the table, 41 Essays, though 39 and 40 are not to be found in the volume. It likewise contains the Religious Meditations and Places of Perswasion and Disswasion. A —P 3, in eights. A 1 blank.

— Another Edition. Edinb. by Andro Hart, 1614. small 8vo.

This appears to be a reprint of the edition of 1613. A to K 6, in eights. Jadis, 7, 2l. 2s.—Editions, Lond. 1619, and 1622. Reed, 1683 and 1772, 16s. each.

— Another edition. Lond. by J. D. for Elizabeth Jaggard, 1624. small 8vo.

This edition likewise contains the Religious Meditations and Places of Perswasion and Disswasion. A—P 3 in eights, A 1 blank.

— Essayes or Counsels, civil and morall, newly enlarged. Lond. 1625. small 4to.

The first edition containing 58 Essays, the only one published in Bacon's life-time. B—X 2 in fours, with title, dedication to the Duke of Buckingham, and table, 5 leaves. Boswell, 264, with MS. notes by Malone, 1l. 5s.

Reprinted 1625, 1629, 1632, 1639, 1664, 1668, 1673, &c. &c.

— Essays, translated from the Latin, by Wm. Willymott, LL.D. Lond. 1720. 8vo. 2 vols. 14s.

The second volume is a translation of 'De Augmentis Scientiarum.'—LARGE PAPER, Williams, 129, morocco, 2l. 3s.

— Essays moral, economical and political. Lond. Bensley, 1798. fcap. 8vo.

LARGE PAPER, in folio, 6 copies printed, one of which is in the British Museum, another in Earl Spencer's library, a third in the Duke of Devonshire's, and a fourth appeared in Payne's Catalogue, 1823, at 8l. 8s.

— Essays edited by Basil Montagu, 12mo. 1845.

Pickering, 1854, on vellum, (only 2 printed,) 7l.

— Saggi Morali, con vn altro suo Trattato della Sapienza degli Antichi, tradotti in Italiano (da Tobia Mathei.) Lond. 1618. 12mo.

A to G 3, with title, 5 leaves of dedication, 'a Don Cosimo de Medici, Gran Duca di Toscana,' by 'Tobia Mathei,' and table of contents. Della Sapienza degli Antichi, A to K 4, in eights. (K 4, containing the errata,) Singer, 3l. 4s. Bindley, pt. i. 877, 2l. 4s.

— Essays moraux: trad. en François par le Sieur Arthur Gorges, Chev. Anglois. Lond. 1619. 16mo.

A copy is in the British Museum.

— Twoo Bookes of the Proficience and Aduancement of Learning, diuine and humane. Lond. 1605. 4to. 10s. 6d.

Contains 118 leaves, and the title. Roscoe, 157, with Dr. Jos. Warton's MS. remarks, 1l. 2s. Lord Bacon enlarged this work into ix. books, and caused it to be translated into Latin—it was afterwards re-translated into English, by Gilbert Wats.

— Second Edition. Lond. 1629. 4to.

Contains A to Tt, pp. 335, and the title.

— Third Edition. Oxford, 1633, 4to.

Contains pp. 335, and the title.

— Another Edition, with the quotations translated. Lond. Pickering, 1825, crown 8vo. 10s. 6d.

The preface and analysis to this edition were written by Basil Montagu, Esq.

BACON. Opera. Tomvs primvs, qui continet de Dignitate & Augmentis Scientiarvm Libros IX. (Cura et Fide Gul. Rawley). Lond. 1623, folio.

First edition, exceedingly scarce, and according to Archbishop Tenison, the 'fairest and most correct edition.' A copy is in the British Museum.

— Of the Advancement and Proficience of Learning, or the Partitions of Sciences, IX. Bookes. Interpreted by Gilbert Wats. Oxford, 1640. folio.

Contains A—Rrr 2, in fours, besides 54 leaves of introductory matter. It has also a title and portrait, engraved by Marshall.

— Another Edition. London. 1674. folio.

— De Sapientia Veterum Liber. Lond. 1609. 12mo.

Contains pp. 129, besides title and introductory matter, 11 leaves. Jadis, 10, 8s. Reprinted 1617, 12mo. 1634. 12mo. All three editions are in the British Museum.

— Wisedome of the Ancients, done into English by Sir Arthur Gorges Knight. Lond. 1619. 12mo.

Contains pp. 175, besides title and introductory matter, 12 leaves. Nassau, pt. i. 89, 5s.

— Instauratio Magna (i. e. Novum Organum, sive Indicia vera de Interpretatione Naturæ.) Londini, Bill. 1620. folio.

First edition, pp. 360. Parasceve ad Historiam Naturalem et Experimentalem, pp. 37, besides an engraved title by Sim. Pass, and 4 leaves, containing preface and dedication to K. James. An epitome in English, by M. D., appeared 1676, folio.

— Editio altera, cum Indice Rerum. Oxonii, 1813. 8vo. 8s.

This edition does not contain the 'Parasceve.' An account of Lord Bacon's Novum Organum Scientiarum has been published in 2 parts, 8vo. by the Society for the Diffusion of Useful Knowledge. [And a translation of the work itself in Bohn's Scientific Library.]

— Historia naturalis et experimentalis ad condendam Philosophiam, sive, Phœnomena Vniversi, quæ est Instaurationis Magnæ Pars tertia. Lond. 1622. 8vo.

— Historia Vitæ et Mortis, quæ est Instavrationis Magnæ Pars tertia. Lond. 1623. small 8vo.

Contains pp. 454, besides title and 'Viventibvs et Posteris Salutem,' 3 leaves.

— The Historie of Life and Death; with Observations naturall and experimentall for the Prolonging of Life. London, 1633, 12mo.

— Another Edition, by William Rawley, D.D. Lond. 1638. 12mo.

Contains pp. 323, besides title, dedication to Sir Edward Mosley, Knight, by Humphrey Mosley, and to the Reader, 5 leaves. There is likewise an engraved title, with his portrait, by G. Glover.

— Another Edition. Lond. 1650. folio.

Contains pp. 64, besides title, 'To the Reader,' 'to the present Age and Posterity greeting,' and preface, 4 leaves. An excellent article on this work, will be found in the Retrosp. Rev. vii. 64—87.

— Historie of the Raigne of K. Henry VII. Lond. 1622. folio, 10s. 6d.

Contains pp. 248. Dedicated to 'Charles Prince of Wales,' with a portrait of the King by J. Payne. Bindley, pt. t. 570, with Lord Bacon's autograph, 6l. 8s. 6d. Reprinted 1629, folio: 1641, folio, pp. 248, with dedication to P. Charles and a table, also a portrait of Bacon, by W. Marshall, 1640: 1676, with Godwin's Lives of Henry VIII., Edward VI., and Q. Mary, folio, 7s. 6d. This admirable historical work is inserted in the first volume of Kennet's History of England; and in 1786, appeared an edition of the life 'now first new written,' in which the native simplicity and genuine dignity of Bacon are totally destroyed.

— Sylva Sylvarum, or a Naturall Historie, in ten Centuries. Published by William Rawley, D.D. Lond. 1627. folio.

Prefixed is a portrait of Bacon, and also an engraved title, by T. Cecill. Reprinted 1635, 1639, 1658, 1670, 1676 (the tenth edition), 1677.

— Discourse of the happy Union of England and Scotland. Lond. 1603. 12mo.

— Sir Francis Bacon his Apologie, in certain Imputations concerning the late Earle of Essex. Lond. 1604. 12mo.

First edition, containing pp. 72, including the title. Jadis, 61, 1l. 1s.

BACON's Apologie. Another Edition. Lond. 1605. 12mo.
Contains pp. 72. Said to be unique. Jadis, 62, 1l. 10s. Reprinted 1642, 4to.
— Charge touching Duels, with the Decree of the Star-Chamber in the same cause. Lond. 1614. 4to.
— Certaine Psalmes, in Verse, by Francis Lord Verulam. Lond. 1625. 4to.
Dr. Cotton mentions two editions of this work, one 'for Street and Whitaker,' the other 'for Hannah Barrett and R. Whitaker.' The Psalms are, Psalm i. xii. xc. civ. cxxvi. cxxxvii. cxlix.
— Apophthegmes, new and old. Lond. 1625, 12mo.
Contains pp. 307, (B to X 2, in eights,) besides title. Jadis, 9, 13s.
— Certaine Miscellany Works, published by William Rawley, D.D. Lond. 1629. 4to.
— Operum moralium et civilium Tomus, Cura et Fide Guil. Rawley, Lond. 1638. fol. With a portrait of Bacon (by S. Pass).
Contents: Historia Henrici VII. Sermones Fideles, sive Interiora Rerum. De Sapientia Veterum Liber. Dialogus de Bello Sacro. Nova Atlantis. Tractatus de Dignitate et Augmentis Scientiarum. Historia Ventorum. Historia Vitæ et Mortis.
— Considerations touching a Warre with Spaine. 1629. 4to.
— New Atlantis. A Worke unfinished. (1635) folio.
Reprinted (1639) folio. (1662) folio. 1660, 8vo. continued by R. H. wherein is set forth a Platform of Monarchical Government.
— Certaine Considerations, touching the better Pacification and Edification of the Church of England. 1640. 4to.
Reprinted with a new preface, Lond., 1689, 4to.
— Three Speeches concerning the Post Nati, Naturalization of the Scotch in England, Vnion of the Lawes of England and Scotland. Lond. 1641. 4to.
Contains pp. 1—28, 55—8, and 57—88, with a title.
— Di^{s}course concerning Church Affairs. Imprinted 1641. 4to.
Published without the author's name.

— Essay of a King. Lond. 1642. 4to.
— XVI Propositions concerning the Reign and Government of a King. Lond. 1647. 4to.
— Remaines, being Essaies and severall Letters, &c. Lond. 1648. 4to.
Contains pp. 103, with title and table, 3 leaves.
— Mirrour of State and Eloquence. Lond. 1656. 4to.
Contains pp. 103, with title and contents, 3 leaves. The running title is 'Bacon's Remaines.'
— Felicity of Queen Elizabeth; and her Times, with other things. Lond. 1651, 12mo.
Contains A, 6 leaves; B—H, in twelves.
— Relation of the Poysoning of Sir Thomas Overbury. Lond. 1651. 8vo. with portrait, by Laur. Lisle.
Lloyd, 46, 10s. 6d.
— History of Winds, translated by R. G. Lond. 1653. 12mo. with portrait by T. Cross.
— Resuscitatio, or Bringing into publick Light severall Pieces of the Works, hitherto sleeping; together with his Lordship's Life, by William Rawley, D.D. Lond. 1657. folio, with a portrait of Bacon.
Reprinted 1661, 1671.
— Opuscula varia Posthuma, Philosophica, Civilia et Theologica. Nunc primum edita, cura et Fide Guilielmi Rawley, una cum nobilissimi Auctoris Vita. Londini, 1658. small 8vo.
pp. 216, besides 18 leaves, containing title, &c.
— Articles of Enquiry touching Metals and Minerals. Lond. 1662. folio.
— Baconiana; or certain genuine Remains of Sir Francis Bacon. Lond. 1679. 8vo.
An Edition 1674. 4to. with portrait.
— Letters written during the Reign of King James the First. (Collected by Robert Stephens) Lond. 1702. 4to. 10s. 6d.

BACON (Lord). Letters and Remains, collected by Robert Stephens. Lond. 1734. 4to. with port. by Vertue, 10s.

— Original Letters, Memoirs, Parliamentary Affairs, State Papers, &c. published by Rob. Stephens, with an Account of the Life of Lord Bacon. Lond. 1736. 4to.

— Letters, Speeches, Charges, Advices, &c. now first published by Thomas Birch, D.D. with a Supplement. Lond. 1763-4. 8vo. 4s.

Bindley, pt. i. 679, 10s.

— Law Tracts, viz. 1. Proposition for compiling an Amendment of our laws. 2. Offer of a Digest of the Laws. 3. Elements of the Common Law of England. 4. Use of the Law. 5. Cases of Treason. 6. Arguments in Law in certain great and difficult Cases. 7. Ordinances in Chancery. 8. Reading on the Statute of Uses. Lond. 1736, 7, or 1741, 8vo. 7s.

Nos. 3 and 4 were printed 1630, 1636, 1639.—No. 5, 1641, 4to. also reprinted in the fifth volume of the Harleian Miscellany. —No. 7, 1623, 1640, 1642, 1656.—No. 8, 1642, 4to. also 1804, with notes by W. H. Rowe. 8vo. 10s.

— Miscellaneous Writings on Philosophy, Morality, and Religion, now first collected into one volume. Lond. 1802. 8vo. 6s. 6d.

— Exemplum Tractatus de Fontibus Juris, and other Latin Pieces of Lord Bacon; translated by James Glassford, Esq. Advocate. Edinburgh, 1823. 12mo.

— Verulamiana; or Opinions on Men, Manners, Literature, Politics, and Theology, by Francis Bacon, Baron of Verulam, &c. &c. To which is prefixed a Life of the Author, by the Editor (P. L. Courtier). Lond. 1803. 12mo. 4s. 6d.

— Memoriæ honoratissimi Domini Francisci, Baronis de Verulamio, Vice-Comitis Sancti Albani, sacrum. Lond. 1626. 4to.

VOL. I.

A tract, 17 leaves, of very rare occurrence, reprinted in the Harleian Miscellany. A copy is in the British Museum.

BACON, John. Liber Regis, vel Thesaurus Rerum Ecclesiasticarum, with an Appendix, containing proper Directions and Precedents relating to Presentations, Institutions, Inductions, Dispensations, &c. Lond. 1786. 4to.

A very valuable and useful work, which has entirely superseded that by Ecton, [and is itself now out of use.] Nassau, pt. l. 368, russia, 2l. 10s.

— Matthew. Abridgment of the Law. Sixth Edition, with considerable additions by Sir Henry Gwillim. Lond. 1807. royal 8vo. 7 vols. 7l. 7s.

A luminous, scientific and much-esteemed work. An edition has since been published by C. E. Dodd, Esq., 8 vols. 8vo. 1832, 12l. First edition, 1736—50, folio. 5 vols. 1l. 1s. Second edition, 1762, fol. 5 vols. 1l. 11s. 6d. Third edition, 1768—70. fol. 5 vols. 1l. 15s. Fourth edition, 1778, 5 vols. and Supplement by Cunningham, 1786, 2l. 12s. 6d. Fifth edition, with considerable additions by Henry Gwillim, 1798, royal 8vo. 7 vols. Sotheby's in 1821, 6l. An edition, Dublin, 1786, 8vo. 5 vols. Sotheby's in 1827, 1l. 4s.

Bacon likewise published a treatise on leases and terms for years, 1798, royal 8vo. 7s.

— Nathaniel. Discourse of the Uniformity of the Government of England, from the first Times till the End of the Reigne of Q. Elizabeth. Lond. 1647-51. 4to. 2 vols. with frontispiece by Marshall. 10s. 6d.

This work is highly praised by the Earl of Chatham in his Letters to his Nephew. It was secretly reprinted in 1672, and again in 1682, for which editions the publishers were prosecuted. 5s. each. Fourth edition, with an advertisement, 1739, folio. 7s. Fifth edition corrected, &c. 1760, 4to. 12s. Heath, 4396, 1l. 1s.

— Sir Nicholas. Right of Succession to the Crown of England in the Family of the Stuarts, exclusive of Mary Queen of Scots, learnedly asserted against Sir Anthony Brown; faithfully published by Nath. Boothe. Lond. 1723. 8vo.

H

BACON. A Remembrance of the worthie Sir Nicholas Bacon. 4to.
Boswell, 3242, 15s.
— John, of Baconthorp. Opus super quatuor sententiarum libros. 4 vols. folio. Mediolani, 1510, 5l. 5s.
— Roger. Libellus de retardantis Senectutis Accidentibus et de Sensibus Conservandis, &c. Oxon. 1590, 8vo. pp. 134.
— Cure of old Age, and Preservation of Youth, translated by Richard Browne; also a physical Account of the Tree of Life, by Edw. Madeira Arrais; translated from the Latin. Lond. 1683. 8vo. 5s.
An excellent article on this, and several other works of the same description, will be found in the Retr. Rev. vii. 64—87.
— Mirror of Alchimy. Also a most excellent Discourse of the admirable Force and Efficacies of Art and Nature (3 pts.). Lond. 1597, 4to.
Contains pp. 84. Reed, 894, 11s. 6d.
— Discovery of the Miracles of Art, Nature and Magick; faithfully translated out of Dr. Dee's own Copy, by T. M. Lond. 1659, 12mo.
— Opus Majus, ad Clementem Quartum Pontifi. Rom., primum edidit S. Jebb, M.D. Lond. 1733. folio. 1l. 1s. LARGE PAPER, 1l. 16s.
Reprinted Venice, 1750, folio. Several of Roger Bacon's pieces still remain in MS.
— The famous Historie of Fryer Bacon, containing the wonderful Things that he did in his Life; also the Manner of his Death; with the Lives and Deaths of the two Conjurors Bungye and Vandermast. Lond. 4to.
Black letter. Reprinted entire in the Miscellanea Antiqua Anglicana, and in Thoms's Early English Fictions. White Knights, 342, mor. 2l. 12s. 6d. Sotheby's in Dec. 1820, 3l. Bindley, pt. ii. 1888, date 1655, 2l. 7s. Fonthill, 3288, date 1661, 3l. 16s. The later impressions were much abridged.

BADDELEY. Memoirs of Mrs. Sophia Baddeley, by Mrs. Steele. [said to be really compiled by A. Bicknell.] Lond. 1787, 12mo. 6 vols.
Duke of York, 3475, 15s. An abridgment of the life of this celebrated actress appeared 1787. 12mo. 2s. 6d.

BADELLY, John, M.D. Narrative of the extraordinary Cure performed by Prince Alexander Hohenlohe on Miss Barbara O'Connor, a Nun, in the Convent of New Hall, near Chelmsford; with a full Refutation of the numerous false Reports and Misrepresentations. Third edition. Lond. 1823. 8vo.

BAERT, ———. Tableau de la Grande Bretagne et de l'Irlande. Paris, 1801. 8vo. 4 vols. 10s. 6d.
An edition, 1796, Earl of Kerry, 82, 1l. 5s.

BAGLEY, George. Guide to the Tongues ancient and modern, being short and comprehensive Grammars of the English, French, Italian, Spanish, German, Latin, Greek, Hebrew, Arabic, Chaldaic, and Syriac Languages, each at one view. Second edition. Shrewsbury, 1809. folio. 12s.

Bagnal's Ghost. See GAYTON, Edmund.

BAGOT, Lewis, successively Bishop of Bristol, Norwich, and St. Asaph. Twelve Discourses on the Prophecies, concerning the first Establishment and subsequent History of Christianity, preached at the Warburtonian Lecture, in Lincoln's Inn. Oxford, 1780. 8vo. 8s.

BAGSHAW, William. De Spiritualibus Pecci, or Notes concerning the Work of God, and some that have been Workers together with God, in the High Peak of Derbyshire. Lond. 1702. 12mo.
A curious work, partly of a biographical kind, written by a nonconformist minister.

BAGWELL, William. The Merchant distressed, his Observations when he was a prisoner for debt in London in 1637. Lond. 1644. 4to.
Bindley, pt. iv. 1080, 12s. Inglis, 134, with port. of Bagwell inserted, 2l. 11s. In the British Museum will be found 'The distressed Merchant, and the Prisoner's Comfort in Distresse.' London, 1645, 4to.

likewise another tract relating to Bagwell, entitled 'A full Discovery of a foul Concealment,' 1652, folio.

— Wits Extraction, conveyed to the Ingenious in Riddles, Observations, and Morals. By W. B. Truth's servant. Lond. 1664, 12mo.

A curious work, with a portrait ' Æt. 66, 1659;' at the back of which is printed a family group seated at table at an evening party; with an explanation, engraved by J. Chantry. Nassau. pt. i. 91, 1*l*. Nassau, pt. ii. 1470, (front. wanting, but port. of Bagwell inserted.) 2*l*. 9s. This writer likewise published Sphynx Thebanus; an Arithmetical Description of both the Globes; and the Mystery of Astronomy. 1655, 8vo. with frontispiece by Gaywood, Towneley, pt. i. 288, 6s. 6d.

Bahar-Danush. *See* SCOTT, Jonathan.

BAILDON, J. Wonder of the world. 4to. 1656. port. by Marshall.
Rodd, 1824, 2*l*. 12s. 6d.

BAILEY, Rev. —. History of Newcastle upon Tyne, and its Vicinity. Newcastle upon Tyne, 1801. 8vo. pp. 612, with 5 plates.

Published anonymously, by subscription.

— James, M.A. Hieroglyphicorum Origo et Natura. Cantab. 1816. 8vo. 3s.

— Nath. Etymological English Dictionary. Lond. 1737. 8vo. 2 vols. 15s.

Best 8vo. edition, containing many words omitted in the previous folio editions. Edit. 1726, 8vo. 2 vols. Bindley, pt. i. 311. 14s. 6d.

— Another edition, by Jos. Nicol Scott. Lond. 1764. folio.

Best edition of this valuable work, formerly in the greatest repute. Dent, pt. i. 318, russia, 4*l*. An edition 1736, folio, Roscoe, 146, 2*l*. 2s.

— Walter, M.D. Discours of certain Bathes or Medicinall Waters in the Countie of Warwicke, neere vnto a Village called Newnham Regis. 1587. 16mo.

A copy of this rare work, with several others written by Bailey, who was physician to Q. Elizabeth, will be found in the British Museum.

— William. Advancement of Arts, Manufactures, and Commerce; or Descriptions of the useful Machines and Models contained in the Repository of the Society for the Encouragement of Arts, Manufactures, &c. Lond. 1772-9. royal 4to. 2 vols. 105 plates, folio.

BAILLIE, Joanna. Series of Plays to delineate the stronger Passions of the Mind, 3 vols., and Miscellaneous Plays, 1 vol. Lond. 1798, 1802, 1812, 1804, 8vo. 4 vols. 1*l*. 10s.

Drury, 310, russia, 2*l*. Fifth edition, 1806-12. 4 vols. 1*l*. 10s.

— Dramas. 3 vols. 8vo. Lond. 1836. 1*l*. 16s.

This may be said to form a sequel to the Plays on the Passions.

— Metrical Legends, 8vo. 7s. 6d. Lond. 1821.

— Dramatic and Poetical Works, with Life, in one volume, 8vo. Lond. 1853. 1*l*. 1s.

— John. Sixty Tables elucidatory of the first part of a Course of Lectures on the Grammar of the Arabic Language. Calcutta, 1801. folio, 1*l*. 1s.

— Lieut. J. Meeut Amel, etc. or Five Books upon Grammar, together with the Principles of Inflection in the Arabic Language; collated from ancient MSS. Calcutta, 1802-5. 3 vols. 4to.

Dr. Adam Clarke observes, 'Of all the publications in this department of Literature, these are the most useful and important.'

— Digest of Mahummedan Law, according to the Tenets of the twelve Imams, compiled under the Superintendence of Sir W. Jones. Calcutta, 1805. 4to. 4 vols. 10*l*. 10s.

A highly valuable work.

— Marianne. Sketch of the Manners and Customs of Portugal and Lisbon, during a residence in 1821, 2, 3. Lond. 1825. 12mo. 2 vols. 15s.

A very faithful and agreeable book.

— Matthew, M.D. Works, to which is prefixed an Account of his Life, by James Wardrop. Lond. 1825. 8vo. 2 vols. 1*l*. 5s.

The fifth edition of this physician's treatise on Morbid Anatomy was published

1818, 8vo. 10s. 6d., and the second edition of a series of Engravings, illustrating Morbid Anatomy, 1812, 4to. at 8*l*. 8s.

— Robert. Letters and Journals, containing an impartial account of public Transactions in England and Scotland, from 1637 to 1662: with an account of the Author's Life, and a Glossary. Edinb. 1775. 8vo. 2 vols. 12s.

A valuable work, published at the recommendation of Dr. Robertson and David Hume. Roxburghe, 7845, 19s.
[A new edition, much enlarged, edited by D. Laing. 3 vols. imp. 8vo. 2*l*. 8s. Edinb. 1841; large paper, 3 vols. 4to. printed for the Bannatyne Club.]

BAILLY, J. S. Letters upon the Atlantis of Plato, and the Ancient History of Asia: intended as a Continuation of Letters upon the Origin of the Sciences, addressed to Voltaire. Lond. 1801. 2 vols. 8vo. 14s.

BAILY, Francis. Doctrine of Interest and Annuities, and of Life Annuities and Assurances, with an appendix. Lond. 1809, 10, 13. 8vo. 2 vols. 2*l*. 2s.

Copies of this valuable work have brought 3*l*. 3s. to 4*l*. 14s. 6d. [There has lately been a surreptitious reprint, under the old date; full of errors.]

— On Leases. 8vo. Lond. 1807.

— Epitome of Universal History, Ancient and Modern. Lond. 1813. 8vo. 2 vols. 1*l*. 1s.

BAINBRIDGE, G. C. Fly-Fisher's Guide. Liverpool, 1816. 8vo. 15s.
Twelve copies, coloured with great care, not intended for sale, 4to. 2*l*. 2s.

— John. Canicularia, una cum Demonstratione Ortus Sirii heliaci, pro Parallelo inferioris Ægypti.— Quibus accesserunt insigniorum aliquot Stellarum Longitudines et Latitudines, ex astronomicis Observationibus Ulug Beigi. Oxon. 1648. 12mo.
This eminent physician and astronomer likewise published another work, entitled 'An astronomicall Description of the late Comet, 1618.' Lond. 1619. 4to.

BAINES, Edward. History, Gazetteer, Directory, &c. of Lancashire. Liverpool, 1825. 8vo. 2 vols.

[Mr. Baines has since published a History of the County, 4 vols. 4to. 1836. 8*l*. 8s.]

BAKER, F. Aug. Sancta Sophia; or Directions for the Prayer of Contemplation, &c. extracted out of the Treatises written by F. Aug. Baker, by S. Cressy. Doway, 1657. 8vo. 2 vols. with portrait of Baker.
Roxburghe, Supplement, 545. 19s. Lloyd, 1117, 1*l*. 1s. Towneley, pt. i. 673, morocco, 2*l*. 8s.

— Dan. Poems. — Hicathrift; Duellum, sive Pugna singularis inter Juvenem quendam fortissimum, cui Nomen Hicathrift, et Gigantem ferocissimum, Lond. 1697. 8vo. 5s.

— David Erskine. Biographia Dramatica, or a Companion to the Play-House, with Additions and Improvements by Is. Reed and Stephen Jones. Lond. 1812. 8vo. 3 vols. in 4.

A severe critique from the pen of Octavius Gilchrist appeared in the Quarterly Review, vii. 282—93; to which Jones replied in a pamphlet entitled Hypercriticism Exposed, 1812. 8vo. Brockett, 316, 1*l*. 8s. Nassau, pt. i. 255, 1*l*. 1s. The former editions of 1764 and 1782, are of very little value.

— George. Catalogue of Books, &c., printed at Strawberry Hill. Lond. 1810. 4to.
Twenty copies printed for presents.

— History and Antiquities of the County of Northampton. Lond. 1822—38. folio. 5 parts forming 2 vols. pub. at 13*l*. 13s. L. P. 27*l*. 6s.
One of the most valuable topographical works ever published, displaying great industry and research. Unfortunately it is left incomplete.

— Henry. Medulla Poetarum Romanorum; or the most beautiful and instructive Passages of the Roman Poets, with translations in verse. Lond. 1787. 8vo. 2 vols. 7s.
Reed, 6551, 8s. 6d.—LARGE PAPER. Drury, 312, 14s. Williams, 132, morocco, 2*l*. 3s.

— The Microscope made Easy, and Employment for the Microscope. Lond. 1743—53. 8vo. 2 vols. with plates, 7s.
The first volume of this valuable and pleasing work has been frequently reprinted. Edwards, 351, 17s. Baker like-

wise published 'A natural History of the Polype,' 1743, 8vo. 4s.

BAKER, J. Lectures on xii. Articles of Christian Faith. 1581. 12mo.
Black letter. Sotheby, June 1855, mor. 1l. 2s.

— J. History of the Inquisition in Portugal, Spain, the East and West Indies, in all its Branches, from the origin of it in the year 1163, to its present state. Westminster, 1736. 4to.
Marq. of Townshend, 1708, 8s.

— James. Picturesque Guide through Wales, 1795. 4to.
Bindley, pt. i. 780, 4 parts, 1l. 15s. Towneley, pt. ii. 283, 3 vols. russia, 2l. 12s. 6d.

— Sir Richard. Meditations and Disquisitions upon the Lord's Prayer. Lond. 1637. 4to.
Williams, 214, 11s. A life of Baker, and a list of his writings, will be found in Dr. Bliss's edition of Ant. à Wood's Athen. Oxon. iii. 148—51.

— Sir Richard. Chronicle of the Kings of England, with two Continuations. Lond. 1730 or 3. folio, 1l. 10s.
The best edition, though the earlier ones, particularly that of 1641, contain many curious documents, and several interesting particulars omitted by Phillips and his followers. First edition, 1641, with front. by Marshall, 15s. Fonthill, 3360, with port. of Charles, 5l. 17s. 6d. Second edition, 1653, 10s. Third edition, (with a continuation by Edw. Phillips,) 1660. Drury, 592, 14s. Fourth edition, 1665, 10s. Fifth edition, 1670. Bindley, pt. i. 393, 10s. 6d. Animadversions were published on this edition by Tho. Blount. Oxford, 1672, 8vo. Towneley, p. i. 264, 9s. Sixth edition, 1674, 6s. Seventh edition, 1679, 6s. Eighth edition, 1684, 6s. Ninth edition, 1696, 6s.

— Richard. Theatrum Redivivum, or the Theatre vindicated, in answer to Mr. Pryn's Histriomastix. Lond. 1662. 8vo.
Nassau, pt. i. 95, 16s. Baker also published Theatrum triumphans; or a Discourse of Plays. Lond. 1670, 12mo. Reed, 8015, 6s. 6d. Boswell, 131, 9s. 6d.

— Thomas. Reflexions upon Learning, wherein is shewn the Insufficiency thereof in its several Particulars, in order to evince the Usefulness and Necessity of Revelation. Lond. 1756. 8vo. 6s.
Best edition of a very ingenious work, at one time one of the most popular books in our language.

— Memoirs of the Life and Writings of Thomas Baker, from the Papers of Dr. Zachary Grey. With a Catalogue of his MS. Collections, by R. Masters. Lond. 1784. 8vo. 4s.

BAKEWELL, Robert. Introduction to Geology. Third edition, enlarged. Lond. 1828. 8vo. 18s.
The former editions 1813, 1815. This writer likewise published an Introduction to Mineralogy and Crystallography, 1819, 8vo.

— Observations made during a Residence in the Tarentaise and various Parts of the Grecian and Pennine Alps, in Savoy, and in Switzerland and Auvergne, in the Years 1820, 21, and 22. Lond. 1823. 8vo. 2 vols. with plates, 14s.

Bakhtyar Nameh; or, Story of Prince Bakhtyar and the Ten Viziers: a series of Persian Tales, from a MS. in the Collection of Sir W. Ouseley. Lond. 1800. royal 8vo. 16s.
Another edition was published with an English Translation. Lond. 1801, royal 8vo. 18s.

Balbulo and Rosina.—Beware the Beare: the strange but pleasing History of Balbulo and Rosina. Lond. 1650. 12mo.
A copy is in the British Museum.

BALCARRAS, Colin Lindesay, Earle of. Account of the Affairs of Scotland relating to the Revolution in 1688. Lond. 1714. 8vo. with a Key, 6s.
A valuable historical document. Reprinted Edinb. 1754, 12mo. Also inserted in the eleventh volume of the Somers Collection of Tracts.

BALDOVINI, Francesco. Cecco's Complaint, translated from Il Lamento di Cecco da Varlungo, by John Hunter. Lond. 1800. 8vo. 2s. 6d.
LARGE PAPER, in 4to. (eight copies printed,) 5s. Reprinted 1805, 8vo. of which edition twenty-five copies were printed on thick paper.

BALDWIN, Archbishop of Canterbury. De venerabili ac divinissimo

Altaris Sacramento Sermo. Ex praeclara Cantabrigiensi Academia, 1521. 4to.

One of the first books printed at Cambridge. In the dedication to Nicholas West, Bishop of Ely, the printer styles himself 'Iohannes Siberch, primus utriusque Linguae in Anglica Impressor.' Baldwin's works were collected and published by Bertrand Tissier in 1662. For an account of his itinerary through Wales, see GIRALDUS CAMBRENSIS.

BALDWIN, George. Political Recollections relative to Egypt; with a Narrative of the ever memorable British campaign in the Spring of 1801. Lond. 1801. 8vo. 6s.

Fonthill, 2865, 18s.

— Tre Opere Drammatiche prese nelle Visioni di Dafini. Lond. 1811. 4to.

Privately printed.

— La Prima Musica. Investigation into Principles, &c. in English and Italian. Lond. 4to. [1801.] 1l. 1s.

Privately printed.

— Thomas. Aëropaidia; containing the Narrative of a Balloon Excursion from Chester, in 1785. Hints on the Improvement of Balloons, &c. Lond. 1786. 8vo. 7s. 6d.

A curious treatise. Fonthill, 2163, 13s.

— William. Treatise of moral Philosophie, contaynyng the Sayinges of the Wyse. Lond. by Edw. Whytchurch. 1547. 16mo.

Black letter. Dedicated to 'Edwarde Beauchampe, Earle of Hertforde,' then, a prologue to the reader. Contains besides, sign. R in eights. A treatise formerly in considerable reputation, reprinted 1550, and n. d. (two editions, one by E. Whitchurch, the other by John Wayland.) Enlarged by T. Palfreyman, and printed 1564, 1575, 1579, 1584, 1587, 1596, n. d. (by Tho. Snodham) 1600, 1610, 1651. Edition 1550, Reed, 2680, 1l. 2s. 1579, Sir M. M. Sykes, 201, morocco, 16s. White Knights, 317, mor. 18s. 1596, Nassau, pt. i. 127, 5s.

— Funeralles of King Edward the Sixt. 1553. Wherin are declared the Causers and Causes of his Death. Lond. by Thomas Marshe, 1560. 4to.

Black letter, pp. 24. On the title is the portrait of the King, which is repeated on the recto of the last leaf. Nassau, pt. i. 871, (date 1558 ?) 4l. 6s. Sir M. M. Sykes, 393, 11l. 11s. Saunders, in 1818, russia, 15l. 15s. Towneley, pt. ii. 1556, 18l. 18s. Bindley, pt. i. 752, (with a single leaf, 'imprynted by Copland,' containing a prayer for K. Edward VI.) 18l. 18s. Perry, the same, 14l. 14s.

Roxburghe, 3309, 19l. 19s. Bibl. Anglo-Poet. 28, russia, 25l.

— Another edition. Lond. 1817. 4to.

Presented to the Members of the Roxburghe Club by the Rev. J. W. Dodd. Dent, pt. ii. 1201, 1l. 10s. Sir M. M. Sykes,. pt. i. 1628, 1l. 16s. Strettell, 364, 2l. 4s. Bindley, pt. iii. 1725, 3l. 19s. Boswell, 3088, 8l. 19s. Another reprint appeared in 4to. 10s. 6d.

BALE, John, Bishop of Ossory. Illvstrivm maioris Britanniæ Scriptorum Summarium. Vesaliæ, 1549. (In fine) Gippeswici in Anglia per Ioannem Ouerton, 1548. 4to. 1l. 1s.

A to 8ss 8, besides title, dedicatory epistle, alphabetical index, and complimentary verses 11 leaves. Rrr and 8ss, consisting of 'additio,' are not found in all copies. First edition, containing 5 centuries. (Supposed to be the first book printed at Ipswich.) This work may be considered as the foundation of English biography, and as such, valuable. Dibdin, 200, russia, 1l. 9s. Bindley, pt. i. 1461, in fine old binding, 5l. 5s.

In the title page is a wood-cut portrait of Bale presenting his book to Edward VI., and at the end of the table of contents is a wood-cut portrait of Wicliffe. (The whole of this volume is incorporated in the next article.)

— Scriptorvm illustrium maioris Brytanniæ Catalogus. Basil. 1557-9. folio. 3l. 3s.

Pars prior, a—z, A—Z, aa to zz, Aa to Aaa, in fours, besides title, &c. — leaves. Pars posterior, pp. 250, with title, &c. 10 leaves, and two indexes, 42 leaves. The last leaf of the work contains the colophon of Oporinus, 1559. LARGE PAPER, Dibdin, 201, 4l. 5s. Best edition containing 14 centuries. On the back of the title-pages to each part, is a wood-cut portrait of Bale, of which a fac-simile is given in the Bibliomania. This work, says Warton, 'perhaps originally undertaken by Bale as a vehicle of his sentiments in religion, is not only full of misrepresentations and partialities, arising from his religious prejudices, but of general inaccuracies, proceeding from negligence or misinformation.' In the British Museum is a copy, with MS. notes by the author, and in the Royal Institution is another with MS. notes by Archb. Parker and Dr. T. Gale.

BALE. Comedy concernynge thre Lawes of Nature, Moses, and Christ, corrupted by the Sodomytes, Pharisees and Papystes most wycked. M.D.XXXVIII. and lately imprented per Nicolaum Bamburgensem. 8vo

Black letter. Contains G 4, in eights. A copy is in the Malone Collection at Oxford. Jolley, 1843 (Brand's copy, wanting title). 8*l*.

— Another edition. Lond. by Thomas Colwel, 1562. 4to.

Black letter. A satirical play against popery, probably, says Warton, the first of the kind in our language. Forster, 1165, 2*l*. 7s. R^ood^a, 499 (sheet A wanting), 4*l*. 6s.

— Tragedye or Enterlude manyfesting the chefe Promyses of God vnto Man by all Ages in the olde Lawe,—M.D.XXXviii. 4to.

Black letter. A copy of this interlude is in the British Museum. It is reprinted in Dodsley's Collection of Old Plays.

— Another edition. Imprynted by John Charlewood, 1577. 4to.

Black letter. 16 leaves. Roxburghe, 4405, 12*l*. Steevens, 1221, 12*l*. 15s. Resold. Jolley, 1843. 20*l*. 10s.

— Brefe Comedy or Enterlude of Johan Baptystes preachynge in the Wyldernesse.—Compiled Anno M.D.XXXVIII. 4to.

Black letter. 18 pages. Reprinted in the first volume of the Harleian Miscellany.

— Brefe Comedy or Enterlude, concerning the Temptatyon of our Lorde and Saver Jesus Christ by Sathan in the Desart. Compyled by Johan Bale, Anno 1538. 8vo.

Black letter.

— Chronycle concernyngge the Examinacyon and Death of Syr Johan Oldecastell, the Lord Cobham, 1544. 8vo.

Black letter. With whole length portrait of Lord Cobham. According to Hearne, 'a lying book, not really in itself worth above twopence.' Hollis, 52, 2*l*. 9s. Bindley, pt. i. 441, 3*l*. 15s.

— Another edition. London, by Anthony Scoloker and Wyllyā Seres. 8vo. 1548.

Black letter. Contains G, in eights.

Reprinted in the second volume of the Harleian Miscellany. Nassau, pt. i, 100, 1*l*. 10s. Inglis, 53, 1*l*. 14s. White Knights, 281, russia, 3*l*. 8s. Roxburghe, 8421, 3*l*. 4s. Strettell, 123, 3*l*. 4s. Denyer, 1, 3*l*. 18s. 6d.

— Another edition. London, 1729. royal 8vo. with port. of Lord Cobham.

Edited by Archdeacon Blackbourne. Nassau, pt. i. 101, 12s. Roxburghe, 8422, 14s. Bindley, pt. i. 442, 16s. Williams, 136, in pig-skin, 1*l*. 4s. Heath, 4309, 1*l*. 9s. Duke of Grafton, 879, 1*l*. 9s. On VELLUM, (of which a copy is in the British Museum,) Dent, pt. i. 177, (with portraits mounted upon vellum inserted,) 6*l*. 6s. Williams, 135, morocco, 9*l*. 12s.

— Mysterye of Iniquyte contayned within the heretycall Genealogye of Ponce Pantolabus, is here both dyclosed and confuted by Johan Bale, An. M.D.xlij. Geneva, by Michael Woode, 1545. 16mo.

Black letter. Contains M, in eights. A copy is in the British Museum. White Knights, 280, russia, 2*l*. 18s. Inglis, 50, 3*l*. 13s. 6d. Horner, 1854, russia, 2*l*. 2s.

— *Vide* Pantolabus.

— A Disclosynge of the Manne of Synne, &c. 12mo. Zurik. O. Jacobson, 1543.

Horner, 1854, mor. 2*l*. 2s.

— Actes of Englysh Votaryes, comprehendynge their vnchast Practyses and Examples by all Ages, from the Worldes Begynnynge to thys present Yeare, collected out of their owne Legendes and Chronycles. Wesel, 1546. 8vo.

Black letter. A copy is in the British Museum. White Knights, 277, with pt. 2, Lond. 1551, russia, 3*l*. 9s.

— Actes of Englysh Votaryes. Lond. by Thos. Raynalde, 1548. 8vo.

Black letter. Contains 86 leaves.

— The First two Partes of the Actes, or unchast Examples of the English Votaryes. Lond. by Abraham Vele, 1550-1. 16mo.

Black letter. 79 leaves, besides the dedication. Nassau, pt. i. 98, 13s. Bindley, pt. i. 464, 1*l*. 13s.

— Another edition. Lond. by John Tysdale, 1560. 16mo.

Black letter. The first part contains N 4, in eights, besides the dedication. The second, V in eights. White Knights, 278, russia, 1l. 1s. Inglis, 52, 1l. 1s. Gough, 250, 1l. 2s. Denyer, 6, 1l. 8s. Horne Tooke, 37, 1l. 11s.

BALE. First Examinacyon of Anne Askewe, lately martyred in Smythfelde by the Romysh Popes Vpholders, with the Elucydacyon of Johan Bale. Marp. in Hessen 1546. 12mo. *See* Confutations.

Black letter. In the British Museum. White Knights, 283, mor. 13s. White Knights, 281, (both parts) 3l. 13s. 6d. and 282, 2l. 12s. 6d. Bindley, pt. i. 463, (both parts) 3l. 13s. 6d. Horner, 1854, both parts, 2l. 14s.

— Lattre Examinacyon of Anne Askewe, lately martyred in Smythfelde by the wycked Synagoge of Antichrist, with the Elucydacyon of Johan Bale. Marp. in Hessen, 1547. 12mo.

Black letter. In the British Museum. Inglis, 51, 2l. 3s. White Knights, 2l. 12s. 6d.

— Confession of the Synner after the sacred Scriptures. Collected by John Bale, 1549. 8vo.

— Dialogue or Comunycacyon to be had at a table betwene two Chyldren, gathered out of the holy Scriptures, by Johan Bale, for the 2 yonge Sonnes, Johan and Paule, 1549. 12mo.

— Laboryouse Journey, and Serche of John Leylande for Englandes Antiquitees. Lond. 1549. 12mo. *See* Leland.

Dent, pt. i. 1248, mor. 2l. 2s. Reprinted at Oxford in the Lives of Leland, Hearne, and Wood, in 1772; at the same time some copies were printed separately.

— Ymage of both Churches after the Reuelacion of Saincte John the Euangelyst. London by me John Wyer, 1550. 4to. 1l. 11s. 6d.

Black letter. The first part contains 84, the second 86, and the third 83 leaves.

— Another edition. Impr. by me Rycharde Wyer, 1550. 12mo.

— Another edition. Lond. by John Daye and Wm. Seres, 16mo.

Black letter. In three parts, introduced with a preface, and adorned with cuts. Part i. contains T in eights. Part ii. contains t 4, in eights. Part iii. Rr, in eighta, all double signatures. White Knights, 279, russia, 19s. Inglis, 54, 1l. 13s. Brand, 15s.

— Another edition. Lond. by Tho. East. 18mo.
Black letter.

— Another edition. Lond. by R. Jugge. 18mo.

Black letter. Nassau, pt. i. 99, 16s.

— Apology of Johan Bale, against a ranke Papyst, Anno Do. M.CCCC.L. A brefe Exposicyon also upon the xxx Chapter of Numeri, which was the fyrst Occasion of thys present Varyance. Lond. by John Daye. 8vo. n.d. (Also an edition 1552.)

Black letter.

— Vocacyon of Johā Bale to the Bishoprick of Ossory in Irelande, his Persecucions in the same, and finall Delyueraunce. Rome, 1553. 8vo.

Black letter. Reprinted in the Harleian Miscellany, vol. vi. A copy is in the British Museum.

— A Declaration of Edmonde Bonner's Articles, concerning the Clergie of London Dyocese. Basil, 1554. 12mo.

A portion of this work, 'A Testimony geuen forth by Fraunces Baldwin Atrebatius, concerning the baudy Behaviour and lecherous Life of Doctor Thomas Martyn,' is reprinted in the fourth number of Morgan's Phœnix Britannicus.

— Another edition. Lond. by John Tysdale, 1561. 16mo.

Black letter. Contains folio 70, besides the preface. A copy is in the Bodleian library. Inglis, 56, 1l. 15s.

— Historye of the Christen Departynge of the reverēde Man D. Martyne Luther, translated into Englishe by Johan Bale. (At end.) Thus endeth the Oracyō or Processe rehearced off Philippe Melanchton at the Buryall of the Reuerende Man, Doctor Martyne Luther, Translated by Johan Bale. Anno M.D.LXVI. 8vo.

Black letter. Contains folio 21. The date is evidently a misprint for 1546. Bale died in 1563.

— Pageant of Popes. Englishe with sundry Additions by J(ohn) S(tudley). Lond. by Tho. Marshe, 1574, 4to.

Black letter. Nassau, pt. i. 372, 16s. Bindley, pt. i. 1079, 17s. 6d. Sotheby's in 1825, 1l. 2s. North, pt. iii. 722, morocco,

1*l.* 4s. Inglis, 137, illustrated and bound in morocco, 4*l.* 8s.

Bale. Expostulation or Complaynte agaynst the Blasphemyes of a franticke Papyst of Hamshyre. Lond. by John Daye, 16mo.

Black letter. Contains C, in eights, the last leaf blank. Dedicated to ' Johan Duke of Northumberland.' Bright 1845, 3*l.* 8s.

— Catechisme, with Dialogue betweene Husbande and Wyfe. Imp. at Wesell, 1545. 8vo.

β¹ and, 10s. 6d.

— *See* HARRISON, John.
LELAND, John.
MANTUANUS, Bapt.
STALBRYDE, Henry.
WRAGHTON, William.

BALES, Peter. Writing Schoolemaster; conteining three Bookes in one; the first, teaching swift Writing: the second, true Writing; the third, faire Writing. Lond. by Thomas Orwin, 1590. 4to.

Black letter. Dedicated 'To Sir Christopher Hatton, Knight.' R 8, in fours. An edition, 'with sundry new editions,' 1597, 12mo. An account of this celebrated person, who was one of the first who introduced short-hand writing into this country, will be found in Dr. Bliss's valuable edition of Wood's Athen. Oxon. i. 655-7.

BALEY. *See* BAILEY.

BALFOUR, Sir James. Practicks, or a System of the more ancient Law of Scotland. Edinb. 1754. folio.

With a preface and a life of the author, by Goodal. Roxburghe, 1054, 10s. 6d.

— Sir Andrew. *See* SIBBALD, Sir Robert, M.D.

— Sir James, Bart. Historical Works, (viz. The Annales of Scotland, from MLVII—MDCXL and Memorialls and Passages of Church and State, from MDCXLI—MDCLII, &c.) Published from the original MSS. preserved in the Library of the Faculty of Advocates (by James Haig.) Edinb. 1824, or Lond. 1825. 4 vols. 8vo. Portrait by Lizars, 1*l.* 1s.

BALGUY, John, D.D. Twenty Sermons on various occasions. Lond. 1750. 8vo. 2 vols. 10s.

The writings of this eminent divine of the church of England are held in considerable estimation, particularly his Essay on Redemption.

— Thomas, D.D. Works, edited by James Drake. Cambridge, 1822. 8vo. 2 vols. 12s.

Sensible and excellent discourses. His work on divine benevolence is a most able answer to ancient and modern sceptics.

BALISTA. Chr. Ouerthrow of the Gowte, written in Latin verse by Chr. Balista, translated by B. (arnaby) G. (ooge). Lond. for Abr. Veale, 1577. 8vo.

BALL, John. Treatise concerning all the principal Grounds of the Christian Religion. Lond. 4to. 5s.

The most popular of all this Puritan Divine's works. It was fourteen times printed before the year 1632, and has been translated into Turkish, by Wm. Seaman. Oxford, 1660. 8vo.

— Thomas, and F. BEATTY. Reports of Cases in the High Court of Chancery, Ireland, 1807-14. Dublin, 1821-3. royal 8vo. 2 vols. 2*l.* 19s. 6d. [Second edit. 1823-4.]

Ballad.—An Answere to a Romish Rime, lately printed and entituled, A proper new Ballad.—Written by that Protestant and Catholike J. R. (hodes). Lond. 1602. 4to.

The Ballad is given in 24 stanzas, Roman type, and the answer by J. R. in 46 stanzas, black letter. 20 leaves. Perry, pt. i. 209, 1*l.* 2s. According to the author's address, there was an answer in prose by Crowley, in 1588.

— A Ballad Book. Edinb. 1824. 12mo.

Thirty copies printed for private distribution, by the editor, C. K. Sharpe, Esq.

Ballads.—A Collection of Old Ballads, corrected from the best and most antient Copies extant, with Introductions historical and critical. Lond. 1726-38. 12mo. 3 vols. with 47 plates.

This collection is, by Dr. Farmer, ascribed to Ambrose Phillips. [The plate of the Swimming Lady at p. 183, in vol. ii. is often wanting.] Dent, pt. i. 178, 4*l.* Duke of York, 3837, 4*l.* White Knights, pt. i. 285, 4*l.* 5s. Roxburghe, 3220, 4*l.* 14s. 6d. Perry, pt. xi. 882, 5*l.* Dibdin, 714, 5*l.* 10s. Gough, 254, 6*l.* 17s. 6d. Bibl. Anglo-Poet. 509, 7*l.* 7s. Strettell, 988, morocco, 7*l.* 7s.

Nassau, pt. 1. 104, 7*l*. 12s. 6d. Sotheby's in May, 1823, 7*l*. 17s. 6d.
— A Collection of Old Ballads. Glasgow, 1755. 12mo.
— Scarce ancient Ballads; many never before published. Aberdeen, 1822. 12mo.
— The Common Place Book of ancient and modern Ballads, and Metrical Legendary Tales, an original Selection, many never before published. Edinburgh, 1824. 12mo.

The ballads in this selection, 'many never before published,' are all modern.

— The Book of British Ballads, edited by Sam. Carter Hall, 2 vols. imperial 8vo. several hundred wood engravings by the best artists. Lond. 1842-4. New edition in 1 vol. Bohn, 1853. 1*l*. 5s.

BALLARD, George. Memoirs of several Ladies of Great Britain, who have been celebrated for their Writings or Learning. Oxford, 1752. 4to.

An entertaining work, comprising notices of the lives and writings of 62 ladies, commencing with Juliana of Norwich, and ending with Constantia Crierson. Bindley, pt. i. 902, 17s. Sir P. Thompson, 127, 1*l*. 8s. Williams, 215, morocco, 1*l*. 14s. Reprinted in London, 1775, 8vo. 10s. 6d. A very large collection of Ballard's epistolary correspondence is in the Bodleian Library.

— G. The History of Susanna, compiled according to the prophet Daniel, amplified with convenient meditations. Sung by the devoted honourer of the divine muses, G. B. T. Harper, for Wm. Hope, 1638.

Dedicated to Ann, Countess of Northumberland, Coll. B to I, in eights; K, two leaves, besides title, &c., nine leaves. Sotheby, May, 1856, 12*l*. 15s.

BALMFORD, James. Dialogue concerning the Unlawfulness of playing at Cards or Tables, or any other Game consisting in Chance. Lond. for Richard Boile. 12mo.

Contains 8 leaves. Addressed to 'Master Lional Maddison, &c. The dedication is dated 1593. In the British Museum are two editions, one with the date of 1623.

BALNAVES, Henry. Confession of Faith concerning how the troubled Man should seek Refuge in God. Edinb. 1584. 8vo.

With a prefatory epistle from John Knox. Roxburghe, 489, 3*l*. 6s. Balnaves likewise published a Treatise concerning Justification. Edinb. 1550, 1584.

BALTHARPE, J. The Straights Voyage, or St. David's Poem. Lond. 1671. 8vo.

Lloyd, 49, 6*l*. 12s. 6d. Perry, 3*l*. 10s.

BALTIMORE, Fred. Calvert, Lord. Tour to the East, in the Years 1763 and 1764. With Remarks on the City of Constantinople and the Turks. Also select Pieces of Oriental Wit, Poetry, and Wisdom. Lond. 1767. 8vo. 5s.

Roxburghe, 7256, 3s. 6d. Baker, 23, (with plates) red morocco, 2*l*. 9s. An edition was printed at Dublin, 1768.

— Gaudia Poetica, Latina, Anglica, et Gallica, Lingua composita, Anno 1769. Augustæ, 1770. 4to. with plates.

Privately printed for presents. It is said that only ten copies were printed. Strettell, 366, 3*l*. 3s. Sir M. M. Sykes, pt. i. 397, morocco, 4*l*. Randolph, 5*l*. 15s. 6d. Reed, 6682, 6*l*. 10s. Bindley, pt. i. 748, morocco, 7*l*. 7s.

— Cœlestis et Inferi. Venet. 1771. 4to.

Bindley, pt. ii. 349, 6s. 6d. Bindley, pt. i. 749, 1*l*. 18s. Reed, 6683, 10s. 6d.

BALZAC, J. L. Guez de. Letters and Remaines. Trans. by Sir R. Baker. Lond. 1655-8. 8vo. 2 vols.

These letters were formerly in much request.

Bamburgh. A Catalogue of the Library at Bamburgh Castle, in Northumberland. 4to. [1799.]

(Privately printed.) A catalogue of a curious and valuable library, collected by Dr. Tho. Sharp, who died in 1792. Bishop of Ely, 450, 2*l*. 15s. Sotheby's in 1826, 6s. 6d.

BAMFIELD (Col. Joseph, Royalist Commander in the reign of Charles I.). Apology, written by himself. 4to.

Privately printed (in Holland) 1687. One of the rarest memoirs relating to the civil war. Bright, 1845, 4*l*.

BAMPFYLDE, John. Sixteen Sonnets. Lond. 1778. small 4to.

These sonnets are highly praised by Dr. Southey, in his specimens, and by the Quarterly Review: they are reprinted in Park's Collection of the Poets.

BAMPFIELD, Francis. All useful Sciences and profitable Arts in one Book of Jehovah Ælokim. Printed, 1677. folio. In two Parts.

Gordonstoun, 808, 8s. Most of the works of this singular character are in the British Museum, and a life of him will be found in Dr. Bliss's edition of Wood's Athenæ Oxon. iv. 126-8.

BAMPTON, Lord. See M'Douall, Andrew, Lord Bampton.

Bampton Lecture. A Collection of the Sermons preached at the Lecture, founded by the Rev. John Bampton, from its foundation in 1780 to the year 1856. Oxford and London, 8vo. 77 vols.

This collection of Sermons is seldom met with complete. Those by Cobb and Tatham were for many years exceedingly scarce, but the latter has been reprinted. Williams, 138, 1780—1821, 44 vols. with some controversial tracts inserted, relating to White's Bampton Lecture, 89l.

1780, J. Bandinel.	1813, J. Collinson.
1781, T. Neve.	1814, W. Van Mildert.
1782, R. Holmes.	1815, R. Heber.
1783, J. Cobb.	1816, J. H. Spry.
1784, J. White.	1817, J. Miller.
1785, R. Churton.	1818, C. A. Moysey.
1786, G. Croft.	1819, H. D. Morgan.
1787, W. Hawkins.	1820, G. Faussett.
1788, R. Shepherd.	1821, J. Jones.
1789, E. Tatham, 2 v. reprinted, 1840.	1822, R. Whately. 1823, C. Goddard.
1790, H. Kett.	1824, J. J. Conybeare.
1791, R. Morres.	1825, G. Chandler.
1792, J. Eveleigh.	1826, W. Vaux.
1793, J. Williamson.	1827, H. H. Milman.
1794, T. Wintle.	1828, T. Horne.
1795, D. Veysie.	1829, E. Burton.
1796, R. Gray.	1830, H. Soames.
1797, W. Finch.	1831, T. W. Lancaster.
1798, C. H. Hall.	1832, R. D. Hampden.
1799, W. Barrow.	1833, F. Nolan.
1800, G. Richards.	1834-1835, No lectures delivered.
1801, G. S. Faber, 2 v.	
1802, G. F. Nott.	1836, C. A. Ogilvie.
1803, J. Farrer.	1837, T. S. L. Vogan.
1804, R. Laurence.	1838, H. A. Woodgate.
1805, E. Nares.	1839, W. D. Conybeare.
1806, J. Browne.	1840, E. Hawkins.
1807, T. Le Mesurier.	1841, No lectures delivered.
1808, J. Penrose.	
1809, J. B. S. Carwithen.	1842, J. Garbett.
	1843, A. Grant.
1810, T. Falconer.	1844, R. W. Jelf.
1811, J. Bidlake.	1845, C. A. Heartley.
1812, R. Mant.	1846, A. Short.
1847, Wa. Shirley.	1853, W. Thomson.
1848, E. G. Marsh.	1854, Hon. S. Waldegrave.
1849, R. Michell.	
1850, E. M. Goulbourn.	1855, J. E. Bode.
1851, H. B. Wilson.	1856, E. A. Litton.
1852, J. E. Riddle.	1857, W. E. Jelf.

Banbury, The Shepherd of. Rules to know of the Change of the Weather. By John Claridge. Lond. 1744. 8vo. 3s. 6d.

A small work of great popularity among the lower orders of the people, said to have been written by John Campbell, LL.D. Reprinted 1827. 8vo.

BANCKS, J. Miscellaneous Works in Verse and Prose. Lond. 1738-9, 8vo. 2 vols. with plates after Hogarth, 14s.

BANCROFT, D. A brief Discoverie of the Untruthes and Slanders against the true Government of the Church of Christ, in a Sermon. February 8, 1588. 12mo. No name or place.

Horner, 1854, mor. 1l. 4s.

— Edward, M.D. Essay on the Natural History of Guiana, in South America. Lond. 1769. 8vo. with a plate. 5s.

Besides natural history, this work may be consulted with advantage on the manners, &c. of the natives. Heath, 2753, 7s. 6d. Willett, 61, 15s.

— Experimental Researches concerning the Philosophy of permanent Colours, and the best Means of producing them by Dyeing, Calico Printing, &c. Lond. 1813, 8vo. 2 vols.

The most scientific work on the subject. The first edition of vol. i. 1794, is now of little value.

— Richard, Ashp. of Canterbury. Survay of the pretended holy Discipline. Lond. 1593. 4to. 15s.

Prefixed is an epistle to the reader, contents, &c. 464 pp. and the errata. Reprinted 1663. 4to. From this and the following work much information respecting the Puritans may be obtained.

— Daungerous Positions and Proceedings, published and practised within this Iland of Brytaine, vnder Pretence of Reformation, and for the Presbyteriall Discipline. Lond. 1593. 4to.

Prefixed are 'An Advertisement to the Reader.—The Contents.' Then a collection of sentences from the scriptures and the fathers. 183 pp. White Knights, 848, 1l. 4s. Sotheby's in 1824, 2l. 6s. Reprinted 1640. 4to. Bindley, pt. i. 1092, 5s. 6d.

BANCROFT, Thos. Two Bookes of Epigrammes and Epitaphs. (481 in number.) Lond. 1639. 4to.
Contains pp. 86. A copious account of this volume will be found in the Restituta, ii. 490—6. Nassau, pt. i. 374, mor. 1l. 11s. Sir M. M. Sykes, pt. i. 399, 2l. Inglis, 139, mor. 2l. 19s. Roxburghe, 3375, 3l. 3s. Towneley, pt. i. 391, 4l. 14s. 6d. Strettell, 363, mor. 4l. 15s. Bindley, pt. i. 744, 4l. 17s. Lloyd, 226, 10l. 10s. Bibl. Anglo-Poet. 80, 20l. afterwards 5l. 5s.

—— Glutton's Feaver. Lond. 1817. 4to.
Presented to the members of the Roxburghe Club, by J. D. Phelps, Esq. Dent, pt. ii. 1204, 12s. Sir M. M. Sykes, pt. i. 1626, 1l. 10s. Boswell, 3037, 4l. Bindley, pt. iii. 1796, 9l. 11s. 6d. (Original edition, 1633, sold 1854, 5l. 2s. 6d.)

—— Heroical Lover. Lond. 1658.
Reed, 6554, 1l. 11s. 6d.

BANDELLO, Matteo. La prima, la seconda, la terza, e la quarta Parte de le Novelle del Bandello. Lond. per S. Harding, 1740. 4to. 4 vols. in 3.
An elegant reprint of the edition of Lucca 1554 and Lione 1578, parte i. 368 leaves; parte ii. 391 leaves, including one containing the register; parte iii. 231 leaves; parte iv. 132 leaves, and 4 of introductory matter, including the title. A copy on LARGE PAPER at the sale of the Mac Carthy library produced 326 fr.

—— The tragicall Historye of Romeus and Juliet, written first in Italian by Bandell, and nowe in English by Ar.[thur] Br.[oke] London, by Richard Tottill, 1562. 4to.
Black letter. In fours extends to fol. 84, besides four leaves of introduction. This edition, with the title of 1587, is reprinted in Malone's Supplement to Shakespeare, 1780; of which reprint about 12 copies were taken off, with new paging, for private distribution. In the British Bibliographer (vol. ii. 113—16) will be found the preface to the edition of 1562, omitted in that of 1587, and also in Malone's reprint.

—— Matteo. Another edition. Lond. by Rob. Robinson, 1587. 4to.

—— A most lamentable and tragicall Historie, which a Spanishe Gentlewoman named Violenta executed upon her Louer Didaco, because he espoused another beying first betrothed vnter her. Newly translated into English Meeter, by T. A. (Thomas Acheley.) Lond. by John Charlewood for Thomas Butter, 1576. 12mo.
Black letter. Not noticed by Ames or Herbert. It is mentioned by Ritson in his Bibliographia Poetica, under Thomas Acheley. A copy was sold at Steevens' sale, No. 1102, with other articles.

BANDINEL, Bulkley, D.D. Catalogue of Books relating to British Topography and Saxon and Northern Literature, bequeathed to the Bodleian Library by Richard Gough. Oxford, 1814. 4to. pp. 459, 1l. 11s. 6d.
The most complete catalogue of English topography extant.

BANIER, Abbé Antoine. Mythology and Fables of the Ancients explained from History. Lond. 1739, 1740. 8vo. 4 vols. 1l. 4s.
A work containing an immense store of important information. Williams, 140, morocco, 4l.

BANISTER, John. Historie of Man sucked from the Sap of the most approved Anatomists, &c. Lond. by John Daye, 1578. folio.
Black letter, with cuts. Horne Tooke, 98, 14s. Banister likewise published several other chirurgical works.

—— John, and Thomas Low. New Ayres and Dialogues composed for Voices and Viols of two, three, and four Parts: together with Lessons for Viols or Violins. Lond. 1678. 8vo.

BANKES, Henry. Civil and Constitutional History of Rome, from its Foundation to the Age of Augustus. Lond. 1818. 8vo. 2 vols.
An excellent article on the early History of Rome, with a notice of this work, will be found in the Quarterly Review, xxvii. 273—308. Drury, 316, extra bound, 1l. 4s. LARGE PAPER, Combe, 99, bds. 18s.

BANKES His Bay Horse in a Trance. See Marocus Extaticus.

BANKS, John. Critical Review of the Life of Oliver Cromwell. Lond. 1760. 12mo. with port. 4s.
Upon the whole, an impartial work, often reprinted.

— Sir Joseph, Bart. Catalogus Bibliothecæ historico-naturalis Josephi Banks, Baroneti, &c. Auctore Jona Dryander. Londini, 1798—1800. 8vo. 5 vols.
An excellent and admirably arranged catalogue, certainly the most comprehensive of the kind ever published. It contains a collation of all the articles in the library, and is illustrated with much curious and important information. 250 copies printed. Vol. i. pp. vii. and 309, and index. Vol. ii. pp. xx. 578, and index. Vol. iii. pp. xxiii. 656, and index. Vol. iv. pp. ix. and 390. Vol. v. pp. 531. Dibdin, 20, 5l. 12s. 6d. Bindley, pt. i. 993, 5l. 17s.

— Thomas C. Dormant and Extinct Baronage of England, from the Norman Conquest to the year 1809. Lond. 1807—9. 4to. 3 vols.
A work of no merit. The greater part of its contents was copied from Dugdale's Baronage, but as many of that writer's most important statements, and all his references to his authorities are omitted, it is of infinitely less value. The account of titles created since Dugdale wrote, is chiefly taken from Collins. An appendix is annexed to the Stemmata Anglicana. Brockett, 466, 3l. 4s. Duke of York, 488, 3l. 11s.—LARGE PAPER, 5l. 5s.

— Genealogical and Biographical History of the Dormant and Extinct Peerage of England, from the Norman Conquest; including the Regal Families anterior to the House of Brunswick. Lond. 1812. 8vo. Vol. i. 10s.
This volume is the only one which appeared of an intended new edition in six octavo volumes, of the Dormant and Extinct Baronage. It commences (p. 1 to 145) with a genealogical account of the Extinct Royal Families of England, which is a useful compilation from Sandford, and other expensive works, though by no means remarkable for accuracy or research. The titles of Peerage treated of, extend in alphabetical order from Abergavenny to Banbury, (p. 148 to the end,) and present the best of the various specimens of the author's genealogical abilities. The elaborate notice of the singular claim to the Banbury Peerage would alone render this volume of some value, as the printed cases, whence it was compiled, may not be easily procured.

— Thomas C. Stemmata Anglicana; or, a miscellaneous Collection of Genealogy. Lond. 1825. 4to. [Afterwards published under the title of Genealogical and Heraldic Gleanings, and as Dormant and Extinct Baronage, vol. iv. 1837.] 4to. 15s. L. P. 1l. 1s.
This volume commences with a treatise on the various dignities of Peerage, and the manner of establishing claims to them. The only valuable part of the work is that entitled 'Barones Rejecti,' being an account of individuals who appear to have held the rank of Barons, but who are not noticed by other writers, which in many instances exhibit proofs of considerable research. The appendix contains 'Additions and Emendations to the author's Dormant and Extinct Baronage, with Indices to the whole work.'

— History of the ancient noble Family of Marmyun; their office of King's Champion, &c. Lond. 1817. 8vo. 10s. 6d. 4to. 1l. 1s.
A very imperfect work. Mr. Banks is the author of some other publications of a similar nature, but they are unworthy of being particularly mentioned.

BANNATYNE, Richard. Journal of the Transactions in Scotland, during the Contest between the Adherents of Queen Mary and those of her Son in 1570-71-72-73. Edinb. 1806. 8vo. 12s.
Bannatyne was secretary to John Knox.

Bannatyne MS. Ancient Scottish Poems. Published from the MS. of George Bannatyne, 1568. Edinb. 1770. 12mo. 4s.
Edited by Sir David Dalrymple, afterwards Lord Hailes. Heath, 1879, 10s. 6d. Roxburghe, 3195, 12s. Strettell, 1006, russia, 17s. A reprint, Leeds, 1815. 8vo. Two hundred copies printed on common paper; and thirty-one on coloured paper.

BANNATYNE CLUB BOOKS. See Appendix.

Banquett of Dainties; for all suche Gestes that loue moderatt Dyate. Lond. by Tho. Hackett. 1566. 8vo.
Black letter, contains pp. 42. This poetical banquet is not noticed by Ames, Her-

bert, or Dr. Dibdin, but an account from an imperfect copy will be found in the Censura Literaria, vol. vii. 55-7. Bibl. Anglo-Poet. 42, morocco (title MS.) 10*l*. 10s. Re-sold by Saunders in 1818, 6*l*. 16s. 6d. Re-sold Bright, 4*l*. 15s.

— Jests. *See* Armstrong, Archee.

— Daintie Conceits. *See* Munday, Antony.

BANSLEY, Charles. Rhyming Satire on the Pride and Vices of Women now a days. Lond. by Thomas Raynalde (about 1540). 12mo.

Black letter, commencing, 'Bo peep, what have we spied.' [Reprinted, but never issued, by the Percy Society, 8vo. 1841, 15s.]

Baptism. Sacra Institutio Baptizandi, Matrimonium celebrandi, Infermos ungendi, Mortuos sepeliendi, acalii nonnulli Ritus Ecclesiastici, juxta usum insignis Ecclesiæ Sarisburiensis. Duaci, 1604. 4to. 10s. 6d.

— Of Baptisme, 1646. *See* LAWRENCE, Henry.

— Ordo Baptizandi, aliaque Sacramenta administrandi, et Officia quædam Ecclesiastica rite paragendi, Jussu Pauli V. pro Anglia, Hibernia et Scotia. Paris, 1657. 12mo. 7s.

— Ordo Baptizandi aliaque Sacramenta administrandi, &c. pro Anglia, Hibernia et Scotia. Lond. 1686. 12mo. 10s.

This book was printed by the special command of James II. in order to form the standard of what he considered the true Catholic religion in this country.

Baratariana; a Collection of Pieces, published during the Administration of Lord Townshend in Ireland, with Supplement. Dublin, 1772-3. 8vo. 3 vols. in 2, with plates.

Nassau, pt. 1. 109, 8s. Garrick, 106, 9s.

BARATTI, Giacomo. Travels into the remote countries of the Abissins or Ethiopia interior, translated by G. D. Lond. 1670. 12mo.

Constable, 39, 6s. 6d. Heath, 2699, 8s.

BARBA, Alvarez Alonzo. Art of Metals, translated by Edward Montagu, Earl of Sandwich. Lond. 1674. 8vo. 3s. 6d.

Reprinted in 'A Collection of valuable Treatises upon Metals, Mines, and Minerals.' 1740. 12mo. The sale of Barba's book was prohibited in Spain, under the penalty of the Inquisition.

BARBADILLO, Don Alonso Geronimo de Salas. Fortunate Fool, translated (from the Spanish) by Philip Ayres. Lond. 1670. 12mo. 5s.

Barbadoes.—Laws of Barbadoes, from 1643 to 1762, by Richard Hall. 1762, 4to. 2*l*. 12s. 6d.

— Public Acts in Force, passed by the Legislature of Barbadoes, from May 11, 1762, to April 8, 1800. By Samuel Moore. 1801. royal 8vo.

Barbara. The Life of St. Barbara. Lond. By Julyan Notary (1518). 4to.

Black letter. Four leaves.

BARBARO, Daniel. Relazione dell' illustrissimo Daniel Barbaro, fatta nel serenissimo Senato doppo la sua Legazione d' Inghilterra ove fu Ambasciatore per la serenissima Republica in Tempo del Re Edvardo VI. nel 1551. 4to.

A copy is in the British Museum.

Barbary. History of Barbary. Lond. 1609. 4to.

Inglis. 140, 3*l*. 2s.

— Three Miseries of Barbary: Plague, Famine, ciuill Warre. With a Relation of the Death of Mahamet the late Emperour: and a briefe Report of the now present Wars betweene the three Brothers. Lond. 4to.

A copy is in the British Museum.

— Late Newes out of Barbary. Lond. 1613. 4to.

A copy is in the British Museum.

— Voyage to Barbary, for the Redemption of Captives in 1720, by the Mathurin-Trinitarian Fathers, 1735. 8vo. With map and plates, 7s.

— Several Voyages to Barbary, with Notes, historical and critical.

BAR 111

The second Edition corrected. Lond. 1736. 8vo. 3s. 6d.
Contains, pp. 146, with Contents. Also Appendix, pp. 158, with six Maps, &c. designed by Captain Henry Boyde.

BARBAULD, Anna Letitia. Selections from the Spectator, Tatler, Guardian, and Freeholder. With a preliminary Essay. Lond. 1804. 12mo. 3 vols. 9s. [New edition, 2 vols. 12mo. 1849. 7s.]
An excellent selection.

— Poetical Works, the Correspondence and other Prose Pieces, with a Memoir. By Lucy Aikin. Lond. 1826. 8vo. 2 vols. 24s.

BARBER, J. T. Tour through South Wales and Monmouthshire. Lond. 1803. 8vo. 15s.
This work is chiefly picturesque, and descriptive of manners. It contains pp. 359, with a Map and twenty Views, engraved from drawings, by the author. Fonthill, 2799, PROOFS, 1l. 12s. Copies are printed in an inferior manner, without plates.

— William. Farm Buildings; or, Rural Economy. Lond: 1805. 4to. with six plates. 10s. 6d.
Barber likewise published a Description of the Mode of Building in Pisé. 1806. 4to.

— T. Picturesque Guide to the Isle of Wight, 8vo. 40 plates. Lond. Bohn, 1834. [New edition, completed to 1850, 45 plates, 10s. 6d.]

BARBERINUS, Maffæus, i.e. Urban VIII. Poemata, cum Vita Auctoris et Annotationibus adjectis, edidit Jos. Brown. Oxon. 1726. 8vo.
Dent, pt. i. 179, russia, 6s. 6d.—LARGE PAPER. Williams, 141, morocco, 1l.

BARBIER, John. Janua Linguarum quadrilinguis, or a Messe of Tongues, Latine, English, French, and Spanish. Londini, 1617. 4to.
Inglis, 523, morocco, 3l. 3s.

— Jos. Game of Chesse-play, being a princely Exercise, whereby the Learner may profit more by reading of this small Book than by playing of a thousand Mates. Lond. 1672. 12mo. with wood cuts.
A Treatise of no merit. Towneley, pt. i.

287, 18s. Marq. of Townshend, 85, 18s. 6d. White Knights, pt. i. 292, morocco, 1l. 2s.

BARBOUR, John. The Actes and Life of Robert Bruce. Edinb. 1620. 8vo.
Black letter. pp. 444. According to Pinkerton the first edition was published in 1616. (?) Reprinted 1648, 1665, 1670, 1671, 1672, 1737, 1758. Edition 1620, Bibl. Anglo-Poet. 21, morocco, 4l. 4s.—1670, Roxburghe, 3242, 2l. 5s. Utterson, 1852, morocco, 5l. 12s. 6d.—1672, Bindley, pt. i. 56, 3l. 18s. —1758, Nassau, pt. i. 376, 9s. Towneley. pt. ii. 188. 13s. Bindley, pt. i. 747, 16s.

— The Bruce; or the History of Robert I. King of Scotland. Written in Scottish Verse by John Barbour. The first genuine Edition, published from a MS. dated 1489; with Notes and a Glossary, by J. Pinkerton. Lond. 1790. 12mo. 3 vols. 15s.
Lloyd, 51, 1l. 1s. Roxburghe, 3243. 1l. 7s.

— The Bruce, published from a MS. dated 1489, with Notes and a Life of the Author, &c. To which is added, Wallace, or the Life of Sir Wm. Wallace of Ellerslie, from a MS. of 1488, by John Wallace Jamieson. Edinb. 1820. 2 vols. 4to.
Two hundred and fifty copies printed. Brockett, 467, 2l. Hibbert, 1l. 18.

BARBUT, James. Genera Insectorum of Linnæus exemplified by various Specimens of English Insects, with Descriptions in English and French. Lond. 1781. 4to. with plates, plain 1l. 1s. coloured, 2l. 12s. 6d.
Contains pp. 371, and 22 plates.—The original drawings. Beckford, 1817, 138, morocco, 7l. 17s. 6d.

— Genera Vermium, with Explanations in English and French. Lond. 1783-8. 4to. Two Parts, with plates, plain, 18s. coloured, 2l. 2s.
Part i. pp. 101, and 11 plates. Part ii. (Testacea.) pp. 76, and 14 plates.

BARCKLEY. See BARCLAY.

BARCLAY, Alexander. Alex. Barkley his Figure of our Mother Holy Church, oppressed by the French King. (Rich. Pynson.) 4to.
From Maunsell's Catal. p. 7.

— Egloges of Alexander Barclay,

Priest, &c. Lond. by Richarde Pynson. folio.
Black letter. Contains 22 leaves with cuts. Dent, pt. i. 312, with the 'Fyfte Eglog,' printed by W. de Worde, 36*l*.

Barclay. Egloges of Alex. Barclay, Priest, whereof the first three containeth the Miseries of Courters and Courte. Lond. by John Herford. 4to. n.
Black letter.

— Egloges of Alexander Barclay, Priest. ⸺nd. by Humphrey Powell (about)48). 4to.
Black letter. Contains P. 2, in fours, pp 116. Inglis, 143, 6*l*. 2s. 6d. Bibl. Anglo-Poet. 894, 15*l*. Bright, 10*l*. 10s.

— Certayne Egloges. Lond. by John Cawood. folio. .
Black letter. D in sixes. Appended to Brant's Stultifera Navis.

— The fyfte Eglog of Alexandre Barclay of the Cytezen and Vplondyshman. Lond. by W. de Worde. 4to.
Black letter. Contains E in sixes. Woodhouse, 5 parts complete, 25*l*. Dent, pt. i. 312, with the Egloges printed by Pynson, 36*l*. Heber, 24*l*. 10s.

— The Introductory to write and to pronounce Frenche, compyled by Alexander Barclay, at the commaundement of Thomas, Duke of Norfolke. Lond. by Robert Copland. 1521. folio.
Black letter. Contains C 4, in sixes.

— *See* BRANDT, Sebastian.
Castle of Labour.
MANCYN, Dominecke.
SALLUST.

A very elaborate account of this elegant writer's productions is given in the 29th section of Warton's History of English Poetry. Further notices, &c. will also be found in Bliss's Wood's A. O. i. 205—9, and Ellis' Specimens, i. 406—9.

— John. Grammatica Latina Johannis Barkley. (Rich. Pynson, 1516.) 4to.

— John Barclay his Argenis, or the Loves of Poliarchus and Argenis, translated by Kingsmill Long. Lond. 1625, folio.
A political allegory, pronounced by the poet Cowper, the most amusing romance ever written. Bindley, pt. i. 195, 5s.

— Argenis, translated by Sir Robert Le Grys, Knight; the Verses by Thomas May, Esq. Lond. 1628-9. 4to.
1628, Gordonstoun, 31*l*, 5s. 6d.—1629, Bindley, pt. i. 1088, russia, 8s. 6d.

— Argenis, translated by Kingsmill Long, Esq. The second edition beautified with pictures, together with a key præfixed to unlock the whole story. Lond. 1636, 4to.
Contains A—Bbb 2 in eights. The cuts are on the letter press. On the back of A 4, is a portrait of Barclay. Roxburghe, 6087, 5s. Nassau, pt. i. 378, 9s.

— The Phœnix, or the History of Polyarchus and Argenis. Translated from the Latin, [by Clara Reeve.] Lond. 1771, 12mo. 4 vols. 12s.

Barclay published an account of the Gunpowder plot, which will be found at the end of his Satyricon and likewise several controversial works relative to England in the reign of James I.

— Icon Animarum; the Mirror of Mindes, translated by T. May. Lond. 1631. 12mo. 5s.
A masterly description of the manners of the several nations of Europe in the beginning of the 18th century, with remarks moral and philosophical on the various tempers of men.

— Description of the Roman Catholick Church, written in the year 1679. (in verse.) Edinb. 1741. 8vo.
Constable, 41, 6s.

— Sketch of the Life of John Barclay of Urie, 1786. 4to.
Published by Sir David Dalrymple Lord Hailes.

— Sir Richard, Knt. Discourse of the Felicitie of Man: or his Summum Bonum. Written by Sir Richard Barkley, Knight. Lond. 1598. 4to.
Reprinted 1603, 1631. This work 'is in fact a garner filled with the most amusing and best histories, and little narrations, told in the author's own words, and occasionally enlarged, but in perfect keeping and consistency.' Retrospect. Review. Edition 1598, Reed, 1774, 6s.—1603, Inglis, 142, 5s.—1631, Nassau, pt. i. 377, 11s.

— Robert. Works. Lond. 1692. folio. 1718. 8vo. 3 vols. 18s.
The celebrated apologist for the Quakers, and one of the ablest writers of that sect: his works are much esteemed.

— Apology for the true Christian Divinity, as the same is held forth and preached by the People, called in scorn, Quakers. Birmingham, 1765. 4to. 18s.
An elegant edition printed by Baskerville. Bindley, pt. i. 920, russia, 1l. 2s. The first edition, 1676, 4to. dedicated to Charles II., has been frequently reprinted, and translated into most European languages.

— Genealogical Account of the Barclays of Urie, 1110—1731, with Memoirs of Colonel David Barclay, and his son Robert Barclay, author of the 'Apology for the Quakers.' Lond. 1812. 8vo. 4s.
Edited by Henry Mill. The original edition appeared Aberdeen, 1740, 8vo.

— William. De Regno et regali Potestate adversus Buchananum, Brutum, Boucherium et reliquos Monarchomachos, Libri sex. Paris, 1600. 4to.
A celebrated treatise denying the authority of the Pope over Sovereigns in Temporals. This learned civilian published several other controversial works.

— Callirrhoe, or the Well of the Spaw. Aberd. 1615, 1670. 8vo.

— Barclaii Gulielmi ex Vita Julii Agricolæ, Auctore Genero, Præmatia.

Bareith.—Memoires de Frederique Sophie Wilhelmine de Prusse, Margrave de Bareith Soeur de Frédéric-le-Grand, ecrits de sa Main. Lond. 1812. 8vo. 2 vols. 12s.
An English translation of these amusing memoirs appeared 1812, 8vo. 2 vols.

BARET, John. Alvearie or Quadruple Dictionarie, English, Latine, Greeke, and French. Lond. 1580. folio, 10s. 6d.
Dedicated to Lord Burleigh. A former edition, containing three languages, English, Latin, and French, appeared in 1573, folio. 1580. Perry, pt. i. 436, 2l. 2s. Bindley, pt. i. 575, 14s. Horne Tooke, 40, 2l. 5s.—1573, Roxburghe, 2161, 1l. 1s.

— Michael. Hipponomie, or the Vineyard of Horsemanship. Lond. 1618. 4to.

BARETTI, Joseph. Italian Library, containing an account of the Lives and Works of the most valuable Authors of Italy. With a Preface, exhibiting the changes of the Tuscan language, from the barbarous ages to the present time. Lond. 1757. 8vo. 6s.

— Account of the Manners and Customs of Italy; with an Appendix. Lond, 1768-9. 8vo. ? '.s. 6s.
'A very entertaining book.' Johnson. Bindley, pt. i. 814, 13s.

— Journey from London to Genoa, through England, ., .tugal, Spain and France. Lond. 1770. 8vo. 4 vols. 10s. 6d.
An entertaining work. Fonthill, 2087, 80s.—4to. 2 vols. Drury, 374, 16s. Fonthill, 418, 1l. 13s.

— Dictionary of the English and Italian Languages. Lond. 1760. 4to. 2 vols. 18s.
The dedication to this dictionary was written by Dr. Johnson. Reprinted 1778, 1790, 4to., and 1820, 8vo. 2 vols. [Republished with large additions, by Davonport and Comelati, 2 vols. 8vo. Lond. 1854. 1l. 10s.]

— Dictionary of the English and Spanish Languages. Lond. 1778. folio.
Reprinted 1794, 1800, in 4to. and 1807, 8vo. 2 vols. Edition 1794, Dent, pt. i. 313, 1l. 6s.—1800, White Knights, pt. i. 352, russia, 1l. 14s. [Republished with large additions and corrections, by Prof. Seoane, Lond. 1837, 2 vols. 8vo. 1l. 8s., and frequently reprinted.]
This writer likewise published many other works, chiefly grammatical.

BARHAM, Henry. Hortus Americanus. Kingston, Jamaica, 1794. 8vo. pp. 212. 5s.

BARKER, Andrew. Report of the two famous Pirates, Capt. Ward and Danseter. Lond. 1609. 4to.
Daborne took the plot of 'A Christian turn'd Turk,' from the above. Nassau, pt. ii. 372.

— Edmund Henry. Classical and Biblical Recreations. Lond. 1812. 8vo. vol. i. (all published) 8s. 6d.
[This laborious scholar edited the 'Classical Journal,' the 'Delphin and Variorum Classics,' 'Stephani Thesaurus Linguæ Græcæ,' and many classical school books for Valpy; and wrote Parriana, Letters on Junius, &c. &c.]

BARKER, Thomas. Art of Angling. Lond. 1651. 12mo.
An edition, 1653, 4to. without the author's name. [It is sometimes adjoined to the Countryman's Recreations, 4to. 1654.] A reprint of the edition of 1651, appeared 1820, and that of 1653 was reprinted at Leeds, 1817, of which one copy was struck off in 4to. Edition 1653. Bindley, pt. iv. 524, 6s. White Knights, pt. i. 158, 8s. Haworth, 919, 1l. 2s.
— Barker's Delight; or, the Art of Angling. The second edition, much enlarged. Lond. 1657 or 1659. 12mo.
Contains pp. iv. and 67. Haworth, 921, date 1659, 17s. Reprinted 1820, of which four copies were printed on yellow paper, and one on vellum.

BARKLEY. See BARCLAY.

BARKSDALE, Clement. Nympha Libethris: or the Cotswold Muse presenting some extempore verses to the Imitation of yong Scholars: in four parts. Lond. 1651. 12mo. pp. 96.
Perry, pt. iv. 316, 2l. 1s. Dent, pt. i. 182, mor. 6l. 15s. Saunders in 1818, 15l. 15s. Bibl. Anglo-Poet. 88, 20l. Gardner, 1854, mor. 4l. Brand, 4l. 10s. A reprint, consisting of 40 copies, was published 1816, by Sir Egerton Brydges. Nassau, pt. i. 117, 15s. Bindley, pt. i. 643, 17s. Strettell, 129, 19s.

— Memorials of worthy Persons. Two Decads, 12mo. Lond. 1661. A third Decad, Oxford, 1662. A fourth Decad, Oxford, 1663. A fifth Decad, entitled 'A Remembrance of excellent Men.' Lond. 1670. 8vo. 2l.
Anthony à Wood says, this work is 'scribled from the sermons preached at their funerals, their lives, and characters occasionally given of them, in public authors.' Nassau, pt. ii. 1465, 2 vols. 1661-3, 1l.
In Dr. Bliss's edition of Wood's Athenæ Oxonienses, iv. 221—5, will be found a biography, with a list of the writings of Barksdale.

Barkshire.—Publication of Guianas Plantation, newly undertaken by the Earl of Barkshire. Lond. 1632. 4to.

BARKSTEAD, or Barksted, Will. Myrrha, the Mother of Adonis, or Lusts Prodigies, a Poem. Lond. 1607. 8vo.

— Hirem, or the Fair Greek, a Poem. Lond. 1611. 8vo.

BARLAAMUS Monachus. Barlaami de Papae Principatu Libellus. Nunc primum Græce et Latine editus, opera Johannis Luidii. Oxoniæ, 1592. 4to. 19 leaves, 6s.

BARLACE, G. Sketch of the Progress of Knowledge in England, with notices of learned men. Lond. 1820. 4to. 1l. 1s. [Of no present value.]

BARLÆUS, Caspar. Britannia Triumphans, sive in inaugurationem Caroli I. Mag. Brit. Franciæ et Hiberniæ Regis, Fidei Defensoris, Poematio. Lugd. Bat. 1626. folio.
A copy is in the British Museum.

BARLEY-BREAKE. See N—. (W.)

BARLEY. Martyrdome of Saint George. Lond. 1614. 4to. with frontispiece.
Dent, pt. i. 309, 3l. 3s. Nassau, pt. i. 379, 12l.

BARLOW, Francis. Multæ et diversæ Avium species. Lond. 1671. 4to.
A copy is in the British Museum.

— Various Birds and Beasts (67) drawn from the Life. Lond. 4to.

— Book of such Beasts as are most useful for Drawing, Graving, or Armes-painting and Chaseing, designed by F. Barlow, and engraved by William Vaughan. 1664.
Thirteen small plates, exclusive of the engraved title.

— Seuerall Wayes of Hunting, Hawking, and Fishing, according to the English manner, &c. invented by Francis Barlow, etched by W. Hollar. Lond.
Barlow published a much esteemed edition of the Fables of Æsop.

— Rev. Frederic. English Peerage. Lond. 1775. 8vo. 2 vols. 7s.
In no estimation as a genealogical work. A former edition appeared in 1778.

— Joel. Columbiad, a Poem. Philadelphia, 1807. 4to. with plates after Smirke's designs, 15s.
Sotheby's in Dec. 1820. 3l. 3s. Reprinted Lond 1809. 8vo. 5s.

— John. Exposition of the first and second Chapters of the second Epistle to Timothy, with a Discourse of spiritual Stedfastness, and five Sermons. Lond. 1632. folio.

Barlow likewise published several sermons, of which an account will be found in Dr. Bliss's edition of Wood's Athen. Oxon. ii. 551-2.

BARLOW, Peter, F.R.S. Mathematical and Philosophical Dictionary; with historical Sketches of the Rise, Progress, and present state of the several Departments of the Sciences. Lond. 1813. royal 8vo. 1l. 1s.

— Essay on Magnetic Attractions and on the Laws of Terrestrial and Electro-Magnetism. Lond. 1822. 8vo. with plates, 8s.

Mr. Barlow, highly distinguished by his scientific labours, was professor of mathematics at the military academy at Woolwich. He wrote several other valuable treatises.

— Stephen. History of Ireland from the earliest period to the present time. Lond. 1814. 8vo. 2 vols. 10s.

— Thomas, Bishop of Lincoln. Several Cases of Conscience learnedly and judiciously resolved. Lond. 1692. 8vo. with portrait by R. White. 4s.

— Genuine Remains, containing divers Discourses, theological, philosophical, historical, &c. Lond. 1693. 8vo. 4s.

Published by Sir Peter Pett. In 1694, Reflections on this work, by Henry Brougham, appeared in 4to.

— Directions for the Choice of Books in the Study of Divinity. Oxford, 1699. 4to. 6s.

A life of this eminent prelate, with a list of his works, will be found in Dr. Bliss's edition of Wood's Athenæ Oxonienses, iv. 333—41.

— William, successively Bishop of Rochester and Lincoln. Vita et Obitus Richardi Cosin, Legum Doctoris, &c. Excudebant Deputati Chr. Barker. 1598. 4to. 3s. 6d.

— Sermon preached at Paules Crosse on the first Sunday in Lent, Martii 1, 1600. With a short Discourse of the late Earle of Essex, his Confession and Penitence, before and at the time of his Death. Whereunto is annexed, a true Copie, in Substance, of the Behaviour, Speache, and Prayer of the said Earle, at the Time of his Execution. 1601. 8vo.

Contains 39 leaves. Nassau, pt. i. 118, 1l. 2s.

— Sum and Substance of the Conference at Hampton Court, Jan. 14, 1603. Lond. 1604. 4to. 10s. 6d.

Reprinted 1625, 1638, and also in the first volume of the Phœnix, 1707. 8vo.

— William, Bishop of Bath. Dialogue describing the originall Ground of these Lutheran Faccions and many of their Abuses, compyled by Syr William Barlowe Chanon, late Byshop of Bathe. Anno 1553. Lond by John Cawoode. 16no

Black letter. Contains L, in eights, half sheets. According to Ant. à Wood, 'thought to have been forged under his name.' Lloyd, 52, (MS. title) 11s. Inglis, 62, 19s. White Knights, 298, mor. 1l. 8s. Horner, 1854, 1l. 6s. Sotheby, Dec. 1854, mor. 2l. 12s. 6d. Brand, 1l. 8s.

— William. Navigators Supply. Lond. 1597. 4to. 10s. 6d.

Contains L 2, in fours, besides dedication to the Earl of Essex and commendatory verses. This eminent mathematician and divine discovered many uses of the magnet and loadstone which were unknown before his time, and was the first inventor of the compass-box, as it is now used at sea.

— Magnetical Advertisements: or divers pertinent Observations and approved Experiments concerning the Nature and Properties of the Loadstone, &c. Lond. 1616. 4to.

This book was animadverted upon by Mark Ridley, a physician, in 1617, in answer to which Barlowe published 'A brief Discovery,' Lond. 1618. 4to.

Barmudas. *See* Bermudas.

BARNABAS. PP. App. Barnabæ et Hermæ Opera, Gr. et Lat. Oxon. 1685. 2[?]nc. 4s.

'A g[...]n'—Dr. Harwood. The editio princeps of this most ancient of all the fathers, was published by Archb. Usher, 1643, 4to. with the Epistles of Ignatius. A translation will be found in Archb. Wake's Epistles of the Apostolical Fathers.

Barnaby, Drunken. See BRATHWAIT, Richard.

Barnard.—Protestant Beadsman. 1822. 12mo.
Only twelve copies printed. Sir M. M. Sykes, 330.

BARNARD, John, D.D. Theologo-Historicus, or the true Life of Peter Heylyn, D.D. Lond. 1683. 12mo. with portrait of Heylyn. 5s.
Written in opposition to Vernon's Life of that author.

Barnard Family.—Copy of a genealogical Account of the Barnard Family, now in the possession of Mr. John Barnard, of Nicoll's Square, Lond. Silver-Flatter.
Privately printed in 1816.

BARNARDINE, of Escalanta.- Discourse of the Navigation which the Portugales do make to the Realms and Provinces of the East Parts of the World. 1579. 4to.
Black letter. Reprinted in the Oxford Collection of Voyages and Travels, vol. ii.

BARNARDISTON, Thomas. Reports of Cases in Chancery, 1740-1. Lond. 1742. folio, 15s.
Lord Mansfield absolutely forbid the citing of Barnardiston's Reports in the Court of Chancery.

— Reports of Cases in the Court of King's Bench, from 12 Geo. I. to 7 Geo. II. Lond. 1744. folio. 30s.

BARNARDISTON. Suffolk's Tears: or Elegies on that renowned Knight, Sir Nathaniel Barnardiston. Lond. 1653. 4to. pp. 70. 1l. 7s.
Nassau, pt. ii. 1175, (with two portraits of him and the plate) 2l. 12s. Saunders in 1818, 4l. Bibl. Anglo-Poet. 685, 12l. 12s. A Sermon at the funeral at Barnardiston was published by Samuel Fairclough, Lond. 1653, 4to.

BARNEFEILDE or Barnefield. See BARNFIELD.

BARNES, Barnabee. Praise of Musike. Oxenforde, 1586. 8vo.
Black letter. White Knights, 3l.

— Divine Centurie of Spiritual Sonnets. Lond. John Windet, 1595. 4to.

Contains pp. 62. Dedicated to 'Tobie (Matthews) Bishop and Comte Palatine of Duresme and Sadberge.' Printed in the Italic letter, with borders round each page. Sir M. M. Sykes, 408, 12l. Bibl. AngloPoet. 78, 3Cl. Heber, 7l. Reprinted in the second volume of the Heliconia.

— Foure Bookes of Offices; enabling privat Persons for the speciall Service of all good Princes and Policies. Lond. 1606. folio.
Contains pp. 210. Dedicated to K. James. Some copies have commendatory verses. A copious description of these volumes will be found in the Restituta, iv. 127—35. Gordonstoun, 248, 7s. 6d. 249, 13s.

— Devil's Charter; a Tragædie, conteining the Life and Death of Pope Alexander the Sixt. Lond. 1607. 4to.
Roxburghe, 4421, 15s. Reed, 7698, 1l. Bindley, pt. i. 1098, 1l. Rhodes, 514, 1l. 4s. Inglis' Old Plays, 11, 3l. 5s. Bright, mor. 2l.

— Parthenophil and Parthenophe. Sonnettes, Madrigals, Elegies and Odes. 4to. Lond.
A brief description of this volume (supposed unique), taken from a copy wanting part of the title, will be found in Beloe's Anecdotes, ii. 777-9. The printer's address is dated 1593.

— Henry. Notes of Cases of Practice in the Common Pleas, from Michaelmas Term 1732 to Hilary Term 1756 inclusive. Third Edition. Lond. 1790. royal 8vo. 18s.

— John. Catholico-Romanus Pacificus. Oxon. 1680. 8vo.
Remitted into Browne's 'Fasciculus Rerum expetendarum et fugiendarum.' An account of this persecuted individual will be found in Wood's Athenæ Oxon. by Dr. Bliss, ii. 500—2.

— Joshua, B.D. Gerania: a new Discovery of a little Sort of People, anciently discoursed of, called Pigmies. Lond. 1675. 12mo. 5s.

— The History of Edward III., together with that of Edward the Black Prince. Cambridge, 1688. folio, with 4 portraits, 1l. 1s.
An elaborate collection of facts, intermixed with long speeches from Barnes' imagination, in imitation of Thucydides. Dent, pt. i. 322, 1l. 13s. Bindley, pt. i. 568, 2l. 2s. Drury, 595, 2l. 2s. Puttick's, 1852, rich old morocco, gilt edges, 9l. 10s.

Barnes edited valuable editions of Anacreon and Euripides.

BARNES, BERNES, or BERNERS, Juliana. The Bokys of Haukyng and Huntyng, and also of Cootarmuris at St. Albons, 1486. folio.

Black letter, 88 leaves. The signatures run a to f in eights, a·i being blank and D only 4 leaves. The treatise upon Coat-Armour, &c. begins on a i and extends to f x in eights. a has six, b five, c, d, and e, eight, and f, 10 leaves. Perfect copies of this work are in the possession of Earl Spencer and the Earl of Pembroke. A perfect copy is estimated by Dr. Dibdin at 420*l*., and a very imperfect one at the Roxburghe sale produced 147*l*., resold at the sale of the White Knights' Library, 394, for 84*l*. A copy very nearly perfect is in the library of Mr. Phelps of Lincoln's Inn.

— Treatyse perteynynge to Hawkynge, Huntynge, and Fysshynge with an Angle: and also a ryght noble Treatise of the Lygnage of Cot Armours, endynge with a Treatise which specyfyeth of Blasynge of Armys. Westmestre, by Wynkyn the Worde, 1496. folio.

Black letter, with wood cuts. The variations of this from the former edition, independent of the orthography, consist of the additions of two wood-cuts upon the first leaf of the ballad of 'Ever gramercy myn owne purse;' the 'treatyse of fysshynge with an angle;' and a substitution on the last leaf, of the arms of England, in place of those of Saint Albans. White Knights, 305, morocco, 60*l*. 18s. resold, wanting C ii and iii, for 46*l*. 4s. Dent, pt. i. 139. morocco, 13*l*. 10s. A perfect copy on vellum with the arms emblazoned is in the Grenville library, now in the British Museum. Another, Haworth, 966, 4 leaves MS. 39*l*. 18s. The treatise on armory has been incorrectly reprinted in the Appendix to Dallaway's Inquiries into the Science of Heraldry. Gloucester, 1793. 4to.

— Booke of Hauking, Huntyng, and Fysshyng, with all the Properties and Medecynes that are necessary to be kept. Lond. by Wylliam Coplande. 4to.

Black letter, with wood cuts, contains m iiij, pp. 96. It is said only one perfect copy of this edition is known. Bibl. Anglo-Poet. 27, 35*l*.

— Booke of Hauking, Huntyng, and Fysshyng, with all the Properties and Medecynes that are necessary to be kept. Part i. Lond. by Robert Toye. Part ii. Lond. by Wyllyam Copland for Robert Toye. Part iii. Lond. by Wyllyam Copland. 4to.

Black letter. The signatures go regularly through all three. Sotheby's in May, 1823, 38*l*. 17s. Dent, pt. ii. 1076, 10*l*. 10s.

— Booke of Hauking, Huntyng, and Fysshyng, with all the Properties and Medecynes that are necessary to be kept. Lond. by Abraham Vele. 4to.

The wood-cuts, folios, &c. similar to that printed by W. Copland. At the end of the Treatise of Huntiug, Lond. by Wyllyam Copland, for Robert Toye. Mason, 11*l*. 16s. A copy is in the British Museum, wanting the title page, and the two leaves of 'measures of blowing.'

— Booke of Haukyng, Huntyng, and Fyshyng, with all the Properties and Medecynes that are necessary to be kept. Lond. by William Coplande, for Rychard Tottell. 4to.

Black letter. Probably the same edition as that with the name of Toye. Inglis, 144, 12*l*.

— Boke of Hawkynge, Huntynge, and Fysshynge, with all the Propertys and Medecynes that are necessary to be kepte. Lond. by me, Hery Tab. 4to.

Black letter. Contains 46 leaves, not numbered, extending to sign. M iiij., sign. J having only two leaves. The text begins on sign. a ij. and each treatise has a distinct colophon. A copy of this edition, supposed unique, is among Cryne's books in the Bodleian Library.

— Boke of Hawkynge, Huntynge, and Fysshynge, with all the Propertyes and Medecynes that are necessary to be kepte. Lond. by John Waley. 4to.

Black letter, with wood-cuts. In this edition the original reading of St. Thomas of Canterbury was restored, it was therefore, probably, published during the short reign of Queen Mary, supposed to be the same edition as that printed by Henry Tab. Haworth, 958, 8*l*.

— Boke of Haukyng, Huntynge, and Fyshing, with all the Properties and Medecynes that are necessary to be kepte, by Dame Juliana

Bernes. Lond. by Wyllyam Powell. 4to.
Black letter. Bibl. Pearson, 202. Haworth, 969, 7l. 5s.

BARNES. Boke of Haukynge, Huntynge, and Fyshing, with all the Properties and Medecynes that are necessary to be kepte. Lond. by William Powell. 1550. 8vo.
Dr. Dibdin, in his Bibliographical Decameron, notices an edition 1586, 4to. printed by E. Allde.

— The Gentleman's Academie, or the Booke of St. Alban's; containing three Bookes: the first of Hawking, the second of Hunting, and the last of Armorie, reduced into a better method by G.(ervase) M.(arkham) Lond. (by Valentine Simmes) for Humfrey Lownes, 1595. 4to.
Black letter. Contains D d, in fours, (fol. 95) inscribed 'To the Gentlemen of England: and all the good fellowship of Huntsmen and Falconers.' The Treatises of Hunting and Armory have separate titlepages. A garbled reprint of the Book of St. Alban's, much altered in the language. Roxburghe, 1733, russia, 9l. 19s. 6d.

— Book containing the Treatises of Hawking; Hunting; Coat-armour; Fishing; and Blasing of Armes, as printed at Westminster, by Wynkyn de Worde, 1496. Lond. 1810. small folio. (or rather 4to.) 5l. 5s.
A 'verbatim, literatim, et punctuatim' reprint under the editorial care of Joseph Haslewood, who has prefixed a very interesting introduction, both biographical and bibliographical, full of curious research. One hundred and fifty copies were printed. Bindley, pt i. 185, 4l. Towneley, pt. i. 8l. 18s. 6d. Brocket, 508, morocco, 10l. A few copies of the Bibliographical Introduction were published separately. Bindley, 429, 16s.

— Treatyse of Fysshynge with an Angle. Wynkyn de Worde. (1532) 4to.
Black letter. A to D iiij. supposed to be unique. Haworth, 963, 19l. 19s.

— Treatise of Fysshynge with an Angle. Lond. 1827, crown 8vo. 5s.
Printed with Baskerville's types, and embellished with fac-simile wood cuts. This is not only the earliest, but by far the most curious essay upon angling which has ever appeared in the English, or perhaps in any other language. In the most important features, Walton has closely followed this production. In piety and virtue — in the inculcation of morality — in an ardent love for their art, and still more, in that placid and Christian spirit for which the amiable Walton was so conspicuous, the early writer was scarcely inferior to his or her more celebrated successor.

— Robert, D.D. Supplicacion vnto Prince H. the viii. The Cause of my Condempnation.—The hole Disputacion betwene the Byshops and Doctour Barnes. Lond. by me, Johan Byddell, 1534. 4to.
Black letter. The whole X 2, in fours, commencing on B 1. Inglis, 64 (no title), 7s. 6d. Horner, 1854 (no title, mor.) 1l. 1s.

— Supplication vnto Kynge Henrye the eyght, with the Declaration of His Articles condēned for Heresy by the Byshops. Lond. by Hugh Syngelton. 8vo.
Black letter.

.— See TINDAL, FRITH, & BARNES.

BARNESTAPLE, Obertus. Maria Stuarta Regina Scotiæ, Dotaria Franciæ, Hæres Angliæ, Hyberniæ, Martyr. Ecclesie, innocens a Cæde Darleana: Vindice Oberto Barnestapolio. Ingolst. 1588. 12mo.
A copy is in the British Museum. Inglis, 898, 1l. 17s. Nassau, pt. i. 120, with a portrait, also 'Summarium de Morte Mariæ Stuartæ.' Ingolst. 1588. 8l.

— Editio altera. Colon. 1627. 8vo. 16s.
In this account Q. Mary is represented as having been persecuted entirely on account of her adherence to the Catholic religion. Reprinted by Jebb in 'De Vita et Rebus gestis Mariæ Scotorum Reginæ.'

BARNEWALL, R. V., and E. H. ALDERSON. Reports of Cases in the Court of King's Bench, from Mich. 58 Geo. III. to Trin. Term, 3 Geo. IV. 1822. Lond. 1818-22. royal 8vo. 5 vols. reduced to 1l.5s.
A continuation of Maule and Selwyn's Reports.

— and C. CRESSWELL. Reports of Cases in the King's Bench, from Mich. 3 Geo. IV. 1822, to East. 11 Geo. IV. 1830. Lond.

1823-35. royal 8vo. 10 vols. 5*l.* 17s. 6d.

— and J. L. ADOLPHUS. Reports of Cases in the K.B. from Trin. T. 11 Geo. IV. to Hil. T. 4 Will. IV., 1834, 5 vols. roy. 8vo. 1831-5, reduced to 1*l.* 10s.

BARNFIELD, Richard. Affectionate Shepherd: containing the Complaint of Daphnis for the Love of Ganymede. Lond. by John Danter, 1594. 4to.

Very rare. Contains pp. 56. Inscribed in a metrical dedication to the 'Ladie Penelope Ritch.' Reed, 6685, 16*l.* 10s. Heber, 14*l.* 14s. A copy, according to Beloe, is in Sion College Library. An edition 1595 is noticed in the Theatrum Poetarum, 1800, p. 323, and one of 1596, in Ritson's Bibliographia Poetica, p. 124-5.

— Cynthia, with certaine Sonnets, and the Legend of Cassandra. Lond. Humfrey Lownes, 1595. 12mo.

Dedicated to William Stanley, Earl of Darby. Reed, 6777, 12*l.* 5s. Heber, 69, 10*l.* An account of this volume will be found in the Restituta, iv. 498—6. It is also appended to the third edition of the Affectionate Shepherd, 1596.

— Encomion of Lady Pecunia; or the Praise of Money; the Complaint of Poetrie for the Death of Liberalitie: *i. e.* The Combat betweene Conscience and Covetousness, in the Minde of Man: with Poems in Divers Humors. Lond. 1598. 4to.

Todd, in his edition of Spenser, notices an edition dated 1605.

— Poems. Auchinleck Press, 1816. 4to.

Presented to the Members of the Roxburghe Club by James Boswell, Esq. Thirty-four or five copies printed. Sir M. M. Sykes, pt. i. 1619, 1*l.* 6s. Dent, pt. ii. 1197, 1*l.* 10s. Boswell. 3028, 4*l.* 6s. Bindley, pt. iii. 1793, 6*l.* 16s. 6d.

Warton speaks highly of Barnfield as a poet, and among his poems will be found that beautiful Ode, commencing

'As it fell upon a day
'In the merry month of May,'

which has been attributed to Shakespeare.

Baro, Bonaventure. Obsidio et Expugnatio Arcis Duncannon in Hibernia sub Thoma Prestono. (1660.)

— Peter, D.D. In Jonam Prophetam Prælectiones xxxix: Conciones tres ad Clerum Cantabrigiensum, habitæ in Templo B. Mariæ: Theses publicæ in Scholis peroratæ et disputatæ: Precationes quibus usus est Author in suis Prælectionibus inchoandis et finiendis. Lond. 1579. folio. 12s.

Baronis, Petri. Stempani de Præstantia et Dignitate Divinæ Legis, Libri duo. Adjectus est alius Tractatus eiusdem Authoris. Lond. ex Officina H. Middeltoni. 8vo.

— De Fide, ejusque Ortu et Natura, plana ac dilucida Explicatio. Adjecta sunt alia quedam ejusdem authoris de eodem Argumento. Lond. apud Rich. Dayum, 1580. 16mo.

— Treatise of God's Prouidence and of Comforts against all kinds of Crosses, &c. Englished by John L. (udham). Lond. by John Wolfe, 1590. 8vo. pp. 541.

Also without date by the same printer. Inglis, 66, 10s. 6d.

A life of this learned divine, with a list of his works, will be found in Wood's Fasti, edited by Dr. Bliss, 1, 203-4.

BARON, Richard. *See* Cordial for low spirits. Pillars of Priestcraft and Orthodoxy shaken.

— Robert, of Aberdeen. Philosophiæ Theologiæ Ancillans, seu Explicatio Questionum Philosophiarum in Dispp. Theologicis occurrentium. Andreap. 1621. 8vo. 12s.

In Watt's Bibliotheca Britannica will be found several other rare pieces by this author, printed at Aberdeen.

— Robert, of Grays Inn. Mirza, a Tragedie' really acted at Persia, in the last Age, illustrated with historicall Annotations. Lond. 8vo.

A—8 (4) in eights. According to Warton, a copy of Jonson's Catiline. Rhodes, 516, 5s. 6d. Bindley, pt. iii. 57, 7s. Bindley, pt. ii. 1969, 13s. 6d.

— EPOTOΠAIΓNION, or the Cyprian Academy. Lond. 1647. 8vo.

Contains pp. 61, also title, dedication to James Howell, to the Ladies and Gentlewomen of England, and complimentary verses, 12 leaves. Prefixed is a frontispiece, also a portrait by Marshall. According to Warton, a sort of poetical romance, formed on the plan of Sidney's Arcadia. Saunders in 1818, 6*l.* 16s. 6d. Bibl. Anglo-Poet. 32, 10*l.* Some copies are dated 1648. Grave, 8, 2*l.* 4s. Nassau, pt. i. 121, (and Mirza) 2*l.* 15s. Bindley, pt. i. 456, 3*l.* 5s. Towneley, pt. ii. 547, 3*l.* 10s. Bright, 2*l.* 2s. Midgley, 4*l.* 4s. Perry, port. and front. 2*l.* 15s. Copies wanting front. and portrait have been sold for 7s. or 8s.

BARON, Robert. Apologie for Paris for rejecting of Juno and Pallas, and presenting of Ates Golden Ball to Venus. With a Discussion of the Reasons that might induce him to favour either of the three. Lond. 1649. 16mo. 15s.

Contains A to G, in eights. (A 1 blank.) Written by the author when eighteen years of age. Sotheby, June, 1856, 1*l.*

— Po^{c}ul^a Castalia. The Author's Motto. Fortune's Tennis-Ball. Eliza. Poems. Epigrams, &c. by R. B. Gent. Lond. 1650. 8vo.

Contains pp. 156, with port. 'Ætat. suæ 17,' by Marshall. Nassau, pt. i. 122, 1*l.* 12s. White Knights, pt. i. 305, 2*l.* 2s. Bibl. Anglo-Poet. 33, 2*l.* 2s. Midgley, 4*l.* 4s.
The imitations, or rather open plagiarisms of this writer are given in the appendix to Todd's edition of Milton's Poetical works.

— Ste$_p$hen. Sermones declamati corā a$_p$lm$_a^p$ Vniuersitate Cātibrigiēsi per venerandum Patrem Fratrem Stephanum Baronis Fratrum Minorum de Obseruātia Nūcupatoru, &c. Tractatulus de Regimine Principū. Lond. per Wynandum [de Worde.] 4to.

Black letter. To G iiij in octaves; the latter tract B 8, both in double columns. Bindley, pt.¹. 875, 1*l.* 5s. Inglis, 67, 1*l.* 19s. Likewise printed at Paris in 12mo.

. Baronetage, The English, 1741. See Wotton, Thomas.

Baronetage of England. See Collins, Arthur.

Baronetage of England, A new. Lond. 1769. 12mo. 3 vols. 10s. 6d.
Published by J. Almon.

Baronetage of England, The new. Lond. 1804. 12mo. 2 vols. with plates by F. Adolpho.
Edited by the Rev. W. Betham.

Baronets. 1. His Majesties Commission touching the Creation of Baronets; whereunto are annexed divers instructions, &c. Lond. 1611.
—2. The Decree and Establishment of the King's Maiestie, upon a Controuersie of Precedence, &c. Lond. 1612.—3. Three Patents concerning the honovrable Degree and Dignitie of Baronets, (pp. 39.) Lond. 1617. 4to. Three Tracts.

Copies are in the British Museum. Gordonstoun, 1277, (Nos. 1 and 3.) 1*l.* 1s. No. 3 is reprinted in the second volume of the Somers Collection of Tracts.

— A Catalogue of the Baronets of this kingdom of England, from the first erection of that Dignity until the 4th of July, 1681, inclusive. Lond. 1681. 12mo.

Contains pp. 148, and 8 pages added in continuation of the catalogue to 1696. Compiled from the Docquet books of the patents.

BARONIUS, Annales Ecclesiastici —A new Essay towards a true Ecclesiastical History, which may serve as a Key to the Annals of Baronius. 4to.

A copy is in the British Museum.

BARRET, Rev. B. Life of Cardinal Ximenes. Lond. 1813. 8vo. 9s.

— Phineas. Tables of the several European Exchanges, &c. Lond. 1772. 4to. 1*l.* 1s.

— Robert. Theorike and Practike of Modern Warres, discoursed in Dialoguewise. Lond. 1598. folio.

Mr. George Chalmers says that Shakespeare evidently alludes to this work in his All's Well that ends Well. Gordonstoun, 282, 13s.

BARRETT, Francis. Magus, or Celestial Intelligencer, being a complete System of occult Philosophy. Lond. 1801. 4to. with engravings, 2*l.* 12s. 6d.

This professor, as he styles himself, of Chemistry, Natural and Occult Philosophy, &c. published Lives of Alchemistical Philosophers, 1815. 8vo. 6s.

— William. History and Anti-

quities of the City of Bristol. Bristol, 1789, 4to.
'A motly compound of real and supposititious history.'—*Park.* Contains pp. xix. and 704, with 31 plates. Nassau, pt. i. 381. 1*l.* 3s. Heath, 4702, 1*l.* 11s. Dent, pt. i. 814, russia, 1*l.* 18s. M. of Townshend, 350, 2*l.* Beckford, 1817, 47, russia, 2*l.* 4s.

— John, D.D. Essay on the earlier part of the Life of Swift. To which are subjoined various Pieces ascribed to Swift, two of his original Letters, and extracts from his Remarks on Bp. Burnett's History. Lond. 1808. 8vo. pp. 232, 5s.
This work is incorporated in Nichols' Edition of Swift. Fonthill, 1661, 9s.

BARRETTO, Joseph, Jun. Dictionary of the Persian and Arabic Languages. Calcutta, 1804. 8vo. 2 vols. 2*l.* 12s. 6d.

— Shums-ool-Loghat; or a Dictionary of the Persian and Arabic Languages, the interpretation being in Persian: compiled by learned Natives, under the inspection of Joseph Barretto, Jun. Calcutta, 1806. 4to. 2 vols. 4*l.* 4s.

BARRETIER. An Account of the Life of John Philip Barretier, who was Master of five Languages at the Age of nine years. Lond. 1744. 8vo. 3s. 6d.

BARREY, Lodowick. Ram-Alley: or Merrie Trickes: a Comedy diuers Times here-to-fore acted by the Children of the King's Reuels. Lond. 1611. 4to.
Reprinted in Dodsley's Collection of Old Plays. Roxburghe, 4422, 8s. 6d. Rhodes, 519, 10s. 6d. Edition, 1635.—Rhodes, 521, 2s.—1639. Bindley, pt. i. 1090, 8s. Farmer, 1*l.* 9s.

Barri or Borri, Christophoro. Cochinchina, containing many admirable Rarities and Singularities of that Countrey, extracted out of an Italian Relation, by Rob. Ashley. Lond. 1633. 4to.
Gordonstoun, 381, 1*l.* Bindley, pt. i. 334, 1*l.* 6s. North, pt. iii. 601, 1*l.* 18s. Reprinted in the second volume of the Churchill Collection of Voyages and Travels.

BARRI, Giacomo. Painter's Voyage to Italy, in which all the famous Paintings and the most eminent Masters are particularized (translated by W. Lodge). Lond. 1679. 8vo.
A curious work, with front. and portraits of artists, etched by the translator. A copy is in the British Museum. Roscoe, 1680. 1*l.* 2s.

BARRI, or BARRY, Girald, Bishop of St. David's. *Vide* GIRALDUS Cambrensis.

BARRIFFE, William. Militarie Discipline; or, the Young Artillery Man. The fourth Edition, newly revised and enlarged by Lieut. Col. Wm. Barriffe. Lond. 1643. 4to.
Contains A—X in fours, and Y 2 leaves, with a portrait of Barriff, 'Ætatis suæ 42,' and a plate of arms, 'Armæ Pacis Fvlcra.' Edition, 1635, Bindley, pt. i. 1107, with port. by Glover, 1*l.* 9s.

— Mars, his Trivmph: or the Description of an Exercise performed the xviii of October, 1638, in Merchant Taylors' Hall, by certain Gentlemen of the Artillery Garden, London. Lond. by J. L. 1639. 4to. 5s.
Contains 28 leaves.

BARRINGTON, Hon. Daines. Miscellanies. (History of the Gwydir Family, by Sir J. Wynne, &c.) Lond. 1781. 4to. 12s.

— Observations on the more ancient Statutes. 5th edition. Lond. 1795. 4to.
A valuable work, with a commentary, of which an excellent notice will be found in the Retrosp. Review, ix. 250—63. The former editions 1766, 1767, 1769, 1775.

— Possibility of approaching the North Pole asserted, with an Appendix, by Col. Beaufoy. Lond. 1818. 8vo. with a map, 5s.
First published in the year 1775, and reprinted in his volume of Miscellanies. They caused the memorable voyage undertaken by Captain Phipps, afterwards Lord Mulgrave. Several papers by this writer will be found in the Archæologia.

— George. Account of a Voyage to, with the History of New South Wales. To which is prefixed a detail of his Life, Trials, Speeches, &c. Lond. 1810. 8vo. 2 vols. with plates.

A work of no authority though frequently printed. Fonthill, 2827, 2828. Voyage, 1795, 10s. 6d. Sequel, 1800, 9s.

BARRINGTON, Sir Jonah. Historic Anecdotes, and secret Memoirs relative to the legislative Union between Great Britain and Ireland. Lond. 1809-15. 4to. five parts. [In 2 vols. royal 4to. *New Titles*, 1835, with 40 portraits, 2*l*. 2s.]
Originally published in demy 4to. at 1*l*. 1s. and in royal 4to. at 2*l*. 2s. each part.

— Personal Sketches of his own Times. Lond. 1827-30. 8vo. 3 vols. 1*l*. 16s.

— John Shute, Lord. Miscellanea Sacra: a new Edition, with large Additions and Corrections. Lond. 1770. 8vo. 3 vols. 15s.
Best edition of a valuable work published by the author's son, the Bishop of Durham. The first edition was published anonymously in 1725, 8vo 2 vols.

— Shute, Bishop of Durham. Sermons, Charges, and Tracts, now first collected. Lond. 1811. 8vo. 9s.

— Political Life of William Wildman, Viscount Barrington, compiled from original Papers. By his brother, Shute, Bishop of Durham. Lond. 1814. 4to. 100 copies, P.P.
Edited by Sir Thomas Bernard. Duke of York, 493, morocco, 1*l*. 11s. An edition 1815. 8vo. printed for sale, 5s.

Barrister, The: or Strictures on the Education proper for the Bar. Lond. 1792. 12mo. 2 vols. 5s.
The greater part of these volumes appeared in the newspaper called 'The World.' Reprinted 1818.

BARRON, William. Lectures on Belles Lettres and Logic. Lond. 1806. 8vo. 2 vols. 10s. 6d.
A valuable work for the student.

BARROS, T. F. W. Atlantic Neptune. Lond. 1780. folio. 2 vols. charts.

BARROW, Isaac, D.D. Works published by Archbishop Tillotson. Lond. 1683-7. folio, 4 vols. with portrait.
Vol. IV. contains Opuscula Latina. Sotheby in 1824, 3 vols. 1*l* 14s. Drury, 597, 3 vols. date 1687-92, russia, 4*l*.

— Works, published by Archbishop Tillotson. Lond. 1716. folio, 3 vols. portrait.
Roxburghe, 490, 1*l*. 16s. Williams, 117, 3*l*. 12s.

— Works, published by Archbishop Tillotson. Lond. 1722. folio, 3 vols. portrait.
Williams, 118, uncut, 3*l*. 8s. Williams, 1724, morocco, 7*l*.—LARGE PAPER. Williams, 119, morocco, 15*l*.

— Works, published by Archbishop Tillotson. Lond. 1741. folio, 3 vols. in 2, portrait, 3*l*. 3s.
The best folio edition. Heath, 853, 2*l*.10s. Bishop of Ely, 230, 2*l*. 15s. Nassau, pt. i. 218, 8*l*. 3s. Marquis of Townsend, 217, 3*l*. 13s. 6d.

— Sermons. Edinb. 1751. 12mo. 6 vols. 2*l*. 2s.
Hollis, 62, 3*l*. 6s.

— Theological Works. Oxford, 1818. 8vo. 6 vols. 2*l*. 17s. [New edition, 8 vols. 8vo. Ox. 1830, 3*l*.17s. 6d.]

— Twenty-two Sermons, selected from the Works of the Rev. Isaac Barrow. Oxford, 1798. 8vo. [New edition, 2 vols. 8vo. Ox. 1830, 17s.]

— Mathematical Lectures, translated by J. Kirkby. Lond. 1734. 8vo. 5s.

— Geometrical Lectures, translated by E. Stone. Lond. 1735. 8vo. 5s.
Lect. Opt. et Geom. 4to. 1674. Roxburghe, Sup. 158, 5s. 6d.
'Barrow had the clearest head with which mathematics ever endowed an individual, and one of the purest and most unsophisticated hearts that ever beat in the human breast.'—*Dr. Dibdin.*

— John. Collection of authentic, useful, and entertaining Voyages and Discoveries, digested in a chronological series. Lond. 1765. 12mo. 3 vols.
This work was translated into French by M. Targe.

— Account of Travels into the Interior of Southern Africa, in the Years 1797 and 1798. Lond. 1801-4. 4to. 2 vols. [Second edition, to which are added 8 coloured plates by Daniell, 2 vols. 4to. 1806. 1*l*. 1s.]
Highly valuable for their variety and extent of information, both political and

scientific. Vol. i. pp. 420, with a map. Vol. ii. pp. 452, with engravings. Gough, 626, 1l. 13s. Fonthill, 342, 1l. 13s. Roxburghe, 7334, 1l. 17s. Earl of Kerry, 195, 2l. 9s. Strettell, 354, 2l. 10s. Fonthill, 242, 2l. 15s. Drury, 377, with coloured plates, 4l. 4s.

BARROW, John, Travels in China. Lond. 1804. 4to.

Contains pp. 622, with engravings. This celebrated traveller was one of the suite to the embassy of the Earl of Macartney. Gough, 627, 1l. 11s. 6d. Strettell, 355, 1l. 12s. Earl of Kerry, 196, 2l. 3s. Drury, 375, 2l. 5s.

— Voyage to Cochin China, in the Years 1792 and 1793: to which is annexed an Account of a Journey made in the Years 1801 and 1802 to the residence of the Chief of the Booshuana Nation. Lond. 1806. 4to.

Perhaps the most valuable of all Mr. Barrow's travels, as it relates to a country not previously known, except by the account of the missionaries. Contains pp. 450, with 21 engravings by Medland, coloured after the original drawings by Alexander and Daniel. Bindley, pt. i. 560, 1l. 8s. Strettell, 347, 1l. 17s. Drury, 376, 2l. 16s. Earl of Kerry, 197, 3l. 17s. In 1809, a pretended French translation by Malte Brun appeared, in which the text of Barrow was completely perverted and corrupted.

— Some Account of the public Life, and a Selection from the unpublished Writings of the Earl of Macartney. The latter consisting of Extracts from an Account of the Russian Empire: a Sketch of the political History of Ireland; and a Journal of an Embassy from the King of Great Britain to the Emperor of China: with an Appendix to each volume. Lond. 1807. 4to. 2 vols. 1l. 1s.

This work forms an excellent accompaniment to Sir G. Staunton's account of Lord Macartney's embassy to China. According to the Quarterly Review, the 'short sketch relating to Russia contains more information than is to be met with in many 4to. volumes.' Bindley, pt. i. 561, 1l. Drury, 378, 1l. 18s.

— Chronological History of Voyages into the Polar Regions. To which are added a Narrative of Captain Buchan's Expedition into the interior of Newfoundland, and a Relation of the discovery of the Strait of Anian, made by Captain L. F. Maldonado, in the year 1588, with an original map of the Arctic Regions. Lond. 1818. 8vo.

Several articles by this writer on the possibility of a North-West Passage, have appeared in the Quarterly Review. Drury, 408, 11s.

BARROWE, Henry. Brief Discoverie of the false Church. As is the Mother such the Daughter is. 1590. 4to. 6s.

Contains 268 pages. Reprinted in 1707. In the British Museum is 'Mr. Henry Barrowe's Platforme,' 1593. 8vo.

BARRUEL, L'Abbé. Memoires pour servir a l'Histoire du Jacobinisme. Lond. 1797-8. 8vo. 4 vols.

A translation by the Hon. Robert Clifford appeared 1798, 8vo. 4 vols. Earl of Kerry, 32, 1l. 1s. Williams, 147, 1l. 10s. An abridgment was likewise published in 8vo. 1 vol.

BARRY, Sir Edward, Bart. Observations on the Wines of the Ancients. Lond. 1775. 4to. 15s.

The substance of this work will be found in Dr. Alex. Henderson's History of Wines, [and more practically in Redding's History of Wines.] Drury, 534, 18s. 6d. Bindley, pt. i. 927, 1l. 1s. Dent. pt. i. 311, 1l. 18s. Fonthill, 1256, 2l. 2s.

— George, D.D. History of the Orkney Islands. Second Edition, by the Rev. James Headrick. Edinburgh, 1808. 4to. with a map and 12 plates, 18s.

The former edition of this highly valuable work appeared at Edinb. 1805, 4to. The additions are of very little moment.

— Captaine Gerat. Discourse of Military Discipline, divided into three Boockes. Bruxells, 1634. small folio. 15s.

This singular and extremely curious work is not noticed by Grose in his history of the English army. Contains pp. 211, exclusive of dedication, &c. There is also an engraved title-page, containing the arms of the Barry family, &c.

— Bishop of Saint David's, Girald. Vide GIRALDUS Cambrensis.

— James. Works of James Barry, Esq., Historical Painter: with some account of his Life and

Writings. Edited by Dr. Fryer. Lond. 1809. 4to. 2 vols.
Bindley, pt. i. 733, 1l. 5s. Duke of York, 499, 2l. 5s.

BARSTON, John. Safeguard of Societe: describing the Institution of Lawes, and Policies to preserue euery Felowship of People by Degrees of Ciuil Gouernmente. Lond. 1576. 16mo.

BARTAS. *Vide* DU BARTAS.

BARTELL, Edmund, Jun. Cromer considered as a Watering Place. The second Edition, much enlarged. Lond. 1806. 8vo.
Contains pp. xiv. and 124, with 3 plates. Fonthill, 797, 16s. The first edition was printed at Holt in 1800.

—— Hints for Picturesque Improvements in Ornamental Cottages, and their Scenery; including some observations on the Labourer and his Cottage. Illustrated by Sketches. Lond. 1804. royal 8vo. 10s. 6d.

Barthelemy, Abbé. Reflections on the ancient Alphabet and Language of Palmyra. Lond. 1755. folio, with plates, 3s. 6d.
Printed on imperial paper, in order to bind up with Wood's Ruins of Palmyra.

—— Travels of Anacharsis the Younger in Greece, during the Middle of the fourth century before the Christian Æra: translated from the French [by Wm. Beaumont.] Lond. 1791. 8vo. 7 vols. with a volume in 4to. containing maps, plates, views and coins.
A faithful and elegant translation of a most interesting work. Hollis. 68, 2l. 12s. An edition 1807, 8vo. 7 vols. and 4to. atlas—another 1817, 8vo. 6 vols. and atlas in 4to.—1796, 8vo. 3 vols. and atlas. Drury, 409, 16s. An abridgment 1797, 8vo. 1 vol.

—— Travels in Italy, with an Appendix, containing several Pieces by the Abbé Winkelmann, Father Jacquier, the Abbé Zarillo, and other learned men. Translated from the French. Lond. 1802. 8vo. pp. 420. 8s.
A highly interesting and attractive volume of travels.

BARTHLET, John. Pedegrewe of Heretiques. Wherein is truely and plainely set out, the first Roote of Heretiques begon in the Church since the Time and Passage of the Gospell, together with an Example of the Ofspring of the same. Lond. by Henry Denham, 1566. 4to.
Black letter. 90 leaves, besides title, epistle to the Earl of Leicester, and Latin verses, 4 leaves. Opposite the title of this curious work is a folio wood-cut of a tree, representing the errors, crimes and fanaticism of the Church of Rome. Sotheby, 1853, 1l. 11s. In a recent catalogue it is marked at 5l. 5s.

BARTHOLOMÆUS Anglicus. *Vide* GLANVILLA.

Bartholomew. The Ordre of the Hospital of S. Bartholomews in Westsmythfielde in London. Lond. by R. Grafton, 1552. 16mo. Black letter.
Contains A—J, in eights. Sir M. M. Sykes, pt. ii. 579, 3l. 5s. Reprinted the following year. [And again, a fac-simile, about 1750, but under the original date, 7s.]

—— Orders and Ordinances for the Government of Bartholomew Hospitall, Orders for Orphan's Portions, &c. with Discourse of the laudable Customs of London. Lond. 1652. 4to. 5s.
Contains pp. 82, including the title and preface.

Bartholomew Faire, or Variety of Fancies, where you may finde a Faire of Wares, and al to please the Minde. Lond. 1641. 4to. with wood cut on title.
This tract was reprinted about 1816, 2s. 6d. The original, King and Lochée's in March, 1810. 1l. 7s.

—— Bartholomew Faire, with the severall Enormities and Misdemeanors, which are there seene and acted. Lond. 1641. 4to.
Nassau, pt. i. 389, 11s.

—— A Bartholomew Fairing, new, new, new, &c. Lond. 1649. 4to.
A mere party pamphlet, in five short acts, never performed. Bindley, pt. i. 1091, 2l. In the British Museum are several other tracts with the title of Bartholomew Fair, most of which have a political tendency.

BARTLETT, Benjamin. Mandu-essedum Romanorum: being the History and Antiquities of the Parish of Manceter (including the Hamlets of Hartshill, Oldbury, and Atherstone) and also of the adjacent Parish of Ansley in the County of Warwick. Lond. 1791. 4to.
This volume forms the first portion of the continuation of Nichols' Bibliotheca Topog. Britannica.

— On the Episcopal Coins of Durham. Newcastle, 1817. 8vo. 5s. 6d.
One hundred and five copies printed. Brockett, 2170.

— Episcopal Coins of Durham, and Monastic Coins of Reading. Darlington.
Brockett, 229, 1l. 11s. 6d. [This tract was first printed in the Archæologia, vol. 5.]

BARTOLOMEO, Fra. Paol. da San. Voyage to the East Indies, with Notes and Illustrations by John Reinhold Forster, LL.D. Lond. 1802. 8vo. 6s.
There are few works which throw more light than this does on the religious antiquities of India. Bartolomeo resided there thirteen years, viz. 1776—89. Fonthill, 2891, 1l. 1s.

BARTOLUS, P. Daniel. The Learned Monk defended and reformed. In two parts. Translated from the Italian by Tho. Salusbury. Lond. 1660. 8vo.
A curious work, with a frontispiece containing the arms of Salusbury quartered with those of Clement, and portrait of the Monk, [rarely found in the book.] Bindley, pt. i. 518, 11s.

BARTON, Benj. Smith, M.D. Fragments of the natural History of Pennsylvania. Philadelphia, 1799. folio. Part i. pp. xviii. and 24.

— Collections for an Essay towards a Materia Medica of the United States. Philadelphia, 1798. 8vo. pp. 49.

— Elements of Botany. Lond. 1804. royal 8vo. 10s.
Contains pp. 344 and 35, with 30 coloured plates. An edition was published at Philadelphia in 1803. 8vo.

— Charles. Elements of Conveyancing, in Theory and Practice. Second Edition, carefully revised, &c. Lond. 1810-22. royal 8vo. 5 vols. 5l.
A highly esteemed work. The former edition, 1802-5, royal 8vo. 6 vols. Brocket, 3523, 1l. 18s. Mr. Barton likewise published 'Historical Treatise of a Suit in Equity,' 1796. 8vo.

— Modern Precedents in Conveyancing, with Explanatory and Practical Notes. 3rd edition, 7 vols. roy. 8vo. 1821.

— Supplement to Modern Precedents, by S. F. T. Wilde, 3 vols. roy. 8vo. 1826.

— Richard. Lectures (6) in Natural Philosophy, designed to be a Foundation for reasoning pertinently upon the Petrifactions, Gems, Chrystals, and Sanative Quality of Lough Neagh in Ireland; and intended to be an Introduction to the Natural History of several Countries contiguous to that Lake. Dublin, 1751. 4to. 15s.
A curious work consisting of 209 pp. besides title, dedication to the learned Universities of Great Britain and Ireland, list of subscribers, the author his friendly address to his countrymen, 12 leaves; also 7 plates (no plate 3, but 2 of 6). Heath, 4786, 2l. 6s.

— Dialogue concerning some Things of Importance to Ireland, particularly to the County of Ardmagh. Some remarks towards a full Description of Upper and Lower Lough Lene, near Killarney. Dublin, 1751. 4to.

— William. View of many Errors and som gross Absurdities in the old translation of the Psalms in English Metre, as also in som other Translations lately published. Lond. 1655. 4to. 6s.
Not noticed in the Athenæ Oxonienses. A copy is in the British Museum, 'A Century of select Hymns.' London, 1659. 12mo. and 'A brief Relation of the Life and Death of William Barton, of Shrewsbury.' Lond. 1664. 12mo. Dr. Cotton, in his List of the various editions of the Bible, notices several editions of Barton's Psalms and Hymns.

— William, P.C., M.D. Vegetable Materia Medica of the United States, or Medical Botany, with coloured engravings. 1821. 4to. 2 vols. 6l. 6s.

BARTON, John. Observations made in his Travels from Pensylvania to Onondago, &c. with an Account of the Cataracts of Niagara, by P. Kalm. Lond. 1751. 8vo. 3s. 6d.

Fonthill, 2784, 10s. Bartram's valuable Journal kept upon a Journey from St. Augustine up the River St. John's, will be found with Stork's Account of East Florida.

— William. Travels through N. and S. Carolina, Georgia, E. and W. Florida, the Cherokee Country, the extensive Territories of the Muscogulges or Creek Confederacy, and the Country of the Chactaws. Philad. or Lond. 1792. 8vo. with plates, 5s.

A most interesting work to lovers of natural history, especially botany. An account of Mr. Bartram will be found in the American Farmer's Letters.

BARTRAM. See BERTRAM.

BARWICK, Edward. Treatise on the Church, chiefly with respect to its Government. Second Edition, considerably enlarged and improved. Lond. 1815. 8vo. 12s.

The former edition appeared at Belfast, in 1813.

— Humfrey. Discourse concerning the Force and Effect of all manual Weapons of Fire, and the Disability of the Long Bowe or Archery, in respect of others of greater force now in use, &c. Lond. for R. Oliffe, 4to.

Written in answer to 'Certain Discourses written by Sir John Smythe, Knt. concerning Weapons,' &c. 1590. Gordonstoun, 233, 18s. 6d.

— Peter. Vita Joh. Barwick, S. T. P. in qua non pauca Arcana Studia pro Regno Britannico, Motibus intestinis collapso, in Lucem proferuntur. Lond. 1721. 8vo. 4s. LARGE PAPER, 7s. 6d.

A work of great interest and amusement, particularly of the period of the restoration of King Charles II. Prefixed are portraits of John and Peter Barwick, by Vertue. An English translation, with notes by Hilkiah Bedford, appeared in 1724. 8vo. 4s. of which there are likewise copies on LARGE PAPER, 7s. 6d. Heath, 4297, 10s. 6d. Williams, 1007, 12s. John Barwick published a Life of Bishop Morton, 1660. 4to. with portrait of Morton, by Faithorne. Williams, 218, russia, 11s.

BAS, William. Sword and Buckler, or serving Man's Defence. Lond. 1602. 4to. Title and 15 leaves.

In six line stanzas. Steevens, 767, 1l. 19s. Sotheby, May 1856 (wanting title), 10l. 10s.

— Great Brittaines summer set bewailed with a shower of tears. A Poem on the Death of Prince Henry, in eight line stanzas, dedicated to Sir R. Wenman. Oxford, 1613. 8vo.

Only four leaves known to exist.

— Three Pastoral Elegies, Lond. 1602. 4to.

Only one copy known, and that is in the Winchester College Library. Bas was the author of an Epitaph on Shakespere, and verses in Walton's Angler.

BASIL, St. the Great. Letter to Gregory Nazaanzen, translated by Richard Sherrie. Lond. by John Day. 16mo.

Black letter. From Maunsell's Catalogue, p. 7.

— Exhortation to his Kinsmen to the Study of the Scriptures, translated by Will. Berker. Impr. by John Cawood, 1557. 8vo.

Black letter.

— Homelye, howe younge Men ought to read Poetes and Oratours. Translated out of Greke. Anno M.D.L.VII. Imprinted by John Cawood. 8vo.

Black letter. A sermon of St. Basil on fasting, is annexed to Cardinal Pole's Treatise on Justification. Lovanii, 1569. And Basil on Solitude, will be found with some tracts of St. Cyprian, 1675. See also BOYD, and STOCKER.

Βασιλικα Δωρα, seu Sylloge Epistolarum, Orationum, et Carminum, regalium, quæ quos Britanniæ Monarchas Authores, quos etiam Editores antehac habuerint, inspicienti statim constabit. Lond. 1640. 8vo. 5s.

Published by Thomas Wykes.

BASILLE, Theodore. *i. e.* Thomas BECON.

Basinello, Triumphs of the Venetian. 1658. 12mo.
Bindley, 1*l.* 10s.

BASINSTOCHIUS, *i. e.* WHITE, R.

BASIRE, Isaac, D.D. Ancient Liberty of the Britannic Church, and the legitimate Exemption thereof from the Roman Patriarchate, discoursed in four Positions. Translated by Richard Watson. Lond. 1661. 8vo. 6s.
The original Latin appeared at Bruges, 1656. 8vo.

BASNAGE, James de Fraquener. History of the Jews from Jesus Christ to the present Time, translated by Thomas Taylor. Lond. 1708. folio. 2*l.* 2s.
Intended as a continuation of Josephus' History. Gough, 243, 18s. Hollis, 231, 1*l.* 10s. Dent, pt i. 323, russia, 1*l.* 14s. An abridgment by Crull, 1708. 8vo. 2 vols.

BASSOMPIERRE, Marshal de. Memoirs of his Embassy to the Court of England in 1626, translated [by J. W. Croker], with Notes [by Sir H. Nicolas.] Lond. 1818. 8vo. 6s.
Notice of these curious and interesting memoirs will be found in the Retrospective Review, xiv. 69—98. Fonthill, 1659, 9s.

BASTARD, Thomas. Chrestoleros. Seven Bookes of Epigrames: written by T. B. Lond. by R. Bradocke, 1598. 12mo.
Contains pp. 184, dedicated to Sir Chas. Blount, Knt. Lord Mountjoy. A copy is in the British Museum, and a notice of it will be found in the Censura Literaria. Steevens, 768, 2*l.* 3s. Perry, pt i. 529, 10*l.* 10s. Bindley, pt. i. 450, 15*l.* 4s. 6d. White Knights, pt i. 312, mor. 17*l.* 17s. Bright, 7*l.* 7s. Ritson mentions an edition with the date of 1584.

— Serenissimo potentissimoque Monarchæ Jacobo Magnæ Britanniæ, Franciæ et Hiberniæ, regi Magnam Britanniam. (Poema) Lond. 1605. 4to.
A copy is in the British Museum. Warton speaks of Bastard as an elegant classic scholar, and better qualified for occasional pointed Latin epigram, than for any sort of English versification. Bright, 1*l.* 1s.

— Sermons. (Five and Twelve.) Lond. 1615. 4to. 2 vols.
For writing a pasquinade entitled Marprelate's Bastardini, to expose the amours in the University and Town of Oxford, Bastard was expelled the University. An account of him will be found in Dr. Bliss's edition of Wood's Athen. Oxon. ii. 227-9.

Bastard, The, a Tragedy. Lond. 1652. 4to. 9s.
Coxeter attributes this play to Cosmo Manuche.

BASTINGIUS, Jeremias. Exposition or Commentarie vpon the Catechisme of Christian Religion, which is taught in the Low Countries, and the Countie Palatine, translated out of Latine into English, with three Tables. Cambridge, 1595. 8vo.
Inglis, 71, 16s. Herbert mentions other editions.

BASTWICK, John, M.D. Letany. 4 parts, Anno 1637. [Secretly printed.] 4to. 10s.
This very singular and once celebrated performance, for which the author was much persecuted, is reprinted in the fifth volume of the Somers Collection of Tracts. An elaborate notice of the work is in the Retrosp. Review, x. 181-98.

— Flagellum Pontificis et Episcoporum Latialium. Lond. 1641. 18mo. with portrait.
For this work, in which the author was supposed to have had the bishops of England in view, Bastwick was thrown into the Gatehouse prison. Bindley, pt. i. 836, 5s. 6d. Bastwick likewise published 'New Discovery of the Prelates Tyranny,' 1641, with his portrait, with four English verses, 10s. 6d. 'The utter Routing the whole Army of Independents and Sectaries.' 1646. with frontispiece by Cross, containing portrait of the author in complete armour. Lloyd, 228, 1*l.*

Batchelor.—The Bacheler's Banquet; or a Banquet for Bachelers: wherein is prepared sundry daintie dishes to furnish their tables, curiously drest, and seriously served in. Pleasantly discoursing the variable humors of women; their quicknesse of wittes, and unsearchable deceits. 1604. 4to.
Black letter, 39 pages. Probably written by Thomas Decker. An edition, 1603,

Roxburghe, 6678, 2*l.* 15s. Nassau, pt. i. 1086, 4*l.* 16s. Reprinted 1660, with a frontispiece.

— Essays from the Batchelor; in Prose and Verse. By the Authors of the Epistle to Gorges Edmond Howard, Esq. Lond. 1773. 12mo. 2 vols. 6s.

A collection of humorous and witty essays, written during Lord Townshend's memorable viceroyalty in Ireland, by Jephson, Courtenay, the Rev. Mr. Boroughs, &c., and originally published at Dublin. The Dublin edition, Reed, 1691, 8s. 6d. Fonthill, 1398, 16s.

BATCHILER, John. Virgin's Pattern: in the exemplary Life and lamented Death of Mrs. Susannah Perwich, of Hackney. Lond. 1661. 12mo.

Prefixed is a portrait of Mrs. Perwich, by T. Cross. Bindley, pt. i. 519, 11s.

BATE, George, M.D. Elenchus Motuum nuperorum in Anglia, simul ac Juris Regii et Parliamentariis brevis Enarratio. Paris, 1649. 12mo. 5s.

A work 'worth reading,' says Bishop Warburton. Reprinted with additions to 1660. Lond. 1661. 8vo.; again with further additions to 1663, 8vo. and with a third part, 1676, 8vo. 4s. It was answered by Rob. Pugh 'Elenchus Elenchi, sive Animadversiones in Elenchum M. Angliæ,' Paris. 1664. 8vo.

— Account of the Rise and Progress of the Troubles in England, translated by A. Lovel. Lond. 1685. 8vo. 3 parts in 1 vol. with a frontispiece, 5s.

Bate in this work is said to lean too much to the side of the Puritans.

— Lives, Actions, and Execution of the prime Actors and principal Contrivers of the horrid Murder of King Charles the First. Lond. 1661. 12mo. 4s.

Not written by the physician Bate, but by 'another far inferior to him in all respects.' Ant. à Wood.

— John. Portraiture of Hypocrisie, liuely and pithilie pictured in her colours. Lond. for John Dalderne, 1589. 16mo.

Black letter. Dedicated to 'Sir Anthonie Therold,' and 'To the Christian Reader,' 192 pages. (182, mispaged 192.) The running title, 'A Dialogue between a Christian and an Atheist.'

— John. Mysteries of Nature and Art in foure severall Parts. 1. Of Water Works. 2. Of Fire Works. 3. Of Drawing, Washing, Limming, Painting, and Engraving. 4. Of sundry Experiments. The second Edition, with many Additions unto every Part. [Lond.] 1635. 4to.

A curious treatise. Title, with engraved border; to the reader, a leaf, then complimentary verses and work A—Qq. in fours. Prefixed is a portrait (scarce) of the author, by G. Gifford, at p. 61 is a separate woodcut representing the horses at work to the engine for a Tyde-water, and at p. 65 another marked D, representing the wheel of an engine. Gordonstoun, 286, 7s. Towneley, pt. i. 400, 1*l.* 5s. The first edition appeared in 1634, and it was reprinted 1638, and in 1654. Roxburghe, 1768, 7s. 6d.

— Julius. Critica Hebræa: or, a Hebrew-English Dictionary, without Points. Lond. 1767. 4to. 1*l.* 5s.

This learned divine of the Hutchinsonian persuasion, published a translation of the Pentateuch, 1783, 'An Hebrew Grammar,' 1751. 8vo. also several valuable tracts chiefly controversial.

BATEMAN, Stephen. Christil Glasse for Christian Reformation. Lond. by John Day. 1569. 4to.

Black letter. A—X 4, with many very curious wood cuts. A copy of this work, which treats on the seven deadly sins, is in the British Museum. An imperfect copy was priced lately in a bookseller's catalogue, 5*l.* 5s.

— Golden Booke of the Leaden Goddes, wherein is described the vayne Imaginations of Heathē Pagans and counterfaict Christians: wyth a Description of their seuerall Tables, what ech of their Pictures signified. Lond. by Thomas Marshe, 1577. 4to.

Dedicated to Lord Henry Cary, Baron of Hunsdon, &c. 72 pages. Shakespeare is supposed to have consulted this book, which may be considered as the first attempt towards a Pantheon, or description of the Heathen Gods. A copy is in the British Museum. Inglis, 148, 11s. Nassau, pt. i. 388, 2*l.* 1s. Bindley, pt. i. 1281, 2*l.* 6s.

— Travayled Pilgreme, bringing

Newes from all Parts of the Worlde, such like scarce harde before. [Lond. by John Denham] 1569. 4to.

Black letter, with 20 wood-cuts. An allegorical-theological romance of the life of man, in verses of 14 syllables, in which are introduced characters and historical incidents relative to the reigns of Henry VIII., Edward VI., Queens Mary and Elizabeth. Sotheby's in April 1821, 29*l*. 18*s*. 6d. resold, Perry, pt. i. 618, 26*l*. 15*s*. 6d.

— Of the Arrivall of the 3 Graces in Anglia, lamenting the Abuses of the present Age. W. Norton. 4to.

Five sheets. Noticed in Herbert's Ames, ii. 882, who also at p. 1021, has the following entry, 'The new Arriual of the three Graces into Anglia, lamenting the Abuses of the present Age,' as printed by Thomas East. 4to.

— Doome warning all Men to Judgement: in maner of a generall Chronicle. Impr. by R. Nubery. 1581. 4to.

Black letter. Contains 437 pages, besides dedication to 'Sir Thomas Bromley, Knt.' 'To the gentle Reader,' commendatory verses, a catalogue of authors, the antiquity of England, and the author's coat of arms, with many cuts of prodigies, monsters, &c. Roxburghe, 491, 9s. and Supplement, 659, 1*l*. 10s. Nassau, pt. i. 389, 2*l*. 16s. Knight, 1847, mor. 2*l*. 2s.

— Joyfull Newes out of Helvetia, from Theophr. Paracelsum, declaring the ruinate Fall of the Papall Dignitie: also a Treatise against Vsurie. By Stephen Batman. Lond. for John Allde, 1575. 8vo.

— Thomas, M.D. Delineations of Cutaneous Diseases, comprised in the Classification of the late Dr. Willan, with a new Series. Lond. 1817. 4to. 12 parts published at 1*l*. 1s. each. [New edition with 72 coloured plates, the colouring superintended by Prof. Carswell, 4to. Lond. Bohn, 1849. 5*l*. 5s.]

This eminent physician published a valuable Synopsis of Cutaneous Diseases, 8th edition, revised by A. T. Thomson, 1836, and other works; and in 1826 appeared some Account of his Life and Character, 8vo. 7s. 6d.

— Atlas of Delineations of Cutaneous Eruptions, illustrative of the 'Practical Synopsis,' by A. Todd Thomson, imp. 8vo. 27 coloured plates. Lond. 1829. 3*l*. 3s.

An abridgment of the previous work.

BATES, Ely. Observations on some important Points of Divinity, chiefly those in Controversy between the Arminians and Calvinists. Extracted from an Author of the 17th century. Second Edition, with Additions. Lond. 1811. 8vo. 6s.

Bates likewise published Rural Philosophy, 1805. Christian Politics, in four parts, 1802—6, and other works.

— G. *See* BATE, George.

— William, D.D. Vitæ selectorum aliquot Virorum, qui Doctrinâ, Dignitate, aut Pietate, inclaruere. Lond. 1681. 4to.

A valuable collection of lives, amounting to thirty-two, mostly taken from scarce tracts. Bp. of Ely, 423, 5s. Heath, 1584, 12s.

— Works, containing some Sermons on the everlasting Rest of the Saints, with a Sermon at his Funeral, by John Howe. Lond. 1700. folio, with portrait by R. White, after Kneller, 1*l*. 1s.

The works of this eminent nonconformist divine were published separately, 1663-99. Another edition of his works, Lond. 1723, folio, with portrait, 1*l*. 5s.

— Works. A new Edition, by the Rev. W. Farmer. Lond. 1815. 8vo. 4 vols. with a portrait, 1*l*. 16s.

Farmer likewise edited an edition of Bates' Harmony of the Divine Attributes, 1815. 8vo. 5s.

BATESON, Thomas. The first and second set of English Madrigalls, to 3, 4, 5, and 6 Voices. Newly composed by Thomas Bateson. Lond. 1604-18. 4to. 2 vols.

See Hawkins' Music, iii. 376. Burney's Music, iii. 347. Bibl. Anglo-Poet. 116.

Bath.—The Manner of Creating the Knights of the Order of the Bath. Lond. 1661. 4to.

Reprinted in the Harleian Miscellany, vol. i. The Statutes of the Order were published 1725, 1744, 1772, 1787, 1812.

— Les Armes des Chevaliers de l'Ordre du Bain, creez le 17me jour de Juin, 1725. J. Sympson, Junr. delin. et sculp. royal fol. 2*l*. 12s. 6d.

A series of one hundred and forty impressions from the plates now fixed at the stalls in Henry VIIth's Chapel, rarely found complete.

Bath.—Plan, Elevations, Sections, and Specimens of the Architecture of the Abbey Church of Bath (10 plates), engraved by James Basire, from Drawings by John Carter. With some Account of the Abbey Church (8 pages). Lond. 1798. atlas folio.
Published by the Society of Antiquaries. North, pt. i. 138, 1l. 18s. Steevens, 1942, 1l. 16s. M. of Townshend, 219, 2l. 5s.

— Bath illustrated by a Series of Views, from the Drawings of John Claude Nattes; with descriptions to each Plate. Lond. 1806. fol.
Published at 7l. 7s. Nassau, pt. i. 220, 1l. 18s. The Views coloured, Duke of York, 3933, 1l. 8s.

— Letters and Papers on Agriculture, Planting, &c. selected from the Correspondence Book of the Society instituted at Bath, for the Encouragement of Agriculture, Arts, Manufactures, and Commerce. Lond. 1780-182—. 8vo. 14 vols.
An abridgment of the first nine volumes appeared in 1808, 8vo. 2 vols.

BATHE, William. Introduction to the true Arte of Musicke. Lond. by Abel Jeffes, 1584. 4to.
Fifth edition, totally different from the following.

— Briefe Introduction to the Skill of Song. Lond. by Thomas Este. 8vo. 1l. 1s.
Rodd, 1824, 3l. 3s. A copy of this edition is in the British Museum. Sir John Hawkins has given extracts from both these productions, but they have little merit.

BATHURST, Ralph, M.D. Life and Literary Remains, by Thomas Warton, M.A. Lond. 1761. 8vo. 5s.

BATMAN. *See* BATEMAN and GLANVILLA.

BATTELY, John. Opera posthuma; viz. Antiquitates Rutupinæ et Antiquitates S. Edmundi Burgi ad annum 1272, perductæ. Oxoniæ, 1745. 4to. with 16 maps and plates, 5s.
An elegant posthumous discourse, says Bishop Nicolson. LARGE PAPER, 8s. Nassau, pt. i. 390, 1l. 14s. A former edition of the Antiquitates Rutupinæ, Oxon. 1711, 8vo. 3s. LARGE PAPER, 5s. Williams, 152, morocco, 18s. An English translation appeared, Lond. 1774, 8vo. 3s.

BATTEUX, Abbé. Course of the Belles Lettres: or, the Principles of Literature, translated from the French. Lond. 1761. 12mo. 4 vols. 9s.
The best edition of the original appeared at Paris, 1774, 8vo. 5 vols.

Battle.—Copye of the Letter following whiche specifyeth of the greatest and meruelous visyoned Batayle, that euer was sene or herde of. And also of the Letter y^t was sent from the great Turke vnto our holy Fad' ye Pope of Rome. Andwarpe by me Johan of Dousborowe. 4to.
Four leaves, without signatures. The former letter was written by Bartholomeus de Clereville, 'in ye castell of ville clere, in ye yere of our lorde m.ccccc.xvij. in the Month of Januarij.' The latter is reprinted in Ames, by Herbert, iii. pp. 1531-2.

— Batayll of Egynge Courte, and the great Sege of Rone. Impr. by John Skot. 4to.
Black letter. 6 leaves.

— The trewe Encountre or Batayle lately don betwene Englade and Scotlande. In whiche Batayle the Scottsshe Kynge was slayne. Empr. by me Richarde Faques. 4to.
Black letter, 4 leaves. White Knights, 1720, 18l. 13s. A reprint of this interesting historical account of the Battle of Flodden Field, in fac-simile, 1809, 4to. 4s. Another reprint, Newcastle, 1822, crown 8vo. 4s. ON VELLUM, six copies printed. Brockett, 472, 1l. 15s.

— Flodden Field, in nine Fits. Lond. 1664. small 8vo.
Steevens, 860, russia, 1l. 8s. Bindley, pt. iii. 1554, 5l. 7s. 6d. Perry, 2l. 15s.

— Famous old Ballad of Flodden Field. York, Tho. Gent. n. d. 12mo.
Nassau, pt. i. 1207, 7s.

— The same, Notes by Jos. Benson, 12mo. Preston, 1773.

— History of the Battle of Flodden, in Verse. Published with Notes by Robert Lambe. Berwick upon Tweed, 1774. 12mo. 4s. LARGE PAPER, 6s.

— Battle of Flodden Field, with

BAT   BAT   131

Notes and Illustrations by Henry Weber. Edinb. 1808. 8vo. 10s.
Best edition. Notes and Illustrations to the Battle of Flodden Field, 8vo. 16 copies printed, 3s. 6d. An edition of the work, Newcastle, 1819. Brockett, 1758, 4s. 6d.

Battle.—Reporte of the Skirmish fought betweene the States of Flaunders and Don Joan, Duke of Austria, with the number of all them that were slayne on both sides, which Battle was fought 1 August, being Lammas Day. Impr. by William Bartlet, 1578. 16mo.
Black letter.

— Dolorous Discourse of a bloudy Battel fought in Barbarie, 4 Aug. 1578. Impr. by Iohn Charlewood for Tho. Man. 16mo.
Black letter. Towneley, pt. i. 344, 1l. 6s. Sir M. M. Sykes, pt. i. 961, 1l. 11s. 6d.

— Discourse of a Battaile fought neere to Cracouia in Pologne, the 25 of December last, betweene Maxamilian, Archduke of Austrich, the Emperours Brother, and Sigismund, Sonne to the King of Sweden, each pretending to be the elect King of Pologne. Translated out of the French. Lond. by Thomas Orwin, 1588. 16mo.
Black letter.

— The Battle of Alcazar, 1594. See Peele, George.

— The Battaile fought betweene Count Maurice and the Archduke of Austria, nere Newport, in Flanders. 1600. 4to.
Black letter, with a plate. Nassau, pt. i. 865.

— Wonderful Battel of Starlings: fought at the City of Cork, in Ireland, the 12th and 14th of October, 1621. Lond. 1622. 4to.
Reprinted in the third number of Morgan's Phœnix Britannicus.

— The great and famous Battle of Lutzen, fought between the renowned King of Sweden and Walstein. Here is also inserted an Abridgment of the King's Life, and Relation of the King of Bohemia's Death, faithfully translated out of the French Copy. Printed 1633. 4to. 7s. 6d.
Contains 45 pages. Reprinted in the fourth volume of the Harleian Miscellany.

— Relation of the Battle of Maxen, with a Treatise on Profiles, the manner of attacking and defending unfortified Heights and Mountains, and positions taken for the defence of Maxen. Translated by an Officer. Lond. 1785. 4to. with plans, 10s. 6d.

— The Battle of Waterloo, also of Ligny and Quatre-Bras, in 1815, illustrated with portraits of Wellington and Blucher, maps and enlarged plans, view of the Field of Waterloo, and 34 etchings from sketches by Capt. Jones. Tenth edition, enlarged and corrected (by John Booth). Lond. 1817. 4to. 4l. 4s. Best edit.
Many of the particulars in this valuable account were furnished by regimental messes, and commanding officers of particular arms of the service, besides all public accounts, both English and Foreign, and communications of privates and non-commissioned officers. At the end is a list of the officers engaged, furnished by authority. INDIA PAPER PROOFS, 5l. 5s.

Battels, All the famous, that have been fought in our age, throughout the Worlde, as well by Sea as Lande. Lond. by Henrye Bynneman. 4to.
Black letter. Written by John Polmon. Reed, 3315, 1l. 5s. Towneley, pt. i. 308, 5l.

— Second Part of the Booke of Battailes, fought in our Age; taken out of the best Authors, and Writers in sundrie Languages. Lond. for Gabriel Cawood, 1587. 4to.
Black letter. A copy is in the British Museum. Inglis, 150, (with the former article,) 1l. 5s.

— The two famous pitcht Battells of Lypsich and Lutzen, with an Elegie upon the Death of Gustavus the Great, composed in heroick verse by John Russell. Cambridge, 1634. 4to. 18s.

BATTY (Barth. of Alost.) Christian

K 2

Man's Closet, the Dutie of Parentes towards their Children, and of Children towards their Parentes. Englished by W. Lowth. By Thomas Dawson and Gregoir Seton, 1581.
Black letter, interspersed with poetry. Sotheby, June 1856, 1l. 12s.

BATTY, Captain. Campaign of the left Wing of the Allied Army in the Western Pyrenees and South of France in the years 1813-14, under Field Marshal the Marquis of Wellington. Lond. 1823. 4to. 2l.
Contains pp. 185, with a plan and plates drawn and etched by Captain Batty. For the other publications of this gentleman, see Scenery.

BAUDIER, Mich. History of the Calamities of Margaret of Anjou, Queen of England. Lond. 1737. 8vo. 5s.
A valuable work, with a preface by the eminent English historian Thomas Carte. The work under the above title, 1755, 12mo. 2 vols. is a translation of the fictitious narrative written by the Abbé Prevost.

BAUDIUS, Dominicus. Monvmentum consecratum Honori et Memoriæ seren. Britanniarum Principis Henrici Frederici. Lugd. Bat. 1612. 4to.
A copy is in the British Museum.

BAUDWIN or BAULDWIN. See BALDWIN.

BAUER, Francis, F.R.S. Delineations of exotick Plants cultivated in the Royal Garden at Kew, drawn and coloured, and the characters displayed according to the Linnæan System. Lond. 1796. folio.
Nos. I. and II., with 20 coloured plates, published by W. T. Aiton.

— Illustrationes Floræ Novæ Hollandæ sive Icones Generum quæ in Prodromo Floræ Nov. Hol. et Insulæ Van-Diemen, descripsit Rob. Brown, 1813. pars I. [See BROWN.]

Bawd.—The London Bawd, with her Character and Life : discovering the various and subtile Intrigues of lewd Women. Lond. 1711. 12mo. 10s. 6d.

BAXTER, Andrew. Inquiry into the Nature of the Human Soul, wherein its Immateriality is evinced from the Principles of Reason and Philosophy. Lond. 1745, 8vo. 2 vols. Appendix, 1750. 1 vol. 16s.
Third and best edition. The appendix is of rare occurrence.
'He who would see the justest and precisest notions of God, and the soul, may read this book; one of the most finished of the kind, in my humble opinion, that the present times, greatly advanced in true philosophy, have produced.'—BISHOP WARBURTON.

— Matho, or the Cosmotheoria Puerilis, in ten Dialogues ; wherein from the Phenomena of the Material World, briefly explained, the Principles of Natural Religion are deduced and demonstrated. Lond. 1745. 8vo. 2 vols. 6s.
This work was originally published in Latin, 1740, 8vo. 2 vols. 3s. The third edition 'corrected and enlarged,' was published 1765, 12mo. 2 vols. 6s. Another, 'accommodated to the capacities and instruction of the youth of both sexes,' by Samuel Whyte, Dublin, 1776, 12mo. 2 vols. 6s. Another work of this author's was published from his MSS. by the Rev. Dr. Duncan of South Warnborough, entitled 'The Evidence of Reason in Proof of the Immortality of the Soul,' 1779, 8vo. Gosset, 354, 8s. 6d.

— Richard. Practical Works. Lond. 1707. folio, 4 vols. with front. and portrait, 10l. 10s.
A rich treasure of controversial, casuistical, positive, and practical divinity. Williams, 121, russia, 21l.

— Works. A new edition, with a Life of the Author by the Rev. W. Orme, 23 vols. 8vo. Lond. 1827—1830. 10l. 10s.

— PRACTICAL WORKS, with an Essay on his Genius, Works, and Times. 4 vols. imp. 8vo. Lond. Bohn, 1838. 2l. 12s. 6d. [Frequently reprinted.]

Saint's Everlasting Rest, Lond. 1653, 4to. with front. 10s. Frequently reprinted.
Confession of Faith, 1655. 4to. 6s.
Reformed Pastor, 1656, 8vo. 5s. Reprinted 1657, 1825.
Reasons of the Christian Religion, 1667, 4to. portrait, with eight English verses, 9s.
Life of Faith, 1670, 4to. front. and port. by White, 10s. 6d. Reprinted 1806, 1817.

Christian Directory, 1675, folio, with port. and frontispiece, 1*l.* 8s. An abridgment by Adam Clarke. Liverpool, 1802, 8vo. 2 vols. 10s.

Breviate of the life of Margaret, wife of Richard Baxter, 1681, 4to. Bindley, pt. ii. 2518, 1*l.* 7s. Bright, 1*l.* 12s.

Treatise of Episcopacy, 1681, 4to. 9s

Paraphrase on the New Testament, 1685, 8vo. with portrait, 6s. Reprinted 1695, 1810.

Catholick Theologie, 1675, folio, with portrait, 15s.

Church History of the Government of Bishops, and their Councils abbreviated, 1680, 4to. 6s. Bindley, pt. 1. 918, 12s.

Poetical Fragments, 1681, small 8vo. pp. 150. Nassau, pt. 1. 129, 4s. Bibl. Anglo. Poet. 66, 3*l.* 3s. Reprinted 1821, 12mo. 4s.

Methodus Theologiæ Christianæ, 1681, folio, with portrait, 15s.

Certainty of the World of Spirits, 1691, 8vo. 3s. A notice of this work will be found in the Retrosp. Rev. v. 87–186.

A copious list of the works of this eminent nonconformist divine will be found in Watt's Bibliotheca Britannica.

— Reliquiæ Baxterianæ. A Narrative of his Life and Times, published by Matthew Sylvester. Lond. 1696. folio, with portrait by R. White, 1*l.* 16s.

The life extracted from this narrative is reprinted in the fifth volume of Wordsworth's Ecclesiastical Biography.

— Abridgment of Baxter's History of his Life and Times, and an Account of the Ministers, &c. ejected after the Restauration, by Edm. Calamy, D.D. with the Continuation. Lond. 1713, 27. 8vo. 4 vols. 1*l.* 16s.

Replete with much useful matter, and many valuable particulars of the history of the times of Charles I. In this second edition of 1713, Baxter's reformed liturgy is inserted.

Calamy, in answer to some objections made to this work, published 'A Defence of moderate Nonconformity, in answer to the Reflections of Ollyffe and Hoadly.' Lond. 1703, 4, 5. 8vo. 3 vols. 12s.

— Thomas. Illustrations of the Egyptian, Grecian, and Roman Costume, in 40 outlines, selected, drawn, and engraved by T. Baxter. Lond. 1810. imp. 8vo.

An edition in 4to. Fonthill, 692, 15s.

— Will. Glossarium Antiquitatum Britannicarum, accedunt Edv. Luidii de Fluviorum, Montium, Urbium, &c. in Britannia Nominibus, Adversaria posthuma. Lond. 1733. 8vo. with portrait by Vertue, 6s. LARGE PAPER, 12s.

A 'curious' work, according to Bp. Nicolson. The first edition, consisting of 350 copies, appeared in 1719, 8vo. 4s. LARGE PAPER. Dent, pt. ii. 193, morocco, 15s. White Knights, pt. 1. 318, russia, 1*l.* Nassau, pt. 1. 130, (with the Reliq. Baxter, 1726) russia, 2*l.* 5s.

— Glossarium Antiquitatum Romanarum, (edente Mos. Williams). Lond. 1731. 8vo. with portrait by Vertue, 4s.

Of this work 250 copies on small, and 120 on large paper, were printed. Some are entitled Reliquiæ Baxterianæ, 1726. LARGE PAPER, 10s. 6d. Heath, 4315, 2*l.*

In some copies will be found ' A View of a Book, entitled Reliquiæ Baxterianæ. In a Letter to a Friend.' Written by Wm. Bowyer, and reprinted in the first volume of Nichols' Liter. Anecd.

BAYARD. The right joyous and pleasant History of the Feats, Gests, and Prowesses of the Chevalier Bayard, the good Knight without Fear and without Reproach. By the Loyal Servant. Lond. 1825. small 8vo. 2 vols. 16s.

An excellent translation (by Miss Coleridge) of a work curious in itself, and in its whole tendency unexceptionably good.

BAYFIELD, Robert. Enchiridion Medicum. Lond. 1655. 8vo. with a portrait, 'Æt. 27,' by Faithorne.

The portrait, for which this work alone is esteemed, was prefixed to the author's subsequent works. Grave, No. 11, 14s.

BAYLE, Peter. Dictionary, Historical and Critical. Lond. 1710. folio, 4 vols. 3*l.* 3s.

'Bayle's Dictionary is a very useful work for those to consult who love the biographical part of literature, which is what I love most.'—DR. JOHNSON.

Marquis of Townshend, 400, 1*l.* 16s. LARGE PAPER, Roxburghe, 9275, 3*l.* 9s. Boswell, 337, 8*l.* 10s.

— The second Edition, carefully collated, &c. To which is prefixed a Life of the Author, by Des Maizeaux. Lond. 1734-7. folio, 5 vols. with port. by James Smith. 6*l.* 6s.

Marq. of Townshend, 401, 4*l.* 7s. Bindley, pt. 1. 375, 4*l.* 10s. Horne Tooke, 43

5*l.* 10s. Sir P. Thompson, 160, 7*l.* 10s. LARGE PAPER, in 10 vols. Dent, pt. i. 324,7*l.* This much-esteemed work is included in 'A General Dictionary Historical and Critical.' Lond. 1734–41, folio, 10 vols. An abridgment in 12mo. 4 vols. appeared in 1826.

— Commentary on these words of the Gospel, Luke xiv. 23, 'Compel them to come in, that my House may be full.' In four Parts. Lond. 1708. 8vo. 2 vols. 6s.

A very shrewd exposure of the folly and wickedness of persecution. When first printed in French, it was pretended to be translated from the English, as the author wished to disguise himself.

BAYLEY, John, F.R.S. History and Antiquities of the Tower of London. Lond. 1821-5. 4to. 2 vols. with plates. Published at 6*l*. 16s. 6d.

A very valuable work. LARGE PAPER, 12*l*. 12s. [These prices now much reduced.]

BAYLY. *See* BAILEY.

BAYLY, Anselm, LL.D. Alliance of Music, Poetry, and Oratory, Lond. 1789, 8vo. pp. 390, 6s.

This writer likewise published several other works, including an Hebrew and English Bible, with Remarks, &c.

— Lewis, Bishop of Bangor. Practice of Piety. The eleventh Edition. Lond. 1619. 8vo.

Upwards of forty editions of this once esteemed work have been published, and it has also been translated into Welsh, French, and other European Languages.

— Thomas, D.D. Royal Charter granted unto Kings by God himself, &c. A Treatise wherein is proved that Episcopacy is Jure Divino. Lond. 1649. 12mo. with port. of Charles II. by Van. Hove, 5s.

Reprinted 1656 and 1680. For this work the author was committed to Newgate.

— Certamen Religiosum, or a Conference between Charles, King of England, and Henry, late Marquess and Earl of Worcester, concerning Religion; at his Majesties being at Raglan Castle. Lond. 1649. 8vo.

To this work, which is considered fictitious, two answers were published, one by Ham. L'Estrange, 1651, 12mo.; the other by C. C. (Christopher Cartwright,) 1651, 4to. It is likewise commented upon by Dr. Pet. Heylin, in his epistle to the Bibliotheca Regia.

— Herba Parietis: or the Wall-Flower, as it grew out of the Stone-Chamber belonging to Newgate. Lond. 1650. fol. with a frontispiece.

Nassau, pt. i. 434, 5s. White Knights, pt. i. 390, 16s.

— End to Controversie between the Roman Catholick and Protestant Religions. Doway, 1654. 4to.

— Life and Death of John Fisher, Bishop of Rochester. Lond. 1655. 12mo. with portrait by R. Vaughan, 10s. 6d.

This life, written by Richard Hall, D.D. of Christ Church, Cambridge, was republished by Tho. Coxeter, 1739. 12mo. with portrait, 5s.

— William. Astronomical Observations. *See* COOK, Capt. James.

BAYMONT. *See* BEAUMONT.

BAYNE, Paul. Commentary on the Epistle to the Ephesians. Lond. 1643. folio, 9s.

This English divine, of considerable eminence at Cambridge, published a commentary on the Colossians, several sermons and other religious works, 1618-37.

BAYNES, Roger. Praise of Solitarinesse, set down in the Form of a Dialogue: wherein is conteyned, a Discourse philosophical of the Lyfe active and contemplative. Lond. Bynneman, 1577. 4to.

Black letter. Gordonstoun, 328, 4*l*. 19s.

— The Baynes of Aqvisgrane, the one Part and one Volume, entitvled Variety: contayning three Bookes, in the Forme of Dialogues, vnder the Titles following, viz. Profit, Pleasure, Honour. Augusta in Germany, 1617. 4to.

A copy is in the British Museum.

Bayning.—Death repealed by a thankful Memorial sent from Ch. Ch. in Oxon, celebrating the noble Deserts of the Rt. Hon. Paul Viscount Bayning. Oxon. 1638. 4to.

Perry, pt. i. 1681, 9s. Bindley, pt. ii. 576, 15s.

Baziliωlogia. *See* HOLLAND, H.

BEACON, Richard. Solon his Follie, or a politique Discourse,

touching the Reformation of Common-Weales conquered, declined or corrupted. Oxford, 1594. 4to.
Dedicated 'To her Maiestie—The author to the reader—The booke vnto the reader,' Besides 114 pages. Steevens, 769, 6s. Perry, pt. i. 641, russia, 8s.

— T. *See* BECON, Thomas.

Beadle of Bridewell's Answer to the Belman of London. Lond. 1610. 4to.
Black letter. Roxburghe, 6680, 1*l*. 5s.

BEAGUE, J. de. History of the Campagnes 1548 and 1549, with an introductory Preface by the Translator (Patrick Abercromby) 1707. 8vo. 7s.
Jadis, 78, morocco, 1*l*. The original was published at Paris, 1556. *See* BEAUGUE.

BEARCROFT, Philip, D.D. Account of Thomas Sutton, Esq. and of his Foundation in Charter House. Lond. 1737. 8vo. 10s. 6d.
Contains pp. xvi. and 276, with three plates. LARGE PAPER. Dent, pt. i. 194, morocco, 1*l*. 1s. Towneley, pt. ii. 41, morocco, 1*l*. Baker, 29, morocco, 2*l*. 6s. Heath, 4643, 1*l*. 6s.

BEARD, Th. Theatre of God's Judgements. Lond. 1597. 4to. 6s.
[First edition, containing 'An account of Christopher Marlowe, and his tragical end.']
Granger says 'Dr. Thos. Taylor was a joint compiler of this volume.' In the third edition, 1631, 4to. from p. 542 to the end is for the first time added. The fourth and generally esteemed best edition, appeared in 1648, small folio, 15s.

— Pedantius, Comœdia olim Cantabrig. acta in Coll. Trin. nunquam antehac Typis evulgata, 1631.12mo. 7s. 6d.
Prefixed is a small whole-length portrait of the author with a rod and a label from his mouth, inscribed 'As in presenti.' Dr. Beard was Oliver Cromwell's schoolmaster.

Beaton and Wischart. The tragicall Death of Dauid Beaton, Bishop of St. Andrewes; with the Martyrdome of George Wischart, Gent. Lond. 1546. 8vo.
Roxburghe, 8736, no date, 14*l*. 5s. Same copy, Heber, pt. ix. 19*l*.

BEATSON, Alexander. Tracts relating to the Island of St. Helena; written during a Residence of five Years. Lond. 1816. 4to.
This work contains little else than statistical, meteorological, and agricultural observations on the island, and plans for its better administration and cultivation. Fonthill, 535, 18s. Beatson likewise published A View of the War with Tippoo Sultaun. London, 1800. 4to. Drury, 536, 10s. 6d. Roxburghe, 8873, 11s.

— Robert, LL.D. Naval and Military Memoirs of Great Britain, from the Year 1727 to the present Time. Lond. 1804. 8vo. 6 vols. 1*l*. 10s.
A former edition appeared in 1790, 8vo. 3 vols. Beatson likewise published a Chronological Register of both Houses of the British Parliament, 1708-1807. Lond. 1808. 8vo. 3 vols.

— Political Index to the Histories of Great Britain and Ireland, third edition, corrected and much enlarged. Lond. 1806. 8vo. 3 vols. 1*l*. 4s.
Best edition of a very useful book, compiled from Sir W. Dugdale's Summons to Parliament, the Historical Register, and a variety of Chronicles and Peerages. Earl of Kerry, 30, 2*l*. 2s. [Since condensed and continued, but with omissions, by Haydn, in his Book of Dignities.]

— Chronological Register of both Houses of Parliament, from the Union in 1708 till 1807. 3 vols. 8vo. Lond. 1807. 1*l*. 4s.

BEATTIE, James, LL.D. Minstrel, with other Poems. To which are prefixed, Memoirs of the Life of the Author, by Alex. Chalmers. Lond. 1811. 12mo. with portrait by Heath and 4 plates.
Many of the poems in this are not to be found in former editions. The first edition of Beattie's poems appeared in 1760; the second, with variations and omissions, in 1766; notices of both will be found in the Censura Literaria. An elegant edition, with plates from the designs of Rich. Westall, appeared in 1816. A third Book of the Minstrel was written by Mr. Merivale, and published 1808. 4to. 4s.

— Account of the Life and Writings of James Beattie, LL.D. including many of his original Letters. By Sir W. Forbes. Edinb. 1806. 4to. 2 vols. with portrait after Sir Jos. Reynolds, 1*l*. 11s. 6d. LARGE PAPER, 3*l*. 3s.
Reprinted 1807, 8vo. 3 vols. and 1824 in 2 vols. The following works written by Dr. Beattie, whom Bishop Warburton pro-

nounced superior to the whole crew of Scotch metaphysicians, are in great request:—

Essays on Poetry and Music, &c, Edinb. 1776. 8vo.
Frequently reprinted. The first edition appeared 1776. 4to. with the Author's Essay on Truth.
Dissertations moral and critical. Lond. 1786. 8vo. 2 vols.
A former edition appeared 1783, 4to.
Evidences of the Christian Religion. London, 1786. 12mo. 2 vols. 6s.
Reprinted 1788, 2 vols. 1814, 1 vol.
Theory of Language, in two Parts, 1788. 8vo.
The first edition appeared with his Dissertations.
Elements of Moral Science, 1790-3. 8vo. 2 vols. Edinb. 1807. 8vo. 2 vols. 16s. 1817. 8vo. 2 vols.
An Essay on Truth, the seventh edition; to which is now added, a Sketch of the Origin and Progress of the Work. Lond. 1807. 8vo.
The first edition appeared in 1770.

BEAUCHESNE, John de, and John BALDON. Booke containing divers Sortes of Hands, as well the English as French Secretary, with the Italian, Chancery, and Court Hands: also the Proportiō of the Capitall of Romaē. Lond. 1570. broad 4to. 1l. 1s.
'I apprehend them,' says Herbert, 'to have been written by Mr. Beauchesne, a schoolmaster in Blackfriars, and cut on wood by Mr. Baldon.' Again 1574, 1590, 1602.

BEAUFORT, Daniel Augustus, LL.D.. Memoir of a Map of Ireland. Lond. 1792. 4to. 1l. 1s.
Contains pp. 218. An exceedingly valuable work, containing a succinct account of the civil and ecclesiastical state of Ireland, and an Index of all the places which appear on the author's map. The map was published by Faden. Marquis of Townshend, 356, with the map coloured, on canvas, in a case, 2l. 6s. Dent, pt. i. 454, with the map col. mor. 1l. 12s.

— Francis. Karamania, or a brief Description of the South Coast of Asia Minor, and of the Remains of Antiquity. Lond. 1818. 8vo. with plates, 14s.
A valuable addition to the maritime geography and antiquities of a part of Asia not described hitherto.

BEAUGUE, Jan de. Histoire de la Guerre d'Ecosse, traittant comme le Royaume fut assailly et en grande Partie occupée par les Anglois, et depuis rendu paisible a sa Reyne, et reduit en son ancien Estats et Dignité. Paris, pour Gilles Corrozet, 1556. 8vo.
According to Bishop Nicolson, the author was present at many of the skirmishes, &c. mentioned in this work. A copy is in the British Museum. Lloyd, 58, 4l. Sotheby's in July, 1821, 1l. 6s. Bright, 1l. 16s. A translation by P. Abercromby was published 1707. See BEAGUE.

BEAULIEU, Luke de. Vie de S. Thomas (à Becket) Archevesque de Cantorbery et Martyr. Paris, 1674. 4to. 1l. 1s.
A copy is in the British Museum.

BEAULNE, Renauld de. Archevesque de Bourges. Oraison funebre de la Royne d'Escosse. Imp. 1588.
Reprinted by Jebb in 'De Vita et Rebus gestis Mariæ Scotorum Reginæ.'

BEAUMONT, Francis. Poems. Lond. 1640. 4to.
Nassau, pt. i. 398, russia, 9s. Bindley, pt. i. 754, 1l. 12s. Reprinted in Chalmers' Collection of the Poets, and in Weber's edition of the works of Beaumont and Fletcher.

— Poems, viz. the Hermaphrodite, the Remedy of Love; Elegies; Sonnets, with other Poems. Lond. 1653. 8vo.
In this collection, made by the printer Blacklock, some pieces are inserted not written by this author. Roxburghe, 3369, 10s. Lloyd, 59, 13s. Sir M. M. Sykes, pt. i. 206, 14s. White Knights, pt. i. 326, 18s. Bindley, pt. i. 631, 2l. 5s.

BEAUMONT, Francis, and John FLETCHER. Poems. The Golden Remains of Francis Beaumont and John Fletcher. The second edition, with the Addition of other Drolleries by severall Wits of these present times. Lond. 1660. 8vo. 1l. 11s. 6d.

— Comedies and Tragedies, published by the Author's originall Copies. Lond. 1647. folio, with portrait of Fletcher, by Marshall.
First collected edition, containing—Plays dedicated by ten comedians to Philip Earl of Pembroke and Montgomery. In this edition, edited by John Shirley, are 36 plays, printed for the first time. Reed,

8655, 17s Marquis of Townshend, 402, 18s. Rhodes, 2665, 1*l*. 11s. Roscoe, 1351, 4*l*. 5s. Drury, 603, (with the Wild Goose Chase, 1652) russia, 6*l*. 6s.
— Fifty Comedies and Tragedies. Lond. 1679. folio, with portrait of Fletcher by Marshall.
Field, 117, 11s. Bindley, pt. i. 184, 1*l*. Roxburghe, 3896, 1*l*. 3s. Garrick, 521, 1*l*. 3s. Reed, 8655*, 1*l*. 5s. White Knights, pt. i. 391, 1*l*. 16s. Goldsmid, 164, 2*l*. 5s. Horne Tooke, 46, with his MS. notes, 6*l*. 16s. 6d.
— Comedies and Tragedies. Lond. 1711. 8vo. 7 vols.
Dowdeswell, 44, 1*l*. 5s.
— Works, with Notes, by Theobald, Seward, and Sympson. Lond. 1750. 8vo. 10 vols. with two ports.
Steevens, 1225, 1*l*. 14s. Reed, 8020, 1*l*. 19s. Garrick, 128, 2*l*. 8s. Roxburghe, 8897, 3*l*. 13s. 6d. Marquis of Townshend, 102, 4*l*. 4s.
— Dramatic Works, with Notes critical and explanatory, by various Commentators. Lond. 1778. 8vo. 10 vols. with portraits of Beaumont and Fletcher, and 54 engravings.
Edited by George Colman. Drury, 422, 2*l*. 1s. Bindley, pt. i. 295, 2*l*. 2s. Dent, pt. i. 195, 2*l*. 2s. Garrick, 127, 2*l*. 15s. Nassau, pt. i. 134, 3*l*. 3s. Steevens, 1226, 5*l*. 10s. Reed, 8021 (with a double set of plates), 6*l*. 8s. 6d.
— Works, with an Introduction and explanatory Notes, by Henry Weber. Lond. 1812. 8vo. 14 vols. with portraits.
This edition was severely censured by Gifford and Oct. Gilchrist. Brockett, 98, 5*l*. 2s. 6d. Sir M. M. Sykes, pt. i. 208, 7*l*. 12s. 6d. Drury, 423, 7*l*. 12s. 6d. Strettell, 76, 8*l*. 8s. A wretched edition, generally accompanied by Ben Jonson, and forming together 4 vols., royal 8vo. printed in double columns, for Stockdale, appeared 1811.
[The best edition is now that edited by the Rev. Alex. Dyce, 11 vols. 8vo. Lond. 1843, £4 4s.]
Original Editions of the Plays.
The Woman Hater. Lond. 1607, 4to. Rhodes, 525, 1*l*. 2s.
The Masque of the Inner Temple and Grayes Inn, 1612. ib. n. d. 4to. Reprinted in Nichols' Progresses of King James I. Towneley, pt. i. 702.
The Knight of the Burning Pestle. ib. 1613. 4to. Rhodes, 528, 16s. Reprinted 1635. 4to. 4s.
Cupid's Revenge. ib. 1615. 4to. Rhodes,

531, 1*l*. 1s. Reprinted, 1630, 1635, 4to.
The Scornfvl Ladie. ib. 1616. 4to. Rhodes, 533, 1*l*. 1s. Field, 98, 1*l*. 1s.
A King and no King. ib. 1619. 4to. with frontispiece. Reed, 7703, 2*l*. 12s. 6d. An edition 1625. Rhodes, 537, 13s.
The Maid's Tragedy. ib. 1619. 4to. Reprinted 1622, 1630. Rhodes, 542, 18s. 1638, 1641, 1650, and 1661, 4to.
Philaster. ib. 1620. 4to. with frontispiece. Jolley, 1843 (wood-cut on title), 8*l*. 10s. Reed, 7705, 24*l*. Sotheby's in April, 1821, 8*l* 8s. no front.
Thierry and Theodoret. ib. 1621. 4to. 1622. Jolly, 1843, 1*l*. 9s. Boswell, 1701, 5s. Rhodes, 547, 15s. Field, 102, 17s.
The faithful Shepheardesse. ib. no date. 4to. 2*l*. 2s. Second edition (1629) 4to. Rhodes, 554, 18s. Third, 1634, 4to.
The two noble Kinsmen. ib. 1684. 4to. Rhodes, 558, 3s. 6d. Roxburghe, 4916, 6s. 6d.
The Elder Brother. ib. 1637. 4to. Rhodes, 559, 4s. Roxburghe, 4913, 2s. 6d.
Monsieur Thomas. ib. 1639. 4to. Rhodes, 563, 4s.
Wit without Money. ib. 1639. 4to Rhodes, 564, 4s. Roxburghe, 4436, 1s. 6d.
The Coronation. ib. 1640. 4to. Claimed by Shirley.
The Bloody Brother. ib. 1639. 4to. Rhodes, 566, 5s. 6d.
Rollo, Duke of Normandy. Oxford, 1640. 4to. The Bloody Brother, with a new title. Rhodes, 567, 3s. Roxburghe, 6915, 2s. 6d.
Rule a Wife and have a Wife. Lond. 1640. 4to. Rhodes, 568, 3s.
The Night Walker. ib. 1640. 4to. Rhodes, 569, 3s. Roxburghe, 4914, 4s. 6d.
The Wild Goose Chase. ib. 1652. fol. 4s.
The Beggar's Bush. ib. 1661. 4to. Rhodes, 572, 5s. This edition appears to have been printed from the original MS., and contains many superior readings to the folio of 1647, which have escaped Beaumont and Fletcher Editors.

BEAUMONT, Sir Harry. A name assumed by Joseph SPENCE.

— J. F. Albanis. Travels through the Rhætian Alps, in the year 1782. Lond. 1792. imperial folio, 2*l*. 2s.
Contains pp. 82, with aquatinta engravings. With COLOURED PLATES, 6*l*. 6s. Saunders in 1818, morocco, 8*l*.

— Select Views in the South of France, with topographical and historical descriptions. Lond. 1794. folio, 1*l*. 11s. 6d.
Beckford, 1817, 307, morocco, 3*l*. 8s.

Dent,' pt. i. 326, morocco, 3l. 5s. Fonthill, 2441, 3l. 13s. 6d.

BEAUMONT, Travels through the Maritime Alps. Lond. 1795. folio, 3l. 3s.

Beckford, 1817, 306, mor. 3l. 10s. Roxburghe, 7255, (with the Rhætian Alps), 7l. 7s. With COLOURED PLATES, Saunders in 1818, mor. 8l. 8s.

— Travels from France to Italy, through the Lepontine Alps. Lond. 1800. folio.

Saunders in 1818, 2l. 10s. With COLOURED PLATES, 7l. 7s. An inferior edition appeared 1806, folio, 1l. 10s.

Beaumont also published Voyage pittoresque aux Alpes-pennines. Genève, 1787, folio, with 12 coloured plates, 1l. 10s. Voyage du Comté de Nice. Genève, 1787, folio, with 12 coloured plates, 1l. 10s. Description des Alpes Grecques et Cottiennes. Paris, 1802-6, 4to. 4 vols. with a folio vol. of plates.

— Sir John, Bart. Bosworth Field, with a variety of other Poems. Lond. 1629. small 8vo.

Title, dedication to the King, Elegy, &c. 11 leaves. Poems, B—O, 208 pp. pages 181 and 182 are missing in all copies. Reprinted in Chalmers' Edition of the Poets. Nassau, pt. i. 221, 7s. Sir M. M. Sykes, pt. ii. 2l. 15s. Reed, 6560. 1l. Jadis, 34, 1l. 1s. White Knights, 324, morocco, 1l. 14s. Bindley, pt. i. 465, 1l. 19s. Towneley, pt. i. 289, 2l. 2s. Lloyd, 60, 2l. 3s. Bib. Anglo-Poet. 25, 2l. 6s. The poem of Bosworth Field was reprinted 1710, 8vo. In the Censura Literaria, will be found a poetical epistle 'To his late Maiesty (James I.) concerning the true Forme of English Poetry,' written by Sir John Beaumont. [which is also found in the above volume.]

— John. Treatise of Spirits, Apparitions, Witchcrafts, and other Magical Practices. Lond. 1705. 8vo.

Written to prove the real existence of witches and apparitions. Roxburghe, 1986, 7s. Heath, 1497, 8s.

— Gleanings of Antiquities. Lond. 1724. 8vo. 4s.

Contains additions to the treatise of spirits, &c.

— Joseph, D.D. Psyche, or Love's Mystery, in 24 Cantos. The second Edition, with Corrections throughout, and four new Cantos, never before printed. Cambridge, 1702. folio. with portrait by White, 10s. 6d.

Pope is reported to have said of this work, 'that there are in it a great many flowers well worth gathering; and a man who has the art of stealing wisely, will find his account in it.' An Edition, Cambridge, 1648, folio, 7s. A notice, with copious extracts, will be found in the Retrosp. Review, xi. 288-307, xii. 229-48.

— Poems in English and Latin, with an Appendix, containing some Dissertations and Remarks on the Epistle to the Colossians. Lond. 1749. 4to. 5s.

Prefixed to this collection of Poems, is an account of the author's life.

— Robert. Love's Missives to Virtue, with Essaies. Lond. 1660. small 8vo.

Contains pp. 120. A notice of this work will be found in the Restituta, iii. 278-81. Reed, 1695, 5s. Lloyd, 61, 5s. Nassau, pt. i. 222, 7s.

BEAUSOBRE, Isaac. History of the Reformation, from the French of M. de Beausobre, by John Macaulay. Lond. 1802. 8vo. vol. i.

Contains pp. 414. The original of this work, written by an eminent Calvinistic divine, was published at Berlin, 1784, 8vo. 4 vols.

— and James LENFANT. Introduction to the Reading of the Holy Scriptures, intended chiefly for young Students in Divinity. Camb. 1779. 8vo.

Inserted in Bishop Watson's Collection of Theological Tracts, who observes, 'This is a work of extraordinary merit; the authors have left scarcely any topick untouched, of which the young student in divinity may be supposed to want information.' An edition, London, 1806, 8vo. 6s.

Beauties of Cambria. *See* Cambria.

Beauties of England, A new Display of the. Lond. 1772. 8vo. 2 vols. with plates.

Nassau, pt. i. 1141, russia, 1l. 5s. The first edition appeared 1767, 8vo. Third edition, 1776, 8vo. 2 vols. Towneley, pt. ii. 50, russia, 15s. An edition, 1787, 8vo. 2 vols. 10s.

Beauties of England and Wales, or Delineations topographical, historical, and descriptive of each county; embellished with Engravings. Lond. 1801-16. 8vo. 18 vols. in 25. The Introduction, by J. N. Brewer, 1818. 1 vol.

Sotheby's, in 1826, in Nos. 15*l*. 15s. Sotheby's in 1825, 26 vols. 17*l*. Sotheby's in March, 1824, 26 vols. hf.-bd., 23*l*. Sotheby's in 1819, 25 vols. half-bound russia, 25*l*. [Of late years at much lower prices.] LARGE PAPER, in royal 8vo. with proof plates. Drury, 424, with Brewer's Introduction, and the Beauties of Scotland, in 32 vols. morocco, 60*l*. 18s. Williams, 160, 26 vols. morocco, 68*l*. 5s. Earl of Kerry, 33, 26 vols. extra bound, 38*l*. 17s. Sotheby's in 1824, 26 vols. bds. 26*l*. 15s. 6d. Sir M. M. Sykes, 1070, 18 vols. in 25, 36*l*. 15s. Dent, pt. 1. 258. Proof Impressions, with numerous duplicates, proofs before the letters, on INDIA PAPER, in russia, 56*l*. 14s.

Collation.

Introduction, by J. Norris Brewer, 1818, pp. xl. 676, and two maps.

Vol. I. BEDFORDSHIRE, BERKSHIRE, AND BUCKINGHAMSHIRE, by J. Britton and E. W. Brayley, 1801, pp. 400, besides title, advertisement, list of books, &c. and index, 10 leaves; also a map to each county, and 6, 14 and 9 plates.

Vol. II. CAMBRIDGESHIRE, CHESHIRE, AND CORNWALL, by the same, 1801, pp. 524, with list of books, &c. and index, 12 leaves; also 3 maps and 8, 6, and 10 plates.

VOL. III. CUMBERLAND, THE ISLE OF MAN, AND DERBYSHIRE, by the same, 1802, pp. 552, with list of books, &c. and index 11 leaves; also two maps, and 10 and 22 plates.

Vol. IV. DEVONSHIRE AND DORSETSHIRE, by the same, 1803, pp. 560, with list of books, &c. and index, 11 leaves; also two maps, and 22 and 11 plates.

Vol. V. DURHAM, ESSEX, AND GLOUCESTERSHIRE, by the same, 1803, pp. 736, with list of books, &c. and index, 12 leaves; also 8 maps, and 7, 20, and 11 plates.

Vol. VI. HAMPSHIRE, THE ISLE OF WIGHT, AND HEREFORDSHIRE, by the same, 1805, pp. 599, with list of books, &c. and index, 12 leaves; also 2 maps, and 16 and 10 plates.

Vol. VII. HERTFORDSHIRE AND HUNTINGDONSHIRE, by the same, 1808, pp. 1—404, · 405*—574,* with advertisement, list of books, &c. 6 leaves, indexes, and additions and corrections, 14 leaves; also three maps, and 17, and 2, plates.

Vol. VIII. KENT, by the same, 1808, pp. 405—612, 611—1366, with title, dedication, list of books, &c. and index, 25 leaves; also 38 plates. Pages 405 to 612 are generally placed at the end of vol. vii.

Vol IX. LANCASHIRE, LEICESTERSHIRE, AND LINCOLNSHIRE, by J. Britton, 1807, pp. viii. and 5—808, with list of books, &c. index and corrections, 16 leaves; also 3 maps, and 14, 5, and 7 plates.

Vols. i. to ix. consist of Nos. 1 to 72, and Nos. 61,* 62,* 63,* 64,* 65.*

Vol. X. Part i. LONDON AND MIDDLESEX, by E. W. Brayley, vol. i. 1810, pp. 680, also list of books, &c. and indexes, 33 leaves, besides a general title, dedication, and advertisement, 3 leaves, also an engraved title containing a vignette.

Vol. X. Part ii. LONDON AND MIDDLESEX, by E. W. Brayley, vol. ii. 1814, pp. 803, and general index, 30 leaves, also general title, advertisement, and notice respecting list of books, 4 leaves. In this part are 23 plates, some containing two views on one plate.

Vol. X. Part iii. LONDON AND MIDDLESEX, by the Rev Jos. Nightingale, vol. iii. 1815, pp. 756, (not including title) and index, 12 leaves, besides general title and advertisement, 2 leaves. In this part are 33 plates.

Vol. X. Continuation of Part iii. LONDON AND WESTMINSTER, by the Rev. Jos. Nightingale, vol. iii. part ii. 1815, pp. 752, with additions and corrections, 3 leaves; list of books, &c. 8 leaves, and index, 24 leaves. In this part are 43 plates.

Vol. X. Part iv. LONDON AND MIDDLESEX, by J. Norris Brewer, vol. iv. 1816, pp. *, 758, list of books, &c. indexes, and additions and corrections, 27 leaves. In this part are 58 plates.

Vol. XI. MONMOUTHSHIRE, by the Rev. J. Evans, 1810, pp. iv and 184, with a list of books, &c. and index 4 leaves, also a map and 11 plates. NORFOLK, by J. Britton, pp. 388, with a map and 21 plates. NORTHAMPTONSHIRE, by J. Britton, pp. 239, with a list of books, &c. and index, leaves, also a map and 7 plates.

Vol. XII. Part i. NORTHUMBERLAND, by the Rev. J. Hodgson, General title, 1813, pp. 256, with a map and 11 plates. NOTTINGHAMSHIRE, by F. C. Laird, pp. 416, with a map and 11 plates.

Vol. XII. Part ii. OXFORDSHIRE, by J. N. Brewer, pp. viii. (including general title to the volume), and 543, with list of books, &c. and index, 11 leaves, also a map and 22 plates. RUTLANDSHIRE, by F. C. Laird, pp. 160, with a map and 4 plates.

Vol. XIII. Part i. SHROPSHIRE, by the Rev. J. Nightingale, 1813, pp. viii. and 388, a list of books, &c. and index, 10 leaves, also a map and 22 plates. SOMERSETSHIRE, by the Rev. J. Nightingale, pp. 389 to 711, with a list of books, and index, 14 leaves; also a map and 11 plates. Prefixed to the vol. is a general title of the date of 1811.

Vol. XIII. Part ii. STAFFORDSHIRE, by the Rev. J. Nightingale, 1813, title, pp. 713—1201, and list of books, &c. and index, 9 leaves; also a map and 12 plates.

Vol. XIV. SUFFOLK, by Mr. Shoberl, 1813, title and dedication, 2 leaves, pp. 423, with a map and 13 plates. SURREY, pp. 307, with a map and 13 plates. SUSSEX, 208 pp. with list of books, &c. and index, 5 leaves, also a map and 10 plates.

Vol. XV. Part i. WILTSHIRE, by John Britton, 1814, pp. viii. and 718, with errata, list of books, &c. and index, 13 leaves; also a map and 18 plates.

Vol. XV. Part ii. WARWICKSHIRE, by J. Norris Brewer, 1814, Title, preface, and list of plates, 4 leaves, pp. 322, with list of books, &c. index, additions and corrections, 11 leaves, also a map and 16 plates. WESTMORELAND, by the Rev. J. Hodgson, pp. 245, with index, 3 leaves, also map and 6 plates. WORCESTERSHIRE, by F. C. Laird, pp. 416, with a map and 15 plates.

Vol. XVI. YORKSHIRE, by John Bigland, 1812, pt. viii. and 988, with index, 10 leaves, also 4 maps and 27 plates.

Vol. XVII. NORTH WALES, by the Rev. J. Evans, 1812, pp. iv. and 970, with a map and 30 plates.

Vol. XVIII. SOUTH WALES, by Thomas Rees, pp. viii. and 917, with a list of books, &c. 13 leaves, and index, and errata, 15 leaves; also a map and 34 plates.

At the end of this volume is an address from the Publisher, and directions for placing the cuts.

Beauties of Nature and Art displayed in a Tour through the World. Lond. 1763-4. small 12mo. 14 vols. with maps and plates, 1l. 5s.

Beauties of Scotland. *See* FORSYTH, Robert.

Beauties of Wiltshire. *See* BRITTON, J.

Beauties of the Irish Press, with Arthur O'Connor's Letter to Lord Castlereagh. Dublin, n. d. [also Lond. 1800.] 8vo.

Very rare: the work was rigorously suppressed by order of government.

Beauty. A Discourse of auxiliary Beauty, or artificiall Handsomenesse, in Point of Conscience between two Ladies. Lond. 1656. 8vo. 5s.

'This work is ascribed to Dr. Gauden by Ant. à Wood, but it seems rather to have been the work of Obadiah Walker. It had a second edition in 1662, under the title of 'A Discourse of Artificial Beauty, with some satyrical Censures on the vulgar Errors of these Times.' Wood, in his first edition, ascribes the work to Bishop Taylor, but this mistake was corrected in the second.'—DR. BLISS.

BEAUVAIS, M. Essay on the Means of distinguishing antique from counterfeit Coins and Medals, translated from the French, with Notes and Illust. by J. T. Brockett. Newcastle, 1819. crown 8vo. 5s.

Two hundred and five copies printed.

BEAVER, John. Roman Military Punishments. Lond. 1725. 4to. with plates.

Valued for the plates, which are by Hogarth.

LARGE PAPER, Steevens, 1564, with additional plates, morocco, 13l. 5s. Nassau, pt. i. 394. With head pieces to the chapters, engraved by Hogarth, and duplicates with variations at the end, in red morocco, 21l. Baker, 756, morocco, 21l.

—— Captain Philip. African Memoranda, relative to an Attempt to establish a British Settlement on the Island of Bulama, 1792. Lond. 1805. 4to. pp. 520.

White Knights, pt. i. 364, 14s.

BEAWES, Wyndham. Lex Mercatoria. Sixth Edition, considerably enlarged by J. Chitty, Esq. Lond. 1813. 4to. 2 vols. 3l. 3s.

Best edition. The former editions are now of little value.

BEBELIUS, John. Critical Remarks on the Epistles, as they were published from several authentic Copies, by John Bebelius at Basil, in 1531. (By Benj. Dawson.) York, 1735. 8vo.

BEC, Jean du, Abbot of Mortimer. History of the Great Emperor Tamerlane. Newly translated out of French into English, by H. M. Lond. 1597. 4to. pp. 265.

Warton observes that probably the story of Tamerlane was introduced into our early drama from this publication. Inglis, 1892, 8s. Sir M. M. Sykes, pt. i. 408, 13s. Gordonstoun, 380, 19s.

BECANUS, Martin. Dissidium Anglicanum de Primatu Regis, cum brevi Præfatione ad Catholicos in Anglia degentes. Mogunt. 1612, 12mo. 10s.

This eminent Jesuit, who was the great friend and supporter of Bellarmin, in his controversies with K. James I. and Archb. Andrews, published Refutatio Apologiæ et Monitoriæ Præfationis Jacobi Regis Angliæ. Mogunt, 1610, 8vo. and several other pieces relating to England, valued at about 10s. each.

[He wrote a great many other works, which were collected in 2 vols. folio. Mogunt. 1633. 3l. 3s.]

BECCARIA, Marquis. Essay on Crimes and Punishments, translated from the Italian; with a Commentary attributed to M. de Voltaire, translated from the French. Lond. 1766. 8vo. 6s. [New edit. 1801. 7s. 6d.]

A celebrated work, which is said to have gone through above fifty editions and translations. The original was published 1764, 12mo.

— Giamb. Treatise on Artificial Electricity. Translated from the Italian. Lond. 1766. 4to. 7s. 6d.

BECCATELLI, Lodovico, Archb. of Ragusa. Life of Card. Reginald Pole, translated from the Italian, with Notes, and an Appendix, by the Rev. Benj. Pye. Lond. 1766. 8vo. 3s. 6d.

An edition of the Life, in Latin, was published. Lond. 1690. 8vo. 3s.

BECHE, H. T. de la. Selection of the Geological Memoirs contained in the Annales des Mines; together with a Synoptical Table of Equivalent Formations. Lond. 1824. 8vo. 18s.

[Sir Henry de la Beche is author of several other geological works, for which see London Cat.]

BECHER, John Joachim. Magnalia Naturæ: or the Philosopher's Stone, lately exposed to public Sight and Sale. Lond. 1680. 4to. pp. 38, 5s.

Reprinted in the seventh volume of the Harleian Miscellany.

BECK, Cave. The Universal Character, by which all Nations may understand one anothers Conceptions. Lond. 1657. 8vo.

A curious work, with a frontispiece, containing, as it is supposed, a portrait of the author, under the figure of the European. Nassau, pt. i. 228, 15s. White Knights, pt. i. 401, russia, 1l. 1s. Towneley, pt. i. 294, 1l. 5s.

BECKE, Edmond. Confutation of the most detestable and anabaptistical Opinion, that Christ dyd not take hys Flesh of the blessed Vyrgyn Mary. Lond. by John Daye, 1550. 4to.

In metre, unknown to Herbert, but noticed by Ritson in his Bibliographia Poetica.

BECKET, Andrew. Shakespeare's himself again; or, the Language of the Poet asserted. Lond. 1815. 8vo. 2 vols.

In little estimation. Bindley, pt. iii. 1102, 13s.

Becket, S. Thomas à, Archbishop of Canterbury. Vita et Processus S. Thome Cantuariensis Martyris super Libertate Ecclesiastica. Paris, Joh. Philip Alemanus. 1495. 4to.

Black letter. A copy is in the British Museum. Towneley, pt. ii. 1476, 17s. Bright, 18s.

— The Lyfe of the blessed Martyr Saynte Thomas. Imprynted by me Rycarde Pynson. 4to.

Black letter, 8 leaves. Strettell, 1239, 9l. 9s. Bindley, pt. ii. 2534, 19l.

— The Life, or the Ecclesiastical Historie of S. Thomas, Archbishope of Canterbury. By A. B. Coloniæ, 1639. 4to.

A copy is in the British Museum. Towneley, pt. i. 467, 12s. White Knights, pt. i. 402, mor. 1l. 3s. Willet, 350, 1l. 15s.

— Epistolæ et Vita Divi Thomæ Cantuariensis, necnon Epistolæ Alexandri III. Pontificis, &c. concernentes Sacerdotii et Imperii Concordiam: Operâ et Studio F. Christiani Lupi Iprensis. Brux. 1682. 4to. 2 parts in 1 vol. 2l. 12s. 6d.

A copy is in the British Museum.
— See BEAULIEU, Luke de.
BRUNÆUS, Ric.
CANDA, Charles de.
COLA, Giov. Battista.
STAPLETON, Thomas.
STEPHANIDES, W.

BECKET, Prophecie concerning the Wars betwixt England, France, and Holland. Lond. 1666. 4to.

In answer to this appeared 'A Letter written to a Friend in Wilts, upon occasion of a late ridiculous Pamphlet,' 1666, 4to.

BECKFORD, Peter. Thoughts on Hunting. Sarum, 1781. 4to. 8s.

First edition. A notice of this work will be found in the Retrosp. Review, xiii. 230–47. Third edition, with front. by Bartolozzi, 4to. Sarum, 1784, 4s. Duke of York, 509, mor. 1l. 1s. Another, Lond. 1796, 8vo. with 20 engravings. 9s. [New edit. plates, Lond. Bohn, 1847. 8s. 6d.]

— Familiar Letters from Italy. Salisbury, 1805. 8vo. 2 vols.

Bindley, pt. i. 315, 6s. Drury, 425, 19s.

— William (of Fonthill). Biographical Memoirs of extraordinary Painters. Lond. 1780. 12mo.

A satirical work, published anonymously, of which a notice will be found in the Retrosp. Rev. x. 172–9. Reed, 3479, 8s. Fonthill, 154 and 1055, 1l. 1s. each. Reprinted 1824, 12mo. 5s.

— An Arabian Tale (Vathek), from an unpublished MS., with Notes critical and explanatory (by Mr. Henley). Lond. 1786. small 8vo. 5s.

Fonthill, 521, 17s. 1934, 10s. 6d. LARGE PAPER, printed for presents, 15s. Fonthill, 3623, 3l. 15s. A new edition, 1809. Third edition, revised and corrected, with an engraved frontispiece, 1815, (and again in 1832), 8vo. 10s. 6d.

'For correctness of costume, beauty of description, and power of imagination, this most Eastern and sublime tale far surpasses all European imitations; and bears such marks of originality, that those who have visited the East will have some difficulty in believing it to be more than a translation.'—*Lord Byron.*

An edition in French (in which language the book was originally written) was published 1815, 8vo. 10s. 6d. LARGE PAPER. Fonthill. 795, 17s. 2108, 1l. 5s.

[Mr. Beckford, in his 80th year, was author of Italy, with Sketches of Spain and Portugal, 2 vols. 8vo. 1835, and Recollections of Alcobaça and Batalha, 8vo. 1835.]

— Wm. (of Suffolk), Account of the Island of Jamaica. Lond. 1790. 8vo. 2 vols. 12s. Vol. i. pp. 464, vol. ii. pp. 405.

A work containing much valuable information. Fonthill, 1024, 1l. 11s. 6d.

— History of France from the most early Records to the Death of Louis XVI. Lond. 1794. 8vo. 4 vols. 24s.

BECKMANN, John. History of Inventions and Discoveries. Translated from the German by William Johnston. Lond. 1815. 8vo. 4 vols. 2l. 2s.

A most interesting and valuable work. The former edition appeared in 1797, 8vo. 3 vols. to which a fourth was added in 1814. [A new edition, revised and continued by Drs. Francis and Griffith, and H. G. Bohn, 2 vols. 1846. 7s.]

BECON, Thomas. The Worckes, diligently perused, corrected, and amended. Lond. by John Day, 1563-4. folio.

Black letter. In 3 parts. Part i. ends on folio DCLXXVIII., the prefixes are 'The names of Authors,' and 'The Preface,' dated 1564. Part ii. on fol. cclxxxxix. Part iii. on fol. ccccxiii. Each part has a separate title. Williams, 124, 5l. 12s. 6d. Horner, 1854, morocco, 15l.

Contents and List of Editions.
PART I.
The Newes out of Heauen, 1541, 8vo.
The Christmas Banket. J. Mayles, 1542, 8vo. Inglis, 69, 1l. 6s. Bibl. Llwyd. 49,* 2l. 12s.
The Potation for Lent, 1542, 8vo. 1543, 8vo.
The Pathwaye unto Prayer, 1542, 8vo. 1543, 8vo. Inglis, 70, 5s.
The Nosegaye.
The Policie of Warre, 1543, entitled, 'The true Defence of Peace,' 8vo.
Dauid's Harpe, 1542, 8vo. Pickering, 1854, mor. 9l. 10s. 1543. 8vo.
The New Yeare's Gift, 1543, 8vo. Reed, 486. 9s. 1560, folio.
The Inuectiue against Swearyng, 1543, 8vo.
The Gouernaunce of Vertue, 1550, 8vo, 1566, 8vo. 1574, 8vo. 1578, 8vo. 1586. 8vo.
The Catechisme.
The Boke of Matrimony, 1542, 1543, FINE, 1848, 2l. 2s. 1546, 8vo. See BULLINGER.
PART II.
The Jewel of Joy.
The Principles of Christen Religion, no date, 12mo.
The fruitful Treatise of Fastyng.
The Castell of Comfort, no date, 8vo. Goldsmid, 95, 7s. 6d. Inglis, 76, 13s.
The Solace of the Soul, 1548, 8vo. 1549, entitled 'The Physicke of the Soule,' 8vo.

The Fortres of the Faythfull, 1560, 12mo. 10s. 6d.
The Christen Knight.
Homely against Whordome.
The Floure of Godly Prayers, no date, 16mo.
The Pomaunder of Prayer. 1582, King and Lochée's, in 1814, 5l. 15s. 1558, 1656, Inglis, 76, 9s. 1578, no date. Inglis, 77, 1l. 1s.
The Sicke Man's Salue, 1561, 8vo. Sir M. M. Sykes, pt. i. 211, mor. 2l. 1574, 1579, 1582, 1587, no date, 1610, 1613, 1619. Inglis, 78, 3s.
This calvinistical devotional tract was, says Gifford, a frequent subject of ridicule with the wits of those days.
The Dialoge of Chrystes Birth.
The Inuective against Whordome (in verse). No date, 12mo.

PART III.
A comfortable Epistle to the afflicted People of God. Strasburgh, 1554, 8vo. Bindley, pt. i. 1364.
An humble Supplication unto God for the restoryng of his Worde.
The Displaying of the Popish Masse. In Latin. Basil. 1559, 8vo. In English. Lond. 1637, 12mo, 2s. 6d.
The common Places of the holy Scripture.
A Comparison betwene the Lord's Supper and the Pope's Masse.
Certayne Articles of Christen Religion, proued and confirmed with the Testimonies and Authorities of the aun-cient Fathers.
The monstrous Marchandise of the Romish Byshops.
The Reliques of Rome, 1553, 8vo. Sotheby's in 1824, 8s. 6d. 1560, 8vo. Inglis, 74, 10s. 6d. 1563, 8vo. White Knights, 3630, mor. 12s. Denyer, 8, 2l. 2s. no date, 8vo. North, pt. i. 215, russia, 9s. Sir M. M. Sykes, pt. i. 202, 13s.
The Diuersitie betwene God's Worde and Man's Iniuncion. No date, 8vo, entitled ' Antithesis.'
The Actes of Christ and of Antichrist. 1577, 12mo. A copy is in the British Museum.
Christe's Chronicle.
The Summarye of the New Testament.
The Demaundes of Holy Scripture.
The glorious Triumphe of God's most blessed Worde.
The Prayse of Death.
[Several of Becon's Works have been republished by the Parker Society. See *Appendix*.]

BECON, Thomas. A new Postil, conteinyng Sermons vpon the Gospells. Lond. 1566. 4to. 10s. 6d.
Reprinted 1567, 9s. Inglis, 152, 17s.

BEDDOES, Thomas, M.D. Hygēia; or Essays moral and medical, on the Causes affecting the personal State of our middling and affluent classes. Lond. 1801-2, 8vo. 3 vols. 1l. 1s.
A sensible and excellent work. A copious list of this eminent physician's various publications will be found in Watt's Bibliotheca Britannica. A Life of him was published by Stock, 1811, 4to.

BEDE, Venerabilis, Opera omnia. Colon. Agrip. 1612. vel 1688. folio, 8 tom. in 4, 5l. 5s.
According to Dr. Henry, the only complete edition. [In 1843 Dr. Giles edited Bedæ Opera Latina, 12 vols. 8vo. 4l. 4s.]

— Opera quædam theologica, necnon historica. Accesserunt Egberti Archiep. Ebor. Dialogus de Ecclesiastica Institutione, et Aldhelmi Liber de Virginitate. Lond. 1693. 4to. 10s. 6d.
Edited by H. Wharton.

— Historia Ecclesiastica Gentis Anglorum. Sine Loco aut Anno, folio. [Sed Argent. Eggesteyn, circa 1473.]
First edition, according to Brunet consisting of 97 leaves, printed in double columns, 40 lines each. *Vide* Panzer, Annal. Typog. i. 83, no. 445. Heber, 45l. In Bohn's Cat. 1841, 5l. 5s. Other Editions, Argent. 1513. folio. Gough, 247, 14s. Antv. 1550. folio, 12s. Lovan. 1566. 12mo. 5s. Heidelb. 1587. 12mo. 4s. Col. Agrip. 1601. 12mo. 3s.

— Ecclesiasticæ Historicæ Genti Anglorum Libri V. tribus præcipuè MSS. Latinis a Mendis haud paucis repurgati: &c. &c. (Per Abrah. Whelocum.) Cantab. 1643. folio, 2l. 2s.
An excellent edition, in which will be found King Alfred's Saxon Version, numerous notes, and a Saxon Chronology. Dent, pt. i. 393, morocco, 2l. 8s. The latter portion of the work, dated 1643, consisting of the Anglo-Saxon laws, is sometimes found separately, 1l. 1s. An edition was published at Paris, 1681. 4to. 7s. 6d.

— Historiæ Ecclesiasticæ Gentis Anglorum Libri V. una cum reliquis ejus Operibus historicis in unam Volumen collectis: cura et studio Joh. Smith. Cantabr. 1722. folio. 3l. 3s.

The best edition, with learned notes and dissertations. King Alfred's Saxon version is also inserted in this edition. Heath, 4508, 3*l.* 3*s.* LARGE PAPER, 3*l.* 13*s.* 6*d.* to 4*l.* 4*s.*

Bede's History of the Church of Englande, translated by Thomas Stapleton. Antwerp, 1565. 4to.
According to Bishop Nicolson, 'A partial translation by a doctor of divinity, in the university of Lovain.' Reed, 3318, mor. 2*l.* 14*s.* Nassau, pt. i. 895, russia, 3*l.* 16*s.*

— Historie of the Church of England. St. Omers, 1622. 8vo. 12*s.*
Dent, pt. i. 200, 13*s.* 'History of the Church of Scotland.' St. Omers, 1622. Nassau, pt. i. 225, 1*l.* 2*s.*

— Ecclesiastical History of the English Nation from the Coming of Julius Cæsar till the Year of our Lord 731, translated into English from Dr. Smith's Edition. To which is added the Life of the Author, also explanatory Notes (by Capt. John Stevens). Lond. 1723. 8vo.
This work, says Dr. Adam Clarke, is scarce—the translation is, in the main, well done, and the notes very useful.
Sotheby's in 1826, 20*s.* Brockett, 104, 1*l.* 1*s.* Williams, 161, morocco, 1*l.* 14*s.*

— History of the primitive Church of England, translated by Hurst; to which are added, a Life of the Saint, and an Appendix of Notes from Stapleton, Cressy, Smith, and Stevens. Lond. 1814. 8vo. 12*s.*

— England's Old Religion faithfully gathered out of Bede, by H. B. Antwerp, 1658. 12mo. 5*s.*

— Epistolæ duæ, necnon Vitæ Abbatum Wiremuthensium et Gerwiensium. Accessit Egberti Arch. Ebor. Bedæ æqualis Dialogus de Ecclesiastica Institutione. Ex antiquis Codd. MSS. in lucem emisit et notis illustravit Jac. Waræus. Dublin, 1664. 8vo. 5*s.*

— Lives of the Abbots of Wearmouth, translated by Wilcock. Sunderland, 8vo. 1818.
Brockett, 3266, 6*s.*

— Axiomata philosophica, Studio M. Joannis Kroeselie. Impensis R. Oliff, 1592. 8vo.

BEDELL, William, Bp. of Kilmore. A Protestant Memorial, or the Shepherd's Tale of the Powder Plot, a Poem in Spenser's Style, published from the original MS. found among the Papers of the late Dr. Dillingham. Lond. 1713. 8vo. 15*s.*
Boswell, 174, 1*l.* 10*s.* A life of this pious and exemplary divine was published by Bishop Burnet, 1685, 8vo. Bishop of Ely, 76, 5*s.* 6*d.* Reprinted 1692, and Dublin, 1736, 1758. The edition 1736 on THICK WRITING PAPER. Williams, 313, morocco, 1*l.* 11*s.* 6*d.*

— Some Original Letters, concerning the Steps taken towards a Reformation of Religion at Venice, on the Quarrel between that State and Pope Paul V. Dublin, 1742. 12mo.
A copy is in the British Museum. Reed, 1700, 11*s.* Among the Lambeth MSS. no. 772, is one by Bishop Bedell in answer to Alabaster, 1604.

BEDFORD, Arthur. Scripture Chronology demonstrated by astronomical Calculations; as also by the Year of Jubilee, and the Sabbatical Year among the Jews. Lond. 1730. folio, 18*s.* LARGE PAPER, 1*l.* 4*s.*
The hypothesis on which this elaborate work is formed, has been set aside by the valuable publication of Dr. Hales. This learned and pious divine published various sermons and treatises, several of which were against Play-houses and music. His Serious Remonstrance, 1709, 8vo. Williams, 162, morocco, 16*s.*

— Hilkiah. Hereditary Right of the Crown of England asserted, &c. Lond. 1713. folio, 5*s.*
The real author of this work was George Harbin, a nonjuring clergyman, and Mr. Bedford was fined 1000 marks, and imprisoned three years for writing, printing, and publishing the same. Bindley, pt. i. 572, 15*s.*

Bedford. The Epitaph of the most noble and valiant Jasper, late Duke of Bedford. Lond. by W. de Worde. 4to.
Consisting of eight pages. A copy is in the Pepysian library of Magdalen College, Cambridge.
An account of the Russells, Earls of Bedford, was published 8vo. by A. L. 16—: a Life of Francis Earle of Bedford, by George Whetstone, 1585. 4to, and a Sermon at his

Funeral, by Tho. Sparke, D.D. Oxon, 1585. 16mo.

— Anecdotes of the House of Bedford, from the Norman Conquest to the present period. Lond. (1796) 8vo. 3s.

Written in answer to 'A Letter to a Noble Lord,' from the pen of the Right Hon. Edmund Burke.

— See Wiffen's House of Russell.

Bedford Level.— Collection of Laws, together with an introductory History thereof, by Charles Nalson Cole. Second Edition, with Additions. Lond. 1803. 8vo. 10s. 6d.

The edition of 1761 is less complete. An account of a considerable number of tracts written on the subject of the surveys of the fens in this part of the country, and the disputes arising thereupon, may be seen in Gough's Brit. Topog. i. 195, &c. Many of the tracts are in the British Museum and London Institution Libraries. *See also* WELLS.

Bedford Marbles.—Outline Engravings of the Woburn Abbey Marbles. Lond. 1822. folio. 180 copies, P.P. 20*l*.

Containing 48 engravings in outline, 28 from the antique, the others from marbles by Chantrey, Westmacott, Thorwaldsen and Canova, after drawings by Corbould; with an appendix containing a dissertation on the Lanti Vase, by Mr. Christie, and on an ancient hymn to the graces by Ugo Foscolo.

Bedford Missal. *See* GOUGH, Rich.

BEDLOE, Captain William. The Life and Death of Captain William Bedloe. Lond. 1681. 8vo. with a portrait by R. White. 18s.

Bedloe's gallantries and rogueries recorded in this volume beggar description. Bindley, pt. ii. 1173, 1*l*. 16s.

A Narrative of the Popish Plot. Lond. 1679, folio, pp. 35, 3s. 6d.; and a tragedy, 'The excommunicated Prince,' according to the title, written by Bedloe, was published 1679, folio, 3s. 6d. *See* Wood's Fasti, ii. 373.

BEDWELL, William. Kalendarivm Viatorivm generale. The Traveller's Kalendar, serving generally for all Parts of the World. Lond. 1614. 8vo.

A copy is in the British Musenm.

— Mohammedis Imposturæ; whereunto is annexed the Arabian Trvdgman. Lond. 1615. 4to. 6s.

Another, entitled 'Mahomet unmasked,' 1642, 4to.

— William. A brief Description of the Towne of Tottenham High Crosse, in Middlesex. To which is added the Tvrnament of Tottenham, by Mr. Gilbert Pilkington. Lond. 1631. 4to.

White Knights, 3362, morocco, 4*l*. 6s. Nassau, pt. i. 396, russia, 18s. Reprinted with Butcher's Stamford, 1717, 8vo. An account of Pilkington's Tournament of Tottenham, will be found in the forty-third section of Warton's History of Poetry.

BEE, Jacob. Diary from 1682-1706. Durham, 1819. 8vo.

Twenty-five copies privately printed by Sir Cuth. Sharp. Brockett, 1685, 4s. 6d.

— Jon.—A (Slang) Dictionary of the Turf, the Ring, the Chase, the Pit, the Bon-ton, and the Varieties of Life, forming the completest and most authentic Lexicon Balatronicum hitherto offered to the notice of the Sporting World, by Jon. Bee, (*i. e.* John Badcock) Esq. Editor of the Fancy, Fancy Gazette, Living Picture of London, and the like of that. Lond. 1823. 12$^{s}_{.}$n$^{.}_{.}$

[This author published books on Stable Economy, &c., in the name of Hinds.]

Bee, The, or Universal Weekly Pamphlet, by a Society of Gentlemen and Booksellers. Lond. 1733-4. 8vo. 8 vols. consisting of 100 Nos.

Edited by Eustace Budgell. Bindley, pt. i. 293, 9s. For another periodical publication entitled The Bee, *see* ANDERSON, James, LL.D.; and in 1759, 8 Nos. 12mo. appeared with the same title, written by Oliver Goldsmith.

BEEARDE, Richard. A godly Psalm of Mary Queen, which brought us Comfort all, Thro God whom we of Deuty praise that give her Foes a Fall. Lond. 1557. 8vo.

A celebration of the accession of Queen Mary. With psalm-tunes, in four parts. Beearde likewise published a poetical broadside, entitled 'Alphabetum Beeardi,' printed by W. Copland. n. d.

BEECHEY, F. W. and H. W. Proceedings of the Expedition to explore the Northern Coasts of Africa in

1821 and 1822, comprehending an Account of the Syrtis and Cyrenaica, of the ancient Cities, composing the Pentapolis, and other various existing Remains. Lond. 1827. 4to. 3*l*. 3s.

BEECHEY, F. W. and H. W. Narrative of a Voyage to the Pacific and Behring's Straits, in 1825-8, 2 vols. 4to. plates. Lond. 1831. 4*l*. 4s.

BEECKMAN, Captain Daniel. Voyage to and from the Island of Borneo in the East Indies. Lond. 1718. 8vo. 5s.

An interesting work, even at this distance of time, reprinted in the eleventh volume of Pinkerton's Collection of Voyages and Travels. Roxburghe, 7805,5s.

BEEDOME, Poems Divine and Humane. Lond. 1641. 8vo.

Reed, 6562, 1*l*. 16s. Bindley, pt. i. 457, 4*l*. 5s. Reprinted in Wit a Sporting, 1657. Bright, 1845, russia, 2*l*. 2s.

Bee Hiue of the Romish Church, translated out of Dutch into English, by Geo. Gilpin, the Elder. Lond. 1580. 16mo. 10s. 6d.

Black letter. Dedicated to 'Master Philip Sidney, Esq. by John Stell, at whose proper costs and charges this worthy book was translated and printed.' North, pt. i. 218, mor. 1*l*. 6s. Sir M. M. Sykes, pt. i. 212, mor. 1*l*. 15s. The Edition, 1579, Bindley, pt. iii. 709, 7s. 6d. Edition 1623, Sotheby's in 1824, 6s. White Knights, pt. i. 406, 3s. . 1580, Sotheby, 1853, 1*l*. 8s.

BEEK, J. Triumph Royal; containing a short Account of the most remarkable Battels, &c. of the House of Nassau. Lond. 1692. 8vo. 5s.

Beer. Warm Beere, farre more wholsome then that which is drunke cold. Cambridge, 1641. 12mo.

Bindley, pt. iii. 2203, 11s. 6d. Reprinted 1724, 8vo.

Beeriad, The, or Progress of Drink. Gosport, 1736. 4to.

Reed, 6686, 6s. 6d. Sotheby's in March, 1823, 7s.

BEEVERELL, James. Les Délices de la Grande Bretagne et de l'Irlande. Leyde, 1707. 12mo. 8 vols. with many plates, 2*l*. 2s.

First edition. Valuable, says the Quarterly Review, as recording perishable features most of which have already passed away. White Knights, 1191. Nassau, pt. i. 229, 1*l*. 1s. Towneley, pt. ii. 52, 1*l*. 11s. M. of Townshend, 692. 2*l*. 3s.

— A Second Edition. Leide. 1727. 12mo. 8 vols.

Dent, pt. i. 590, 13s. 6d. Bindley, pt. i. 2093. 1*l*. 9s. Drury, 427, 1*l*. 13s. Sotheby's in 1823, 2*l*. 12s. 6d. Edwards, 626, mor. 5*l*. The plates only in 4to. Williams, 220, 13s.

Beggar.—History of the Blind Beggar of Bednal Green. Lond. n. d. 4to.

Sir M. M. Sykes, pt. i. 426, russia, 14s. Saunders in 1818, 1*l*. 1s. There is a play with the same title, by Jo. Day, 1659, 4to.

— The Begger's Ape, a Poem. Lond. 4to. with a frontispiece.

Reed, 6687, 1*l*. 8s. Nassau, pt. i. 397, 8*l*. 10s. Towneley, pt. i. 390. Brand, (cut short,) 1*l*, 5s., date 1627. Jolley, 1843, (cut) 2*l*. 15s. Utterson, 1852, cut, 1*l*. 3s.

— The Supplication of Beggars. *See* FISH, Simon.

— Praise of Antiquity and Commodity of Beggery, Beggers, and Begging, a Poem. Lond. 1621. 4to. with a frontispiece.

Bindley, pt. iii. 2271, 3*l*. 9s.

BEHMEN, Jacob. Works, to which is prefixed the Life of the Author. With Figures illustrating his Principles. Left by the Rev. William Law, M.A. Lond. 1764-81. 4to. 4 vols. plates, 4*l*. 4s.

— The Life of one Jacob Boehmen: wherein is contained a perfect Catalogue of his Workes. Lond. 1644. 4to. 5s.

Another life of this celebrated mystic was published by Francis Okely, 1780, 8vo. 2s. 6d.

BEHN, Mrs. Aphra. Plays. The Second Edition. Lond. 1716. 2 vols. 8vo. with portrait by Vander Gucht.

This edition contains 15 plays, seven in Vol. i. and eight in Vol. ii. Field, 119, date 1702-16. 1*l*. 9s.

— Plays. Lond. 1724. 12mo. 4 vols. with portrait, by R. White, after T. Riley.

In this edition the Prologues and Epilogues are omitted. Nassau, pt. i. 230, 1*l*. 17s.

Original Editions, as published in 4to.
Forced Marriage, 1671.
The amorous Prince, 1671.
The Dutch Lover, 1673.

Adelazar, 1677.
The Town Fop, 1677.
The Rover, part. i. 1677.
The Debauchee, 1677.
Sir Patient Fancy, 1678.
The feigned Courtezans, 1679.
The Rover, part. ii. 1681.
The City Heiress, 1682.
The false Count, 1682.
The Roundheads, 1682.
The young King, 1683.
The luckey Chance, 1687.
The Emperor of the Moon, 1687.
The Widow Ranter, 1690.
The younger Brother, 1696.
Bindley, pt. i. 741, 1l. 5s. Roxburghe, 4442, &c. (except the Debauchee) 2l. 3s.

Mrs. Behn likewise published:
Poems. Lond. 1684, 8vo. 4s. Miscellany being of a Collection of Poems, by several hands, 1685, 8vo. 4s. Lycidus, or the Lover in Fashion, translated by Mrs. A. Behn, 1688, 4to. 4s. Lover's Watch, 1686, 8vo. with front. 4s. Histories and Novels, 1698, 1718, 8vo. 1722, 1735 (eighth edition) with Life by Gildon, &c. 12mo. 2 vols. 10s. 6d.
To her also are attributed love letters between a Nobleman (Ford Lord Grey) and his sister (the Countess of Berkley.)

BEHRENS, Geo. Henning. Natural History of Hartz Forest, in Germany, translated by John Andree. Lond. 1730. 8vo. 3s. 6d.

BEKINSAU, John. De supremo et absoluto Regis Imperio. Lond. Berthelet, 1546. 8vo. 1l.
Dedicated to King Henry VIII. Reprinted in the first volume of Monarchia S. Romani Imperii, &c. by Melchior Goldastus Hamensfeldius. Franc. 1621, folio. Dr. Dibdin mentions a doubtful edition of the date of 1537. *See* Wood's Athenæ, vol. i. 307. Bright, 1l. 1s.

BEKKER, Balthazar. World bewitched; or an Examination of the common opinion concerning Spirits. Lond. 1695. 12mo. vol. i. (no more published) 15s.
' The best account of the power of devils, is that given by the celebrated and persecuted Dr. Bekker, in his work entitled ' Le Monde enchanté.' 4 vols. 12mo.'—*Retrosp. Review.*

Bel.—Adam Bel, Clym of the Cloughe, and Wyllyam of Cloudesle. Lond. by William Copland. 4to.
This very ancient, curious, and popular performance is reprinted from a copy in the Garrick collection of plays, in the British Museum, in Ritson's Pieces of ancient popular Poetry.

— Adam Bel, Clym of the Cloughe, and Wyllyam of Cloudesle. No printer's name or date. 4to.
Contains pp. 18. Bibl. Anglo-Poet. 3, (2 leaves MS.) 3l. resold at Saunders' in 1818, 1l. 18s.

— Adam Bell, Clim of the Clough, and William of Cloudesle. Lond. by James Roberts, 1605. 4to.
To this reprint, consisting of 17 leaves, was affixed ' The second part,' a very inferior and servile production. A copy is in the Bodleian. 1652, by T. Cotes. Utterson, 1852, (from Heber) mor. 5l. 15s. 6d., re-sold, Gardiner, 1854, 3l. 4s.

— Adam Bel, Clim of the Cloughe, and William of Cloudesle. Lond. 1668. 4to.
Roxburghe, 3408, 4l.

— Adam Bell, Clim of the Clough, and young William of Cloudesley. The second Part. Lond. 1616. 4to.
This edition differs considerably from the former one, printed in 1605.

BEL, William. The Testament of William Bel, Gentleman, left written in his owne Hand; with Annotations at the End, and Sentences by his Sonne, Francis Bel. Doway, 1632. 12mo.
A copy is in the British Museum.

BELCAMP, Jo. V. Consilium et Votum pro ordinanda ac stabilienda Hibernia. Lond. 1651. folio.
A copy is in the British Museum.

BELCHIER, Dabridgecourt. Hans Beer Pot, his invisible Comedie of See me and See me not: acted in the Low Countries, by an honest Company of Health-Drinkers. Lond. 1618. 4to.
Phillips and Winstanley have erroneously attributed this piece to Thomas Nash. A copy is in the British Museum. Inglis' Old Plays, 12, 4l. 1s. Sotheby's in April, 1821, 5l. 2s. 6d.

Belfast. — Historical Collections. Belfast, 1817. 8vo. 7s.
A meagre collection of annals, useful only as a book of reference.

— Select Papers of the Literary Society of Belfast. 1809, &c. 4to. Fasc. i. ii. iii. iv. 3s. each.

BELFOUR, John. History of Scotland, from the earliest accounts to the present time. Lond. 1770. 8vo. 5s.
A useful epitome.

Belgicke Pismire and Souldier. *See* SCOT, Thomas.

Belgium. *See* RUTLAND, Duke of.

Belianis of Greece.—The Honour of Chivalrie, set downe in the most famous Historie of Don Belianis. Lond. 1598. 4to.
Only the first part. An edition unknown to Ames, Herbert, or Dr. Dibdin. Stanley, 747, 7l. White Knights, 7l.

— Honour of Chivalry, or the famous and delectable History of Don Belianis of Greece, translated out of Italian. Lond. 1650. 4to.
Black letter. Steevens, 1156, 11s. An edition 1671, 4to. 2 parts. Goldsmid, 4408, 6s. 6d.—1673, (by Kirkman.) Goldsmid, 404, 13s. 6d.—1683, (by Shirley.) Goldsmid, 405, 1l. 1s.—1694, Roxburghe, 6364, 1l. 6s.—1703. 4to. 2 parts. Nassau, pt. i. 1285, 9s. White Knights, 369, 10s. Goldsmid, 406, (the continuation) russia, 3l. 4s.

BELING, Richard. Vindiciarum Catholicorum in Hibernia, Rerum in Hibernia gestarum ab Anno 1641 ad Annum 1649. Paris, 1650. 12mo.
A rare book published under the name of Philopater Irenæus, unknown to Nicolson, and most bibliographers. Gordonstoun, 1767, 5l.

— Innocentiæ suæ impetitæ per Reverendissimum Fernensem, (Nic. French) Vindiciæ. Paris, 1652. 12mo.
Beling's account of the transactions of Ireland, during the period of the rebellion, is esteemed more worthy of credit than any written by the Romish party.

— Annotationes in Johannis Poncii Librum, cui Titulus, Vindiciæ Eversæ: accesserunt Belingi Vindiciæ. Paris, 1654. 8vo.

BELKNAP, Jeremy, A.M. History of New Hampshire. Philadelphia, and Boston, 1784-92. 8vo. 3 vols. 2l. 2s.
Vols. I. and II. are historical. Vol. III. relates to climate, soil, produce, &c.

BELL, —. The Confession, Obstinacy, and Ignorance of Father Bell, a Romish Priest, wherein is declared the manner of his Tryal, Condemnation, and Execution on Monday, Dec. 10, 1643. 1643. 4to.
Nassau, pt. ii. 1325, 11s.

— Andrew, D.D. Elements of Tuition. Lond. 8vo. 3 parts, 1808. 7s. 6d.

— Benjamin. System of Surgery. Edinb. 1801. 8vo. 7 vols. 1l. 1s.
The former editions appeared Edinb. 1783-6, 8vo. 6 vols. 1792, 6 vols. 1796, 7 vols. Bell published several other surgical works.

BELL, Charles. Essays on the Anatomy of Expression in Painting. Second Edition. Lond. 1824. 4to. with plates. 2l. 12s. 6d.
The former edition 1806, 4to. Sir M. M. Sykes, pt. i. 409, 1l. 10s. Duke of York, 715. 1l. 14s.

— Anatomy of the Brain, explained in a Series of Engravings. Lond. 1811. 4to. 2l. 2s.
A former edition appeared in 1802, 4to. Mr. Bell has likewise published other valuable works, the principal of which are
Engravings from Specimens of Morbid Parts, preserved in the Author's Collection in Windmill Street, and selected from the Divisions inscribed Urethra, Vesica, Ren morboso et læsa. Lond. 1813. folio, 1l. 16s.
A description of Bell's Museum has been published, 4to. 2s.
System of Operative Surgery, founded on the Basis of Anatomy. Lond. 1814. 8vo. 2 vols. 1l. 18s.
A former edition appeared in 1807.
Engravings, explaining the Course of the Nerves. Lond. 1817. 4to. 1l. 1s.
Illustrations of the great Operations of Surgery, Trephine, Hernia, Amputation, Aneurism, and Lithotomy. Lond. 1821. large 4to. with 21 plates, 3l. 15s. plain, or 5l. 5s. coloured.
Engravings of the Arteries. Third Edition. Lond. 1824. 8vo. plain 15s. coloured 1l. 1s.
The first edition appeared in 1801.
THE HAND, its Mechanism, etc., (a Bridgewater Treatise), 8vo. Lond. 1833.

— George Joseph. Commentaries on the Laws of Scotland, and on the Principles of Mercantile Jurisprudence. Fourth Edition. Edinb. 1821. 4to. 2 vols. 1l. 1s.

— Henry. Historical Essay on the Original of Painting. Lond. 1728. 8vo. 4s.

BELL, Henry Nugent. Huntingdon Peerage: to which is prefixed a genealogical and biographical History of the illustrious House of Hastings, including a Memoir of the present Earl and Family. Lond. 1820. (Second edition, with portraits, 1821.) 4to. 1*l*.1s.

Contains pp. 403, with a portrait of the Earl of Huntingdon. The genealogical account of the family is wholly recomposed from the most authentic sources, and the singular circumstances attending the establishment of the claim to the title of Huntingdon, which had been unclaimed for nearly thirty years, are detailed with more spirit and vivacity than truth. To the unsold copies a new title page was affixed in 1821, with the addition of a Genealogical Table, and portraits of the Countess of Huntingdon, Jane Shore, Lady Jane Grey, Henry Hastings of the Woodlands, and the Author.

— Major James. Chronological Tables of Universal History, brought down to the end of the Reign of George III. Lond. 1820. royal folio, 1*l*. 10s.

[Quite superseded by the Oxford Chronological Tables.]

— John. Gratiarum Actio ob profligatam Hispanorum Classem, que Ecclesie Dei in vtroque Britanniæ Regno extremam Vastitatem minata est. Edinb. 1590. 16mo.

A poem, in Latin elegiac verse, consisting of six leaves, dedicated by the author Johanes Belus, to Mr. Robert Bruce, M. in Edinburgh.

— of Antermony. Travels from St. Petersburg, in Russia, to divers parts of Asia. Glasg. 1763. 4to. 2 vols.

'The best model for travel-writing in the English language.'—*Quart. Review.* Drury, 539, 1*l*. 2s. Gough, 634, 1*l*. 4s. Bindley, pt. i. 594, 1*l*. 4s. Sir P. Thompson, 124, 1*l*. 11s. 6d. Heath, 2547, 2*l*. 12s. 6d. Fonthill, 311, 3*l*. 3s. Reprinted Dublin, 1764, 8vo. 2 vols. Edinb. 1788, 8vo. 2 vols. Edinb. 1806, 8vo. 2 vols. and also in the seventh volume of Pinkerton's Collection of Voyages and Travels.

— John, New Pantheon; or, Historical Dictionary of the Gods, Demi-Gods, Heroes, and Fabulous Persons of Antiquity, &c. Lond. 1790. 4to. 2 vols. in 1. with plates.

An excellent and useful compilation. Dent, pt. i. 456, 1*l*. 5s.

— Theatre. } Theatre.
   Poets.   } *See* Poets.
   Fugitive Poetry. } Poetry.

— John. Principles of Surgery. Edinb. 1801, 6, 7. 4to. 3 vols. with 160 plates, 1*l*. 16s.

— John and Charles. Anatomy and Physiology of the Human Body; and the Anatomy and Physiology of the Brain and Nerves, the Organs and the Senses, and the Viscera, by Charles Bell. Fifth Edition. Lond. 1822. 8vo. 3 vols. [Sixth edition, 1829] 1*l*. 7s.

Mr. John Bell likewise published engravings of the Bones, Muscles, and Joints. Third Edition, 4to. 1*l*. 11s. 6d.

— Robert. Treatise on the Election Laws, as they relate to Scotland, in the Parliament of the United Kingdom of Great Britain and Ireland. Edinb. 1812. 4to. 2*l*. 5s.

— Dictionary of the Law of Scotland. Second Edition. Edinb. 1815. 8vo. 2 vols. 1*l*. 4s.

— System of the Form of Deeds used in Scotland. Edinb. 1811. 8vo. 7 vols. 4*l*. 10s.

Best edition. The seventh volume, intended as a supplement to former editions, is sold separately. Mr. Bell has published several other Scotch Law Books.

— Thomas. Survey of Popery. Lond. 1596. 4to.

Bindley, pt. i. 1080, 1*l*. 7s.

— Anatomie of Popish Tyrannie. Lond. 1603. 4to.

Black letter. Interesting for the notices it affords of many distinguished Jesuits in England, during the reign of Elizabeth. Reed, 3320, 8s. Bell published other works relative to Popery, several of which were in the Gordonstoun Library, nos. 147 to 153. In the Bodleian Library is 'The dolefvl Knell of Thomas Bell,' by B. C. (Father Parsons.) Roane, 1607, 8vo.

— Thomas. Roma Restituta, sive Antiquitatum Romanarum Compendium absolutum, ex optimis Authoribus in Usum studiosæ juventutis collectum. Glasg. 1672. 8vo. 5s.

A very brief compendium, highly extolled by contemporary versifiers. After the fourth book is a 'Coronis de Scotorum Stratagematis.' Reprinted Lond. 1677. 12mo.

BELL, Wm. D.D. Enquiry into the Divine Missions of John the Baptist and Jesus Christ. Lond. 1761. 8vo. 5s.

Williams, 16s, 12s. The works of this writer are recommended by Bishop Watson.

Bella Scot-Anglica.—A Brief of all the Battells and Martial Encounters which have happened 'twixt England and Scotland from all Times to this present. Lond. 1648. 4to. 6s.

BELLAMY, George Anne. Apology for her Life, written by herself. To which is annexed, her original Letter to John Calcraft, Esq., advertised to be published in October, 1767, but which was then violently suppressed. Lond. 1785. 12mo. 6 vols. with portrait by Bartolozzi, and frontispieces, 15s.

Vol. vi. was published subsequently, and is frequently wanting. Duke of York, 3058, 5 vols. 18s. An edition was published Dublin, 1785, in 2 vols. In 1785, appeared 'Letters addressed to Mrs. Bellamy, occasioned by her Apology, by Edward Willet,' 8vo. Reed, 8615, 6s. 6d.

—— John. History of all Religions. A new and enlarged Edition. Lond. 1813. 12mo. 5s.

This writer published two numbers of a new translation of the Bible, which met with very little encouragement.

—— Thomas. Philanax Anglicus: or, a Christian Caveat for all Kings, Princes, and Prelates, how they entrust a Sort of pretended Protestants of Integrity, or suffer them to commix with their Government. Lond. 1663. 8vo. 5s.

A curious account of this work will be found in Dr. Bliss's edition of Wood's Athen. Oxon. iv. 139.

BELLARMIN, Robert. Responsio ad Librvm inscriptvm 'Triplici nodo triplex Cuneus.' 1608. 4to. 5s.

This answer to King James appeared under the fictitious name of Matthæus Tortus.

—— A trve Relation of the last Sicknes and Death of Cardinall Bellarmine, who died in Rome the seauenteenth Day of September, 1621: by C. E. of the Society of Jesus. 1622. 12mo.

Bindley, pt. iii. 298, 4s.

'Bellarmin was one of the best controversial writers of his time: few authors have done greater honour to their profession or opinions, and certain it is, none have ever more ably defended the cause of the Romish church, or contended in favour of the Pope with greater advantage.'—Dr. Bliss.

BELLAY, William de. Instructions for the Warres, translated (from the French) by Paule Iue, Gent. Lond. 1589. 4to. 7s. 6d.

Black letter. Contains 312 pp. besides dedication, &c.

Belle Assemblée, La, from the Commencement in 1806 to the present Time. Lond. royal 8vo.

Published monthly, (at 3s. 6d. per part) with portraits and plates of costume, and which for future ages will form a valuable record of the costume of part of the last, and present century. [Discontinued in 1832.]

BELLCHACHIUS, Ogerius. Sacrosancta Bvcolica Elizabeth Britanniæ, Franciæ, et Hiberniæ Reginæ dicata. Lond. 1583. 4to.

A copy is in the British Museum.

BELLENDENUS, Gulielmus. Caroli primi et Henriettæ Mariæ, Regis et Reginæ Magnæ Britanniæ, &c. Epithalamivm. Paris, 1625. 4to.

A copy is in the British Museum.

—— Ciceronis Consul, Senator, Senatusque Romanus, 8vo. plate by Gualtier. Paris, 1612. Dedicated to Prince Henry.

Bridges, 1726, 2l. 12s. 6d. Duke of Grafton, 3l.

—— Cicero's Prince, the Reasons and Counsels for Settlement and good Government of a Kingdom, collected out of Cicero's Works. Lond. 1668. 12mo.

Bindley, pt. i. 644, 3s. White Knights, pt. i. 849, morocco, 7s.

—— De Statu prisci orbis Libri tres. Editio secunda, longè emendatior. Lond. 1787. 8vo. 15s.

With an elaborate and learned preface by the editor, Dr. Parr, and portraits of Burke,

Fox, and North, to each of whom sections are dedicated. Drury, 428, russia, 16s. Sir M. M. Sykes, pt. i. 215, morocco, 1l. 2s. Horne Tooke, 49, 1l. 5s.
The 'Præfatio,' separately, 1788, 8vo. Bindley, pt ii. 2246. with the portraits of Burke, Fox, and North, and the cancelled leaf, 13s. pt. iii. 76, with the cancelled leaf, 6s. 6d.

— A free translation of the Preface to Bellendenus (by the Rev. Wm. Beloe). Lond. 1788. 8vo. 3s. 6d.
Hollis, 1013, 8s. Horne Tooke, 514, 12s. 6d. This celebrated preface gave rise to the following tracts:—
Remarks on the new Edition of Bellendenus, with some Observations on the extraordinary Preface. 1787. 8vo.
Animadversions on the political part of the Preface to Bellendenus. 1788. 8vo.
In olentem Bellendeni Editorem Carmen Antamoellæum. With an Epistle dedicatory to the free translator of the celebrated Preface to Bellendenus. 4to.
The Parriad, addressed to the Editor of Bellendene, upon his elegant but illiberal Preface. By William Chapman, A.M. 1788. 4to.

Bellendenus, de tribus Luminibus Romanorum libri XVI. folio. Paris, 1634. 2l. 12s. 6d.
'This celebrated work is posthumous, and relates to Cicero only.'—*Bibl. Parriana.*

BELLERS, Fettiplace. Delineation of universal Law. Lond. 1754. 4to. 6s.
An excellent outline. A former edition appeared 1740. 4to. 3s. Mr. Bellers likewise published 'On the Ends of Society,' 1759. 4to.

— Fulke, Sermon, July 24, 1655, at the Interment of John Lamotte, Esq. Ald. of London. Lond. 1656. 4to. with portrait by Faithorne.

BELLEWE, Richard. Les Ans dv Roy Richard le second. Lond. 1585. 8vo. 10s. 6d.
This book forms a substitute for the year book of that reign, which is wholly omitted.

BELLICARD, M. Observations upon the Antiquities of Herculaneum. Lond. 1753. 8vo. with 42 plates, 6s.
An ingenious work, containing some particulars which had escaped the observation of former writers.

BELLIN, Nicholas. Essai géographique sur les Isles Britanniques. Paris, 1757. 4to. 7s.

BELLOMAYUS, Joannes. Gradus Comparationum cum Verbis anomalis simul cum eorum Compositis. Lond. by me John Toye, 1531. 4to.
The only piece known printed by John Toye. It consists of eight leaves, and has John Scot's device at the end. Dr. Dibdin enumerates three other editions printed by W. de Worde, 1526, 1527, and 1530.

BELLON, P. Irish Spaw; being a Short Discourse on Mineral Waters in general, &c. Dublin, 1684. 8vo.
A copy is in the British Museum. Nassau, pt. i. 238, 1l. 10s.

BELLOPOELIUS, Petrus. De Pace inter invictissimos Henricum Galliarvm et Edvardvm Angliæ Reges Oratio. Londini in Ædibus Guill. Powell, 1552. 4to.
Contains K 5, in fours. Dedicated to John Duke of Northumberland.

Bellora and Fidelio. *See* GREENE, Robert.

BELLOT, James, French Methode, Lond. 1588. 8vo.
Bindley, pt. i. 671, 15s. Not mentioned by Dr. Dibdin, who, however, notices that James Bellot had licence to print 'The Englishe Skoolmaster.'

Bellum Grammaticale, a Discourse of grete War and Dissention between two worthy Princes, the Noun and the Verb, contending for the chiefe Place or Dignity in Oration, turned into English by William Haywarde. Lond. 1576. 8vo.
Wood mentions an edition of the date of 1574, and states that he was informed that Dr. Leonard Hutten was the author of the Trag. Com. called Bellum Grammaticale.

Bellum Grammaticale; sive Nominum Verborumque Discordia civilis. Lond. 1635. 12mo.
Acted before Queen Elizabeth in Christ Church, Oxford, on Sunday, the 24th of Sept. 1592. An edition 1638. Roxburghe, 3649, 5s.—Edinb. 1698. Bindley, pt. i. 843, 10s.—London, 1729. Nassau, pt. i. 239, 4s.

BELLUS. *Anglice* BELL.

Belman.—The Belman of London. *See* DECKER, Thomas.

— Merry Bell-man's Out-Cryes, or the Cities O Yes! being a mad merry Ditty, both pleasant and witty, to be cry'd in Prick-Song

Prose, through County and City. Printed in the Year of Bartledum Fair, 1655. 4to.
King and Lochée's in March 1810, 15s.
— The Bell-Man's Treasury, containing above a hundred several Verses, fitted for all Humours and Fancies, and suited to all Times and Seasons. Lond. 1707. 8vo. front. 18s.
Perry, 13s. 6d.

BELOE, Rev. William. Anecdotes of Literature and scarce Books. Lond. 1807-12. 8vo. 6 vols.
A work containing much bibliographical information, and extracts from curious works. Bindley, pt. i. 411, 1l. 13s. Nassau, pt. i. 233, 1l. 14s. Drury, 429, 1l. 15s. Brockett, 112, 2l. Strettell, 97, 2l. 18s.
Mr. Beloe likewise published 'Miscellanies,' 1795, 12mo. 3 vols. 7s. 6d. Fonthill, 3561, 1l. 16s. And also translations of Herodotus, Coluthus, Aulus Gellius, &c. [also Julia, or Rash Follies' 1798, 4to. P.P.]

— Sexagenarian; or, Recollections of a literary Life. Lond. 1817. 8vo. 2 vols. 1l. 1s.
[Second edition, 1818, in which much is suppressed, 10s. 6d.]
These volumes for presumption, misstatement, and malignity, have rarely b en exceeded, or even equalled. Nassau, pt. i. 234, 7s, Strettell, 98, with a MS. Key, 1l. 11s. 6d. Bindley, pt. i. 410, with a MS. Key, 1l. 18s.

BELSHAM, Thomas. Memoirs of the late Rev. Theophilus Lindsey, A.M., with a brief Analysis of his Works; also, a General View of the Progress of the Unitarian Doctrine in England and America. Lond. 1812. 8vo. 12s.
This writer has published many other works, which are held in estimation by those of the Unitarian persuasion.

— William. Essays, philosophical, historical, and literary. Lond. 1789-91. 8vo. 2 vols. 10s. 6d.
Reprinted 1799.

— History of Great Britain from the Revolution 1688, to the Conclusion of the Treaty of Amiens in 1802. Lond. 1805. 8vo. 12 vols. best edition, 2l. 12s. 6d.
In little estimation. An edition 1796, 4to. 5 vols. Sir M. M. Sykes, pt. i. 414, 1l. 1798, 8vo. 10 vols. Dent, pt. i. 204, 1l. 12s.

BELTRAMI, J. C. Pilgrimage in Europe and America, leading to the Discovery of the Sources of the Mississippi, and Bloody River, &c. Lond. 1828. 2 vols. 8vo.

BELUS. *Anglice* BELL.

Bel-vedere, or the Garden of the Muses. *See* BODENHAM, John.

BELZONI, G. Narrative of the Operations and recent Discoveries within the Pyramids, Temples, Tombs, and Excavations in Egypt and Nubia. Lond. 1820. 4to. with a portrait.
A much esteemed and highly valuable work. Dent, pt. i. 457, 1l. 7s. Sir M. M. Sykes, pt. i. 415, 1l. 1s. In illustration of this narrative a series of 44 plates, followed by a Supplement containing 6, was published. Duke of York, 718, with the coloured plates, 6l. 2s. 6d. Drury, 540, russia, with the coloured plates, 5l. 2s. 6d.
A third edition of the narrative was published 1822, 8vo. 2 vols. 1l. 8s.

BEMETZRIEDER, ——. Music made easy to every Capacity, in a Series of Dialogues, translated by Giffard Bernard. Lond. 1778. 4to. 3s. 6d.
Another work by Bemetzrieder, entitled Compendium of a new Method of Music, 1783, 8vo. also, A complete Treatise of Music, 1800, 4to.

BENDISH, Sir Thomas. Newes from Tvrkie, or a true Relation of the Passages of Sir Thomas Bendish, Ambassador, with the grand Seignieur at Constantinople. Lond. 1648. 4to.
A copy is in the British Museum.

BENDLOE. *See* BENLOE.
BENEDICT. *See* BENNET.
BENEDICTUS, Abbas Petroburgensis. *Vide* HEARNE, Thomas.

BENESE, Sir Richard de. Boke of Measurynge of Lande. Lond. by Thomas Colwell [1562]. 16mo.
Black letter, G in eights, introduced with 'The Preface of Tho. Paynell, Chanon of Marton.' Bindley, pt. iv. 1059, 3s. According to the British Museum Catalogue there were two editions printed by Tho. Colwell. An edition, imprinted by R. Wyer, 16mo. Inglis, 82, 9s. 6d. White Knights, pt. i. 415, russia, 14s. Another edition, Southwark, by James Nicholson, 16mo.

Bengálí Selections, with Translations and a Vocabulary, by G. C. Haughton. Lond. 1822. 4to. 1*l*. 10s.

BENGELIUS, John Albert. Introduction to his Exposition of the Apocalypse; with his Preface, and the greatest part of the Conclusion of it: and also his marginal Notes on the Text, which are a Summary of the whole Exposition, translated from the High-Dutch, by John Robertson, M.D. Lond. 1757. 8vo. 5s.

An esteemed work.

BENGER, Miss. Memoirs of Anne Boleyn, Queen of Henry VIII. Lond. 1821. 8vo. 2 vols. 16s.

— Memoirs of Mary Queen of Scots, with Anecdotes of the Court of Henry II. Lond. 1822. 8vo. 2 vols. 24s.

Taken principally from Chalmers' Life of this unfortunate Princess.

— Memoirs of Elizabeth Stuart, Queen of Bohemia, Daughter of King James I. Lond. 1825. post 8vo. 2 vols. 1*l*. 4s.

This authoress has likewise published Memoirs of Mrs. Elizabeth Hamilton, 8vo. 2 vols. 1*l*. 1s. and of Mr. John Tobin, 1820, 8vo. 12s. Her historical memoirs are of no great value. (These prices are all now considerably lower.)

Ben Gorion. *Vide* JOSEPH Ben Gorion.

BENJAMIN, Rabbi. Travels of Rabbi Benjamin, Son of Jonah of Tudela; through Europe, Asia, and Africa, from the ancient Kingdom of Navarre, to the Frontiers of China. Translated from the Hebrew, with a Dissertation and Notes, by the Rev. B. Gerrans. Lond. 1783. 12mo. 5s.

A very faithful translation of a curious but fictitious narrative, written to lift up the sinking spirits of his countrymen. It will be found in Harris and Pinkerton's Collections of Voyages and Travels, [and in Bohn's 'Early Travels in Palestine.']

BENLOE, Wm. Reports en les Regnes de Henry VIII., Edward VI., philip et Mary, et Elizabeth. 1661. 5s.

In this edition there is a vacancy, viz. pp. 44 to 83, and the 4 pages preceding 44 are wrongly numbered.

— and William Dalison. Reports des divers Pleadings et Cases en le Court del Common-bank, en le Regnes de les Roys Henry VII., Henry VIII., Edward VI., et les Reines Mary et Elizabeth. Lond. 1689. folio, 15s.

BENLOWES, Edward. Sphinx Theologica, seu Musica Templi, ubi Discordia Concors. Cantab. 1626. [also 1628] 8vo.

— A Buckler against the fear of Death, or pious and profitable Meditations and Consolations, front. Cambridge, 1640. 12mo.

Jolley, 1843, 2*l*. 14s.

— Honorifica Armorum Cessatio, sive Pacis et Fidei Associatio Feb. 11. An. 1643. 8vo.

— Theophila, or Love's Sacrifice, a Divine Poem. Lond. 1652. folio.

This very extraordinary and rare Book is seldom found complete.

Collation.

Title. A. 2 leaves. ¶ 2 leaves. ¶¶ 2 leaves. ¶¶¶ 2 leaves. B 6 leaves. C 6 leaves—but between C and C 2 should be inserted (c) 2 leaves, and (d) one leaf. It will be found by this arrangement, that all the catchwords agree. C—N, 6 leaves each; sheet O, seven leaves, pages 123, 124, being double; the first set not containing engraved verses at the bottom of page 123, and the second set containing them; the latter very rare. P—V, 6 leaves; X—Nn, 2 leaves each. The paging 1—268 commences on sheet D.

Engravings and Decorations.

1. Portrait of Benlowes, surrounded by a wreath of laurel, beautifully etched (by Barlow).
2. Opposite A 2. A Lady in a Winter habit, with a mask on, engraved by Hollar.
3. Canto I. The Prelibation to the Sacrifice (sig. D, p. 1.) an engraving with eight verses at the bottom, commencing
"The Author musing, here survay."
4. Canto 2. The Humiliation, with eight verses, commencing
"Satan caused Eves, Eve Adams fall."
5. At page 25. A wood-cut, (size of the page) Adam and Eve, and the Tree of Knowledge. This cut first occurs in Barker's Bible, 1633, folio.

6. P. 37, Canto 3. The Restauration, with eight verses, commencing "Here Angels tender from the Skie."
7. P. 50, Canto 4. The Inamoration, with eight verses, commencing "The Soule against Temptation fights."
8. P. 67, Canto 5. The Representation, with eight verses, commencing "View here the Author's high Designe." This plate is printed at the back of the letter-press of p. 65.
9. Canto 6. The Association, with eight verses, commencing, "Here Abraham, David, Daniel stand."
10. Canto 7. The Contemplation, without verses. (An angel, with an emblem of eternity in his hand, Theophila looking upwards in an attitude of adoration.)
11. Canto 8. The Admiration, without verses. (Theophila supported by two Angels ascending.) The other half of the Engraving representing the Fall of the Wicked into Hell.
12. P. 122–3. An Emblematical Female Figure of Astronomy.
13. Canto 9. The Recapitulation, (A Portrait of Theophila treading on a serpent; a palm-branch and book in her right hand, &c.) This plate is larger than the others, and is very rare.
14. P. 161. Ludus Literarius Christianus, Anthreno-Tripsis seu Crabronum tritur Edw. Benlosii. An Engraving surrounded by a border of flowers, with seven verses at bottom, very rare.
15. Canto 10. The Abnegation. The Author looking up to the Heavens, from which a hand, with an emblem of Eternity, surmounted by a Crown, also a figure in armour, with a cloak, in the foreground.
16. Canto 11, at the End, p. 206. The Spring, an Engraving by Hollar, on the Letter-press.
17. P. 209. Typus Orbis Terrarum, (the two Hemispheres,) on the Letter-press.
18 and 19. P. 210, 212. Two small Engravings on the Letter-press.
20. Canto 12. The Segregation, a faint Etching, very rare. The author in the country, discoursing with a shepherd, &c.
21. Canto 13. The Re-invitation. A Female Figure, in an attitude of Prayer. In the corner, on a scroll, Theophila's Love Sacrifice, by Edw. Benlowes, Esq. Lombart sculp. with six Latin and six English verses, signed Jer. Collier.
22. On p. 245. A wood-cut of Q. Elizabeth praying.
23, 24. At end of the volume, two singular Engravings, one by T. Cecill, A.D. 1632, the other with a Monogram.

The above collation was made from a copy supposed perfect, but on comparing it with another, formerly Mr. Inglis's, the following additional engravings were found. This copy, it is said, cost the proprietor 60*l*.
1. An Etching. Subject; St Matthew, ch. 21, verse 28.
2, 3, 4, 5. The Four Seasons, by Hollar, 3 quarter length; the regular set.
6. An Engraving; the day of Judgment. In the corner at bottom "Vanitas vanitat omnia Vanitas," &c.
7. The author in the Country conversing with a Shepherd. The same subject as in plate 20, but a different engraving.
8. A curious emblematical engraving allusive to the vanity of the world; being the bust of a female, a Cupid issuing from the forehead, the breast formed by globes, &c. very rare.
9. An Engraving with a legend in the left corner, at the top, "the Extravagant Shepherd."
10. A folded Engraving, at the left corner at bottom, "Ianbattest Iaspers In, et Fe."
11. An Engraving intituled "A curious piece of antiquity on the Crucifixion of our Saviour and the two Thieves."

Inglis, 198, morocco, 4*l*. 18*s*. Bibl. Anglo-Poet. 18, 8*l*. 19, 8*l*. 8*s*. Bindley, pt. ii. 189, 12*l*. 5*s*. Nassau, pt. i. 437, (said to be the most perfect copy in existence) 26*l*. 5*s*.
[Several of the plates which occur in Jno. Davies's Extravagant Shepherd, folio, 1654, are sometimes found in Benlowe's Theophila.]

BENLOWES, E. Summary of divine Wisedome. Lond. 1657. 4to.
In verse. Bindley, pt. iv. 1076.
— Oxonii Encomium. Oxon. 1672. folio.
Four sheets, mostly in Latin verse.
— Quarleidis. *Vide* Quarle's Emblems, 1635.
A life of Benlowes, with a list of his works, will be found in Dr. Bliss's edition of Wood's Fasti, ii. 358-9.

BENNET, Saint. The Rule of Seynt Benet. Imprinted by Richarde Pynson, 1516. folio.
Black letter, contains sign. G 7. A Treatise relating to the rule of St. Bennet will be found in 'Diuers fruytful Ghostly Maters,' printed by Caxton.
— Rule of St. Benedict, by C. F. Douay. 1638.
Dedicated to 'Mrs. Anne Carie, daughter to the Lord Viscount Faukland.' Another work, entitled 'Life and Miracles of St. Benedict,' 1638, 12mo. with plates. Heath, 1601, 9*s*. 6*d*.

BENNET, Benjamin. Memorial of the Reformation, and of Britain's Deliverances from Popery and arbitrary Power, with a Defence. Lond. 1721-3. 8vo. 2 vols. 9s.
— Christian Oratory; or the Devotion of the Closet displayed. Lond. 1725. 8vo. with portrait, by J. Pine, 6s.
The work of a dissenting minister of considerable note, frequently reprinted. An edition 1732, 8vo. 2 vols. Williams, 165, 2l. A new edition, with an Appendix, 1811, 8vo. 2 vols. 12s.
— Chr. Theatri Tabidorum Vestibulum et Tabidorum Theatrum. Lond. 1654-6. 8vo. 2 vols. with portrait by Lombart, 7s.
— George. Olam Haneskamoth; or a View of the Intermediate state. Carlisle, 1800. 8vo. 7s. 6d.
Highly commended by Bp. Horsley, who pronounces it 'a work of various erudition and deep research.'
— H. Treasury of Wit: being a methodical Selection of about twelve hundred, the best, Apophthegms and Jests; from Books in several Languages. Lond. 1786. 12mo. 2 vols. 10s. 6d.
Nassau, pt. i. 235, 9s.
[A compilation by John Pinkerton.]
— John. Madrigalls to fovre Voyces, newly pvblished by John Bennett, his first Works. Lond. 1599. 15s.
This volume, dedicated to Ralph Asheton, Esq. contains xvii songs.
— Thomas. Paraphrase. with Annotations upon the Book of Common Prayer. Lond. 1708. 8vo. 3s. 6d.
This eminent English divine likewise published an Essay on the xxxix Articles, 1715, 8vo. 4s., and many other religious treatises, chiefly controversial. His History of Forms of Prayer, Camb. 1708, 8vo. Williams, 164, 1l. 15s.
BENNO, Cardinal. Life of Hildebrand, called Gregory the 7th, translated by Thomas Swinerton, under the name of Joh. Roberts. Lond. by W. de Worde, 1588. 4to.
Reprinted in 12mo. for John Byddell, the same year. A copy of which is in the Bodleian Library. See Dr. Bliss's Edition of Wood's Athen. Oxon.
BENSE, Peter. Analogo-Diaphora, seu Concordia discrepans, et Discrepantia concordans trium Linguarum Gallicæ, Italicæ et Hispanicæ. Oxon. 1637. 8vo.
BENSON, George, D.D. Paraphrase and Notes on six of the Epistles of St. Paul, and on the seven Catholic Epistles; to which are annexed several critical Dissertations. London, 1752-6. 4to. 2 vols. 2l. 2s.
Best edition of a work written in continuation of Locke's attempt to illustrate the Epistles, and with Pierce's work, completes the design. Hollis, 189, 1l. 5s. Gosset, 714, 1l. 16s. Williams, 221, 3l. 9s.
— History of the First Planting of the Christian Religion. London, 1756. 4to. 3 vols.
Best edition of a work of very considerable research, full of important matter. Gosset, 715, 1l. 4s. The first edition appeared in 1735, 4to. 2 vols. Hollis, 188, 10s.
— Reasonableness of the Christian Religion as delivered in the Scriptures. The third Edition. Lond. 1759. 8vo. 2 vols.
'The author not only advances many arguments in proof of the truth of the Christian Religion, but obviates in a familiar way the chief objections of the Anti-revelationists.'—*Bishop Watson.*
An edition, 1743. Williams, 167, 8s.
— History of the Life of Jesus Christ, taken from the New Testament: to which is added, Memoirs of the Author. London, 1764. 4to. with port. by J. McArdell, 1l. 1s.
The creed of this learned writer, which was Arian, verging to Socinian, prevented him, says Mr. Orme, from doing justice to his subject. Williams, 222, 2l. 12s. 6d.
— Thomas. Vocabularium Anglo-Saxonicum, Lexico Gul. Somneri magna parte auctius. Oxoniæ, 1701. 8vo. 15s.
Bishop of Ely, 108, 1l.
— Wm. Letters concerning Poetical Translations, and Virgil's and Milton's Arts of Verse. Lond. 1739. 8vo. 4s.
Published without the author's name.

BENSON, Robert, M.A. Sketches of Corsica, a Journal written during a Visit to that Island in 1823, with an Outline of its History and Specimens of the Language and Poetry of the People. Lond. 1825. 8vo. 10s. 6d.
This interesting work is spoken of with much approbation by Sir Walter Scott in his life of Napoleon.

BENT, William. Meteorological Journals and Extracts, from 1786 to 1808, kept in London. 8vo.

— Literary Advertiser, or List of New Publications from the Commencement in January, 1802, to the present time. Lond. 4to.
Published monthly. [Mr. Bent is also editor and publisher of the London Catalogue.]

BENTHAM, Edward. Reflections upon the Study of Divinity, to which are subjoined, Heads of a Course of Lectures. Oxford, 1774. 8vo. 4s.
A work containing many judicious observations: the heads of lectures exhibit, perhaps, as complete a plan of Theological studies as was ever delivered.

— Orationes Funebres, Græcæ. Oxon. 1746. 8vo.
Best edition. A very elegant work, with an index and valuable notes. Dent, pt. ii. 47, russia, 11s. Frequently reprinted.

— George. Outline of a New System of Logic. Lond. 1827. 8vo.

— James, M.A. History and Antiquities of the Conventual and Cathedral Church of Ely, 673—1771. Cambridge, 1771. royal 4to.
Vol. i. A—Ee 4, pp. 224, besides title; dedication two pages, list of subscribers, four pages; preface, five pages; contents and errata, three pages.—Vol. ii. Ff—Oo 2, pp. 225—92. Appendix and index *70 pages besides the title page, and an inventory of two pages. The list of plates with directions to the binder form pages 290, 291, 292. In Davis' Olio, will be found Cole's Notes on this work. Nassau, pt. i. 399, russia, 4l. 4s. Towneley, p. ii. 272, 4l 10s. Bindley, pt. i. 722, russia, 4l. 18s. Heath, 4632, russia, 5l. Baker, 169, morocco, 6l. 16s. 6d. Towneshend, 361, russia, 8l. 15s. Fonthill, 8308, morocco, 8l. 17s. 6d. Dent, pt. i. 458, with the Supplement, 1817, 2 vols. russia, 7l. 15s. Drury, 543, with the Supplement, 2 vols. in hogskin, 8l. 15s. A few copies were taken off on large paper.

— Supplement to the first edition of Mr. Bentham's Ely, by William Stevenson. Norwich, 1817. imperial 4to.
One hundred and eighty copies were printed in imperial and twenty-five on elephant paper, with proofs on India paper. Imperial 4to. Fonthill, 590, 3l. Title, dedication, preface, contents, and list of subscribers xii. pp. Memoirs of Bentham, 20 pages. Addenda, half-title. An acknowledgment, &c. two pages; addenda, 28 pages; supplement, 92 pages; notes, &c. preceded by a half-title, 154 pages (sign. T and U are repeated with asterisks); appendix, &c. *54 pages; catalogue of the plates and errata, 1 page.

— History of Ely. The second edition, edited by W. Stevenson. Lond. 1812. imperial 4to.
Of this edition, 250 copies were printed on imperial, and 25 on elephant paper. Vol. i. Title, dedication, advertisement, original dedication, preface, and contents, memoirs of Bentham, with the pedigree (folded) after which the work, 224 pp. Vol. ii. title, an inventory, then the work, pp. 225—92, after which appendix, *70 pages. Addenda, Title, the Editor's thanks, and contents, then the addenda 28 pages, with directions to the binder, and errata on a separate slip. This edition has also several plates more than the former one.

— Supplement to the second edition, by William Stevenson. Norwich, 1817. imperial 4to.
The variations in the supplement to the second edition, consist of a slight alteration in the title, and the omission of the memoirs of Mr. Bentham, the addenda and plates 2 and 15; in other respects the work is the same. Only 84 copies of this supplementary volume were printed.

— Jeremy. Works published under the superintendence of his executor, John Bowring. 11 vols. 8vo. Edinb. 1843, &c. 5l. 5s.

— Introduction to the Principles of Morals and Legislation. A new edition, corrected by the Author. Lond. 1823. 2 vols. 8vo. with port. by Worthington, 1l. 1s.
'In this work the author has given to the public his enlarged and enlightened views, and has laboured for all nations, and for all ages yet to come.'—*Edinb. Review.* The first edition was printed in 4to. 1780, and republished in 1789.

List of (some of) Mr. Bentham's Works.

Fragment on Government, being a Critique on Blackstone's Commentaries, 1776, 8vo. Second edition enlarged 1823, 8vo. 8s.
View of the Hard Labour Bill, 1778, 8vo. 3s.
Defence of Usury, 1787, 3s. 6d. Second edition, Dublin, 1791. Third edition, with a protest against Law Taxes, 1816, 12mo. 7s.
An Essay on the usefulness of Chemistry, translated from the Swedish of Bergman, 1783. 8vo.
Draught of a Code for the Organisation of the Judical Establishment in France, 1791, 8vo. pp. 242.
Panopticon, or the Inspection House, 1791, 12mo. 3 parts in 2 vols. 14s.
The 3 plates are seldom found in the work.
Essay on Political Tactics, 1791, 4to. 5s.
To the National Convention of France, 'Emancipate your Colonies,' 1793, 8vo. pp. 48.
Supply without Burden, or Escheat vice Taxation, with a Protest against Law Taxes, 1796, 12mo. 3s.
Pauper Management, 1797, 8vo. pp. 288.
Published in Young's Annals of Agriculture.
Letters (Two) to Lord Pelham, 1802, 8vo. pp. 80 and 72.
Plea for the Constitution, 1803, 8vo. 3s. 6d.
Scotch Reform, 1808, 8vo. 6s.
Chrestomathia, 1816-7, 8vo. 2 parts, 15s.
Parliamentary Reform Catechism, 1817, 8vo. 8s.
Ditto, with Additions, by Wooler, 8vo. 4s.
On Codification and Public Instruction, 1817, 8vo. 8s.
'Swear not at all,' 1817, 8vo. 3s. 6d.
A Table of the Springs of Action, 1817, 8vo. 3s. 6d.
Church of Englandism and its Catechism examined, 1818, 8vo. 1l.
Radical Reform Bill, 1819, 8vo. 4s.
The King against Sir C. Wolesley, Bart. &c. 1820, 8vo. 1s.
The King against Edmonds, &c. 1820, 8vo. 1s.
Observations on the restrictive and prohibitory commercial System, 1821, 8vo. 2s.
Art of packing special Juries, 1821, 8vo. 10s. 6d.
On the Liberty of the Press, 1821, 8vo. 1s.
Three Tracts relative to Spanish and Portuguese Affairs, 1821, 8vo. 1s. 6d.
Letter to Count Toreno, on the Spanish Penal Code, 1822, 8vo. 5s.
Not Paul but Jesus, by Gamaliel Smith, 1823, 8vo. 12s.
Truth versus Ashurst, 1823, 8vo. 6d.
Book of Fallacies, 1824, 8vo. 12s.

Observations on Peel's Police Magistrates' Salary Raising Bill, 1825, 8vo. 2s. 6.
Mother Church relieved by Bleeding, 1825, 8vo. 1s.
Rationale of Reward, 1825, 8vo. 12s.
Indications respecting Lord Eldon, 1825, 8vo. 3s.
Postscript to ditto, 1826, 8vo. 1s.
Rationale of Judicial Evidence, 1827, 8vo. 5 vols. 3l.
Introduction to the Rationale of Evidence, 8vo. pp. 148.
Defence of Economy against Burke. In Pamphleteer, No. XVI.
Defence of Economy against Rose. In Pamphleteer, No. XX.
Leading Principles of a constitutional Code for any State. In Pamphleteer, No. XLIV.
Codification proposal, 1827, 8vo.

Apologie de l'Usure. Paris, 1790, 8vo.
Lettres sur la liberté du taux de l'intérêt de l'argent publiées par De Lessert. Paris, 1790. 8vo.
Panoptique, Memoire sur un nouveau principe pour construire des maisons d'inspection et nommément des maisons de force. Paris, 1792. 8vo.
Esquisse d'un ouvrage en faveur des Pauvres, publiée par Ad. Duquesnoy. Paris, An. X. 8vo.
Traités de Legislation civile et penale, publiés par Et. Dumont. Paris, 1802. 8vo. 3 vols. Second edition, Par. 1820. 8vo. 3 vols. Spanish translation, with Commentaries by Ramon de Salas. Madrid, 1821. 8vo. 3 vols. Second edition, Paris, 1825. 18mo. 6 vols. Two Russian translations and an Italian translation.
Théorie des Peines et des Recompenses, publiée par Et. Dumont. Londres. 1811. 8vo. 2 vols. Second edition, Paris, 1818. 8vo. 2 vols. Third edition, Paris, 1826. 8vo. 2 vols. Spanish translation, Paris. 18mo. 4 vols.
Tactique des Assemblees Legislatives, publiée par Et. Dumont. Geneve, 1815, 8vo. 2 vols. Second edition, Paris, 1822, 8vo. 2 vols. Spanish translation, Paris.
Essais de Jérémie Bentham sur la situation politique de l'Espagne. Paris, 1823. 8vo.
Essai sur la classification des principales branches d'art et science, publié par G. Bentham. Paris, 1823. 8vo.
Traite des Preuves Judiciaires, publié par Et. Dumont. Paris, 1823. 8vo. 2 vols. Spanish translation, Paris, 1825. 18mo. 4 vols. English translation, London, 1825. 8vo.
De l'Organisation Judiciaire et de la Codification, publiée par Et. Dumont. Paris, 1828. 8vo.

158

BENTIVOGLIO, Guido, Cardinal. Historicall Relations of the United Provinces and of Flanders, rendered into English by Henry [Carey] Earle of Monmouth. Lond. 1652. fol. 6s.
Prefixed is a portrait by Faithorne, of the Earl of Monmouth.

— History of the Wars of Flanders, Englished by Henry [Carey] Earle of Monmouth. Lond. 1678. folio, 6s.
Contains pp. 26 and 387, with a map of the 17 provinces and above 20 figures. To this edition is a continuation from 1671 to 1675. Roxburghe, 7945, 11s. The former edition appeared 1654, to which is prefixed a portrait of the Earl.

— Collection of Letters to divers Persons of eminence, during his Nunciature in France and Flanders. In Italian and English. Lond. 12mo. 4s.

BENTLEY, John. Halifax. *See* BENTLY, William.

— Genealogical Table of the Royal Families of England from the Norman Conquest to the year 1790. Lond. 1790. folio, 8s.

— Historical View of the Hindu Astronomy. Lond. 1825. 8vo. with plates, 14s.

— Richard, D.D. Emendationes in Menandri et Philemonjs Reliquias, ex nupera Editione Joannis Clerici. Accedit Epistola de Johanne Malela Antiocheno. Cantab. 1713. 8vo.
Combe, 662, 5s. 6d. D. of Grafton, 329, 8s. Williams, 169, 9s.

— Proposals for printing a new edition of the Greek Testament, and St. Hierom's Latin Version. Lond. 1721. 4to.
Bindley, pt. i. 917, with tracts relating to the proposals, 10s. 6d.

— Remarks upon a late Discourse of Free Thinking, (by Collins) in a Letter to F[rancis] H[are,] D.D. by Phileleutherus Lipsiensis. Camb. 1743, 8vo. 6s.
Best edition of a most valuable work which should be studied by every man who is desirous of forming just notions of biblical criticism. The edition 1737. Williams, 169, 9s. Bentley's remarks on Free Thinking are reprinted in Bishop Randolph's Enchiridion Theologicum.

— Dissertation upon the Epistles of Phalaris, with an Answer to the Objections of the Hon. Charles Boyle, to which are added Dr. Bentley's Dissertation on the Epistles of Themistocles, Socrates, Euripides, and others, and the Fables of Æsop; as originally printed, with occasional Remarks on the whole. Lond. 1777. 8vo. 10s. 6d.
A highly esteemed work. Drury, 436, 16s. Heath, 194, 19s. Edwards iii. 1l. 8s. Williams, 170, 1l. 11s. 6d. Reprinted 1816, 8vo. [and again in 1836, under the superintendence of Mr. Dyce, in connection with his Boyle Lecture, &c. In all 3 vols. 8vo. being the commencement of an edition of Bentley's Works, never completed.]
For the various tracts published on this controversy, see PHALARIS.

— Eight Sermons preached at the Hon. R. Boyle's Lecture. Oxford, 1809. 8vo. 7s. 6d.
The first Boyle Lecture preached. An edition, Camb. 1724. Williams, 168, 10s. 6d. 1735, Bindley, pt. i. 434, 10s.

— Bentleii et doctorum Virorum Epistolæ, partim mutuæ. Accedit Richardi Dawesii ad Joannem Taylorum Epistola singularis. Londini, 1807, 4to.
Edited by the late Dr. C. Burney. One hundred and fifty copies were struck off on large and fifty on small paper, all for private distribution. Prefixed are portraits and facsimile autographs of Bentley and Grævius. LARGE PAPER, Drury, 544, russia, 2l. 19s. Sir M. M. Sykes, pt. i. 418, 2l. 19s. Gough, 640, 8l. 18s. 6d. Combe, 333, 1l. 11s. 6d. Sotheby's in 1825, 3l. 6s. Reprinted Lips. 1825, 8vo. Drury, 435, 11s.
In the British Museum is a very large collection of tracts written by, and against this celebrated critic, many of which are of very rare occurrence. [Bentley's Correspondence, including these letters, was, in 1842, edited by Dr. Wordsworth; *only* 250 *copies printed*, 2l. 10s.]

— Life of, by Bp. Monk. 4to. port. 1l. 1s. Second edition, 2 vols. 8vo. Lond. 1833, 1l. 1s.

— Thomas. Monvment of Matrones: containing seuen seueral Lamps of Virginitie, or distinct Treatises; whereof the first fiue concerne Praier and Meditation, the other two last, Precepts and Examples, as the woorthie works, partlie of Men, partlie of Women. Printed by H. Denham [1582] 4to. 3 vols.

Brand, 8*l*. 18s. 6d. Woodhouse, 1803, 10*l*. 5s. Hawtrey, 1853, in 1 vol. 8*l*. 18s. 6d. resold Sotheby, June 1855, 19*l*. 19s. Inglis, 156, supposed to be the only perfect copy in existence, 15*l*. [now in the Grenville Library, British Museum.]

Each of these lamps has a distinct title-page. On the back of the first, or general title-page, is 'A Praier upon the poesie prefixed,' then follow in order ' To Queen Elizabeth.—Lampas Virginitatis.—To the Christian Reader.—Facies militantis Ecclesiæ.—Rob. Marbeck ad lectorem.—Argumentum libri.—The names of sundrie famous Queens, &c.—What ceremonie euerie woman ought by God's word to vse in the time of praier, publike or priuate." Then ' The first Lampe of Viginitie,' on 49 pages. 'The second Lampe,' on 252 pages. 'The third Lampe,' continued from the second to p. 362. At the end is a neat cut of the last judgment, on the back of which begins a table for the three lamps. ' The fourth Lampe' continued from the third to p. 1009, with the same cut of the last judgment and a table. ' The fifth Lampe,' on 213 pages, with a table at the end. ' The sixt Lampe' on 115 pages. 'The seuenth Lampe,' continued from the sixth, to p. 331.

BENTLY, William. Hallifax and its Gibbet-Law placed in a true Light, together with a Description of the Town: to which are added, the unparallel'd Tragedies committed by Sir John Eland and his grand Antagonists. Lond. 1708. 8vo. 5s.

This work was written by Dr. Samuel Midgley, when in prison for debt; but published after his death by Bently, who affixed his name as the author. An edition 1712, 12mo. with frontispiece. Heath, 4588, 15s. [1761] with a frontispiece. Fonthill, 2552, 1*l*. 6s. Sir M. M. Sykes, pt. i. 219, russia, 10s.

Benwel Village.—A most pleasant Description of Benwel Village in the County of Northumberland, by Q. Z. [Dr. Ellison] Newcastle-upon-Tyne, 1726. 12mo.

A ludicrous performance, written by Dr. Ellison. pp. 582, with two indexes and errata, 4 leaves. Bindley, pt. ii. 2229. 1*l*. 13s. Perry, pt. i. 1369, morocco, 1*l*. 13s. Brockett, 124, morocco, 1*l*. 13s. Nassau, pt. i. 956, russia, 1*l*. 17s. Towneley, pt. ii. 211, 1*l*. 17s. White Knights, pt. i. 1297, 2*l*. Thorpe, 1888, 2*l*. 2s.

BENYOWSKY, Mauritius Augustus Count de. Memoirs and Travels, consisting of his military Operations in Poland, his Exile into Kamschatka, his Escape and Voyage from that Peninsula through the Northern Pacific Ocean touching at Japan and Formosa, to Canton in China, with an Account of the French Settlement he was appointed to form upon the Island of Madagascar. Lond. 1790. 4to. 2 vols. with port. and plts.

Amidst much that is trifling, and more that is doubtful, this work contains some curious and authentic information relating to Kamschatka and Madagascar; what he states on the subject of his communications with Japan, is very suspicious. Roxburghe, 7170, 1*l*. 18s. Fonthill, 3076, 5*l*. 7s. 6d.

Beracoth.—Massaceth Beracoth, Titulus Talmudicus, in quo agitur de Benedictionibus, Precibus & Gratiarum Actionibus, adjectâ Versione Latinâ. Oxon. 1667. 8vo.

Published by Sam. Clarke 'In usum studiosorum literarum Talmudicarum in Æde Christi.'

BERCHERUS, Gulielmus. Epitaphia et Inscriptiones lugubres. Lond. 1566. 4to.

Contains E in fours. A copy is in the British Museum. Dr. Dibdin mentions an edition of the date of 1554.

BERCHTOLD, Count Leopold. Essay to direct and extend the Inquiries of patriotic Travellers. To which is annexed, a List of English and Foreign Works intended for the Instruction and Benefit of Travellers; and a Catalogue of the most interesting European Travels which have been published, in different Languages, from the earliest Times down to September 8th, 1787. Lond. 1789. 8vo. 2 vols. 7s.

BERDMORE, Samuel, D.D. Specimens of Literary Resemblance in the Works of Pope, Gray, and other celebrated Writers, with critical Observations. Lond. 1801. 8vo. 4s.

BERENGER, Richard. History of the Art of Horsemanship. Lond. 1771. 4to. 2 vols. in 1. plates.

Dent, pt. i. 459, 14s. 6d. Duke of York, 721. morocco, 1l. 10s.

BERGERAC, Cyrano de. Satyrical Characters and Handsome Descriptions in Letters, translated from the French, by a Person of Honor. Lond. 1658. 8vo.

An account of this singular and amusing work will be found in the Retrosp. Review, i. 279-87. Nassau, pt. i. 242, 4s.

— History of the World in the Sun and Moon, done into English by Tho. St. Serf, Gent. Lond. 1659. 12mo.

Towneley, pt. i. 291' 6s. 6d.

— Comical History of the States and Empires of the Worlds of the Moon and Sun; newly englished by A. Lovell. Lond. 1687. 8vo. 5s.

Prefixed is a front. by Van Hove. An interesting analysis of this curious production will be found in Dunlop's History of Fiction, iii. 334.

— Voyage to the Moon, with some Account of the Solar World, done from the French, by S. Derrick. Lond. 1753. 12mo. 4s.

To this philosophical romance on the system of Descartes, Swift is supposed to have been greatly indebted; the journey to the moon being the origin of Swift's Brobdignag, and that to the sun suggesting the voyage to Laputa.

BERGMAN, Torbern. Physical and Chemical Essays, translated from the Latin, with Notes and Illustrations, by Edm. Cullen, M.D. Lond. 1788-91. 8vo. 3 vols. 10s. 6d.

An excellent work. Several other treatises by this celebrated Swedish chemist and natural philosopher have been translated into English, viz. Outlines of Mineralogy, by William Withering, M.D. Birm. 1783. 8vo. A Dissertation of Elective Attractions. Lond. 1785, 8vo. &c.

BERINGTON, Rev. Joseph. Memoirs of Gregorio Panzani; giving an Account of his Agency in England, 1634-6, translated from the Italian original, with an Introduction and a Supplement. Lond. 1793. 8vo. 1l. 11s. 6d.

[The Supplement, beginning after page 261. is often deficient.]

Bindley, pt. i. 429, 11s. The Rev. C. Plowden published Remarks on this work. Liege, 1794, 8vo. 5s.

— History of the Lives of Abeillard and Heloisa; comprising a period of eighty-four years, from 1079 to 1163; with their genuine Letters, from the Collection at Amboise. The 2nd edition. Birm. 1788. 4to. 1l. 1s.

A valuable and accurate work, composed from authentic materials.

— History of the Reign of Henry II. and of Richard and John his Sons; with the Events of this Period, from 1154 to 1216. In which the Character of Thomas à Becket is vindicated from the Attacks of George Lord Lyttelton. Birmingham, 1790. 4to. 1l. 1s.

Roscoe. 485, 1l. 6s.

— Literary History of the Middle Ages. Lond. 1814, 4to.

Hollis, 191, 1l. 2s. Drury, 547, mor. 1l. 7s. Brockett, 484, 1l. 8s.

— Simon. Dissertations on the Mosaical Creation, Deluge, Building of Babel, and Confusion of Tongues. Lond. 1750. 8vo. 5s.

The production of a Roman Catholic writer, displaying considerable research, though held in little estimation.

BERKELEY, George, Earl of. Historical Applications, and occasional Meditations upon several Subjects, written by a Person of Honour. Lond. 1670. 12mo. 10s. 6d.

A little book, valuable for its merit, as well as its rarity. A third edition appeared in 1680, 8vo.

— Geo. Bishop of Cloyne. Works; to which is added, an Account of his Life, and several of his Letters to Thomas Prior, Esq., Dean Gervais, and Mr. Pope. Lond. 1784. 4to. 2 vols. with port. by Cooke.

Nassau, pt. i. 400, russia, 2l. 18s. Heath, 1674, russia, 3l. 13s. 6d. An edition 1820, 8vo. 3 vols. Drury, 438, 2l. 2s.

— Alciphron, or the minute Philosopher, in seven Dialogues; containing an Apology for the Christian Religion against Free-Thinkers. Lond. 1732. 8vo. 2 vols.

An argumentative dialogue, containing a powerful refutation of the doctrines of Atheism, Fatalism, and the Disbelief of Revelation. Bindley, pt. i. 294, 9s. Williams, 171, 1l. 1s.

— Siris, a Chain of philosophical

Reflections and Inquiries respecting the Virtues of Tar Water in the Plague; Farther Thoughts on Tar Water. Lond. 1747, 52. 8vo.
These tracts excited at the time of their publication much interest, and gave rise to various publications on the subject, some supporting the Bishop's tenets, others refuting them. An excellent notice of the work will be found in the Retrosp. Review, xi. 239-52.

— George. Principles of Human Knowledge. Lond. 1776. 8vo.
A truly original and masterly work. Gosset, 438, 17s. Reprinted 1820, 7s. The first edition appeared in 1734.

— Memoirs of George Berkeley, D.D. late Bishop of Cloyne, in Ireland. The second Edition, with Improvements. Lond. 1784. 8vo. 3s. 6d.
The former edition appeared in 1776.

— George Monck. Poems, with a Preface by the Editor (his Mother), consisting of some Anecdotes of Geo. Monck Berkeley, and several of his Friends. Lond. 1797. 4to.
Privately printed, with a portrait of Berkeley, from a painting by the Rev. W. Peters. Bindley, pt. i. 737, 1l. 3s.

— Literary Relics, containing original Letters from King Charles II., King James II., the Queen of Bohemia, Swift, Berkeley, Addison, Steele, Congreve, the Duke of Ormond, and Bishop Rundle; to which is prefixed, an Inquiry into the Life of Dean Swift. Lond. 1789. 8vo. 6s.

— John. Collectanea Historica complexa ipsius Negotiationem Anni 1647, cum Olivario Cromwel, Ireton, & aliis Exercitus Præfectis pro Revocatione Caroli I. in Regni Administrationem. Lond. 1699. 8vo.

— Memoirs of Sir John Berkley, containing an Account of his Negotiation for restoring King Charles the First. Lond. 1702. 8vo.
Roxburghe, 8479, 12s. An edition appeared 1699, 8vo. pp. 93. 5s. which is reprinted in the ninth volume of the Harleian Miscellany.

Berkeley Peerage — An Address to the Peers of the United Kingdom of Great Britain and Ireland, from Mary, Countess of Berkeley. Lond. 1811. 8vo. 3s. 6d.
On this claim the following have appeared:—
1. Minutes of Evidence taken before the Committee for Privileges, on the Earl of Berkeley's Pedigree, in the Year 1799; ordered to be reprinted 8th March, 1811. folio, pp. 85.
2. Case of William Fitzhardinge Berkeley, on his Petition to the King, to be summoned to Parliament for the Earldom of Berkeley, Feb. 1811. folio, pp. 4, with a pedigree of the Earldom of Berkeley.
3. Minutes of Evidence given before the Committee of Privileges, to whom the Petition of William Fitzhardinge Berkeley, claiming as of Right to be Earl of Berkeley, was referred. Ordered to be printed 8th March, 1811. folio, pp. 876.
4. Appendix to the Minutes of the Committee of Privileges on the Berkeley Peerage of the 7th June, 1811. Ordered to be printed 7th June, 1811. folio, pp. 6.
5. Index of the Names of Witnesses examined, folio, pp. 3.
The above five, Marq. of Townshend, 2628, 1l. 7s.
6. A Narrative of the Minutes of Evidence respecting the Claim to the Berkeley Peerage, as taken before the Committee of Privileges in 1811; together with the entire evidence of the Persons principally concerned; to which are added, fac-similes of the Banns, and Register of the Marriage; extracted from the Parish Books of Berkeley. To the whole is prefixed, a Sketch of the Proceedings of the Committee on the Earl of Berkeley's Pedigree, in the year 1799. Lond. 1811. 8vo. pp. 276, with a preface and Introduction, pp. 18, 5s.

Berkeley.—Pedigree and Descent of Norborne Berkeley, Esq. from John Lord Botetourt, who was summoned to Parl. 33 Edw. I.—The Case of Norborne Berkeley, Esq. in Relation to the Barony of Botetourt. folio.
Copies are in the British Museum.

— Abstracts and Extracts of Smyth's Lives of the Berkeleys, illustrative of ancient Manners, and the Constitution; including all the Pedigrees in that ancient Manuscript. To which are annexed, a copious History of the Castle and

Parish of Berkeley, consisting of Matter never before published. By Thomas Dudley Fosbrooke, M.A. F.R.S. Lond. 1820. 4to. 10s. 6d.

BERKENHOUT, John, M.D. Synopsis of the natural History of Great Britain and Ireland. Lond. 1795. 8vo. 2 vols. 10s.
The former editions appeared 1767-70, 8vo. 3 vols.; 1789, 8vo. 2 vols.

— Biographia Literaria; or a Biographical History of Literature: containing the Lives of English, Scottish, and Irish Authors, from the Dawn of Letters in these Kingdoms to the present Time, chronologically and classically arranged. Vol. I. From the Beginning of the fifth to the End of the sixth Century. Lond. 1777. 4to. 18s.
Of this judicious and useful compilation, only one, out of three volumes, was published.

BERKLEY, Hon. Capt. George. Naval History of Britain, from the earliest Periods of which there are any Accounts in History to the Conclusion of the Year 1756. Lond. 1757. folio. 12s.
Written by Sir John Hill, M.D.

— Sir William. The lost Lady, a Tragy-comedy. Lond. 1689. folio.
Reprinted in the first edition of Dodsley's Collection of Old Plays. Rhodes, 2668. 3s. Berkley likewise published 'A Discourse and View of Virginia,' folio. Particulars respecting him will be found in Dr. Bliss's edition of Wood's Athen. Oxon. iii. 1111-12.

Berkshire.—Looke up and see Wonders : a miraculous Apparition in the Ayre, lately seen in Barkshire at Bawlkin Green near Hatford, April 9, 1628. Lond. 1628. 4to. with wood cut. 18s.
A copy is in the British Museum.

BERMUDA. A plaine Description of the Barmvdas, now called Sommer Ilands. Lond. 1613. 4to.
Jadis, 260, morocco, 5l. 5s. A copy is in the British Museum, also Orders and Constitvtions ordained by the Gouernour and Company, 6 Feb. 1621. 1622. 4to.

— Bermuda or Summer Islands, Acts of Assembly passed in, from 1690 to 1713. Lond. 1719. folio.

— Laws of Bermuda, from 1690 to 1736. 1719, 37, 2 parts.

BERNARD, Saint. Medytacōns. Westmester by Wynkyn de Worde, 1496. 4to.
*Loscombe, 1854, 4l. 8s.
A copy is in the Royal Collection. Dr. Dibdin notices another edition by W. de Worde, 1545. 4to.*

— A goodly Treatyse called a Notable Lesson, otherwise the Goldem Pystle. Impressus Anno Dom. 1530. 4to.
The last leaf has the marks of W.C. and Wynkyn de Worde. Dr. Dibdin notices several other editions of the translation of S. Bernard's Epistle, viz. by W. de Worde, no date ; by Thomas Godfray, no date ; Sotheby, June, 1856, mor. 1l. 5s. and by Robert Wyer, 1531. Horner, 1854, 4l. 6s.

— Treatyse of well Liuynge, translated by Thomas Paynell. Lond. by Thomas Petyt. 8vo.
Contains fol. cxcviii, besides dedication to Mary, daughter of K. Henry viii. and a table. Another edition by John Byddell. n. d. 12mo.

— Hive of sacred Honiecombes, translated by Antonie Batt, Monke. Doway, 1631. 18mo. with front.
Towneley, pt. i. 450, 6s.

— Complaint or Dialogue, betwixt the Soule and Bodie of a damned Man. *See* CRASHAW, W.

BERNARD, Jean. Discours des plus memorables Faictz des Roys et Grands-Seigneurs d'Angleterre depuis 500 Ans ; avec les Genealogies des Roynes d'Angleterre et d'Ecosse ; plus une Guide des Chemins d'Angleterre. Paris, 1579, or 1587.
Sotheby's in July, 1821. 1l. 2s.

— Edward. De Mensuris et Ponderibus antiquis Libri tres. Editio altera purior, et duplo locupletior. Oxon. 1688. 8vo. 5s.
A useful work, originally published with Dr. Pocock's Commentary on Hosea.

— Librorum MSS. Academiarum Oxoniensis et Cantabrigiensis, et celebrium per Angliam, Hiberniamque Bibliothecarum Catalogus, cum Indice alphabetico. Oxon. 1696-7. folio, 2 pts. in 1 vol. 15s.

Prefixed is a very learned preface and copious index. An account of Bernard will be found in Dr. Bliss's edition of Wood's Athen. Oxon. iv. 701—10.

BERNARD, John. Oratio de vera Animi Tranquilitate. Lond.1568.4to.

Dedicated 'Petro Osburno.' Contains 118 leaves, besides prefixes commendatory. A translation by Anth. Marten. 1570. 8vo.

— Nicholas, D.D. Penitent Death of John Atherton, late Bishop of Waterford in Ireland, who was executed at Dublin, 5 Dec. 1640. Lond. 1641. 4to.

Reprinted Dublin, 1641. 4to. Lond. 1642. 12mo. Nassau, pt. i. 119, 7s. Inglis, 61, 8s. Fonthill, 613, 18s. Lond. 1651, 12mo. Lond. 1709, 8vo.

— Life and Death of Dr. James Usher, late Archbishop of Armagh. Lond. 1656. 4to. with port. 3s. 6d.

An account of Bernard, with a list of his writings, will be found in Wood's Fasti Oxonienses.

— Richard. Key of Knowledge for the Opening of the secret Mysteries of St. John's mysticall Revelation. Lond. 1617. 4to. with a frontispiece, 8s.

— Looke beyond Luther: or an Answere to that Question, where this our Religion was before Luther's Time. Lond. 1623. 4to.

Bernard likewise published 'A Guide to Grand Jurymen.' Lond. 1627. 12mo.

— The Isle of Man, or the legal Proceeding in Man-shire against Sin. Lond. 1627. 18mo.

A religious allegory, frequently reprinted. 1629, Nassau. pt. i. 248, 17s. 1663, Bindley, pt. i. 605, 4s. 6d. Bristol, 1808, 12mo. 2s.

— The Bible Battels, or the sacred Art Military. Lond. 1629. 12mo.

— Thesaurus Biblicus, sive Promptuarium Sacrum. Lond. 4to. with portrait by W. Hollar.

An enlarged edition was published, Lond. 1664, folio, 12s. Bernard published other works, a list of which will be seen in Watt's Bibliotheca Britannica.

— Sir T. Life of Sir F. Bernard. Lond. 1790, 8vo.

Privately printed. Bindley, pt. i. 431, 1l. 1s.

BERNARDI, Major John. Life of Major John Bernardi. Lond. 1729. 8vo. with portrait by G. vr. Gucht. Lloyd, 118, 4s. Towneley, pt. i. 472, 9s.

BERNERS, or BERNES. See BARNES-
— John Bourchier Lord. See ANTONINUS. Arthur of Little Britain; Castle of Love; FROISSART; Huon of Bourdeaux.

BERNIER, Francis. History of the late Revolution of the Empire of the Great Mogul, and concerning the extent of Hindostan. Lond. 1671-2. 8vo. 4 vols. in 2.

A notice of this excellent work will be found in the Retrosp. Review, N. S. i. 245 —68. Dent, pt. i. 207. russia, 18s. Bindley, pt. i. 506, 1l. 5s. White Knights, 424, 1l. 5s. Roxburghe, 7289, 2l.

— Travels in the Mogul Empire, translated from the French by Irving Brock. Lond. 1826. 8vo. 2 vols. 18s.

'A good translation of this excellent old traveller.'—*Quart. Rev.* 'A more curious and entertaining work than Bernier's Travels can hardly be imagined; the lively style of the author, combined with his intelligence, and the extraordinary nature of the scenes of which he was an eye-witness, render his work altogether more like a glowing romance than a detail of real events.' Bernier's Voyage to the East Indies is also reprinted in the Oxford Collection of Voyages and Travels, vol. ii. and in Pinkerton's Collection, vol. viii.

BERNOULLI, James. Doctrine of Permutations and Combinations, and some other useful Mathematical Tracts. Published by Francis Maseres, Esq. Lond. 1795. 8vo. pp. 606. 12s.

— John. Sexcentenary Table. Lond. 1779. 4to. 5s.

Published by the Board of Longitude.

BERRIMAN, John. Critical Dissertation upon 1 Tim. iii. 16. Lond. 1741. 8vo. 4s.

In this work are noticed several glaring and unpardonable blunders in the impressions of the Bible during the seventeenth century. A copy is in the British Museum, with the author's MS. notes.

— William, D.D. Christian Doc-

trines and Duties explained and recommended, in forty Sermons, &c. Lond. 1751. 8vo. 2 vols. 10s.
In considerable estimation. Dr. Berriman published several other works.

BERRY, William. Introduction to Heraldry. Lond. 1810. 8vo. 9s.
Contains pp. 158, besides preface, pp. 3.

— History of the Island of Guernsey, with Particulars of the neighbouring Islands of Alderney, Serk, and Jersey. Lond. 1815. 4to. with a map and plates.
Fonthill, 244, 14s. Drury, 551, russia, 1l. 9s.

— Genealogia Antiqua, or Mythological and Classical Tables; compiled from the best Authors on fabulous and ancient History. Lond. 1816. folio.
Contains pp. 87, besides index, pp. 10. Dedicated to Lord Grenville.

— Encyclopedia Heraldica, or Complete Dictionary of Heraldry. Lond. 1828. 4to. 3 vols. with plates, 4l. 4s. or LARGE PAPER, 5l. 5s.
[A Supplementary or 4th volume was published in 1840, at 2l. 2s.]
A valuable Heraldic work, as it embraces the greater part of the contents of Edmondson and other writers, with original matter.
[Mr. Berry also published the following County Genealogies, in small folio, some at 5 or 6 guineas per volume; but all now reduced to the annexed prices:—Berkshire, Buckinghamshire, and Surrey, folio, 1837, 2l. 2s. Essex, folio, 1841, 1l. 1s. Hampshire, folio, 1833, 2l. 2s. Hertfordshire, folio, 1844, 1l. 1s. Kent, folio, 1830, 3l. 3s. Sussex, folio, 1830, 2l. 2s.]

BERT, Edmund. Treatise of Hawkes and Hawking, diuided into three Bookes. Lond. 1619. 4to.
Contains pp. 109, besides the title. Haworth, 933, 13s. Inglis, 157, 1l. Sir M. M. Sykes, 1l. Best, 1l. 10s.

BERTHELSONE, Andreas. English and Danish Dictionary. Lond. 1754. 4to. 10s. 6d.
Wolff in 1779 published a Danish and English Dictionary.

BERTHOLDUS, Andr. Vertues and strange Vse of a new Terra sigillata, lately found in Germanie, translated by B. G. Lond. 1587. 8vo.
A copy is in the British Museum. Reprinted 1589.

BERTHOLLET, C. L., M.D. Elements of the Art of Dyeing, translated from the French by William Hamilton, M.D. Lond. 1791. 8vo. 2 vols. 12s.
Another translation, by Dr. Ure, with a Description of the Art of Bleaching, was published 1824, 8vo. 2 vols. 1l. 4s. The following have likewise appeared: An Essay on Chemical Statics, translated by B. Lambert. Lond. 1804, 8vo. 2 vols. 10s. Researches into the Laws of Chemical Affinity. Lond. 1804, 8vo. 4s. Essay on the new Methods of Bleaching by means of oxygenated muriatic acid, translated by Rob. Kerr. Edinburgh, 1790, 12mo. 2s. 6d.

BERTIN, —. China, its Costumes, Arts, and Manufactures, edited from the Collections of M. Bertin, with additions, &c. Lond. 1812. 8vo. 4 vols. with plates, plain, 3l. 3s. coloured, 4l 4s.

BERTIN, Captain Joseph. Game of Chess. Lond. 1735. 12mo. 4s.
Captain Bertin is entitled to the praise of having invented the three pawns' gambit usually ascribed to Cunningham.

BERTRAM or RATRAM, Monk of Corby in the Ninth Century. De Corpore et Sanguine Domini Liber. Lond. 1688. 8vo. 5s.
Best edition, with a new English translation by Wm. Hopkins, and an historical dissertation and appendix by Dr. Peter Allix. A former edition appeared 1686. 4s.

— Boke of Barthrā Priest, intreatinge of thee Bodye and Bloude of Christe, wrytten to greate Charles the Emperour, and set forth vii. C. Yeares agoo, and imprinted An. Dni. M.D.XLIX. Lond. by Thomas Raynalde. 8vo. 10s.
Black letter. Contains C in eights. On the back of the title is 'The Lyfe of Barthram Pryeste by Johannes Thrythemyus.' Dr. Dibdin notices another edition by Anth. Kytson, 1549. 8vo. An edition 1548, Inglis, 85, 12s. Horner, 1854, mor. 1l. 13s.

— Booke of Bertram the Priest, first translated and printed in English 1546, and nowe newly reuiued, corrected, and published by T(homas) W(ilcox) 1581. Lond. 1582. 8vo.

— Another translation by Sir Humphrey Lynde. Lond. 1623. 8vo.
Reprinted with additions 1686. 12mo.

with a portrait of Charles the Great, King of France. 4s.

— Another translation, by William Guild. Aberdeen, 1624. 12mo.
A copy is in the British Museum

BERTRAM, Car. Britannicarum Gentium Historiæ antiquæ Scriptores tres —Ricardus Corinensis—Gildas Badonicus—Nennius Banchorensis— recensuit, Notisque et Indice auxit Car. Bertramus. Hauniæ, 1757. 8vo. with a frontispiece and map.
Bindley, pt. i. 834, 11s. White Knights, pt. i. 429, 19s. Nassau, pt. i. 329, 1l. 5s. Constable, 51, 1l. 8s. Towneley, pt. ii. 55, 1l. 7s. Bishop of Ely, 102, 1l. 16s. Fonthill, 3014, 2l. 4s.

BERTRAND, M. Historical Relation of the Plague at Marseilles in the Year 1720. Translated from the French MS. by Anne Plumtre. Lond. 1805. 8vo. 6s.
A notice of this excellent history, and of the writers on the Plague, will be found in the Retrosp. Review, vii. 219—39.

— de Moleville, A. F. Histoire d'Angleterre depuis la premiere Invasion des Romains jusqu' à la Paix de 1763. Paris, 1815. 8vo. 6 vols.

— Chronological Abridgment of the History of Great Britain. Lond. 1811. 8vo. 4 vols. 16s.
Earl of Kerry, 28, 1l. 16s.

— Private Memoirs relative to the last Year of the Reign of Lewis XVI. late King of France. Lond. 1797. 8vo. 3 vols. with five portraits, 10s. 6d.
Earl of Kerry, 28, 1l. 4s.

— Annals of the French Revolution, translated by R. C. Dallas. Lond. 1800. 8vo. Two Parts, in 9 vols.
Earl of Kerry, 26, 3l. 1s. Fonthill, 1425, with the private Memoirs of Lewis XVI. 12 vols. morocco, 7l. 10s.

— Costume of Austria. *See* Costumes.

BERWICK, Marshal Duke of, Memoirs of the, written by himself, with a Continuation, 1716-34, &c. Translated from the French. Lond. 1779. 8vo. 2 vols. 10s. 6d.

— Rev. Edw. Lives of Marcus Valerius Messala Corvinus, Titus Pomponius Atticus, Caius Asinius Pollio, Marcus Terentius Varro, and Cneius Cornelius Gallus, with Notes and Illustrations. Lond. 1813-14. small 8vo. 7s.

Mr. Berwick has likewise published Memoirs of the Life of the elder Scipio Africanus, 1818, small 8vo. 7s. And the Life of Apollonius of Tyanæus, 8vo. 1810, 5s.

BESARDUS, John Bapt. Observations on Lute Playing. Lond. 1610. folio.

BESSE, Joseph. Collection of the Sufferings of the People called Quakers, for the Testimony of a good Conscience. Lond. 1753. folio, 2 vols. 1l. 10s.

BEST, George. Discovrse of the (three) late Voyages of Discouerie for the finding of a Passage to Cathaya by the Northweast, vnder the Conduct of Martin Frobisher, Generall. With a particular Card therevnto adioyned of Meta incognita. Lond. 1578. 4to.
Dedication to 'Sir Christopher Hatton, Knight,' then the printer's preface. The first voyage on 52 pages; the second on 39 pages; and the third on 68 pages. Jadis, 270, with fac-simile drawings of the two maps, 8l. 10s. Steevens, 1877, 2l. 18s. North, pt. iii. 585. The third and last Voyage into Meta Incognita was also printed in 16mo. *See* ELLIS, T.

— Thomas. Art of Angling. To which is added, the complete Fly-Fisher. Lond. 1787. 12mo. First edition. 5s.
Frequently reprinted.

Beswick.—Life of Lavinia Beswick, alias Fenton, alias Polly Peachum. Lond. 1728. 8vo. 10s. 6d.
A copy is in the British Museum.

BETAGH, William. Voyage round the World. Lond. 1728. 8vo. 4s.
Reprinted in the first volume of Harris's Collection of Voyages and Travels. The Account of Peru will likewise be found in the fourteenth volume of Pinkerton's Collection.

BETHAM, Matilda. Biographical Dictionary of the celebrated Women of every Age and Country. Lond. 1804. 8vo. with a frontispiece containing five portraits, 7s. 6d.

BETHAM, Peter. *See* PUBLILIA.
— Rev. William. Genealogical Tables of the Sovereigns of the World, from the earliest to the present Period. Lond. 1795. folio.
A useful work, but much less valuable than Anderson's elaborate compilation, containing 716 Genealogical Tables, with an Index, pp. 5. Dedicated to the King. Roscoe, 296, 1*l.* 7s. Roxburghe, 9130, russia, 2*l.* 8s. FINE PAPER, fifty printed, 3*l.* 3s.

— Baronetage of England, or the History of the English Baronets, and such Baronets of Scotland as are of English Families. Ipswich and Lond. 1801-5. 4to. 5 vols.
A very incorrect and imperfect work. Sir M. M. Sykes, pt. i. 421, bds. 3*l.* 3s.

— Sir William. Irish Antiquarian Researches. Dublin, 1826-7. 8vo.
Parts I. and II. pp. 442, and Appendix, pp. 55. (All published.)

BETHUNE, Philip. The Counsellor of Estate, translated by Edward Grimeston. Lond. 1634. 4to.
Prefixed is a portrait of Charles I. by Marshall. Gordonstoun, 234, 9s. 6d.

BETS, John. Genealogy of the York and Lancaster Families. *See* HALL, Edward.

BETTERTON, Thomas. History of the English Stage. [By Wm. Oldys.] Lond. 1741. 8vo. with portrait.
Reed, 8025, 12s. Roxburghe, Supplement, 549, 9s. 6d. 550, 8s. In 1710, appeared a Life of Betterton, by Gildon, with his Amorous Widow, a comedy, and a portrait of Betterton, 8vo. Reed, 8247, 4s. Roxburghe, 3298, 5s. 6d. 9291, 8s.

BETTIE, W. Historie of Titana and Theseus. Lond. 1686. 4to.
Black letter, containing sign. G 2. A notice of this curious work will be found in the British Bibliographer, ii. 436-7. Steevens, 1196, 12s.

Betty-Land.—The present State of Betty-Land. Lond. 1684. 8vo.
White Knights, 438, 8s.

BEVAN, Joseph Gurney. Life of the Apostle Paul, as related in the Scriptures, with select Notes, critical, explanatory, and relating to Persons and Places. Lond. 1807. 8vo. 6s.
This work is interesting, as affording some explanation of the theological sentiments of the Quakers. Mr. Bevan likewise published 'A Refutation of some of the more modern Misrepresentations of the Quakers, with a Life of James Nayler.' Lond. 1800, 8vo. and other works.

BEVER, Thomas, LL.D. History of the Legal Polity of the Roman State: and of the Rise, Progress, and Extent of the Roman Laws. Lond. 1781. 4to. 18s.
Dr. Bever also published a Discourse on the Study of Jurisprudence and the Civil Law. Oxford, 1766, 4to.

BEVERIDGE, William, Bishop of St. Asaph. Works. Lond. 1729. folio, 2 vols. with portrait.
Edited by Is. Kimber, who has prefixed a life of the Bishop. Sotheby's in 1821, 2*l.* 12s. 6d. Williams, 125, morocco, 7*l.* 17s. 6d.

— Works. Lond. 1820. 8vo. 6 vols. 3*l.* 3s.

— Works, with a Memoir of the Author, and a critical Examination of his Writings, by Thomas Hartwell Horne, M.A. Lond. 1824. 8vo. 9 vols. 5*l.* 8s.
Well edited and handsomely printed. The greater part of the impression was destroyed by fire.

— Works. 10 vols. 8vo. 1848.
See Library of Anglo-Catholic Theology, APPENDIX.

— Grammatica Syriaca, et de Linguarum Orientalium Præstantiâ et Utilitate. Lond. 1658. 8vo.
Williams, 174, mor. 11s.

— Συνοδικον sive Pandectæ Canonum SS. Apostolorum et Conciliorum ab Ecclesia Græca receptorum, &c. per. Gul. Beveregium. Oxon. 1672. folio, 2 vols. 2*l.* 12s. 6d.
A work in universal estimation, with learned notes.

CONTENTS.
Vol. I.
Canones Apostolorum et Conciliorum.
Anonymi cujusque Canonis Epitome.
Theodori Balsamonis, }
Joannis Zonaræ } Scholia.
Alexii Aristeni }
Josephi Ægyptii Arabica Paraphrasis, cum Interp. Lat.
Vol. II.
Dionysii et aliorum Canones, cum Scholiis Theodori Balsamonis et Jo. Zonaræ.

Ex {S. Gregorii Theologi de sacris
Metris Libris
Amphilochii—Iambis legendis.
Gennadii et Tarasii Epistolæ.
Alexii Aristeni Epistolarum Canon. Synopsis.
Matthæus Blastares de Rebus quæ in Canonibus comprehenduntur.
Anonymus de Synodo quæ Photium restituit.
Acta Octavæ Synodi Constantinopoli.
— Codex Canonum Ecclesiæ Primitivæ vindicatus ac illustratus. Lond. 1678. 4to. 6s.
— New Edition, 2 vols. 8vo. See Library of Anglo-Catholic Theology, APPENDIX.
— Thesaurus Theologicus, or a compleat System of Divinity, summed up in brief Notes upon select Places of the old and new Testament. Lond. 1710-11. 8vo. 4 vols.
Gossett, 450, 1l. 7s. Bp. of Ely, 50, 1l. 4s. Reprinted, Lond. 1816. 8vo. 2 vols. 12s. and Oxford, 1820, and Lond. 1828, 8vo. 2 vols. 1l. 4s.
— Private Thoughts upon Religion, and a Christian Life. Lond. 1713. 8vo. 2 vols. 7s. 6d.
Frequently reprinted in 1 vol. 8vo. or 12mo.
— Exposition of the xxxix Articles. Lond. 1716. 8vo. with port. 5s.
An edition was published 1711, in folio, with port., 10s. 6d. [Frequently reprinted.]
— Institutionum chronologicarum Libri II. unà cum totidem Arithmetices chronologicæ Libellis. Lond. 1705. 4to. 5s.
According to Ant. à Wood, Dr. John Hudson abridged Beveridge's Introduction to Chronology, and printed two impressions for the use of his pupils.
— Sixteen Sermons abridged from the Works, by the Rev. H. G. Glasse. To which are added ten original Discourses. Lond. 1805. 8vo.
Williams, 175, 10s.
— Sermons selected and abridged by the Rev. John Dakins. Lond. 1815. 8vo. 2 vols. 1l.

BEVERLEY, Peter. Historie of Ariodanto and Jeneura, Daughter to the King of Scottes, in English Verse. Lond. by Tho. East. 16mo.
Black letter. Gordonstoun, 296, morocco, 6ll. 10s. Roxburghe, 3l. 3s. 31l. 10s. Heber,
1l. 7s. 6d. Another edition, 1600, 12mo.
See Warton's Poetry, iv. 310, note 1.

— R. History and present state of Virginia. Lond. 1722. 8vo. with a front. and 14 engravings by Gribelin, copied from De Bry, 1l. 1s.
This work contains many pertinent remarks. A former edition, 1705. Fonthill, 3202, 9s.

BEVIN, Elway. Instruction of the Art of Musicke, to teach how to make Descant of all Proportions that are in use. 1631. 4to. 5s. 6d.
This writer was a musician eminently skilled in the knowledge of practical composition.

Bevis of Hampton, or Southampton. Sir Beuys of Southampton, the Son of Guy Erle of Southampton [Rich. Pynson] 4to.
An abstract of this romance from the Caius Coll. MS., and the edition printed by Pynson, will be found in the second volume of Ellis' Specimens.
— Sir Beuys of Hampton. Lond. by W. Coplande. 4to.
Black letter. A to S 8, in fours. A copy is in the Garrick Collection in the British Museum. Heber, 12l. 15s.
— Syr Bevis of Hampton. Lond. by Thomas East. 4to.
Black letter. 33 leaves. A copy is in the Bodleian Library.
— Sir Bevis of Hampton, with 15 wood cuts. C. W. for W. Lee. n. d. 4to.
Black letter, only one copy known, with title MS., Gough, 3l. 8s., resold, Utterson, 1852, 22l. 10s.
— Sir Bevis of Hampton, newly corrected and amended. Lond. Richd. Bishop, 4to. n. d.
Black letter. Heber, 10l.
— Sir Bevis of Hampton (ante 1622), 4to.
Black letter. Of this edition only one copy is known.
— Sir Bevis of Hampton. Lond. 1622. 4to.
Black letter, with cuts. Steevens, 1190, 3l. 13s. 6d. resold Roxburghe, 3230, 7l. 7s. again Sir M. M. Sykes, pt. ii. 74, 10l. 10s.
— Sir Bevis of Southampton. Lond. 1689. 4to.
Sir M. M. Sykes, 1506, 7s. Nassau, pt. i. 402, 8s. North, pt. iii. 738, 1l. 9s. Goldsmid, 272, 4l. 6s. See Abbotsford Club, APPENDIX.

BEWICK, Thomas. History of Quadrupeds. The Figures engraved on wood, by T. Bewick. Newcastle, 1790. 8vo.

First edition. Steevens, 1520, 1*l*. 8s. Roxburghe, 1795, 1*l*. 8s. Bindley, pt. i. 297, 1*l*. 5s. Brockett, 188, mor. 2*l*. 2s. ROYAL, Steevens, 1521, 2*l*. 5s. Brockett, 137, mor. 5*l*. 7s. 6d. A copy on EXTRA THICK ROYAL PAPER was sold at Evans' for upwards of 10*l*.

Second edition, 1791. DEMY, Lloyd, 63. 1*l*. 9s. Roscoe, 1783, 2*l*. 17s. ROYAL, Dent, pt. i. 209, 1*l*. 2s. Nassau, pt. ii. 1455, 2*l*. 2s. Williams, 176, mor. 3*l*. 15s.

Third Edition, 1792. DEMY, 18s. ROYAL, 1*l*. 10s.

Fourth Edition, 1800. DEMY, 12s. ROYAL, Earl of Kerry, 630, russia, 3*l*. 3s. IMPERIAL, (the first on this size paper) 2*l*. 8s. Edwards, 452, russia, 4*l*. 10s.

Fifth Edition, 1807. DEMY. Brockett, 145, mor. 1*l*. 4s. ROYAL, 1*l*. 11s. 6d. IMPERIAL, 2*l*. 2s.

Sixth Edition, 1811. DEMY, 16s. Brockett, 146, mor. 1*l*. 1s.

Seventh Edition, 1820. DEMY, 1*l*. 1s. ROYAL, 1*l*. 10s. IMPERIAL, 2*l*. 2s.

Eighth Edition, 1824. DEMY, 1*l*. ROYAL, 1*l*. 10s. IMPERIAL, 2*l*. 2s.

— Figures of Quadrupeds and Tail Pieces taken off without the Letter Press. Newcastle, 1818. 4to. 2*l*. 12s. 6d.

Twenty-four or five copies printed. Brockett, 183, morocco, 6*l*. 2s. 6d. On INDIA PAPER (twelve copies). Brockett, 168. 4*l*. 4s. A second edition, without the tail pieces, appeared 1824.

— History of British Birds. The Figures engraved on wood by Bewick. Newcastle, 1797-1804. 8vo. 2 vols.

First edition. The last leaf of vol. i. is sometimes found blank, sometimes with the third edition of the Quadrupeds advertised, and others with the fourth edition. Query, If there have not been more than one edition of the same date? Roscoe, 1784, 5*l*. 5s. ROYAL. Williams, 177, morocco, 5*l*. 7s. 6d. Nassau, pt. i. 1456, 6*l*. 6s. Earl of Kerry, 631, russia, 6*l*. 10s. Brockett, 139, morocco, 7*l*. Some copies were printed on thicker royal. IMPERIAL, 6*l*. 6s.

Second Edition, 1804, 2 vols. DEMY, 1*l*. 11s. 6d. ROYAL. Brockett, 144, mor. 3*l*. 19s. IMPERIAL. Edwards, 755, russia, 6*l*. 10s.

Third Edition, 1809. DEMY. 1*l*. 10s.

Fourth Edition, 1816. DEMY. Brockett, 147, morocco, 2*l*. 8s.

Fifth Edition, 1821. DEMY. Brockett, 160, 1*l*. 14s. ROYAL. Brockett, 159, 2*l*. 2s. IMPERIAL. Brockett, 158, 3*l*. 1s.

A new and enlarged Edition, 1826. DEMY, 1*l*. 16s. ROYAL, 2*l*. 5s. IMPERIAL, 3*l*. 8s.

— Supplement to the History of British Land and Water Birds. Newcastle, 1822. 8vo.

This supplement is intended to complete the first four editions.

DEMY, 6s. ROYAL, 8s. IMPERIAL, 12s.

— Figures of British Land Birds (with the Vignettes), engraved on wood by T. Bewick. To which are added, a few foreign Birds, with their vulgar and scientific Names. Newcastle, 1800. royal 8vo. 12s.

These are the cuts to the first volume with a few foreign birds added. The second was not published to correspond. Brockett, 141, morocco, 3*l*. 5s.

— Figures of British Land and Water Birds, together with a few Figures of Foreign Birds. Newcastle, 1817. demy 4to. 2*l*. 12s. 6d.

Twenty-five copies printed, without any letter press. Brockett, 182, morocco, 5*l*. Some few sets of the figures and vignettes have been taken off on India paper on slips, for mounting. Another edition appeared in 1825.

— Cuts of the Supplement to the British Land and Water Birds, without the letterpress. Newcastle, 1821. 4to. 12s.

— Select Fables, with Cuts designed and engraved by Thomas and John Bewick, and others, previous to the Year 1784: together with a Memoir and a descriptive Catalogue of the Works of Messrs. Bewick. Newcastle, 1820. 8vo.

Brockett, 154, 13s. ROYAL. Brockett, 153. 1*l*. 11s. 6d. IMPERIAL. Brockett, 151, 1*l*. 7s. Twelve copies with the cuts and tail pieces taken off on INDIA PAPER. Brockett, 152. 5*l*. 5s.

Vignettes to Bewick's Various Works. Newcastle, 1827. 8vo. 2*l*. 2s. 4to. 2*l*. 12s. 6d.

[This 4to. volume of *Vignettes* was published as a companion to the Figures of *Quadrupeds and Birds*, which together are sometimes bound in 2 vols. mor. 8*l*. 8s.]

— Fables of Æsop, forming the fifth volume of his works. *Vide* ÆSOP.

A descriptive and critical catalogue of works illustrated by Thomas and John Bewick, with Life, by E. J. Selwyn, was published by J. G. Bell. Lond. 1851, royal 8vo. 10s. 6d. 77 pp. and Appendix, 4 l.

BEWICKE, Robert. Tables of the several European Exchanges. Lond. 1802. 4to. 2 vols. 1l. 1s.

Published at 4l. 4s.

BEZA, Theodore. Tragedie of Abraham's Sacrifice translated into English by A[rthur] G[olding]; finished at Powles Belchamp, in Essex, the 11th Day of August 1575. Lond. by Vautrowllier, 1577. 18mo.

Black letter, with wood cuts. Forster, 1166, 10l. 5s. King and Lochée's, in 181—, 21l.

— Sermons (xxxi) vpon the three first Chapters of the Canticle of Canticles, translated out of French by John Harmar. Oxford, 1587. 4to.

In this work the fashion of curled locks is condemned in terms similar to those used by Prynne. Inglis, 158, 5s. Boswell, 282, 6s.

— Cordial for a sick Conscience, translated into English by H. A(ires). Lond. 1593. 8vo.

A poetical tract, consisting of 24 leaves, unknown to Herbert or Ritson, noticed in the British Bibliographer, ii. 283-7.

— Codex Cantabrigiensis. *See* Evangelia.

The following Works of Beza are many of them of rare occurrence.

Admonition to the Parliament. Roan, 1558. 8vo. Herbert also notices another edition, 1560. 8vo.

Briefe Declaration of the chiefe Poyntes of Christian Religion. Geneua, 1556. 16mo. From Maunsell's Catalogue, p. 9. Another edition, with a Treatice of Election, &c. by Anthonie Gilbie. 'Imprinted by Dauid Moptid and John Mather.' 16mo.

An Oration made Tuesday the ix Day of September, 1561, in the Noonnery of Poyssi. Lond. by R. Jugge, 1561. 8vo. Contains E 4, in eights. Bindley, pt. i. 1364. 4l. 14s. 6d. (with other tracts).

Ane Answer made the 4th day of Septembre, 1561, to the Cardinal of Lorraine, in the Name of the reformed Churches, &c. Edinburgh, by Robert Lekprevik, 1562. 8vo.

Life and Death of M. John Calvin, with his last Will and Catalogue of his Works. Lond. by H. Denham, 1564.

8vo. Bindley, pt. i. 604, (with Life of Luther, 2l.) Inglis, 86, 17s.

Quæstionum et Responsionum Christianarum Libellus. Lond. 1571. 16mo. 7s. Reprinted 1580.

Quæstionum et Responsionum Christianarum Pars altera. Lond. 1577. 8vo. A translation of this part was published by John Field, 1580. 8vo.

Booke of Christian Questions and Answers, translated into Englishe by Arthur Goldinge. Lond. 1577. 8vo. Contains 90 leaves, besides the dedication to 'Lorde Henry, Earle of Huntingdon, Baron Hastinges.' Reprinted, 1578. An edition, 1586. Inglis, 87, 12s.

Sum of the Christian Faith, translated by Robert Fyll. Lond. 1572. 16mo. 7s. Black letter. Herbert and Dr. Dibdin notice other editions, 1563, 1585, and without date.

Confessio Christianæ Fidei et eiusdem Collatio cum Papisticis Hæreisbus. Lond. 1575. 8vo. Contains X 4, in eights. Reprinted 1581.

Display of Popish Practices, or patched Pelagianisme, translated by Will. Hopkinson. Lond. 1578. 4to.

Little Catechisme. Lond. 1578. 8vo. From Maunsell's Catalogue, p. 29.

Judgment concerning a threefold Order of Bishops, &c. (1580). *See* Strype's Annals, ii. 629. Ant. à Wood says, 'this was done as it was supposed by Field in order to make Episcopacy shake, and to incline the people to change the government of the church by bishop, into that of elder.'

Treatise of the Plague, turned into English by John Stockwood. Lond. (1580.) 8vo. Dedicated to Sir Henry Sidney.

Treasure of Truth, turned into English by John Stockwood. Lond. 1581. 8vo. Herbert in his edition of Ames's Typographical Antiquities, notices a former edition entitled Treatise of Truth, translated by Whittingham. Geneva about 1556.

The Psalms truly opened by Paraphrases in Prose, from the Latin, by Ant. Gilbie. Lond. 1581. 18mo.

Discourse of the true and visible Marks of the Catholic Church, translated by Tho. Wilcox. Lond. 1582. 16mo. Again without date.

Christian Meditations vpon eight Psalmes of the Prophet David, &c. translated out of Frenche by I. S. Lond. 1582. 16mo. Reprinted 1589. An edition by Chr. Barker, no date. Williams, 130, 18s.

Confutation of the Pope's Canons, translated by Tho. Stocker. Lond. 1585. 16mo. Reprinted 1587.

Two very learned Sermons, together with a short Sum of the Sacrament of the Lord's Supper, by T. W. (Thomas Wilcocks.) Lond. 1588. 8vo.

Confession of Faith, with a Confutation of superstitious Errours contrarie thereunto, translated out of French by Rob. Fyll. Lond. 1569. 8vo. Inglis, 88, 7s.

Paraphrastical Explanation of 14 holie Psalms, englished by Ant. Gilbie. Lond. 1590. 24mo. pp. 77, and a table.

Two Epistles, translated by R. Vaux. Lond. 1598. 8vo.

Maister Beza's Hovshold Prayers, for the Consolation and Perfection of a Christian Life. Lond. 1607. 18mo. black letter, within borders.

Bhagvat-Geeta. *See* WILKINS, Charles.

Bhascara Acharia. *See* TAYLOR, John.

BIANCHA, John. Dissertation on the Case of Catherina Vizzani, a young woman born in Rome, who for eight years passed in the Habit of Man, was killed for an Amour with a young Lady, &c. Lond. 1651. 12mo.

A translation from the Italian.

BIBLIA Sacra Polyglotta, complectentia Textus originales, Hebræum cum Pentateucho Samaritano, Chaldaicum, Græcum, Versionemque antiquarum Samaritanæ, Græcæ, LXX. Interp. Chaldaicæ, Syriacæ, Arabicæ, Æthiopicæ, Persicæ, Vulg. Lat. quicquid comparari poterat. Cum Textuum et Versiorum Orientalium Translationibus Latinis. Cum Apparatu, Appendicibus, Tabulis, variis Lectionibus, Annotationibus, Indicibus, etc. Edidit Brianus Walton, S.T.D. Lond. 1657. folio, 6 vols. with portrait by Lombart.

[This should be accompanied by Castelli Lexicon Heptaglotton, folio, generally bound in 2 vols.] The 8 vols. 30l. and upwards.

'All the preceding Polyglots were eclipsed in use and excellence, if not in splendour and size, by that which is called the English and London Polyglot.'—*Carpzovius.*

The last leaf but one of the preface is cancelled in many copies, in which mention is made of the Protector in these words: 'Primo autem commemorandi quorum favore chartam a vectigalibus immunem habuimus, quod quinque adhinc aunis (1652) a concilio secretioro primò concessum, postea a serenissimo D. PROTECTORE ejusque consilio, operis promovendi causa, benignè confirmatum et continuatum erat, quibus, &c. In the loyal copies the clause is altered, and the words 'Sereniss. PRINCEPS D. CAR. LUDOV. pr. PALATIN.' are found. In some copies are found a dedication to 'King Charles II. (reprinted 1811, folio) and 'An advertisement to the Subscribers, and others, unto whom any copies of the first volume of the Bible shall be delivered,' [dated Sept. 4, 1654, on a 4to. leaf,] which latter has been reprinted by Todd, in his life of Walton, p. 68, and by Dr. Dibdin in his Introduction to the Greek and Latin Classics, pp. 22-3.

In the Apparatus Criticus is a treatise entitled 'Explicatio Idiotismorum, seu Proprietatum Linguæ Hebraicæ et Græcæ quæ sæpius in Scripturis occurrant,' in which the author asks, in what manner the sense of scripture is to be determined. Over the fourth and fifth answers (in most copies) a paper, containing other fourth and fifth answers, is pasted.

The Polyglott, 6 vols. Duke of Grafton, 2, 38l. 13s. Copies with Castell's Lexicon. Bp. Randolph, 38l. 43l. 38l. 38l. 17s. Roscoe, 55l. with the dedication to King Charles II. 41l. Gosset, 50l. 45l. Willet, 28l. 53l. 11s. Edwards, 80l. morocco, 61l. Heath, 42l. with the dedication, ruled with red lines and bound in morocco by Roger Payne, 73l. 10s.

LARGE PAPER, 12 copies printed, all with the royal preface. Copies of which are in the Royal Library, British Museum, St. Paul's, St. John's, Camb. Shrewsbury School Library, Lambeth, and in Lord Spencer's Collection.

To complete, says Mr. Horne, the London Polyglott, the following publications should be added. 1. Paraphrasis Chaldaica in Librum priorem et posteriorem Chronicorum, Auctore Rabbi Josepho, cum Versione Latina a Davide Wilkins. Amst. 1715, 4to. 2. Dr. Castell's Lexicon Heptaglotton. The purchaser should also procure Dr. John Owen's Considerations on the Polyglott, 1659. 18mo. Bishop Walton's reply, entitled 'The Considerator Considered,' &c. 1659. 18mo. and a most important work, Walton's Introductio ad Lectionem Linguarum Orientalium, &c. Lond. 1654. 18mo. Of the latter work one hundred copies were reprinted 1815, in folio, of which 97 were destroyed by fire in March 1822. Of the three copies saved one was presented by Mr. Bagster to the British Museum, one to the Rev. H. J. Todd, and the other remained in the publisher's possession. [The prolegomena has been edited, with variorum notes, by Archd. Wrangham, 2 vols. 8vo. Cantab. 1828. 9s. LARGE PAPER, 18s.]

For further information respecting this valuable Polyglott, consult Horne's Crit. Introd. to the Scriptures, ii. appendix, 28—30. Todd's Memoirs of Bishop Walton. Clarke's Bibliogr. Dictionary, i. 248 —70. Butler's Horæ Bibl. i. 138—49. Dr. Dibdin's Introduction to the Classics. 1827, vol. i. pp. 20—35.

In 1797, the Rev. Josiah Pratt issued 'A Prospectus, with Specimens of a New Polyglott Bible, in Quarto,' and in 1799, another ' Prospectus, with Specimens of an octavo Polyglott Bible;' but for want of encouragement the design has not been carried into execution. A similar fate has attended 'The Plan and Specimen of Biblia Polyglotta Britannica,' published and circulated by the Rev. Adam Clarke, LL.D. in 1810, in folio, reprinted in the Classical Journal, iv. 493—7.

Biblia Sacra Polyglotta, Textus Archetypos, Versionesque præcipuas ab Ecclesia antiquitūs receptas complectentia. Lond. 1817-28. 4to. 5l. 5s. 8vo. 4 vols. 4l. 9s.

This Polyglot, published by Mr. Bagster, comprises the original Hebrew text of the Old Testament, the Samaritan Pentateuch, the Septuagint Greek Version of the Old Testament, the Vulgate Latin, and the authorised English version of the entire Bible, the original Greek text of the New Testament, and the venerable Peschito or old Syriac Version of it. A good account of the Plan of it may be seen in Todd's Memoirs of Bishop Walton, i. 365—9.

Biblia Sacra Polyglotta, Gallice, Italice, Hispanice, et Germanice, Versiones præcipuas ab Ecclesiis Christianis hodie receptas, aut vulgo approbatas, complectentia. Lond. 4to

Of this edition no perfect copy exists; the whole were destroyed by fire in March, 1822, at Mr. Bagster's, excepting 23 copies of the New Testament.

Biblia Sacra Polyglotta. Lond. 1828. folio, 8l. 8s.

This work bears the title of 'Bagster's London Polyglott Bible,' and presents 8 Languages at each opening of the volume. It comprises the Samaritan Pentateuch, the Septuagint Greek version of the Old Testament, the Vulgate Latin, Diodati's Italian, Scio's Spanish, Ostervald's French, Luther's German, and the authorised version of the English Bible, the original Greek text of the New Testament, and also the venerable Peshito, or old Syriac version.

Biblia Hebraica (sine punctis) accurante Nath. Forster. Oxon. 1750. 4to. 3l. 3s.

This is the first edition of the Hebrew Bible, except that in the Polyglot, printed in England. It has, however, been highly censured by Masch, though Dr. Adam Clarke pronounces it to be 'the most elegant and correct of the Anti-Masoretic Bibles.' LARGE PAPER, in 2 vols. 5l. 5s.

— The Old Testament, English and Hebrew, with Remarks critical and grammatical on the Hebrew, and Corrections of the English, by Anselm Bayly, LL.D. Lond. 1774. royal 8vo. 4 vols. 3l. 10s.

An useful edition of the Masoretic Hebrew text for those desirous of learning Hebrew. The Hebrew is printed in long lines on the left hand page; and the authorised English version on the right hand page, divided into two columns. The critical notes, which are few, are placed under the English text.

— Vetus Testamentum Hebraicum, cum variis Lectionibus, edidit Benj. Kennicott. Oxonii, 1776-80. folio, 2 vols. 7l. 17s. 6d.

This edition of the Hebrew Bible is, according to the learned Dr. Henry Owen, 'a work which contains, with all its imputed defects, a vast treasure of Hebrew learning; which, judiciously applied, will contribute more to rectify and restore the Hebrew text than all the methods hitherto practised.' It has also been pronounced by one of the most wary of German critics to be 'a first rate and even unique ornament of a theological collection.' Sir M. M. Sykes, pt. i. 471, morocco, 8l. 8s. Gossett, 500, russia, 9l. 19s. 6d. For a further account of this splendid work see Bishop Marsh's Divinity Lectures, part ii. pp. 105-8. Monthly Review, vol. lv. 92—100, lxiv. 178—82, 321—8, and lxv. 121—81. To Dr. Kennicott's Hebrew Bible, M. de Rossi published an important supplement in 4 vols. 4to. printed at Parma, 1784-7, entitled, Variæ Lectiones Veteris Testamenti.—See KENNICOTT, B.

Biblia Hebraica, or the Hebrew Scriptures of the old Testament, without Points, after the Text of Kennicott, with various Readings, and English Notes, by B. Boothroyd, D.D. Pontefract, 1810—16. 4to. 2 vols. 3l. 13s. 6d.

This edition, according to Mr. Horne, 'is peculiarly interesting to the Hebrew scholar and critic, as it contains, in a condensed form, the substance of the most valuable and expensive works. The type is very clear, and the poetical parts of the Hebrew Scriptures are printed in hemistichs, according to the arrangement proposed by Bp. Lowth, and adopted by Abp. Newcome.' There are copies ou Large Paper in royal quarto.

Biblia Hebraica, ad Editionem Vanderhooght, à J. S. C. F. Frey. Lond. 1812. 8vo. 2 vols. 2l. 2s.

This edition is in no estimation, and is said to be very incorrect. It is entirely superseded by D'Allemand's edition of Van der Hooght. 8vo. London, Duncan, 1828, *frequently reprinted*, (Bohn, 1852), 10s. 6d.

Biblia Hebraica, Versibus, Capitibus, et Sectionibus interstincta. Lond. 1822 and 1826. 12mo. 1l. 1s.

Another edition was printed without the points, 1l. 1s. Both are on the basis of Vanderhooght's, and owe their character for accuracy to the talent and assiduity of Messrs. H. Jacob and J. D'Allemand. The various readings of the Hebrew and Samaritan Pentateuch are given, together with the Masoretic notes, termed Keri and Ketib. To some copies an English version will be found opposite, in others a French, &c. An English and Hebrew edition of the Old Testament was published by Bagster, 1826, 12mo. 1l. 11s. 6d.

Bible (The) in the Arabic Language. Newcastle-upon-Tyne, 1811. 4to. 18s.

This edition was superintended by the late Arabic professor, the Rev. J. D. Carlyle. Twelve copies were printed in large folio, for presents; one of these is deposited in the British Museum. Adam Clarke, 18l. 18s. Another elegant edition, Newcastle-upon-Tyne, 1816, 4to.

Biblia Vetus Testamentum Syriace, edidit Samuel Lee, A.M. Lond. 18²³. 4to.

This edition was printed under the patronage of the Church Missionary Society, and at the expense of the British and Foreign Bible Society. Three MSS. were collated for this edition, viz. one brought by the Rev. Dr. Buchanan from Travancore, in the East Indies; another belonging to the Rev. Dr. Adam Clarke; and the Syriac Pentateuch, in the Library of New College, Oxford.

— Vetus Testamentum Græcum, ex Versione LXX. Interpretum. In S. Biblia Græca Scholia, &c. Novi Testamenti Libri omnes Græce. Lond. 1653. 4to. 3 vols. in 1. 10s. 6d.

This edition, printed by Roger Daniel, which professes to follow accurately the Roman edition of 1586, has been severely handled by Walton, Bos, Masch, and Harles. According to Mr. Horne, the editors have altered and interpolated the text in several places, in order to bring it nearer to the Hebrew text, and the modern versions. Drury, 557, 15s. Heath, 427, 28s. LARGE PAPER. MacCarthy, 47 fr. Reprinted, Cambridge, 1653, 8vo.

— Vetus Testamentum Græcum, juxta Exemplar Vaticanum. Cantab. 1665. 12mo.

This Cambridge edition was twice printed, first by John Field in 1665, and then by John Hayes in 1684, with the original date of 1665. Prefixed is a learned preface of 19 pages, written by the celebrated Bishop Pearson. Drury, 444, with the Greek Testament, Apocrypha, and Liturgy. 19s.

— Vetus Testamentum Græce, ex antiquiss. Codice MS. Alexandrino descriptum, Cura et Studio Joan. Ernesti Grabe. Oxonii. 1707—19. folio, 4 tom. in 2 vols. 1l. 11s 6d.

'Editio omnium editionum splendidissima, emaculatissima, commendatissima ob Typorum Elegantiam,' &c. *Reimannus.* LARGE PAPER. 3l. 3s. An edition in 8vo. 4 vols. in 8. 1l. 11s. 6d.

— Vetus Testamentum Græcum, cum variis Lectionibus, edente Rob. Holmes, et Jac. Parsons. Oxon. 1798—1827. folio, 5 vols.

A truly valuable and splendid edition of the Septuagint version. Vol. i. consisting of 3 parts, was published 1798, 1801, 1804. Vol. ii. comprising all the historical books from Joshua to the second book of Chronicles inclusively; the several fasciculi of which were published in the following order, viz.: Joshua in 1810; Judges and Ruth in 1812; 1 Kings in 1813; and the five remaining books in the four succeeding years. The third and fourth volumes, containing the book of Job to the Prophet Jeremiah, were published 1819—25; and the remaining, or fifth volume, which contains the Apocryphal books, between the years 1825 and 1827. For critiques on this magnificent undertaking *see* Bishop Marsh's twelfth Lecture; Eclectic Review, ii. part i. 85—90, 214—21, 267—74, 337—48; Classical Journal, ix. 475—9, xix. 367—72; Horne's Introduction to the Scriptures, ii. appendix, 37—8.

— Vetus Testamentum Græcum, juxta Exemplar Vaticanum, ex Editione Lamb. Bos. Oxon. 1805. 8vo. 5 vols.

An elegant, accurate, and commodious edition, printed in columns.

— Vetus Testamentum e Codice MS. Alexandrino. qui Londini in Bibliotheca Musei Britannici asservatur, Typis ad similitudinem ipsius Codicis Scripturæ fideliter descriptum, Cura et Labore Henrici Herveii Baber, A.M. Lond. 1816-28. imperial folio, 4 vols

This edition exhibits a faithful fac-simile of the celebrated Alexandrian manuscript, the earliest existing of the Scriptures; it was printed at the public expense, under the control of the Trustees of the British Museum. The three first volumes comprise the entire text of the septuagint; and the fourth contains the notes and the prolegomena.

On PAPER, 250 copies were printed, and on VELLUM ten copies, and which are thus disposed: The library of King George III. The Imperial library at Vienna. The Bibliothèque du Roi at Paris. The Abp. of Canterbury. The Duke of Devonshire. This copy is five inches taller than any of the others. Earl Spencer. John Dent, Esq. Sir M. M. Sykes, Bart. Archdeacon Usher. Rev. H. H. Baber. The publication price of the work complete upon VELLUM, is 184 guineas, and on paper, 36*l*. 15s.

The New Testament, which completes this edition of the Scriptures, was published by Woide, *vide* Test. Nov. Gr. Woide. 1786.

— Vetus Testamentum Græcum, secundum Exemplar Vaticanum Accedunt variæ Lectiones e Codice Alexandrino, nec non Introductio J. B. Carpzovii. Oxon. 1817. 8vo. 6 vols. 1*l*. 7s.

A handsomely printed and accurate edition. The introduction is extracted from the second and third chapters of Carpzovius' Critica Sacra. Part iii. LARGE PAPER, 4*l*. 4s. Drury, 446, russia, 8*l*. 8s. Williams, 186, with Griesbach's Testament, morocco, 16*l*. 5s. 6d.

— Vetus Testamentum Græcum. Lond. 1819. 8vo.

An elegantly executed volume, correctly printed after the editions of Holmes and Bos.

— Vetus ac Novum Testamentum Græcum, cum variis Lectionibus Millii et Griesbachii. Lond. 1826. 12mo. 1*l*. 6s.

Copies of this edition, published by Mr. Bagster, have also been printed with the authorised English version on the opposite page, 1*l*. 16s.

— Vetus Testamentum juxta Exemplar Vaticanum. Glasguæ, 1822. 18mo. 3 vols. 18s. and Lond. 1 vol. 12mo. 1827. 18s.

This very neat edition was printed at the university press, at Glasgow.

Biblia Latina.—Sacræ Bibliæ Tomus. Lond. Excudebat Thomas Bartholetus. 1535. 4to.

The first Latin Bible printed in England. Copies are in the British Museum and Bodleian libraries.

[It is not the whole of the Bible; for contents, *see* Ames, by Dibdin, vol. iii. p. 291.]

— Testamenti Veteris Biblia Sacra, Latini recens ex Hebræo facti, brevibusque Scholiis illustrati ab Imm. Tremellio et Franc. Junio: accesserunt Libri Apocryphi, Latini redditi et Notis quibusdam aucti, a Fr. Junio. Lond. 1580. 8vo. 10s. 6d.

First London edition of this version was made under the direction of the Elector Palatine, Frederick III. Reprinted with Beza's Testament, 1581, 8vo. 1585. 8vo. 1593, folio, 12s. 1640, with an engraved title page, by Marshall, 12mo. 5s. 1650, 12mo. 1661, 8vo. 1680, 12mo.

Biblia Sacra ex Sebastiani Castellionis Interpretatione ejusque postrema Recognitione. Lond. 1724. 12mo. 4 vols. 15s.

This edition of Castalio's Bible is printed without the notes usually accompanying the work.

This version was attacked both by Catholics and Protestants. Castalio published a defence of himself and his work in 1562, 12mo.

Biblia Sacra Vulgata. Lond. 1826. 12mo. 18s.

Bagster's esteemed edition.

— Annotationes in Vetus Testamentum, et in Epistolam ad Ephesios, incerto Autore: e Bibliotheca Johannis Archiep. Eboracensis in Lucem erutæ. Cantab. 1653. 8vo.

A copy is in the British Museum.

— Disquisitiones criticæ de variis per diversa Loca et Tempora Bibliorum Editionibus. Lond. 1684. 4to. 5s.

BIBLE (Holy)—*English versions.*

— (WYCLIFFE). Holy Bible, containing the Old and New Testaments, with the Apocryphal Books, in the earliest English versions, made from the Latin vulgate, by John Wycliffe and his followers (with a glossary), edited by the Rev. Josiah Forshall and Sir Frederick Madden. 4 vols. royal 4to. 1850. Oxford University Press. 5*l*. 15s. 6d.

Particularly valuable as a specimen of the English language in the fourteenth century.

— (COVERDALE). BIBLIA. The Bible, that is, the holy Scripture of the Olde and New Testament, faithfully & truly translated out of Douche and Latyn in to Englishe. 1535. folio.

Black letter, printed in double columns, in a foreign secretary-gothic type, with wood-cuts, by Hans Sebald Beham. This first Protestant translation of the whole Bible is considered as the joint production of Tyndal and Coverdale. [It is not satisfactorily settled where this volume was printed; some say, by *Froschover, at Zurich;* others by *Egenholf, at Frankfort;* while others suggest *Cologne* or *Lubec.* There is no perfect copy yet (1857) known to exist. Copies, nearly perfect, are in the Earl of Leicester's library (no map); Earl Spencer's, with the map, but no title; Earl of Jersey's (map), *title faulty;* Bodleian (*no map*); Trin. Coll., Dublin (*no map*); British Museum (no map), the *title faulty.* Another, in the Grenville Coll., of which the *title*, 4 leaves, and also the map, are in fac-simile by Harris. Mr. Dunn Gardiner's copy, formerly Lea Wilson's, *with the original map*, but the title and first leaf in fac-simile by Harris, sold, in 1854, for 365*l*.; Dent, part i. 630, title and two following leaves in fac-simile, 89*l*. 5s.; Sotheby (Hawtrey), July, 1853, 16 leaves in fac-simile, 111*l*.; another, Sotheby, Aug., 1857, the map, title, preliminary leaves, six leaves in Genesis and last seven of Revelations in fac-simile by Harris, 190*l*.; Duke of Sussex, in 1844, pt. i. No. 1425, the map and title in fac-simile by Harris, but wanting the whole of the preliminary matter; the copy damaged and stained, 130*l*. Other copies, more or less imperfect, have been sold at sums varying from 30*l*. to 60*l*.]

Collation. Wood-cut title; dedication to K. Henry VIII. 5 pp. 'A prologe to the reader,' 6 pp.; 'The bokes of the hole Byble,' 2 pp. 'The contentes of the boke of Genesis,' 1 page. The first book of Moses, &c. fol. i.— xe. (then should follow a map, headed 'The descripcion of the londe of promes, called Palestina, Canaan, or the holy londe'). 'The second parte of the Olde Testament,' Josua, &c. to Hester, fol. li—cxx. Job, &c. to 'Salomon's balettes,' fol. i—lii. 'All the Prophetes in Englishe,' fol. li—cii. 'Apocripha,' fol. li—lxxxiii. falsely numbered lxxxi. Then follows a blank leaf. 'The Newe Testamente,' fol. li—cxiii. on the reverse of the last is 'Prynted in the yeare of oure Lorde M.D.XXXV. and fynished the fourth daye of October.' A full page contains 57 lines.—The dedication, prologue, and contents of Genesis are printed in a different type; there are separate title pages to the five portions formed of the woodcuts which decorate the book, exclusive of the general title.

For an account of this version, the variations in the Dedication, &c., *see* Lea Wilson's List of his Collection of Bibles, &c. 4to. privately printed, 1845. No. 1. Dr. Cotton's List of Editions of the Bible, 8vo. *Oxford,* 1852, pp. 8, and 274. Ames' Typ. Antiq. by Herbert, iii. 1544—5. Bibl. H leiana, i. no. 155. Bibl. Spencer. i. 78—91. Abp. Newcome's Histor. View, 29—33. Lewis' History of the English Translations of the Bible, 91—104. Horne's Introduction to the Scriptures. Anderson's Annals of the English Bible, 2 vols. 8vo. 1845. Preface to Bishop Wilson's edit. of the Bible, 1785. Bagster's Reprint of the volume, &c. &c.

Mr. Bagster, in 1838, issued a reprint (in the Roman letter) of this edition, 4to., copies on LARGE PAPER in folio. Mr. Eyton's copy, most superbly bound in morocco, with clasps, sold, Pickering, 231, March, 1854, 31*l*. 10s.

— (COVERDALE). BIBLIA, the Byble: that is the holy Scrypture of the Olde and New Testament, fayth-fully translated in to Englyshe, 1536. folio.

This is the same as that of 1535, *with a different title.* Two copies known: Gloucester Cathedral and Earl of Jersey, *with the map. See* Cotton, p. 11, 275.

— (COVERDALE). BIBLIA, The Byble, that is the holy Scrypture of the Olde and Newe Testamēt fayth-fully translated in Englysh, and newly oversene and corrected. Southwarke, for Jas. Nycolson. 1537. folio.

Collation. Title. Epistle unto the King, by Coverdale, (with name of Queen Jane), 5 p. Prologue, 6 p. The bokes of the Holy Bible, 2 p. Contents of Genesis, 1 p. Genesis to Ruth, i—cxvi (for cxvii). Title to Second part, 1 l. 1 Sam. to Hester, li—c. Job to Canticles, i—lx. Title, 'All the

Prophetes in Englishe.' Isaiah to Malachi, ii—ciii. Title to Apocripha. Esdras to Maccabees, ii—lxxxix. Blank leaf. Title to New Test. St. Matthew to Revelation, ii—cxix. Tables of Epistles, &c. 4 p. A full page contains 57 lines.
This edition is rarer than the first (1535). Copies are in the Bodleian, Baptist Museum Bristol and Lincoln Cathedral libraries. See L. Wilson, no. 2. Cotton, pp. 12—276. Knight, 1847, very imperfect (a fragment), 8*l*. 16s.

— (COVERDALE) The Byble, that is the holye Scrypture of the Olde and Newe Testamente, faythfully translated in Englysh, and newly oversene and correcte. Southwarke, by James Nycolson, 1537. 4to.
Collation. Title, in red and black, comprehending 20 lines enclosed within an arabesque border; contents, 2 pages; Coverdale's address to the King and 'unto the Christen reader', 9 p. Almanac and Calendar, 4 p. The text, fol. i—xcvii. Title. The second part, cxviii (for xcviii)—ccxxvii. Title. The thyrde part of the olde Testament, &c. Job to Malachi, fol. ii—clxxix. 'The new Testament,' with a fresh set of numerals, concluding at fol. cxxiiii., then two leaves of a table, closing the volume at cxxvi. A full page contains 59 lines.
See Lea Wilson, no. 3. Cotton, p. 12, 276. Anderson. Ames, by Dibdin, iii. 51, 52. Bibl. Harl. no. 288. Ædes Althorp. i. 61-2. A copy is in the Douce Collection, now in the Bodleian.
It is stated that Nicolson printed another edition in 1541, of which the Duke of Sussex possessed an imperfect copy. *Vide* Sale Cat. Pt. I. No. 516. 4*l*.

— (MATTHEW). The Byble, which is all the holy Scripture: in which are contayned the Olde and Newe Testament truely and purely translated into Englysh by Thomas Matthew. 1537. folio.
Black letter, with marginal annotations and wood-cuts in several parts. The Canticles are printed in red and black; the running titles, signatures, marginal notes, &c. are all in the Gothic letter. This Bible, evidently of foreign workmanship, was printed by Grafton and Whitchurch either at Hamburgh, Lubec, Malborow, or Paris. It varies but little from Tyndale's and Coverdale's translation; and the few emendations and additions which it contains were supplied by John Rogers (the first martyr in Queen Mary's reign), who superintended the publication, assuming the name of Matthew. Copies are in the British Museum, Lambeth, Bodleian, St. Paul's, and other libraries. Sotheby's in June, 1822, 19*l*. 19s. Denyer, 18, front. and concluding leaf, M$.) 23*l*. 12s. Sir M. M. Sykes. pt. i. 613, 78*l*. 15s. Duke of Sussex (imperfect), 22*l*. 10s. Fletcher, May, 1845 (2 leaves of table and imprint MS., other leaves mended, 105*l*. Gardner, 1854 (Lea Wilson's copy), 150*l*. Sotheby's, Aug. 1857, 23*l*.
Collation. Title, in red and black, within a wood engraving, at the bottom in large characters 'Set forth with the Kinges most gracyous licence;' 'A calendar and almanac for 18 years, beginning 1538,' 4 pages; 'An exhortation to the study of the holy Scripture,' 1 page; 'The summe and content of all the holy Scripture,' 2 pages; dedication to K. Henry VIII., 3 pages; 'To the Chrysten readers,' and a 'Table of the pryncipal matters,' together 26 pages; 'The Names of all the bokes of the Byble,' &c. dated MDXXXVII. 1 page, on the reverse of which is a wood engraving of Adam and Eve in Paradise. Genesis to Salomon's Ballet, fol. i—ccxlvii. A title, 'The Prophetes in Englysh, in black and red, between 16 wood cuts; on the reverse, a large wood cut between R. G. & E. W. [Richard Grafton and Edward Whitchurch]. 'Esay,' &c. to Malachy, fol. i—xciv.;' at the end W. T. [William Tyndale]. 'The volume of the bokes called Apocripha,' &c. in red and black, between 15 wood cuts; 'Esdras,' &c. to 2 Maccabees, fol. ii —lxxxi. One blank leaf. 'The Newe Testament—M.D.XXXVII.' in red and black, within the same wood-engraving as that to the O. T. St. Matthew to Revelations, with tables of the Epistles, &c. fol. ii—cxi. On the next and last leaf is the imprint with the date of M.D.XXXVII. A full page contains 60 lines.
See Lea Wilson, no. 4. Cotton, 12. 277. Bibl. Harl. no. 155. Ames by Dibdin, iii. 434—6. Dibdin's Libr. Comp. 30—1. Dibdin's Ædes Althorp. i. 62-3. Bp. Tomline's Chr. Theol. ii. 9. Abp. Newcome's Hist. View, 34—42. Lewis's History, 105—12. Horne's Introd. ii. appendix, 60—1.

— (MATTHEW). The Bible, by Thomas Matthew (1538), folio.
A reprint of the edition of 1537, with some variation. [*See* Lewis's History. Dr. Cotton says, no such edition of this year has yet been *ascertained*. A copy of this presumed edition, but wanting the title, was in the library of S. Ewer of Hackney, sold by Sotheby, Nov. 24, 1808].

— (TAVERNER). The most sacred Bible, translated into Englyshe and newly recognised with great diligence after most faythful exemplars, by Richard Taverner. Lond.

by John Byddell for Thomas Barthlet, 1539. folio.

Black letter. First edition of Taverner's Bible. Copies are to be found in the British Museum, Bodleian, and other libraries. Denyer, 19, (title wanting, and ending with the second boke of the Maccabees) 8*l*. 8*s*. Sotheby (Steevens), Aug. 1857. 36*l*. Pickering, 1854, wanting title and 5 leaves, 21*l*. *Collation.* Title. A dedication to the king. An exhortation to the study of the holy Scripture, 2 p. The summe and content of all the holy Scripture, 2 p. The names of all the bokes, &c. A briefe rehearsall declarynge how long the world hath endured, &c. 2 p. A Table of the principal matters, 22 p. Genesis to Solomon's song, fol. i.—ccxxx. Then follows on a separate leaf, 'The boke of the Prophetes, Esaye,' &c. Esaye to Malachy, fol. ii—lxxxxi.; on a separate leaf, 'The volume of the bokes called Apocripha.' Esdras, &c. folio i—lxxv. A blank leaf. After which the title of the new Testament, within an architectural compartment. St. Matthew, &c. fol. ii—ci. Tables of Epistles, &c. 3 leaves, not numbered; on the last is the date of M.D.XXXIX. This edition has no wood cuts. In the margin are notes, references, and pointing hands; the running titles, and titles of chapters, are in Roman letters. A full page contains 68 lines.

See Lea Wilson, no. 5. Cotton, 15, 278. Ames, by Dibdin, iii. 894-5. Bibl. Harl. no. 160. Beloe's Anecdotes, ii. 312. Dibdin's Lib. Comp. 30—1. Abp. Newcome's hist. View, 46—8. Lewis' History, 130-4. Horne's Introduction, ii. appendix, 63—4. Anderson's Annals.

Dr. Cotton thus briefly notices, 'Bible recognised by Richard Taverner. London, by John Bydell, for Tho. Berthelet, 1539, 4to. and an imperfect copy of the Bible, as set forth by Abp. Cranmer. Southwark, by J. Nicolson, 1539 ? 4to. is described in Dr. Dibdin's edition of Ames' Typographical Antiquities, iii. 57-8.

— ("THE GREAT," or CRUMWELL'S). The Byble in Englyshe, truly translated after the veryte of the Hebrue and Greke textes, by ye dylygent studye of dyuerse excellent learned men, expert in the forsayde tonges. Prynted by Rychard Grafton and Edward Whitchurch, [Paris and Lond.], Apryll, 1539. fol.

Black letter, with wood cuts, printed under the correction of Coverdale and auspices of Thomas, Lord Crumwell, (whose arms are on the Title), containing some improvement of Matthew's translation. It is generally called the Great Bible, and is supposed to be the same which Grafton and Whitchurch were secretly printing at Paris in 1538, when, being interrupted by the Inquisition, they finished it in London, 1539. This edition has been styled the first edition of *Cranmer's* Bible, but *erroneously*]. Copies are in the British Museum, Lambeth, St. Paul's, and other libraries, and one on VELLUM is in the library of St. John's Coll. Cambridge, specially printed for Lord Crumwell. Lea Wilson's copy was fine and perfect. as is the Grenville copy. Sotheby (Pickering), Aug. 1854, (imperfect), 12*l*. Gardner (Lea Wilson's copy), 121*l*.

Collation. Title in red and black, on the reverse 'the names of all the books;' 'Kalendar and almanac' (beginning 1539) four pages; 'An exhortacyon,' &c. 1 page; 'The summe and contents,' 2 pages; 'A Prologue,' &c., 1 page; 'A description,' &c. 2 pages; Genesis, fol. 1—lxxxiiii; 'The second part of the Byble,' &c. in black and red, between 16 wood cuts. Joshua, &c. fol. ii—cxxiii. blank leaf. 'The thirde parte.' &c. between 16 different wood cuts. Psalms to Malachi, fol. ii—cxxxiiii.; 'The volume of the bookes, called Hagiographa,' in black and red, within the same title as at the beginning, on the reverse is an address to the reader; Esdras, &c. fol. ii—lxxx. falsely numbered lxi; 'The Newe Testament,' &c. in black and red, between nine larger wood cuts; St. Matthew, &c. fol. ii—ciiii, the last two containing tables of the epistles and gospels. On the last is '—Fynished in Apryll, anno M.CCCCC.XXXIX.' A full page has 62 lines. The engraved title pages are said to have been designed by Hans Holbein. This edition is readily distinguished from the six succeeding ones, by having the Holbein frontispiece to the Apocripha, and *not* to the New Testament; and by the several wood cuts having on each side of them a pillar or border, which were omitted in the subsequent editions.

See Lea Wilson, no. 6. Cotton, 15, 279. Bibl. Harl. i. no. 159. Ames by Dibdin, iii. 438-40. Beloe's Anecdotes, ii. 313. Bp. Tomlins's Chr. Theol. ii. 11. Abp. Newcome's hist. View, 43—5. Lewis' History, 122—9. Horne's Introduction ii. appendix, 62-3. Anderson's Annals.

— ("THE GREAT," or CRUMWELL'S). The Byble in Englyshe, truly translated after the veryte of the Hebrue and Greke Textes, the diligent studye of dyuers excellent lerned men, experte in the fore saide Tongues. Lond. by Thomas Petyt and Roberte Redman, for Thos. Berthelet, Apryll, 1540. folio.

[This volume is a reprint or second edition of that of April, 1539, *erroneously* called the First of Cranmer's.] Copies are in the British Museum, St. Paul's, Emanuel College. Cambridge, and other libraries.

Collation.—Title, and the following prefixes, viz. an almanacke for xxx. yeres, a kalendar for the 12 months, 2 l.; the names of the bokes, and contents of the chapters, and a short prologue, 1 l.; Genesis to Job, fol. 1—ccxiiij.; The Psalter of David to the end of the books called Hagiographa, fol. 1—CCxxvij. (folio C lxii is omitted.) The new Testament ends on fol. C.ij. then follows a table, 2 l.

See Lea Wilson, no. 13. Cotton, 17-280. Ames by Dibdin, iii. 233, 309-11. Dibdin's Lib. comp. 31. Lewis' History, 139-40. Anderson.

— (MATTHEW). The Bible, in Five Parts or Volumes. Lond. by Rob. Redman, 1540. 16mo.

Imperfect copy at St. Paul's, London. *See* Ames by Dibdin, iii. 235, iv. 58-9. Dr. Cotton, 17. Anderson, Annals.

— (CRANMER, 'THE GREAT.') The Byble in Englyshe,—with a prologe thereinto, made by Thomas [Cranmer] archbysshop of Cantorbury. Printed by Edward Whytchurche, or R. Grafton, Apryll, 1540. folio.

FIRST EDITION OF CRANMER'S BIBLE.— The preface is reprinted in the third volume of 'The Fathers of the English Church.' A copy is in the British Museum, printed on vellum, which formerly belonged to King Henry VIII., having been a presentation copy from Antony Marlar, a citizen of London, who bore all the expense of the six folio editions of the Bible, printed by Grafton and Whitchurch in 1540 and 1541. *See* Anderson's Annals, ii. 131, 142, 152. For other copies, *see* Cotton, p. 17.

Collation.—Title, with the arms of Crumwell, red and black. Kalendar and Almanack, 4 p. An exhortacyon, 1 p. The summe and content, 2 p. A prologe, 1 p. A descripsion, 2 p. The prologe, 6 p. Names of the books, 2 p. In all, 10 l. Genesis to Deut. ii—lxxxviiii. Seconde part, ii—cxxiii. Third part, ii—cxxxiii (called 132). Hagiographa, ii—lxxx. The New Testament, ii—civ. A full page contains 62 lines. Some copies have the name of Richard Grafton in place of Edward Whytchurche, but have no other difference. *See* Lea Wilson, no. 7.—Dr. Cotton, 16.

[Mr. Lea Wilson possessed five other editions, printed by Grafton and Whitchurch, of which he gives the collation and their variations; also to be found in Dr. Cotton's List, 280-4, who gives, on p. 285, a synoptical table of the variations of the seven folio editions between 1539 to Dec. 1541.]

— (CRANMER). The Byble in Englyshe, &c. *as before.* Rychard Grafton. July, 1540. folio.

Collation.—Title, names of the books, 1 p. Calendar and Almanac, 4 p. Prologue, 6 p. Text, pt. 1, 1—lxxxiiij. Pt. 2, ii—cxxiij. Pt. 3, ii—cxxxij. Pt. 4, ii—lxxx. New Testament, ii—cij. Tables of Epistles, 2 p. 62 lines in a full page.

— (CRANMER). Edwarde Whitchurch, 28 May, 1541. folio.

Collation.—Title, Calendar, &c. 4 p. Prologue, 6 p. Text, pt. 1, 1—lxxxiiij. Pt. 2, ii—cxxij. Pt. 3, ii—cxxxiii (for 132). Pt. 4, ii—lxxx. New Testament. ii—ciiij (for 103). Tables of Epistles, 1 p. 62 lines in a full page.

— (CRANMER). Rycharde Grafton. O. T. title 1540, end December, 1541. folio.

Collation.—Title, names of the Books, 1 p. Calendar, 4 p. Exhortation, 1 p. Summe and content, 2 p. Prologue, 1 p. Description, 2 p. Prologue, 6 p. Text, pt. 1, i—lxxxiiij. Pt. 2, ii—cxxiij. Pt. 3, ii—cxxxij (for 133). Pt. 4, ii—lxxx. New Test. ii—cij. Tables of Epistles, 2 p. 62 lines in a full page.

— (CRANMER). ' *Oversene and perused by Cuthbert* (TUNSTAL) *byshop of Duresme, and Nicolas* (HEATH) *bisshop of Rochester*.' Edwarde Whitchurch, O. T. title 1541, end November, 1540. folio.

Collation.—Title, Calendar, &c., 4 p. Prologue, 6 p. Text, pt. 1, i—lxxij. Pt. 2, ii—cviij. Pt. 3, ii—cxvi. Pt. 4, ii—lxxij. (for 70). New Test. ii—xcij. (for 93). Tables of Epistles, 1 p. 65 lines in a full page.

— (CRANMER). Edwarde Whitchurch. November, 1541. folio.

(*Same title as Nov.* 1540, *but a distinct edition*). *See* Cotton, 284.

Collation.—Title, Calendar, 4 p. Prologue, 6 p. Text, pt. 1, i—lxxij. Pt. 2, ii—cviij Pt. 3, ii—cxvi. Pt. 4, ii—lxxij (for 70). New Test. ii—xcij. (for 93). Tables of Epistles, 1 p. 65 lines in a full page.

Knight, 1847 (the corners of 4 leaves MS.) 31*l*. Sotheby (Stevens) Aug. 1857, 90*l*. The New Testament titles of the editions April, 1540, and July, 1540, have the arms of Crumwell; in the other editions they are effaced.

See Lea Wilson, nos. 8-12. Cotton, 281-4. Bibl. Harl., nos. 161-163. Dibdin's Lib. Comp. 31. Ædes Althorp. 1-63. Lewis' History, 134-7. Ames, by Dibdin, iii. 440, 1, 2; 484-5. Anderson's Annals, &c. &c.

— (CRANMER). The Byble in Englyshe, &c. after the Translacion appointed to be read in the Churches. Lond. by Edward Whitchurche, xxix December, 1549. folio.

A reprint of Cranmer's edition of 1541, with his prologue, in black letter, which, according to Dr. Cotton, was certainly printed at two different presses. Some copies appear with the name of Rich. Grafton as the printer, others, Grafton and Whitchurch. Copies are in the Bodleian, Exeter Coll. [on yellow paper], All Soul's Coll. Libraries, Oxford, in the Baptist Museum, Bristol, and many other collections. Sotheby (Stevens), Aug. 1857, imperfect, 12l. 15s. Duke of Sussex, pt. 1, 1430, 21l. Pickering, 23l. 10s. Gardner, 1854, 44l.

Collation.—Title, in black, within a woodcut containing the king's arms at the top; Cranmer's prologue, 7 pages; 'The summe and content of all the holy Scripture,' &c. 2 pages. 'An exhortacion to the studye,' &c. 1 page: Genesis to Deuteronomy, fol. i—xcviii. 'The seconde parte of the Byble,' &c. in a compartment made up of xi wood cuts; Josua to Job, fol. ii—cxlii. ; 'The thyrde parte,' &c.; Psalms to Malachy, fol. ii—cxlviii.; 'Apogrypha. The fourth parte of the Bible ;' Esdras, &c. fol. ii—xcvi; 'The newe Testament,' &c. between 10 wood cuts, on the reverse begins 'A Table,' which occupies 3 pages; St. Matthewe, &c. fol. i—cxvi. A full page contains 57 lines.

See Lea Wilson, no. 16. Dr. Cotton, 21-286. Bibl. Harl. no. 166. Ames by Dibdin. iii. 467, 494. Brit. Bibl. ii. 11. Lewis' History, 181-2. Anderson's Annals.

— (MATTHEW). The Byble, nowe lately with greate industry and Diligëce recognised (by Edm. Becke). Lond. by Jhon Daye and William Seres, 17 Aug. 1549. folio.

Black letter, with wood cuts throughout. This edition contains Tyndal's prologues. At the beginning of the psalms is a woodcut, occupying the whole breadth of the page : and before each gospel is the figure of the writer, executed in a different style from the other cuts. To that of St. Mark is affixed the engraver's mark I.F. Copies are in the Lambeth, British Museum, Bodleian, and other Libraries. Bp. Randolph, 372 (one leaf wanting), 6l. 10s. Willett, 291, russia, 10l. 10s. Sir M. M. Sykes, pt. 1. 614, russia, 31l. 10s. resold Wilks, 1847, 29l. 10s. Gardner, 1854, 40l. Pickering, 1854, 16l. Sotheby (Stevens), Aug. 1857, 22l.

Collation.—Title, in red and black, within a border of 14 wood cuts. On the reverse is 'An Almanac for xxix years;' 'Calendar,' 2 leaves; 'An exhortation,' &c. 'The summe and content,' &c. 1 leaf; 'Dedication by Edm. Becke,' 3 pages; 'A description & successe,' &c. 1 page; 'A Table of the principal matters,' &c. 'A perfect supputation of the yeres from Adam unto Christ,' &c. together 12 leaves ; 'A prologe,' 'A register,' 2 leaves. All these pieces occupy 20 leaves. Genesis to Deuteronomy, fol. i—lxxxvi, lxxxviij (marked Fo. 86). 'The seconde parte of the Byble' within a compartment composed of historical cuts; Josua to Hiob, fol. ii—cxliii. 'The thyrd part;' title as before. Psalter to Malachi, fol. ii — cxlv, followed by a blank leaf. In this part are two leaves not numbered, between fol. xlviii and xlix. Title as before. 'The volume of the bokes called Apocripha,' &c. on the reverse is an address to the reader; Esdras, &c. fol. ii—lxxvi. 'The newe Testament,' in a compartment, with the four Evangelists at the corners. 'William Tyndale unto the Christen Reader,' &c. fol. ii—cxxi. Table, two leaves. Fol. lxxxv. is omitted. The titles, notes and references are wholly in the Gothic character, and a full page contains 65 lines.

See Lea Wilson, no. 15. Cotton, p. 21-288. Ames by Dibdin, iv. 57-8. Bibl. Harl. no. 167. Lewis' History, 177—9. Anderson's Annals.

— (MATTHEW). The Byble, whych is all the holy Scripture. By Thomas Matthewe, 1537. Lond. by Thomas Raynalde and William Hyll, 31 October, 1549. folio.

Black letter. Reprinted (faultily) from the edition of 1537, with some alterations, and published by Edmund Becke. The numbering of the leaves is very clumsy and confused through the whole of the volume: the types are rude and much battered, and the composition is very faulty. Copies are in the Lambeth and St. Paul's Libraries. Pickering, 1854, 31l.

Collation.—The title; a calendar and almanac for xii yeares, 4 pages; 'An exhortation,' 1 page; 'The summe and contente, &c. 2 pages; 'A description and successe,' &c. 2 pages ; 'To the reader,' 1 page. 'A table of principal matters,' 27 pages. 'The names of all the bokes,' &c. 'A brief rehersal of the yearen passed,' &c. 'Unto the reader W. T.' 3 pages ; Genesis to Job, folio i—ccliiii. falsely numbered ccxliiii.; Psalms to Malachi, fol. i—ccxvi. falsely numbered ccxix. The Apocrypha, fol. ccxvii—cccxl. Title of the New Testament, in black within a compartment ; St. Matthew to the Acts, fol. ii—lxxvi. Tyndal's prologue to the Epistle to the Romans, 4 leaves not numbered. The Epistle to the Romans, &c. fol. i—xlviii (for 57). Tables of Epistles, &c. 3 l. A full page contains 58 lines, occasionally 54.

See Lea Wilson, no. 14. Cotton, 21-287. Bibl. Harl. no. 168. Ames, by Dibdin, iii. 570. Dibdin's Lib. Comp. 32. Lewis' History, 180-1. Anderson's Annals.

— (TAVERNER). The Bible, in Five Parts or Volumes. Lond. by Jhon Day and Wylliam Seres, 1549. 16mo.

This edition is thus divided: 1. The Pentateuch. 2. The Boke of Josua to the Boke of Hiob. 3. The Psalter—The Boke of the Prophet Malachi. 4. The Bokes called the Apocrypha—The thyrd Booke of the Machabees. (The first translation of that book in English.) 5. The new Testament. Each part has a title page and a colophon. *See* Ames, by Dibdin, iv. 58—9. The second and fourth part Williams, 194, morocco, 7l. 2s. 6d. Part 2. Sir M. M. Sykes, pt. i. 223, 3l. 13s. 6d.

There exists doubts as to whether more than one edition of this Bible was printed in parts, in 12mo.—no perfect set being known to exist. Mr. Wilson has examined a copy of vol. 1, containing the Pentateuch, dated 1551, and from which he reprinted the preface. (List, p. 131*.) He possessed vols. 2 and 4, dated 1549; [L.]t, no. 17, and pp. 129* and 130*)—also vol. 3, dated 1550. Parts 2 and 4 are in the British Museum. Part 4 is in the Bodleian, and at Lambeth. The Duke of Sussex, pts. 2 and 4.

Dr. Cotton, p. 21; he also notices two other editions of the Bible in 1549, 4to. one printed for John Cawood, the other by Richard Grafton. A copy of the latter is in the Baptist Museum, Bristol.

— (CRANMER). The Bible in Englishe, accordinge to the translacion that is appointed to be rede in the Churches. Prynted by Ed. Whytchurche, 1550. 4to.

In the Douce collection is a perfect copy. The Duke of Sussex possessed an imperfect one; and in St. Paul's library are two copies, both imperfect. The Museum. Mr. Lea Wilson, perfect.

Collation.—Title. Abp. Cranmer's prologue, 7 pages. The Summe and cōtent of all the holy Scripture, 2 pages. Names of all the Bookes, 1 page—in all, 6 leaves. Gen. to Deuter. i—lxxxvii. Blank leaf. The seconde parte, &c. Joshua to Hiob, i—cxxxii. The Thyrde parte, &c. The Psalter to Malachy, i—cl. The volume of the Bookes called Hagiographia, i—lxxxviii. The Newe Testament, i—cxi. A Table to find the Epistles, &c. 1 leaf. A full page contains 60, 61, or 62 lines.

See Lea Wilson, no. 18. Cotton, p. 23-289. Ames by Dibdin, 111-495. Lewis' Hist. p. 183.

— (COVERDALE). The whole Byble, faythfully translated into Englyshe, by Myles Coverdale, and newly oversene and correcte. M.D.L. Prynted for Andrewe Hester (Zurich, Froschover) 16 Aug. 1550. 4to.

In Skipton's Travels, among the Church. ill Collection, vol. vi. 462, this edition is said to be 'printed at Zurich, by Christopher Forshower, 16 August, 1550.' Dr. Cotton observes that 'perhaps the preliminary pieces were printed in London: but the body of the work is unquestionably of foreign typography.' [Mr. Anderson has proved the place where this book was printed, by adducing a copy preserved in the Public Library at Zurich, which bears on the title page, 'Imprinted at Zurich, bey Christopher Froschover,' in the printers' autograph]. Hollis, 193, (title MS. morocco, 9l. 5s. Knight, 1847, (title MS. and short) 30l. Puttick, 1852, (title to Test. Almk. Calendar, and Tables wanting), 31l. Sotheby (Gardner), 1854. (Lea Wilson's copy), 38l. Sotheby (Stevens), Aug. 1857. Preliminary pieces, fac-simile, 28l. 10s.

Collation. Title, within an architectural compartment; 'The bokes of the hole Byble,' 1 page; dedication to King Edward VI. 4 pages; 'Myles Coverdale to the Christen reader,' 5 pages; almanac for fourteen years, beginning 1550, and calendar, 4 pages. Genesis to ii. Maccabees, fol. i—ccccxciv; St. Matthew, &c. fol. i—cxxi; Tables, 8 leaves, not numbered. The Apocrypha begins on fol. cccc. and a full page contains 50 lines.

See Lea Wilson, no. 19. Cotton, p. 23-289. Ames by Dibdin, iii. 535-6. Lewis' History, 182-3. Anderson's Annals.

— (MATTHEW). The Byble: set furth according to y⁰ Coppy of Thomas Mathew's Translaciō [by Edm. Becke]. Lond. by Jhon Daye, 23 Maye, 1551. folio.

Though stated on the title to be *Mathewe's* translation, it is, with the exceptions of a few chapters [pointed out by Mr. Lea Wilson, *vide* List, p. 39], in reality TAVERNER's, of 1539, with trivial variations by Ed. Becke, and the addition of the Third Book of Maccabees (for the first time added). The New Testament is Tyndale's, with his prologues, and has marginal notes, references, and pointing hands. Every part is in the Gothic letter, and at the beginning of each Gospel is a wood cut. Copies are in the British Museum, Lambeth, St. Paul's, and Bodleian Libraries. Denyer, 21, (a little

N 2

imperfect,) 4*l.* 12s. 6d. Sotheby's in 1824, (title and index wanting), 20*l.* Gardner, 1854, 45*l.* Sotheby (Stevens), Aug. 1857, with variation on back of title, 15*l.* 5s.

Collation. Title, within a compartment, having the king's arms and initials at the top, and John Daye's device or rebus at the bottom ; ' To the Christen reader.' ' A Table of the principal matters,' &c. ' A gatheryng of certain harde wordes,' &c. ' An exhortation to the studye of the Holy Scripture.' ' The summe and content of all the Holy Scripture.' ' A supputation of yeres.' &c. ' The names of all the bookes,' &c. ' A regyster,' &c. ' A descripcion and successe of the kynges of Juda & Hierusalem,' &c. W. Tyndal's prologue. These preliminary pieces occupy 19 leaves, besides the title. Genesis to Deuteronomy, fol. i—lxxxiiii. 'The second parte.' Josua to Job, fol. ii—cxvii. 'The thirde parte.' Psalms to Malachi, fol. i—cxlii. ' The volume of the bokes called Apocripha,' on the reverse, 'a prologe to the reader.' iii Esdras, to iii Maccabees, fol. ii—lxxxiiii. 'The newe Testament, &c. Anno M.D.LI.' Tyndal's prologue to Revelations, fol. l—xcviiii. Tables of epistles, &c. 2 leaves. A full page contains 67 lines.

See Lea Wilson, no. 20. Cotton, p. 27-290. Ames by Dibdin, iv. 65-6. Bibl. Harl. no. 170. Beloe's Anecdotes, ii. 315. Lewis' History, 189-90. Ædes Althorp. 1164-5. Anderson's Annals.

Dr. Cotton mentions a doubtful edition. London, by John Daye, 1551, 12mo. probably that begun in 1549. See *ante.*

— (MATTHEW). The Byble,— truly and purely translated into Englishe, and now lately with great industry and diligence recognysed. Lond. by Nich. Hyll *(for others),* 1551. folio.

The volume contains Tyndal's prologues; has marginal notes and references, and capital letters down the page, but no wood cuts or Roman characters. The colophon of a copy in the library of Trinity College, Oxford, runs thus, ' Imprynted at London by Nicolas Hyll, dwelling in Saynct John's Streate, at the coste and charges of certayne honest menne of the occupacyon, whose names be upon their bokes.' The names of not fewer than eight booksellers are found each by itself, upon this edition, viz. Rd. Kele, Thomas Petyte or J. Petyt, Rob. Toye, Abr. Veale, John Walley, John Wryghte or Wyghte. Bindley, pt. i. 384 with the Common Prayer, 1552, and old Version of Psalms, 1567, 7*l.* 17s. 6d. Pickering, 12*l.* 15s.

Collation. Title, in black and red, within a compartment formed by two large wood cuts at top and bottom, with four smaller on the sides ; on the reverse is an almanac, beginning 1549. ' A Table for the ordre of the Psalms.' ' The order how the rest of holy Scripture is to be read.' ' The Kalender.' ' An exhortation unto the study,' &c. ' The summe and content of the holy Scripture.' ' To the Christian readers.' ' A description & successe of the Kynges of Juda and Jerusalem.' ' A table of the principal matters.' ' A perfit supputacion of the yeares,' &c. ' A prologue, shewing the use of the Scripture.' ' The names of the bokes of the Byble.' ' A register, or a briefe rehearsall of the names,' &c. These preliminary pieces occupy 19 leaves, exclusive of the title. Genesis to Deuteronomy, fol. i—cxii ; ' The seconde parte of the Byble,' &c. between 11 wood cuts ; Josua to Job, fol. ii—clv. ' The thirde parte,' &c. ; Psalms to Malachi, fol. ii—cxc. 'The volume of the bokes called Apocripha,' between ten wood cuts ; fol. ii—cii. ' The Newe Testament,' &c. St. Matthew, &c. fol. ii—cl., the last of which is not numbered. On the reverse of the last is the colophon. A full page contains 55 lines.

See Lea Wilson, no. 21. Cotton, p. 27-291. Ames, by Dibdin, iii. 513, 571, 575, iv. 282-3, 271. 370. Bibl. Harl. no. 169. Lewis' History, 187-8, 192—4. Anderson's Annals.

— (CRANMER). The Bible. London. N. Hyll, for Abraham Veale, 1552. 4to.

Herbert, in his ' Ames,' erroneously assigns this book to Nicolson of Southwark. A copy in the Public Library, Cambridge.

See Lea Wilson, no. 22. Cotton, p. 28 and 292.

— (CRANMER) The Byble in English, accordyng to the Translaciō that is appointed to be read in Churches. Lond. by Edw. Whytchurche, 1553. folio.

Probably copied from the first edition of 1540 : since here, as in that, the Apocryphal books are entitled Hagiographa.

It has been said that Queen Mary destroyed many copies of this edition.

Collation.—Title in black. Names of the books, &c. 1 l. Genesis to Deut. i—lxxxviij. Josua to Hiob, ii—cxxxiiij. Psalter to Malachy, ii—clij. Hagiographa, ii—lxxxvij. New Test. on the back Table to find the Epistles, 3 pages. Matthew to Revelation, i—cxvi. A full page has 58, sometimes 59 lines. Copies are in St. Paul's, Worcester Coll., Bodleian, Glasgow Univ., and the Earl of Bridgewater's Libraries. Pickering, 27*l.* 10s. Sotheby (Stevens), Aug. 1857. Title fac-simile, 16*l.* 5s.

See Lea Wilson, no. 23. Cotton, p. 29—293. Ames, by Dibdin, iii. 498-9. Lewis' History, 197. Anderson's Annals.

— (COVERDALE). The whole Byble, faithfully translated into Englyshe by Myles Coverdale. Lond. by Richard Jugge, 1553. 4to.

The Zurich edition of 1550, with a new title-page, almanac, &c.

Collation. — Title, 1 l. Bokes of the whole Byble, 1 p., Coverdale's dedication, 4 pp. Coverdale's prologue, 5 pp. Table and Kalendar, 2 pp. Proper Psalmes, 2 pp. The rest as 1550.

Copies are in St. Paul's, Balliol Coll., Exeter Coll., and other Libraries, also in the Baptist Museum, Bristol.

See Cotton, p. 29-294. Ames, by Dibdin, iv. 246-7. Bibl. Harl. no. 291. Lewis' History, 196-7. Anderson's Annals.

— (CRANMER). The Bible in Englishe, accordig to the Translation of the great Byble. Lond. by R. Grafton and Edw. Whitchurch, 1553. 4to.

The type of this edition, printed in double columns, is remarkably small. In the margin are references and indications of the portions appointed to be read as lessons in the church. A full page has 62 lines, and there are neither prologues, heads of chapters, notes, nor wood cuts. Some copies have only Grafton's name as printer. In St. Paul's Library, and the Baptist Museum, Bristol. Inglis, 16l, morocco, 11l. 10s.

Collation. — Title, 1 l. Names of the Books, 1 l. Genesis to Maccabees, 1—ccclxxxij. New Test. ii—xcij. Table to find the Epistles, 2 l.

See Lea Wilson, no. 24. Cotton, p. 29-293. Ames by Dibdin, iii. 478, 498. Bibl. Harl. no. 290. Ædes Althorp. i. 65. Anderson's Annals.

— (GENEVAN). The Bible and holy Scriptures, translated according to the Ebrue and Greke, and conferred with the best Translations in divers Langages. With most profitable Annotations upon all the harde Places, and other Thinges of great Importance. Geneva, by Rouland Hall, 1560. 4to.

The first edition of the Genevan version, which was for many years the most popular one in England, and it went through about fifty editions in the course of thirty years. From the peculiar rendering of Genesis iii. 7, the editions of this translation have been commonly known by the name of 'Breeches Bibles.' The translators were Bp. Coverdale, Anthony Gilby, William Whittingham, Christopher Woodman, Thomas Sampson, and Thomas Cole; to whom some add, John Knox, John Bodleigh, John Pullein, and others. Sotheby's in June, 1822, 7l. 17s. 6d. Wilks, 1847, 16l. 5s. Horner, 1857, 29l. 10s. Sotheby (Stevens), 10l. 10s.

Copies are in the Lambeth, British Museum, Mr. Offor, St. John's Coll., and Balliol Coll. Libraries, the latter an exceedingly fine one, printed on LARGE PAPER. [A similar copy in the Public Library of Cambridge].

Collation. On the back of the title is 'The order of all the books,' &c. An Epistle to Queen Elizabeth, 4 pages. 'To our beloved in the Lord,' &c. 2 pages. Genesis to 2 Maccabees, folio 1—474. The description of the Holy Land, with a map. Then follows a title, 'The newe Testament,' &c. 'The holy Gospel,' &c. fol. 2—122. 'A Table of the interpretation of proper names,' 7 pages. 'A Table of the principal things contained in the Bible,' 17 pages and a half. 'A perfite supputation of the yeares and times from Adam unto Christ,' 2 pages. 'The order of the yeres from Paul's conversion,' 1 page. The book is printed in two columns, a full page containing 63 lines. At Numbers chap. xxxiii. is a map of the journeys of the Israelites; at Joshua, xv. a smaller one, of the divisions of the land of Canaan for the twelve tribes; at the end of Ezechiel, a map of the temple and citie restored; before the Acts, a map of places mentioned therein.

See Lea Wilson, no. 25. Cotton, p. 31-294. Ames, by Dibdin, iv. 410-1. Bibl. Harl. no. 292. Dibdin's Cassano Catalogue, 193-4. Anderson's Annals.

— (GENEVAN). The Bible. Geneva, O. T 1562—N. T. 1561. folio. No printer's name.

This edition is printed in the Roman letter; each page has 65 lines.

Collation. — Title to O. T. dated 1562. Epistle to Q. Elizabeth, 3 pp. To our beloved brethren, 2 pp. Genesis to Maccabees, 5-432. Newe Test. title, date 1561. A map Description of the holie land. Text, 2-111. Tables, &c. 24 pages. There are detached maps in Numbers and Joshua, and a large folded plan of the city and temple at the end of Ezechiel. Map of Holie Land before St. Matthew, and another before the Actes.

See Lea Wilson, no. 28. Cotton, p. 31-297. Herbert's Ames, iii. 1603, who observes, in all probability this edition was issued by John Bodleigh, one of the English refugees at Geneva; to whom and his assigns Queen Elizabeth granted a patent for printing this version during the term of seven years, from Jan. 8, 1561. The Dedication is dated from Geneva, 10 April, 1561.

— (CRANMER). The Bible. Lond. by Jhon Cawoode, 1561. 4to.

Copies are in the British Museum and Lambeth libraries. The Earl of Leicester's only perfect copy known. Sotheby (Stevens), Aug. 1857. Title fac-simile, and wants preliminary pieces, 11*l*.

Collation. Title and preliminary pieces, — leaves; Genesis to Job, fol. 1—cciii; 'The thirde parte of the Byble;' Psalms to Malachi, fol. i—cxxxiii. The volume of the bookes called 'Hagiographa;' Esdras, &c. folio cxxxv—ccxiv; 'The Newe Testamente'; St. Matthew, &c. fol. li—cii; the two last, containing tables, are not numbered. The type is a small Gothic, a full page containing 61 lines. [Lea Wilson says 53 lines].

See Lea Wilson, no. 26. Cotton, p. 32-295. Ames by Dibdin, iv. 400.

Dr. Dibdin notices an edition of Cranmer's Bible printed by Cawood, 1561, in folio.

— (CRANMER). The Bible in Englishe, according to the Translacion that is appointed to be read in Churches. Lond. by Richarde Harrison, 1562. folio.

A copy is in the Baptist Museum at Bristol. Sotheby (Stevens), Aug. 1857, 22*l*.

Collation.—Title, &c.; Kalendar, 4 pages; Cranmer's prologue, 6 pages; 'A description and successe of the kings,' &c. 2 pages; Genesis to Deuteronomy, folio i—xc; on the reverse of the last is 'The second part of the Bible,' &c.; Josua to Job, fol. i—cxxxviii. on the reverse of the last, 'The third part,' &c. Psalms to Malachi—clvi. in the Psalms the folios are not marked, and Proverbs commence on fol. xxxv. b. 'The fourth part,' &c. Esdras, fol. i—lxxxviii. 'The newe Testament,' on the reverse is a table to find the Epistles, &c. 3 pages; map, &c. 2 pages; St. Matthew, &c. folio i—cxviii, erroneously marked cxviiii. A full page contains 58 lines. The heads of chapters, as far as Judges, chapter viii., are in a different letter from those of the rest of the volume. [According to Cotton, there should be four maps in the volume.]

See Lea Wilson, no. 27. Cotton, p. 32-296. Bibl. Harl. no. 171. Beloe's Anecd. ii. 325. Ames, by Dibdin, iv. 559-60. Lewis' History, 213-14. Anderson's Annals.

— (CRANMER). The Bible in Englyshe, of the largest and greatest Volume, according to the Translation apoynted by the Queenes Maiesties Injunctions to be read in all Churches within her Maiesties Realme. Rouen, by C. Hamilton, at the Coste and Charges of Richard Carmarden, 1566. folio.

Denyer, No. 122, (front. and two leaves, MS.) 17*l*. 17*s*. Sotheby (Stevens), Aug. 1857, 24*l*. Pickering, pt. 2, 294 (Lea Wilson's copy, *very fine, on thick paper*), 64*l*. Copies are in the British Museum and Bodleian libraries.

Collation.—Title, 1 l. The order how H. S. to be read. Proper Lessons. Almanacke for 30 years, beginning 1561, &c. &c. together 21 leaves. Gen. to Deut. i—lxxxviij. Joshua to Hiob, i—cxxxiiij. Psalms to Malachi, i—cl. The Apocripha, ii—xc. The New Test. i—cxiii. Table of Epistles, 1 l. A full page has 56 lines. The Third Book of Maccabees is inserted in the contents, but is not contained in the Volume. The Volume has Initial letters cut in wood, some of remarkable beauty. The engraver's initials, I. M. (Jehan Mallart), are to be seen in the wood cuts of the title.

See Lea Wilson, no. 29. Cotton, p. 33-297. Bibl. Harl. no. 172. Lewis' History, 214-7. Ames, by Herbert. iii. 1614-15. Lewis' History, 214. Dibdin's Ædes Althorp. i. 65-66. Beloe's Anecdotes, ii. 315. Anderson's Annals.

Dr. Dibdin briefly notices an edition by Rich. Grafton, 1566. 8vo. No copy known. *See* note in Cotton, p. 33; and Mr. Beriah Botfield notices a 4to. edition by Seres, 1567. Cathedral Libraries, p. 308.

— (THE BISHOPS'). The Holie Bible, conteynyng the Olde Testament and the newe. Lond. by Richard Jugge, 1568. folio.

FIRST EDITION of Parker's, or 'The Bishops' Bible,' rarely found in a perfect state. It contains three portraits, engraved on copper, viz. Queen Elizabeth (on the title), Lord Leicester, and Cecil, Lord Burleigh. Pickering, pt. 2, 1854 (Lea Wilson's copy), 60*l*. 10*s*.

Collation. Title, a copper-plate engraving; 'The summe of the whole scripture,' 1 leaf; 'A Table of the genealogie from Adam to Christ,' 11 pages, the initial letter contains Abp. Parker's arms, &c. beneath which is the date 1568; 'A table of the books,' &c. 2 pages; then a blank page; 'Proper Lessons,' &c. 2 pages; 'Proper Psalms,' &c. on 4 pages; a calendar, 12 pages: Abp. Parker's preface, in the Roman letter, 6 pages; Cranmer's preface, in Gothic letter, 5 pages; 'A description of the yeres,' &c. 1 page; 'The order of the books,' &c. 1 page, reverse blank; Genesis, &c. fol. i—cxxviii; on a separate leaf, 'The second part of the Byble,' &c. underneath is the portrait of Lord Leicester, in armour, within an oval; 'The booke of Josuah,' &c. fol. ii.—clxxxv.; on a separate leaf, 'The thirde parte,' &c. beneath is a wood cut, on the reverse is 'A prologue of St. Basill the great, upon the Psalmes,' with Lord Burleigh's arms in the initial D. At the beginning of the first psalm is the portrait of Lord Burleigh standing between two pillars. 'The Psalmes,' &c. fol. ii—cciii. On a separate leaf 'The volume of the bookes called Apocrypha,' &c. beneath is a wood cut; 'The thirde book of Esdras,' &c. fol. ii—cxviii. Then title of the new Testament, being a wood engraving somewhat similar in design to the frontispiece of the old Testament, on the reverse is 'A preface,' &c. with Abp. Parker's arms in the initial letter; St. Matthew, &c. fol. ii—clvii. (misprint clix.) On the reverse of this last is the colophon, and Jugge's device, but no date. A full page of text has 57 lines, and the whole number of engravings, including the title, portraits, and maps, is 143.

See Lea Wilson, no. 30. Cotton, p. 34-298. Ames, by Dibdin, iv. 256. Dibdin's Lib. Comp. 30-1. Beloe's Anecdotes, ii. 316. Bibl. Harl. no. 173. Tomline's Chr. Theol. ii. 15-16. Censura Literaria. Abp. Newcome's Histor. View, 78-90. Lewis' History, 235-53. Dibdin's Ædes Althorp. i. 66-7. Horne's Introduction, ii. appendix 67. Strype's Life of Parker. Anderson's Annals. From a note in the 'Book Rarities of Cambridge,' we learn that, in 1571, this volume was sold for 27s. 8d.

— (CRANMER). The Bible in Englyshe. Lond. by R. Jugge and J. Cawood, 1568. 4t°.

Copies are in Trinity Coll. Cambridge, All Soul's College, and Duke of Sussex's Libraries. *See* Cotton, p. 35-300. Lewis' History, 217-18.

— (CRANMER). The Bible, Lond. by John Cawood, 1569. 4to.

Copies are in the Lambeth Library, in that of Earl Spencer, and in the Baptist Museum, Bristol.

See Lea Wilson, no. 31. Cotton, p. 35 [There are two other editions of Cranmer's Bible printed by Cawood, (date 1569), described by Lea Wilson, nos. 32 and 33.]

— (BISHOPS'). The Holi Bible. Lond. by R. Jugge, 1569.4to.

Second edition of The Bishops' Bible. *See* Lea Wilson, no. 34. Cotton, p. 35-300. Ames, by Dibdin, iv. 256-7. Bibl. Harl. no. 294. Lewis' History, 253-6.

Pickering, 1854 (Lea Wilson's copy), 23l. 10s. Sotheby (Stevens), Aug. 1857, wanting 25 leaves, 2l. 4s.

— (GENEVAN). The Bible and Holy Scriptures, translated according to the Ebrue and Greke. Geneva, John Crespin, 1569 and 1570. 4to.

A copy of this Genevan version, 1570, is in the Bodleian Library. Herbert in his Ames briefly notices an edition of 1568 [one copy known in the library of Mr. Pinchard of Taunton]. Dr. Cotton and Lea Wilson think the editions of 1569 and 1570 to be one and the same. Dr. C. also notices a doubtful edition of this version 1570, in folio; also an edition, 1575, 4to. *See* Lea Wilson, nos. 35, 36. Cotton, p. 35-301.

— (BISHOPS'). The Bible. Lond. by Richard Jugge, 1570. 4t°.

— (BISHOPS'). The holie Bible. Lond. by Richarde Jugge, 1572. folio.

Second edition in folio. In this reprint of the Bishops' Bible, are two versions of the Psalter, that of the Great Bible in black letter, and a new one in Roman. Abp. Parker's prefaces are reprinted in vol. vii. of the Fathers of the English Church. At the commencement of the Epistle to the Hebrews is a wood-cut, representing the story of Leda and the swan, and many other of the Initials are subjects from Ovid's Metamorphoses. Two copies are in the Bodleian, and others in the British Museum, Lambeth, Pub. Lib. Cambridge, Bp. Daly, &c. &c..

This edition varies in many particulars from that of 1568. The title, the prefixes are nearly the same, altogether 25 leaves. Genesis, &c. fol. i—cxii; Josuah, &c. fol. cxiii—cclxx); Psalms, &c. fol. ii.—clxxxix (for cxc; Esdras iii. &c. fol. ii—cv. The new Testament, fol. ii—cxxxviii. 2 more leaves of table unnumbered. The colophon with the date 1572, is on the recto of the last. The engravings throughout the whole volume, including the titles, portraits, and maps, are only 30 in number. Denyer, 25, with the port. of Lord Burleigh without the letter B. 6l. 16s. 6d. Sotheby, 1850, (Title and 4 leaves damaged), 26l. Pickering, pt. 2, 42l. 10s. Sotheby (Stevens), Aug. 1857, 25l. 10s.

See Lea Wilson, no. 37. Cotton, p.37-302. Beloe's Anecdotes, ii. 317. Bibl. Harl. 174. Ames by Dibdin, iv. 258-9. Lewis' History, 257—9. Dibdin's Cassano Library, 191-2. Anderson's Annals.

— (BISHOPS'). The holy Byble. Lond. by Richard Jugge, 1573. 4to.

A very fine copy, bound in 5 vols., is in the Library at Lambeth, probably the presentation copy to Queen Elizabeth.

See Lea Wilson, no. 38. Cotton, p. 37. Bibl. Harl. i. 195. Ædes Althorp. i. 68.

— (BISHOPS'). The Bible. Lond. by Richard Jugge, 1574. folio.

A copy is in the Baptist Museum, Bristol. [At Josua, ch. 24, is a folded map of Canaan, dated 1574, which is from the same

block that was used for the map in Coverdale's Bible of 1535. Lea Wilson.]
See Lea Wilson, no. 39. Cotton, p. 39. Bibl. Harl. i. no. 175. Lewis' History, p. 260. Another edition, by John Judson, 1575, folio.

— (BISHOPS'). The Bible. Lond. by Richard Jugge. 1575. 4to. [or small folio].
This edition was a joint undertaking, copies being known to exist as '*Printed by R. Jugge,' B. Kele, J. Walley, L. Harrison, J. Judson, W. Norton, F. Coldock.*
See Lea Wilson, nos. 40, 41, 42. Cotton, p. 39. Bibl. Harl. no. 177.
Cotton mentions an edition of the Genevan version, 4to. 1575, as in Dr. Gifford's collection, and one by C. Barker, 8vo. 1575.

— (GENEVAN). The Bible and Holy Scriptures conteined in the olde and newe Testament, translated according to the Ebrue and Greke, 'printed in Edinburgh, Be Alexander Arbuthnet,' 1579. N.T. Printed by Thomas Bassandyne, 1576. folio.
A copy of this first edition of the Scriptures from the Scottish press is in the Advocates' Library at Edinburgh, Earl of Morton, Earl Spencer, Bp. Daly, &c. &c.
Collation.—Title, 1579. The names and order of all the books. Dedication to K. James VI. Romane and Hebre Calendar. An Almanack. Rules for double Calendar. Description and successe. How to take profit—in all 18 pages. The old Testament consists of 503 double pages ; the New of 125 double pages. Table of proper names, &c. 27 pp. Maps at Numbers, ch. 23 ; Joshua, ch. 15. Folded plan of the temple at Jerusalem at the end of Ezechiel. The Third book of the Maccabees was announced, but never added. It is handsomely printed with a sharp Roman letter, and is seemingly the same in the text, in the notes, in the marginal references, and the whole disposition of the several parts, as the Geneva Edition of 1561.
See Lea Wilson, no. 45. Cotton, p. 43,303. Ames, by Herbert, iii. 1499, 1818. Dr. Dibdin's Ædes Althorp. i. 68-70, and his Libr. Comp. 31-2. Bibl. Harl. 1. no. 178. Beloe's Anecdotes, ii. 329-31. Lincoln Nosegay, no. 5. Lee's Memorials of the Bible Societies of Scotland, p. 28. Anderson's Annals.

— (GENEVAN, TOMSON'S). The Bible. Lond. by Chr. Barker, 1576. folio.
This edition of the Genevan version is very neatly printed in long primer Roman, with the arguments in Latin. The Old Testament consists of 365, the Apocrypha, 84, and the New Testament, 115 leaves.
See Lea Wilson, no. 44. Cotton, p. 40. Lewis' History, 264-71, and Horne's Introduction ii. appendix 66. Dr. Cotton notices another edition of this version by Chr. Barker, 1576. 4to.

— (BISHOPS'). The Bible. Lond. by Richard Jugge, 1576. 4to.
See Lea Wilson, no. 43. Cotton, p. 40. Bibl. Harl. no. 296.

— (GENEVAN, TOMSON'S). The Bible. Lond. by Chr. Barker, 1577. small folio.
Copies are in the libraries at Oriel and St. John's Coll. Cambridge. The Duke of Sussex possessed the copy formerly belonging to Queen Elizabeth. Sold at his sale for 9*l.* 12*s.* A description of it is given in Strutt's View of the Manners of England, vol. ii. p. 89. An edition in 4to. is noticed in the Bibl. Harl. no. 297.
See Lea Wilson, no. 46. Cotton, p. 41.

— (BISHOPS'). The Bible. Lond. by R. Jugge, 1577. 4to:
This edition is specially noted by the Rhemist translators, in their Annotations to the New Testament of 1582.
See Cotton, p. 41. Mr. Wilson had an imperfect copy of an octavo edition of this date, *vide* List, p. 131*. Also Ames, by Dr. Dibdin, iv. p. 261-2.

— (GENEVAN). The Bible. Lond. by Christopher Barker, 1578. folio.
In this edition are two versions of the Psalms ; the Genevan, printed in Roman letter ; and that of the Great Bible, printed in Gothic similar to the rest of the volume. The preface is reprinted in vol. viii. of the Fathers of the English Church.
See Lea Wilson, no. 47. Cotton, p. 42. Bibl. Harl. no. 179. Beloe's Anecdotes, ii. 701. Lewis' History, 271-3.

— (BISHOPS'). The Holy Bible. Lond. by Assignement of Chr. Barker, 1578. folio.
This edition, called the Dotted Bible, is printed page for page with that of 1574.
See Lea Wilson, no. 48. Cotton, p. 42.

— (GENEVAN). The Bible. Lond. by Chr. Barker, two impressions, 1579. 4to.
Barker printed other editions of this version, viz. 1580, folio and 4to. two editions, one on LARGE PAPER. 1581, folio and 4to. (Bibl. Harl. no. 298), and 8vo. (Ædes Althorp. i. 70-1). 1582, folio. 1583, n.v. folio (Hawtrey, 1853, 6*l.* Lea Wilson, very

fine copy), and 4to. (B. Harl. nos. 180 and 181). Lewis' History, 275-6. Bp. of Ely, 227, 1*l*. 5s. Williams, 867, 2*l*. 5s. (The third part of the Bible, 16mo.) 1586, 4to. and 8vo. 1587, 4to. 1588, 4to.

See Lea Wilson, nos. 49-55, 59-62. Cotton.

— (GENEVAN). The Bible. Lond. by the Deputies of Chr. Barker, 1588. 4to.

Other editions by the same—1589 folio [?] and 4to. Bindley, pt. i. 911, 11s. 6d. 1590, 4to. Bindley, pt. i. 912, on yellow paper, 15s. 6d. 1592, folio and 4to. 1593, 8vo. 1594, 4to. 1596, 4to. and 8vo. 1597, 4to.

— (GENEVAN, TOMSON'S). The Bible. Lond. by the Deputies of Chr. Barker, 1592. folio.

1595, folio and 4to. 1597, small folio. 1598, 4to. 1599, 4to and 8vo. Of the 4to. dated this year Lea Wilson had *six* different editions. Denyer, 16, 1*l*. 1s. Williams, 230, with the Boeke of Psalmes, morocco, 4*l*. 8s.; there is also another by Barker's deputies, 1599, printed at Amsterdam in 1633.

— (BISHOPS'). The Bible. Lond. by Chr. Barker, 1584. folio and 4to.

Sotheby's in June, 1822, russia, 2*l*. 12s. 6d. *See* Bibl. Harl. no. 182. Ædes Althorp. i. Another edition, 1585, folio. *See* Lea Wilson, nos. 56-58.

— (BISHOPS'). The Bible. Lond. by the Deputies of Chr. Barker, 1588. folio.

[Lea Wilson had a LARGE PAPER copy of this edition.] Dr. Cotton notices 'The third part of the Bible,' as printed by the Deputies of Chr. Barker, 1591; and again in 1598, 16mo. Other editions by the Deputies of C. Barker, 1591, fol. 1595, fol. (The Psalms according to Cranmer's version.) White Knights, 578, 2*l*. 15s. Brit. Museum, on LARGE PAPER. 1598, folio. Bibl. Harl. no. 184.

See Lea Wilson; Cotton; Lewis' History, 260-2.

— (GENEVAN). The Bible. Cambridge. John Legate. 1591. 8vo.

See Lea Wilson, who says, 'The volume is not paged, and 'I have never seen or heard of another copy of this beautiful edition, which is the earliest at present known printed at Cambridge.'

— (GENEVAN TOMSON'S). The Bible, with Tomson's version of the New Testament. 4to. circa 1600.

Without date, place, or printer's name; but supposed to have been printed at Dort, from the figure of a goose on the title page of the Psalms, and at the end of the volume.

— (GENEVAN). The Bible. Lond. by Robert Barker. 1600. 4to.

See Bibl. Spencer, v. 71.

EDITIONS.— 1601, 4to. and 8vo. 1602, folio. Lea Wilson, LARGE PAPER. 1603, 4to. and 8vo. 1605, 4to. 1606, folio, 4to. and 8vo. Bibl. Spencer. vii. 192. 1607, 4to. and 8vo. Bibl. Spencer. v. 72. 1608, 4to. and 8vo. 1610, 4to. and 8vo. 1611, 4to. 1613, 4to. 1614, 4to. 1615, 4to. Roxburghe, 14, 18s.

— (GENEVAN and TOMSON'S). The Bible. Lond. by Robert Barker, 1601. 4to.

EDITIONS.—1602, folio. 1603, 4to. 1606, 4to. 1607, folio. 1608, 4to. 1609, 4to. 1610, folio, 4to. and 8vo. 1611, folio. 1615, 4to. 1616, folio (the last of this version printed in England). Bindley, pt. 1. 387, mor. 7*l*. 10s.

— (BISHOPS') The Bible. Lond. by Robert Barker, 1602. folio.

Bindley, pt. i. 385, 2*l*. 2s. Gardner, 1854, 9*l*. 10s. An edition, 1606, folio.

See Lewis' History, 262-3.

— (ROMANIST VERSION). The holie Bible, faithfvlly translated into English ovt of the avthentical Latin. By the English College of Doway. Doway, by Lavrence Kellam, 1609-10. 4to. 2 vols.

This translation of the old Testament with that of the new Testament printed at Rhemes, by John Fogny, 1582, forms the first edition of the English Romanist version, which alone is used by the Romanists of this country. Annotations to the old Testament are subjoined, which are ascribed to Thomas Worthington; the translators were William (afterwards Cardinal) Allen, Gregory Martin, and Richard Bristow.

See Lea Wilson, no. 105. Cotton, p. 58-304.

— (GENEVAN and TOMSON). The Bible. Edinburgh, by Andro. Hart, 1610. fol.

This [second edition printed in Scotland] was much admired, and it continued long to be accounted a high recommendation to be 'conform to the edition printed by Andro. Hart.' It follows the Geneva translation in the old Testament, but the new is that which was first published in 1576, by Laurence Tomson, with annotations said to be taken from Beza, Joachim Camerarius, and P. L. Villerius. Other editions: Edinb. 1613, folio. Amst. 1617, folio (according to the edition of Edinb. 1610.) Amst. 1633, 4to. for Tho. Crafoorth for J. Fred. Stam. Amst. 1640, 4to. by Tho. Stafford. Mr. Wilson had two editions of this date, slightly differing. Amst. 1644, folio, by T.

Stafford. Concerning the numerous Amsterdam editions, both with and without notes, imprinted about 1630-40, consult Archbishop Laud's Life and Troubles.

See Lea Wilson, no. 106. Cotton, p. 59-70. 305.

—— (KING JAMES, OR AUTHORIZED). The holy Bible, conteyning the old Testament and the new: newly translated out of the originall Tongues, and with the former Translations diligently compared and revised by his Maiestie's speciall Comandement. Lond. by Robert Barker, 1611. folio.

BLACK LETTER. First edition of the authorised translation now in use, commonly called King James's Bible.

[Two impressions, both printed with large type, issued with this date. The *first* may be known by its having a large wood cut coat of arms of King James on the recto of the leaf commencing 'The Genealogies of the Holy Scripture,' and other variations pointed out in Cotton's List, p. 60, and in Notes and Queries no. 249. Aug. 5, 1854. The second issue may be readily identified by the arms being wanting, their absence filled in with a letter-press title [within two black lines.] "The Genealogies of holy Scripture, by J: S.," and by the remarkable typographical blunders in the dedication to King James, where in line 4 the word OF is printed OE, and the name of CHRIST is printed CHRIST, &c., &c. The second issue is often to be found with a title dated 1613, the new Test. title bearing 1611.]

Collation.—First impression. Engraved title by C. Boel. Letter press title within wood cut border. Dedication to the King ("To THE MOST,") 3 pages, the first one 27 lines, the catch word *-lation*. The Translators to the Reader, 2 pages, the first commencing with an ornamental letter Z, the last finishing with the word Amen. Calendar, January to Dec. 12 pages. An Almanac for xxxix yeares [1603 to 1641], one page. To find Easter for ever, one page [*i.e.* the two on one leaf.] The Table and Kalendar expressing the order of Psalmes and Lessons, 1 p., on the back of which Proper Lessons to read for the first Lessons [on Sundays.] Lessons proper for Holy Dayes, 1 p.; on the back, Proper Psalmes on certaine dayes, &c. continued on the next page *Septuagesima* ending *Munday and Tuesday in Whitsun Weeks*, and the catch word "The." The names and orders of the bookes wholly printed in *black*, then follow the Royal arms, occupying the whole page, on the back of which the top line is "The Genealogies of the Holy Scriptures" continued, 16 leaves—in all, 17 leaves.] The Dedication ending (∴). Introductory matter, with Genealogies, form 34 leaves. Map of Canaan, by J. More and Jo. Speede, dated 1611. Gen. 1 to Maccabees 2, xv. cccccvi. New Test. wood cut title as before. Matth. i. to Revelations xxii., Aa vi.

The collation of this edition given by Cotton and Lea Wilson refer to the *second issue* of 1611, and differs but slightly in the preliminary matter, the Dedication having a distinguishing mark ¶ TO THE MOST; it also answers for the editions of 1617 (N.T. INPRINTED). 1634, 1640 (N.T. 1639)—in all which, as well as the two issues of 1611, the Psalms commence on Bbb 4. But in a small type Black letter edit., printed by Barker in 1613, they commence on Kk. Denyer, 28, imperfect, 5*l.* 5*s.* Williams, fine copy, wanting titles and map, 9*l.* 9*s.* Pickering, pt. 2, 25*l.* 10*s.* Horner, 1854, 2nd issue, 4*l.* 8*s.* Crawford, 2nd issue, 10*l.* 15*s.*

See Selden's Table Talk. Horne's Introduction, ii. appendix, 67—74. Todd's Vindication of our authorised Translation and Translators of the Bible. Also, Lea Wilson, no. 112. Cotton, 60 and 305. Anderson.

—— (ROYAL VERSION). The Bible. Lond. by R. Barker, 1612. 4to.

The first quarto edition of the authorised version, printed in the Roman letter.

EDITIONS.— 1613, folio and 4to. 1614, two 4to editions and 8vo. The Third part of the Bible, 1614, 16mo. (1616, folio. Gardner, 9*l.*) and 4to. 1617, folio. 1618, 12mo.

—— (ROYAL VERSION). The Bible. Cambridge, by T. and J. Buck, 1629. folio, with copper plate title.

White Knights, 580, 1*l.* 3*s.*

[In this beautiful edition the text has undergone a complete revision. See *Lea Wilson*, no. 139.]

In an edition of the Bible printed in the reign of Charles, the text of Ps. xiv. 1, ran "The fool hath said in his heart *there is a God.*" For which error, according to Nye (in his Defence of the Canon of the New Testament), the printers were fined 3,000*l.* and all the copies suppressed.

—— The Bible. Lond. 1632. 8vo.

North, pt. iii. 495, Simon de Passe's copy, in blue velvet, with silver clasps, &c. 4*l.* 19*s.* resold, Williams, 195, 8*l.*

In an edition of the Bible, Barker and Lucas, 1632, called the "Wicked Bible," according to Dr. Heylin in his Life of Laud, book iii. p. 228, the word "not" was omitted in the 7th commandment. The printers were called before the High Commission, fined deeply, and the whole impression destroyed.

[A copy of this edition was exhibited to the Society of Antiquaries, by Mr. Henry

Stevens, June 21, 1855, which he had bought in Holland for 50 guineas.]

— The Bible. Edinburgh, by Robert Young, 1633. 8vo.
[First edition of the authorized version in Scotland. There were two editions, both in 8vo., issued in this year at Edinburgh, one by "*Robert Young*," the other by "*The Printers to the King's most excellent majesty*."]
This Bible is printed in double columns, and bears a great resemblance to some London editions of the same period.
Pickering, pt. 2, 11*l*. 10s. Lea Wilson, no. 148. Cotton, p. 67.

— (ROMANIST VERSION). The Bible. Rouen, by John Cousturier, 1635. 2 vols. 4to.
The Douay version of the Old Testament. The Rhemish New Testament published by John Cousturier, 1633, 4to., generally accompanies this edition.

— The Bible. Cambridge by Buck and Daniel, 1638. folio.
A handsome edition containing a very material error of the press, by substituting *ye* for '*we* may appoint over this business,' in Acts vi. 3. This error has been without foundation imputed to the Independents, and sometimes to the Presbyterians. It appeared in many other editions prior to 1685. Bindley, pt. 1. 388, mor. 5*l*. 15s. 6d. Copies, with the Prayer, of the edition of 1638, are not uncommon on LARGE PAPER. Gardner, 7*l*. 15s.
See Lea Wilson, no. 161. Cotton, 69.

— The Bible. Edinburgh, 1638.
A very small edition, printed by Young.

— The Bible. London. by Robert Barker—and by the assignes of John Bill, 1638, 12mo.
Although this Bible bears a London imprint, it was really executed in Holland some years later. It is disfigured by numerous gross and disgraceful errors.
See Lea Wilson, no. 162. Cotton, 69.
An edition of the Royal text, with annotations, Amsterdam, 1642. folio.

— (ROYAL VERSION). The Bible. Amsterdam, by Joost Broerss, 1642, folio.
Another edition, Amst. printed for C. P. 1644, 16mo.

— The Bible. Edinb. 1642.
A neat pocket Bible, printed in parts by Evan Tyler.

— The Bible, with marginal Notes, shewing Scripture to be the best Interpreter of Scripture. By John Canne. Amsterdam, 1644. 4to.

The marginal references of this learned Brownist are generally very judicious and apposite. The later editions, which pass under the name of Canne's Bible, are full of errors, and crowded with references, which do not belong to the original author.
EDITIONS.— London, 1647, 2 vols. 8vo. London, 1662, 12mo. London, 1664, 8vo. London, 1671. Amsterdam, 2 vols. 12mo. London, Bill and Newcomb, 1668. London, 1700, 4to. Cambridge, Basket, 1720, 4to. Edinburgh, 1727 and 1754.

— The Bible. Cambridge, by John Field, 1648. 4to.
Roxburghe, 16, 12s. An edition, Lond. by Barker, 1646. Williams, 196, in silk, 2*l*.—Another, Cambridge by Daniel, 1648, 18mo. Williams, 197, in fish skin, 3*l*. 15s. Another, Edinb. by Evan Tyler, 1649. 12mo. Another, the Royal translation, with the Genevan notes. Lond. 1649. 4to.

— The Bible, in Short-hand, by Jeremiah Rich. 1650. 12mo. with port. and front. by Cross.
White Knights, 452, morocco, 9s.

— The Bible. Cambridge, by John Field, 1653. 24mo.
This edition, says Mr. Horne, is usually called the Pearl Bible, from the very small type with which it was printed, but is disgraced by very numerous errata, some of which are of importance. An imitation of it was made in Holland in 1658; but the genuine edition is known by having the four first psalms on a page without turning over. White Knights, 445, morocco, with silver clasps, 1*l*. 13s. Williams, 198, morocco, 4*l*. 9s.
D'Israeli, in his Curiosities of Literature, has an article on 'Pearl Bibles and Six Thousand Errata,' from which the following instances are copied.—Rom. vi. 13. 'Neither yield ye your members as instruments of *righteousness* unto sin,' for *unrighteousness*.—1 Cor. vi. 9. 'Know ye not that the unrighteous *shall inherit* the kingdom of God,' for *shall not inherit*. 'This *erratum* served as the foundation of a dangerous doctrine, for many libertines urged the text from this corrupt Bible, against the reproofs of a divine.'
[*See* also a melancholy but curious account of the wretched state of the Bibles and Testaments printed in Scotland during the 17th and 18th centuries, in Dr. Lee's Memorial, Edinb. 1824, 8vo.]

— The Bible. Cambridge, by J. Field, 1657. small 8vo.
Bindley. pt. 1. 414, 13s. 6d. Dent, pt. 1. 218, illustrated with plates by Van Langeren, in old morocco, 3*l*. 13s. 6d. Other editions, same year, 12mo. and 18mo.

The Bibles printed during the time of the Commonwealth have been generally reputed to be full of errors:— In a tract entitled 'The London Printer his Lamentation; or the Press oppressed or overpressed, 1660.' 4to. (reprinted in the Harleian Miscellany), it is said, that Bill and Barker had contrived to get into their possession 'ever since the sixth of March 1655, the manuscript copy of the last translation of the Holy Bible in English, attested with the hands of the venerable and learned translators in King James's time.' And that having thus secured themselves from instant detection, they published editions filled with 'egregious blasphemies and damnable errata.'—*Dr. Cotton.*

— The Dutch Annotations upon the whole Bible, together with their Translation according to the direction of the Synod of Dort, 1618. By Theodore Haak. Lond. 1657. folio. 2 vols.

This work, dedicated to Cromwell, is very similar in plan and character to the Assembly's Annotations. An account of the work, and of the translators, &c. will be found in Dr. Bliss's edition of Wood's Athen. Oxon. iv. 279. Gosset, 2455, 1*l.* 7s.

— The Bible. Lond. by J. Field, 1658. 24mo.

Exceedingly incorrect, and badly printed. In the same year, bearing Imprint. *Lond. by J. Field*, was printed in Holland, one of the most correct and beautiful editions of the Bible, seldom found in good preservation. Williams, 199, in fish skin, 4*l.* 16s. Roxburghe, 17, 3*l.* 17s.

— The Bible. Cambridge, by John Field, 1660. 2 vols. royal folio, with chorographical cuts by John Ogilby.

This edition, which may be considered as an unrivalled specimen of the press of the time, was severely censured by Bishop Wetenhal in 'Scripture authentic and Faith certain,' 1696. In Acts vi. 3, the word Ye was substituted for We.

Roxburghe, 18, morocco, 6*l.* 15s. Grave, 402, morocco, 3*l.* 13s. 6d. Bindley, pt. i. 389, with the Prayer, morocco, 5*l.* 15s.— LARGE PAPER. Edwards, 813, illustrated with plates by Hollar, morocco, 21*l.* Williams, 869, morocco, 11*l.* Pickering, pt. 2, 15*l.*

An edition by Field, 1660. 12mo.

Another by Field, 1661. 8vo. Hollis, 76, mor. 3*l.* 13s. 6d.

Another, by Field, 1663. 4to. Duke of Grafton, 20. with the Common Prayer, morocco, 5*l.* 16s.

Another by Field, 1666. 4to. 1*l.* 1s.

Another by Field, 1666. folio. Duke of Grafton, 21, morocco, 6*l.* 6s.

Another by Field, 1668. 4to. Bishop of Ely, with Prayer, and Jackson's Index Biblicus, 1*l.* 14s.

Others, with Genevan Notes. Amst. S. Swart, or Lond. 1672, 1679. folio.

From the time of Field to the end of the seventeenth century, several curious flat Bibles were printed in 4to., which are denominated *Preachers or preaching Bibles*, from the use made of them in the pulpit during that period.

— The Bible. Cambridge, by John Hayes, 1674. folio.

Roxburghe, 19, 2*l.* Jadis, 861. King James II.'s copy, splendidly bound in velvet, with the crown, the royal initials, and embossed ornaments on the sides, 49*l.* 7s. resold Knight, 1847. 32*l.* 10s.

An edition, with additional parallel texts. Cambr. 1677. 4to.

— The Bible. Cambridge, by J. Hayes, 1678. folio.

Published by Anthony Scattergood, D.D. with the addition of many parallel texts, which are still reprinted in the margin of the large bibles.

— The Bible. Royal version, with Canne's notes, 1682. 12mo. No place or printer's name.

One of the most valuable of the earlier pocket editions.

'In 1683 our authorised translation was corrected, and many references to parallel texts added by Dr. Scattergood.'—*Horne.*

— The Bible, 1683—5. See POOLE, Matthew.

— The Old and New Testaments, with Annotations and parallel Scriptures, &c. by Sam. Clarke, A.M. Lond. 1690. folio, 2*l.* 10s.

'The selection of parallel texts is admirable; and the notes, though very brief, are written with great judgment. The work was recommended, in very high terms, by Drs. Owen and Bates, as well as Mr. Baxter and Mr. Howe. It is also recommended by Bishop Cleaver to the attention of the younger clergy. The author was a nonconformist.'—*Horne.* Reprinted Lond. 1760, fol. with plates, 8*l.* 8s. Glasg. 1765, fol. 1*l.* 10s. &c.

In various editions of the Bible printed between the year 1690 and the commencement of the present century, an error will be found in 1 Tim. iv. 16, where we read, 'Take heed unto thyself and *thy* doctrine,' instead of *the* doctrine.

— The Bible, in Short-hand, by

Wm: Addy, engraved by J. Sturt. (Lond. 1695) 18mo. with portrait of Addy, by Sturt, 10s. 6d.

— The Bible, with marginal Notes, shewing the Scripture to be the best Interpreter of Scripture, (by John Canne.) Lond. by Charles Bill. 1698. 12mo. 10s. 6d.
Reprinted Lond. 1700. 4to. 1*l*. 10s.

— The Bible. Lond. 1701. Large folio.
'A very fine edition, published under the direction of Abp. Tenison, with additional marginal references, chronological dates, and an index by Bishop Lloyd, and accurate tables of Scripture weights and measures by Bishop Cumberland. This edition is, however, said to abound with typographical errors.'—*Horne.* Dowdeswell, 143, ruled, and bound in russia, 5*l*. 15s. 6d. It was likewise printed in 1699. 4to.

— The Bible. Printed in the Year 1708. folio. 1*l*. 10s.
The authorised translation, with the annotations which accompany the Geneva Version. Reprinted 1715.

— The Bible, 1709—29. *See* WELLS, Edward, D.D.

— The Bible, 1710. *See* HENRY, Matthew.

— The Bible. Oxford, 1711. 8vo.
Remarkable, says Mr. Tutet, for this mistake in Isaiah, chap. lvii. ver. 12. 'I will declare thy righteousness and thy works, for they *shall* profit thee.'

— The Bible. Edinb. by James Watson, 1715. 8vo.
A rare and coveted edition, says Dr. Dibdin. Roxburghe, 24, 3*l*. 15s. An edition, Edinb. 1714. 4to. Bibl. Harl. no. 325. Another, Edinb. 1716. White Knights, 448, morocco, with silver clasps, 17s. Williams, 201, morocco, 1*l*. 16s. Another, Edinb. 1717. Roxburghe, 25, 2*l*. 7s.

— The Bible. Belfast, James Blood, 1716. 8vo.
First edition of the Scriptures printed in Ireland. An error occurs in a verse of Isaiah. 'Sin no more' *is printed* 'Sin on more.' *The error was not discovered until the entire impression (8000 copies) were bound, and partly distributed.*

— The Bible. Oxford, by J. Baskett, 1717. folio, 2 vols. front. by Sturt, and vignette on the title by Burghers; the LARGE PAPER copies with a front. by Du Bosc, and vignette engravings by Vander Gucht.
A most magnificent edition, called 'The Vinegar Bible,' from an error in the running title at Luke, chap. xx., where it reads 'the parable of the vinegar,' instead of 'the parable of the vineyard.' Williams, 870, ruled, mor. 12*l*. 12s. Dent, pt. 1. 331, with a set of plates, proofs before the letters, from Macklin's edition, 16*l*. 16s. There are two copies of this most magnificent book printed upon vellum, one in the Royal, the other in the Bodleian Library. LARGE PAPER. Sotheby, March, 1856, morocco ruled, 9*l*. 15s.

— The Bible. Edinburgh, by J. Watson, 1722. 8vo.
According to Mr. Horne, one of the most valuable of the earlier pocket editions.

— The Bible. 1727—67. *See* PATRICK, LOWTH, ARNALD, and WHITBY.

— The Bible, with critical and explanatory Annotations, compiled from Grotius, Lightfoot, Poole, Calmet, and others. Lond. 1735. folio, 3 vols. with plates, 2*l*. 10s.

— The Bible. John Baskett. Lond. folio, 1738.

— The Bible, with an Exposition, in which several mis-translations are rectified, by J. Marchant. Lond. 1743-5. folio. 2 vols.

— The Bible, 1748—63. *See* GILL, John, D.D.

— The Bible. Printed in the year 1750. 12mo. 4 vols.
The Anglo Romish version, with some alterations in the text and many in the notes, published from the copy of Dr. Chaloner, titular Bishop of Debra, and one of the vicars apostolic of the Romish Church in England.

— The Bible. Mark Baskett. Lond. small 4to. 1752.
Although this volume bears a London imprint, it was really printed at Boston, by Kneeland and Green, and is the first edition of the Scriptures printed in America. See *Thomas' History of Printing in America.*

— The Family Bible, by S. Smith. Lond. 1752-3. folio, 2 vols. with plates, 1*l*. 1s.

— The Universal Bible, with Notes, &c. by S. Nelson, D.D. Lond. 1758-60. fol. 2 vols. with plates. 1*l*. 1s.

— The Bible. 1759. *See* GOADBY, —.

— The Royal Bible, by Leonard Howard. Lond. 1761. fol. 2 vols. 1*l*. 1s.

— The Bible illustrated and explained, by the Rev. John Butley. Second edition. Lond. 1761. 4to. 2 vols.

— The Family Bible, with explanatory Notes, by Francis Fawkes, M.A. Lond. 1761-2, 4to. 2 vols.
Garrick, 778, 18s.

— The British Bible, illustrated with Notes, in a manner entirely new, by James Millar. Lond. 1762. fol. 1*l*. 1s.

— The Bible. Cambridge, by Bentham, 1762. 4to. and LARGE PAPER, folio.
This edition, with the exception of about six copies, was destroyed by fire, at Dod's the publisher's warehouse. Sotheby's in 1821, mor. 6*l*. 8s. 6d. LARGE PAPER. Sotheby, 1857 (Queen Charlotte's copy), red morocco, 6*l*. 6s.

— The Bible. Cambridge, 1763. royal folio.
From Baskerville's press. One of the most beautiful books ever printed. Constable, 278, morocco, 7*l*. 7s. Williams, 371, morocco, 8*l*. 10s. Heath, 443, morocco, 9*l*. Roxburghe, 26, 10*l*. 15s. Gardner, 9*l*. A few copies on LARGE PAPER. Duke of Sussex.

— The Christians Commentary, by William Rider, A.B. Lond. 1763. folio, 3 vols. 1*l*. 4s.

— A new and literal Translation of all the Books of the Old and New Testament, with Notes critical and explanatory. By Anthony Purver. Lond. 1764. folio. 2 vols.
This singular work was printed at the expense of Doctor Fothergill, the Quaker. Purver was originally a shoemaker, and taught himself Hebrew, Greek, and Latin, in order that he might translate the Bible. Gosse, 1483, 2*l*. 2s.

— The Bible. 1764. 12mo. 5 vols.
The Romish version of the Old and New Testament, corrected by Dr. Chaloner.

— The Bible, 1765. *See* HAWEIS, T.

— The Bible [O. T. only], with explanatory Notes by John Wesley, M.A. Bristol, 1765. 4to. 3 vols. 3*l*. 3s.

— The grand Imperial Bible, by Luke Phillips. Lond. 1766. 4to. 1*l*. 1s.

— The Bible, with marginal References. Oxford, 1769. 4to. 4*l*. 4s. and folio.
The 'standard edition,' from which all subsequent impressions have been executed. It was made under the direction of the Vice-Chancellor and delegates of the Clarendon Press at Oxford. A full account of Dr. Blaney's Collation and Revision was communicated by him to the Gentleman's Magazine, xxxix. 517—9. The folio edition is very scarce, owing to the destruction of a large part of the impression by a fire in the warehouse in London. Sotheby's in June, 1822. 9*l*. 9s. Gosset, 495, 4*l*. 14s. 6d.
[Mr. Horne notices a remarkable omission in Revelations xviii. 22, which occurs only in the 4to edition.]

— The Bible, with Annotations. Birmingham, by J. Baskerville, 1769. folio, 2*l*. 12s. 6d.
[A spurious edition.]

— The Bible, with Annotations. Birmingham, by Boden and Adams, 1769. folio.
[A spurious edition.] The annotations differ from those in the former edition.

— The Bible, wherein the Mistakes in the present Translation are corrected, with Notes. Aberdeen, 1769. folio, 2 vols.

— The Bible, 1770. *See* DODD, W., LL.D.

— The complete Family Bible, with Notes, by the Rev. —— Cruden. Lond. 1770. fol. 2 vols. 1*l*. 1s.
'The compiler of this indifferently executed commentary is not to be confounded with Mr. Alexander Cruden, author of the well-known Concordance to the Holy Scriptures.'—*Horne*.

— The Bible, with practical Observations, by the Rev. Mr. Ostervald. Edinb. 1770. 8vo.
Translated at the desire of, and recommended by the Society for propagating Christian Knowledge.

— The Bible, with Notes. Birmingham, by J. Baskerville, 1772. folio, 2*l*. 2s.
[A spurious edition.]

— The Bible, with Notes and Observations by Richard Wynne. Lond. 1772. 8vo. 6s.

— The Bible, with a commentary and Notes. Bristol, by William Pine, 1774. 18mo. 1l. 5s.

— The Christian's Divine Library, illustrated with Notes theological, historical, practical, and critical, by Henry Southwell, D.D. Lond. 1774. folio, 2 vols. 1l. 1s.

— The Bible, with Annotations. Lond. 1775. folio, 15s.

The Genevan version.

— The Bible. Lond. 1776. 32mo.

Pashams edition. White Knights, 449, morocco, 1l. 5s. Stanley, 117, morocco, 3l. 6s. Williams, 205, ruled, morocco, richly tooled, 4l. 5s.

— The Bible, with Notes explanatory, selected from the Works of several Authors. Lond. 1777. folio, 1l. 1s.

— The Self-interpreting Bible, by John Brown. Edinb. 1778. 4to. 2 vols. 1l. 5s.

So called from the copiousness of its marginal references. Frequently reprinted.

— The Bible, in verse, by John Fellows. London, 1778. 4 vols.

— The Bible. Philadelphia. R. Aitkin, 1782. 12mo.

The first edition openly admitted to be printed in America.

— The Bible, authorized version, with explanatory notes by Pope Clement XIV. (Ganganelli). Lond. T. Kearsley. 1784. folio.

The notes in this edition are falsely ascribed to Ganganelli—they have a freethinking tendency. Duke of Sussex, 966, 30l. Sotheby, 1853, 5l. 10s. Gardner, 1854, 15l. 15s.

— The Bible, with a Commentary by the Rev. James Cookson. Lond. 1784. folio, 1l. 1s.

— The Bible, with Notes, by Thomas Wilson, D.D. Lord Bishop of Sodor and Man, and various Renderings, collected from other Translations, by the Rev. Clement Cruttwell, the Editor. Bath, 1785. 4to. 3 vols. 4l. 4s.

This edition contains a new translation (by the editor) of the apocryphal third book of Maccabees, which had not appeared in an English Bible since Becke's edition of 1551. The text and marginal references are printed with equal beauty and correctness. Steevens, 98, blue turkey, 7l. 7s. Gosset, 728, 6l. 8s. 6d. LARGE PAPER (twelve copies printed), Dent, pt. i. 332, morocco, 31l. 10s. Stanley, 119, morocco, 58l. 16s. Sir M. M. Sykes, pt. i. 615, morocco, 64l. 1s. Heathcote, 1805, in 6 vols. 78l. 10s.

— The Bible, with original Notes, &c. &c. by Thomas Scott. Lond. 1788-92. 4to. 4 vols. 4l. 4s.

First edition, published in numbers. Frequently reprinted.

— The Bible. Lond. 1790. 12mo. 1l. 1s.

A neat edition, published by Scatcherd and Whittaker.

— The Bible (Douay—Rhemish), newly revised and corrected. Dublin, H. Fitzpatrick. 4to. 1791.

This, the fifth edition, is regarded as the standard of the Romanist version, and has been reprinted in various sizes.

— The Bible, faithfully translated from the corrected Texts of the Originals, with various Readings, explanatory Notes, and critical Remarks by the Rev. Alex. Geddes, LL.D. Lond. 1792, 7, 1800. 4to. vol. i. ii., and Remarks, vol. i.

The following are necessary to form a complete collection of Geddes' translation: Prospectus. Glasgow, 1786. 7s. 6d. Appendix, London, 1787. 3s. 6d. Proposals, ib. 1788. 1s. 6d. General Answer to the Queries, &c. ib. 1790. 1s. 6d. Bible, vols. I. and II. containing the historical books from Genesis to Chronicles, and the Book of Ruth, ib. 1792, 7. Address to the Public. ib. 1793. 1s. Critical Remarks on the Hebrew Scriptures, vol. i, ib. 1800. 1l. 1s. The Rev. John Earle published Remarks on the prefaces prefixed to the first and second volumes of this translation,12mo.2s. 'A literary phenomenon of a curious nature; a priest of the Romish Church, resident in England, translating the scriptures into our native tongue, and publicly maintaining, against two Protestants, Dr. Vices. Knox, and the writer in the Monthly Review for January, 1797, the great utility of a new English translation, in preference to that made a hundred and eighty years ago.'—*Abp. Newcome.* Of the Doctor's heterodox commentaries and version, the reader, says Mr. Horne, may see an ample examination and refutation in the 4th, 14th, 19th,

and 20th volumes of the British Critic. This examination is attributed to Bp. Horsley.
Gosset, 727, 3 vols. 2l. 12s. 6d. LARGE PAPER, Duke of Grafton, 23 and 88, 3l. 5s.

— The Bible. Oxford, 1792. 8vo.
'Remarkable for a mistake in St. Luke, chap. xxii. 34, where St. *Philip* instead of St. *Peter* is named as the disciple who should deny Christ.'—*Dr. Cotton.*

— The Christian and British Family Bible, by Wright. Lond. 1792. folio, 1l.

— The Bible, ornamented with Engravings by James Fittler, from celebrated Pictures by old Masters. Lond. 1795. royal 8vo. 2 vols.
Printed by Bensley, and published by Bowyer. Sir M. M. Sykes, pt. i. 226, mor. 3l. 6s. Bindley, 417, mor. 4l. 5s. LARGE PAPER, in 4to.

— The Bible. Lond. 1795. royal 4to. with plates, 2l. 2s.
Heptinstall's superb edition.

— The Bible. Lond. 1796. 12mo. 1l. 1s.
Bowyer's Cabinet edition. LARGE PAPER. Williams, 206, an unique copy, ruled, with titles painted, the first leaf of every chapter gilt, &c. &c. morocco, 7l. 7s.

— The Bible, 1796. 12mo. 5 vols. 1l. 1s.
The vulgate version.

— The Bible, with Ostervald's Arguments and Observations. Lond. 1799. royal 4to. 1l. 5s.

— The Bible, with Engravings from Pictures and Designs by the most eminent Artists. Lond. 1800. folio, 7 vols.
Macklin's splendid edition, published in 70 Numbers, at 1l. 1s. each. The Apocrypha, 1816, published at 18l. 18s. Beckford in 1817, 300, (with the Apocrypha,) 35l. 14s. Roxburghe, 27, blue turkey, 43l.

— The Bible. Lond. 1800. 32mo.
Corrall's edition. White Knights, 450, mor. 1l. 1s.

— The Bible, with explanatory Notes on the most interesting Passages, by the Rev. Henry Cox Mason, M.A. &c. Lond. 1800. 4to. 18s.

— The Bible. Notes by the editor [T. Parsons]. Bristol, 1802. 32mo. 1l. 1s.
Edwards' diamond Edition, and the smallest ever printed.

— The Bible. Lond. J. Reeves, 1802. crown 8vo. 10 vols.
Reeves' edition. Another Edition, ROYAL OCTAVO, 9 vols. Earl of Kerry, 63, mor. 5l. 10s. QUARTO, Drury, 555, mor. 6l. 6s. PRINTED ON VELLUM, in 4to. In a bookseller's catalogue for 1820, marked 105l. afterwards offered at 52l.
Beautiful editions, with short explanatory notes and philological scholia. According to Mr. Horne, Mr. Reeves' notes are selected with great judgment from the labours of Patrick, Lowth, Whitby, and others; and his mode of printing the text is admirable. The historical parts, which are in prose, are printed in contiguous paragraphs, and the poetical parts are divided into verses. Each book is divided into sections, conformable to the natural divisions of the several subjects; and to facilitate reference, the chapters and verses are distinctly pointed out in the margin. A'n edition, without notes, 8vo. 4 vols. 14s. FINE PAPER, 18s.

— A new Translation of the Bible; an Attempt to preserve the Holy Scriptures from their Disrepute with Free-Thinkers, and their Misapplication to certain Tenets, by a new and correct Translation of controverted Passages, illustrated with Notes and the Opinion of the Ancients, by Robert Tomlinson. Lond. 1803. 8vo. 7s.

— The Bible, with Notes and Annotations. Liverpool, 1804. folio, 1l. 1s.

— The Bible, translated from the Latin Vulgate, first published at the English College at Douay; newly revised and corrected according to the Clementin edition, with Annotations. Edinb. 1805. 8vo. 5 vols. 1l. 10s. L. P. 2l. 2s. Again, 4 vols. Dublin, 1811.
[The first American edition of this version was printed at Philadelphia, 1805. 4to.]

— The Bible. Lond. 1806. 4to. 3l. 3s.
Notwithstanding the great labour and attention bestowed by Dr. Blayney on his edition, Oxford, 1769, it must now yield the palm of accuracy to the very beautiful and correct one printed by Woodfall, and published by Messrs. Eyre and Strahan in 1806 [only one erratum has been detected], again in 1813, very correct, 4to. LARGE PAPER, in imperial 4to. 4l. 4s.

— Bible. Oxford, 1807. 4to. 2 vols. 8vo. 3s.

An edition esteemed for its accuracy. LARGE PAPER, in imperial 4to. Stanley, 120, morocco, 11l. 5s.

— The Old Covenant, commonly called the Old Testament, translated from the Septuagint. The New Covenant, translated from the Greek. By Charles Thomson. Philadelphia, 1808. 8vo. 4 vols.

The first English version of the Septuagint. This translation is faithfully executed. The notes which accompany the text are very brief, but satisfactory.

— The Bible, illustrated from the Works of the most approved Commentators. 1809. 2 vols. 4to.

LARGE PAPER, Drury, 441, russia, 2l. 10s.

— The Bible, with a Commentary by Thomas Coke, LL.D. Lond. 1806. 4to. 6 vols. 3l. 13s. 6d.

— The Bible, with short Notes, by several learned and pious Reformers, as printed by Royal Authority, at the Time of the Reformation, with additional Notes and Dissertations. Lond. 1810. 4to. with maps, tables, and vignette engravings, 1l. 11s. 6d.

This edition, which is entitled The Reformers' Bible, was edited by the Rev. Thomas Webster. The notes to the Old Testament are reprinted from those appended to the English version of the Bible, published at Geneva; the annotations to the New Testament are translated from the Latin of Theodore Beza.

— The Bible, printed from the most correct Copies of the present authorised Translation, including the marginal Readings and parallel Texts; with a Commentary and critical Notes, by Adam Clarke, LL.D. Lond. 1810-26. 4to. 8 vols.

A highly elaborate work. Mr. Horne observes, the literary world in general, and biblical students in particular, are greatly indebted to Dr. Clarke for the light he has thrown on many very difficult passages. LARGE PAPER. Re-issued, on completion, in 8 vols. 4to. 1825; again in 4to. 6 vols. London, Tegg, 1844; also in 6 vols. imp. 8vo. 1844.

— The Bible. Edinb. 1811. 12mo.

Copies on LARGE PAPER (small octavo) are, says Dr. Dibdin, much more beautiful than the vaunted diamond letter Bible of Richlieu, 1656, 8vo. Williams, 209, ruled and bound in morocco, 8l. 10s. 6d. 210, mor. 11l. 5s.

— The Family Bible, with Notes and practical Reflections, by the Rev. Is. Saunders. Lond. 1811. 4to. 2 vols. with plates, 2l. 2s.

Complete in thirteen parts.

— The Devotional Family Bible, with Notes and Illustrations, partly original and partly selected, by the Rev. John Fawcett, D.D. Lond. 1811. 4to. 2 vols. 2l. 2s.

'This work is wholly designed for family use, to which it is excellently adapted; but the marginal renderings and parallel texts have been entirely omitted.'—Horne.

Earl of Kerry, 187, russia, 4l. Some copies are printed in royal quarto, 3l. 8s.

— The Bible, with Notes, critical, philological, and explanatory, by John Hewlett. Lond. 1811. 4to. 3 vols. with plates, 3l. 13s. 6d. without plates, 3l.

This edition contains the Apocrypha. LARGE PAPER. Earl of Kerry, 189, in 6 vols. with 120 engravings, morocco, 16l. 16s.

An edition of the notes, without the text, appeared 1816. 8vo. 5 vols. 1l. 5s.

— The Bible, with Notes from various Commentators, by S. Clarke. Lond. 1811. folio.

An indifferent compilation, published in numbers.

— The Bible, with a Commentary, by George Burder. Lond. 1811. 4to. 2 vols.

Some copies are printed in royal quarto.

— The Bible, translated from the Latin Vulgate, with useful Notes, &c. by the Rev. G. L. Haydock. Manchester. T. Haydock, 1811-14. folio, 2 vols.

A reprint of Dr. Chaloner's text of the Douay and Rhemish version. A revised edition in 8vo. Dublin, T. Haydock, 1822.

— The Royal Standard devotional Family Bible. Yarmouth, 1811-16. 4to. 3 vols.

— The Bible, with Notes, &c. &c. by the Rev. Joseph Benson. Lond. 1811-18. 4to. 5 vols.

'An elaborate and very useful commentary.'—*Horne.*
— The complete Family Bible, with illustrative Notes, by the Rev. John Styles of Brighton. Lond. 1812. 4to. 2 vols.
— The Bible. Lond. 1813. 4to. 3*l.* 3*s.*
A beautiful and accurate edition, printed by Woodfall. It has been recommended, says Mr. Horne, by the General Convention of the Protestant Episcopal Church in the United States of America, to be adopted as the *Standard Edition,* to which future editions of the English Version of the Holy Scriptures (for the use of the members of that church) are to be made conformable. ROYAL 4to. 4*l* 4*s.*
— The Bible. Lond. 1814. medium 8vo.
A beautifully printed book, executed by His Majesty's Printers.
— The Bible. Lond. 1814. 24mo. 1*l.* 1s.
Printed with diamond type by Corrall for Messrs. Eyre and Strahan.
Brockett, 309, morocco, 1*l.* 7s.
— A revised translation and interpretation of the Holy Scriptures, after the Eastern Manner, by David Macrae. Glasgow, 1815. 4to. 1*l.* 10s.
A former edition appeared at Glasgow, 1799, 8vo. 9s. It has been reprinted in 8vo. 3 vols.
'In this work the author has certainly succeeded in introducing very many approved renderings; but he has also marred exceedingly that venerable simplicity and dignity which are so eminently conspicuous in the authorised version.'—*Horne.*
— The Bible, illustrated with Engravings by Charles Heath, from the Designs of Westall. Oxford, 1815. 3 vols. imp. 8vo.
A very elegant edition. The plates have been twice engraved.
Brockett, 4891, morocco, 5*l.* An unique copy on the largest paper, with three sets of plates, viz. etchings, proofs, and proofs on INDIA PAPER, in 3 vols. folio, morocco, North, part i. 303.
— The Bible. Cambridge, by J. Smith [1815]. 8vo.
LARGE PAPER (three copies printed).
— The Bible. Lond. 1816. 24mo. Printed by Eyre and Strahan.
'This pocket edition, published by Bagster, contains a new selection of upwards of sixty thousand references to passages that are really parallel.'—*Horne.*

A copy, printed on INDIA PAPER, Williams, 211, morocco, 6*l.* 6s.
— The Bible. Dublin, 1816. 4to.
The Anglo-Romish version, 'corrected, revised and approved of by the most Rev. Dr. Troy. R. C. Archbishop of Dublin.' For a review of the dangerous and obnoxious tenets in this edition, see the British Critic, N. S. viii. 296-308.
— The Bible, with Notes explanatory and practical, taken from the most eminent Writers of the Church of England, prepared and arranged by G. D'Oyly, D.D. and the Rev. R. Mant, Bishop of Down and Connor. Oxford, 1817. 4to. 3 vols. with maps and outline engravings.
This work, which may be pronounced a library of divinity, was published under the sanction of the venerable Society for Promoting Christian Knowledge. Upwards of 30,000 copies have been sold. Of the labour attending this publication, some idea may be formed, when it is stated, that the works of upwards of 160 authors, amounting to several hundred volumes, have been consulted for it. There is a useful concordance in 4to. edited by the Rev. T. W. Bellamy, M.A., which is usually bound up with this commentary: and in the year 1818, the Rev. Dr. Wilson, published an index, much more complete than that annexed to the work.
Nassau, pt. i. 406, 3*l.* LARGE PAPER, in royal 4to. Earl of Kerry, 188, 6*l.* 16s. 6d. Bindley, pt. i. 915, 18*l.* 10s. Williams, 232, ruled with red lines, red morocco, 16*l.*
Reprinted, Cambridge, 1822, 4to. 3 vols. 3*l.* 13s. 6d.; and several times since.
— The self-interpreting Bible, by John Brown. A new Edition, with considerable Additions by the Rev. Thomas Raffles. Lond. 1817. 4to. 2 vols. with engravings.
Best edition, published in parts. This work, which is exceedingly useful to preachers, for its marginal references and its practical reflections, was first published in 1778, and has gone through repeated editions. INDIA PROOFS. Sotheby's in 1824, 2*l.* 16s.
— The Bible, with Notes, &c. prepared and arranged by the Rev. G. D'Oyly, D.D. and the Rev. Rich. Mant, Bishop of Down and Connor. New York, 1818-20. 4to. 2 vols.
'To this reprint, edited by the Right Rev. J. H. Hobart, D.D. bishop of the Protestant Episcopal church in the State

of New York, numerous additional notes selected from the writings of upwards of thirty of the most eminent divines not noticed by Drs. D'Oyly and Mant. Many other notes are likewise selected from several of the authors cited by Doctors D'Oyly and Mant.'—*Horne.*

— The Bible, with historical Prefaces, by E. Nares, D.D., with the plates as used to Macklin's edition. Lond. 1818. folio. 3 vols.

Sotheby's in 1821, 6*l.* 6*s.*

— The Bible, newly translated from the original Hebrew, with Notes critical and explanatory, by John Bellamy. Lond. 1818-41. 4to. Parts I. to VIII. only have appeared.

'The arrogant claims of the author, and his extravagancies of interpretation, have been exposed in the Quarterly Review, xix. 250-80, 446-60, and xxiii. 287-325; in the Eclectic Review, N. S. x. 1—20, 130-50, 280-89; in the Anti-Jacobin Review, liv. 97-103, 193-207, 305-16; in Mr. Whittaker's Enquiry into the Interpretation of the Hebrew Scriptures, and Supplement. Cambridge, 1819-20; in Professor Lee's Letter to Mr. Bellamy, Cambridge, 1821; and last, though not least in value, in Mr. Hyman Hurwitz's Vindiciæ Hebraicæ.'— *Horne.* In answer to the Quarterly Review, Bellamy published 'A Reply,' 1818. 8vo. and see Sir James Bland Burges' 'Reasons in Favour of a new Translation of the Scriptures.' 1819. 8vo.

— A new family Bible, and improved Version, with Notes critical and explanatory; and short practical Reflections on each Chapter, by the Rev. B. Boothroyd, D.D. Pontefract, 1818, 21, 3. 4to. 3 vols.

'This improved English version of the Bible will be found a valuable help to the critical understanding of the sacred Scriptures.'—*Horne.*

— The Bible, with a centre Column of original References. Lond. 1819. 12mo. 1*l.* 4*s.*

'The most elegant and useful of all the pocket editions of the entire English Bible with parallel references, is that published by Mr. Bagster, and certainly a new selection of upwards of sixty thousand references to passages that are really parallel.' —*Horne.*

— The Bible, with alternate Pages of Biblical Concordance. Lond. 1820. 12mo.

Published by Bagster. Williams, 1941, morocco, 2*l.* 19*s.*

— The Old and New Testament, arranged in historical and chronological Order, with copious Indexes, by the Rev. Geo. Townsend. Lond. 1821-5. 8vo. 4 vols. 3*l.* 13s. 6d.

This very elaborate performance is characterised by Archdeacon Nares, as being 'digested with such skill, and illustrated with such notes, as prove the author to have studied his task with deep attention and distinguished judgment.'

Williams, 212, morocco, 5*l.* 10*s.* Second edition, corrected, &c. Lond. 1826—7. 8vo. 4 vols.

— The Bible. Oxford, 1821. minion 8vo.

'One of the most commodious and correct editions that has ever been printed.'— *Horne.*

— See HAWKER (Robert).

— The Bible, with original Notes, practical Observations, and copious Marginal References. By Thomas Scott. Lond. 1822. 4to. 6 vols.

Fifth and best edition, stereotyped; the largest work ever submitted to that process. Mr. Horne deems it 'an act of bare justice to state, that he has never consulted this elaborate commentary in vain on difficult passages in the Scriptures. And in every instance, especially in the Pentateuch, he found, in Mr. Scott's Commentary, brief but solid refutations of alleged contradictions, which he could find in no other similar work extant in the English Language.' Reprinted, 3 vols. imp. 8vo, 1850. Bohn, 1*l.* 16*s.*

— The Bible, arranged and adapted for Family Reading, with Notes, practical and explanatory. By a Layman of the Church of England. 1824. 4to. 3*l.* 3*s.*

— The Holy Bible, translated from the Latin Vulgate, with Annotations, References, and an historical and chronological Index. The whole revised and diligently compared with the Latin Vulgate. Dublin and Lond. 1825. 8vo.

This, says Mr. Horne, is the latest and most easily accessible edition of the Anglo-Romish version of the Bible. It has been altered for the better, and made conformable to our Protestant authorised version, in several instances, which had been stigmatised by Romanists as heretical. *See*

Hamilton's Observations on the Present State of the Roman Catholic English Bible, pp. 19—21.

— The Cottage Bible and Family Expositor, with practical Reflexions and short explanatory Notes, by Thos. Williams. Lond., Simpkin and Marshall, 1825-7. 8vo. 3 vols. 1*l*. 1s.

'This unassuming but cheap and useful commentary on the Holy Scriptures, though professedly designed for persons and families in the humbler walks of life, is not unworthy the attention of students of a higher class, who may not be able to purchase more bulky or more expensive commentaries. The fine paper copies are handsome library books.'—*Horne.*

— The Bible. Oxford, 1827. 8vo.

This elegant pocket edition is, says Mr. Horne, from its type and size, known by the appellation of the Oxford ruby octavo Bible.

— The Comprehensive Bible; containing the authorized Version, with the various Readings and marginal Notes, a general Introduction, &c. &c. &c. Lond. 1827. crown 4to. 1*l*. 10s. Reprinted 1846.

This valuable Bible contains 4000 notes, which by a simple index used to illustrate 40,000 passages. Not one note is of a doctrinal or controversial nature, but comprise illustrations of Jewish and Eastern manners, customs, rites, and ceremonies. DEMY PAPER, with larger type, 2*l*. 5s. ROYAL PAPER, 3*l*. 10s. SUPER ROYAL cream-coloured WRITING PAPER, 8*l*. 15s.

— Bible Pictorial, illustrated with woodcuts of historical events, landscapes, &c., and with notes by J. Kitto and others, Lond. 1837, 4 vols. royal 4to. 4*l*. 4s. Reprinted in 3 vols. imp. 8vo. 2*l*. 2s.

— The Bible in Welsh.—Y Beibl Cys-segr-lan. Sef yr hen Destament, a'r Newydd, 2 Tim. iii. 14, 15. Testament newydd ein Harglwydd Jesu Grist, Rom. i. 16. Lond. by Christopher and Robert Barker, 1588. fol.

Black letter. Contains 555 leaves. This, the first edition of the Bible in Welsh, contains the Old Testament, the Apocrypha and the New Testament—has contents to each chapter—is distinguished into verses throughout — has some marginal references—has prefixed a Latin dedication to Queen Elizabeth, 'Gulielmus Morgan,'—has a calendar, one or two tables besides, and is numbered not by pages, but by leaves. The dedication [by W. Morgan Bp. of Llandaff and St. Asaph] is reprinted in Llewelyn's Account of the British Versions and Editions of the Bible. Sotheby's in 1824, 5*l*. 18s. Duke of Sussex (1844), pt. 1, no. 1847. 59*l*. Pickering (1854), pt. 2, no. 241, 28*l*. 10s.

— The Bible in Welsh. Lond. by Norton and Bill, 1620. folio.

Black letter. Old Testament and Apocrypha, Eeee 3. New Testament, Y 2. The second edition of the Bible in Welsh, usually called Parry's Bible. Prefixed is a calendar, and a Latin dedication to King James, by Richard Parry, bishop of St. Asaph, which is reprinted in Llewelyn's Account of the British or Welsh Versions and Editions of the Bible. This, says Ant. à Wood, is the translation now used in Wales, and is one of the best translations extant, and much better than the English. Duke of Sussex, pt. 1, no. 1848. Pickering, 1854, pt. 3, 4*l*. 15s. A copy of this, as well as the editions 1677, 1717, are in the British Museum.

— The Bible in Welsh, 1630. 8vo.

The first edition in a portable size, printed at the expense of one or more citizens of London. Reprinted 1654, 5000 copies; 1677, or 1678, 8000 copies; 1689 or 1690; 1718; 1727.

— The Bible in Welsh. Oxford, 1690. folio.

Printed under the inspection of Bishop Lloyd.

— The Bible, in Welsh. Cambridge, 1746. royal 8vo. 18s.

A very excellent edition. Other editions 1752, 1769, or 1770.

— The Bible in Welsh. Carmarthen, 1779. 4to.

This Bible (including a Welsh Concordance) is, in many respects, a good one; though supposed to contain, in two or three passages of the reflections, at the end of the chapters, a tincture of Sabellianism.

— The Bible in Welsh. Lond. 1799. 8vo.

This edition consisted of ten thousand copies of the Welsh Bible, Common Prayer, and singing Psalms, besides two thousand extra copies of the New Testament.

— The Bible in Welsh. Oxford, 1821. crown 8vo.

According to Mr. Horne, one of the most beautiful specimens of typography, printed at the expense of the Society for Promoting Christian Knowledge.

Several editions of the Welsh Bible have been published by the Bible Society, 8vo. 12mo. and 24mo.

— The Bible in the Manks Version. Whitehaven, 1775. 4to.

Printed at the expense of the Society for promoting Christian Knowledge. In 1819 a beautiful and accurate octavo edition of the Manks Bible was published by the British and Foreign Bible Society.

— The Bible in the Gaelic Tongue. Edinb. 1807. 8vo. 2 vols.

The several books of the Old Testament were translated and published in detached portions or volumes 1783, 1787, and 1801. The New Testament, 1796.

— The Bible in the Gaelic Tongue. Edinb. 1826. 4to.

This, which may be considered as the standard edition of the Gaelic Bible, was revised by a committee of clergymen, appointed by the General Assembly of the Church of Scotland. Several editions of the Gaelic Bible have been published by the Bible Society, 8vo. and 12mo.

— The Books of the Old Testament, translated into Irish, by William Bedel, late Bishop of Kilmore. Lond. 1685. 4to. 2*l*. 2s. Reprinted in Dublin, 1827.

Printed at the expense of the Hon. Robt. Boyle. The New Testament was translated by William O'Domhnuill. Lond. 1681. 4to. An edition of the Old Testament with the New Testament, translated by William O'Domhnuill. 1690. 8vo. 10s. 6d. These bibles are said to abound with errors, grammatical and typographical.

— The Bible in Irish. Lond. 1817. 8vo.

Several editions of the Bible in Irish have been published by the British and Foreign Bible Society, &c. viz. in the Roman character, 8vo. and in the vernacular, 8vo. and 24mo.

— A Table of the principal Matters contained in the Bible. Lond. (1548) 16mo.

Contains M 6, in eights. Frequently printed.

— A briefe and compendiouse Table, in the Maner of a Concordaunce, gathered and set furth by Henry Bullinger, Leo Jude, Conrade Pellicane, and by the other Ministers of the Church of Tigure. 1550. 12mo.

In this work appeared 'The third boke of the Machabees.' Copies are in the British Museum and Bodleian libraries. Reprinted 1563. 8vo. T 2, in eights. *See* Wilson's List, p. 291.

— A briefe Summe of the whole Bible, &c. translated by Anth. Scoloker. Lond. 1575. 16mo.

— Fort-Royal of the Scriptures, or the Vade Mecum Concordance. Lond. 1649. 12mo.

Williams, 715, 13s.

— A brief Description of an Edition of the Bible in the original Hebrew, Samaritan, and Greek, with the most ancient Translations of the Jewish and Christian Churches (1652), folio.

A copy is in the British Museum.

— Propositions concerning the printing of the Bible in the original and other learned Languages. 1653. folio.

A copy is in the British Museum.

— Annotations upon all the Books of the Old and New Testament, by the Assembly of Divines. Lond. 1657. folio, 2 vols.

Third and best edition of the 'Assembly's Annotations,' so called from the circumstance of its having been composed by members of the Assembly of Divines, who sat at Westminster during the great rebellion. An account of the authors is in Calamy's Life of Baxter. The work is pronounced by Job Orton to be valuable, though rather long, and to contain much excellent criticism. Dr. Z. Grey, on the other hand, speaks of it very disrespectfully.

The first edition, 1645. folio, 9s. Second, 1651. folio, 2 vols. 1*l*. 1s. Additional Annotations, or a Collection of all the several Additions to the third (above the first and second) impression. Lond. 1658. 8vo. 4s.

— An Account of the Translation of the Bible into the Lithuanian Tongue. Oxford, 1659. 4to.

A copy is in the British Museum.

— An exact Catalogue, or Collection of our English Writers on the Old and New Testament. Lond. 1663. small 8vo. 3s. 6d.

Sotheby's in 1823, date 1668, 7s. 6d.

— Critical Enquiries into the various Editions of the Bible (by Father Simon), 1684. 4to.

Bishop of Ely, 669, 10s.

— Ex Nihilo Omnia; or the Saints Companion. Being a Scripture—Memorial of divine Distichs upon the Holy Bible, in English and Latin. Lond. 1698. 12mo.

Contains pp. 144. Bibl. Anglo-Poet. 248, 9s. 6d.

— The History of the Bible, translated from the French by R. G. Printed in the year 1747. folio.
Translated from the French of David Martin by Richard Gough, the antiquary, when eleven years of age. Twenty-five copies only were printed.

— Critical Notes on some Passages of Scripture, comparing them with the most ancient Versions, and restoring them to their original Reading or true Sense. Lond. 1747. 8vo.
These notes, published anonymously, were written by Nicholas Mann. According to Mr. Horne, they contain some good illustrations of confessedly difficult passages of scripture.

— The Question truely stated, and calmly considered, whether or no there be any just Reasons for a new Translation of the Bible, or a Review of our Liturgy, Articles and Canons. Lond. 1751. 8vo. 2s. 6d.
A moderate, candid, and sensible tract.

— A Dictionary of the Holy Bible. Lond. 1759. 8vo. 3 vols. 12s.
An abridgment of Calmet, Stackhouse, and other illustrators of the Bible. Williams, 203, morocco, 2l. 7s.

— A List of various Editions of the Bible and Parts thereof in English, from the Year 1526 to 1776, from a MS. (no. 1140) in the Archiepiscopal Library at Lambeth, much enlarged and improved. Printed by Bowyer, 1776. 8vo. 3s. 6d.
This List, commonly called Dr. Ducarel's List, was made by Mark Cephas Tutet, and 250 copies, were privately printed for presents only, at the expense of the Archb. of Canterbury. Another edition, 1778, printed on one side only for presents (8vo. 37 leaves, 250 copies), 5s. Bindley, pt. ii. 1883, 1l. 10s. Gosset, 515, 16s.
This list, with additions, will be found in Cruttwell's edition of the Bible with Bp. Wilson's Notes, and in Archbishop Newcome's Historical View of the English Biblical translations, printed at Dublin, 1792. 8vo.
[Other lists of editions of the Bible may be found in Lewis' History of the Translations of the Bible, folio, 1731; 1739, 8vo.; 1818, 8vo. Cotton's Editions of the Bible, second edition, 1852, 8vo. Lea Wilson's Catalogue of English Bibles (privately printed), 1845, 4to. and in the Appendix to Anderson's Annals of the English Bible, 2 vols. 8vo. 1845.]

— The Reasons for revising by Authority our present Version of the Bible, briefly stated, and impartially considered. Lond. 1790. 8vo.
'An anonymous work, justly entitled to the attention of the public.'—*Abp. Newcome.* Some copies are dated Cambridge, 1788.

— Candid Examination of the assumed Divine Authority of the Bible. 1796. 4to.
Horne Tooke, 57, 1l. 1s.

— Compendium of the Holy Scriptures. 1809. 3 vols.
Earl of Kerry, 95, 1l. 11s. 6d.

— An Index to the Bible. Lond.
This useful index, by Dr. Priestley, is printed in various sizes to bind up with Bibles.

— Reasons why a new Translation of the Bible should not be published without a previous Statement and Examination of all the material Passages, which may be supposed to be misinterpreted. Durham, 1816. 8vo.
Written by Thomas Burgess, D.D., subsequently Bishop of Salisbury.

— Scripture Genealogy from Adam to Christ. Lond. 1817. royal 4to.
This collection of 36 engraved tables is an improvement upon those of Speed.

— Scripture Harmony, or Concordance of Parallel Passages; being a Commentary on the Bible, from its own resources: consisting of an extensive collection of References from the most esteemed Editors and Commentators. Lond. 1818. 18mo. 18s.
Of this work the Rev. T. H. Horne speaks as follows. 'The contents of this useful compilation are comprised in three particulars, viz. 1. The Chronology, in which Dr. Blayney is followed, his being deemed the best fitted for general utility. 2. The Various Readings, in the giving of which great care has been bestowed. And 3. The

Scripture References—a laborious compilation of half a million of scripture references, chiefly from Canne, Brown, Scott, Dr. Blayney, and the Latin Vulgate, and other Writers, who have devoted their services to this useful mode of illustrating the Scriptures.'

An edition of the Scripture Harmony is printed in 4to. 1*l*. 4s. royal 8vo. 1*l*. 4s. or with the text on opposite pages, 1*l*. 16s.

— An Index to the Bible, in which the subjects are alphabetically arranged.

This very useful index, by some attributed to the Rev. Mr. Simeon, is printed in 8 forms, viz. royal 4to. 2s. Demy 4to. 2s. Royal 8vo. 2s. Demy 8vo. 2s. Foolscap 8vo. 1s. 6d. Demy 12mo. 1s. 6d. Royal 18mo. 1s. 6d. Small size 24mo. 1s. 6d. The first edition appeared in 1811.

— Reasons why a new Translation of the Bible should be published. 1819. 8vo.

Of no great value.

— Scripture Atlas. 4to.

This atlas, published by Mr. Leigh, is, according to Mr. Horne, 'executed in a superior style, and has had a very extensive sale. Mr. Wyld's Scripture Atlas (30 cold. maps) is a neat publication.' 10s. 6d.

— The Bible, in various Foreign Languages.

Those marked * were printed for the Foreign and British Bible Society.

*Amharic, 4to. *Arabic, 8vo. *Chinese. *Danish, 8vo. *Dutch, 8vo. *French, 24mo. sm. 8vo., royal 8vo. Bagster (J. F. Ostervald), 9s. An edition, 1819. royal 24mo. *German, 24mo. 18mo. and 8vo. Bagster (Luther), 9s. Greek, Septuagint. Bagster, small 8vo. 9s. *Greek, modern, 8vo. *Hebrew, 12mo. and 8vo. Bagster, small 8vo. 18s. *Italian (Diodati), 24mo. 16mo. and 8vo. Bagster (Diodati), small 8vo. 9s. Latin. Bagster (Vulgate), small 8vo. 9s. Malay, in Roman Character, 8vo. *Persian, 8vo. *Portuguese (Pereira), 8vo. (D'Almeida) 8vo. Bagster, small 8vo. 9s. *Raratongan, 8vo. *Spanish, 8vo. and 12mo. Bagster. (Philipe Scio de S. Miguel). small 8vo. 9s. *Swedish, 24mo. and 8vo. *Syriac, small 4to. *Tahitian, 8vo. *Turkish, 4to.; an edition by Wm. Seaman. Oxford, 1666. 4to.

For other versions printed at the expense of the society abroad and by affiliated institutions, *see* the Reports and brief Views, published by the British and Foreign Bible Society.

— The Images of the Old Testament, lately expressed, set forthe in Ynglishe and Frenche, with a playn and brief Exposition. Lyons by Johan Frellon, 1549. small 4to.

The cuts are from the designs of Holbein. A copy is in the British Museum. Gordonstoun, 1264, morocco, 2*l*. 3s.

— Icones Veteris Testamenti. Illustrations of the Old Testament, engraved on wood from designs by Holbein, with introduction by T. F. Dibdin. Pickering, 1830. 90 cuts by John and Mary Byfield.

— The true and lyuely historyke Pvrtreatvres of the woll Bible (with the Arguments of eche Figure, translated into English Metre by Peter Derendel). Lyons by Jean of Tournes, 1553. 8vo.

One hundred and four leaves, with woodcuts by Bernard Salomon (le Petit Bernard). A collection of well-finished wood cuts, with four lines to each in explanation of the subject, written in a barbarous and almost unintelligible jargon. White Knights, 453, morocco, 5*l*. 5s. Bindley, pt. iii. 1542, 6*l*. 6s. Rogers, 1856, vellum, 8*l*. 15s.

— A volume of plates to the Bible, with Descriptions by Slatyer. 4to.

Bindley, pt. iv. 150, 1*l*. 5s.

— Series of Engravings from Scripture. Are to be sould by R. Peake.

Bindley, pt. ii. 1221, with MS. English verses opposite to each plate, 1*l*. 13s.

— Pictures of the Old and New Testaments, shewing the most notable Histories, in 150 Copper plates, by most famous and principal Masters. The text in French and English. Amsterdam, 4to.

— Scripture illustrated by Engravings referring to Natural Science, Customs, Manners, &c. By the editor of Calmet's Dictionary of the Bible. (C. Taylor), 1802. 4to.

'Many otherwise obscure passages of the Bible are in this work happily elucidated from natural science, &c. Though it does not profess to be a complete natural history of the Scriptures, yet it illustrates that interesting subject in very many instances.' —*Horne.*

— A Series of Eighty-one Designs, by Thurston and Craig, engraved on wood by Bewick. Lond. 1810. royal 4to.

—— A Set of Engravings, from the Designs of Corbould and Riley, adapted to illustrate the Old and New Testaments. Lond. 1818. royal 4to. 1*l*. 1s.

—— Scripture Costume exhibited in a Series of Engravings, drawn under the Superintendance of Benjamin West, P.R.A. by R. Satchwell, with biographical Sketches and historical Remarks on the Manners and Customs of eastern Nations. Lond. 1819. elephant 4to.

—— Sixty Illustrations and Embellishments of the Holy Scriptures, from superior designs by eminent Masters, engraved in outline and tinted, with Descriptions in French and English. Lond. 1824. 12mo. 7s. 6d.

Published by Bagster.

Bible Society.—Twenty-three Reports of the British and Foreign Bible Society. Lond. 1805-7. 8vo.

—— Memorial for the Bible Societies in Scotland : containing Remarks on the Complaint of his Majesty's Printers against the Marquis of Huntley and others. With an Appendix, consisting of many original Papers. Edinburgh, 1824. 8vo. 12s.

Contains pp. xxxii. 256 & 96. The sale of this book, written by Dr. Lee, was prohibited by the Court of Session in Scotland. In it will be found much curious bibliographical information relating to the early literature of Scotland.

BIBLIANDER, Theod. Consultation, by what Meanes the cruell power of the Turks both maye and ought for to be repelled of the Christian People [translated from the Latin]. Basill, 1542. 16mo.

Black letter. Contains V in eights. White Knights, pt. i. 457. 11s. A copy of the date of 1513? is in the British Museum.

Bibliographical Dictionary and Miscellany. *See* CLARKE, Adam, LL.D.

Bibliographical Memoranda ; in Illustration of old English Literature. Bristol, 1816. 4to.

One hundred copies printed. Edited by J. Fry. Sir M. M. Sykes, pt. i. 1195, 1*l*. 8s. Strettell, 1018, 1*l*. 5s.

Bibliographical Miscellanies ; being a Selection of curious Pieces in Verse and Prose. Oxf. 1813. 4to.

One hundred copies printed. Edited by Philip Bliss, D.D. Nassau, pt. i. 414, 18s. Bindley, pt. i. 742, 10s. 6d.

Bibliosophia ; or Book Wisdom. Lond. 1810. 12mo.

An anonymous and vapid attempt at wit, by the Rev. James Beresford. Sir M. M. Sykes, pt. i. 221, 2s. Strettell, 120, 6s.

Bibliotheca Anglo-Poetica ; or, a descriptive Catalogue of a Collection of early English Poetry, in the possession of Longman and Co. illustrated by occasional Extracts and Remarks critical and bibliographical, compiled by A. F. Griffiths. Lond. 1805. royal 8vo.

This extremely useful catalogue of the rare and curious collection, made by T. Park, and added to by Tho. Hill, is deserving of a place in every good library, from the interesting information which it affords of the works of our early poets. Nassau, pt. i. 2052, 1*l*. 5s. Sir M. M. Sykes, pt. iii. 750, 1*l*. 18s. Brockett, 313, 1*l*. 9s.—LARGE PAPER. (50 printed.) Nassau, pt. i. 2053, 3*l*. 5s. Dent, pt. i. 1350, russia, 1*l*. 16s.

—— Annua, or the Annual Catalogue for 1699, &c. Lond. 1700-1. 4to. 3 Nos.

A copy of Nos. 1 and 3 is in the British Museum.

—— Biblica. *See* PARKER, Samuel.

—— Fanatica ; or the Phanatique Library. 1660. 4to.

Contains pp. 8. A ridiculous attack on the republicans and commonwealth men, reprinted in the eighth volume of the Harleian Miscellany.

—— Litteraria ; a Collection of Inscriptions, Medals, Dissertations, &c. Lond. 1722-4. 4to. 10 nos. in 1 vol. 10s. 6d.

A very valuable literary journal published by Dr. Jebb, Mr. Wasse, Dr. Wotton,

Dr. Jortin, Dr. Pearce, and others. Brockett, 491, 14s.

Bibliotheca Militum; or, the Souldiers Publick Library. Lond. 1659. 4to. 7s.
Contains pp. 6. A cutting satire against the republicans, reprinted in the seventh volume of the Harleian Miscellany, and in the fifth number of Morgan's Phœnix Britannicus.

— Parliamenti; Libri Theologi, Politici, Historici, qui prostant venales in Vico vulgo vocato Little-Britain. Done into English for the Assembly of Divines. Anno Domini, 1653. 8vo. 6s.
Contains pp. 12. A bold and pertinent attack on the hypocritical leaders during the time of the commonwealth. Reprinted in the seventh volume of the Somers' Collection of Tracts.

— Parliamenti: Classis secunda. Done into English for the Assembly of Divines. Anno Domini, 1653. 4to.
A copy of this and the former tract are in the British Museum.

— Regia. *See* CHARLES I.

— Topographica Britannica. *See* NICHOLS, John.

— Universalis, or an historical Accompt of Books, and Transactions of the learned World, begun A.D. M.DC.LXXXVIII. Edinburgh, 1688. 18mo.
A copy is in the British Museum.

Bibliotheque Angloise, ou Histoire Littéraire de la Grande Bretagne. Amst. 1717-27. 18mo. 15 vols. 1l. 1s.
A species of review edited by Michael de la Roche and Arnaud de la Chapelle.

— Angloise, Nouvelle, par M. de Joncourt. A la Haye, 1756-7. 12mo. 3 vols. 5s.

— Britannique, ou Histoire des Ouvrages des Savans de la Grande Bretagne, 1733-46, avec la Table. A la Haye, 1733, &c. 12mo. 25 vols. 1l. 1s.

— Britannique, rédigee par Auguste Pictet et F. G. Maurice.

Genève, 1796-1845. 8vo. 140 vols. Tables jusqu'en 1815. 4 vols.
Each year of this journal is divided into 7 vols. viz. Littérature, 3 vols.; Sciences et Arts, 3 vols.; Agriculture, 1 vol.

BICHAT, Xavier. Physiological Researches on Life and Death, translated from the French, by F. Gold. Lond. 1815. 8vo. 9s.
The works of this celebrated French physician are much esteemed.

BICKERSTAFF, Isaac. *i.e.* Sir Richard STEELE.

BICKERSTETH, Rev. Edward. Scripture Help, designed to assist in reading the Bible profitably. Tenth Edition. Lond. 1823. 8vo.
' A practical introduction to the reading of the Scriptures, frequently reprinted. The sale of upwards of 15,000 copies of the large editions, and of more than 100,000 copies of the 18mo. abridgment, sufficiently attest the high estimation in which this manual is deservedly held.'—Horne. This excellent author has published many other works, a list of which will be found in the London Catalogue.

BICKHAM, George. First Principles of Heraldry. Lond. (1742) 8vo.
A work of no value, consisting of pp. 12. The title as well as the whole book is engraved.

— Universal Penman. Lond. 1743. folio.
A neatly engraved work, with numerous head and tail pieces. Bindley, pt. 1. 586, 17s. 6d.

— British Monarchy, or a new chorographical Description of all the Dominions subject to the King of Great Britain. Lond. 1748. folio. 15s.
Consisting of 190 plates. Nassau, pt. i. 440, 1l. 13s. Dent, pt. i. 334, date 1734, russia, 2l.

— Deliciæ Britannicæ; or, the Curiosities of Kensington, Hampton Court, and Windsor Castle delineated. The second edition, with additions. Lond. 1742. 12mo.
Contains pp. viii. and 184 (B—N 4), with 9 plates.

— Musical Entertainer, a Collection of Songs set to Music, with engraved Head pieces. 2 vols. folio.
The engraved head-pieces consist of hu-

morous, fanciful, and local views. Sotheby's in 1825, 2*l*. 2s.

BICKNELL, Alexander. Life of Alfred the Great, King of the Anglo-Saxons. Lond. 1777. 8vo. 5s.
Edwards, 39, 7s.

— History of Edward the Black Prince, with a short View of the Reigns of Edward I. II. and III. and a summary Account of the Institution of the Order of the Garter. Lond. 1777. 8vo. with Portrait of the Black Prince, 5s.
This writer published several other historical compilations, of little value, and less reputation.

BICKNOLL, Edmund. Swoorde against Swaryng. Lond. for William Towreolde. 8vo.
Black letter. Inglis, 89, 9s. 6d.

BIDDLE, John. Confession of Faith, touching the Holy Trinity, according to Scripture. Lond. 1658. 8vo.
A life of this celebrated Socinian writer, with a list of his works, will be found in Dr. Bliss's edition of Wood's Athen. Oxon. iii. 598—603.

— Joannis Bidelli Vita. Lond. 1682. 12mo.
'The author was, as I have been informed, one Joh. Farrington, J. C. T. of the Inner Temple.'—*Ant. à Wood.*

BIDDULPH, Rev. Thomas T. Baptism a Seal of the Christian Covenant; or Remarks on Dr. Mant's Tract on Regeneration. Lond. 1815. 8vo.
Contains pp. 255. A notice of this work will be found in the Quarterly Review, xv. 475—511.

— Practical Essays on the Liturgy of the Church of England. Lond. 1822. 8vo. 3 vols. 1*l*. 5s.
According to the Quarterly Review, 'These Essays have been read with pleasure and improvement, by many, whose opinions do not altogether accord with those of Mr. Biddulph.' The former editions 1799, 12mo. 5 vols. 1810, 8vo. 3 vols.

— Divine Influence; or the operation of the Holy Spirit traced from the Creation of Man to the Consummation of all things. Lond. 1824. 8vo.

Contains pp. 263. According to the Quarterly Review, this essay is principally taken from Dr. Vices. Knox's Christian Philosophy.

— Theology of the early Patriarchs, illustrated by an Appeal to subsequent Parts of the Holy Scriptures. Bristol, 1825. 8vo. 2 vols. 1*l*. 1s.

— William. *Vide* LAVENDER, (T.)

BIDLAKE, John, D.D. Sermons on various Subjects. Lond. 1808. 8vo. 3 vols. 18s.
Dr. Bidlake published several very pleasing volumes of poems, which are recommended by Dr. N. Drake.

BIDPAI. Kalila and Dimna, or the Fables of Bidpai, translated from the Arabic, by Knatchbull. Oxford, 1819. 8vo. 10s. 6d.

BIELFELD, Baron de. Elements of universal Erudition, containing an analytical Abridgment of the Sciences, Polite Arts, and Belles Lettres, translated from the German by William Hooper, M.D. Lond. 1770. 8vo. 3 vols. 9s.
Dr. Hooper translated Letters containing original Anecdotes of the Prussian Court, 1761-70. 12mo. 4 vols. 7s. 6d.

BIENVILLE, T. de, M.D. Nymphomania; or a Dissertation on the Furor Uterinus, &c. translated from the French, by E. S. Wilmot, M.D. Lond. 1775. 8vo. 5s.

BIESTON, Roger. Bayte and Snare of Fortune. Lond. by John Wayland, folio.
Black letter. Sometimes found attached to 'Lydgate's Siege of Troy.'
Contains 10 leaves. Written in the octave stanza. On the last leaf is an acrostic of the author's name Rogervs Bieston. Inglis, 200, 17s, Sir M. M. Sykes, pt. i. 617, 3*l*. 10s.

BIGELOW, Dr. American Medical Botany. Boston, 1817. royal 8vo. 3 vols. (6 parts), with 60 coloured plates.

BIGLAND, John. Geographical and Historical View of the World. Lond. 1810. 8vo. 5 vols. Published at 3*l*. 13s. 6d.

A highly useful work for juvenile students. This writer likewise published History of Spain, 1810, 8vo. 2 vols. Sketch of the History of Europe, 1783—1810, 1811, 8vo. 2 vols. History of England, 1815, 8vo. 2 vols. and various other works.

— Ralph. Observations on Marriages, Baptisms and Burials, as preserved in Parochial Registers. Lond. 1764. 4to. 5s.

Contains pp. 96. A very curious book, containing much valuable information for the genealogist.

— Historical, monumental, and genealogical Collections, relative to the County of Gloucester. Lond. 1791-2. folio. 2 vols. 3l. 3s.

This work is not completed. Bindley, pt. i. 378, 5l. 5s.

Vol. i.—Title; half sheet, with a quotation from Warton; dedication to the Duke of Norfolk; preface, 2 pages; history, &c. 631 pages; and directions for placing the 23 detached plates in vol. i. Vol. ii.—Title; quotation as in vol. i.; history, 252 pages, ending with the catchwords 'clxxxi. Newington.' In this volume, consisting of ten numbers, there are 11 detached plates.

[As this work was never completed, and the 'City of Gloucester' is one of its deficiences, it is desirable to add 'Fosbrooke's City of Gloucester,' which was compiled from Bigland's papers and printed in folio for the express purpose. *See* FOSBROOKE.]

BIGOD or BYGOD, Sir Francis. Treatise concerning Impropriation of Benefices. Lond. 1571. 4to.

'Written after the breach which K. Henry 8 made with the Pope, his marriage with Anne Bolleyn, and the birth of Q. Elizabeth, as 'tis conjectured by circumstances. The epistle, dedicated to K. Henry 8, is reprinted at the end of Sir Henry Spelman's work on Tithes.'—*Ant. à Wood.*

Bija Gannita. *See* STRACHEY, Edward.

BIJOU, The, or Annual of Literature and the Arts, 12mo. 2 vols. Lond. 1828-30. 12s. each, with the engravings on India paper, 1l. 1s.

These volumes are embellished with Engravings after Sir Thomas Lawrence, P. R. A. Stothard, Wilkie, and others. They contain translations of two letters of Cicero, one by his Majesty, and the other by the late Duke of York—also an interesting letter by Sir Walter Scott, Bart., descriptive of a family picture by Wilkie.

BILL, Anna. Mirror of Modestie. Lond. 1621. 8vo.

Prefixed is a portrait of Ann Bill, with ornaments of Music, &c. Then follows 'Monument of Mortalitie, with front. by S. Pass. Mirror of Modestie, with portrait of Anna Bill, 1621. Vaile of Modesty, Verses to the Memory of Anna Bill, with the plate 1621.' Bindley, pt. ii. 1719, 3l. 16s.

BILLINGS, Joseph. *See* SAUER, Martin.

— Peter. Folly predominant, or the Town taken in with the palpable Deceptions and frothy Orations of four public Orators, three of which suddenly springing up like Mushrooms, must as soon decay. Lond. 1755. folio.

A very uncommon tract, with portraits of Henley, Foote, Macklin, and Stevens. Reed, 904, 1l. 4s.

BILLINGSLEY, Martin. Pens Excellencie, or the Secretary's Delight. Lond. 1618. 4to. with portrait by W. Hole, 7s.

This writer likewise published a Copy Book, 4to. with portrait, 'æt. 27, 1623,' by J. Goddard.

BILLINGSLY, Nicholas. Brachy-Martyrologia: or a Breviary of all the greatest Persecutions which have befallen the Saints and People of God from the Creation to our present times; paraphrased (in verse). Lond. 1657. 8vo.

Contains pp. 228. Dedicated to Jeremy Martin, M.D. A notice of this work will be found in the Restituta, iv. 454-7. Bindley, pt. i. 449, 2l. 11s. Bibl. Anglo-Poet. 52, 3l. 3s. Nassau, pt. i. 250, 3l. 3s. Midgley, 2l. 18s. Perry, 2l.

— ΚΟΣΜΟΒΡΕΦΙΑ, or the Infancy of the World. Lond. 1658. 8vo.

Contains pp. 206. Dedicated to Francis Rous. A notice of the work will be found in the Brit. Bibl. ii. 643-6, and Restituta iv 458-62. Bindley, pt. i. 448, 2l. 7s. Bibl. Anglo-Poet. 53, 3l. 3s. Midgley, 2l. 16s. Perry, 1l. 8s.

— Treasury of Divine Raptures. Lond. 1667. 8vo.

This little work consisting of pp. 240, was intended as the first portion of an extensive alphabetical collection, but no more ever appeared. Nassau, pt. i. 351, russia, 1l. 13s. Bibl. Anglo.-Poet. 54, 3l. 10s. Midgley, 2l. 3s.

BILLINGTON, Mrs. Memoirs of Mrs. Billington, from her Birth. Lond. 1792. 8vo. with a portrait, a small oval, by A. v. Assen. 10s. 6d.

An infamous attack on this celebrated vocalist, published with a view, it is supposed, of extorting money. Perry, pt. iv. 533, 13s. An answer, with the life and adventures of Richard Daly, Esq. and an account of the Irish Theatre, appeared in 1792, 8vo.

Bills of Mortality.—Collection of the yearly Bills of Mortality, with Graunt's Observations. Sir W. Petty on the Growth of the City of London. Corbyn Morris on the past Growth and present State of the City of London. Lond. 1759. 4to.

Edited by Thomas Birch, D.D. In 1665 appeared 'Reflections on the Weekly Bills of Mortality, for the Cities of London and Westminster,' 4to. in 24 leaves.

BILLYNS, Wm. Five Wounds of Christ, a Poem from an ancient Parchment Roll. Published by W. Bateman. Manchester, 1814. 4to.

Black letter, with fac-similes. Forty copies printed. Saunders in 1818, with a duplicate set of the plates in colours, morocco, 3l. 5s.

BILSON, Thomas, Bishop of Winchester. Difference betweene Christian Subiection and vnchristian Rebellion. Oxford, 1585. 4to. 9s.

Reprinted Lond. 1586, 16mo. Certain Observations collected out of this treatise, 1641, will be found reprinted in the fourth volume of the Somers' Collection of Tracts.

— Perpetval Government of Christes Church. Lond. 1593. 4to. 5s.

Black letter, contains pp. 414. Reprinted 1610, 4to. A Latin translation appeared 1611. 4to.

— Treatise of the Sufferings and Victory of Christ in the Worke of our Redemption. Lond. 1598. 8vo. 5s.

'These sermons preached at Paul's Cross, made great alarms among the puritanical brethren.'—*Ant. à Wood.* This eminent divine likewise published 'A Survey of Christ's Sufferings and Descent into Hell.' Lond. 1604. folio. Gordonstoun, 14l. 6s. 6d.

Bilson.—The Boy of Bilson. *See* FOWLES, Susanna. PERRY, William.

BINET, F. Stephen. Lives and singular Virtues of the Saints, Eleazar Count of Salran, and Delphina, his wife; both Virgins and married. Lond. 1630. 8vo.

BINFIELD, William. Travels and Adventures, with an accurate Account of the Dog-Bird. Lond. 1753. 12mo. 2 vols. 6s.

BINGHAM, Jos. A.M. Works, containing the Origines Ecclesiasticæ, or Antiquities of the Christian Church; a Scholastical History of Lay Baptism; the French Churches' Apology for the Church of England; a Discourse concerning the Mercy of God to penitent Sinners. Lond. 1726. folio. 2 vols.

An invaluable treasure of Christian antiquities. Gosset, 788, 1l. 15s. Bp. of Ely, 231, 1l. 16s.

— Origines Ecclesiasticæ; or the Antiquities of the Christian Church. Lond. 1710-22. 8vo. 10 vols.

A Latin edition was published at Halle, 1724-9, in 10 vols. 4to. with a preface by the learned Budæus. An abridgment of this work, by A. Blackmore. Lond. 1722. 8vo. 2 vols. 8s.

— Origines Ecclesiasticæ. Edited by his grandson, the Rev. Rd. Bingham. Lond. 1829. 8 vols. 8vo.

New edition, with his other works; an account of the author, by the Rev. Rd. Bingham, and the quotations at length in the original languages, and index. Edited by the Rev. J. R. Pitman. Lond. 1840. 9 vols. 8vo. 5l. 8s. 1855, 10 vols. 8vo. 5l. 5s. An edition, 2 vols. imperial 8vo. Bohn, 1l. 11s. 6d.

'Bingham is a writer who does equal honour to the English clergy, and to the English nation, and whose learning is only to be equalled by his moderation and impartiality.'—*Quarterly Review.*

— P. Reports in the Court of Common Pleas, from Trinity Term 3 Geo. IV. 1822, to Trin. Term, 4 Will. IV. Lond. 1824-1834. royal 8vo. 10 vols. 2l. 5s.

New cases in the Common Pleas and other Courts, Trin. T. 4 Will. IV. to Mich. T. 4 Vict. 1840. roy. 8vo. 6 vols. 2l.

BINGLEY, Rev. Wm. Tour round North Wales. Lond. 1800.

8vo. 2 vols. with views in aquatinta by Alken.

In this work the language, manners, customs, antiquities, and botany, are particularly attended to and well described. Bindley, pt. i. 482, 13s. Towneley, pt. ii. 37, 9s. Fonthill, 2192, 2l. 2s.

Another edition, 1804. 8vo. 2 vols. Towneley, pt. ii. 38, 12s.

— Animal Biography, or Anecdotes of the Animal Creation; arranged according to the System of Linnæus. Lond. 1803. 8vo. 3 vols. 15s.

One of the most entertaining books in the English language, frequently reprinted.

— Memoirs of British Quadrupeds. Lond. 1809. 8vo. 2 vols. with 70 plates.

At the sale of Nassau's library, pt. i. 253, a copy on large paper, with coloured plates, produced 1l. 11s. 6d. This author has published several other works.

BINNING, Hugh. Works; viz. Sermons on the Catechism, &c. Edinb. 1735. 4to. 8s.

Best edition. Williams, 233, 1l. 3s.

BIOCHIMO, —. Royall Game of Chesse Play, illustrated with almost an hundred Gambetts. Lond. 1656. 12mo. with portrait of Charles I. by Stent.

A translation of Greco, by Dr. Budden. Nassau, pt. i. 132, no portrait, 13s. Stanley, 91, 1l. 7s. White Knights, 463, mor. 1l. 7s.

Biographia Britannica: or the Lives of the most eminent Persons of Great Britain and Ireland. Lond. 1747-66. folio, 7 vols. vol. 6 being in two parts.

An indispensable work in every English historical library. Steevens, 1801, 7l. 10s. Bindley, pt. i. 376, 8l. 12s. Dent, pt. i. 338, russia, 7l. 10s. Heath, 1524, 10l. Hollis, 234, 10l. 10s. Brockett, 287, russia, 11l. 1s. 6d. Marquis of Townshend, 412, 12l. 5s. Edwards, 36, russia, 17l. LARGE PAPER— Stanley, 52, 27l. 16s. 6d. Roxburghe, 9277, 23l.

— enlarged by Andrew Kippis, D.D. and others. Lond. 1777-93. folio. Vols. 1 to 5.

An exceedingly valuable work, which it is necessary to possess, as well as the former edition. Bindley, pt. i. 377, 2l. 9s. Drury, 797, 2l. 9s. Brockett, 288, 2l. 3s. Duke of York, 2700, 3l. 3s. Sir M M. Sykes, pt. i. 6118, 3l. 15s. Steevens, 1802, 4l. 7s. 6d. Roscoe, 271, 5l. 5s. Edwards, 37, russia, 6l. A portion of a sixth volume (Featley to Foster) was printed, of which, it is said, only two copies exist.

Biographia Classica. A new Edition corrected and enlarged by Edward Harwood, D.D. Lond. 1778. 12mo. 2 vols.

Nassau, pt. i. 256, 15s. A former edition appeared 1740, 12mo. 2 vols. 5s.

Biographia Ecclesiastica; or, the Lives of the most eminent Fathers of the Christian Church. Lond. 1704. 8vo. 2 vols. 9s.

Williams, 253, 1l. 16s.

Biographia Gallica; or, the Lives of the eminent French Writers of both Sexes, from the Restoration of Learning under Francis I. to the present Time. Lond. 1752. 12mo. 2 vols. 6s.

An entertaining collection of anecdotes (not lives) relating to most of the noted writers of the French nation.

Biographical Collections; or, Lives and Characters, from the Works of the Rev. Mr. Baxter and Dr. Bates; with various Additions interspersed. Together with Abstracts of their Funeral Sermons. Lond. 1767. 12mo. 2 vols. 6s.

Memoirs of a considerable number of eminent divines (chiefly among the puritans) of the last age.

Biographical Dictionary, A new and general. Lond. 1798. 8vo. 15 vols.

Steevens, 1595, 4l. White Knights, pt. i. 464, russia, 5l. 5s. An edition 1784, 8vo. 12 vols. 1l. 16s.

— See CHALMERS, Alexander.

Biographical Dictionary of the Living Authors of Great Britain and Ireland. (A to C by Wm. Upcott, the remainder by Fred. Shoberl.) Lond. 1816. 8vo. 6s.

As accurate a list of the works of the authors living in 1816, as could possibly be compiled.

Biographical Magazine, or historical Library. Lond. 1776. 4to. with portraits.

Nassau, pt. ii. 1560, 1l. 6s. Another

work, entitled Biographical Magazine, containing 140 portraits, 1794, 8vo. Sotheby's in 1825, 15s.

Biographical Magazine, containing Portraits, with Lives and Characters of eminent Persons, 2 vols. roy. 8vo.
Twenty-four Nos. complete. Brockett, 318, 1l. 16s.

Biographical Mirrour. *See* HARDING.

Biographie Moderne: Lives of remarkable Characters during the French Revolution. Lond. 1811. 8vo. 3 vols. 12s.
Two editions of this work, one in 1801, the other with alterations, &c. in 1806, were published at Paris, but immediately suppressed. This is a translation of the edition of 1806. Earl of Kerry, 74, 1l. 6s.

Biographium Fœmineum; the Female Worthies. Lond. 1766. 12mo. 2 vols. 6s.

Biography.—Contemporary Biography. Lond. 1824. 3 vols. post 8vo. with 150 engraved portraits, 2l. 2s.

BION. Bionis et Moschi quæ supersunt, Gr. et Lat. cum Notis Jo. Heskin. Oxon. 1748. 8vo. 4s.
A very elegant and correct edition. Heath, 3458, 7s. 6d. Williams, 254, mor. 1l. 1s.

— Bionis et Moschi Idyllia, Gr. illustrabat et emendabat Gilbertus Wakefield. Lond. 1795. 8vo.
A beautiful and correct edition, printed without accents, fc. 8vo. demy 8vo. and royal 8vo. LARGE PAPER in 4to. Drury, 462, mor. 15s. 6d. Sir M. M. Sykes, pt. i. 230, 1l. Williams, 255, mor. 1l. 7s. Brockett, 494, morocco, 1l. 11s. 6d.

— Bionis, Moschi et Tyrtæi quæ supersunt, Gr. et Lat. Edinb. 1807. 18mo.
A beautifully printed edition.

— The Idyllia, and other Poems that are extant of Bion and Moschus; transl. from the Greek into English verse. To which are added a few other Translations, with Notes critical and explanatory. 12mo. 6s. 6d.
For other editions and translations of Bion see ANACREON, MUSÆUS, Poetæ Minores Græci, THEOCRITUS.

BION, Nic. Construction and Uses of Mathematical Instruments, by Edm. Stone. Lond. 1758. folio, 18s.
A very excellent and esteemed work. The second Edition contains au Appendix, which makes it greatly preferable to that of 1723, folio.

BIONDI, Gio. Franc. Storia della Guerre civili d'Inghilterra. Venezia, 1637, 41, 47. 4to. 3 vols. 10s. 6d.

— History of the civill Warres of England, betweene the Houses of Lancaster and Yorke, englished by Henry, Earl of Monmouth. Lond. 1641-6. folio, 2 parts in 1 vol. with front. by Elstracke. 10s. 6d.
An 'elegant history.'—*Bp. Nicolson.*

—Eromena, or Love and Revenge, englished by John Hayward. Lond. 1632. folio.
Gordonstoun, 316, 7s. 6d.

— Banished Virgin, englished by John Hayward. Lond. 1635. folio.
Gordonstoun, 317, 5s. Bindley, pt. i. 396, 5s.

— Coralbo, a new Romance. Lond. 1655. folio.
Prefixed is a portrait of the Duke of Newcastle on horseback. Sotheby's in December, 1822, 10s. 6d.

BIRCH, Thomas, D.D. Life of the Hon. Robert Boyle. Lond. 1741. 8vo. 5s.
Reprinted 1744, of which a copy, with MS. notes by the author, is in the British Museum. Edition 1744, Bindley, pt. i. 423, 7s.

— Heads of illustrious Persons of Great Britain, engraven by Houbraken and Vertue, with their Lives and Characters, by Thomas Birch. Lond. 1743-52. folio, 2 vols.
Vol. i. pp. 160, with title and contents, 2 leaves, and 80 portraits, of which 71 are by Houbraken. Vol. ii. pp. 56, with title and contents, 2 leaves, and 28 portraits, of which 23 are by Houbraken. Sir M. M. Sykes, pt. i. 1533, 8l. 8s. LARGE PAPER, (200 copies struck off, 100 before, 100 after the small paper copies.) Dent, pt. i. 340, russia, 18l. Fonthill, 1484, 18l. 18s. Roxburghe, 9282, 25l. 4s. Nassau, pt. i. 1964, russia, 26l. 15s. 6d. Edwards, 47, russia, 27l. 6s. Heath, 1526, 34l. 13s. An edition,

with retouched impressions of the plates, appeared 1813, on small and large paper.

BIRCH (T.) Inquiry into the Share which K. Charles I. had in the Transactions of the Earl of Glamorgan, afterwards Marquis of Worcester, for bringing over a Body of Irish Rebels to assist that King in the Years 1645 and 1646. Lond. 1747. 8vo.
Reprinted 1756, with an Appendix. Heath, 4462, 5s. 6d. Bindley, pt. i. 328, 4s.

— View of the Negotiations between the Courts of England, France, and Brussels, from 1592 to 1617, extracted chiefly from the MS. State Papers of Sir Thomas Edmondes, Knt. Lond. 1749. 8vo. 5s.
Heath, 4438, 9s. 6d.

— Life of the Rev. John Tillotson, Archb. of Canterbury. Lond. 1752. 8vo. 5s.
A copy is in the British Museum, with a few MS. notes by the author. LARGE PAPER, Reed, 4819, 1l. 2s. Williams, 256, mor. 2l. Second edition, corrected and enlarged, 1753, 8vo. Bindley, pt. i. 331, 7l. Williams, 257, mor. 1l. 6s. In 1755 appeared Remarks upon this Life, 8vo. 1s. 6d.

— Memoirs of the Reign of Queen Elizabeth, from the Year 1581 till her Death. Lond. 1754. 4to. 2 vols.
Dr. Birch has formed his narrative of the most striking facts in the numerous letters of the Bacon family, though, as might be expected, the letters are much abbreviated. Bindley, pt. i. 903, 2l. 5s. Heath, 4432, 3l. 9s. Nassau, pt. i. 408, 2l. 15s. Fonthill, 854, 2l. 2s. Marq. of Townshend, 175, 3l. 3s. Reed, 3329, 2l. 3s.

— History of the Royal Society of London. Lond. 1756. 4to. 4 vols.
Reviewed by Dr. S. Johnson in the Literary Magazine. Drury, 562, 2l. 8s. Sir P. Thompson, 135, 18s.

— Life of Henry, Prince of Wales. Lond. 1760. 8vo. 6s.
An excellent and just account of this book will be found in Lodge's Memoir of Prince Henry. Fonthill, 2257, 18s. THICK PAPER. Williams, 258, mor. 1l. 17s. Reprinted at Dublin, 1760, 8vo. Birch likewise published a Life of John Ward, LL.D. Lond. 1766, 8vo.

— William. Delices de la Grande Bretagne: a Series of Views (36 in number) with Descriptions. Lond. 1791. oblong 4to.
In little estimation. Roxburghe, 8568, 1l. 13s. Bindley, pt. i. 728, first impressions, 3l. 5s.

BIRCH (Wm.). Songe betwene the Quene's Majestie and Englande. Lond. by William Pickeringe.
Reprinted in the tenth volume of the Harleian Miscellany, from a copy, supposed unique, in the Library of the Society of Antiquaries, London.

BIRCHEDUS. *Anglice* BIRKHEAD.

BIRCKBEK, Simon. The Protestant's Evidence. Lond. 1657. folio.
This book was valued by Selden and other learned men, says Ant. à Wood. A former edition appeared 1634, 4to.

BIRD, John. Ostenta Carolina: or the late Calamities of England, with the Authors of them. Lond. 1661. 4to. 6s.

— Samuel. Lectures vpon the 8th and 9th chapters of the second Epistle to the Corinthians, and upon the 11th Chapter of the Epistle vnto the Hebrewes, and upon the 38th Psalme. Cambridge, 1598. 16mo. 2 vols. in 1.
Nassau, pt. i. 259, 18s. Bird likewise published a 'Dialogue between Paule and Demas.' Lond. 1580, 8vo. 89 leaves, with an epistle to the reader.

— William. Magazine of Honour, or a Treatise on the several Degrees of the Nobility of this Kingdom. Printed for William Sheares, 1642. 8vo. pp. 158. 2s. 6d.
Although this treatise contains little more than the argument of Mr. Serg. Doddridge in the disputed question regarding the Barony of Abergavenny, it is well deserving of perusal by persons interested in the history of the peerage. Towneley, pt. i. 286, 9s. The volume has had several title-pages.

BIRD. *See* BYRD.

Birds.—A proper new Boke of the Armony of Byrdes. Lond. by John Wyght. 12mo.
This curious little volume, consisting of 8 leaves, written in the Skeltonic manner, is reprinted in the fourth volume of Dr. Dibdin's edition of Ames, p. 379-84.

— Ornithologia Nova: the History of Birds. Birm. 1743. 12mo. 2 vols.

This work is adorned with 400 figures of birds, very neatly engraved on wood, in a style superior to any other work of the period. Nassau, pt. i. 2471, 1l. 10s. Dent, pt. i. 1077, russia, 1l. 8s. Some copies bear the imprint of London, 1745. Bindley, pt. ii. 309, 1l. Stanley, 101, mor. 4l. 5s.

BIRKBECK, Morris. Notes on a Journey in America, from the Coast of Virginia to the Territory of Illinois. Lond. 1818. 8vo.

A notice of this work, and likewise of the author's Letters from Illinois, will be found in the Quarterly Review, xix. 54-78.

BIRKENHEAD, Sir John. The Assembly Man, written in the year 1647. Lond. 1662-3. 4to.

Contains pp. 22, with a front. by Faithorne, supposed to have been intended for Hugh Peters, or some active zealot of that period. Towneley, pt. ii. 1558, 15s. 6d.

This once admired character of an Assembly Man, meant to be the representative of that celebrated body of divines who met at Westminster for the establishment of church discipline upon the Presbyterian plan, was reprinted 1684, 1704, and in the fifth volume of the Harleian Miscellany.

— Paul's Church Yard. Libri Theologici, &c. 4to.

Centuria prima, 8 pages. Centuria secunda, 8 pages. A cutting satire against the republicans during O. Cromwell's Protectorate. Reed, 5383, 9s.

— Two Centuries of Paul's Church-Yard, 12mo.

This second edition, to which was added 'Bibliotheca Parliamenti,' is reprinted in the ninth volume of the Harleian Miscellany. Paterson observed that 'the spirited humour of this little book was admirable, and worthy the pen of a Butler.' Towneley, pt. ii. 53, 16s. Inglis, 91, 17s.

Birkenhead's News from Pembroke and Montgomery will be found in the fifth volume of the Harleian Miscellany, and according to Ant. à Wood, this wit and royalist wrote an anniversary poem on the nuptials of John, Earl of Bridgwater, 22 July, 1652.

BIRKHEAD, Henry. Poemata in Elegiaca, Iambica, Polymetra Antitechnemata et Metaphrases, membratim qvadripertita. Oxon. 1656. 12mo.

Birkhead, according to Ant. à Wood, 'was accounted an excellent Latin poet, a good Grecian, and well vers'd in all human learning.' Nassau, pt. i. 258, 1l.

— & Hen. Stubbe. Otium Literarum ; sive Miscellanea quædam Poemata, &c. Oxon. 1656. 8vo. 4s.

Stubbe's Deliciæ Poetarum Anglicanorum were reprinted 1658, 8vo. and had at the end added to them Elogiæ Romæ et Venetiarum.

— Oxford Verses on the Death of Sir Bevill Grenville. 1684. 4to.

Prefixed is a portrait by Faithorne. Reed, 6688, 1l. 8s.

Birmingham. Views (Eight in aquatint, after P. H. Witton, jun. by W. Ellis) of the Ruins of the principal Houses destroyed during the Riots of Birmingham, 1791, with Letter-press Descriptions in English and French. Lond. 1792. oblong 4to.

BIRNIE, William. The Blame of Kirkburial, tending to persuade Cemiterial Civility. Edinb. 1606. 4to.

[A new edition by W. B. D. Turnbull, 4to. Edinb. 1833.] Eyton, 1848, printed on vellum, unique, 2l. 5s.

Birth of Mankind. See RAYNALD, Thomas.

Births.—Two most strange Births. Lond. 1608. 4to.

An account of this curious black letter tract of eight leaves will be found in Oldys' catalogue of pamphlets affixed to the Harleian Miscellany, no. 529.

BISANI, Alexander. Picturesque Tour through Part of Europe, Asia, and Africa. Lond. 1793. 8vo.

In this work will be found plates after Athenian Stuart's designs. Nassau, pt. ii. 1172, 6s. Dent, pt. ii. 1069, mor. 9s.

BISACCIONI, El Conde Mayolino. Gverras civiles de Inglaterra tragica Muerte de su Rey Carlos. Escrita en Toscano—trad. en Lengva Castellana por Don Diego Felipe de Albornoz. Barcelona, 1673. 4to. 4s.

BISCOE, Richard, D.D. History of the Acts of the holy Apostles confirmed from other authors, and considered as full Evidence of the

Truth of Christianity. Lond. 1742. 8vo. 2 vols. 15s. [In 1 vol. 8vo. Ox. 1840, 9s.]

'This learned and elaborate work contains the substance of Dr. Biscoe's Sermons preached at Mr. Boyle's Lecture between the years 1736 and 1738. Dr. Doddridge frequently refers to it as a work of great utility, and as showing, in the most convincing manner, how incontestably the Acts of the Apostles demonstrate the truth of Christianity.'—*Horne*.

BISHOP, John. Beautifull Blossomes gathered by John Byshop, from the best Trees of all Kyndes. Lond. for Henrie Cockyn, 1577, 4to.

Contains 154 leaves, and the errata. Prefixed are The Author vnto his Booke, the Authour vnto the Reader, and a Table. At page 61 is the remarkable story on which Walpole's Mysterious Mother is founded. Reed, 4l. 16s. Brand, 4l. 10s. North, 8l. 8s.

— Garden of Recreation, collected out of the most auncient and best Writers in all Ages by John Bishoppe, Gentleman. Lond. for Henrie Cockin, 1578. 4to.

The former book, with a new title-page.

— Matthew. The Life and Adventures of Matthew Bishop, of Doddington, in Oxfordshire, containing an account of several Actions by Sea, Battles, and Sieges by Land, in which he was present, from 1701 to 1711, interspersed with many curious Incidents, entertaining Conversations, and judicious Reflections; written by himself. Lond. 1744. 8vo. 6s.

An amusing piece of autobiography, written by a common sailor, ably noticed in the Retrosp. Rev. N. S. ii. 42, &c.

— Samuel, Poetical Works, with Life by the Rev. Thomas Clare. Lond. 1796. 4to. 2 vols.

Bindley, pt. 1. 738, 7s. This writer likewise published Sermons, chiefly upon practical subjects, 1798, 8vo. 4s.

— William. Reformation of a Catholic deformed, by Will. Perkins. Printed 1604—7. 4to. 2 vols.

A life, with a list of the works of this Roman Catholic priest, who was in 1622 created Bishop of Chalcedon by the Pope, will be found in Dr. Bliss' edition of Wood's Athenæ Oxoniensis, iii. 356-7.

Bishop.—The Boke of the Descrypcyon of the Images of a very Chrysten Bysshop and of a counterfayte Bysshop. Impr. by Wyllyam Marshall. 8vo.

Contains v vij. in eights. The preface consists of ten unnumbered pages. This book, which is quoted by Prynne in his Lordly Prelacie, pp. 337-8, as 'a very rare one,' is a biting and coarse satire against the Roman Catholic Bishops—certain texts of scripture being chosen and commented upon.

— The Forme and Maner of makyng and consecrating Bishoppes, Priestes, and Deacons. Lond. 1552. folio.

Reprinted 1559, &c. The first edition appeared 1549. Wilkes, 1847, 15l. Horner, 1854. mor. 4l. 14s. 6d. *See* Archbishops. An edition 1629, reprinted in Sparrow's Collection of Articles, &c. 1671, and frequently since separately. [Included in some editions of the Common Prayer Book.]

— The sum of the Actes & Decrees made by dyuers Byshopes of Rome, 1538. Translated out of Latyn into Englyshe, and imprinted in ye House of Thomas Gybson. 12mo. 16 leaves.

Black letter. Bindley, pt. iii. 852, 16s. 6d. Inglis, 444, 17s. White Knights, 3737, 1l. 2s.

— Lord Bishops none of the Lord's Bishops. Lond. 1640. 4to.

Bindley, pt. ii. 2528, 11s. In the British Museum is a very large collection of Tracts relating to the Bishops, 1640, &c.

— An Apology for the ancient Power of the Bishops to sit and vote in Parliaments. Lond. 1660. 4to.

Written by the Rev. Jeremiah Stephens, the learned coadjutor of Sir Henry Spelman, in his Collection of the Councils. In Moule's Bibl. Heraldica will be found a list of the tracts, &c. on this celebrated controversy.

— The proceedings and Trial of the Bishops in the Court of King's Bench, Anno Dom. 1688. Lond. 1689. folio, 6s.

Prefixed is a frontispiece, containing their portraits, by White.

— *See* SALMON, N.

BISMARK, Count von. Lectures

on the Tactics of Cavalry. Translated from the German, with Notes. By Major N. Ludlow Beamish. Lond. 1827. 8vo. pp. 402, with plates.
This translation is considered superior to that of Major Fred. Johnston's.

BISPHAM, Thomas. Iter Australe, a Reginensibus Oxon, An. 1658 expeditum. Oxon. 1660. 4to.
'An ingenious Latin poem, dedicated to Tho. Barlow, provost of Qu. Coll. Oxford.'—Ant. à Wood.

BISSE, Thomas, D.D. Beauty of Holiness in the Common Prayer Lond. 1721. 8vo. 3s. 6d.
A copy on large paper, Williams, 259, morocco, 1l. 9s. Another work, 'Decency and Order in Publick Worship,' 1723, 8vo. LARGE PAPER, ruled with red lines, Williams, 260, morocco, 1l. 2s.

BISSELUS, Jo. Mariæ Stuartæ viventis et morientis, acta, 8vo. Ambergæ, 1675. port.
Sotheby, 1829, 1l. 16s.

BISSETT, Robert, LL.D. History of the Reign of George III. A new Edition completed (to his death). Lond. 1825. 8vo. 6 vols.
The edition 1803, 8vo. 6 vols. Earl of Kerry, 29, 2l. 9s. Dr. Bissett likewise published a life of Edmund Burke, 1798. 8vo. 1 vol. and 1800, 8vo. 2 vols.

BITAUBÉ, P. J. Joseph, a Poem, translated from the French, (by the Rev. W. Beloe.) Lond. 1783. 12mo. 2 vols. 5s.

BIZZARI, Petri. Varia opuscula ac Poemata, 8vo. Ven. Aldi, 1565.
The first tract is dedicated to Queen Elizabeth, the second to Mary Queen of Scots, the third to the Duke of Bedford; poems to the nobility and gentry of that period are interspersed. Sykes, 4l. 10s. Hibbert, 3l. 4s. Renouard, 4l. 4s.

BLACK, John. Life of Torquato Tasso, with an account of his Writings. Edinb. 1810. 4to. 2 vols. with port. by Raimbach.
A very valuable and elaborate work. Drury, 564, 1l. 2s. Roscoe, 274, 2l. 4s.

— Joseph, M.D. Lectures on the Elements of Chemistry, published by John Robinson, LL.D. Edinb. 1803. 4to. 2 vols. 1l. 10s.
Dr. Black, as a chemist, opened that path of discovery which has since been prosecuted with such splendid success.

BLACK, W., M.D. An Historical Sketch of Medicine and Surgery, from their Origin to the present Time; and of the principal Authors, Discoveries, Improvements, Imperfections, and Errors. Lond. 1782. 8vo. 5s.

— William. Privileges of the Royal Burrows. Edinb. 1707. 12mo. 5s.

BLACKADDER, J. Life and Diary of Lieut.-Col. J. Blackadder, of the Cameronian Regiment, &c., who served under the Duke of Marlborough, and afterwards in the Rebellion of 1715, in Scotland. By Andrew Crichton. Edinburgh, 1824. 12mo. with portrait, 5s. 6d.

BLACKALL, Offspring, Bishop of Exeter. Works, w'th a Preface by Archbishop Dawes. Lond. 1723. folio, 2 vols. with portrait by Vertue, 1l. 5s.

— Discourses on our Lord's Sermon on the Mount. Lond. 1717. 8vo. 8 vols. with portrait by V. Gucht.
Drury, 466, 1l. 1s. Williams, 262, morocco, 5l. 18s.

BLACKMORE, A. Ecclesiæ Primitivæ Notitia; or, a Summary of Christian Antiquities, Index Hæreticus, and an Account of the first eight Councils. Lond. 1722. 8vo. 2 vols. 10s.

BLACKBURNE, Francis, Archdeacon of Cleveland. Works Theological and Miscellaneous, with Life by his Son. Cambridge, 1804. 8vo. 7 vols. with portrait, 1l. 4s.

— The Confessional; or a full and free Inquiry into the Right, Utility, Edification, and success of establishing systematical Confessions of Faith and Doctrine in Protestant

Churches. Third Edition. Lond. 1770. 8vo. 5s.

'The author of this work, who is well known to be a very learned clergyman of the Church of England, takes so much notice of all the writers who opposed his sentiments, that there is no need to give a particular enumeration of the several pamphlets which were written against it.'—*Bp. Watson.* Williams, 263, 15s.

BLACKBURNE, Francis. Historical View of the Controversy concerning an intermediate state. Lond. 1772. 8vo. 7s. 6d.

— Remarks on Johnson's Life of Milton; to which are added, Milton's Tractate of Edvcation and Areopagitica. Lond. 1780. 12mo. 6s.

Privately printed, at the expense of Archd. Blackburne, without his name.

BLACKER, Valentine. Memoir of the Operations of the British Army in India during the Mahratta War of 1817, 18, 19. Lond. 1821. 4to. with an atlas of 45 plates.

Published at 4*l*. 14s. 6d. Duke of York, 734, 2 vols. mor. 3*l*. 3s.

Black-Friars. 1. The doleful Even Song, or a true Narration of that Calamity which befell Mr. Drurye, a Jesuite, and the greater Part of his Auditory, by the Downefall of the Floore of an Assembly in the Black-friers on Sunday, the 26 of Octob. last. 2. Something written by occasion of that Accident in the Black Friers. 3. A Word of Comfort, by I. R. P. Lond. 1623. 4to. Three Tracts.

Copies are in the British Museum. The first tract, Nassau, pt. i. 411, 2*l*. 3s. The second, King and Lochée's, in March, 1810, 6s. The three tracts. Bindley, pt. ii. 761, 13s.

BLACKET, Joseph. Remains, with Life by Pratt. Lond. 1811. 8vo. 2 vols. 10s.

BLACKETT, Sir W. Memoirs of Sir W. Blackett, cr. 8vo. Newcastle, 1819.

Two hundred and sixty copies printed. Brockett, 2170.

Blackguardiana; or, Dictionary of Rogues, Bawds, &c. 8vo. (by Jas. Caulfield) Lond. 1795, with portraits.

Lloyd, 179, 12s. 6d. Bindley, pt. i. 422, 2*l*. 2s.

BLACKLOCK, Thomas, D.D. Poems, with an Essay on the Education of the Blind. To which is prefixed an Account of his Life and Writings, by Henry Mackenzie, 1793. 4to. 10s. 6d.

Incorporated in Chalmers' Collection of the British Poets.

BLACKMAN, John. Collectarium Mansuetudinum et bonorum Morum Regis Henrici VI. ex Collecti e Magistri Joann^{is} Blakman. [Lond. by Robert Copland.] 4to.

Black letter, with wood cuts, consisting of ten leaves. Gough, 1106, 3*l*. 8s. Reprinted by Hearne in his edition of Otterbourne.

BLACKMORE, Sir Richard, M.D. A Paraphrase on the Book of Job, the Songs of Moses, Deborah, and David, and on four select Psalms, some Chapters of Isaiah, and the third Chapter of Habakkuk. Lond. 1700. folio. 1716. 12mo.

A metrical translation of some little merit as poetry, but little as a version of the original text. The edition 1716, on large paper. Nassau, pt. i. 263, 10s.

— Creation, a Philosophical Poem in seven Books. Lond. 1712. 8vo. 4s.

Addison observes, 'This work was undertaken with so good an intention, and executed with so great a mastery, that it deserves to be looked upon as one of the most useful and noble productions in our English verse:' and Dr. Johnson says, 'if he had written nothing else it would have transmitted him to posterity among the first favourites of the English Muse.'

Sir Richard Blackmore likewise published other Poems, viz. Prince Arthur, Alfred, King Arthur, a Satire on Wit, Eliza, &c., and several Medical works. His poem of the Creation, with life by Dr. Johnson, is inserted in Chalmers' Collection of the Poets.

BLACKSTONE, Henry. Reports of Cases in the Courts of Common Pleas and Exchequer Chamber, from Easter Term, 28 Geo. III. 1788, to Hilary Term, 36 Geo. III. inclusive.

The third Edition, corrected, with additional Notes and improved Indexes. Lond. 1801. royal 8vo. 2 vols. [4th edition, Lond. 1827, 2 vols. royal 8vo.] 2*l.* 16*s.*
Best edition. The former editions appeared in folio, 1791, 1*l.* 10*s.* and 1796, 2 vols. each.

BLACKSTONE, Jo. Specimen Botanicum quo Plantarum plurium rariorum Angliæ indigenarum Loci natales illustrantur. Lond. 1746. 8vo. 3*s.*
This writer likewise published 'Fasciculus Plantarum circa Harefield sponte nascentium.' Lond. 1737, 8vo.

— Sir William, Knt. LL.D. Great Charter, and Charter of the Forest, with other authentic Instruments; to which is prefixed an introductory Discourse concerning the History of the Charters. Oxford, 1759. royal 4to.
Bindley, pt. i. 924, 8*s.* Dent. pt. i. 466, 14*s.* 6*d.* Steevens, 1752, 1*l.* 2*s.* Gough, 1*l.* 5*s.* Marquis of Townshend, 1*l.* 10*s.*

— Commentaries on the Laws of England.
Of these Commentaries Sir Wm. Jones observed, 'they are the most correct and beautiful outline that ever was exhibited in any human science.'

List of Editions.
1st Edition. Oxford, 1765—9. 4to. 4 vols. 2*l.* 2*s.* [Sundry passages, strongly advocating the liberty of the subject, were expunged in subsequent editions.]
2d Edition. Oxford, 1768, 4to. 4 vols. Horne Tooke, 66, with MS. notes by Tooke, 6*l.* 18*s.* 6*d.* 3d Edition, and 4th Edition, each 4 vols. 8vo.
5th Edition. Oxford, 1773, 8vo. 4 vols.
6th Edition. Lond. 1774, 4to. 4 vols. with port. by Hall. Heath, 1661, 1*l.* 11*s.* 6*d.*
7th Edition. Oxford, 1775, 8vo. 4 vols.
8th Edition. Oxford, 1778, 8vo. 4 vols.
Continued by Ri. Burn, LL.D. Lond. 1783, 8vo. 4 vols.
By Ri. Burn, LL.D. and John Williams. Lond. 1787, 8vo. 4 vols. Edwards, 602, 16*s.*
By the same. Lond. 1791, 8vo. 4 vols.
With Notes and Additions by Edw. Christian. Lond. 1793-4, 8vo. 4 vols. with portraits of the Judges.
By Ed. Christian, 1800, 8vo. 4 vols.
By Ed. Christian, 1803, 8vo. 4 vols.
By E. Christian. Lond. 1809, 8vo. 4 vols.
By J. F. Archbold. Lond. 1811, royal 8vo. 4 vols.
By J. Williams. Lond. 1822, 8vo. 4 vols.
By J. T. Coleridge. Lond. 1825, 8vo. 4 vols. with a portrait.
By J. Chitty. Lond. 1826, royal 8vo. 4 vols.
By Lee, Hovenden, and Ryland, Lond. 1829, 6vo. 4 vols.
By Hovenden and Ryland, Lond. 1836, 8vo. 4 vols.
By Hargrave, Sweet, Couch, and Welsby, Lond. 1844, 8vo. 4 vols.
By Stewart, Lond. 1844-9, 8vo. 4 vols.
By Mr. Sergt. Stephen, Lond. 1848-9, 8vo. 5 vols.
23rd Edition, by James Stewart, Lond. 1854, 8vo. 4 vols.
By Robert Malcolm Kerr, Lond. 1857, 8vo. 4 vols. 2*l.* 2*s.*

———

An Abridgment, by William Curry, 8vo. 1796, 5*s.* 1809, 10*s.*
An Abridgment, by John Gifford, 1821, 8vo. 15*s.*
An Analysis, by Baron Field, 1811, 8vo. 8*s.*
An Epitome for the Use of Schools, by N. Wanostrocht, LL.D. 12mo. 10*s.* 6*d.*
A translation of all the Greek, Latin, French, and Italian sentences and quotations in Blackstone's Commentaries, and also those in the notes of Christian, Archbold and Williams, 8vo. Lond. 1823.

Tracts on the subject of Blackstone's Commentaries.
Remarks, by James Sedgwick, 1800, 4to. 12*s.* 1804, 8vo. 7*s.*
Vindication of, against Sedgwick, by Wm. Hen. Rowe, 1806, 8vo. 6*s.*
A Reply to Dr. Priestley. Remarks on the fourth volume of the Commentaries, 1769, 8vo.
Letters by Philip Furneaux, D.D. The second edition, with Additions and an Appendix, 1771, 8vo. 4*s.*
Fragment on Government, by Jeremy Bentham, 1776, 8vo. 3*s.* 1823, 8vo. 8*s.*
A Letter to Dr. Blackstone, occasioned by a Passage in his Commentaries concerning the Character of the Ecclesiastics of the present Age. 8vo. 6*d.*

— Tracts, chiefly relating to the Antiquities and Laws of England. Lond. 1771. 4to. 1*l.* 1*s.*
Best edition.
CONTENTS.—An analysis of the Law of England. An essay on collateral consanguinity. Considerations on copyholders. Observations on the Oxford press. An introduction to the great charter. Magna charta, charta de foresta. The former edition, 1762, 8vo. 2 vols.
An argument of Sir W. Blackstone in the Exchequer Chamber, in the case of Perrin and Blake, will be found in Har-

grave's Law Tracts, and his Memoir concerning the authenticity of Dr. Littleton's roll, containing an ancient copy of magna charta, is printed in Gutch's Collectanea Curiosa.

— Reports of Cases determined in the several Courts of Westminster Hall, from 1746 to 1779. Lond. 1781. folio, 2 vols. 3*l*. 3s.

These reports were not generally received by the profession with that approbation which has followed all the other writings of this great author. An edition, Dublin, 1781, 8vo. 2 vols. 2*l*. 2s. [An edition with additional notes, &c., by C. H. Elsley, Lond. 1828, 2 vols. royal 8vo.]

— Biographical History of Sir Wm. Blackstone. Lond. 1782. 8vo. 4s.

A compilation stolen principally from the account given by Mr. Clitherow, in his preface to the learned Judge's reports.

BLACKWALL, Anthony. Introduction to the Classics. Lond. 1740. 12mo. 2s. 6d.

A valuable little book.

— The Sacred Classics defended and illustrated. Lond. 1727-31. 8vo. 2 vols. with portrait by Vertue, 6s.

Williams, 264, morocco, 1*l*. 9s. A second edition, 1737, 8vo. 2 vols.

This work, according to Dr. Doddridge, 'gives many well-chosen instances of passages in the classics, which may justify many of those in Scripture that have been accounted solecisms. They illustrate the beauty of many others, and contain good observations on the divisions of chapters and verses, by which the sense of scripture is often absurd.'

'Blackwall was a strenuous advocate for the purity of the Greek style of the New Testament, which he vindicates in his first volume. The second volume, which is most valuable, contains many excellent observations on the division of the New Testament into chapters and verses, and also on various readings. The work was translated into Latin by Christopher Woll, and published at Leipsic in 1736, 4to.'—*Horne.*

BLACKWELL, Elizabeth. Herbal containing 500 Cuts of the most useful Plants which are now used in the Practice of Physick. Lond. 1737. folio, 2 vols. plain, 25s. coloured, 3*l*. 3s.

This work, which in its day was highly esteemed, is now in little request. Some copies are dated 1739 or 1751. 1739, Williams, 372, LARGE PAPER, with coloured plates, 5*l*. 15s. 6d.

— George, Arch-priest of England. A large Examination taken at Lambeth, according to his Majestie's Direction, Point by Point, of George Blackwell. Lond. 1607. 4to.

Gordonstoun, 193, 7s.

— Answers upon sundry his Examinations, together with his Approbation, &c. Lond. 1607. 4to.

Consisting of 21 leaves. A life of this divine will be found in Dr. Bliss's Edition of Wood's Athenæ Oxon. ii. 122-4, and most of his writings will be found in the British Museum.

— Examination de M. Geo. Blackwell, faicte à Lambeth, avec lettre aux Catholiques Romains d'Angleterre, &c., 12mo. Amst. 1609. 15s.

— Quæstio in G. Blacvellum Angliæ Archipresbyterum a Papa designatum. 1609. 4to.

Bindley, pt. iii. 1440, 11s.

— John. Compendium of Military Discipline. Lond. 1726 or 9.

With plates by Hogarth. Baker, 41, mor. 11s. Yates in 1827, 2*l*. 12s.

— Sir Ralph. The Honour of Merchant Tailors. Lond. 4to.

Black letter, with a portrait of Blackwell. A work of the same class, if not written by the same hand, with the well-known history of Sir Richard Whittington.

— Thomas. Enquiry into the Life and Writings of Homer. Lond. 1735. 8vo. 5s.

A production which displays more erudition than genius, and more affectation than elegance. Roxburghe, 9163, 11s. LARGE PAPER. Fonthill, 644, 16s. Heath, 1541, 1*l*. 1s. Baker, 41, with the proofs, 1747, 2*l*. 4s. Williams, 265, mor. 11*l*. 8s. Reprinted 1736, and in 1747, 8vo. appeared Proofs of the Enquiry translated into English. The third edition of the work appeared in 1757.

— Letters concerning Mythology. Lond. 1748. 8vo. 4s.

A pompous trifle, of which a second edition, or rather a new title-page, appeared in 1757.

— Memoirs of the Court of Augustus. Edinb. and Lond. 1753—63, 4to. 3 vols.

This work was most ably reviewed by Dr. Johnson in the Literary Magazine. Earl of Kerry, 192, 3*l*. 18s. Sir P. Thompson. 134, 2*l*. LARGE PAPER, Roxburghe, 7774, 4*l*. 8s. An edition appeared Basil, 1794, 8vo. 7 vols.

Blackwood's Edinburgh Magazine, from the Commencement in 1817 to 1857 inclusive, 82 vols. Edinb. 8vo.

Published monthly. Some copies of October, 1817, contain Hogg's Chaldee Manuscript, which was afterwards suppressed.

BLACKWOOD, Adam. De Conjunctione Religionis et Imperii ad illustriss. Principem D. Mariam Scotiæ Reginam. Paris. 1575. 8vo. 10s. 6d.

BLACKWOOD, Adami Blacuodæi adversus Geo. Buchanani Dialogum de Jure Regni apud Scotos pro Regibus Apologia. Pictav. 1581 4to.

Bindley, pt. i. 1475, 9s. 6d.

— Editio secunda, per Auctorem recognita. Paris. 1588. 8vo.

— Sanctorum Precationum Prooemia, quibus addita sunt ejusdem Argumenti varii Generis Odæ cum aliis quibusdem Poematüs. August. Pictav. 1598. 12mo.

Gordonstoun, 176, 1*l*. 1s.

— Martyre de la Reyne d' Escosse. Edinb. 1587. 8vo. Anvers. 1588. 8vo.

'A most virulent invective against Queen Elizabeth.'—*Bishop Nicolson*. Blackwood's works, with his portrait by J. Picart, appeared at Paris, 1644. 4to. from which edition this tract is reprinted in the second volume of Jebb de Vita, &c. Mariæ.

— Christopher. Expositions and Sermons upon the ten first Chapters of St. Matthew. Lond. 1659. 4to.

BLACOW, Richard. Letter to William King, LL.D. Principal of St. Mary Hall, in Oxford; containing a particular Account of the treasonable Riot in February 1747. Lond. 1823. 8vo. 1s. 6d.

BLACUODÆUS, *Anglice*, BLACKWOOD.

BLAGDON, Francis Wm. Modern Discoveries; translated, &c., from the Works of the most eminent Authors. Lond. 1802-3. 18mo. 8 vols. 1*l*. 1s.

— Brief History of ancient and modern India, from the earliest Periods to the Termination of the Maratta War. Lond. 1805. atlas folio, with coloured plates by Daniell.

Sotheby's in June, 1822. 4*l*. 11s. Fonthill, 768, 6*l*. 5s.

— The European in India, from Drawings by C. Doyley, Esq. with Preface and History by T. W. Blagdon and Capt. Williamson. Lond. 1813. royal 4to.

— Flowers of Literature. Lond. 1802—9. 7 vols. 12mo. 1*l*. 10s.

BLAGE, Thomas. Schole of Wise Conceytes. 4to. 1569.

A book of Æsopian fables. Ritson's Bibl. Poet. 13*l*. 1572. Sotheby, 1851, 4*l*. 4s. Jolley, 1844, 8*l*. 8s.

BLAGRAVE, John. Mathematical Jewel. Lond. 1585. folio.

A very curious work with wood-cuts by the author. A copy of this work, as well as Blagrave's Baculum familliare, 1596, and Astrolabium Vranicum, 1566, are in the British Museum. A life of him will be found in Dr. Bliss's edition of Wood's Athen. Oxon. ii. 96-8.

— Jos. Planispherium Catholicum. Londini, 1658. 4to.

In the title are portraits of Blagrave and Palmer by D. L(oggan).

— Epitome of the Art of Husbandry. Lond. 1669. 12mo. 5s.

Reprinted 1679 and 1685. In this work will be found brief experimental directions for the right use of the angle.

BLAINE, Delabere P. Outlines of the Veterinary Art. New Edition. Lond. 1816. 8vo. 2 vols.

This writer has likewise published several other esteemed works, [especially an Encyclopædia of Rural Sports, 8vo. 1852, 2*l*. 10s.]

BLAINVILLE, M. de. Travels through Holland, Germany, Switzerland and other Parts of Europe, but especially Italy. Translated

from the French, by Turnbull and Guthrie. Lond. 1743 or 1757. 4to. 3 vols. with maps, &c.
These travels, though praised by Dr. Johnson, are now held in little estimation. Reed, 3332, 1l. 2s.

BLAIR, Arn. *See* WALLACE, Sir William.

— Hugh, D.D. Sermons, with Life, by James Finlayson, D.D. Edinb. and Lond. 1777-1801. 8vo. 5 vols.
These excellent sermons have passed through innumerable editions.

— Lectures on Rhetoric and Belles Lettres. Lond. 1798. 8vo. 3 vols.
Frequently reprinted. The first edition appeared 1783, 4to. 2 vols. with a portrait. Heath, 134, 1l. 11s. 6d. William, 284, 1l. 8s. An acount of Blair's Life and Writings was published by John Hill, LL.D. 1807. 8vo. 6s.

— James. Our Saviour's divine Sermon on the Mount, contained in the Vth, VIth, and VIIth Chapters of St. Matthew's Gospel, explained; and the Practice of it recommended in diverse Sermons and Discourses. To which is prefixed a Paraphrase on the whole Sermon on the Mount. Lond. 1740. 8vo. 4 vols. 1l. 5s.
Best edition of these valuable Sermons, with a recommendatory preface by Dr. Waterland. Williams, 266. 2l. 267, mor. 2l. 9s. The former edition appeared 1722, 8vo. 5 vols.

— John, LL.D. Lectures on the Canon of the Scriptures. Lond. 1785. 4to. 6s.
A work of considerable learning and research.

— John. The Life and Acts of Sir William Wallace, maintainer of the liberty of Scotland, in verse. Glasgow, 1713. 16mo. 1l. 1s. [3 vols. 12mo. Perth, 1790.]

— Chronology and History of the World, illustrated in LVI Tables, with 14 Maps, and a Dissertation of the Rise and Progress of Geography. Lond. 1768. folio.
Heath, 2143, 4l. 10s. The first edition of this valuable and highly useful work appeared 1756. Roxburghe, 7360, 1l. 15s.

and Supplement, 707, 15s. An edition, 1779, Drury, 796, russia, 3l. 15s. Other editions with continuations have appeared 1790, 1808, 1815, 1820. The fourteen maps were published separately.
[A new edition in royal 8vo., prepared by Mr. John Sharpe with the assistance of Sir Henry Ellis, was published in 1844, 2l. 2s.; and another, considerably enlarged and improved, and continued to its date, by Mr. J. W. Rosse, was published in 1857 by Henry G. Bohn, 10s.]

— Patrick. Botanical Essays in two Parts. Lond. 1720. 8vo. 4s.
A most ingenious work, relating chiefly to the sexes of plants, with 4 plates. This writer likewise published Pharmaco-Botanologia. Lond. 1723-8, 4to. extending only to the letter H.

— Robert. The Grave, a Poem, with 12 plates by Schiavonetti, after Blake. Lond. 1808. large 4to. port.
Duke of York, 738, 1l. some copies were printed in folio. This much esteemed poem has passed through numerous editions, and is reprinted in Chalmers and other Collections of the Poets.

BLAKE, Robert. Arrivale and entertainment of the Ambassador Alkard and his associate Mr. Rob. Blake from the Emperor of Morocco. 1637. 4to. port.
Gordonstoun, 4l. 18s.

— Wm. Silver Drops, or serious Things; with Letters concerning the Lady's Charity School, at Highgate. 12mo.
Contains pp. 293 (A—T 3) with 4 plates. Nassau, pt. 1. 267, 8s.

— Wm. Artist. Poetical Sketches, by W. B. 70 pages, 8vo. 1783.
Very scarce, written between his twelfth and twentieth year.

— Songs of Experience, 17 plates, 12mo. n. d.

— Songs of Innocence and of Experience, 2 vols. 8vo. 1789-94.
Sotheby, 1855, mor. 12l. 5s.

— The Same. 1 vol., imp. 4to., coloured by the artist, 54 engraved pages, Bohn's Cat. 10l. 10s.

— Book of Thiel, 8 engraved pages. 1789. 4to.
Sotheby, 1854, 3l. 2s.

— America, a Prophecy, 18 designs. Folio. Lambeth, 1793.
Sotheby, 1855, 2l. 7s

BLAKE, Wm. Gates of Paradise, 16 engravings for children, 12mo. Lambeth, 1793.
— Vision of the Daughters of Albion, in verse, 6 leaves. 1793. small folio.
— Book of Ahania, 3 designs. 1795.
Sotheby, 1855, 1*l.* 13*s.*
— Europe, a Prophecy. Lambeth, 1794. Folio. 17 plates, including title and front.
— Marriage of Heaven and Hell. 27 pages, 1800.
Sotheby, Dec. 1854, 4*l.* 16*s.*
— Jerusalem, the emanation of the Giant Albion. 100 engraved pages, folio.
Sotheby, Dec. 1854, 4*l.* 16*s.*
— A Descriptive Catalogue of Pictures painted by himself. 1809. 12mo.
— Illustrations to the Book of Job. 21 plates, folio. 1826. 3*l.* 3*s.* Proofs, 5*l.* 5*s.*
Sotheby, Dec. 1854, 2*l.* 8*s.*
— Illustrations to Comus. 8 original designs.
Sotheby, 1855, 4*l.* 6*s.*
— Milton, a poem, in 12 books, 50 engraved pages, coloured by the artist, 4to. 1804. Bohn's Cat. 10*l.* 10*s.*
— Illustrations to Dante. 7 plates, imp. fol., India proofs, 1*l.* 16*s.*
— *See* Blair's Grave; Young's Night Thoughts; and Malkin's Life of a Child.

BLANCHARD, W. T. Complete Instructor of Short-Hand. 1786. 4to.
Best edition of a valuable treatise. The former appeared 1779.

Blanchardin and Eglantine.—The Hystorye of Kynge Blanchardyn and Queen Eglantyne his Wyfe. Impr. by Caxton, 1485, fol.
This work consists of 54 chapters, with a table. Only one copy of this curious romance, and that imperfect, is known to exist. It was purchased by Earl Spencer at the sale of the Roxburghe Library, 6360, for 215*l.* 5*s.*
— The most pleasaunt historye of Blanchardine, sonne to the King of Friz and the faire lady Eglantine, Queene of Tormaday. By P. T. G. Gent. Lond. Wm. Blakewall, 1595. 4to.
Heber, 7*l.* 17*s.* 6*d.*

BLANCOURT, Handiequer de Art of making Glass, translated from the French. Lond. 1699. 8vo.
A useful treatise. Dent, pt. i. 227, 8*s.*

BLAND, Wood, Brewster, and Pennant. Discovery of New Britaine, in August, 1650, from Fort Henry to the Falls of Blandiana (with large map and one plate), 4to. 1651.
Sotheby, May, 1846, 5*l.* 17*s.* 6*d.* Sotheby, June, 1856 (no map or plate), 6*l.* 15*s.*

— Rev. Miles. Algebraical Problems, producing simple and quadratic Equations, with their Solutions. Lond. 1812. royal 8vo. 15*s.*
A work of considerable utility, frequently reprinted. A key was published 1827, 8vo. 9*s.*

— Revd. Robert. Translations chiefly from the Greek Anthology. with tales and miscellaneous poems. Lond. 1806. small 8vo. 5*s.*
— Collections from the Greek Anthology, and from the pastoral, elegiac, and dramatic poets of Greece. Lond. 1813. 8vo. 10*s.*
This is an enlarged edition of the previous work.
— New edition by J. H. Merivale. Lond. 1833. 8vo. 10*s.*
Each of these three editions contain matter not common to the others.

— Robt. M.D. Proverbs chiefly taken from the Adagia of Erasmus, with Explanations; and illustrated by Examples from the Spanish, Italian, French and English Languages. Lond 1814. crown 8vo. 2 vols.
Bindley, pt. i. 467, with a few MS. remarks by the author, 1*l.* 2*s.*

— Tobie. Baite for Momus, so called upon Occasion of a Sermon at Bedford, injuriously traduced by the factious. Lond. 1589. 4to.
Black letter. Contains pp. 38, with an epistle to the reader, and a wood-cut of St. George killing the dragon, on the back of the title. Inglis, 164, 7*s.* 6*d.* Gordonstoun, 157, 10*s.* 6*d.*

BLANDFORD, Marquis of. Catalogus Librorum qui in Bibliotheca Blandfordiensi reperiuntur, cum duobus Supplementis (by Rob. Triphook). Londini, 1812. 4to.

The privately printed catalogue of the White Knights Collection, since sold by auction, by Mr. Evans. Brockett, 747, 1*l*. 6s.

BLANDY, Mary. Trial of Mary Blandy, for the Murder of her Father. Lond. 1752. folio.

Reprinted 1752, in 8vo.

The following Tracts on this unhappy affair have appeared:

The Tryals and History of Mary Blandy and Eliz. Jeffreyes. 1752. 4to. with ports. Roxburghe, 1025, 19s.

Miss Mary Blandy's own Account of the Affair between her and Mr. Cranstoun. 1752. 8vo.

A candid Appeal to the Publick, by a Gentleman at Oxford. 1752. 8vo.

A Letter from a Gentleman to Miss Mary Blandy, with her Answer thereto, 1752. 8vo.

The secret History of Miss Blandy, from her first Appearance at Bath, to her Execution at Oxford. 1752. 8vo.

Memoirs of William Henry Cranstoun, Esq. 1752. 8vo. portrait.

An impartial Enquiry into the Case of Miss Blandy, with Reflections on her Trial, Defence. Repentance, Denial and Death. 1753. 8vo.

The fair Parricide, a Tragedy of three Acts, founded on the late melancholy Event. 1752. 8vo.

Captain Cranstoun's Account of the Poisoning the late Mr. Blandy, declared solemnly by him before he died at Furnes, in Flanders, on the 30th of November last. 1753. 8vo.

The genuine Lives of Capt. Cranstoun and Miss Mary Blandy. By a Gentleman, who was a Spectator at her Trial and Death, and afterwards accompanied the Captain in his Travels through France. 1753. 8vo. with a p'int.

[The female Parricide, a Tragedy, by Edward Crane, of Manchester. 1761. 8vo.

Roxburghe, 1026. Nine Tracts, 17s. Baker, 42. Six Tracts, 1*l*. 10s.

— William. Castle, or Picture of Pollicy. Lond. Daye. 1581. 4to.

Black letter, 30 leaves, besides 4 of prefixes, including the title. This curious tract contains an account of the exploits of 'M. John Noris, Generall of the army of the States in Friseland.' A copy is in the British Museum.

BLAQUIERE, Edward. Letters from the Mediterranean. Lond. 1824. 8vo. 2 vols.

These volumes chiefly relate to the civil and political state of Sicily, Malta, Tunis and Tripoli, and contain much valuable information. The author has likewise published several works on Greece, in support of the attempts to rescue it from the Ottoman power.

BLAXTON, John. English Usurer, or Usury condemned by the most learned and famous Divines of the Church of England, &c. Lond. 1634. 4to. with a frontispiece.

At the end are verses by George Wither. Nassau, pt. i. 413, 10s. Gordonstoun, 219, 19s. Towneley, pt. i. 389, 1*l*. 1s.

BLAYNEY, Allan. Festorum Metropolis. The metropolitaine Feast of the Birth-day of our Saviour Jesus Christ, annually to be kept holy by them that call upon him in all Nations. Lond. 1654. small 8vo.

A copy is in the British Museum. Bibl. Anglo-Poet. 260.

— Benjamin, D.D. Dissertation, by Way of Inquiry, into the true Import and Application of the Vision related Dan. ix. 20. to the End. Oxford, 1775. 4to.

A learned tract, in which some of Professor Michaelis'opinions are controverted.

— on Jeremiah. *See* JEREMIAH.

— Lord. Narrative of a forced Journey through Spain and France, with a Sequel. Lond. 1815-16. 8vo. 3 vols.

A severe critique on this work appeared in the Quart. Rev. xiv. 112--20, and xv. 183—7.

Blazon of Coloures in Armoryes and Ensignes military, translated (oute of a little Frenche Booke printed at Parys, 1546) by me R(ichard) R(obinson). Lond. by R. I. for Iohn Wolfe (1583).

A long description of this very rare book will be found in the British Bibliographer, i. 125—82.

BLENERHASSETT, Thomas. A revelation of the true Minerva.

London, T. Dawson for T. Woodcoke, 1582. 4to.
Evans, Dec. 6, 1821, fine copy, 9l. Heber, 4l. 12s. 6d.

BLENERHASSETT, Thomas. A Direction for the Plantation of Ulster, 1610. 4to.
Blenerhassett was one of the writers in the Mirror for Magistrates.

BLESENSIS, Peter. Bathoniensis Archidyaconi. Epistolæ quorum primum pertinet ad regem Angliæ. Folio. edit. prima. n.d. 2l. 2s.
(Reprinted in his works.)

BLETERIE, J. P. R. de la. Life of Julian the Apostate. Lond. 1746. 8vo.
A curious and well written performance.

BLIGH, Richard. Reports of Cases heard in the House of Lords on Appeals and Writs of Error in 1819-20. Lond. 1823-5. royal 8vo. 3 vols. and vol. iv., pt. 1. New Series, 1827-36, royal 8vo. 10 vols. vol. xi. pts. 1, 2, and 3.
These reports are in continuation of those by Mr. Dow, and are still in the course of publication.

— William. Narrative of the Mutiny on Board the Bounty; and the subsequent Voyage of Part of the Crew in the Ship's Boat from Tofoa, one of the Friendly Islands, to Timor, a Dutch Settlement in the East Indies. Written by Lieut. William Bligh. Lond. 1790. 4to. with charts, 7s.
Fonthill, 309, 14s.

— Voyage to the South Sea. Lond. 1792. 4to. with port. by J. Condé. 12s.
Bindley, pt. l. 565, 15s. Drury, 567, 17s. Roxburghe, 7172, 1l. 1s. Fonthill, 3098, 2l. 11s.

BLITH, Walter. English Improver, or a new Survey of Husbandry, &c. Lond. 1649. 4to.
'A well known and very ingenious work.' —*Quart. Review.* Subsequent editions, with additions, were entitled 'The Improver Improved.' The third impression, 1652, with portrait and plates, 10s.

BLOISSE. See BLOSIUS.

BLOME, Richard. Description of the Island of Jamaica, with the other Isles and Territories of America to which the English are related, with the State of Algiers. Lond. 1672. 12mo. with maps.
White Knights, pt. i. 472, 19s. Nassau, pt. i. 271, 7s. The edition 1678, 8vo. with port. Roxburghe, 7349, 8s.

BLOME, R. Britannia, or a Geographical Description of England, Scotland, and Ireland, and the Isles and Territories thereto belonging. Lond. 1673. folio with arms of subscribers and maps, also a plan of London before the fire, by W. Hollar.
A 'most entire piece of theft out of Camden and Speed.'—*Bp. Nicolson.*
Roxburghe, 8654, 5s. LARGE PAPER, Dent, pt. i. 342, with maps and arms coloured, 1l. Towneley, pt. ii. 177, with the plates coloured, 1l. 3s.

— Alphabetical Account of the Nobility and Gentry of England and Wales. Lond. 1673. folio.
This useful list, consisting of pp. 120, occurs at the end of Camden's Britannia, 1673. The arms are in number eight hundred and twelve.

— Essay to Heraldry; in two Parts. Lond. 1684. 8vo. pp. 259.
Contains pp. 259, with a dedication to George Earl of Berkeley, a table and plates. An edition, entitled Art of Heraldry, 1685, 1693. 12mo.

— Gentleman's Recreation, consisting of Horsemanship, Hawking, Hunting, Fowling, Fishing, &c. Lond. 1710. folio, with plates.
Marquis of Townshend, 418, 2l. Edition 1686. (Preferable on account of the impressions.) Roxburghe, 1735, 2l. 6s. LARGE PAPER, Dent, pt. i. 343, morocco, 5l. 10s.

— History of the Bible. See ROYAUMONT.
'Richard Bloome, a kind of an arms painter, (but originally a ruler of books and paper), who has since practised, for divers years, progging tricks in employing necessitous persons to write in several arts, and to get contributions of noblemen.'— *Ant. à Wood.*

BLOMEFIELD, Rev. Francis. History of the ancient City and Burgh of Thetford. Fersfield, 1739. 4to.
Title; dedication, 2 pages; contents, 2 pages: history, A—Zz, 184 pages; appendix, 12 pages. This work is inserted in the author's first volume of his history of

Norfolk. Towneley, pt. ii. 273, 5s. Bindley, pt. i. 1292, 1l. 1s. Nassau, pt. i. 415, 12s.

BLOMEFIELD, Rev. Francis. Collectanea Cantabrigiensia; or, Collections relating to Cambridge University, Town, and County. Norwich 1750. 4to.

'Contains 268 pages, besides the title. The author began his Collectanea with an account of Ely Roll, Luton, and Caddington Churches in Bedfordshire, and Atwood Church, in Buckinghamshire, which were printed in 28 quarto pages, including Gerton in this county, which forms p. 6 of the present edition; but choosing to confine himself to Cambridgeshire, he cancelled these pages, and added Cantabrigiensia to his title.'—*Gough*.

Towneley, pt. ii. 274, 2l. 10s. Heath, 4634, 14s. Nassau, pt. i. 416, 15s. Marq. of Townshend, 374, 3l. Some copies bear the date of 1751. Bp. of Ely, 206, 7s. 6d. Dent, pt. i. 467, 8s. Reed, 3334, 10s. 6d. Bindley, pt. i. 1114, 11s. 6d.

—— Essay towards a Topographical History of the County of Norfolk, continued by the Rev. Charles Parkin. Fersfield, &c., 1739—75. fol., 5 vols.

Dowdeswell, 146, russia, 12l. 5s. Dent, pt. i. 344, russia, 14l. 14s. Marquis of Townshend, 419, 17l. 10s. Towneley, pt. ii. 321, russia, 18l. 18s. Heath, 4618, russia, 18l. 18s.

Collation.—Vol.i.1739,Title; list of subscribers, 4 pages (*scarce*); introduction, 3 pages; History, A—9 K, 771 pages; indexes, pp. 772—808. *Plates*, besides those on the letter-press. 1. Monumental figures at p. 68. 2. The prospect of Bukenham Castle, p. 261. 3. Monument, with the portrait of Thomas Lord Richardson, at p. 683, also separate pedigrees of the family of Blomefield, at p. 74 (*scarce*); of Holland, p. 232; of Wright, p. 368; of Jernegan, on 4 pages, between pp. 660 and 661; of William, Lord Richardson, p. 684. Pages 765 to 770 contain the pedigree of the family of Wodehouse, and in some copies pp. 33 to 48 inclusive, are wanting.

Vol. ii. Fersfield, 1741, or Norwich, 1745. Title; dedication to John Nuthall, Esq.; (*scarce*) the history, &c. 913 pages—pages 770 to 780 omitted. *Plates*. 1. A plan of Norwich, with references on a separate folded sheet at p. 1, (*both scarce*). 2. Monument of Bp. Hall, p. 414. (This plate is positively no part of the book. The error has been perpetuated from Dawson Turner's illustrated copy, collated by Upcott.) 3. The Ichnography of Norwich Cathedral, p. 489. 4. The Seals of Norwich Cathedral, p. 584. 5. Monument of Aug. Briggs, Esq. p. 641. 6. Monument of Edmond Hobart, Esq. p. 643. 7. Monument of Richard Manby, p. 749. 8. Fac-simile of a Grant of the Town of Hexham, p. 848. A Pedigree of the family of Briggs faces p. 640.

Vol. iii. Lynn, 1769. Title, preface, and errata, 8 pages; the history, A—10. K 2, 870 pages; indexes, 8 pages. *Plates*. 1. Portrait of Sir Henry Spelman, Knt. p. 464. 2. Brass of the Fountaine Family, p. 522. 3. Monument of Erasmus Earle, p. 532. 4. Monument of Thomas Marsham, Esq. p. 593. 5. Effigies of Catherine Schuldham, p. 661. 6. Portrait of James Calthorpe, p. 762. 7-8. The East and West Fronts of Houghton Hall, p. 798. pedigree of the Family of Bedingfield, at p. 482.

Vol. iv. Lynn, 1775. Title; list of subscribers, 2 pages; the history, &c. pp. 794. *Plates*. 1. Forty-three shields of arms, at p. 60. 2. Portrait of John Dethick, p. 217. 3. The south-east prospect of Cromere Church, p. 304. 4. Monument of Robert Wiggett, p. 383. 5. Monument of Rice Wiggett, p. 383. 6. Monument of William Bulwar, p. 459. 7. Plan of the town of King's Lynn, p. 574. 8. A south-east view of King's Lynn, p. 576. 9. A chronological table of the Mayors of Lynn Regis, p. 586. 10. A view of Lynn Market Cross, p. 594. 11. A map of Marsh Land in Norfolk, p. 691. 12. St. Peter's Church at Walpole, p. 716. 13. Tomb of Thomas Winde, Esq. p. 780.

Vol. v. Lynn, 1775. Title; the history, &c. pp. 783—1709. *Plates*. 1. View of the seat of Richard Milles, p. 996. 2. North view of North Elmham Church, p. 1000. 3. South-west prospect of Snettisham Church, p. 1315. 4. Arms and seals in the Priory Church of Horsham St. Faith's, p. 1358. 5. View of Yarmouth, p. 1589. The pedigree of the family of L'Estrange, on two folded sheets, faces p. 1265. Some sets have reprinted titles, dated alike.

—— Essay towards a Topographical History of the County of Norfolk, continued by the Rev. Charles Parkin. Lond. 1805—10. royal 8vo. 11 vols.

Duke of York, 744, 5l. 5s. Sir M. M. Sykes, pt. i. 427, 5l. 7s. LARGE PAPER in 4to.

Collation.—Vol. i. pp. xvi. and 548; index, 2 pages, and 9 plates, and pedigrees.

Vol. ii. pp. 569, index, 3 pages, and 4 pedigrees and plates.

Vol. iii. pp. viii. and 672, not including index, with a folded sheet plan of the City of Norwich, and an explanation to face the plan.

Vol. iv. 580 pp. besides two titles, contents, index, and 7 plates and pedigrees.

Vol. v. pp. 527, besides title, and an index of three pages.

Vol. vi. Title; preface, 7 pages; history, 521 pp. not including the index, and 6 plates and pedigrees.
Vol. vii. pp. 520, besides title. an index of 3 pages, and 6 plates and pedigrees.
Vol. viii. pp. 548, besides title, an index of 4 pages, and 9 plates and pedigrees. At p. 553 is a chronological table of the Mayors of Lynn Regis.
Vol. ix. pp. 527, besides the title, an index of 4 pages, and 5 plates.
Vol. x. pp. 479, besides the title, an index of 4 pages, and a pedigree and two plates.
Vol. xi. Two titles; history, 402 pages; indexes, 80 pages; some remarkable occurrences, &c. 3 pages; list of subscribers, 11 pages; directions to the binder, 3 pages; and a view of Yarmouth at p. 255.

BLOMFIELD, Charles James, Bishop of Chester (late Bishop of London). Dissertation upon the traditional Knowledge of a promised Redeemer, which subsisted before the Advent of our Saviour. Cambridge, 1819. 8vo. 4s. 6d.

— Twelve Lectures on the Acts of the Apostles; to which is added a new Edition of Five Lectures on the Gospel of St. John, as bearing Testimony to Jesus Christ. Lond. 1828. 8vo. 10s. 6d.

The former edition of the Lectures on Saint John appeared 1828, 12mo. 2s.

BLONDEL, David. Treatise of the Sibyls, translated by J. Davies. Lond. 1661. folio, 5s.
Roxburghe, 6*l*. 0, 9s. 6d.

— Pindar and Horace compared, translated by J. Davies. Lond. 1680. 8vo. 4s.

Another translation by Sir Edward Sherburne, 1696, 8vo. 4s.

BLONDEVILLE. See BLUNDEVILLE.

BLOOD, Thomas. Remarks on the Life and Death of the famed Mr. Blood. Lond. 1680. folio.

Reprinted in the eighth volume of the Somers Collection of Tracts, and in Smeeton's Collection, 4to.

Blood for Blood; or, Murthers revenged, briefly set forth in thirty tragical Histories, to which are added five more, being the sad Product of our own Times, viz., Charles the Martyr, and four others. Lond. 1661. 8vo. with front.

Sotheby's in May, 1848, 15s.

BLOOMFIELD, Ezekiel. Lectures on the Philosophy of History, accompanied with Notes and illustrative Engravings. Lond. 1820. 4to. 20s.

— Robert. Farmer's Boy, a rural Poem. Lond. 1805. 12mo. 5s.

Frequently reprinted. An elegant edition, 1800, 4to. with wood cuts by Bewick, 5s. LARGE PAPER, 10s. 6d.

In illustration of this poem, a selection of views was published by Messrs. Storer and Greig, 1806, 8vo. 4s.

— Rural Tales, Ballads, and Songs. Lond. 1802. 12mo. 4s.

An elegant edition in 8vo. was published 1802, with wood cuts by Bewick, 5s. LARGE PAPER, 4to. 8s. This celebrated poet has likewise published Wild Flowers, 1806. Miscellaneous Poems, 1806. The Banks of Wye. May Day with the Muses, 1822. 12mo. Remains in Poetry and Prose, 1824. fscap. 8vo. 2 vols. 12s.

— Rev. S. T. Recensio synoptica Annotationis sacræ, being a critical Digest and synoptical Arrangement of the most important Annotations on the New Testament, exegetical, philological, and doctrinal. Lond. 1827. 8vo. 8 vols.

'One of the most important works in sacred literature which has been offered to the attention of Bible students for many years.'—*Horne.*

BLORE, Edward. Monumental Remains of noble and eminent English Persons. Lond. 1825. imperial 8vo. 5 pts. with 30 plates, 3*l*. 15s.

An elegant work, which it is to be regretted did not meet with sufficient encouragement. Quarto, 6*l*. 6s. INDIA PAPER proofs, 9*l*. (Since much reduced.)

— Thomas. History and Antiquities of the County of Rutland. Stamford (1811). royal folio. vol. 1, part ii. 3*l*. 3s. LARGE PAPER, 4*l*. 4s.

This work merits great praise, and deservedly ranks very high among such publications. Only this part has been published.

— History of the Manor and Manor House of South Winfield, in Derbyshire. Lond. 1793. 4to.

No. iii. of the Miscellaneous Antiquities,

in continuation of the Biblioth. Topogr. Brit. Bindley, pt. i. 909, 6s. Drury, 568, 7s.

BLORE, Robert. Account of the Public Schools, Hospitals, and other charitable Foundations in the Borough of Stamford. Stamford, 1813. 8vo.
B—3 A 3, besides title, introduction and contents.

BLOSIUS, F. Mirrour for Monkes. Paris, 1676. 18mo. with front. and plates.
White Knights, pt. i. 473, mor. 1l. 5s.

BLOUNT, Charles. Miscellaneous Works. Lond. 1695. 12mo. 4s.
The works of this writer are held in some little estimation with the Deists.

— Edward. Ars Aulica, the Courtier's Arte. Lond. 1607. 16mo. 5s.

— Horæ Subsescivæ. Observation and Discovrses. Lond. 1626. 8vo. 6s.

— See CONESTAGGIO, Jerome. GARZONI.

EARLE, John, Bishop of Salisbury.

— Sir Henry. Voyage into the Levant. Third Edition. Lond. 1638. 4to. 5s.
Of little value or authority; reprinted in the Oxford and Pinkerton's Collections of Voyages and Travels. Nassau, pt. i. 419, 7s. The first edition appeared 1636, 4to. Fonthill, 2612, 1l.; reprinted 1637, 1650, 1669, Nassau, pt. i. 276, 5s.

— Tho. Journey to Jerusalem in 1669. 12mo. 1672. 10s. 6d.

— English Academie of Eloquence. Lond. 1654. 12mo.
The title engraved by W. Faithorne contains portraits of Lord Bacon and Sir P. Sidney. 1656. Nassau, pt. i. 273, 1l.

— Boscobel, or the compleat History of his sacred Majesties most miraculous Preservation after the Battle of Worcester. The third edition, with Additions. Lond. 1680.
Best edition. Part i. 81 pp. Part ii. 90 pp. also five plates. 'Pen'd,' says A. à Wood, 'with great truth and fidelity.' Baker, 44, russia, 2l. 3s. A notice of the work and its various editions will be found in the Retrosp. Review, xiv. 47—68. The edition 1660. Bindley, pt. i. 616, 13s. Towneley, pt. ii. 52, 16s. Williams, 270, with portraits of Charles II, Mrs. Jane Lane, Richard Penderell, and the plan, morocco, 4l. 14s. 6d.—1682. with port. of Charles II., ground plot and plan. Jadis, 72, morocco, 2l. 8s.—1692. Nassau, pt. i. 290, 17s.— 1725. Roxburghe, 8475, 1l. 16s.—1745. White Knights, pt. i. 511, 9s.

— Glossographia, or Dictionary of hard words. Lond. 1719. 8vo. 5s.
The best edition. It was first printed in 1656; reprinted 1670, 1671, 1674, 1679, 1691, 1707.

— Law Dictionary and Glossary of obscure Words and Terms, in ancient Law, Records, &c., by W. Nelson. Lond. 1717. folio, 5s.
Best edition. The former editions, 1670, 1691.

— A world of Errors discovered in the New World of Words, folio. 1673. See PHILLIPS (Ed.)

— Fragmenta Antiquitatis; or, ancient Tenures of Land, and jocular Customs of Manors, with considerable Additions, by H. M. Beckwith. Lond. 1815. 4to. 2l. 12s. 6d.
Best edition of a very popular work. FINE PAPER, 3l. 8s. The original edition, Lond. 1679, 8vo. Heath, 4558, 7s. New Edition, with Alterations, Additions, &c. by Josiah Beckwith. York, 1784. 8vo. Roxburghe, 977, 1l. 10s. Supplement, 553, 16s. Dent, pt. i. 229, russia, 11s. Nassau, pt. i. 276, 1l.

— Art of making Devises. See ESTIENNE (Henry).

— Thomas Pope. Censura celebrium Authorum; sive Tractatus in quo varia Virorum doctorum de clarissimis cujusque Seculi Scriptoribus Judicia traduntur. Lond. 1690. fol. 10s. 6d.
Heath, 222, 18s. An erudite work, much esteemed by the curious, reprinted at Geneva, 1694, 4to. and again 1710 and 1718.

— Natural History: containing many not common Observations. extracted out of the best modern Writers. Lond. 1693. 8vo. 3s. 6d.

— De Re Poetica; or Remarks upon Poetry, with Characters and Censures of the most considerable Poets, whether antient or modern. Lond. 1694. 4to.

Contains pp. 392. Bibl. Anglo-Poet. 73, 1l. 5s. Heath,221, 3s. 6d. Reed, 6690, with MS. additions by Mr. Wm. Oldys, 3l. 11s.

— Essays. Lond. 1697, 8vo. 5s.
Mr. Chalmers observes, that 'in point of learning, judgment, and freedom of thought, these essayes are in no way inferior to those of the celebrated Montaigne.'

BLOW, John. Amphion Anglicus. Lond. 1700. folio, with portrait by R. White.
Nassau, pt. i. 445, 6s. Towneley, pt. ii. 839, 1l. 1s.

Blue Blanket.—Historical Account of the Blue Blanket, or Craftsmen Banner, with the Prerogatives of the Crafts of Edinburgh. Edinb. 1780. small 8vo. with cuts.
Nassau, pt. i. 1576, 6s.

BLUMENBACH, J. F. Manual of the Elements of Natural History: translated from the tenth German Edition, by R. T. Gore. New Edition. Lond. 1826. 8vo. 14s.
A translation of the author's system of comparative Anatomy, with additions by W. Lawrence, appeared 1807. 8vo. 12s.

BLUMENTHAL, Mme. de. Life of General de Zieten, translated from the German by the Rev. B. Beresford. Berlin, 1803. 8vo. 2 vols. 9s.

Blundell (or Ince) Gallery.—Engravings and Etchings of the principal Statues, Busts, Bas-Reliefs, Sepulchral Monuments, Cinerary Urns, &c., in the Collection of Henry Blundell, Esq., at Ince. 158 plates. 1809. imperial folio.
Privately printed. Fifty copies were struck off for presents. (Sometimes bound in 2 vols., vol. i. 77 plates, vol. ii. 81 plates. A copy is in the British Museum. Combe, 1052, with a MS. memorandum of the plates, morocco, 33l. 12s. 6d.)

BLUNDELL, H. Account of the Statues, Busts, Bas-Reliefs, Cinerary Urns, and Paintings at Ince. Liverpool, 1803. 4to., privately printed, front. and six plates. 2l. 2s.

BLUNDEVILLE, Thomas. Three Treatises, the one called the learned Prince, the other the Fruites of Foes, the thyrde the Porte of Rest. Lond. by Wyllyam Seres, 1561. small 4to.

The first is written in four-lined stanzas, and contains C 3, in fours; the second, likewise in four-lined stanzas, with a separate title page, contains E 2 in fours; the third tract, which also has a separate title-page, is in prose, and contains K in fours. The whole are taken from Plutarch. Bibl. Anglo-Poet. 51, 12l. 12s. resold by Saunders in 1818, for 5l. 15s. 6d. Reprinted, according to Herbert, 1568, 1580, 8vo. and n.d. 1609.

— Treatise declaring howe many Counsels, and what Maner of Counselers a Prince that will gouerne well ought to haue. Lond. by William Seres (1570). 16mo.
This treatise, dedicated to the 'Erle of Leycester,' contains Q in fours. It was first written in Spanish by Federigo Furio, and afterwards translated into Italian, by Alfonso D'Ulloa. Sotheby, June, 1856, fine copy, 2l. 11s.

— Methode of wryting and reading Hystories, according to the Precepts of Francischo Patritio, an Accontio Tridentino. Lond. 1574. 16mo.
This treatise, dedicated to the 'Erle of Leycester,' contains H in fours. Bright, 1845, 2l. 2s.

— Briefe Description of vniuersal Mappes and Cardes, and of their Vse; and also the Vse of Ptholemey his Tables. Lond. 1589. 4to.
Black letter. Dedicated to Mr. Francis Windam. F 2, in fours, with the mariner's quadrant to fold. Inglis, 167, 11s.

— His Exercises containing sixe Treatises. Lond. 1594. 4to. 10s. 6d.
Each tract has a separate title-page, but the folios are continued to 350, with tables and projections. Reprinted 1597, 4to. with the addition of 'A briefe Description of vniversal Maps and Cards,' &c.

— Art of Logike. Lond. 1599. 4to. 10s. 6d.
Contains, Preface 'To the Reader. A Postscript. The Contents,' 170 pages.

— Booke containing the ryding and breakinge greate Horses. Lond. by William Seres. 4to.
Contains besides prefixes, F 4 in eights. At the end are 50 wood-cuts of the halter and various sorts of bitts.

— The foure chiefest Offices belonging to Horsemanship. Lond. 1580. 4to. 7s. 6d.

The last three tracts have distinct title-pages, &c. The first treatise contains 22 leaves; the second, 80; the third, 22; the last, 86; besides their several prefixes. Reprinted 1597 and 1609. First edition, 1565-6. Inglis, 165, imperfect, 10s. Edition, 1597. Gardner, 1854. mor. 2l. 7s.

BLUNDEVILLE, Thos. The Theoriques of the seven Planets. Lond. 1602. 4to. 10s. 6d.

Blundeville likewise published 'The Making, Description and Use of the Two Instruments for Sea-men to find out the Latitude.' Lond. 1602. 4to.

BLUNT, Charles. Essay on Mechanical Drawing. Lond. 1811. royal 4to. 3l. 3s.

— H. See BLOUNT, Henry.

— Rev. J. J. Vestiges of ancient Manners and Customs discoverable in modern Italy and Sicily. Lond. 1823. 8vo. 9s. 6d.

Contains pp. 293. Drury, 476, 18s.

— Veracity of the Gospels and Acts of the Apostles, argued from the undersigned Coincidences to be found in them, when compared, 1. with each other, and 2. with Josephus. Lond. 1828. 8vo.

An admirable supplement to Dr. Lardner's Credibility of the Gospel History, and to Dr. Paley's Horæ Paulinæ. A list of various other works of this able divine will be found in the London Catalogue.

— Leonard. Asse upon Asse, a Poem, 8vo.

Steevens, 1047.

BOADEN, James. Inquiry into the Authenticity of various Pictures and Prints, which, from the Decease of the Poet to our own Times, have been offered to the Public as Portraits of Shakspeare. Lond. 1824. 8vo. with five portraits, 15s. LARGE PAPER, in 4to. 1l. 11s. 6d.

— Memoirs of the Life of John Philip Kemble, Esq., including a History of the Stage from the Time of Garrick to the present Period. Lond. 1825. 8vo. 2 vols. with portrait after Sir T. Lawrence. 28s.

Mr. Boaden likewise published Memoirs of Mrs. Siddons, 8vo. 2 vols. with a portrait after Sir Thomas Lawrence; Life of Mrs. Inchbald, 2 vols. 8vo. 1833, portrait.

Memoirs of Mrs. Jordan, 2 vols. 8vo. 1831. port.

BOARDMAN, Thomas. Dictionary of the Veterinary Art. Lond. 1805. 4to. with 39 plates, 1l. 1s.

BOATE, Gerard. Ireland's Natural History, published by Samuel Hartlib. Lond. 1652. 12mo. 3s. 6d.

'A work excellent in its kind; as not only full of truth and certainty, but written with much judgment, order and exactness.' —Nicolson. Bindley, pt. 1. 600, 5s. 6d.

— Natural History of Ireland, in three parts, by Dr. Gerard Boate, Thomas Molineaux, M.D. and others. Dublin, 1726. 4to.

Towneley, pt. ii. 143, 11s. Bindley, pt. 1. 729, 15s. Heath, 4778, 18s. An edition, Dublin, 1755. 4to. Marquis of Townshend, 375, 1l. 11s. 6d. Another, Dublin, 1799, 4to.

BOAYSTUAU, Peter. Theatrum Mundi, whereunto is added a Worke of the Excellencie of Mankynd. Englished by John Alday. Lond. 1574. 16mo.

Black letter. Contains 287 pages, besides title, dedication to Sir Wm. Chester, Knt. the printer to the reader; Peter Boaystuau to the reader; and table. Burton was probably acquainted with this work, as there are many passages in his Anatomy of Melancholy which bear a strong resemblance. Boswell, 227, 3s. 6d. Bindley, pt. 1. 461, 4s.—An edition without date, Steevens, 773, 4s. 6d. Inglis, 93, 8s. Another, 1581. Sotheby's in 1824, 19s.

BOBBIN, Tim. See COLLIER, John.

BOCCACCIO, Giovanni. Il Decamerone. Londra, 1725. 4to. 14s.

An accurate edition. 'Ristampato secondo l'Edizione dell' Anno 1527, da P. Rolli.' Drury, 570, morocco, 1l. 7s. LARGE PAPER, in folio, 1l. 11s. 6d. Stanley, 488, red mor. 15l. An edition of the Decamerone, Lond. 1727, 12mo. 2 vols. 10s. 6d.

— Decamerone (da Vincenzio Martinelli, colla Prefazione dell' Editore, e Vita di Boccaccio, Tavola ed Osservazioni). Lond. 1762. royal 4to. 18s.

A fine edition, containing pp. xvi. and 574, 'Tavola,' 8 pages, and 'Osservazioni,' 35 pp. also a port. of Martinelli, engraved by F. Bartolozzi.

— Il Decamerone. Lond. 1792. 4to. 1l. 1s.

A reprint of Martinelli's edition.

There are several editions bearing the imprint of London, which were printed abroad.

BOCCACCIO, Giovanni. Il Decamerone, con un Discorso critico da Ugo Foscolo. Lond. 1825. crown 8vo. 3 vols. with a portrait and ten engravings by Fox, from designs by Stothard, 2*l*. 12s. 6d.

'In this new and beautifully printed edition of the Decameron, the text has been carefully revised by Signor Foscolo, whose prefatory essay on the genius of Boccaccio will afford great pleasure and instruction to the admirers of the old Italian novelist.'

LARGE PAPER, in demy 8vo. 4*l*. 14s. 6d. ON INDIA PAPER, 6*l* 6s. One copy was taken off upon VELLUM, Hibbert, 48*l* 6s. resold at Hanrotts, 21*l*. Stothard's Illustrations are sold separately, 1*l*. Proofs, 2*l*. India Paper Proofs, 3*l*.

— Decameron, translated into English. Lond. 1625, 1620. folio, two parts, woodcut titles. (First English translation.)

Part i. 1625. Bindley, pt. i. 191, 1*l*. 13s. Part ii. 1620. White Knights, 767, russia, 1*l*. 10s. Bindley, pt. i. 190, 1*l*. Gordonstoun, 313, 1*l*. 4s. Two Parts, 1625, 1620. Garrick, 527. 1*l*. 13s. Nassau, pt. i. 446, with both the titles and wood-cuts, 2*l*. 11s.

— Novels and Tales. Lond. 1684. folio, with portrait by White, 9s.

Another, Lond. 1712, 8vo. Goldsmid, 693, 7s. Roxburghe, 6305, 1*l*. 4s.

— The Decameron, translated from the Italian. Lond. 1741. 8vo. 10s. 6d.

White Knights, 481, morocco, 3*l*. Nassau, pt. i. 277, 10s. Dr. Mosely, 2*l*. 10s,

— The Decameron, translated from the Italian, with remarks on the Life and Writings of Boccaccio, and an Advertisement (by E. Dubois). Lond. 1804. 8vo. 2 vols. 16s.

ROYAL PAPER, 1*l*. 11s. 6d. Reprinted 1820, 8vo. 10s. 6d. 18[22], 18mo. 4 vols. 7s.

[Nearly all the English translations of Boccaccio are more or less imperfect, wanting Novel X. of the *third* day, and X. of the *ninth* day. The edition published as one of Bohn's extra volumes is complete, but some passages are in French or Italian.]

— The Boke called de John Bochas descriuinge the Falle of Princis Princessis and other Nobles, trāslated ito Englissh, by John Lydgate, &c. Lond. by Richard Pynson 1494. folio.

First translation, in black letter, consisting of 214 leaves, with wood-cuts. There are two sets of signatures, each running in eights; the first extends to V, the second to H, which has only three printed leaves. The prologue occupies 3 leaves, a i being blank. Copies are in the Bodleian, in Heber's, and in Earl Spencer's library Towneley, pt. i. russia, 27*l*. 16s. 6d.

— Another Edition. Lond. by Richarde Pynson, 1527. folio.

This edition has double columns, running titles, and the leaves numbered, with catch-words, regularly every page to folio xxxviii., afterwards only at the close of every signature, and even then sometimes omitted. It contains fol. ccxvi. Dent. pt. i. 345, russia, 9*l*. 1854. 22*l*. 10s.

— Another Edition. Lond. by R. Tottel, 1554. folio.

Black letter, with wood-cuts. Prefixed are a table of contents, and 'The Prologe of John Lydgate,' at the end of which is a cut of the author. The poem is divided into nine books, with a cut before each of them, and ends on fol. ccxix. To this edition is annexed 'The Daunce of Machabree,' which finishes on fol. CCxxiii Towneley, pt. i. 428, 2*l*. 12s. 6d. White Knights, 772, 3*l*. 3s. Alchorne, 92, 3*l*. 9s. Bibl. Anglo-Poet. 416, 6*l*. 6s.

— Another Edition. Lond. by John Wayland, 1558. folio, 2*l*. 2s.

This edition in black letter, without cuts, seems to have been printed at two presses. The first seven books contain 'folio Clxiiii, besides the title and table of contents on sig. x, six leaves, and the first prologue on three leaves more, not numbered, though part of sig. A. The eighth and ninth books with a fresh set of signatures, contain fol. xxxvii; and many copies have another leaf with the title 'A Memorial of such Princes,' &c. at the back of which is 'The copy of the Queenes Maiesties Letters Patentes.' Roxburghe, 3261, morocco, 13*l*. 2s. 6d. Field, 1735, russia, 3*l*. 3s..

— Another Edition. Lond. by John Wayland. folio.

Black Letter. A copy of this edition is in the British Museum. Nassau, pt. i. 447, 1*l*. 12s. Roscoe, 1829, 2*l*. 18s Sir M. M. Sykes, pt. ii. 260, russia, 3*l*. 13s. 6d.

'The work is not improperly styled a set of tragedies. It is not merely a narrative of men eminent for their rank and misfortunes. The plan is perfectly dramatic, and partly suggested by the pageants of the times. Every personage is supposed to appear before the poet, and to relate his respective sufferings: and the figures of these spectres are sometimes finely drawn. The book never was popular here, because it had no English examples.'—*Warton.*

BOCCACCIO. Philocopo, or disport of divers noble personages, 12mo. Imp. by Bynneman, 1567.
Farmer, 1*l.* 1s.

— Philocopo, etc. composed in Italian, by M. Iohn Bocace, turned into English, by H. G. 12mo. Lond. by Abell Jeffes, (for Thomas Woodcocke.) 1587.
Dedicated to 'M. Wm. Rice, Esq.' L, in eights. Townsley, pt. 1. 290, 2*l*. 1s.

— Amorous Fiammetta, done into English, by B. Giouano del M. Temp. (i.e. Barthol. Young, of the Mid. Temple). With Notes in the Margine, and with a Table in the Ende of the cheefest Matters. Printed by I.(ohn) C.(harlwood for Thomas Newman) 1587. 4to.
Dedicated to 'Sir William Hatton, Knight. To the noble & gallant Dames of the Cittie of Castale, in Mon Ferrato: Gabriel Giolito.—The authour his Prologue. Fiammetta speaketh.' 123 leaves. Inglis, 169, 5*l*. 15s. 6d. Roxburghe, 6308, 10*l*. 10s. Same copy, 1838, 5*l*. 5s.

— A pleasaunt and delightfull History of Galesus, Cymon, and Iphigenia, describing the Fickleness of Fortune in Love, translated out of Italian into English verse, by C. T. (Christopher Tye). Printed by Nicholas Wyer. 12mo.
Black letter, in stanzas. Extremely rare.

— A notable Historye of Nastagio and Trauersari, no less pitiefull than pleasaunt, translated out of Italian into English Verse, by C. T. Lond. by Thomas Purfoote, 1569. 12mo.
Black letter. According to Warton, 'Tye has unluckily applied 'to this tale, the same stanza which he used in translating the Acts of the Apostles.'

— Sigismonda and Guiscard. *See* WALTER, William.

— De Præclaris Mulieribus, translated from Bocasse, by Henry Parcare, Knight, Lord Morley. Lond. 1789. 8vo.

VOL. I.

A translation of the Preface, and a Specimen of the work only, in Waldron's Literary Museum, 1789.

BOCAGE, Madam du. Letters concerning England, Holland, and Italy. Lond. 1770. 12mo. 2 vols. 5s.
An entertaining work.

BOCCALINI, Trajan. Advertisements from Parnassus, translated into English, by H. Carey, Earl of Monmouth. Lond. 1656 or 7. folio, with portrait of the Earl, by Faithorne, 5s.
Reprinted 1669, 1674, with the Politick Touchstone, and in 1706, with a preface by Hughes, the Poet. Other works by this writer have been translated into English, viz. Newes from Parnassus. Helicon, 1622, 4s. and The new-found Politicke, 1626, 4to. 6s.

BOCCO, Paulus. Icones et Descriptiones rariorum Plantarum Siciliæ, Melitæ, Galliæ et Italiæ. Oxon. 1674. 4to. 8s.
Edited by Morison.

BOCCUS.—The History of Kyng Boccus and Sydracke. Translated by Hugo of Caumpeden oute of Frenche in to Englisshe. Lond. by Thomas Godfray. (1510?) 4to.
Black letter. B. to S. 4, in the second alphabet, with title and table of contents. A romance in verse, consisting of questions and answers, 362 in number. Steevens, 774. (no title) 2*l*. 19s. Roxburghe, 3272, 30*l*. resold White Knights, 550, 35*l*. 14s. Heber, 24*l*. 10s.
See Warton's Poetry, ii. 408. Ames, by Dibdin, iii. 20. Ritson's Bibl. Poet. 501. Wood, by Bliss, i. 104, 465.

— The Boke of Demaundes, of the Scyence of Philosophye and Astronomye, betwene Kynge Boccus and the Phylosopher Sydracke. Printed by Robert Wyer. 12mo.
Contains D in fours. This tract has neither preface nor introduction: but it consists of 24 questions, with their answers in prose.
In the British Museum is 'Certayne Questyons of Kynge Boethus of the Maners. Tokyns, and Condycions of Man, with the Answeres made to the same, by the Phylosopher Sydrac. Printed by Rob. Wyer.' 12mo. Black letter.

— A Booke of Medicines of King

Q

Bocchus. Lond. by Rob. Redman. 4to.

BOCHART, Samuel. Hierozoicon, sive bipertitum Opus de Animalibus, S. Scripturæ. Lond. 1663. folio, 2 vols. 1*l*. 1s.

'His Geographia Sacra hath made him famous in the learned werld, as also his Hierozoicon; for both which, eminent authors do in a high manner celebrate his name.'—*Ant. à Wood.*

BOCHAS. *See* BOCCACCIO.

BODENHAM, John. Politeuphuia. Wits Commonwealth. Lond. 1598. 8vo.

A collection of sententious extracts from the ancient moral philosophers, &c. frequently reprinted. The eighteenth edition was printed 1661. An edition 'newly corrected and amended.' 1644. Another, 1699. Palladis Tamia, Wits Treasury, by F. Meres, forms a second part.

— Wits Theater of the little World. Lond. 1598. 16mo.

Reprinted 1599. Gordonstoun, 308, 1*l*. 15s. Nassau, pt. ii. 1252, 1*l*. 1s. Perry, pt. iv. 459, 5s. 6d. 460, 1*l*. 13s.

— Bel-vedere, or the Garden of the Muses. Lond. 1600. 16mo.

A collection of mere sentences, from most of the principal poets living and dead, consisting of pp 236, besides the table of contents, &c. [R. in eights.] Sir M. M. Sykes, pt. i. 289. (one leaf MS.) 3*l*. Perry, pt. iv. 315, 5*l*. pt. i. 533, 6*l*. 6s. Steevens, 1127, with additions and a MS. index, 11*l*. 15s. Bindley, pt. i. 455, 13*l*. 2s. 6d. Bibl. Anglo-Poet. 55, 25*l*. Heber, 1*l*. 10s. Major Pearson's copy with MS. mem. by Park, resold Jolly, 1843, 6*l*. 2s. 6d.

— Garden of the Muses. Lond. 1610. 8vo.

Contains pp. 250. Mr. Oldys doubted the existence of this edition, in which the editor's proemium is omitted. It consists of pp. 250. Nassau, pt. i. 278, 2*l*. 15s. Sir M. M. Sykes, pt. i. 240, 2*l*. 18s. Sotheby's in 1821, morocco, 4*l*. and 6*l*. 6s. Bibl. Anglo-Poet. 56, 21*l*.

— England's Helicon. Lond. 1600. I. R. for John Flasket, 4to.

This first edition consisting of 192 pp. contains 150 poems. The arms of Bodenham are on the back of the title page. The writers of which, are Shakspere, Spenser, Breton, Sir P. Sydney, Drayton. Green, &c., &c. A copy with slips placed over the name of Sir P. Sydney at the close of the poems of 'Astrophel, his song of Phillida and Corydon,' giving its authorship to *N. Breton*, with other similar corrections. Sold, Sotheby, May 28, 1856, 31*l*.

— England's Helicon, or the Muse's Harmony. Lond. 1614. 8vo.

Second edition. Roxb. 24*l*. 13s. 6d.

— England's Helicon, with a biographical and critical Introduction, by Sir E. Brydges, and the Variations and Additions of the two Editions. Lond. 1812. 8vo.

Reprinted entire in the British Bibliographer, at which time one hundred and twenty copies were printed off separately. 200 copies in 8vo. at 1*l*. 1s., and 50 copies in 4to. at 2*l*. 2s.

BODERIE, Antoine Le Fevre de la. Ambassades en Angleterre sous le Regne d'Henri IV. & la Minorité de Louis XIII. depuis les Années 1606 jusqu'en 1611. Paris, 1750. 12mo. 5 vols. 10s. 6d.

BODIN, John. The six Bookes of a Common-Weale, out of the French and Latine copies, done into English by Richard Knolles. Lond. 1606. folio. 7s.

This work of Bodin's, says Gifford, was once read at our universities. It is dedicated to Sir Peter Manwood, Knight.

BODIUS, *Anglice*, BOYD.

BODLEY, Sir Thomas. Oratio funebris habita in Schola Theologica in Obitum clariss. Equitis Tho. Bodley. Oxon. 1613. 4to.

This oration, written by Is. Wake, is reprinted in Dr. Will. Bates's Vitæ selectorum aliquot Virorum. Lond. 1681. 4to. In the British Museum Catalogue it is attributed to Richard Corbet, Bishop of Norwich.

— Ivsta Fvnebria Ptolemæi Oxoniensis, Thomæ Bodleii Equitio avrati, celebrata in Academiâ Oxoniensi, Mensis Martii 29, 1613. Oxon. 1613. 4to.

A copious collection of funereal verses by Archbp. Laud, Robert Burton, author of the Anatomy of Melancholy, Isaac Casaubon, &c. Bindley, pt. ii. 1227, 1*l*. 2s.

— Bodleiomnema; seu Carmina et Orationes in Obitus ejus. Oxon. 1613. 4to.

Bindley, pt. i. 1469, 1*l*. 1s.

— The Life of Sir Thomas Bodley, the honourable Founder of the Publick Library in the University of Oxford. Written by himself. Oxford, 1647. 4to.

Bindley, pt. ii. 2538, 4l. 5s. Sir M. M. Sykes, pt. i. 437, 18s. Nassau, pt. i. 2380, inlaid with a portrait and view of the library inserted, 3l. 18s.

This tract, consisting of 20 pp. including the title and epistle to the reader, is reprinted in the fourth volume of the Harleian Miscellany.

— Litteræ D. Tho. Bodleio τω πάνυ ex Morbo decumbenti, missæ. Oxon. 1658. 4to.

Published from the originals in the Bodleian library.

— Reliquæ Bodleianæ. 1703. *See* HEARNE, Thomas.

Bodleian Library.—Ecloga Oxonio-Cantabrigensis, tributa in Libros duos: Opera et Studio T. I. [Thomas James.] Lond. 1600. 4to.

Contains pp. 284, including two title-pages. Liber prior continet catalogum confusum librorum manuscriptorum in illustissimis bibliothecis, duarum florentissimarum academiarum Oxoniæ et Cantabrigiæ. Liber posterior, catalogum eorundem distinctum et dispositum secundum quatuor facultates, observato tam in nominibus, quam in operibus ipsis, alphabetico literarum ordine.

— Catalogus universalis Librorum in Bibliotheca Bodleiana. Accessit Appendix Librorum recens allatorum. Oxon. 1635-6. 4to. 5s.

This catalogue was prepared by Dr. Thomas James. The first edition appeared in 1605, the second with additions in 1620. In it is inserted all the MSS. then in the Bodleian Library. The appendix was written by John Rouse.

— Catalogvs Interpretum S. Scriptvræ, jvxta Nvmerorvm Ordinem, qvo extant in Bibliotheca Bodleiana: olim a D. Jamesio in usum Theologorum concinnatus, nunc verò alterâ fere Parte auctior redditus, &c. Oxoniæ, 1635. 4to.

Contains pp. 55.

— A Nomenclator of such Tracts and Sermons as have beene printed or translated into English upon any Place or Booke of Holy Scripture. Now to be had in the most famous and publique Library of Sir Thomas Bodley, in Oxford. 1642. 18mo.

A curious little work, published by John Vernueil or Vernulius, formerly in some request, as two editions were published within a short time.

— Catalogus Librorum impressorum Bibliothecæ Bodleianæ, a Tho. Hyde. Oxon. 1674. folio. 6s.

Contains pp. 766, including the title, dedication, preface and errata, with the same portraits of the founders, on the letter press, at the beginning of each division, as are in Wood's Hist. Univ. Oxon. Prefixed to this catalogue is a print by M. Burghers, containing the portraits of Sir T. Bodley, Wm. Earl of Pembroke, Abp. Laud, Sir Kenelm Digby and John Selden.

— Catalogus impressorum Librorum Bibliothecæ Bodleianæ. Oxonii, 1738. folio. 2 vols. in 1.

Vol. i. title; preface, signed Rob. Fysher; Hyde's address, 6 pages; the catalogue, 611 pages [A—7 P 2]. The portraits of Sir Thomas Bodley, Wm. Earl of Pembroke, Abp. Laud, Sir Kenelm Digby, and John Selden, designed and engraved by M. Burghers, on one plate, are prefixed. Vol. ii. half-title, the catalogue, I—ZYPE, 714 pages: errata, 1 leaf.

Bindley, pt. i. 1330, 1l. 10s. LARGE PAPER.

[This Catalogue of 1738 is now entirely superseded by the following: Catalogus Librorum impressorum Bibliothecæ Bodleianæ, 4 vol. fol. Oxon. 1843—50. 6l. 10s.]

— Nvmmorvm Antiqvorvm Scriniis Bodleianis reconditorvm Catalogvs, cvm Commentario, Tabvlis aëneis, et Appendice cura Wise. Oxonii. 1750. folio. 15s.

Title; Latin dedication, signed Franciscus Wise; preface, p. v—xiv; half-title, and elenchus operis on the reverse; the catalogue, A—Rrrr 2, 343 pages; index, 13 pages. On pages 251—95, are twenty-three plates of coins, also twenty nine plates of coins and other embellishments engraved by M. Burghers and J. Green are on the several pages of letter-press.

— Bibliothecæ Bodleianæ Codicum Manuscriptorum Orientalium Catalogus. Pars I. a Joanne Uri. Oxon. 1788, 1l. 10s. Pars II. ab Alex. Nicoll, A.M. Oxon. 1821. 18s.

Pars III. Arabicos complectens ed. E. B. Pusey, Ox. 1835. 2l. 2s.

Bodleian. Notitia Editionum, quoad Libros Hebr. Gr. et Lat., quæ vel primariæ vel Sæc. xv. impressæ, vel Aldinæ, in Bibl. Bodl. adservantur. Oxon. 1795. 8vo. 5s.

This valuable notitia is ascribed to Dr. Randolph, the late Bishop of London, and the Rev. Dr. Wm. Jackson. It contains pp. 64, including the title and contents. A new edition is now preparing by the Rev. Dr. Bandinel.

— Codices MSS. et impressi, cum Notis MSS. olim D' Orvilliani, qui in Bibliotheca Bodleiana adservantur. Oxon. 1806. 4to. 8s.

Some copies were struck off in folio.

— Catalogus MSS. qui a cel. E. D. Clarke comparati in Bibl. Bodl. adservantur. Inseruntur Scholia quædam inedita in Platonem et in Carmina Gregorii Nazianzeni. Ox. 1812, 1815. 4to. 2 Parts. 12s. 6d.

Part I. by Professor Gaisford. Part the second, containing the Oriental MS., was edited by Alex. Nicoll, A.M.

— A Catalogue of the Books relating to British (including Welsh, Scottish and Irish) Topography, and Saxon and Northern Literature, bequeathed to the Bodleian Library in the Year MDCCXCIX. by Richard Gough, Esq. F.S.A. Oxford, 1814. 4to. 1l. 11s. 6d.

Title; extract from Gough's will, and a notice of the mode of arrangement, signed B. Bandinel; the catalogue and index pp. 459.

— Catalogus Librorum impressorum quibus Bibliotheca Bodleiana aucta est Annis 1825, 6, 7. folio.

Published annually.

*** The following Bodleian and Oxford Catalogues published of late years, complete the list.

CATALOGUS Dissertationum Academicarum quibus nuper aucta est Bibl. Bodl. 1834. fol. 1l.

CATALOGUS MSS. Borealium præcipue Islandicæ Originis, qui nunc in Bibl. Bodl. adservantur. 1832. 4to. 4s.

CATALOGUS Codicum MSS. qui in Bibl. Bodl. adservantur. Pars. I. Codices Græci. 4to. 1853. 1l.

CATALOGUS Codicum MSS. qui in Collegiis Aulisque Oxoniensibus hodie adservantur. Confecit H. O. Coxe, A.M. 2 vols. 1852. 4to. 2l.

CATALOGUE of Early English Poetry and Works illustrating the British Drama, collected by Edmond Malone, Esq., and now preserved in the Bodleian Library. 1836, folio, 4s.

CATALOGUE of the Printed Books and Manuscripts bequeathed by Francis Douce, Esq. to the Bodleian Library. 1840. fol. with Plates. *Plain*, 1l. 5s.; *coloured*, 2l. 2s.

CATALOGUE of the Manuscripts bequeathed unto the University of Oxford by Elias Ashmole, Esq. M.D., &c. By W. H. Black. 1845. 4to. 1l. 10s.

— *See* OXONIANA.

— Letters written by eminent Persons in the 17th and 18th Centuries: to which are added, Hearne's Journies to Reading and to Whaddon Hall, and Lives of eminent Men, by John Aubrey, Esq. The whole now first published from the Originals in the Bodleian Library and Ashmolean Museum; with biographical and literary Illustrations by Jno. Walker. Lond. 1813. 8vo. 2 vols. in 3.

Vol. i. pp. xxiii. and 304. Vol. ii. pt. i. pp. 352. Vol. ii. pt. ii. pp. 353—668.

Strettell, 779, 1l. 7s. Brockett, 1831, 1l. 2s.

BODMER, Jno. Jas. Noah: attempted from the German, in twelve Books. By Joseph Collyer. Lond. 1767. 12mo. 2 vols. 5s.

A miserable translation.

BODRUGAN, Nicholas, otherwise ADAMS. An epitome of the Title that the Kynges Maiestie of England hath to the Souereigntie of Scotlande, continued vpon the auncient Writers of both Nations from the Beginyng. Lond. by Richard Grafton, 1548. 12mo.

Collation h in 8's; preface 7 pp. addressed to K. Edward 6th.

Black letter. A copy is in the British Museum. White Knights, 492, 8l. 15s.

BOECE. *See* BOETHIUS.

BOEMUS, Joannes. Manners and

Customs of all Nations, translated by E. Aston. Lond. 1611. 4to. 5s.
Reed, 3335, 11s. For another translation of this work, see WATERMAN, *William.*

BOERHAAVE, Herman. Aphorisms concerning the Knowledge and Cure of Diseases, translated into English, with Observations and Explanations. Lond. 1735. 8vo. 5s.
On this work Van Swieten wrote an excellent commentary, which has been translated into English, in 18 vols. 8vo.

— Elements of Chemistry, translated by P. Shaw. Lond. 1753. 4to. 2 vols. 10s. 6d.
An excellent translation of a work once in the highest estimation. Many other works, written by this most illustrious Physician and Professor at Leyden, have been translated into English.

BOETHIUS, A. M. T. S. De Consolatione Philosophiæ. Glasguæ, 1751. 8vo. 3s. 6d. 4to. 5s.
A correct edition, Williams, 278, morocco, 10s.

— Consolationis Philosophiæ Libri, Anglo-saxonice redditi ab Alfredo Rege, ex Recensione Christ. Rawlinson. Oxon. 1698. royal 8vo. with a head of Junius by Burghers, after Vandyke.
Bindley, pt. i. 823, 1l. 3s. Dent, pt. i. 235, morocco, 1l. 7s. Williams, 277, morocco, 2l. 15s.

— The Boke of Consolacion of Philosophie, by Boecius (translated by Geoffrey Chaucer and printed by Caxton). folio.
'This book is in Latin and English; the Latin not cited at length, but only a few verses or lines of a period, and then the whole of that period in English; and so on alternately, Latin and English throughout, as in the subsequent editions of Chaucer; and not the Latin and English side by side, as in Cawood's edition of this book, 1556.' —*Ames.* This edition has neither signatures, numerals, catchwords, nor capital initials; the leaves are 93 in number. A full page contains 29 lines. Copies are to be found in the British Museum, Bodleian Library, Magdalen College Library, Oxford, and in Earl Spenser's and the Grenville Collection. *See* Ames, by Dibdin, i. 308—6. Bibl. Spencer. iv. 310—12. White Knights, 774, imperfect, russia, 22l. 11s. 6d. Alchorne, 173, imperfect. 53l. 11s. Gardner, 1854 (2 leaves fac-simile), 70l.

— The Boke of Comfort, translated into Englesse Tonge. Enprented in the exempt Monastery of Tavestok in Denshyre, by me Dan Thomas Rychard, Monke, 1525. 4to.
The first book printed at Tavistock, containing R 7, in eights. It was rendered into English by John Walton, Canon of Osney, and Sub-dean of York, at the request of Elizabeth Berkeley, and was finished in the year 1410. According to Wanley, 'The printing composer who set the types of this book seems to have been either a Dutchman or a German.' A copy is in the Bodleian Library. Gough, 685, 27l. 6s. re-sold, being imperfect, for 14l. 3s. 6d. Mason, 17l. Heber, 63l. *See* Wood's Athen. Oxon. by Dr. Bliss, i. 48.

— Boetius de Consolationae Philosophiæ, translated by George Coluile, alias Coldewel. Lond. by John Cawode, 1556. 4to.
Black letter, containing F f 2, in fours, dedicated to Queen Mary. The Latin is printed in italics, on the inner margin. White Knights, 552, russia, 2l. Reprinted 1561, 4to. and again without date. Warton mentions an edition of the date of 1566, 4to.

— Five Bookes of Philosophicall Comfort, translated by J. T. Lond. 1609. 12mo.
Not noticed by Dr. Adam Clarke. Contains fol. 1609, dedicated to the Countesse of Dorset, Dowager. Bindley, pt. i. 646, 6s.

— Consolation of Philosophy, in English verse, by H. Conningesbye, 12mo. 1664. 10s. 6d.

— Of the Consolation of Philosophy, made English and illustrated with Notes by the Right Hon. Richard (Graham) Lord Viscount Preston. Second Edition corrected. Lond. 1712. 8vo. 3s.
A good translation, originally published in 1695. 8vo.

— Consolation of Philosophy, translated into English, by W. Causton. Lond. 1730. 8vo. 3s. 6d.

— Consolation of Philosophy, translated, with Notes and Illustrations, by the Rev. Philip Ridpath. Lond. 1785. 8vo. 5s.
An excellent translation with very useful notes, and a life of Boethius, drawn up with

great accuracy and fidelity. Roxburghe, 1297, 9s. 6d.

BOETHIUS. Consolation of Philosophy, translated by R. Duncan. Edinb. 1789. 8vo.

— The Metres of Boethius on the Consolation of Philosophy. Lond. 1792. 8vo. 3s.
A pitiful performance.

— Hector. Episcoporum Murthlacen. & Aberdonen. Vitæ Prelo Ascensiano, 1522. 4to.
'The chief ecclesiastical history of the diocese of Aberdeen.'—*Nicolson*. It contains 40 leaves including the title; the last blank. An imperfect copy is in the British Museum. [Reprinted by the Bannatyne Club.]

— Scotorum Historiæ a prima Gentis Origine. Typis et Opera Jodoci Badii, 1526. folio.
First edition, consisting of only 17 books, of a work abounding with fictions of every denomination.

— Scotorum Historiæ cum Continuatione Jo. Ferrerii, Lib. XIX. Paris. 1575. (or 1574) folio, 1l. 11s. 6d.
Best edition. A copy is in the British Museum. Roxburghe, 8686, date 1574, 3l.

— Hystory and Croniklis of Scotland, translatit by John Bellendene. Edinb, by me Thomas Dauidson, folio, 1536.
Black letter. The prefixes on F, in sixes. The history has a fresh set of signatures, and the leaves numbered to Fo. cc.l. White Knights, 4012, morocco, 64l. 1s. Roxburghe, 8687, 65l. Towneley, pt. i. 429, moroccc, 85l. ON VELLUM, three copies known, one of which is in the library of the University of Edinburgh. [Another in the library of the Duke of Hamilton, and the third at Ham House.] Boece's History was epitomized, continued to the year 1586, mostly by Fr. Thynne, Lancaster herald, and printed with Holinshed's Chronicle, 1587.

— History and Chronicles of Scotland. Edinb. 1821. 4to. 2 vols. with cuts.
Of this reprint two hundred copies were struck off, and one or more ON VELLUM.

BOGAN, Zachary. Homerus EBPAIZΩN, sive Comparatio Homeri cum Scriptoribus Sacris, quoad Normam Loquendi. Subnectitur Hesiodus OMHPIZΩN. Oxonii, 1658. 8vo.
A learned philological work. Williams, 911, mor. 1l. 7s. Heath, 3396, 1l. 11s. Perry, pt. ii. 135, 1l. 5s.
Zachary Bogan likewise published 'A View of the Threats and Punishments recorded in the Scriptures, alphabetically composed.' Oxford, 1653, 12mo. 4s. 'Meditations of the Mirth of a Christian Life.' Oxford, 1653, 8vo. and 'Help to Prayer.' Oxford, 1660, 8vo.

BOGATZKY, C. H. V. Golden Treasury for the Children of God. 1754. 8vo.
This work has gone through numerous editions.

Bogg Witticisms, or Dear Joy's Common Places. 1682. 8vo.
Inglis, 205, 19s.

BOGUE, David, D.D. Essay on the Divine Authority of the New Testament. Portsea, 1801. 8vo.
A very valuable little work. Gosset, 813, 5s. Frequently reprinted, the latter editions with additions.

— and BENNETT, James. History of Dissenters, from the Revolution in 1688 to the Year 1808. Lond. 1808, &c. 8vo. 4 vols. 2l. 2s.
According to the Quarterly Review, Messrs. Bogue and Bennett are any thing rather than impartial writers.

Bohemia.—History of the Bohemian Persecution, from 894 to 1632. Lond. 1650. 12mo. 5s.
In the British Museum are several works relating to Bohemia, particularly about the years 1619—20. An account of the Bohemian and Moravian Brethren, translated from the German, was published at Bradford, 1822, 12mo. 2s. 6d.

BOHUN, Edmund. Character of Q. Elizabeth. Lond. 1693. 8vo. with portraits of Elizabeth and Mary. 6s.
This short system of her policies was translated into French, and printed à la Haye, 1695, 8vo. Bohun, who was a political and miscellaneous writer of the 17th century, published many other works, chiefly compilations, now in little or no estimation.

— Wm. Privilegia Londini: or, the Rights, Liberties, Privileges,

Laws, and Customs of the City of London. Third Edition, with Additions. Lond. 1723. 8vo. 6s.
This writer likewise published several other law books.

BOIARDO, Matteo Maria. Orlando Innamorato, riformato da Lodovico Domenichi. Dublin, 1784. 8vo. 3 vols. 18s.
Many copies of this edition, which was printed at the expense of Dr. Hill, at the press of the College of Dublin, were destroyed by fire.

[ORLANDO INNAMORATO, with an essay by A. Panizzi. Lond. 1831. 8vo. 5 vols. *generally adjoined to the same editor's* ARIOSTO Orlando Furioso, with English Notes and Illustrations. 4 vols. Lond. 1834. together 9 vols. 2l. 12s. 6d.]

— Orlando inamorato. The three first Bookes done into English heroicall verse, by R(obert) T(ofte). Lond. 1598. 4to.
Steevens, 597, 12s. but now worth considerably more. [A translation or rather resumé of *Berni's* Boiardo, in prose, interspersed with verse, was made by Wm. Stewart Rose. Lond. 1823. post 8vo. 10s. 6d.]

— Sonetti e Canzone, edited by A. Panizzi (only 50 printed), 4to. 1835.
Pickering, 1854, 4l. 4s.

BOILEAU—DESPREAUX, Nicolas. Les Œuvres. Glasg. 1749. 12mo. 2 vols. 7s. 6d.
A neat edition, printed by Foulis.

— Poesies, avec des Notes par M. de Levizac. Londres, 1800. 12mo. 4 vols.
Of the works of this writer the following translations have appeared: The Art of Poetry. Lond. 1683, 8vo. 2s. Lutrin, a mock heroic Poem, 1708, 8vo. 3s. The Works, by Ozell, and others, 1712, 8vo. 2 vols. 5s. Posthumous Works, 1713—14, 8vo. 3 vols. Satires, 1806, 8vo.

BOISGELIN, Louis de. Ancient and Modern Malta, with an Appendix, containing a number of authentic State Papers, &c. Lond. 1804 or 5. 4to. 3 vols. with a map and other engravings.

The first part of this work is descriptive, and contains an interesting account of Malta and the Maltese; the rest is historical. Fonthill, 823, 1l. 10s. Drury, 575, russia, 1l. 10s. Brockett, 501, 1l. 19s.

— Travels through Denmark and Sweden: to which is prefixed a Journal of a Voyage down the Elbe from Dresden to Hamburgh: including a compendious historical Account of the Hanseatic League. Lond. 1810. 4to. 2 vols. with 13 views after Dr. C. Parry, 1l. 5s.
Some copies have coloured plates. Drury, 576, 2l. 2s.

BOIS-GUIBERT, Pierre le Pesant de. Histoire de Marie Regne d'Ecosse. Paris, 1675. 12mo. 3 vols. 9s.
[A translation by Freebairn, 8vo., Edinb. 1725.]

BOISIUS, *Anglice*, BOYS.

BOLD, Henry. Wit a sporting in a pleasant Grove of new Fancies. By H. B. Lond. 1657. small 8vo.
Contains pp. 116, with a portrait, æt. 32. Bibl. Anglo-Poet. 63. Bindley, pt. iii. 2191, 6l. 18s. Heber, 2l. 15s.

— Poems Lyrique, Macaronique, Heroique, &c. Lond. 1664. small 8vo.
Contains pp. 250. Dedicated *to* 'Colonel Henry Wallop,' after which are some commendatory verses. Bibl. Anglo-Poet. 62, 6l. 6s. Bindley, pt. i. 647, 5l. 10. Perry, 3l. 4s. In the British Museum is 'St. George's Day, sacred to the Coronation of His Majesty Charles II. Lond. 1661.' folio.

— Latine Songs, with their English: and Poems. Lond. 1685. 8vo.
Contains pp. 176. Nassau, pt. i. 279, 19s. Bindley, pt. i. 648, 1l. 9s. pt. iii. 1151, 15s. Bibl. Anglo-Poet. 64, 1l. 11s. 6d. A short account of Bold will be found in Wood's Athenæ Oxonienses.

BOLINGBROKE, Henry Saint John, Viscount. Works, published by David Mallet. Lond. 1754. 4to. 5 vols.
Left as a legacy to David Mallet, for traducing the memory of Alex. Pope. Roscoe, 676, 4l. 8s. Heath, 1675, 4l. Marquis of Townshend, 382, 5l. 7s. 6d. Drury, 577, with the Letters, 7l. 7s. An edition Lond. 1786. 11 vols. 8vo. Lond. 1809. 8vo. 8 vols. 2l. 12s. 6d. [Reprinted at Boston, U.S. 1844. in 4 vols. 8vo. 2l. 2s.]

Bolingbroke. Philosophical Works. Published by David Mallet. Lond. 1754. 8vo. 5 vols. 1*l*. 1s.

—— Letters and Correspondence, with State Papers, explanatory Notes, and a Translation of the foreign Letters, &c. by the Rev. Gilbert Parke. Lond. 1798. 4to. 2 vols.

Heath, 1676. 1*l*. 4s. FINE PAPER, 2*l*. 2s. An edition, 1798, 8vo. 4 vols. Pope published an edition of Bolingbroke's Patriot King clandestinely, a copy of which, at the sale of Mr. Bindley's library, pt. i. 692, produced 1*l*. 10s. Pope likewise printed a surreptitious edition of his Lordship's letters on the spirit of patriotism, revised, subdivided, altered, and, in short, remodelled according to his own ideas. Nearly the whole impression, consisting of 1500 copies, were burnt by his Lordship.

—— Henry. Voyage to the Demerary, containing a statistical Account of the Settlements there, and those on the Essequibo, the Berbice, and other contiguous Rivers of Guayana. Lond. 1807. 4to.
'The book of a very ingenious man.'— *Quart. Review.* Fonthill, 366, 11s.

BOLTON, Edmund. Elements of Armories. Lond. 1610. 4to. 7s.
Contains 210 pp. dedicated to 'Henrie, Earl of Northampton,' &c. by E. B., after which are commendations by W. Segar, and 5 others, and an address to the reader. Sir P. Thompson, 325, 9s. Bindley, pt. ii. 1200, 11s. LARGE PAPER, with the arms emblazoned, Sir M. M. Sykes, pt. i. 439, 1*l*. 17s. This work consists of a dialogue between two knights, Sir Evstace and Sir Amias. It is written in a very pedantic style; but many curious examples are brought forward, and illustrated by woodcuts, spiritedly executed.

—— Nero Cæsar, or Monarchie depraued, an historical Work. Lond. 1624. folio, with engraved title by Delaram, 10s. 6d.
Sir P. Thompson, 173, 16s. Bindley, pt. i. 573, 10s. 6d. After the first publication there were some additions made to the work, and a new title-page struck off, with the date 1627. The copies bearing date 1624, have not the blanks for the coins filled up; those of 1627 have.

—— Hypercritica: or, a Rule of Judgment for writing or reading our Histories. 8vo. Lond. 1722.
This highly esteemed and sensible treatise, written in 1617, will be found in Nic. Triveti Annalium Continuatio, and in vol. ii. of Ancient Critical Essays upon English Poets and Poesy. Dr. Bliss observes, that 'a MS. in the Bodleian [Rawl. Misc. i.] containing part only of the Hypercritica, differs considerably with that from which Dr. Hall printed his edition.' A long account of Bolton will be found in the Biographia Britannica.

—— James. Filices Britannicæ: An History of the British proper Ferns, with Descriptions. Leeds and Huddersfield, 1785—90. 2 parts. 4to. 2*l*. 2s. with 46 coloured plates.
Part i. pp. 59, with 31 coloured plates. Part. ii. pp. 60—81, and plates coloured 32—46.

—— History of Fungusses growing about Halifax. Huddersfield, 1788—91. 4to. 4 vols. with 182 plates. 2*l*. 2s., or coloured, 4*l*. 4s.
Vol. i. Pages and Plates coloured, 44. Vol. ii. 45—92. Vol. iii. 93—138. Vol. iv. Appendix or Supplement, 139—82. Towneley, pt. ii. 137, 4*l*. 14s. 6d.

—— Natural History of British Song Birds. Lond. 1794—6. 4to. 2 vols. with 80 coloured plates. [New edition. Lond. 1845. 4to. the plates highly finished, in colours. 3*l*. 3s.]
Sotheby's in 1826, 2*l*. 7s. Towneley, pt. ii. 325, 2*l*. 10s.

—— Sir Richard. Justice of Peace for Ireland, enlarged and corrected by Michael Trovers, 1750. 4to. 10s. 6d.
A former edition appeared, Dublin, 1683, folio. In Harris' Hibernica will be found Sir R. Bolton's Declaration, setting forth how, and by what means, the laws and statutes of England came to be of force in Ireland, with Serjeant Mayart's answer to Sir R. Bolton.

—— Robert. Worke of the foure last Things, Death, Judgment, Hell, and Heaven: with an Assise Sermon, and Notes on Justice Nicolls, his Funerall. Together with the Life and Death of the Author. Published by E(dward) B(agshawe). Lond. 1633. 4to. with portrait by Payne, 1632. 15s.

Williams, 235, 1l. 11s. 6d. This learned and eminent puritan scholar likewise published, A Discourse about the state of true Happiness. Lond. 1611, 4to. 5s. A sixth edition appeared 1631. Instructions for the right comforting afflicted Consciences. Lond. 1631, 4to. 6s. Helps to Humiliation. Oxford, 1631, 12mo. Carnal Professor. Lond. 1634. 12mo. Sermons. Lond. 1625, 33, 35, 40, 4to. 4 vols. 1l. Threefold Treatise: The Saints sure and perpetual Guide, &c. Lond. 1634, 4to. Devout Prayers upon solemn occasions. Lond. 1638, 12mo. Discourse concerning Usury. Lond. 1637, 4to. The last Visitation, Conflicts and Death of Mr. Tho. Peacock, 1646. His life was published 1641, 4to.

BOLTON, Samuel, D.D. Dead Saint speaking to Saints and Sinners living. Lond. 1657. folio, with portrait by W. Faithorne, 10s. 6d.

— Solomon. Extinct Peerage of England. Lond. 1769. 8vo.
A very useful work, consisting of pp. 315, with a preface and index. Heath, 1622, 7s. 6d. Roxburghe, 8671, 10s. 6d.

BOLTS, William. Considerations on India Affairs. Lond. 1772—5. 4to. 2 Parts in 3 vols.

Bombay.—Transactions of the Literary Society of Bombay. Lond. 1819, 20, 23. 4to. 3 vols. with plates.
Vol. i. 2l 12s. 6d. Vol. ii. 3l. 3s. Vol. iii. 3l. 13s. 6d. (all published.)

BOMBET, L. A. C. Lives of Haydn and Mozart; with Observations on the Genius of Metastasio, and the present State of Music in France and Italy. Translated from the French, with Notes by the Author of the Sacred Melodies. Lond. 1817. 8vo.
A valuable, authentic, and interesting volume of musical biography. Strettell, 1586, 14s.

BOMBIN, Paul. Vita et Martyrivm Edmvndi Campiani, Martyris Angli Societate Iesv. Antverp. 1618. 12mo.
A copy is in the British Museum. Sotheby's in July 1821, 2l. Cellotti, 3l. 18s. Reprinted, according to Ant. à Wood, at Mantua, 1620, 8vo.

Bon.—John Bon and Mast Person. Lond. by John Daye and Willyā Seres. 4to.
A bitter satire, consisting of four leaves, against the *real Presence*, written by one Luke, a physician, of which only one copy is said to exist. It has been reprinted in fac-simile, 1807, 8s., of which 25 copies were struck off upon vellum. Brockett, 1796, 8s. 6d. Constable, 524, 6s. Nassau, pt. i. 2329, 10s. Sir M. M. Sykes, pt. ii. 92, morocco, 1l. 13s. Towneley, pt. i. 388, 11s.

Bon Ton Magazine, or Microscope of Fashion and Folly. Lond. 1791. 8vo. 4 vols.

BONA, John. Guide to Eternity, extracted out of the Writings of the holy Fathers and ancient Philosophers. Lond. 1709. 18mo. 3s.
Frequently reprinted.

BONARELLI, Guidub. de. Filli di Sciro, Favola pastorale. Glasg. 1763. small 8vo. 5s.

— Filli di Sciro, translated into English by J. S. (probably James Shirley). Lond. 1655. 4to.
Inglis' Old Plays, 121, 8s. Roxburghe, 5752, 13s.

BONAVENTURE, Saint. Legēda maior beatissimi Patris Francisci a Bonavētura. Paris. in Offic. Claudii Cheuallon, venund. Lond. 8vo.
Contains a to m 4 in eights.

— Speculum Vite Christi; or the Myrroure of the blessed Lyf of Jhesu Cryste. Emprynted by Wyllyam Caxton. Folio, with woodcuts.
Compiled from the Latin of Bonaventure De Meditatione Vite Cristi. The English translator is supposed to be John Morton, an Augustine friar. The volume ends on the reverse of sign. t iiij in eights, A 1 being blank. On sign. 8 commences a short treatise of the sacrament of Christ's body. A copy is in Earl Spencer's library. Roxburghe, 212, two leaves wanting. 45l. See Ames, by Dibdin, i. 320—2. Bibl. Spencer. iv. 326-7. Warton's Poetry, 8vo. ii. 426.

— Speculum Vite Cristi (cum Tractatu breve de Sacramento et Oratione ejusdem Sacramenti) Westmonasterii, 1494. folio.
This volume, consisting of pp. 168 and 16, was printed by W. de Worde.

— Vita Christi. Lond. by W. de Worde, 1517. 4to.
Black letter. To D d 5, without W. de

Words's device, in fours and eights, with cuts. White Knights, 1106, 8l. Gardener, 1854, fine copy, 14l. Another edition, by W. de Worde, 1525. 4to. consisting of lxiiij leaves, with numerous cuts. Another 1530, 4to. D d 6, with cuts.

BONAVENTURE, Saint. The Myrrour of the blessyed Life of Jhesu Cryst, translated into English, 1410. Emprinted by Richard Pynson. folio, with cuts.

Contains sign. r iiij in eights. Both W. de Worde's and the present impression are copies from Caxton's publication of the same work. There is an edition by Pynson, in 4to.

— His Lessons, entitled Alphabetum Religiosorum [translated by Richard Whitford]. Lond. by W. de Worde, 1532. 4to.

— The Life of S. Francis. Douay, 1610. 8vo, 10s. 6d.

Dr. Dibdin notices an edition of the Life of St. Francis, printed by Pynson.

BOND, John. King Charles his Welcome Home. Lond. 1641. 4to. with wood-cut portrait, 12s.

Bond likewise wrote England's Reioycing for the Parliament's Retvrne. Lond. 1641. 4to. The Poets Recantation having suffered in the Pillory. ib. 1642. 4to.

Ant. à Wood mentions several of the name of John Bond, one who published commentaries on Horace and Persius, 'a polite and rare critic, whose labours have advanced the commonwealth of learning very much.' Another, author of 'A Door of Hope,' 1641, and other religious treatises, 'an impudent, canting, and blasphemous person, who by his doctrine did lead people to rebellion, advance the cause of Satan much, and in fine by his, and the endeavours of his brethren, brought all things to ruin, merely to advance their unsatiable and ambitious desires.'

— William. Supernatural Philosopher, or the Mysteries of Magick. Second Edition. Lond. 1728. 8vo. with 2 portraits and 3 plates. 6s.

Defoe's Life of Duncan Campbell, with a new title-page.

BONDE, Cunelgus. Scutum Regale. Lond. 1660. with front. and port.

Inglis, 20s, 14s.

— Guilielmus. De Julii Clovii clari admodum Pictoris Operibus. Lond. 1733. folio.

Of very uncommon occurrence. Bindley, pt. i. 755, 5l. 7s. 6d.

BONEFONIUS, Joh. Carmina, edente Maittaire. Lond. 1720. 12mo. 3s.

— Belinda; or, the Kisses, translated, and accompanied with the original Latin. Lond. 1798. 8vo. 4s. 6d.

Boni Ominis Votum. *See* WITHER, George.

BONNEL, James. Harmony of the holy Gospels. Lond. 1705. 8vo. 3s. 6d.

BONNER, Edmund, Bishop of London. The Declaration of the Bishop of London, to be published to the Lay People of his Diocese, concerning the Reconciliation.

A broadside dated Lond. 12 Feb. 1554.

— Commyssion sent to the bloody butcher (Bishop of London) and to all Fryars by H. M. H. Prince Satan. 12mo.

Black letter. Brand, 163. 17s.

— Commemoration or Dirige of Bastard Bonner, usurped Bishop of London, 1569. 12mo.

Bindley, 3l. 13s. Heber, pt. iv. No. 43. 10l.

— Articles (37) to be enquired of in his general Visitation, exercised by him in the City and Dioc. of Lond. an. 1554.

On these articles, reprinted by Bishop Burnet in his History of the Reformation, Jo. Bale 'has commented with a great deal of raillery.'

— Jniunctions geuen in the Visitatiō of Edmunde, Bishop of London. Lond. by John Cawood, 15⁵5. 4to.

Nine leaves.

— Homelies not onely promised before in his Boke, intituled, A necessary Doctrine, but also now of late adioyned, &c. Anno. M.D.LV. Lond. by John Cawood. 4to.

T 2, in fours.

— A ꝓofitable and necessary Doctrine, pwith certayne Homelies, adioyned thervnto. Lond. in Ædibus Joannis Cawodi, 1555. 4to.

Ccc, in fours. 'This doctrine or catechism is said to have been composed by his chaplains, John Harpesfield and Henry Pendleton, and to be taken out of the Institution of a Christian Man, set out by K. Hen. 8, only varied in some points.'—*Ant. à Wood.* Bindley, pt. i. 1097 (Doctrine and Homelies), 3*l.* 16s. Williams, 237, both parts, morocco, 4*l.* 10s. Sir M. M. Sykes, pt. iii. 708. Sotheby, 1843, fine old mor. 6*l.* 6s. Horner, 1854, 2 vols. mor. 6*l.* 6s. Other editions, without date Sir M. M. S kes, pt. i. 442, 1*l.* 18s. Wilkes, 1847. mor. 5*l.* 15s"

Another edition, at the end of which is a 'Tetrastichon, in immodicam præsentis temporis pluuiam.' Also, 'A Dialogue betwene man and the Ayre of lyke effecte.' Then 'Domine salue fac.' &c. 4to. Dr. Dibdin notices other of Bonner's Works. Also his Catechism, 4to. *See* catalogue of Dr. Lort's books, 1086. Bishop Bonner's Catechism, 1555. 4to.

In Fox's Acts and Mon. of the Church, and Bp. Burnet's History of the Reformation, will be found much by and relating to Bishop Bonner.

See AUALE, Lemeke.
BALE, John.
BROOKE, T.
HARPESFIELD, John.
KNELL, T.

BONNER Richard. Treatise of the right Worshipping of Christ in the Sacrament. Lond. for Gualther Linne, 1548. 8vo.

From Maunsell's Catalogue, p. 22. *See* Strype's Eccl. Mem. ii. 146.

BONNET, Charles. Philosophical and critical Inquiries concerning Christianity, translated by J. L. Boissier. Lond. 1787. 8vo. 5s.

Several other works by this eminent natural philosopher, have been translated into English.

BONNEVAL. Memoirs of the Bashaw Count Bonneval, from his Birth to his Death. Lond. 1750. 8vo. 6s.

An entertaining work, containing much secret history of Europe, told after the manner of romance.

BONNEY, Henry Kaye, D.D. Life of Jeremy Taylor, Bishop of Down, Connor and Dromore. Lond. 1815. 8vo. with portrait, 7s.

Dr. Bonney likewise published Memoirs of T. F. Middleton, Bishop of Calcutta, and also Historic Notices of Fotheringay. Oundle, 1821. 8vo. Brockett, 348, 5s. 6d. 349, LARGE PAPER, 6s. 6d.

BONNOR, T. Views of the interior and exterior of Gloucester Cathedral: drawn and engraved by T. Bonnor, in 1796, and reprinted in 1815. 8vo.

Contains pp. 37, with 12 plates. The ichnography of the cathedral accompanies the letter-press. Some impressions of the plates were taken off in quarto, and a small number of the same size on India paper.

— Interior and exterior Views of Goodrich Castle, on the Banks of the Wye, drawn and engraved by T. Bonnor, 1798, and reprinted in 1815. 8vo.

Contains pp. 57, with an engraved page, and 13 plates. Some copies of the plates were taken off in quarto; and a limited number of the same size on India paper.

BONNYCASTLE, John. Treatise on Algebra. Second Edition. Lond. 1823. 8vo. 2 vols. 1*l.* 5s.

Bonnycastle likewise published several other excellent elementary treatises, which have been frequently reprinted.

— R. H. Spanish America. Lond. 1818. 8vo. 2 vols. with maps, 12s.

BONWICKE, Ambrose. Pattern for young Students in the University, set forth in the Life of Mr. Ambrose Bonwicke, sometime Scholar of St. John's College, Cambridge. Lond. 1729. 12mo. 4s.

This little volume was generally ascribed to Bowyer, the learned printer, though it was in reality the production of Ambrose's father. The preface was written by Bowyer.

Book.—Book of St. Albans. *See* BARNES.

— The Book of good Maners, translated out of the Frensshe into Englisshe. (Imprinted by William Caxton, 1487.) folio.

The prologue begins on sign. a l. and on the last leaf (the fifth after sign. h v.) we have Explicit & hic est finis per Caxton, &c. &c. Laus Deo. *See* Ames by Dibdin, i. 263-6.

The same, printed by Wynkyn deWorde, 1507, 4to.

The same, translated in 1486, and imprynted by R. Pynson, 1494, folio, only Mr. Heber's copy known. Sold imperfect for 4*l.* 4s.

— A Boke of diuers ghostly

236   BOO   BOO

Maters. Emprynted at Westmynstre, folio.

This volume, printed by Caxton, consists of three treatises: the first (A—M, in eights) is entitled 'The Treatyse of the vij Poyntes of true Loue and euerlastyng Wysdom drawen of the Boke that is wryten in Laten named Orologiū Sapiēcie.' The second (A—D, in eights) 'A Treatyse shewynge the xij Profites of Tribulacyon.' The third (20 leaves, a and b in eights, c in fours) relates to the Rule of St. Bennet. The whole volume consists of 148 leaves. Willett, 1777. 194*l*. 5s. A copy is in Earl Spencer's library.

See Ames, by Dibdin, i. 330—2. Bibl. Spencer. iv. 329—31.

— Book of the citye of Ladyes. Imp. by Henry Pepwell, 1521. 4to.

Bindley, MS. title, and wanting the three first chapters, 3*l*. 19s.

— Booke of Canons concerning some parte of the discipline of the church of England. Daye, 1571. 4to.

Black letter, 16 leaves.

— Book of Christian Prayers, Q. Elisabeth. *See* PRAYERS.

— Book, The, which is called the body of the policie. Imp. by J. Skot, 1575. 4to.

Black letter. Woodhouse, 1803, 5*l*. 7s. 6d.

— The Booke of Death, or howe a Christian Man ought to behaue himselfe in the Danger of Death: and how they are to be comforted whose deare Frends are departed out of this World. Translated out of High Dutch, by Miles Couerdale. Lond. 1579. 16mo.

From Maunsell's Catalogue, p. 42.

— The Blacke Booke. Printed by T(homas) C(reede). 1604. 4to.

Black letter. Steevens, 770, 1*l*. 8s. Roxburghe, 6671, 3*l*. 13s. 6d. Reed, 1779, 4*l*. 14s. 6d. Bindley, pt. i. 897, 6*l*. 8s. 6d. Saunders in 1818, 7*l*. 17s. 6d.

— Book of Kings. *See* HOLLAND.

— The first and second Booke of Discipline; together with some Acts of the generall Assemblies, clearing and confirming the same: and an Act of Parliament. 1621. 4to.

Gordonstoun, 161, 13s.

— The Booke of Bulls, baited with two Centuries of bold Jests and nimble Lies. Lond. 1636. 12mo.

— A Book of the Continuation of Forreign Passages, that is of Peace between the Common-wealth and the Netherlands, England and France, from Generall Blake's Fleet, the Turks in Argier consent to deliver up all the English Slaves, and desire for Peace, with Account of the battering their Castle, setting their Fleet on Fire, Attempt on the Island of Jamaica, with Narrative of various Engagements, with the Spaniards, &c. Lond. for T. Jenner, 1657. 4to. 1*l*. 1s.

A curious historical tract, with plates, by Pass, of the taking the Spanish West India Fleet, Map of the Island of Jamaica, Blake's Engagement with the Turks of Tunis, Portraits of the Queen of Sweden, Alexander VII., Lewis XIII., &c. Hollis, 203, 6s. Towneley, pt. i. 318, 5*l*. 5s. Saunders in 1818, 5*l*. 5s. Longman, mor. 6*l*. 6s.

— Book of Fortune. 1672. folio.

Perry, pt. i. 651, 4*l*. 4s.

— Book of Rates now used in the Sin Custom House of the Church and Court of Rome, with the Pardons for all Manner of Villanies and Sums to be paid. 1674. 4to.

Dent, pt. i. 346, 13s.

— The Book of Fun, or the Quintessence of Wit and Mirth, with frolicsome Stuff from all the jolliest Authors, &c. Lond. 1759. 12mo. 6s.

— The Book of Life, a bibliographical Melody, dedicated to the Roxburghe Club. 1820. 8vo.

Fifty-five copies privately printed for presents, by R. Thomson. Sir M.M. Sykes, pt. i. 242, 7s.

BOOKER, John. The Bloody Almanack, to which England is directed to foreknow what shall come to passe. Lond. 1643. 4to.

Nassau, pt. ii. 807, 8s. King and Lochée's, in March, 1810, 16s. 6d.

— No Mercurius Aquaticus, but a Cable Rope double twisted for John Taylor the Water Poet. 1644. 4to.

Nassau, pt. i. 425, 1*l*. 1s. Booker likewise published another tract against the

BOO BOO 237

Water Poet, entitled 'A Rope treble-twisted for John Taylor.' London, 1644, 4to.

— Bloody Irish Almanack. Lond. 1646. 4to.
This piece, which contains some memorable particulars relative to the war in Ireland, is the only work of Booker worth the reader's notice. Towneley, pt. i. 315, 5s. Many of Booker's publications are in the British Museum.

— Dutch Fortune Teller, discovering XXXVI Questions, which old and young, married Men and Women, Bachelors and Maids, delight to be resolved of. 1677. folio.
Nassau, pt. i. 448, 15s. An edition, no date, 8vo.

— L. Historical Account of Dudley Castle. 8vo. 7s. 6d. LARGE PAPER, 15s.

Books.—Critical Observations on Books, Ancient and Modern, Nos. 1 to 16, with several appendixes, forming 5 vols. 8vo. 1776 and 1813, rare, 2l. 2s. (Bohn's Cat. 1847.)
Dr. Parr ascribes this work to John Howes, of Norwich.

BOONE, Rev. T. C. Book of Churches and Sects; or the Opinions of all Denominations of Christians differing from the Church of England, traced to their Source. Lond. 1826. 8vo. 14s.

— J. S. Essay on the Study of modern History. Lond. 1821. 8vo. 8s.
A spirited and luminous work.

BOORDE. See BORDE.

BOOT, Arnold, M.D. Animadversiones sacræ ad Textum Hebraicum veteris Testamenti. Lond. 1644. 4to. 6s.
A learned work.

— Ger. et Arnold. Philosophia naturalis reformata; id est, Philosophiæ Aristotelicæ Examinatio et Confutatio, et novæ ac verioris Introductio. Dublin, 1641. 4to.

BOOTE, R. Historical Treatise of an Action or Suit at Law. Sixth Edition, with considerable additions, by John Adams, Serjeant at Law. Lond. 1823. 8vo. 9s. 6d.
The former editions of this valuable and esteemed work appeared 1766, 1781, 1795, 1805, and 1814.

BOOTH, Abraham. Works, with his Life. Lond. 1813. 8vo. 3 vols. with portrait, 18s.
The writings of this popular Baptist minister are much esteemed by those of his sect. His Pædobaptism Examined is considered by them as unanswerable.

— Barton. Memoirs of the Life of Barton Booth, with his Character. Lond. 1733. 8vo. with portrait by Vander Gucht, 4s.
Other lives of this celebrated actor were published by Theophilus Cibber, 8vo. 4s. and by Benjamin Victor, 8vo. 4s.

— David. Analytical Dictionary of the English Language. New edition, to which is added an introduction and an index, with an Appendix. Lond. 1836. 4to. 1l. 1s.
The introduction to this dictionary was first published Edinb. 1806, 8vo. Horne Tooke, 81, 8s. 6d.

— George. Nature and Practice of real Actions in their Writs and Process, both original and judicial. Second Edition corrected, with the Notes of Serjeant Hill. Lond. 1811. royal 8vo. 16s.
The first edition appeared London, 1701, folio, some of which have the date of 1704.

— John. Lexicon of the primitive Words of the Greek Language. Lond. 1817. 8vo. 9s.

— Robert. Encomivm Herovm, Carmine ΑΧΡΟΣΤΙΚΩ 'tentatvm. Lond. 1620. 4to.
A copy is in the British Museum.

BOOTHBY, Sir Brooke. Tears of Penelope. Lond. 1795. small folio, with engravings after the designs of Fuseli.

— Sorrows sacred to the Memory of Penelope. Lond. 1796. folio.
Towneley, pt. ii. 345, 7s. Fonthill, 1785, 1l.

— Fables and Satires, with a Preface on the Æsopean Fable. Edinb. 1809. post 8vo. 2 vols. 10s. 6d.

BOOTHBY, Richard. Description of Madagascar. Lond. 1646. 4to.
Bindley, pt. i. 1274, 18s. Jadis, 278, 2l. 5s. Inglis, 176, 3l. 15s. North, pt. iii. 587, russia, 1l. 8s. Reprinted in the Oxford Collection of Voyages and Travels, vol. ii. In the British Museum is a tract entitled 'A true Declaration of the intollerable wrongs done to Richard Boothby, Merchant of India, by two lewd Servants to the hon. East India Company.' London, 1644, 4to.

BOOTHOUSE, Samuel. Remonstrance of several national Injuries and Indignities perpetrated by the Dey of Tunis, in Barbary. Lond. 1653. 4to.
A copy is in the British Museum.

BOOTHROYD, B. The History of the ancient Borough of Pontefract. Pontefract, 1807. 8vo. in two parts. 15s.
Pp. xvi. 496, and xxiv. with a frontispiece, and five plates, viz. at p. 162, 166, 317, 364, and 443.

BOQUINE, Peter [of Heidelberg]. Defence of the old and true Profession of Christianitie, against the new counterfeite Sect of Iesuites, translated by T. G. Lond. 1581. 8vo.
Dedicated to F. Russell, Earl of Bedford.

BORDE, Andrew, M.D. Boke of the Introduction of Knowledge. Lond. by W. Copland. 4to. with wood cuts.
A curious and interesting work, divided into 37 chapters, containing many genuine traits and characteristic notices of various countries. Bindley, pt. i. 895, 13l. 13s. Copland printed two editions, one extending to Niiij, printed at the sign of the Rose Garland in Flete Strete, 7l. 2s. 6d. Heber; the other printed in Lothbury. A—Bb, 2 leaves each, and Cc, with 3 leaves. From this last the reprint of 1814 was made. See Ames by Dibdin, iii. 158—60. British Bibliographer, iv. 19—30. Ritson's Bibl. Poet. 136. Warton's Poetry, 8vo. iii. 354—61.

— Boke of the Introduction of Knowledge. Lond. 1814. 4to. Edited by W. Upcott.
Of this reprint 100 copies were printed. Brockett, 504, 9s. ON VELLUM, (four copies printed). Sir M. M. Sykes, pt. i. 444, 7l. 7s.

— Pryncyples of Astronomye. Lond. by Robert Copland. 16mo.
A treatise on *Astrology*, in xiii chapters. A copy is among Bishop Moore's books in the public library at Cambridge.

— Breviarie of Health. Lond. by W. Middleton, 1547. 4to.
'The first written of that faculty in English,' says Fuller. Herbert is of opinion that Middleton printed an edition before 1547, in 12mo. Reprinted 1548, 1552. Towneley, pt. i. 402, 1l. 4s. Sir M. M. Sykes, pt. i. 445, 1l. 3s. Inglis, 175, 15s. 1556, Nassau, pt. i. 426, 2 pts. 1556—7, 15s. 1557, 1575, 1587, Goldsmid, 142, 15s. 1598.

— Regimente, or Dietary of Health. Imprinted by me Thomas Colwel, 1562. 16mo.
Inglis, 210, 4s. 6d. 1564, White Knights, 507, mor. 9s. 1567, Perry, pt. i. 468, 9s. Bindley, pt. i. 460, 11s. 1576. Two editions by Robert Wyer, without dates, are in the British Museum.
'Of Borde's numerous books the only one that can afford any degree of entertainment to the modern reader is the Dietarie of Helthe; where, giving directions as a physician, concerning the choice of houses, diet, and apparel, and not suspecting how little he should instruct, and how much he might amuse a curious posterity, he has preserved many anecdotes of the private life, customs, and arts of our ancestors.'—*Warton.*

— Merie Tales of the Madmen of Gotham, gathered together by A. B. of Physick Doctor.
According to Ant. à Wood, 'Printed at London in the time of K. Hen. 8, in whose reign and after, it was accounted a book full of wit and mirth by scholars and gentlemen. Afterwards, being often printed, is now sold only on the stalls of balladsingers.' An edition, London, 1630, 12mo. is in the Bodleian library. This physician has the reputation of being the original Merry Andrew; to him is ascribed 'A Historie of the Mylner of Abyngton,' 4to. and John Scogin's Jests. *See* Warton's Poetry, section XLI. Wood's Ath. Oxon. by Dr. Bliss, i. 170—82.

Border Antiquities. *See* SCOTT, Sir Walter, Bart.

BOREMAN, Robert, D.D. Παιδεια θραιμβος, the Triumphs of Learning over Ignorance, and of Truth over Falsehood. Lond. 1653. 4to.
Reprinted in the first volume of the Harleian Miscellany.

— Mirrour of Mercy and Judgement, or an exact and true Narrative of the Life and Death of Freeman Sonds. Lond. 1655. 4to.

Reprinted with Sir George Sondes' own account at Evesham (1792), small 8vo. and in the tenth volume of the Harleian Miscellany. Rob. Boreman likewise published The Churchman's Catechism, London, 1651, 4to. A Mirrour of Christianity and a Mirrour of Charity; or a true and exact Narrative of the Life and Death of Alice Dutchess Dudley, &c. London, 1669. 4to. Sermon on Philip iii. 20; London, 1669. 4to. A Panegyrick and Sermon at the Funeral of Dr. Comber. London, 1654. 4to. An Antidote against Swearing. London, 1662. 8vo.

BORGIA, Cardinal. Letters from the Cardinal Borgia and the Cardinal York. Lond. 1801. 4to.

Privately printed by Sir J. C. Hippisley, Bart. Duke of York, 2922, 11s.

BORFET, Abiel. Postliminia Caroli II. The Palingenesy, or Second-Birth of Charles the Second to his Kingly Life; upon the Day of his first, May 29. Lond. 1660. 4to.

A copy is in the British Museum.

BORINGDON, Lord. Some Account of Lord Boringdon's Accident and Death. Lond. 1818. 4to. with portrait, 5s.

Privately printed. Dent. pt. i. 472, with portrait on India paper, 15s.

BORLACE, Edmund, M.D. Latham Spaw, in Lancashire; with some remarkable Cases and Cures affected by it. Lond. 1670. 8vo. 3s. 6d.

— Reduction of Ireland to the Crown of England. Lond. 1675. 8vo. 4s.

'A short but instructive work.' *Nicolson.* Roxburghe, 8816, 1*l.* 5s. Dent, pt. ii. 1313, 12s. Bindley, pt. i. 653, 3s. 6d.

— History of the execrable Irish Rebellion. Lond. 1680. folio.

Bp. of Ely, 237, 11s. 6d. Heath, 4765, 19s. 6d. According to Ant. à Wood, 'much of this book is taken from another entitled The Irish Rebellion. London, 1646, 4to. written by Sir John Temple, Knt.' Dr. Borlase also wrote Brief Reflections on the Earl of Castlehaven's Memoirs. London, 1682. 8vo. 3s. 6d.

BORLASE, William, LL.D. Observations on the Antiquities of the County of Cornwall. Oxford, 1754. folio. with 24 plates, 15s.

Title; dedication to Sir John St. Aubyn of Clowance, Bart. 2 pages; to the reader, list of subscribers, particular antiquities where explained, 8 pages; table of contents, 4 pages; history, &c. pp. 1—414.

— The same. The second edition revised, with several Additions by the Author; to which is added a Map of Cornwall, and two new plates. Lond. 1769. folio.

Lloyd, 259, 1*l.* 2s. Bingley, pt. i. 380, 1*l.* 11s. 6d. Title; dedication, to Sir John St. Aubyn, Bart.; to the reader, 5 pages; contents, 6 pages; history, &c. [B—6 B 2] 464 pages. *Plates.* New Map, p. 1; Map, p. 11; Pl. vii. p. 117; Pl. x. p. 164; Pl. xi. p. 173; Fig. 1. The Wringcheese, &c. p. 173; Pl. xiii. p. 174; Pl. xiv. p. 177; Pl. xv. p. 198; Pl. xvi. p. 199; Pl. xvii. p. 206; Pl. xviii. p. 208; Pl. xx. p. 219; Pl. xxi. p. 223; Pl. xxii. p. 224; Pl. xxiii. p. 259; Pl. xxiv. p. 287; Pl. xxv. p. 293; Pl. xxviii. p. 316; Pl. xxix. p. 346; Pl. xxx. p. 352; Pl. xxxi. p. 354; Pl. xxxii. p. 356; Pl. xxxiii. p. 358; Pl. xxxiv. p. 379; Pl. xxxv. p. 391; Pl. xxxvi. 396. The other plates are on the letter press. The new map, pl. xxii. & xxviii. are not in the edition of 1754. *See* Savage's Librarian, ii. 193—225.

— Natural History of Cornwall. Oxford, 1758. folio, with a map and 28 plates.

This volume is much scarcer than the Antiquities of Cornwall, there having been only one edition of it. Title; dedication, 4 pages; an introductory explanation, 6 pages; list of subscribers, 4 pages; table of contents, 3 pages; natural history, [B— 40] 326 pages; errata, and directions for placing the plates, 2 pages. *See* Savage's Librarian, iii. 241—64. Copies of the Natural History and Antiquities, 1758—69. 2 vols. Sir P. Thompson, 162, 4*l.* 5s. Drury, 809, russia, 4*l.* 4s. Heath, 4708, 5*l.* 15s. 6d. Beckford, in 1817, 83, mor. 7*l.* 17s. 6d. Dent, pt. i. 480, russia. 8*l.* 8s. Of the Natural History some copies were struck off on LARGE PAPER.

— Observations on the antient and present State of the Island of Scilly. Oxford, 1756. 4to. 8s.

This work was reviewed by Dr. Johnson in the Literary Magazine. Heath. 4711, 2*l.* 3s. Reed, 8338, 2*l.* Marquis of Townshend, 385, 2*l.* 4s. Bindley, pt. i. 726, 10s.

BORN, Baron Inigo. Travels through the Bannat of Temeswar, Transylvania and Hungary, in 1770. By Baron Inigo Born. To which is added, J. J. Ferber's Mineralogical History of Bohemia. Translated from the German, with some explanatory Notes, and a Preface on the Mechanical Arts, the Art of Mining and its present State and future Improvement, by R. E. Raspe. Lond. 1777. 8vo. 5s.

A very valuable mineralogical tour, likewise containing some curious notices respecting the tribes inhabiting Transylvania and the adjacent districts.

— New Process of Amalgamation of Gold and Silver Ores, and other metallic Mixtures, translated by R. E. Raspe. To which are added, a Supplement and an Address to the Subscribers. Lond. 1791. 4to.

A valuable work, consisting of pp. 290, with twenty-two copper plates.

BOROUGH, William. Discovrs of the Variation of the Cumpas, or magneticall Needle. Lond. 1581. 4to. 7s.

Black letter, reprinted 1585, 1596, 4to.

BOROUGHS, John. Impetus Juveniles et quædam sedatioris aliquantulum Animi Epistolæ. Oxon. 1643. 8vo.

Most of the epistles are written to Philip Bacon, Sir Francis Bacon afterwards Lord Verulam, Tho. Farnabie, Tho. Coppin, Sir H. Spelman, &c.

— Sir John. Soveraignty of the British Seas, proved by Records, History, and the municipall Lawes of the Kingdom. Written in the Year 1633. Lond. 1651. 12mo. 5s.

Dent, pt. i. 237, 10s. 6d.

Boroughs of Great Britain. *See* OLDFIELD, T. H. B.

BORTHWICK, William. Inquiry into the Origin and Limitations of the Feudal Dignities of Scotland. Edinburgh, 1775. 8vo.

This tract is intended to exhibit a view of the limitations of the ancient dignities of Scotland. Boscobel. Brockett, 354, 9s.

— Remarks on British Antiquities, viz. 1. The Origin and Ceremony of judicial Combats. 2. The Solemnities of ancient Writs. 3. The ancient and modern Use of Armorial Figures. 4. The Form of Funeral Service. Edinburgh, 1776. 8vo. 3s. 6d.

Brockett, 355, 8s. 6d.

BORUWLASKI. — Memoirs of the celebrated Dwarf, Joseph Boruwlaski, a Polish Gentleman. Written by himself. Lond. 1788. 8vo. with portrait by W. Hincks. 4s.

— Memoirs of the Life and Travels of Count Boruwlaski. Durham, 1820. 8vo.

Brockett, 357, 5s.

Bos, Lambert. Ellipses Græcæ, ex Edit. G. H. Schaeferi. Subjiciuntur B. Weiskii Pleonasmi Linguæ Græcæ, necnon G. Hermanni Dissertatio de Ellipsi et Pleonasmo in Græca Lingua. Lond. 1825. 8vo.

Drury, 470, morocco, 1l. 3s. An edition Glasg. 1813, 8vo. Oxon. 1813, 8vo. Drury, 489, 6s. 6d.

[Greek Ellipses abridged and translated into English from Schaffer's edition by Seager. London, 1830, 8vo. 7s.]

— Antiquities of Greece, with the Notes of Frederick Leisner, translated by Percival Stockdale. Lond. 1772. 8vo. 6s.

A work intended principally for the use of schools. Heath, 2195, 15s. 6d.

Bos, L. V. Het Leven van Maria Stuart Koninginne van Schotland. Amst. 1647, 12mo.

BOSANQUET and PULLER. Reports in the Common Pleas and Exchequer Chamber, and in the House of Lords, 36 Geo. III. to 44 Geo. III. Lond. 1800-4. folio. 3 vols. 1l. 1s.

An edition 1814. royal 8vo. 3 vols. 1l. 1s. New reports in the C. P. 44 Geo. III. to 47 Geo. III. Lond. 1806-8, 2 vols. roy. 8vo. 1l. 1s.

[New edition of the two series, 5 vols. royal 8vo. Lond. 1826, 2l. 2s.]

For Continuations of these Reports, *see* Taunton, Broderip, and Bingham.

Boscobel. *See* BLOUNT, Thomas.

BOSMAN, William. Description of Guinea. Lond. 1705. 8vo. 5s.

Roxburghe, 7322, 6s. Fonthill, 2848, 15s. Reprinted 1721, 8vo. Dent, pt. i. 239, 5s. and also in Pinkerton's Collection of Voyages and Travels, vol. xvi.

BOSSET, C. P. de. Essai sur les Medailles antiques des Iles de Céphalonie et d'Ithaque. Lond. 1815. 4to. 15s.

— Proceedings in Parga, and the Ionian Islands. Lond. 1819. 8vo. 6s.
Excellent articles on Parga, will be found in the Edinburgh and Quarterly Reviews.

BOSSEWELL. *See* BOSWELL.

BOSSU, M. Travels through Louisiana, transl. by J. R. Forster, with Notes. To which is added a systematic Catalogue of all the known Plants of English North-America, together with an Abstract of Articles contained in Peter Loefling's Travels through Spain and Cumana in South America. Lond. 1771. 8vo. 2 vols. 10s. 6d.
This work forms a portion of the Linnean Voyages.

BOSSUET, J. B. Eveque de Meaux. Le veritable Genie du Christianisme, ou Œuvres choisies. Lond. 1802-4. 8vo. 3 vols.

— Discours sur l'Histoire Universelle, a Monseigneur le Dauphin. Lond. 1807. 8vo. avec port. par Audinet.
An elegant edition of this valuable epitome of Ancient History. A corresponding edition of the Oraisons Funebres et Discours. Lond. 1807. 8vo.

— Exposition of the Doctrine of the Catholick Church. Lond. 1685. 4to. 4s.
This translation is attributed, on very slight grounds, to Dryden.

— History of the Variations of the Protestant Churches. Antwerp. 1742. 8vo. 2 vols.
[Reprinted, Dublin, 1829, 2 vols. 8vo. 14s.]
This work was refuted by several able writers.

— History of France, from Pharamond to Charles IX. translated from the French. Edinburgh, 1762. 12mo. 4 vols. 7s. 6d.

— View of Universal History, translated by James Elphinston. Lond. 1778. 12mo. 2 vols. 5s.
Another entitled Introduction to Universal History, in two Parts, by Richard Spencer. Lond. 1729-30. 8vo.

VOL. I.

— Select Sermons and funeral Orations, with an Essay on Pulpit Eloquence. Lond. 1801, 8vo. 5s.
A life of Bossuet has been published by Charles Butler. Lond. 1812. 8vo. 7s.

BOSSUT, John. General History of Mathematics, from the earliest Times to the Middle of the eighteenth Century, translated from the French: to which is affixed a chronological Table of the most eminent Mathematicians. Lond. 1803. 8vo. 6s.

BOSTOCK, John, M.D. Treatise on Physiology. 1824-7. 8vo. 3 vols.
[Second edition, 1828-30, 8vo. 3 vols. Fourth edition, 1844. 8vo. 10s. 6d.]

BOSTON, Thomas. Whole Works; to which is subjoined the Marrow of modern Divinity illustrated, with many valuable Notes. Edinburgh, 1767. folio. 1l. 5s.
The works of this popular and learned Scotch divine were published separately, and some of them have been frequently reprinted, particularly his 'Human Nature in its fourfold state.'

— Memoirs of his Life, Time and Writings. Edinb. 1776. 8vo.
Reprinted Edinb. 1813. 8vo. An abridgment by Pritchard appeared 1811, 12mo. 2s. 6d.

Boston. — Transactions of the American Academy of Arts and Sciences. Boston, 1785-1818. 4to. 4 vols. New Series, 1833-48. 3 vols. 4to.

BOSWELL, Sir Alexander. ClanAlpin's Vow, 8vo. Edinb. 1811. Lond. 1817.
Bind[ly], pt. i. 683, 11s.

— Edward. Civil Division of the County of Dorset. Sherborne (1795). 8vo.
Title; advertisement, errata and addenda, 2 pages; dedication to George Lord Rivers; list of subscribers, 8 pages; the civil division, &c. pp. i—xxii; list of fees, 6 pages; preliminary observations, &c. 4 pages; the names, &c. pp. 1—107; appendix, 64 pages; index, 3 pages; and general index, 22 pages. Between pp. 8 and 9 of the appendix are 4 pages of opinions on the Kingston case. Prefixed is a folded map of Dorsetshire. Hollis, 118, 6s. 6d.

— H. Description of a Collection of picturesque Views and Representations of the Antiquities of England and Wales. Lond. fol. (1785). with plates, copied from Grose.

BOSWELL, J. Method of Study; or, an useful Library. Lond. 1738. 8vo. 2 vols.
In little estimation. Gosset, 846, 6s. 6d.
— James. Account of Corsica. Glasgow, 1768. 8vo.
First and uncastrated edition. Drury, 491, 7s. 6d. Heath, 2311, 14s.
— Journal of a Tour to the Hebrides, with Samuel Johnson, LL.D. Lond. 1785. 8vo.
Bindley, pt. i. 307, 8s. Fonthill, 71, 11s. Roxburghe, 7215, 15s. Second Edition, revised and corrected, 1785, 8vo. Reprinted 1807, 1813.
— Life of Samuel Johnson, LL.D. with additional Notes and Illustrations, by F. P. Walesby, Esq., of Wadham College. Oxford, 1826. 8vo. 4 vols. 1l. 12s.
Of this edition 50 copies were printed on LARGE PAPER, at 4l. 4s. First edition, 1791, 4to. 2 vols. with port. after Sir Joshua Reynolds. Roxburghe, 9314, 1l. 11s. 6d. Marq. of Townshend, 389, 2l. 10s. Williams, 240, 2l. 12s. 6d.—A supplement to the first edition, 4to. was published in 1793, at one guinea! Second edition, 1793 8vo. 3 vols. Bindley, pt. i. 301, 15s. Dent, pt. i. 242, 1l. 1s. Fonthill, 79, 1l. 14s.—Third edition with additions, 1799, 8vo. 4 vols. Bindley, pt. iii. 16, 1l. 1s. Stanley, 59, 2l. 16s.—1804, 8vo. 4 vols. Bindley, pt. i. 302, 1l. 2s. Drury, 492, 1l. 10s.—1807, 8vo. 4 vols. Bindley, pt. i. 303, 1l. 1s.—1811, 8vo. 4 vols. Bindley, pt. i. 304, 1l. 3s. Of late there have been innumerable editions in 8vo. 12mo. 18mo. &c. An edition edited by J. W. Croker, Lond. 1831. 5 vols. 8vo. 2l. 12s. 6d.; republished with additions and corrections, in 10 vols. fcap. 8vo. Lond. 1835, 1l. 10s.
— James, Jun. Memoir of the late Edmond Malone, Esq. Lond. 1814. 8vo. 5s.
This sketch originally appeared in the Gentleman's Magazine. A few copies, with some additions, were afterwards printed for private distribution.
— John. Workes of Armorie, devyded into three Bookes. In Ædibus Richardi Totelli, 1572. 4to.
The first book contains 17 leaves; the second 136; and the third, 30 leaves or folios; with numerous cuts. Dedicated to Sir W. Cecil, Baron of Burghleigh. Sir M. M. Sykes, pt. i. 447, 12s. White Knights, 572, mor. 1l. The dedication copy, on LARGE PAPER, is in the library of Wm. Currie, Esq. This deservedly valued work was reprinted 1597. Boswell, 302, 13s. Bindley, pt. i. 1275, 1l. Inglis, 179, 1l. 3s. Marq. of Townshend, 3465, 2l. 2s. An edition 1610, Boswell, 299, 8s. 6d.

BOSWORTH, Rev. J. Elements of Anglo-Saxon Grammar, with copious Notes. Lond. 1823. 8vo.
An excellent work, intended to divest the Saxon Grammar of the useless Latin incumbrances adopted by preceding writers.
[This author also published a Dictionary of the Anglo-Saxon Language. Lond. 1838, roy. 8vo. 1l. 10s.; or with a philological preface on the connection of the Germanic tongues, 2l. 2s.]

— William. The chast and lost Lovers lively shadowed in the Persons of Arcadius and Sepha, &c. &c. Lond. 1651. 8vo.
Contains pp. 127, without introduction, &c. Prefixed is an anonymous portrait, æt. 30, 1637, by G. Glover. Inglis, 212, 1l. 9s. Bindley, pt. i. 466, 1l. 13s. Nassau, pt. i. 294, 1l. 16s. Bibl. Anglo-Poet. 65, 3l. 13s. 6d.

Botanist's Guide through the Counties of Northumberland and Durham. Newcastle-upon-Tyne, 1805. 8vo. 2 vols. 10s.
The following anonymous botanical publications are held in some estimation, viz. Botanist's Calendar and Pocket Flora's, Lond. 1797, 12mo. 2 vols. 10s. Tract, relative to Botany, translated from different languages. 1805, 8vo. 5s. Elements of the Science of Botany, as established by Linnæus. 1809, 12mo. 2 vols. 10s. Conversations on Botany. 1817, 12mo. The Botanist's Companion. 1820, 12mo. 2 vols. 10s.

BOTERO, Giov. Of the Greatness and Magnificence of Cities, translated by Robert Peterson. Lond. 1606. 4to. 5s.

BOTT, Edmund. See CONST, Francis.

BOTTARELLI, F. Italian, English, and French Pocket Dictionary. To which is prefixed a new compendious Italian Grammar. Lond. 1777. 3 vols. 12s.
[Reprinted as Bottarelli and Polidori. Lond. 1826, 1l. 1s.]

BOTTOM the Weaver. The merry

conceited Humors of Bottom the Weaver. Lond. n.d., 4to.
An interlude taken from Shakespeare's Midsummer Night's Dream, by some attributed to Robert Cox, Comedian. An edition 1661. Sotheby's in November, 1826, 1*l.* 4s.

BOUCHARD, Alain. Chroniques et Annales des Pays d'Angleterre et Bretaigne. Paris, 1531 folio.
Best edition of a work classed by Du Fresnoy and Debure among romances. Willett, 417. russia, 21*l.* First edition, published anonymously. Paris, 1514. folio. White Knights, 4*l.* 14s. Reprinted Caen, without date, folio. Caen, 1518. folio. Paris, 1528. folio. Caen, 1532. folio. Paris, 1541. 4to.

BOUCHER, Rev. Jonathan. View of the Causes and Consequences of the American Revolution, in thirteen Discourses. Lond. 1797. 8vo. 4s.
This writer likewise published a valuable supplement to Dr. Johnson's Dictionary, A to G, 1807. 4to. 5s.

BOUCHET, Jean. Annales d'Aquitaine, Faits et Gestes des Rois de France et d'Angleterre, &c. augmentées de plusieurs Piéces rares et historiques, recueillies par Abraham Mounin. Poitiers, 1644. folio.
Best and most complete edition. First edition, Poitiers, 1525. folio. Reprinted Poict. 1531. folio. Poict. 1585. folio. Paris, 1537. folio. Sir M. M. Sykes, pt. i. 627. morocco, 1*l.* 3s. Paris, 1540. folio. Poict. 1557. folio.

BOUCHETTE, Jos. Topographical Description of Lower Canada. Lond. 1815. 8vo.
[Dictionary of Lower Canada, 1832 4to. 1*l.* 8s. British Dominions in North America, 2 vols. 4to. 1832, 2*l.* 12s..6d.]

BOUGAINVILLE, Lewis de. Voyage round the World, 1766—9. Lond. 1773. 4to.
Bindley, pt. i. 566, 7s. Roxburghe, 7161, 16s.

— History of a Voyage (to the Malouine) or Falkland Islands, made in 1763 and 1764, under the command of M. de Bougainville: and of two voyages to the Streights of Magellan, with an account of the Patagonians. Translated from Dom Pernety's historical Journal, written in French. Lond. 1773. 4to. 7s.

BOUHOURS, Dominick. Life of St. Francis Xavier, of the Society of Jesus, translated by Dryden. Lond. 1688. 8vo. 5s.
Fonthill, 1609, 18s.

BOUILLON, Jean. Histoire de la Vie et dv Pvrgatoire de St. Patrice, Archev. et Primat d'Hybernie. Lyon, 1674. 12mo. 15s.
A copy is in the British Museum.

BOULAINVILLIERS, Henri Comte de. Etat de la France. Lond. 1727-8. folio, 3 vols. avec une carte. 15s.
Willett, 419, 1*l.* 2s. Heath, 2329, 1*l.* 6s. Towneley, pt. ii. 500, 1*l.* 7s. Boulainvilliers likewise published 'Histoire des anciens Parlements de France.' Lond. 1737. folio, of which an English translation appeared 1739. 8vo. 2 vols. 5s. and Vie de Mahomed, Lond. 1730. 8vo. 3s.

BOULANGER, N. A. Recherches sur' l'Origine du Despotisme Oriental. Lond. 1763. 12mo. 5s.
An English translation, Amst. 1764. 12mo. 5s. Both editions were printed at the private press set up by John Wilkes at his residence in Great George Street, Westminster.

BOULAY de la Meurthe. Tableau Politique des Regnes de Charles II. et de Jacques II., derniers Rois de la Maison de Stuart. Paris, 1822. 8vo 2 tom.
This work (according to the preface) was surreptitiously printed at La Haye.
M. Boulay also published 'Essai sur les Causes qui, en 1649, amenérent en Angleterre l'Etablissement de la Republique; sur celles qui devaient l'y consolider; sur celles qui l'y firent périr. 1799.'

BOULTER, Hugh, D.D., Lord Primate of all Ireland. Letters, containing an Account of the most interesting Transactions which passed in Ireland from 1724 to 1738. Oxford, 1769-70. 8vo. 2 vols. 10s. 6d.

BOULTON, Samuel. Medicina magica tamen Physica. Lond. 1665. 12mo. 4s.
A former edition of this curious work appeared 1656. 12mo.

BOUQUET, Henry. Account of the Expedition against the Ohio Indians, in the year 1764. Lond. 1766. 4to. with plates by Benj. West, 5s.

BOURCHIER, Thomas. Historia Ecclesiastica de Martyrio Fratrum Ordinis D. Francisci, qui partim in Anglia sub Henrico VIII, partim in Belgio, partim et in Hybernia, Tempore Elizabethæ regnantis Reginæ passi sunt, 1536-82. Paris, 1582. 8vo. 1*l.* 1s.

Copies are in the British Museum and in the Bodleian libraries. Reprinted Ingolst. 1583. 12mo. Paris, 1585, 1586. 8vo.

BOURDALOUE, Louis. Practical Divinity. 12mo. 4 vols. 1*l.* 4s.

A translation of some select sermons written by this celebrated Jesuit, was published in 8vo. 7s. 6d.

BOURDE' de Villehuet. Manœuverer or Skilful Seaman, translated by the Chevalier de Sauseuil. Lond. 1788. 4to. with 13 plates, 10s. 6d.

BOURGET, Dom. John. History of the Royal Abbey of Bec, near Rouen in Normandy, translated from the French (by Dr. Ducarel). Lond. 1779. 8vo. with plates, 5s.

This work is usually appended to Gough's Alien Priories.

BOURGH, John Lord. The most horrible and tragicall Murther of John Lord Bourgh, Baron of Castell Connell; committed by Arnold Cosby, the 14 of January. Printed by R. R. 1591. 4to.

Bindley, pt. iv. 598, 5*l.* 18s.

BOURGOANNE, Chev: de. Travels in Spain, to which are added, copious Extracts from the Essays on Spain of M. Peyron. Translated from the French. Lond. 1789. 8vo. 3 vols. with 12 plates, 15s.

An accurate and correct picture, written in a clear and distinct manner. It is reprinted in the fifth volume of Pinkerton's Collection of Voyages and Travels.

BOURGOING, J. F. Modern State of Spain, translated from the French. Lond. 1808. 8vo. 4 vols. with atlas in 4to.

An excellent work, treating fully of the manufactures, the civil, political, and religious state of Spain, manners, literature, &c.

BOURIGNON, Antonia. Apology for M. Antonia Bourignon, in four Parts. Lond. 1699. 8vo. 4s.

At the end of the volume is a list of the works of this female enthusiast. The following translations have been published. Light of the World, 1696. 8vo. On Solid Virtue, 1699. 8vo. Light risen in Darkness, 1703. 8vo. Gospel Spirit, 1707. 8vo. Warning against the Quakers, 1708. 8vo. Academy of learned Divines, 1708. 8vo.

BOURKE, Thomas. History of the Moors in Spain, from their Invasion of that Country till their final Expulsion from it. Lond. 1811. 4to. 21s.

BOURN, Samuel, of Norwich. Sermons and Discourses. Lond. 1760, 3, 77. 8vo. 6 vols. 18s.

Recommended by Job Orton as a specimen 'of a good style for sermons.' Sermons on the Christian Religion. Lond. 1755. 8vo. Williams, 285. 15s.

— Thomas. Gazetteer of the most remarkable Places in the World, with brief Notices of the principal historical Events, and the most celebrated Persons connected with them. Third Edition. Lond. 1822. 8vo. 18s.

The first edition appeared in 1807.

BOURNE, Rev. Henry. History of Newcastle upon Tyne. Newcastle upon Tyne, 1736. folio, 12s.

Contains pp. viii, not including list of subscribers, 3 pages and 246 (B-Rrr.) The last paged leaf was reprinted in 1757, but is bound only in a few copies. Appendix, 5 pages. A folded plan of Newcastle faces the title. Towneley, pt. ii. 322, 1*l.* 1s. Nassau, pt. i. 450, 1*l.* Heath, 4577, 1*l.* 7s. Sir P. Thompson, 172, 3*l.* 4s. LARGE PAPER, *very rare*. The dedication copy, extensively illustrated, sold at Brockett's sale for 54*l.* 12s.

— Henry. Antiquitates vulgares: or, the Antiquities of the Common People. Newcastle, 1725. 8vo.

Roxburghe, 8587, 8s. Reprinted with additions, by John Brand, Newcastle, 1777, 8vo. [and afterwards incorporated in Brand's Popular Antiquities, 2 vols. 4to. or 3 vols. post 8vo.]

— Vincent. Miscellaneous Poems;

consisting of Originals and Translations. Lond. 1772. 4to. 10s.

Roscoe, 1427, 10s. 6d. Dent, pt. i. 474, morocco, 15s. 1734. 1743. Editio tertia. 1750. Heath, 1771, 8s. Oxford, (with his Letters) 1808. 2 vols. 12mo. 7s. 6d. Oxford, 1826, crown 8vo. 9s. [Cambridge, 1838, 18mo. 2s. 6d., or LARGE PAPER, 3s. 6d. with Life by Jas. Mitford. Lond. 1846, 12mo. 5s.]

Cowper thinks Bourne 'a better Latin poet than Tibullus, Propertius, Ausonius, or any of the writers in his way, except Ovid, and not at all inferior to him.'

— William. Regiment for the Sea. Lond. by Tho. Hacket (1574). 4to. 10s. 6d.

First edition. Inglis, 184, 17s. Reprinted (1577.) 1584. 1587. Bindley, pt. i. 1121, 2l. 12s. 1592. and 1596.

— Inuentions or Deuices very necessary for all Generalles and Captaines, or Leaders of Men, as well by Sea as by Land. Lond. 1578. 4to.

Inglis, 296, 3s.

— Treasure for Traueilers, in five Books. Lond. 1578. 4to.

A curious work, containing 'very necessary matters for all sorts of travellers by sea or land.' Inglis, 184, 2l. 15s. Towneley, pt. i. 387, russia, 4l. 4s., fine copy.

— Arte of Shooting in great Ordnaunce. Lond. 1587. 4to. 4s.

BOURNON, M. Le Comte de. Traité de Minéralogie. Lond. 1808. 4to. 3 vols.

In 1813 appeared Catalogue de la Collection minéralogique du Comte de Bournon. 8vo. with a folio volume of plates, 1l. 1s.

— Count de. Descriptive Catalogue of Diamonds in the Cabinet of Sir A. Hume, Bart. 1815. 4to. 1l. 1s.

BOURRIT, M. T. Relation of a Journey to the Glaciers in the Dutchy of Savoy, translated from the French, by C. and F. Davy. Norwich, 1775. 8vo. 6s.

BOUTCHER, William. Treatise on Forest Trees. Edinb. 1775. 4to. 7s. 6d.

BOUTERWEK, Fred. History of Spanish and Portuguese Literature. Lond. 1823. 8vo. 2 vols. 1l. 1s.

[The Spanish Literature reprinted in Bogue's European Library, 12mo. 3s. 6d.]

BOUVET, Father J. Life of Canghy, the present Emperor of China. Lond. 1699. 8vo. 3s. 6d.

Bouvet likewise wrote 'The present Condition of the Muscovite Empire till the Year 1699.' Lond. 1699. 8vo. Heath, 2544, 8s.

BOVET, Richard. Pandemonium, or the Devil's Cloyster, being a further Blow to modern Sadduciam, proving the Existence of Witches and Spirits. Lond. 1684. 8vo. with front. by Sturt.

Nassau, pt. i. 297, 10s.

BOURGES. Voyez BEAULNE.

BOWACK, John. The Antiquities of Middlesex. Lond. 1705-6. folio.

Part I. title; dedication to Hans Sloane, M.D.; to the reader, errata and advertisement, 4 pages; the antiquities, [B—G] 22 pages. Part II. Title to the second part; title as before; dedication to Henry Lord Bishop of London; the antiquities [H—Q 2] pp. 25—59; advertisement and errata, 1 page. Part III. was announced, but never published. Dent, pt. i. 348, 2l.

BOWDEN, John. Epitaph Writer; consisting of upwards of 600 original Epitaphs. To which is prefixed, an Essay on Epitaph Writing. Chester, 1791. 12mo. 3s. 6d.

BOWDICH, T. Edward. Mission from Cape Coast Castle to Ashantee, with a statistical Account of that Kingdom, and geographical Notices of other Parts of the Interior of Africa. Lond. 1819. 4to. with plates.

Of little value or interest. Drury, 737, 1l. 13s.

Mr. Bowdich likewise published An Analysis of the natural Classification of Mammalia, for the Use of Students and Travellers. Paris, 1821. 8vo. pp. 115, with 15 plates, 15s.

Introduction to the Ornithology of Cuvier. Paris, 1821. 8vo. pp. 86, and 17 plates, 15s.

Elements of Conchology. Paris, 1821-2, 8vo. Part. i. pp. 74, with 19 plates. Part ii. pp. 38, with 9 plates, 1l. 11s. 6d.

Excursions in Madeira and Porto Santo, during the Autumn of 1823, while on his third Voyage to Africa. Lond. 1825. 4to. 2l. 2s.

— Mrs. Fresh-Water Fishes of Great Britain, royal 4to. with 47 coloured drawings beautifully executed. Lond. 1828. Published by subscription in 12 parts at 1*l*. 1s. each.

BOWDLER, John, Jun. Select Pieces in Prose and Verse. Lond. 1816. 8vo. 2 vols. 12s.
'The peculiar value of these volumes, is the combination of talent, of taste, and of piety which they exhibit.'—*Quarterly Review.*

— Thomas. Sermons on the Nature, Offices, and Character of Jesus Christ. Lond. 1818. 8vo. 2 vols. 1*l*. 1s.

— Mrs. Practical Observations on the Revelation of Saint John, written in the year 1775. Second Edition. Bath, 1800. 12mo. 5s.
This work is expressly designed for those who have not leisure or inclination to examine the prophetical meaning of the apocalypse. The first edition was published anonymously in 1787. Several other esteemed works by this lady have appeared, particularly a volume of Sermons on the Doctrines and Duties of Christianity, which has gone through upwards of twenty editions.

BOWEN, Thomas. Account of the Origin, Progress, and present State of Bethlehem Hospital. Lond. 1783. 4to. 5s.

BOWER, Alexander. Life of Luther, with an Account of the early Progress of the Reformation. Lond. 1813. 8vo. 7s. 6d.
Bower likewise published a life of Dr. James Beattie. Lond. 1804. cr. 8vo.

— History of the University of Edinburgh. Edinb. 1817. 8vo. 2 vols. 1*l*. 4s.

— Archibald. History of the Popes, from the Foundation of the See of Rome to the present Time. Lond. 1748-66. 4to. 7 vols. 4*l*. 4s. LARGE PAPER, 6*l*. 6s.
The publication of this work gave rise to much controversy. Most of the tracts pro and con will be found in the British Museum. Drury, 738, 3*l*.

— Edmond. Dr. Lamb revived, or Witchcraft condemned in Ann Bodenham. Dr. Lambs Darling; an exact Relation of the Contract and Engagement made between the Devil and Mistris Anne Bodenham. Lond. 1653. 4to. Two Tracts.
First tract. Roxburghe, 1993, 11s. Bindley, pt. iv. 173, 13s.

— John. Description of the Abbeys of Melrose and Old Melrose, with their Traditions. 1813. 8vo. 5s.

Bowes.—True Report of the horrible Murther committed in the House of Sir Jerome Bowes, 20th Feb. 1606. Lond. 1606. 4to. 1*l*. 11s. 6d.
[Life of Andrew Robinson Bowes and the Countess of Strathmore, by Jesse Foote. Lond. 8vo. n.d.

— Bowes Correspondence, see *Surtees Society Appendix*.]

BOWLE, John. Letter to Bishop Percy, concerning a new and classical Edition of Don Quixotte. Lond. 1777. 4to. 3s. 6d.

BOWLES, Rev. Wm. Lisle. Paulus Parochialis; or, a plain and practical View of the Object, Arguments, and Connection of St. Paul's Epistle to the Romans: in a Series of Sermons, adapted to Country Congregations. Bath, 1826. 8vo.
This writer edited an edition of Pope's Works, and published several volumes of sonnets and poems.
[Also a History of Bremhill, Wilts. Lond. 1828, 8vo. Life of Bishop Ken. Lond. 1830, 2 vols. 8vo.]

BOWLKER, Richard. Art of Angling improved in all its Parts, especially Fly Fishing. Worcester (1746), 12mo.
First edition. Haworth, 795, russia, 1*l*. 1s. Frequently reprinted. The Third Edition was printed at Birmingham with Baskerville's types.

BOWMAN, Hildebrand. Travels into Carnovirria, Taupincera Olfactaria, and Auditante, in New Zealand, &c. Lond. 1778. 8vo. 5s.
An imitation of Gulliver's Travels. Fonthill, 2771, 10s.

BOWREY, Tho. Dictionary English and Malayo, Malayo and English. Lond. 1701. 4to. with a map.
Townley, pt. ii. 261, russia, 1*l*. 12s. Dent, pt. i. 475, 1*l*. 2s.

— Dictionary of the Hudson's Bay Indian Language. 1701. folio.

— Grammar of the Malay Tongue, compiled from Bowrey's Dictionary, and other authentic Documents. Lond. 1800. 4to. with a map, 7s. 6d.

BOWRING, John, and Harry S. VAN DYK. Batavian Anthology; or Specimens of the Dutch Poets; with Remarks on the poetical Literature and Language of the Netherlands. Lond. 1824. fcap. 8vo. 7s. 6d.

Mr. Bowring (now Sir John) has also published Ancient Poetry and Romances of Spain, 1824. fcap. 8vo. 10s. 6d. Servian Popular Poetry, 1827. fcap. 8vo. 8s. Specimens of the Polish Poets. 1827, 8s. Specimens of the Russian Poets, 2 vols. 15s. Poetry of the Magyars, fcap. 8vo. 1830, 10s. 6d. Cheskian Anthology, History of the Poetry of Bohemia, fcap. 8vo. 1832, 7s. German Lyric Poets, fcap. 8vo. 1822. 5s. Minor Morals for Young People, 3 vols. fcap. 8vo. with plates by Cruikshank, 1839, 18s.

Bowyer.—The gallant Caualiero Dicke Bovvyer, newly acted. Lond. 1605. 4to.

The running title of this dramatic piece is 'The History of the Tryal of Cheualry.'

BOWYER, William. Origin of Printing. Second and much improved Edition. To which was afterwards added a Supplement. Lond. 1776, 81. 8vo. 10s. 6d.

The first edition appeared in 1774, to which an appendix was added in 1776.

— Miscellaneous Tracts, by the late William Bowyer, and several of his learned Friends; including Letters on literary Subjects, by Mr. Markland, Mr. Clarke, &c. &c. collected and illustrated with occasional Notes by John Nichols. Lond. 1785. 4to. port. 1l. 1s.

Sir M. M. Sykes, pt. i. 451, 1l. 13s.

— Critical Conjectures and Observations on the New Testament, collected from various Authors. Lond. 1812. 4to. 1l. 10s.

Best edition of this valuable work, intended as a companion to the author's edition of the Greek Testament. Edition, 1772, 8vo. 4s. Third edition, 1782, 4to. Bindley, pt. i. 916, 1l. 11s. 6d. Sir M. M. Sykes, pt. i. 451, 16s. Heath, 805, 1l. 13s.

— Anecdotes. *See* NICHOLS, John.

BOXHORNIUS, Mar Zuirius. Originum Gallicarum Liber : accedit antiquæ Linguæ Britannicæ Lexicon Britannico-latinum, cum adjectis et insertis Adagiis Britannicis Sapientiæ Veterum Druidum Reliquiis. Amst. 1654. 4to. 18s.

A copy is in the British Museum.

Boy Bishop. In Die Innocencium Sermo pro Episcopo Puerorum. [Lond. by Wynkin de Worde.]

This contains about 25 pages in black letter, double columns. At the end is a wood-cut of the crucifixion, and the mark of W. C. and W. de Worde.

— Episcopus Puerorum in Die Innocentium; or Discoverie of an antient Custom in the Church of Sarum, of making an anniversarie Bishop among the Choristers. By Dr. John Gregory. Lond. 1649. 4to. with cuts.

Sir M. M. Sykes, pt. i. 1018, 5s. Nassau, pt. i. 1477, russia, 4s. An edition, 1671, White Knights, 1551, 5s. This tract, which forms the fifth of his opera posthuma, and is included in his works, published 1684 (*see* GREGORY), was written in explanation of a stone monument still remaining in Salisbury-cathedral, representing a little boy habited in episcopal robes, with a mitre upon his head, a crosier in his hand, &c., and the explanation was derived from a chapter in the ancient statutes of that church entitled De Episcopo Choristarum. A long account of the Boy Bishop will be found in Hawkins' History of Music, vol. ii.

BOYCE, Samuel. Poems on several Occasions. Lond. 1757. 8vo. 5s.

LARGE PAPER. Garrick, 292, 12s. 6d.

— William, Mus. D. Anthems. Lond. 1788. folio, with portrait by J. K. Sherwin, 1775.

[*Also* Cathedral Music, 3 vols. folio.]

An account of Dr. Boyce will be found in Burney's Music. iii. 619—21.

BOYCE. *See* BOETHIUS.

BOYD, And. Ad avgvstissimvm Monarcham Carolum in Scotiam redeuntem, Carmen panegyricum. Edinb. 1633. 4to.

A copy is in the British Museum.

BOYD, Hugh. Miscellaneous Works, with an Account of his Life and Writings by L. D. Campbell. Lond. 1800. 8vo. 2 vols. 9s.

Boyd is one of the reputed authors of the Letters of Junius. Fonthill, 2896, 1l. 11s. A copy of this writer's Indian Observer. Calcutta, 1795. Bindley, pt. i. 641, 13s. 6d

— Hugh Stuart. Select Passages from the Writings of St. Chrysostom, St. Gregory, Nazianzen and St. Basil: translated from the Greek. Lond. 1810. royal 8vo. 10s.

— Mark Alex. Sketch of the Life of Mark Alexander Boyd. 1787. 4to.

By Sir David Dalrymple, Lord Hailes.

— Robert. Bodii in Epistolam Pauli Apostoli ad Ephesios Prælectiones supra CC. Lond. 1652. fol. 1l. 1s.

It consists of pp. 1296, with life by Andrew Rivet, preface by Principal Baillie, and Latin verses by David Leech, Zachary Boyd and others. Reprinted Geneva, 1660, folio. An English translation of these Prælections, which contain some good critical remarks, as well as many eloquent passages, was published in 4to. by the author's son.

— Monita de Filii sui primogeniti Institutione. Accessit Hecatombe Christiana. Edinb. 1701. 8vo.

An edition of the Hecatombe Christiana was published, Edinb. 1627, 8vo.

— R., Dr. Office, Powers and Jurisdiction of his Majesty's Justices of the Peace and Commissioners of Supply. Edinb. 1787. 4to. 2 vols.

Boyd also published Judicial Proceedings before the Court of Admiralty and Supreme Consistorial or Commissary Court of Scotland. Edinb. 1779. 4to.

— Zachary. Garden of Zion. Glasgow, 1644. 4to.

Roxburghe, 3339, 3l. 3s. Pickering, 1854, 8l. 7s. 6d. Boyd likewise published The Battle of the Soul in Death. Edinb. 1619, 1629, 8vo. Oratio panegyrica ad Carolum Regem, pridie quam in Scotia coronatur. Edinb. 1633. 4to. Crosses, Comforts, Counsels. Glasg. 1643. 8vo. Two Oriental Pearls, Grace and Glory, the godly Man's Choice, and a Cordial of Comforts for a wearied Soul. Edinburgh, 1718, 12mo.

BOYDE, H. Voyage to Barbary. Lond. 1736. 8vo.

Heath, 2723, 3s. 6d.

BOYDELL, John. Collection of Prints, engraved after the most capital Paintings in England, published by J. Boydell, with a Description of each picture in English and French. Lond. 1769. atlas folio. 9 vols.

Vol. i. contains 50 plates.—Vol. ii. 64 plates.—Vol. iii. 78 plates.—Vol. iv. 87 plates.—Vol. v. 60 plates.—Vol. vi. 60 plates.—Vol. vii. 52 plates.—Vol. viii. 60 plates.—Vol. ix. 50 plates, making in the whole 571 prints. Fonthill, 3774, halfbound russia, 75½ guineas.

— Views of Seats, Castles, and romantick Places in North Wales. 1792. folio.

Paoors. Dent, pt. i. 350. 1l. 5s.

— The History of the River Thames. (By William Coombe.) Lond. 1794-6. folio. 2 vols.

These volumes contain coloured plates, from drawings by J. Farington, R.A. engraved by J. E. Stadler.

Vol. i. Title, and dedication to Horace Earl of Orford; preface, table, and list of plates, 8 pages; the historical part, 312 pages.—Vol. ii. Title; list of plates and table, 2 pages; history, 294 pages.

Dent, pt. ii. 145, russia, 3l. 16s. Baker, 271, 4l. 10s. Beckford, in 1817. 197, 6l. 8s. 6d. Nassau, pt. i. 657, russia, 7l. 17s. 6d. Roxburghe, 6640, russia, 8l. 18s. 6d. Fonthill, 568, russia, 16l. 16s. 1734, 5l.

Many copies of the plates were taken off in bistre, and are of less value than those in colours.

— Picturesque Scenery of Norway. 1820. folio. 2 vols. with coloured plates, 5l. 5s.

Sotheby's in 1823. 3l. 11s.

— Illustrations of holy Writ, designed and engraved by Isaac Taylor. royal 4to. 6l. 6s.

Some copies in imperial 4to. Proofs on INDIA PAPER, 8l. 8s.

— Thirty-nine Views in London and its Environs, drawn and engraved by John and Thomas Boydell. Size 17¼ by 10¾ inches.

— Catalogue raisonné d'un Recueil d'Estampes, d'après les plus Tableaux qui soient en Angleterre. Lond. 1779. 4to. 6s.

BOYDELL. *See* GUERCINO. Gallery at Houghton.

BOYER, Abel. Political State of Great Britain, 1711-40. Lond. 8vo. 60 vols.
A monthly publication containing a history of all parties, ecclesiastical and civil, with abstracts of pamphlets, &c. relative to Great Britain and Europe. A copy is in the British Museum. Marquis of Townshend, 264, (vol. 39 wanting), 12l. 12s. Willett, 1920. 25l. Heath, 4406, 43l. 1s.

— Theater of Honour and Nobility, both in English and French. Lond. 1729. 4to. 12s.
Contains pp. 259, with a front. engraved by P. Fourdrinier. and plates.

— History of Queen Anne. Lond. 1735. folio. with portrait of the Queen by V. Gucht, plans and medals. 10s. 6d.
This work is esteemed a very good chronicle of this period of English history. Another entitled 'The History of the Reign of Q. Anne digested into Annals.' Lond. 1703-13. 8vo. 11 vols. 10s. 6d.
Boyer likewise published a History of William III. 1702. 8vo. 3 vols. and a Life of Sir W. Temple, 1714. 8vo. with portrait.

— French and English Dictionary. Lond. 1816. 4to. 2 vols. 1l. 16s.
Best edition of this esteemed work. An abridgment in 8vo. (frequently reprinted) and now united to Deletanville, 12s.

— Peter. History of the Vaudois. Lond. 1690-2. 12mo. 2 vols. 10s. 6d.

BOYLE, Charles. *See* ORRERY, Earl of.

— Robert. Works, to which is prefixed the Life of the Author [by Thomas Birch, D.D.] Lond. 1744. folio. 5 vols.
Fonthill, 1347, 8l. 1s. Willett, 428, 5l. 5s. LARGE PAPER. Garrick, 529, 3l. 3s. Dr. Birch's Life of Boyle was likewise published separately, 1744. in 8vo.

— Another Edition. Lond. 1772. 4to. 6 vols.
Best edition. Sir M. M. Sykes, pt. i, 450, russia, 4l. 10s. Dent, pt. i. 477, russia, 4l. 11s. Nassau, pt. i. 569, russia, 6l. Duke of Grafton, 405, 6l. 10s. Drury, 743, 7l. 7s. Heath, 1677, 9l. 9s.

— Philosophical Works abridged, by Dr. Shaw. Lond. 1725. 4to. 3 vols. 1l. 1s. 1738. 4to. 3 vols.

— Theological Works epitomiz'd by Richard Boulton. Lond. 1715. 8vo. 3 vols. 12s.

— Captain Robert. Voyages and Adventures in several Parts of the World. Lond. 1728. 8vo.
A fictitious narrative, written by W. R. Chetwood, frequently reprinted. Fonthill, 2598, date 1728. 10s.

Boyle Lecture.—A Defence of natural and revealed Religion, being a Collection of the Sermons preached at the Lecture founded by the Hon. Robert Boyle (1691-1732), with the Additions and Amendments of the several Authors and general Indexes. Lond. 1739. folio. 3 vols. 2l. 12s. 6d.
'If all other defences of religion were lost, there is solid reasoning enough (if properly weighed) in these three volumes to remove the scruples of most unbelievers.' —Bp. Watson.

List.

1692. By Richard Bentley, 4to. frequently reprinted in 8vo.
1693-4. by Richard Kidder, folio. 18s. 8vo. 3 vols. 16s.
1695-6. by John Williams, 4to. 4s.
1697. by F. Gastrell, 8vo. 2 vols. 6s.
1698. by J. Harris, 4to. 4s.
1699. by Sam. Bradford, 4to. 4s.
1700. by Offspring Blackall, 8vo. 3s. 6d.
1701. by George Stanhope, 4to. 4s. 6d.
1704-5. by Samuel Clarke, 8vo. 2 vols. 4s.
1706. by John Hancock, 8vo. 2s. 6d.
1707. by W. Whiston, 8vo. 3s.
1708. by John Turner, 8vo. 3s. 6d.
1709. by Lilly Butler, 8vo. 3s.
1710. by Josiah Woodward, 8vo. 3s.
1711-12. by William Derham, 8vo. 4s.
1713-14. by Benj. Ibbot, 8vo. 2 vols. 5s.
1717-18. by John Leng, 8vo. 3s.
1719-20. by John Clarke, 8vo. 2 vols. 5s.
1721-2. by Robert Gurdon, 8vo. 3s.
1724-5. by Thomas Burnett, 8vo. 2 vols. 7s.
1730-2. by William Berriman, 8vo. 2 vols. 6s.
1736-8. by Richard Biscoe, 8vo. 2 vols. 15s.
1739-41. by Leonard Twells, 8vo. 2 vols. 5s.
1747-9. by Henry Stebbing, 8vo. 3s. 6d.
1763. by Ralph Heathcote.
1766-8. by William Worthington, 8vo. 2 vols. 7s.
1769-71. by Henry Owen, 8vo. 2 vols. 7s. Bindley, pt. ii. 2031, 9s. 6d.
1778-80. by James Williamson, 8vo. 3s. 6d.

1802-4. by William Van Mildert, 8vo. 2 vols. 1*l.* 4s.
1821. by William Harness, 2 vols. 8vo.
1846-7. by F. D. Maurice, 8vo.
Only those printed before 1736, are comprised in the collection in 3 vols. folio.
[These Lectures are only printed occasionally, and at long intervals.]

BOYLE Lectures, by the Rev. Gilbert Burnet. Lond. 1737. 8vo. 4 vols. 1*l.* 4s.

BOYS, Edward. Sermons. Lond. 16—. 4to. with port. æt. 66. (by Faithorne) 7s.

— John, (Dean of Canterbury). Workes; containing an Exposition of all the Scriptures used in our Liturgy, &c. Lond. 1622, [also 1630], folio, with a doubtful portrait by J. Payne. 10s. 6d.
Another work entitled Remains. Lond. 1631. 4to.

— John. Veteris Interpretis cum Beza aliisque recentioribus Collatio in quatuor Evangeliis et in Actis Apostolorum. Lond. 1655. 8vo.
An ingenious and learned work, by one of the translators of the Bible, temp. James I.

— John, (of Hode-court). Æneas his Descent into Hell. Lond. 1661. 4to.
Contains pp. 248. Bindley, pt. i. 1297. 2s. 6d. 1820. 7s. 6d. Nassau, pt. ii. 1588, 6s. Bibl. Anglo-Poet. 896, 3*l.* 3s. LARGE PAPER. Nassau, pt. i. 590, morocco, 19s.

— Thomas, A.M. Tactica sacra: an Attempt to develope, and to exhibit to the Eye, by tabular Arrangement, a general Rule of Composition prevailing in the holy Scriptures. Lond. 1824. 4to. 10s. 6d.
'An ingenious attempt to extend to the epistolatory writings of the new Testament the principles of composition so ably illustrated by Bishop Jebb. The work consists of two parts: the first contains the necessary explanations; and the second comprises four of the epistles arranged at length in Greek and English examples.'—*Horne*. Mr. Boys likewise published A Key to the Book of Psalms, 1825. 8vo. 8s. 6d.

— William. Testacea minuta rariora: a Collection of the minute and rare Shells lately discovered in the Sand of the Sea Shore near Sandwich, considerably augmented, and all their Figures accurately drawn, as magnified with the Microscope, by Geo. Walker. Lond. (1784.) 4to. 15s.
Contains pp. 38, including title, dedication, and introduction, with 8 plates.

— Collections for a History of Sandwich, in Kent, with Notices of the other Cinque Ports and Members, and of Richborough. Canterbury, 1792. 4to. 1*l.* 16s.
Contains pp. viii and 877. besides list of subscribers, with an additional list, 5 pages; list of plates and contents, 2 pages, also an index, &c. 4 pages, and a second errata and addenda, 1 leaf. 'The editor has collated a copy with four additional pages, containing the original list of subscribers, with a notice respecting the arrangement of the volume, headed 'Collections for a History of Sandwich, Part the First;' but he believes that it was generally cancelled, when the volume was completed.'—*Upcott*. There are copies on LARGE PAPER, 2*l.* 12s. 6d.

BOYSE, Rev. Joseph, of Dublin. Works; being a complete Collection of his Discourses, Sermons, and other Tracts. Lond. 1728. folio. 2 vols. in 1. 1*l.* 1s.
'Boyse has been called the dissenting Scott, but much more polite. His language is plain, animated, and nervous; his matter is excellently digested.'—*Doddridge*.

Brabant and Flanders.—Discourse on the Husbandry of Brabant and Flanders. Lond. 1645. 4to. 5s.
This discourse, which has always been looked upon as an excellent work in husbandry, was published by Hartlib. It was written by Sir R. Weston, and reprinted 1655. It is remarked in the Philosophical Transactions, that England has profited in agriculture to the amount of many millions by following the directions in this little treatise.

BRACKENRIDGE, H. M. Voyage to South America, in 1817-18. Lond. 1820. 8vo. 2 vols. 14s.
In the Edinburgh Review, xxxii. 231-48, is a notice of this author's Views of Louisiana. Pittsburgh.

BRACTON, Henr. de. De Legibus et Consuetudinibus Angliæ Libri quinque. Lond. 1569. folio.
According to Sir Wm. Jones, 'the best of judicial classics.' Fol. 444, besides title, 'T. N. Candido lectori. 8.' next 'Varietates

lectionis,' then an index. Willett, 427, 1*l*. 18s. Towneley, pt. ii. 508, 2*l*. 12s. 6d. LARGE PAPER. Nassau, pt. i. 658, 4*l*. 11s. Duke of Grafton, 126, 3*l*. 13s. 6d. Sotheby's in 1828, russia, 6*l*. Reprinted Lond. 1840. 4to. Marq. of Townshend, 1869, 1*l*. 3s. Brockett, 508, 1*l*. 18s.

BRADBURY, John. Travels in the Interior of America, in 1809-10-11 ; including a Description of Upper Louisiana, Kentucky, Indiana, and Tennessee. Lond. 1817. 8vo. 6s.

— Thomas. Works, consisting of LIV Sermons. Lond. 1762. 8vo. 3 vols.

Williams, 287, 1*l*. 17s. These sermons, chiefly political, written by a facetious preacher among the dissenters, were reprinted 1772, 8vo. 3 vols. 15s.

BRADDON, Lawrence. Essex's Innocency and Honour vindicated. Lond. 1690. 4to. with a plate.

White Knights, 1562, 5s. Braddon likewise published An Enquiry into, and Detection of the barbarous Murther of the late Earl of Essex. 1684. 4to. The Tryal of Laurence Bradqon and Hugh Speke, Gent. upon an Information of High misdemeanor, Subornation, and spreading false Reports. 1684. folio. Bishop Burnet's late History charg'd with great Partiality and Misrepresentations. 1725. 8vo. Towneley, pt. i. 283, 5s. 6d.

BRADFORD, John. Copye of a Letter sent to the Erles of Arundel, Darbie, Shrewsbury, and Pembroke, declarig the Nature of Spaniardes, and discouering the most detestable Treasons, whiche they haue pretended moste falselye against Englande. Whereunto is added a tragical Blast of the papistical Trōpet for Mayntenaunce of the Popes Kingdome in Englande, by T. E. (1555). 16mo.

'The title-page and preface seem to have been prefixed after the work was printed, for there is another title, without mentioning 'The Tragical Blast,' and a preface signed 'Thy louinge frende John Bradeforte.' The author, John Bradford, tells us that in King Edward's time he served Sir William Skipewithe, in Lincolnshire, and writes as from abroad.'—*Herbert.*

— Hurt of hearing Masse. Lond. by Wyllyam Copland. 16mo.

Contains Fii, in eights. Reprinted 1580, 16mo. F 4, in eights. With Two notable sermons on Repentance, 1555, in 1 vol. Sotheby, 1853, 2*l*. 5s.

This protestant Martyr likewise published—

A Letter sent to Master A. B. from I. B. in which is set forth the Authoritie of Parentes vpon their Children ; with an Addition of a Sermon of Repentance. Anno 1548. 8vo. The letter consists of nine leaves, the sermon of leaves.

Complaynt of Veritie, an exhortation of Mathewe Rogers unto his children, &c., &c., in verse. Lond. 1559. 8vo. *See* Wood's Athen. Oxon. by Dr. Bliss, i. 59. Bright, 1845. 17*l*.

A godly Meditacion of John Bradforth. By Coplande, 1560. Towneley, pt. i. 357. In Maunsell's catalogue, p. 84, is Jo. Bradford, his godly Meditations, which he vsed being in prison, entituled his Beades.'

All the Examinacions of M. John Bradforde ; wherevnto is annexed his priuate Talk and Conflicte in Prison after his Condemnacion. Anno Domini, 1561, 8vo. 10s. 6d. It is introduced with ' The Oryginal of his Lyfe,' 114 leaves.

Godlie Meditations vpon the Lordes Prayer, the Beleefe and ten Commaundementes, with other comfortable Meditations, Praiers, and Exercises. Whereunto is annexed a Defence of the Doctrine of God's eternal Election and Predestination. Lond. 1562. 16mo. 10s. 6d. Contains Q 6, in eights. The treatise on Election and Predestination was also published separately, 1562.

Godly Meditations vppon the ten Commaundements, the Articles of the Fayth, and the Lords Prayer. Whervnto is ioyned a Treatise against the Feare of Death : also a Comparison betweene the old Man and the new; the Lawe and the Gospie. &c. 1567. Lond. 8vo. 10s. 6d. Contains 96 leaves, besides the preface.

Two notable Sermons, the one of Repentance, and the other of the Lordes Supper. Lond. 1574. 8vo. 5s. Reprinted 1581, 1599. The sermon on repentance was likewise published separately, 1558. Roxburghe, supplement, 597.

Treatise against the Feare of Death ; whereunto are annexed certaine sweete Meditations of the Kingdom of Christ, of Life everlasting, and of the blessed State and Felicity of the same. Lond. 1563, 24mo. Two other editions without date, one printed by W. Powell, the other for H. Singleton.

An Answer to a Letter, whether it be lawfull to be present at the Popish Masse, and other superstitious Church Seruice. Lond. 16mo.

The Life, Martyrdom, and Selections from the Writings of John Bradford will be found in vol. vi. of the Fathers of the English Church, and many of his letters,

&c. are printed in Fox, and other martyrologies.
[See Parker Society *Appendix*, Bradford.]

BRADFORD, Rev. Wm. Sketches of the Country, Character, and Costume, made during the Campaign, and on the Route of the British Army, in Portugal and Spain, in 1808 and 1809; accompanied with incidental Illustration and Description on each Subject. Lond. 1809. folio, with 56 coloured plates.

Duke of York, 1000, 3*l*. 7s. 1497, 2*l*. 15s. Dent, pt. i. 481, 2*l*. 2s. White Knights, 778, 6*l*. 16s. 6d. This work was published in 24 Numbers at 10s. 6d. small, and 16s. large paper.

BRADLEY, Charles. Sermons preached in the Parish Church of High Wycombe. Lond. 1819. 8vo.

[For several other volumes of this author's Sermons, see London Catalogue.]

— James, D.D. Astronomical Observations made at the Royal Observatory at Greenwich, 1750—62, with a Continuation by the Rev. N. Bliss. Oxford, 1798, 1805. folio. 2 vols. 2*l*.

In 1795 was printed Proceedings of the Board of Longitude, in Regard to the Recovery of the late Dr. Bradley's Observations; with some other Papers relative thereto, folio, pp. 22. See for continuations, GREENWICH OBSERVATORY.

[His Astronomical Observations, by Büsch, 4to. Oxford, 1838. 4s. 6d. Works and Correspondence, by Rigaud, 4to. Oxford, 1832, 1*l*. 12s.]

— John. View of the Truth of Christianity, with the History of the Life of Apollonius Tyanæus, &c. Lond. 1699. 4to. 5s.

— Richard. Historia Plantarum succulentarum (Anglice et Latine). Lond. 1716—27. 4to.

An unfinished work, consisting of five Decades, with 50 plates.

— Philosophical Account of the Works of Nature. Lond. 1721. 4to. 5s.

Pp. 194, with 28 plates. Fonthill, 275, 14s.

— Survey of the ancient Husbandry and Gardening, collected from Cato, Varro, Columella, Virgil, and others, the most eminent Writers among the Greeks and Romans; wherein many of the most difficult Passages in those Authors are explained. Lond. 1725. 8vo. with cuts. 5s.

This writer, who was Professor of Botany in the University of Cambridge, published many other works on Agriculture, Botany, &c. His Dictionarum Botanicum, 8vo. 2 vols. is said to be the first attempt of the kind in this country.

BRADSHAW, Henry. Holy Lyfe and History of Saynt Werburge, very frutefull for all Christen People to rede. Imprinted by Richarde Pynson. 1521. 4to.

Black letter, containing pp. 224, s iv. in fours and eights alternately, beginning with ¶ iiij. then a viij. Two copies are in the Bodleian. Reed. 6972, 18*l*. Woodhouse, 31*l*. 10s. Bibl. Anglo-Poet. 895, 63*l*. resold by Saunders in 1818, for 42*l*. Heber, 19*l*. 5s.

— Lyfe of Saynt Radegunde. Impr. by Richard Pynson, 4to. n. d.

Black letter, containing by signatures e 6, eights and fours alternately. Woodhouse, in 1803, 851, 17*l*. 17s. Heber, 21*l*. 10s. For further particulars respecting this writer, see Warton's History of Poetry, 8vo. iii. 13—24. Wood's Athen. Oxon. by Dr. Bliss, i. 13—19. Savage's Librarian, ii. 75—9. Ames, by Dr. Dibdin, ii. 491—9.

— John. The President of Presidents; or an Elegie on the Death of John Bradshaw (1659), folio.

In the British Museum are several tracts relating to Bradshaw, President of the Regicides.

— Thomas. Shepherds Starre, now of late seene and at this Hower to be observed merveilous orient in the East, which bring glad Tydings to all that may behold her Brightness. Lond. by Robert Robinson, 1591. 4to. pp. 60.

In verse. Dedicated to 'Robert Deuerex, Earle of Essex, and unto Thomas, Lord Burgh.' Unknown to Ames or Herbert, but mentioned by Ritson in his Bibliographia Poetica. Bibl. Anglo.-Poet. 84, morocco, 30*l*. Resold by Saunders in 1818 for 10*l*. 10s. and again by Bright, 9*l*. 5s.

— William. English Puritanism, containing the main Opinions

of the rigidest Sort of those that went by that Name in England. Lond. 1605.

This is valuable, as showing the difference between the principles of the ancient and modern nonconformists. This eminent puritan divine published several other works.

BRADSTREET, Anne. The tenth Muse lately sprung up in America. Lond. 1650. small 8vo.

Consisting of pp. 222. Nassau, pt. l. 302, 9s. Bibl. Anglo-Poet. 67, 1l. 5s. Perry, pt. 1. 539, 1l. 6s. Bindley, pt. 1. 1544, 1l. 15s. Towneley, pt. 1. 679, morocco, 3l. 15s. Fraser, 1852, 2l. 3s. [Second edition, Boston, U.S. 1678.]

— Captain. Life and uncommon Adventures of Captain Dudley Bradstreet. Dublin, 1755. 8vo.

A copy is in the British Museum. Nassau, pt. 1. 1990, morocco, 1l. 1s.

BRADWARDINE, Thomas, Archbishop of Canterbury. De Causa Dei, contra Pelagivm, et de Virtute Cavsarvm ad suos Mertonenses, Libri tres: Opera et studio D. Henr. Savilii. Lond. 1618. folio, 1l. 11s. 6d.

This scarce and curious work is, says Dr. Adam Clarke, 'accused by the Catholics as holding out the same doctrine which has since been termed Protestantism.'

Bradwardine, who was nearly contemporary with Chaucer, published several skilful mathematical works.

BRADWELL, Stephen. Watchman for the Pest. Lond. 1625. 4to.

This writer likewise published Helps for svddain Accidents endangering Life, 1633, 12mo. and Physick for the Sicknesse commonly called the Plague, 1636, 4to.

BRADY, John. Clavis Calendaria, or Analysis of the Calendar, illustrated with ecclesiastical History and classical Anecdotes. Lond. 1812. [third edition, 1816.] 8vo. 2 vols. 1l. 1s.

An abridgment of this useful work appeared 1814, 12mo. 10s. Brady likewise published Varieties of Literature, post 8vo. 8s.

— Nicholas, D.D. Sermons, chiefly upon practical Subjects. Lond. 1730. 8vo. 3 vols. 10s. 6d.

Brady was the translator, in conjunction with Tate, of the present version of the Psalms. He likewise translated the Æneid of Virgil into English verse, 4 vols. 8vo.

— Robert, M.D. Introduction to the old English History, comprehended in three several Tracts. Lond. 1684. fol. 10s. 6d.

This volume generally accompanies the author's history of England. LARGE PAPER. Sir M. M. Sykes, pt 1. 680, morocco, 3l. Dr. Brady had previously published A full and clear Answer to a Book written by Wm. Petit, Esq. with some Animadversions upon Jani Anglorium Facies nova. Lond. 1681, 8vo. 8s.

— History of England, from the first Entrance of the Romans to the Death of Richard the Second, with an Appendix of Official Documents, Lond. 1685, 1700. folio, 3 vols. in 2, 2l. 2s. [Or with the Introductory Volume, 4 vols. in 3, 3l. 3s.]

This Tory history is commended by Lordkeeper Guildford and the Historian Hume; the latter of whom is said to have been chiefly indebted to Brady for the facts and principles of his celebrated work.

— Historical Treatise of Cities and Burghs or Boroughs. Lond. 1690. folio, 5s.

Reprinted 1704, folio, 1777, 8vo. Heath, 4407, 12s.

BRAGGE, Francis. Practical Discourses on the Parables of our Saviour. Lond. 1706. 8vo. 2 vols. 7s.

These discourses, frequently reprinted, are still in estimation. Bragge likewise published a work on the Miracles, 1706, &c. 8vo. 2 vols. 7s.

[His works were published collectively at Oxford, 1833, 5 vols. 8vo. 1l. 12s. 6d.]

— The Passion of our Saviour, to which is added a Pindarick Ode on the suffering God, 12mo.

Engraved by Sturt. Nassau, pt. 1. 2506, 1l. 10s.

BRAHE, Tycho. Propheticall Conclusion of the new and much admired Starre of the North, 1572. Lond. 1632. 4to. 10s. 6d.

A curious tract relating to Gustavus Adolphus, consisting of 18 leaves (A—E 2) with portraits of Brahe and Gustavus Adolphus, and plate. Another tract entitled Astronomicall Conjectur, 1632, 4to. is in the British Museum.

B[raidshaigh] (J. A.). Virginialia, or Spiritual Sonnets in praise of the most glorious Virgin Marie, printed with Licence, 1632. 4to.
Bright, russia, fine, 6*l*. 6*s*.

BRAINERD, David. Life of D. Brainerd, Missionary from Scotland to the Indians. 1765. 8vo.
Bindley, pt. ii. 1310, 10s.

BRAITHWAIT, R. *See* BRATHWAIT, Richard.

BRAITHWAITE, John. History of the Revolutions in the Empire of Morocco upon the Death of the late Emperor Muly Ishmael. Lond. 1729. royal 8vo.
A work containing valuable information on the physical and moral state of the people, written by one who was an eyewitness of the events he describes. Heath, 2721, 4s. Dent, pt. i. 250, russia, 10s. 6d. Fonthill, 2252, 1*l*. 11s. 6d.

BRAMHALL, John, Archbishop of Armagh. Works (with Life by Dr. Vesey, Bishop of Limerick, afterwards Archbishop of Tuam). Dublin, 1677. folio, 1*l*. 1s.
Williams, 373, 2*l*. reprinted by the Library of Anglo-Cath. Theology in 5 vols. 8vo. Oxford, 1842-45. Many of this eminent prelate's works were published separately.
'The Consecration and Succession of Protestant Bishops justified,' &c. Gravenhagh, 1658, 8vo. Brockett, 376, 2*l*.

BRAMWELL, George. Analytical Table of the private Acts, 1 Geo. II. 1727, to 5 Will. IV. 1834. Lond. 1812-34. royal 8vo. 2 vols. 1*l*. 10s.

BRANCH, Lady Helen. Epicedivm, a funerall Song, vpon the vertuous Life and godly Death of the Lady Helen Branch (by Sir William Harbert). A Commemoration of the Life and Death of Dame Helen Branch (by I. P.).— An Epitaph of the vertuous Life and Death of Dame Helen Branch. Lond. Thomas Creede, 1594. 4to. Three tracts in 1 vol.
A notice of this work, believed to be unique, will be found in the Restituta, iii. 297—300. Bibl. AngloPoet. 246, 60*l*. Sir M. M. Sykes, pt. i. 1159, 17*l*. 5s. Heber, 10*l*. *See* SILVESTER (Josh.).

BRANCHE, T. Principia Legis et Equitatis. Fourth Edition, with Additions, and the Latin Rules and Maxims translated by John Richardson. Lond. 1824. 12mo. 6s.
This work contains more law and more useful matter than any one book of the same size which can be put into the hands of the student. *See* Preston on Abstracts, i. 214.

BRAND, Adam. Journal of the Embassy from the Emperors of Muscovy, &c. over Land unto China, by Everard Isbrand, their Secretary in the years 1693, 1694 and 1695, translated from the High-Dutch. Lond. 1698. 8vo. *See* IDES (E. Y.)
Roxburghe, 8890, 9s.

— John. Description of Orkney, Zetland, Pightland, Firth and Caithness. Edinb. 1701 or 3. 8vo.
A curious and interesting account. Jadis, 85, 9s. Baker, 49, 17s. Bindley, pt. i. 510, 1*l*. 1s. Heath, 4728, 1*l*. 11s. 6d. Roxburghe, 8780, 1*l*. 11s. 6d. Reprinted in the third volume of Pinkerton's Collection of Voyages and Travels.

BRAND, John, M.A. History and Antiquities of the Town and County of Newcastle upon Tyne. Lond. 1789. 4to. 2 vols.
Vol. I. engraved title; pp. xvi. and 676; index, errata, and list of plates, 24 in number, 4 pages. Vol. II. engraved title; the history continued, with an appendix and addenda, 724 pages; index, omissions, errata; and list of plates, 10 in number, 8 pp. Roxburghe, 8642, russia, 1*l*. 13s. Bindley, pt. i. 723, 2*l*. 6s. Towneley, pt. ii. 275, russia, 2*l*. 6s. Nassau, pt. i. 592, russia, 2*l*. 12s 6d. Beckford in 1817, 156, russia, 3*l*. 6s. Brockett, 512, with printed additions, russia, 3*l*. 16s.

— Observations on Popular Antiquities, chiefly illustrating the Origin of our vulgar Customs, Ceremonies and Superstitions. Arranged and revised, with Additions, by Henry Ellis. Lond. 1813. 4to. 2 vols.
An able article on this entertaining and instructive work, will be found in the Quarterly Rev. xi. 259-85. Brockett, 513, russia, 3*l*. 13s. 6d. LARGE PAPER. Drury, 4685, russia, 5*l*. 7s. 6d. Sir M. M. Sykes, pt. i. 458, 4*l*. Strettell, 359, russia, 4*l*. 7s.
[Republished, with considerable additions, in *Bohn's Antiquarian Library*, 3 vols. post 8vo. 1848, 15s.]

BRANDE, William Thomas. Manual of Chemistry. Second Edition. Lond. 1821. 8vo. 3 vols. [Sixth edition, 2 vols. 8vo. 1848. 2*l*. 5s.]
Drury, 503, 2*l*. 1s. The first edition appeared 1819, 8vo. 1 vol. LARGE PAPER. Sotheby's in 1823, 1*l*. 2s. Mr. Brande has likewise published Descriptive Catalogue of the British Specimens deposited in the Geological Collection of the Royal Institution. Lond. 1816. 8vo. 9s. Outlines of Geology, being the Substance of a Course of Lectures at the Royal Institution in 1816. Lond. 1817. 8vo. 7s. 6d. Tables, in Illustration of the Theory of definite Proportionals. Lond. 1828. 8vo. pp. xix. and 88.

[BRANDE'S Dictionary of Science, Literature, and Art. Lond. 1853. royal 8vo. 3*l*. For his many other works, *see* London Catalogue.]

BRANDER, Gustavus. *See* British Museum.

BRANDON, Saint.—The Lyfe of Saynt Brandon. Lond. by W. de Worde. 4to.
A copy of this life of the Irish Saint, supposed unique, is in the Rt. Hon. Thomas Grenville's library. It consists of 10 leaves, without numbers, signatures, or catchwords, having 33 lines on a full page.

— H. and C. Dukes of Suffolk. Vita et Obitus dvorvm Fratrum Suffolciensium Henrici et Caroli Brandon Ducum illustrissimorum. Adduntur Epitaphia, &c. Lond. R. Grafton, s.a. (1552). 4to.
Copies of this piece of English biography, published by Tho. Wilson, LL.D. are in the Bodleian Library, British Museum, the Grenville Library, and in Earl Spencer's Collection at Althorp. Bright, 6078, 5*l*. 2s. 6d.

— Richard. Confession of Richard Brandon, the Hangman, concerning his beheading Charles the First (with frontispiece). 1649.— Last Will and Testament of Richard Brandon, Headsman and Hangman to the pretended Parliament. 1649. 4to.
Copies of both these tracts are in the British Museum, Nassau, pt. i. 594, 1*l*. 13s. Dent, pt. i. 800. (The Confession with King Charles his Speech on the Scaffold) 1*l*. 7s.

— Sam. Tragicomœdi of the vertuous Octavia. Lond. 1598. 12mo.
Annexed is an epistle from Octavia to M. Antony, and his answer. Roxburghe, 4506. 3*l*. 17s. Jolley, 1843. 12*l*. 15s.

Brandon Cause.—A true Narrative of the Proceedings in the several Suits in Law that have been between the Rt. Hon. Charles Lord Gerard of Brandon, and Alexander Fitton, E$_{sq}$. Hague, printed 1663. 4to. pp. 46.

BRANDT, Gerard. History of the Reformation, and other Ecclesiastical Matters, in and about the Low Countries. Lond. 1720-3. folio, 4 vols. with portraits.
Lord Hardwicke said that the Dutch language was worth acquiring, if it were only to enjoy the pleasure of reading this history. Marq. of Townshend, 428, 2*l*. 12s. 6d. Bishop of Ely, 229, 2*l*. 12s. 6d. Sotheby's in 1824, 4*l*. 5s. Willett. 7*l*. 10s. LARGE PAPER. An abridgment was published 1725. 8vo. 2 vols. 8s.

BRANT, Sebastian. Shyp of Folys of the Worlde, translated out of Laten Frenche and Doche into Englysshe Tonge, by Alexander Barclay Preste. Lond. by Rycharde Pynson, 1509. folio.
Black letter, with numerous cuts, 277 leaves, numbered 1 to CCLXXIIII folios [folios 57, 58, 59, 67, and 68 are repeated, and folio 58 again repeated ; folios 132, 174, 288 are omitted] besides dedication, and table, four leaves. The Latin is uniformly printed in the Roman type, and the English in the Gothic. A copy is in the Grenville Library. Inglis, 196, (two leaves MS.) 6*l*. 16s. 6d. Sir P. Thompson, 176 (no title), 16*l*. Sotheby's in 1821, 28*l*. Dent, pt. i. 321, morocco. date 1508? 30*l*. 9s. Bibl. Anglo-Poet. 15, 105*l*.

— Another Edition. Lond. by John Cawood, 1570. folio.
Black letter, pp. 676, with cuts. This second edition contains some of Barclay's smaller pieces, and is, on that account, to be greatly preferred to the more rare one from Pynson's press,[but has not the Balade to the Virgin Mary, which is in the edition 1509]. A copy is in the Grenville Library. Towneley, pt. ii. 324, 4*l*. Nassau, pt. i. 659, 5*l*. Roscoe, 1396, 5*l*. 12s. 6d. Constable, 282, 6*l*. Gordonstoun, 298, 6*l*. 6s. Perry, pt. i. 859, 8*l*. 5s. White Knights, 386, 8*l*. 12s. Roxburghe, 3294, 9*l*. 19s. 6d. Bibl. Anglo-Poet. 16, 12*l*. 12s. resold by

Saunders in 1818, 5*l*. 5*s*. Fonthill, 3248, 13*l*. 13*s*. Knight, 1847, FINE, 11*l*. 5*s*. Crawfurd, 1854, mor. 8*l*. 10*s*.

This work was first written in German, thence translated into Latin, and then into French. The design was to ridicule the prevailing follies and vices of every rank and profession, under the allegory of a ship freighted with fools, and in his metrical translation, Barclay has given a variety of characters drawn exclusively from his own countrymen, and added his advice to the various fools, which possesses at least, the merits of good sense and sound morality.

BRANT, Sebastian. The grete Shyppe of Fooles of this Worlde (translated by H. Watson). Lond. by W. de Worde, 1517. 4to. with wood cuts.

In prose. A to GG 6, fours and eights alternately, besides 6 leaves with the prologue, prolude and table before sign. A. A copy is in the possession of Francis Douce, Esq. Roxburghe, 3293, 64*l*. Heber. Dr. Dibdin in his Tour, ii. 249-50, notices a copy ON VELLUM, of 'The Shyppe of Fooles, Lond. by Wynkyn de Worde, 1509.' 8vo. with cuts, as being in the Royal Library at Paris.

BRASBRIDGE, Joseph. Fruits of Experience, or Memoir of Joseph Brasbridge: written in his eightieth and eighty-first years. Lond. 1824. 8vo. with portrait.

The auto-biography of a silversmith of Fleet-street, severely handled in Blackwood's Edinburgh Magazine.

— Thomas. Poore Man's Jewell, that is to say, a Treatise of the Pestilence: vnto which is annexed a Declaration of the Vertues of the Hearbes Carduus Benedictus, and Angelica. Lond. 1578. 8vo.

Reprinted 1580, 1591. Brasbridge likewise published Quæstiones in Officia M. T. Ciceronis. Oxon. 1615. 8vo. and an Interpretation of Abdias the Prophet. 1574. 8vo.

BRASIER, Rich. Last Will and Confession of the Christian Faith, made in the 4 Yeare of the Raigne of King Edward the 6. Lond. by John Day. 8vo.

From Maunsell's Catalogue, p. 23.

BRASSE, Rev. J. Greek Gradus; or a Greek, Latin, and English Prosodial Lexicon. Lond. 1827. 8vo. Revised by the Rev. F. E. J. Valpy. 8vo. 1842. 15*s*.

— Samuel. Ship of Arms vseful for all Sorts of People in this woful Time of War, fashioned by a plain Country-Farmer. Lond. 1653. 12mo.

A privately printed volume consisting of 240 pages, dedicated to the Lady Elwes, Wife to Sir Jervace Elwes, Knight, after which is an address to the Commons of England, another to the Reader, and some commendatory verses. The author states that having lavisht out 80 years in jollity and pleasure, he was induced, during a long illness, to write this book chiefly for the use of himself and familiar friends.

BRATHWAIT, Richard. Golden Fleece. Whereunto bee annexed two Elegies, entitled Narcissvs Change and Æson's Dotage, with Sonnets, &c. Lond. 1611. sm. 8vo.

Pp. 112, dedicated to M. Robert Bindlosse, Esquire. At sign. E 3, is the following title, 'Sonnets or Madrigals. With the Art of Poesie annexed thereunto by the same Author.' The Art of Poesie, however, is wanting, and no copy has yet been discovered extending beyond G 8, which ends with the catchword 'The.' Bibl. Anglo-Poet. 45, 2*l*. 2*s*. Heber, pt. 4. 20*l*.

— Poets Willow: or the passionate Shepheard: with sundry delightfull and no lesse passionate Sonnets: &c. Lond. 1614. sm. 8vo.

A copy of this work, written in lyric and anacreontic measures, consisting of 48 leaves (pp. 83, and 12 of title, dedication, &c.), is in the Bodleian library. Heber, pt. 4, 205.

— The Prodigals Teares: or his Fare-well to Vanity, &c. Lond. 1614. small 8vo.

An excellent tract, written in good style, and abounding with sound morality, consisting of 138 pp. besides title, dedication, and last leaf to the reader, 6 more. A copy is in the Bodleian library.

— Schollers Medley, or an intermixt Discovrse vpon Historicall and Poeticall Relations. Lond. 1614. 4to. 1*l*. 10*s*.

The running title of this work, which consists of 63 leaves (pp. 118), title, &c. 8 more, is 'A Survey of History.' A copy is in the Bodleian library.

— Survey of History; or, a Nursery for Gentry. Lond. 1638. 4to.

Second edition, consisting of 221 leaves: the title containing a portrait of the author in the centre, is from the burin of Wm. Marshall. Roxburghe, 7369, 13*s*. Stanley,

17, 16s. Lloyd, 439, 16s. 6d. Dowdeswell, III. 17s. Bindley, pt. i. 1106, 19s. Nassau, pt. i. 598, 1l. 1s. According to Ant. à Wood, some copies bear the date of 1652. Towneley, pt. i. 898, date 1651, 2l. 5s.

BRATHWAIT, R. Strappado for the Diuell. Epigrams and Satyres alluding to the Time, with diuers Measures of no lesse Delight. By Μισοσυκος, to his Friend Φιλοκρατις. Lond. 1615. 12mo.

The second part of the volume is entitled Loves Labyrinth: or the True-Louers Knot; &c. By Richard Brathwayte. The whole consists of 182 leaves. Bibl. Anglo-Poet· 47, 8l. 8s. Strettell, 127, 2l. 17s. White Knights, 597, 3l. 19s. Inglis, 216, 2l. 12s. 6d. Roxburghe, 3372, 2l. 12s. 6d. Nassau, pt. i. 312, 5l. 10s. Roxburghe Supplement, 554, 1l. 5s. Midgley, 2 parts, with whole-length port. 6l. Utterson, 1852, 2l. 12s. 6d. Bright, mor. 3l. 4s.

— Solemne Ioviall Disputation, Theoreticke and Practicke briefely shadowing the Law of Drinking, &c. &c. Oenozythopolis, at the Signe of Red-eyes, 1617.—The Smoking Age, or the Man in the Mist; with the Life & Death of Tobacco, &c. Oenozythopolis. At the Signe of Teare-Nose, 1617. 8vo.

Prefixed are two curious engraved titles by Marshall, with leaves explanatory. The late Mr. Bindley considered this work as one of the scarcest books in England, and the plates by Marshall are the earliest production of that engraver. Gordonstoun, 1423, 4l. 10s. Nassau, pt. i. 1881, morocco, 9l. Bindley, pt. ii. 1345, 6l. 6s. Towneley, pt. i. 475, 3l. 16s. Hibbert, same copy, 8l. 8s. Bright, 3l.

— The good Wife: or a rare one amongst Women. Whereto is annexed an exquisite Discourse of Epitaphs; including the choicest thereof ancient or moderne. Lond. 1618. small 8vo.

Containing 156 pages. At sign. C 2 is a fresh title-page, 'Remains after Death:' 1618.—'Taking this volume altogether, I think it one of the most curious as well as one of the scarcest books of the period to which it belongs.'—*Dr. Bliss.* The Remains after Death, 1618. Bibl. Anglo-Poet. 48, (13 pages MS.). 10l. 10s. Midgley (13 leaves MS.). 4l. 17s. 6d. Perry, same copy, 2l. 18s. (Malone's, now in the Bodleian Library, the only perfect copy known.) Brydges' Restituta, iii. 196—203.

VOL. I.

— Description of a good Wife: or, a rare one amongst Women. Lond. 1619. small 8vo.

Bibl. Anglo-Poet. 46. Midgley (MS. title), 4l. 8s. *See* HANNAY, Patrick.

— A new Spring shadowed in sundry Pithie Poems. Mvsophilvs. Lond. G. Eld for F. Baylie, 1619. 4to.

Contains E in fours, last leaf blank. Jolley, 1843, 3l. 12s. resold Utterson, 4l. 6s. mor.

— Essaies vpon the Five Senses, with a pithie one vpon Detraction, &c. Lond. 1620. 12mo.

The Character of "a Shrew" at the end of the volume, which consists of 76 leaves, is omitted in the second edition. Gordonstoun, 330, 16s. 6d.

— Essaies vpon the Five Senses, revived by a new Supplement; &c. The second Edition revised and enlarged by the Author. Lond. 1635. 12mo. 12s.

After the Essays on the five senses, ending p. 81, is a second title, 'A Continuation of these Essayes,' &c.; and after p. 229, a third title, as 'The Distinct Titles of these Contemplations,' &c. The whole consists of 167 leaves. Nassau, pt. i. 313, 1l. 13s. Reprinted in the Archaica from an incomplete copy. The omissions, &c. however, will be found stated in Brathwait's Barnabees Journal, 1820, i. 168–74, 322–9.

— Shepheards Tales. Lond. 1621. 8vo.

Consisting of 25 leaves. A continuation of these Tales or Eclogues was printed with 'Natures Embassie.'

— Natvres Embassie: or, the Wilde mans Measvres: Danced naked by twelve Satyres, with sundry others continued in the next Section. Lond. Richard Whitaker, 1621. 8vo.

Containing pp. 264, title, &c. 8 more. At p. 73, is another title, 'The Second Section of Divine and Morall Satyres;' at p. 173, 'The Shepheards Tales;' at p. 215, 'Omphale, or, the Inconstant Shepheardesse;' at p. 237, 'His Odes: or Philomels Teares,' (pages 79 and 80 are repeated, 95, 96, 191, and 192 are omitted). A copy is in the Bodleian Library, and the Grenville Library. Steevens, 782, 1l. 3s. Lloyd, 197, 6l. Bibl. Anglo-Poet. 43, 8l. 8s. Midgley, MS. title, 5l. 15s 6d. Bright, 2l. 4s. 'His Odes: or Philomels Tears,' were reprinted at Lee Priory, 1815, 8vo. 8s. 6d.

— Times Cvrtaine drawne, or the

Anatomie of Vanitie. With other choice Poems, entituled: Health from Helicon. Lond. 1621. 8vo.

Consisting of pp. 214, dedicated to the univ. of Oxford; to John Earl of Bridgewater. At sign. I ' Panedone: or Health from Helicon: Ded. to Sir Thomas Gainsford, Knight.' A copy is in the Bodleian Library. Bibl. Anglo-Poet. 49, 12*l*. Midgley, 6*l*. Utterson (mended), 2*l* 2s.

BRATHWAIT, R. Britain's Bath. 1625.

Mention is made of this work in a marginal note attached to the dedication of the Snrvey of History, 1638, and another 'The Hunts-mans Raunge,' is noticed in the margin of the English Gentleman, 1630, p. 198.

— English Gentleman. Lond. 1630. 4to.

This volume has a fine frontispiece by Ro. Vaughan, with a folding broad-side as an explanatory draught. After p. 456, is a sheet without pagination, Nnn* (4th leaf blank): then follows a new title, 'Three choice Characters of marriage;' &c. The whole volume consists of p. 487, without the dedication to Tho. Viscount Wentworth. Strettell, 360, 15s. Dowdeswell, 113, 1*l*. 4s. Nassau, pt. i. 596, 1*l*. 13s. Inglis, 299, 1*l*. 14s. North. pt. iii. 632, russia, 1*l*. 17s.

— English Gentleman. The second Edition: revised, corrected, and enlarged. Lond. 1633. 4to. Frontispiece by Vaughan.

Nearly a paginary reprint of the first edition, with the text revised and corrected, but not enlarged. It consists of 240 leaves, and has the frontispiece by Vaughan. Lloyd, 438, 6s. Towneley, pt. i. 397, 2*l*. 5s.

— English Gentleman; and Gentlewoman, with a Ladies Love-Lectvre and a Svpplement lately annexed, and entituled the Tvrtles Trivmph. The Third Edition revised, corrected, and enlarged. Lond. 1641. folio, 1*l*. 10s. Frontispiece by Marshall.

This volume has an engraved title-page by W. Marshall, with a broadside explanatory. Each of the Four Articles, The English Gentleman, the English Gentlewoman, a Ladies Love Lecture, and the Turtles Triumph, have distinct titles. The three choice characters in the preceding editions are omitted in this. Bindley, pt. i. 395, 1*l*. 6s.

— Times Treasury; or Academy for Gentry. Lond. 1652. folio.

This is the English Gentleman, 1641, with a new title-page, and a few additions or alterations. The volume is dedicated to William Earle of Stafford, instead of Philip Earle of Pembroke, and has also a dedicatory address to Elizabeth (Dowager) Covntesse of Strafford, together making 4 leaves, (the general title, and that to the English Gentleman, 1641, being cancelled). At the end of the volume will be found 'A Character of Honour,' of 4 leaves only, a head title. In other respects the editions are the same. Nassau, pt. i. 660, 12s.

— English Gentlewoman, drawne out to the full Body. Lond. 1631. 4to.

This volume has a frontisp. by Will. Marshall, with a folding broadside explanatory. After the printed title are 22 leaves of dedications and a table. After p. 221 of the work, is 'the Character of A Gentlewoman,' 4 leaves, not paged, the 'Embleme,' and 'Vpon the Errata,' 2 more, then an 'Appendix vpon a former supposed Impression of this title,' 5 leaves. Dowdeswell, 112, 1*l*. 2s. Nassau, pt. i. 596, 2*l*. 8s. Stanley, 16, with the English Gentleman, 1630, 4*l*. 4s. Another edition will be found with the English Gentleman, 1641, fol.

— Whimzies: or, a new Cast of Characters. Londi 1631. 12mo.

The dedication to Sir Alex. Radcliffe, is signed Clitus Alexandrinus. In the work occurs a second title, viz. 'A Cater Character throwne out of a Boxe by an experienc'd Gamester.' The whole volume consists of 117 leaves. Bindley, pt. iv. 864, 12s. Reed, 3362, 19s.

— Anniversaries upon his Panarete (Mrs. Frances Brathwait). Lond. 1634. 8vo.

Contains sign. A, B, C, 24 leaves, or 48 pages. In 1635 appeared Anniversaries upon his Panarete continued. Bright (uncut), 2*l*. 2s.

— Raglands Niobe: or Elizas Elegie. Imprinted by F. K. 1635. 12mo.

An Elegy to the Memory of Lady Elizabeth Herbert, wife of Edward Somerset Lord Herbert, &c. consisting of 14 leaves.

— Arcadian Princesse; or, the Triumph of Ivstice: Prescribing excellent Rules of Physicke, for a sicke Iustice. Digested into fowre Bookes, and faithfully rendred to the originall Italian copy, by Ri. Brathvvait, Esq. Lond. 1635. 18mo.

A translation from Mariano Silesio, a Florentine, interspersed with various Poesies.

Collation.—Front. by Marshall, verses upon, Title, Epistle dedicat. to H. Somerset, Earle of Worcester, &c. Testimonies & Summary of the Contents, 13 leaves.—The Arcadian Princesse (Part i.) 254 pp. pages 191 and 192 (*bis*). (Part ii.) 250 pp. and Life of Silesio, 8 pp. Strettell, 127, 6s. 6d. Boswell, 377, 7s. Lloyd, 196, 16s. Bindley, pt. i. 649, 1*l*. 1s. Nassau, pt. i. 318, 1*l*. 3s. White Knights, 598, 1*l*. 7s.

BRATHWAIT, R. Lives of all the Roman Emperors, being exactly collected from Iulius Cæsar unto the now reigning Ferdinand the second. Lond. 1636. 12mo.

Prefixed is an engraved title, by W. Marshall. The volume consists of pp. 384, besides dedications and table.

— Spiritval Spicerie: containing sundrie sweet Tractates of Devotion and Pietie. Lond. 1638. 12mo.

Jacobus Gruythrodius, a German, was the author of this dialogue. At p. 228 is a new title, 'A Christian Dial,' written by Joh. Justus Lanspergius, a Carthusian; at p. 324, 'The Passionate Pilgrim;' at p. 345, a head-title, 'Holy Memorials, or heavenly Memento's.'

— Psalmes of David the King and Prophet, and of other holy Prophets, paraphras'd in English, by R. B. Lond. 1638. 12mo.

This little volume has an engraved title by Marshall, at the bottom of which is a small oval, containing a portrait subscribed Quamquam ô (intended for Rich. Brathwait). The volume consists of 300 pp.

— Ar't asleepe Husband? A Boulster Lecture; stored with all Variety of witty Jeasts, merry Tales and other pleasant Passages, &c. By Philogenes Panedonius. Lond. 1640. 12mo.

This volume, consisting of pp. 330, should contain a front. by W. Marshall and a print at p. 246, also found in the Two Lancashire Lovers. Inglis, 34, 1*l*. 1s. Marq. of Townshend, 52, 1*l*. 1s. North, pt. i. 87, russia, 1*l*. 12s. Nassau, pt. i. 314, 3*l*. 6s. Stanley, 675, 4*l*. 16s. Gardner, 1854, fine copy, mor. 5*l*.

— Two Lancashire Lovers: or the excellent History of Philocles and Doriclea. By Musæus Palatinus. Lond. 1640. 8vo.

This volume, consisting of pp. 268, has an engraved title, and also a print at p. 247, same as in 'Ar't asleepe Husband?' p. 246. Nassau, pt. i. 316, 1*l*. 5s.

— Penitent Pilgrim. Lond. 1641. 21mo. 15s.

This volume, consisting of pp. 445, has an engraved front. by W. Marshall. Bright, FINE PAPER, rich old mor. 6*l*. 8s. 6d.

— Mercurius Britannicus. Tragi-Comœdia Lutetiæ. Summo cum Applausu publice acta. Sine Loco aut Anno. 4to.

Consisting of four sheets. Roxburghe, 3651, 4s.

— Mercurius Britannicus: or, the English Intelligencer, a tragic comedy, at Paris acted with great applause. Reprinted with sundry additions. Printed in the yeare 1641. 4to.

This piece is wholly political: the subject of it being entirely on the ship-money, one of the great points which occasioned the troubles of K. Charles I. Several of the judges are attacked in it under feigned names; particularly Justice Hutton and Justice Croke, under those of Hortensius and Corvus Acilius; also Prynne, who is introduced under the character of Prinper. Roxburghe, 4505, 4s. Rhodes, 639, 10s. 6d.

— Astræa's Tears. An Elegie vpon the Death of Sir Richard Hutton, Knight. Lond. 1641. 12mo.

This volume has a front. in Marshall's style, containing an excellent portrait of the judge in his robes, extremely rare. The work concludes at sign. E 4; then a new title for 'Panaretees Triumph; or Hymens heavenly Hymne.' The whole contains 55 leaves [sign. H 2]. Nassau, pt. i. 817, 1*l*. 19s. Bindley, 5*l*. 10s. W. Knights, 5*l*. 10s. Woodhouse, 4*l*. 14s. 6d. Heber, no portrait, but uncut, 1*l*. 19s.

— Barnabees Journall (and Bessie Bell, both in Latin and English Verse) by Corymbæus. [Lond. circa 1648—50.]

First edition, containing sign. A—Ee, in eights, with a frontispiece by Marshall materially differing from the later editions, they having been modernized, &c. White Knights, 299, morocco, 8*l*. 10s. Nassau, pt. i. 305, 7*l*. Garrick, 86, (bad copy, no frontispiece), 1*l*. 4s. Bibl. Anglo-Poet, 57, (five leaves reprinted) 5*l*. Dent, pt. i. 248, 3*l*. 18s. A copy in March, 1815, was sold for 16*l*. 16s. Heber, mor. 6*l*. 6s. Sotheby, 1857, fine, no portrait, 7*l*.

— Drunken Barnaby's four Journeys to the North of England, in Latin and English Verse, &c. to which is added Bessy Bell. Lond. 1716. small 8vo.

Second edition, consisting of 83 leaves and two plates. An index and some introductory matter were added to this edition, which has been repeated in the subsequent ones. White Knights, 300, morocco, 15s. Nassau, pt. i. 306, 16s. Lloyd, 53, 4s. Bindley, pt. i. 1755, 10s.—Third Edition. Lond. 1723, small 8vo. 102 leaves. with six cuts. Bibl. Anglo-Poet. 59, 1l. 5s. White Knights, 301, 6s. Nassau, pt. i. 307. 7s. Reed, 6557, 15s. 6d. Roscoe, 1376, 2l. 2s. Drury, 504, 11s. Stanley, 416, 1l. 2s. Gossett, 315, 11s. 6d. Roxburghe, 6697, 10s. 6d. Towneley, pt. i. 354, 18s. FINE PAPER. Nassau, pt. i. 308, 19s.—An Edition, Dublin, 1762, 8vo. 72 leaves.—Fourth Edition, Lond. 1776, sm. 8vo. 102 leaves, with six copper plates. At the end of this edition only there is 'Lucus Chevinus—Chevy Chase,' separately paged, and alternately Latin and English, extending to 16 leaves. This translation is modern and anonymous. Bibl. Anglo-Poet. 60. 18s.—White Knights, 302, 6s.—Fifth Edition, Lond. 1805, 8vo. 98 leaves, with seven new vignettes and tail-pieces. Prefixed is an advertisement relative to the supposed author, Barnaby Harrington, and his Journal. White Knights, 303, 8s. Nassau, pt. i. 309, 6s. LARGE PAPER. Bibl. Anglo-Poet. 69, 18s. Goldsmid, 233, 1l. 1s. This edition was partially collated with the earlier copies.—Sixth Edition. Lond. 1808, 8vo. 98 leaves. Drury, 505, 8s.—Seventh Edition. Lond. 1818. Nassau, pt. i. 311, 2 vols, 2l. 4s. Bindley, pt. i. 1756, 10s.—A new edition. Lond. 1822, 12mo. with four lithographic prints, 3s. 6d.

BRATHWAIT, R. Barnabæ Itinerarium, or Barnabee's Journal, with a Life of the Author, a Bibliographical Introduction to the Itinerary, and a Catalogue of his Works. Edited from the first Edition, by Joseph Haslewood. Lond. 1820. sq. 12mo. 2 vols.

Of this excellently edited reprint only one hundred and twenty-five copies were printed. Drury, 506, 2l. 4s. Brockett, 83, 2l. 2s.

— Mustur Roll of the evill Angels embatteld against S. Michael. Faithfully collected out of the most authentike Authors. By R. B. Gent. Lond. 1655. 24mo.

A curious work, consisting of pp. 94. In 1659 it appeared with a new title-page, 'Capitall Hereticks, or the evill Angels embattel'd against St. Michael.'

— Lignum Vitæ. Libellus in quatuor partes distinctus: &c. Lond. 1658. 12mo.

This volume, consisting of pp. 579, has an engraved title by Vaughan. Bindley, pt. i. 865, 2l.

— Honest Ghost, or a Voice from the Vault, an Age for Apes. Lond. 1658. 12mo.

Contains pp. 332, with two prints by Vaughan, one inscribed 'The honest Ghost,' the other 'An Age for Apes.' Heath, 1822, 2l. 16s. Strettell, 125, 2l. 15s. Nassau, pt. i. 315, 2l. 17s. White Knights, 2017, 2l. 18s. Dent, pt. i. 249, 4l. 4s. Towneley, pt. i. 441, 7l. 17s. Bibl. Anglo-Poet, 50. 10l. Midgley, 6l. Sotheby, 1854, 4l. There are copies on THICK PAPER which sell high.

— To his Majesty upon his happy Arrivall in our late discomposed Albion. Lond. 1660. 4to.

A copy of this poem, consisting of eight leaves, is in the British Museum.

— The Captive-Captain: or the Restrained Cavalier; &c. Lond. 1665. 8vo.

The characters are of a prison; jaylor; his wife; a porter; the centry; fat prisoner; lean prisoner; restrained cavalier; &c. The volume consists of 98 leaves. Bindley, pt. iii. 37, 1l. 19s. Heber, 1l. 8s.

— Tragi-Comœdia, cui in titulum inscribitur Regicidium, Perspicacissimus Judiciis acuratiùs perspecta, pensata, comprobata. Lond. 1665. 8vo. 6s.

At p. 159, Bedlamum Novum. Scena Britannia. (Pars Secunda.) The volume consists of 192 pp.

— Comment upon the Two Tales of Sir Jeffray Chavcer, Knight. The Miller's Tale, and The Wife of Bath. Lond. 1665. 8vo.

Consisting of p. 199. Towneley, pt. ii. 63, 11s.

— Some Rules and Orders for the Government of the House of an Earle. Lond. 1821. 4to. with portrait.

This tract forms No. 6 of the Miscellanea Antiqua Anglicana.

Brawl.—The new Brawle, or Turnmill-Street against Rosemary-Lane: a mock Comedy. Lond. 1654. 12mo.

A copy is in the British Museum.

BRAY, Thomas, D.D. Bibliotheca Parochialis; or a scheme of such theological and other Heads as seem requisite to be perused by the reverend Clergy. Lond. 1707. 8vo. 5s.

— Papal Usurpation and Persecution, to which is appended a translation of Perrin's History of the old Waldenses and Albigenses, and other works. Lond. 1712. fol. 5s.

Intended as a supplement to Fox's Book of Martyrs. In 1746 appeared 'Publick Spirit illustrated in the Life and Designs of the Rev. Tho. Bray, D.D.' 8vo. 4s.

— William. Sketch of a Tour into Derbyshire and Yorkshire; including Part of Buckingham, Warwick, Leicester, Nottingham, Northampton, Bedford, and Hertfordshires. Lond. 1783. 8vo.

Pp. 400, besides title, two prefaces, list of the nine plates engraved by J. Carter, errata, and iter. Fonthill, 2126, 1l. 5s. Beckford in 1817, 124, 11s. 6d. Dent, pt. i. 252, 8s. Edwards, 637, 7s. Heath, 4160. 10s. 6d. The first edition was published anonymously, 1778, 8vo. and the work is reprinted in vol. 11 of Pinkerton's Collection of V°yages and Travels.

— Collections relating to Henry Smith, Esq. some time Alderman of London; the Estates by him given to charitable Uses; and the Trustees appointed by him. Lond. 1800. royal 8vo.

[Privately printed, Bray, 5l. 2s. 6d. A continuation of these Pedigrees has been privately printed by Mr. Jos. Gwilt, vide Manning.]

BRAYBROOKE, Richard, Lord. History of Audley End, to which are appended notices of the town and parish of Saffron Walden, in the county of Essex. Lond. 1836. 4to.

LARGE PAPER, folio. 50 copies printed, not for sale.

BRAYLEY, Edward Wedlake. A Series of Views of the most interesting Remains of the ancient Castles in England and Wales, engraved by W. Woolnoth; accompanied by historical Descriptions. Lond. 1823. royal 8vo. 2 vols.

Published at 5l. QUARTO, at 7l. 8s. INDIA PROOFS, 10l. 10s.

A concise Account of Lambeth Palace, by E. W. Brayley and W. Herbert. Lond. 1806, 4to.

Delineations, historical and topographical, of the Isle of Thanet and the Cinque Ports, illustrated with (108) Engravings by W. Deeble. London, 1817—18, fsc. 8vo, 15 nos. in 2 vols. 15s. Demy 8vo. 1l. 1s. Royal 8vo. with proof plates on India paper, 1l. 11s. 6d.

—Topographical Sketches of Brighthelmstone and its Neighbourhood. Lond. 1825, 12mo.

An Inquiry into the Genuineness of Prynne's 'Defence of Stage Plays,' &c. together with a Reprint of the said Tract, and also of Prynne's 'Vindication.' Lond. 1825, 8vo. (50 printed.)

Historical and descriptive Accounts of the Theatres of London. Lond. 1826. 4to. 2l. 2s.

[Brayley's History of the County of Surrey, 400 plates, 5 vols. royal 8vo. 3l. 3s., 5 vols. 4to. 6l. 6s., 5 vols. royal 4to. India proofs, 12l. 12s.]

BRAY-THWAITUS, Willihelmus. Siren cœlestis centum Harmoniarum, duarum, trium, et quatuor Vocum. Lond. 1638. 4to.

A copy is in the British Museum.

Braze Nose Garlande. 8vo. 1811.

Only 20 copies printed. Boswell, 3082.

BREDOW, G. G. A compendious View of universal History and Literature in the Series of Tables, from the German: to which is added, a Table of Painters, arranged in Schools and Ages, compiled from the French notes of Matthew Von Bree, &c. By Major James Bell. Lond. 1823. folio. 1l. 10s.

Sir Matthew Von Bree's Chronological Chart of the most celebrated Painters, translated and arranged, with the Addition of the English, &c. by Major Bell. Plain, 7s. 6d. Coloured and framed, 12s.

BREDWELL, S. Razing the Foundations of Brownisme, Lond. 1588. 4to.

BREE, John. Sketch of this Kingdom during the 14th Century, with a particular Account of the Campaign of K. Edward III. in 1345 and 1346. Lond. 1791. 4to. vol. 1. 5s.

This is rather a collection of materials for a work on the subject than a treatise, but as those materials are chiefly taken from the best sources, though unskilfully arranged, the volume is of considerable value. The editor, however, possessed no other qualifications for his task than zeal.

BREKELL, John. Essay on the Hebrew Tongue, to show that the Hebrew Bible might be originally read by Vowel Letters without the Vowel Points. Lond. 1758. 8vo. 5s.

A sensible little work, written on the Anti-Masoretic system. Brekell, who was an Unitarian Minister at Liverpool, published a volume of Discourses, 1765. 8vo.

BREME, Thomas. Mirrour of Friendship : both how to know a perfect Friend and how to choose him. Translated out of Italian. Lond. 1584. 16mo.

Black letter. Not noticed by Ames or Herbert, Gordonstoun, 322, with a Caveat against Fortune, by T. B. 1l. 10s.

BREMOND, M. S. Pilgrim, a pleasant Piece of Gallantry, translated by P. Belon, Gent. Lond. 1680. 12mo. 4s.

'The triumph of Love over Fortune, by S. Bremond,' 1678. White Knights, 599, mor. 9s.

BREMONT, S. Hattigé ou les Amours dv Roy de Tamarin, Nouvelle. Cologne, 1676. 12mo. 6s.

The secret history of the amours of Charles II. and the Duchess of Cleveland.

BRENTIUS, John. Exposition vpon the syxte Chapter of Saynte John, transl. into English by Richard Shirrye. Lond. 1550. 8vo.

Sotheby, 1855, mor. 1l. 2s.

The following works written by this reformer have been published in England :

Homelye of the Resurrection of Christe, transl. by Tho. Sampson. 1550. 8vo.

Treatise of the Argumentes of the old and new Testament, by John Calcaskie. 1550. 8vo.

Newes from Ninive to Englande brought by the Prophete Jonas, transl. by Tho. Timme. 1570. 8vo.

Exposition on Hester, transl. by John Stockwood. 1584. 8vo.

BRENTON, Edward Pelham. Naval History of Great Britain from 1783 to 1822. Lond. 1823. 8vo. 5 vols. with portraits, views, &c.

Published at 4l. 10s. [New edition in 2 vols. 8vo. 1l. 11s. 6d., 1836.] 'A refutation of the Statements of Admiral Sir George Montagu.' 1823. 8vo. 3s. 6d.

BRERELY, John. The Protestants Apologie for the Roman Church. 1608. 8vo. 6s.

This work was written by James Anderson of Lancashire, under the assumed name of Brerely. See St. AUGUSTIN'S Religion. 1620.

— Life of Luther. St. Omers, 1624. 4to.

Bindley, pt. i. 1284, 1l. 8s.

BRERETON, Henry. Newes of the present Miseries of Rushia, occasioned by the late Warre in that Countrey. Lond. 1614. 4to.

A copy of this black letter tract is in the British Museum. In it will be found, 'memorable occurrences of our owne nationall forces English and Scottes, under the pay of the now King of Swethland.' Gordonstoun, 379, 1l. 19s.

— John. Relation of the Discoverie of the north Part of Virginia. Lond. 1602. 4to.

Twelve leaves. A copy is in the British Museum. Bindley, pt. i. 1298. Jadis, 5l. 15s. 6d.

BREREWOOD, Edward. De Ponderibus et Pretiis vetervm Nummorvm, eorumq ; cum recentioribus Collatione, Liber unvs. Lond. 1614. 4to.

Heath, 2, 5s. 6d. Republished by Walton, in the preliminary Dissertations to the Polyglott.

— Enquiries touching the Diversity of Languages and Religions through the chief Parts of the World. Lond. 1674. 8vo. 5s.

There is considerable learning in this small work, partly biblical and partly relating to church history. A copious analysis of the work will be found in Oldys' British Librarian, 159—62. The former editions appeared 1614. 4to. — 1622. 4to. Williams, 241, 1l.—1635. 4to. Brerewood likewise published,

A Treatise on the Sabaoth, with Nic. Byfield's Answer, and Brerewood's Reply. Oxf. 1630—2. 4to. Williams, 242, date 1631, 14s.

Tractatvs dvo, quorum primus est de Metoris, secundus de Oculo. 1631. 8vo.

Commentarii in Ethica Aristotelis. Oxon. 1640. 4to. The original MS. is now in Queen's Coll. library.

Patriarchal Government of the ancient Church. Oxford, 1641. 4s.

A Life of Brerewood will be found in Wood's Athenæ Oxonienses.

Bretagne.—Les grandes Croniques de Bretagne. *See* BOUCHARD, Alain.

— Nouveau Theatre de la Grande Bretagne. *See* KIP.

BRETON, Nicholas. A Small Handful of fragrant Flowers, selected and gathered out of the sacred Scriptures. By N. B. Lond. Richard Jhones, 1575. 12mo.

Bindley, pt. iii. 1135, 14*l*. resold Perry, pt. i. 558, 10*l*. 12s. 6d.; resold Jolley, 1843, mor. 17*l*. supposed unique. Reprinted in the first volume of the Heliconia.

— Floorish upon Fancie: to which are annexed, the Toyes of an idle Head. Lond. Richard Jhones, 1577. 4to.

Bindley, pt. i. 743, 42*l*. resold, Perry, pt. i. 597, 28*l*. 17s. 6d. Heber, 14*l*. 14s.—Again, 1582, 4to. A—O ii. in fours, which edition is reprinted in the first volume of the Heliconia.

— Workes of a young Wyt trust vp with a Fardell of prettie Fancies: whereunto is ioned an odde Kinde of Wooing with a Banquet of Comfettes. Lond. 1577. 4to.

A curious little work, containing picturesque descriptions of the manners of the times, &c. Steevens, 997. Roxburghe, 3170. White Knights, 3173.

— Arbor of amorous Deuices. Lond. 1597. 8vo.

— Brittons Bowre of Delights, contayning many Deuices of rare Epitaphes, pleasaunt Poems, Pastoralls, and Sonnets. Lond. Johnes, 1591. 4to.

This edition was disowned by Breton in 'The Pilgrimage to Paradise,' 1592. Perry, pt. i. 598, 26*l*. 15s. 6d. Heber, 16*l*. 5s. resold Jolley, 1843, 31*l*. Hayley, at Evans', 28*l*. Ritson mentions an edition 1597. 4to. Farmer, 1*l*. 13s.

— The Countess of Pembrook's Passion. 4to. Lond 1592.

A MS. copy of this poem occurs in the Harleian Collection, no. 1303.

[This is really the Countess of Pembroke's 'Love,' as contained in the next article.]

— Pilgrimage to Paradise, joyned with the Countess of Pembroke's Love. 4to. Oxford, Barnes, 1592.

Heber, 10*l*.; resold, Jolley, 1843, 30*l*. Two poems dedicated 'To the Countess of Pembroke, with an address to the Gentlemen students and scolers of Oxford.'

— Marie Magdalens Loue, a practical Discourse on John 20, 1—18. A solemne Passion of the Soules Loue. Lond. 1595. 16mo.

The first tract, E 7, in eights; the latter, in six-line stanzas, continued to G 8. At the end 'Nicholas Britten.' An edition of the latter tract, 1598. 4to. is in a volume bequeathed by Bp. Tanner to the University of Oxford.

— Pleasant Quippes for Upstart New-fangled Gentlewomen, 1595. *See* Quippes.

— The Will of Wit. The Author's Dream. Dispute of the Scholar and Soldier. The Miseries of Mavilla. The Praise of Woman. Dialogue between Anger and Patience, and his Physicians Letter. Lond. 1597. 4to.

These pieces are in prose, intermingled with verse. Another edition, 'Wil of Wit, Wit's Will or Wils Wit, chuse you whether. Newly corrected and amended, being the fift Time imprinted.' Lond. 1606. 4to. 18 leaves. Forster, 147, 7*l*.

The Miseries of Mauillia, the most vnfortunate Lady that ever lived, 4to. This is supposed to be a portion of a volume commencing with Breton's Will of Wit, Wit's Will, or Will's Wit, 1606. A long description is given, from an imperfect copy, in the Brit. Bibl. i. 353—8.

— Wits Trenchmone in a conference had betwixt a scholler and an Angler. Lond. printed by J. Robarts for N. Ling. 1597. 4to.

Wheatley, March 1838, 10*l*. 5s. supposed unique. This work is supposed to have suggested the idea to Is. Walton.

— Auspicante Jehova. Marces Exercise. Lond. printed by T. Este, 1597. 12mo.

Bright (unique), 19*l*.

— Melancholike Humours, in Verses of diuerse natures. Lond. 1600. 4to.

Contains A—F, 23 leaves. Heber (with Britton's Boure of Delights, 1597), 12*l*. 5s. Reprinted at the Lee Priory private press, with a critical preface by Sir E. Brydges, Bart. 1815. 4to.

— Pasquill's Mad-cap and Madcappe's Message, 4to. Lond. 1600.

'A satyrical piece in stanzas, of considerable merit.'—*Warton.* Another edition. Pasquil's Mad-cappe thrown at the Corruption of these Times, with his Message to Men of all Estates. Lond. 1626. 4to. Gordonstoun, 305, 12*l*. 12s. Bindley, 8*l*. 2s. 6d.

BRETON, Nicholas. The second Part of Pasquil's Mad-cap, intituled the Fooles Cap : with Pasquils Passion : began by himself, and finished by his Friend Morphorius. Lond. 1600. 4to.

— Pasqvils Passe, and passeth not. Lond. 1600. 4to.
A poetical tract, consisting of 23 leaves. The fourth leaf of sheet B is blank. White Knights, 3329, morocco, 5*l*. 18s. Perry, pt. i. 599, 8*l*. 18s. 6d. Jolley, 1843, 9*l*. 5s.

— Longing of a blessed Heart, with an Addition vpon the Definition of Love. Lond. 1601. 4to.
A poetical tract, consisting of 24 leaves. Steevens, 784, 1*l*. Sir M. M. Sykes, pt. i. 548, 5*l*. Bibl. Anglo-Poet. 37, 9*l*. 9s. Jolley, 1843, 6*l*. 16s. 6d. Bright, fine, 8*l*. 10s. 6d. Reprinted at the Lee Priory Press 1814. 4to.

— A diuine Poeme, diuided into two Partes : the Rauish't Soule, and the blessed Weeper. Lond. 1601. 4to.
A poetical tract, consisting of 24 leaves, dedicated to the Countess of Pembroke. Sir M. M. Sykes, pt. i. 547, 4*l*. 6s. Bibl. Anglo-Poet. 36, 15*l*. Steevens, 785, 1*l*. 2s. Jolley, 1843, 7*l*. 2s. 6d. Bright, 10*l*. 15s. Reprinted in vol. ii. of the Excerpta Tudoriana. Some copies were struck off separately.

— Old Mad-cappes new Gallymawfry, made into a merrie Messe of Mingle-mangle out of these three idle conceited Humours following : I will not ; 2. Oh the merrie Time ; 3. Out of Money. 1602. 4to.

— The Mother's Blessing. Lond. 1602. 4to.
A copy of this poetical tract is in a volume bequeathed by Bp. Tanner to the University of Oxford.—Another Edition. Lond. 1621. 4to. Catchword A 'Be.' Bindley, pt. iv. 721, 5*l*. 5s. Gordonstoun, 300, 10*l*. 15s. Sir M. M. Sykes, pt. i. 551, 4*l*. 4s. Perry, 5*l*. 17s. 6d. Heber, 3*l*. 3s. Sotheby, 1851, 3*l*. 12s.

— The Plot of the Play, called 'England's Joy.' To be playd at the Swan this 6 of Nov. 1602.

Reprinted in the Harleian Miscellany, vol. x.

— Passion of a discontented Minde. Lond. 1602. 4to.
1601. Gardner, 1854, very poor, 5*l*. 10s. supposed unique, 1602. Malone's (in the Bodleian), 4to. 1621. Heber, 4to.

— A trve Description of Vnthankfulnesse ; or an Enemie to Ingratitude. Lond. 1602. 4to.
A copy of this tract is in a volume bequeathed by Bp. Tanner to the University of Oxford.

— The Soules Harmony. Lond. 1602.
Jolley, 1843, 16*l*. unique.

— Wonders worth the Hearing which being read or heard in a Winters Evening by a good Fire, or a Summer's Morning in the green Fields, may serve both to purge Melancholy from the Mind and grosse Humour from the Bodey. Lond. 1602. 4to.
In prose.

— Dialogue full of Pithe and Pleasure, between three Philosophers, Antonio, Meandro, and Dinarco, upon the Dignitie or Indignitie of Man. Lond. 1603. 4to.
Black letter, in prose, 19 leaves. Jolley, 1843, 4*l*.

— A mad World my Masters, mistake me not. Or a merry Dialogue betweene two Trauellers, the Taker and Mistaker. Lond. 1603. 4to.
A long conversation between two old friends, who meet after they have both travelled in various countries. Gordonstoun, 301, 5*l*. An edition 1635, to which is subjoined 'The Mirrour of Compliments.' Gordonstoun, 302, 3*l*. 3s. Inglis, 395, 3*l*. 3s.

— Wits private Wealth, stored with choice Commodities to content the Minde. Lond. 1603.
A collection of choice maxims, in the manner of Rochefoucault, rather coarse in their diction. Reprinted 1612, and 1639. A curious collection of choice sayings, 1639. Brand, 8*l*. 9s. Jolley, 1843, 3*l*. 5s.

— A Poste with a Packet of Letters. Lond. 4to.

— A Poste with a Packet of mad Letters. Lond. 1603. 4to.
An edition, 1607. Reed, 3114.—1633. 4to.

Dedicated by Nicholas Breton to Maximilian Dallison, of Hawlin, Kent. 1634. Bindley, 3*l*. 3s.—1637, both parts. Garrick, 2383.—1685. Nassau, pt. i. 600, 11s.

BRETON, Nicholas. Grimello's Fortunes. Lond. 1604. 4to.
Bryant, 183, 8*l*. 8s.

— An Olde Man's Lesson and a Young Man's Love. Lond. 1605. 4to.
In the preface to this interlude, Breton acknowledges himself to have been only the editor. Gordonstoun. 303, 5*l*. 7s. 6d. Garrick, 477. Rhodes, 646, 3*l*. 13s. 6d. Perry, 5*l*. 5s. Bright, 3*l*. 10s. 1607. Jolley, 1843, 3*l*. 12s.

— Honest Counsaile, a merrie Fitte of a poetical Furie: good to be read, better to follow. Lond. 1605. 4to.
In verse. Inglis' Old Plays, 6, 7*l*. 10s. Heber, 3*l*. 12s.

— I pray you be not angry, for I will make you merry, a pleasant and merry Dialogue between two Travellers as they met on the Highway. Lond. 1605. 4to.
In black letter. An edition 1632. Gordonstoun, 306, 5*l*. 5s. Heber, 1*l*. 11s.

— Soules immortall Crowne; consisting of seaven glorious Graces. 1. Virtue. 2. Wisedome. 3. Love. 4. Constancie. 5. Patience. 6. Humilitie. 7. Infiniteness. Lond. 1605. 4to.
A poetical tract consisting of 34 leaves, within wood-cut borders, dedicated to K. James, by Ber. N. Gent. i. e. Nicholas Breton. Reed, 6697, 1*l*. 10s. Steevens, 786, 2*l*. 14s. Sir M. M. Sykes, pt. i. 549, 3*l*. l.lloyd, 440, 7*l*. 7s. Bibl. Anglo-Poet. 38, 10*l*. Perry, 6*l*. 18s. 6d. Bright, 3*l*. 3s.

— The Honour of Valour. Lond. C. Pursett, 1605. 4to.
Heber, p. iv. 171 (with Ravisht Soule), 8*l*.

— Sir Philip Sydneys Ourania, that is, Endimions Song and Tragedie, containing all Philosophie. Lond. 1606. 4to.
[According to Mr. Hunter, this is by the Rev. Nath. Baxter, tutor to Sir Philip Sydney.]
Contains pp. 104. Perry, 3*l*. 6s. Jolley, 1843, 3*l*. 4s. Inglis, 300, 2*l*. 6s. Roscoe, 1339, 1*l*. 6s. Sir M. M. Sykes, pt. i. 550, 2*l*. 2s. Bindley, pt. iii. 2027, 8*l*. An edition, 1655, 4to. pp. 102, dedicated to 'Maria Pembrokiana.' North, pt. iii. 698, russia, 2*l*. 4s. Bibl. Anglo-Poet. 40, morocco, 5*l*. 5s. Utterson, mor. 3*l*. 4s. Midgley, 3*l*. 13s. 6d.

— Praise of vertuous Ladies. Lond. 1606. 4to.
Black letter, in prose, Aaa to Ccc, in fours. On Ccc 3 and 4, is a dialogue between anger and patience, eighty copies reprinted at the Lee Priory private press, 1815, 8vo. 5s.

— A Murmurer. Lond. printed by R. Raworth, 1607.
Jolley, 1843, 7*l*. unique.

— Barley Break, or a Warning for Wantons. Lond. 1607. 4to.
Bindley, 7*l*. 7s. Nassau, 6*l*. 3s. 6d. Utterson, 1852, poor, 2*l*. 10s. This appears to have been poetical, and occurred in Farmer's Catalogue.

— Cornv-copiæ; Pasquil's Night Cap, or an Antidot for the Headache. Lond. 1612. 4to.
[Supposed to have been first published as early as 1600, but no copy has been found.]
Written by Nicholas Breton, and not by Samuel Rowlands. See Collier's Poet. Decam, i. 329. Gardner, 1854, 3*l*. 10s. An edition 1623. Bindley, pt. i. 1201, 4*l*. 4s.— Reprinted, 1819, 8vo. 5s.

— I would and would not. Lond. 1614. 4to.
A poetical tract of 22 leaves, consisting of 174 stanzas, attributed by George Steevens to Nicholas Breton, whose inverted initials B. N. appear at the end of the address to the reader.
Roxburghe, 8*l*. 18s. 6d. Heber, 6*l*. Miller, 1854, 5*l*.

— Characters upon Essaies, morall and diuine. Lond. 1615. 12mo.
These Essays, 16 in number, are inscribed to Sir Francis Bacon, afterwards Lord Verulam. A 16, B 16, C 8, and D 6 leaves. Sir M. M. Sykes, 347, 1*l*. 10s. Jadis, 19, 1*l*. 2s. Lloyd, 1*l*. 17s. Pickering, 1854, 2*l*. 14s. Reprinted in the first volume of the Archaica.

— The Good and the Badde; or Descriptions of the Worthies and Unworthies of this Age, where the Best may see their Graces, and the Worst discerne their Basenesse. Lond. 1616. 4to.
In prose, pp. 60, also title, dedication to 'Sir Gilbert Houghton, Knight,' and preface, six more. Gordonstoun, 304, imperfect, 1*l*. 1s. Nassau, pt. i. 1712. Utterson, 1852, 2*l*. 10s. Reprinted in the first

volume of the Archaica. Another edition entitled 'England's selected Characters,' &c. 4to. 1643. Miller, 1854. 8*l*.

BRETON, Nicholas. The Crossing of Proverbs, 2 parts. Lond. 1616. 12mo.
No perfect copy known. Heber had only the 2nd part, imperfect, IV. 111, 1*l*. 4s.

— The Hate of Treason, with a touch of the late treason. Lond. 1616, 4to.
Heber, 3*l*. unique.

— The Mother's Blessing. Lond. 1621, 4to.
Heber, 3*l*. 3s.

— Strange Newes out of divers Countries never discovered till of late by a strange Pilgrime in those Parts. Lond. 1622. 4to.
In prose and verse, with wood-cut in the title. Jolley, 1843 (2 leaves wanting), 5*l*.

— A solemn Passion of the Soules Love (in verse,) 12mo. 12 leaves, by G. Purslowe, 1623.
Sotheby, May 1856, unbound, 18*l*. supposed unique.

— Fantasticks : serving for a perpetuall Prognostication. Descants of the World, the Earth, Water, Ayre, &c. 1626.
Black letter. In prose. Garrick, 2383. Bright, 5*l*. 14s. Jolly, 1843, FINE, 7*l*. 7s.

— The Figures of Three, Foure, Five, Sixe, and Seven : by N. Breton and others. 1626.

— The Figvre of Fovre. The second Part. Lond. 1636. 12mo.
A copy of this tract, consisting of 20 pp. not numbered, is in the Bodleian library. The initials N. B. are affixed to the preface.

— The Figure of Foure, being a new booke, containing many merry conceites, which will yield both pleasure and profit to all that read or hear it, the last part. Lond. W. Gilbertson, 1654. 12mo.
Sotheby, 1856, edges uncut, 11*l*.

— The Court and the Country, or a brief discourse on between the Courtier and Countryman. Lond. 1618, 4to.
Heber, 1*l*. 18s. Mentioned by Winstanley.
In 'The Phœnix Nest,' 1593, are five, and in 'England's Helicon,' 1600, eight poems; and in Nichols' Progresses, vol. ii. 1788, is a Character of Q. Elizabeth; all written by Nicholas Breton.
Among the Royal MSS. 17 C xxxiv. is Nic. Breton's 'Invective against Treason,' and in 18 A LVII. his 'poem upon the praise of vertue.' Likewise in a volume bequeathed by Bp. Tanner to the University of Oxford, are 'The Passions of the Spirit,' and 'Excellent Vercis worthy Imitation of every Christian in their Conversation,' MSS. by Nic. Breton.
In 1578 was licensed to Richard Jones, 'The Payne of Pleasure.'
In 1602 (27 Oct.) was enter'd to James Shawe, 'A merry Dialogue betwixte twoo Trauellers, Lorenzo and Dorindo, by Nicholas Britton.' Qy. if not the same as 'A Mad World my Masters,' 1603, or 'I pray you be not angry,' 1605. Heber, 1*l*. 18s.
An unpublished poem, in six cantos, from an early MS., will be found at p. 177 of Mr. Halliwell's description of MSS. in Plymouth library, 4to. 1853.

BRETONNEAU, F. Vie de Jacques II. Roy de la Grand Bretagne. Paris, 1703. 12mo. with port. by Edelinck. 5s.
Bretonneau's James II. 1704. Dent. pt. i. 253, mor. 12s. 6d.

BRETT, Arthur. The Restauration, or a Poem on the Return of Charles II. to his Kingdoms. Lond. 1660. 4to.
This person, who, according to Ant. à Wood, 'was a great pretender to poetry,' likewise published Threnodia, on the Death of Prince Henry Duke of Glocester. Oxford, 1660, 4to.; and Patientia victrix: or the Book of Job, in lyric verse. Lond. 1661, 8vo.

— Richard, D.D. Iconum sacrarum Decas, in quâ è subjectis Typis compluscula sanæ Doctrinæ Capita enuentur. Oxon. 1603. 4to.
Brett 'was a person famous in his time for learning as well as piety, skill'd and vers'd to a criticism in the Latin, Greek, Hebrew, Chaldaic, Arabic, and Æthiopic tongues.'—*Ant. à Wood.* He was one of the translators of the Bible in 1604.

— Samuel. Narrative of the Proceedings of a great Councel of Jews assembled in the Plain of Agedy in Hungaria, on the 12th of October 1650. Lond. 1655. 4to.
Assembled 'to examine the scriptures concerning Christ.' Reprinted in the first volume of the Harleian Miscellany, and in the first volume of the Phœnix.

BRETT, Thomas, LL.D. Dissertation on the ancient Versions of the Bible, in a Letter to a Friend. The second Edition, prepared for the Press by the Author before his Death, and now printed from his own MS. Lond. 1760. 8vo.

Gosset, 876, 6s. 6d. Reprinted in Bishop Watson's Collection of Theological Tracts, who observes, ' It is an excellent Dissertation, and cannot fail of being very useful to such as have not leisure to consult Dr. Hody's Book de Bibliorum Textibus; Bp. Walton's Prolegomena to his Polyglot, &c. The first edition came out in 1742, several years after it had been composed.'

This eminent divine and controversial writer likewise published,

An Account of Church Government and Governors. Lond. 1710. 8vo. Best edition, 4s.

A Collection of the principal Liturgies used by the Christian Church in the Celebration of the holy Eucharist: with a Dissertation upon them. Lond. 1720. 8vo. 7s. and many other tracts, sermons, &c.

BRETTERGH, Katherine. Death's Advantage little regarded, and the Soules Solace against Sorrow, in two funerall Sermons at Childwal in Lancashire, at the Burial of Mistris Bretteygh, with the Life of the said Gentlewoman. Lond. 1602.

Inglis, 217, russia, 10s.

— Discovrse of the christian Life and Death of Mistris Katherin Brettergh. Lond. 1606. 12mo.

A copy of this, as well as the following, are in the British Museum.

A funeral Sermon on Mrs. Brettergh. By Wm. Harrison. Lond. 1605. 12mo.

A funeral Sermon on Mrs. Brettergh. By W. Leigh. Lond. 1606. 16mo.

BRETTINGHAM, Matthew. Plans, Elevations and Sections of Holkham, in Norfolk, the Seat of the Earl of Leicester. Lond. 1761. atlas folio.

This volume consists of a title, dedication to the Duke of Cumberland, preface, and 34 plans, &c. in bistre. In the preface is the following notice, ' That the present publication may be acceptable to the dilettanti, I have printed most of the designs in the colour his Lordship intended them (in bistre): a few other books are in printer's ink.' Fonthill, 1852, 1l. 4s.

— Another Edition. To which are added the Ceilings and Chimney-Pieces; and also a descriptive Account of the Statues, Pictures and Drawings not in the former Edition. Lond. 1773. atlas folio. 1l. 11s. 6d.

This volume consists of a title, dedication to the Baroness Clifford, preface and explanation, pp. x and 24. The Plans, &c. in printer's ink, 1—69, likewise duplicates, marked 24*. 27*. 27**. Fonthill, 2l. 16s.

BREVAL, John Durant. Remarks on several Parts of Europe. Lond. 1723-38. folio. 4 vols. in 2, with plates. 15s.

Heath, 2380, 1l. 5s. Roxburghe, 7184, 1l. 7s. LARGE PAPER. Fonthill, 453, 2l. 2s.

In 1734, appeared, The History of the House of Nassau, particularly with Regard to that Branch of it that inherited the Estates of Orange. 8vo. 5s.

BREVIARIUM ABERDONENSE (*Aberdeen*), 2 vols. small 8vo. Edinb. Walter Chepmen, 1509-10.

Only four copies known, and those imperfect; but out of the four, one might be completed. A reprint of 500 copies, 2 vols. 4to. 1852-3, has been made, 220 of which were subscribed for by the Bannatyne and Maitland Clubs, the remainder were published at 5l. 5s., by Mr. Toovey.

— ABINGDONENSE (*Abingdon*), 2 vols. small 4to. Abingdon. Johannis Scholaris, 1528.

The only portion known is Pars æstivalis, which is in Emmanuel College.

— EBORACENSE (*York*), 8vo. 1493. Venetiis. Johan. Hannam.

Coll. Temporale, p. 1. Calendarium, Psalterium, p. 209. Commune, p. 265. Sanctorale, p. 301, only one copy known. Other editions. Paris, Regnault, 1526, 12mo. Paris, Regnault, Impensis Jo. Gauchet, 1526 ? 12mo.

— HEREFORDIENSE (*Hereford*), In clarissimo Rothomagen. Emporio: Impensis et cura Ingelberti Haghe, 1505. 16mo.

A description of this volume will be found in Herbert's Ames, iii. 1821.

Only three copies of Pars æstivalis known.

— SARISBURIENSE (*Salisbury*), Venetiis Raynaldum de Novimagio, 1483. 8vo. 2 vols.

A copy on VELLUM, Mac Carthy, 51 fr., now in the Royal Library of Paris, 357

leaves, printed in double columns, 40 lines to a page.
Panzer notices an edition by this printer in folio.

Other editions.

PARIS. P. Levet, 2 vols. 8vo. 1494. One on vellum, Trin. Col. Dublin.—VENET. Joan. Hertzog, 12mo. 1495.—LOUVAIN. T. Martin Alost, 8vo. 1499.—PARIS. Folio, 1499. Foster, March, 1857. Printed on vellum, 46*l*.—LONDON. Impensis Margaretæ Comitissæ Richmondiæ, R. Pynson, 4to. Mac Carthy. Printed on vellum (date cut off), now in the Spencer library.—Richd. Pynson, folio, 1500. Mac Carthy. Printed on vellum.—PARIS? Wynkyn de Worde, 12mo. 1507.—LONDON. Wynkyn de Worde, 4to.1509.—PARIS. 8vo. 1510.—Kerver,12mo 1514.—Kerver, 4to. 1514.—PARIS. 4to. and 12mo. 1515.—Byrkman, folio, 1516.—PARIS. Folio, 1519 (Harleian Catalogue.)—Regnault, 4to. 1519.—Regnault and Byrkman, 4to. 1519.—ANTWERP. F. Byrkman, 1526.—PARIS. Regnault, 8vo. May 18, 1528, and 8vo. and 4to. 1528.— PARIS. 2 vols. 8vo. 1528.—Jehan Petit, 12mo, 1528.—T. Kerver, 16mo. 6 calend. Novr. 1530 (Herbert's Ames, p. 1828). — Kerver, Vidua. 12mo. 1530. — Chevallon, folio, 1531.— Chevallon and Regnault, folio, 1531.— Regnault, 2 vols. 4to. 1533.—Regnault, 12mo. 1533.— Regnault, 2 vols. 4to. 1535. — Regnault, folio, 1535. — LONDON. E. Wytchurch, 2 vols.16mo. 1541.—Grafton and Wytchurch, 2 vols. 12mo. 1544. — R. Grafton, small 8vo. 1544. An edition date, 1551. qy. place and printer.—LONDON, 4to. 1554.—PARIS. 8vo.1554.—Regnault Vidua, 8vo. and small 4to. 1554.—LONDON, 2 vols. 4to. 1554.—PARIS. 2 vols. 8vo. 1554-5. — Regnault Vidua, 2 vols. 12mo.1555.—LONDON. Kyngston and Sutton, 2 vols. 4to. 1555. Sotheby, April, 1857 (1555-6) 2 vols. 31*l*.—Grafton, 4to. 1555.—PARIS. 8vo. and 12mo. 1555.—LYONS. 8vo. 1555.—PARIS. 8vo. and 12mo. 1556.—LONDON. Kyngston and Sutton, 4to. 1556. Sotheby, April, 1857, imperfect, 15*l*. 10s.—PARIS. Merlin, 12mo. 8vo. and 4to. 1556.—Le Blanc pro Merlin, 8vo. 1556. Sotheby, April, 1857 (1556-7), 2 vols. imperfect, 15*l*.—PARIS, fol. 1556.—ROUEN, 8vo. 1556.—Valentin, 2 vols. 16mo. 1556.—PARIS. Le Blanc, pro Merlin, 12mo. 1557.

Several Editions exist without date, as ROUEN. M. Morin, 2 vols. 12mo. Bodl. Lib. on vellum.—PARIS. Jo. Amori.

BREVINT, Daniel, DD. Missale Romanum; or the Depth and Mystery of Roman Mass. Oxford, 1672. 8vo. 5s.

Reprinted 'with several pages transpos'd to the injury of the book,' 1673. 8vo. A biography of this divine, who 'was a person of great reading, zealous for the church of England; and for his life and learning truly praiseworthy,' will be found in Wood's Athen. Oxon.

BREWER, Anthony or Tony. Lingua: or the Combat of the Tongue and the five Senses for Superiority. Lond. 1607. 4to.

Published anonymously. Winstanley has attributed this comedy to Anthony Brewer; and tells us that Oliver Cromwell once acted the part of Tactus in it, from which he first imbibed his sentiments of ambition. Reprinted n. d. 4to.—1617. 4to. Rhodes, 651, 7s. 6d.—1622. 4to. Hollis, 688, 6s. 6d.—1632. 4to. Rhodes, 652, 2s. 1657. 8vo. Nassau, pt. i. 2038, 8s. Dent, pt. i. 1272, 8s. Bindley, pt. ii. 1386. 7s. and in Dodsley's Collection. To this writer, who appears to have been held in high estimation by the wits of his time, are ascribed The Country Girle, a Comedie. Lond. 1647. 4to. Retr. Rev. n. s. ii. 14-23. Rhodes, 654. 6s. This play was published by John Leanerd in 1677, as his own, under the title of 'Country Innocence.'—The Love-sick King, an English tragical History: with the Life and Death of Cartesmunda the fair Nun of Winchester. Lond. 1655. 4to. Rhodes, 655, 15s. This play was revived in 1680, and published under the title of the Perjured Nun. Of late The Merry Devil of Edmonton, by T. B., has also been attributed to Brewer.

— George. Maxims of Gallantry, or the History of the Count de Verney. By G—e B—r. Printed for the Author, 1793. 8vo.

The licentious descriptions in this work excited such severe censure from the Reviewers, that the author recalled and destroyed most of the impression.

— J. N. Beauties of Ireland; being original Delineations topographical, historical, and biographical of each county. Lond. 1826. 8vo. 2 vols.

Published at 2*l*. 8s. LARGE PAPER, Proofs, 3*l*. 12s.

Introduction to the Beauties of England and Wales. Lond. 1818. 8vo.

The Picture of England. Lond. 1820. 12mo. 2 vols.

A descriptive and historical Account of various Palaces and public buildings. Lond. 1810. 4to.

Histrionic Topography; or the Birthplaces, Residences, and Funeral Monuments of the most distinguished Actors. Lond. 1818. 8vo. with 15 engravings, 12s.

A Select Catalogue of
NEW BOOKS AT REDUCED PRICES,

PUBLISHED OR SOLD BY

HENRY G. BOHN,

YORK STREET, COVENT GARDEN, LONDON.

THE COMPLETE CATALOGUE OF NEW BOOKS AND REMAINDERS, IN 100 PAGES, MAY BE HAD GRATIS.

*** *All the Books advertised in the present Catalogue are neatly boarded in cloth, or bound.*

FINE ARTS, ARCHITECTURE, SCULPTURE, PAINTING, HERALDRY, ANTIQUITIES, TOPOGRAPHY, SPORTING, PICTORIAL AND HIGHLY ILLUSTRATED WORKS, ETC., ETC.

BARBER'S ISLE OF WIGHT. 42 fine Steel Plates, and Dr. MANTELL'S GEOLOGICAL MAP. 8vo, gilt, cloth, 10s. 6d.

BARRINGTON'S FAMILIAR INTRODUCTION TO HERALDRY, in a Series of Lectures; illustrated by numerous Drawings of Armorial Bearings, Badges, and other Devices, 20 plates, containing several hundred subjects fcap. 8vo, gilt cloth (pub. at 7s. 6d.), 5s.
——— the same, with the plates mostly coloured, gilt cloth (pub. at 10s. 6d.), 7s.

BULWER'S LEILA; or the Siege of Granada; and Calderon the Courtier, 8vo., illustrated by 16 beautiful Line Engravings by CHARLES HEATH, cloth, gilt edges, (pub. at 1l. 1s.), 10s. 6d
——— the same, morocco extra, gilt edges, 1l.

BILLINGTON'S ARCHITECTURAL DIRECTOR, being an improved Guide to Architects, Draughtsmen, Students, Builders, and Workmen, to which is added a History of the Art, &c., and a Glossary of Architecture. New Edition, enlarged, 8vo, 100 plates, cloth lettered (pub. at 1l. 8s), 10s. 6d. 1848

BOOK OF BRITISH BALLADS. edited by S. C. HALL; every page richly embellished with very highly-finished Wood Engravings, after Designs by CRESWICK, GILBERT, FRANKLIN, CORBOULD, &c., Imperial 8vo, cloth gilt edges (pub. at 2l. 2s.), 1l. 5s.

BOOK OF COSTUME, from the earliest period to the present time. Upwards of 700 beautiful Engravings on Wood, by LINTON. 8vo (pub. at 1l. 1s.), gilt cloth, gilt edges, 10s. 6d. 1847

BOOK OF GEMS, OR THE POETS AND ARTISTS OF GREAT BRITAIN. 3 vols. 8vo. 150 exquisite Line Engravings after TURNER, BONINGTON, LANDSEER, ROBERTS, MULREADY, etc. etc.; also numerous Autographs (pub. at 4l. 14s. 6d.) Cloth elegantly gilt, 2l. 5s., or in morocco 3l. 3s.

BOOK OF GEMS, OR THE MODERN POETS AND ARTISTS OF GREAT BRITAIN. 8vo. 50 exquisitely beautiful Line Engravings after TURNER, BONINGTON, etc. etc. (pub. at 1l. 11s. 6d.), cloth elegantly gilt, 15s., or morocco, 1l. 1s.

BLUNT'S BEAUTY OF THE HEAVENS; a Pictorial Display of the Astronomical Phenomena of the Universe; with a Familiar Lecture on Astronomy. Illustrated by 104 Plates, many coloured Broad 8vo., cloth gilt, 1l. 1s. 1850

BOTTA AND FLANDIN'S GREAT WORK ON NINEVEH; published at the expense of the French Government. MONUMENS DE NINIVE, découverts et décrits par P. E. BOTTA, mesurés et dessinés par E. FLANDIN. 5 vols. large folio, (in 90 livraisons), containing 400 Engravings, (pub. at 90l.), 36l.

BOOK OF SHAKSPEARE GEMS. A Series of Landscape Illustrations of the most interesting localities of Shakspeare's Dramas; with Historical and Descriptive Accounts, by WASHINGTON IRVING, JESSE, W. HOWITT, WORDSWORTH, INGLIS, and others. 8vo, with 45 highly-finished Steel Engravings (pub. at 1l. 11s. 6d.), gilt cloth, 14s.

B

BOOK OF WAVERLEY GEMS. A Series of 64 highly-finished Line Engravings of the most interesting Incidents and Scenes in Walter Scott's Novels, by HEATH, FINDEN, ROLLS, and others, after Pictures by LESLIE, STOTHARD, COOPER, HOWARD, &c., with illustrative letter-press, 8vo. (pub. at 1l. 11s. 6d.), cloth, elegantly gilt, 15s.

BROCKEDON'S PASSES OF THE ALPS. 2 vols. medium 4to. Containing 109 beautiful Engravings (pub. at 10l. 10s. in boards), half-bound morocco, gilt-edges, 3l. 13s. 6d.

BRITTON'S CATHEDRAL CHURCH OF LINCOLN, 4to, 16 fine plates, by LE KEUX, (pub. at 3l. 3s.), cloth, 1l. 5s. Royal 4to, Large Paper, cloth, 1l. 11s. 6d. 1837
This volume was published to complete Mr. Britton's Cathedrals, and is wanting in most of the sets.

BRYAN'S DICTIONARY OF PAINTERS AND ENGRAVERS. New Edition, corrected, greatly enlarged, and continued to the present time, by GEORGE STANLEY, Esq., complete in one large volume, impl. 8vo, numerous plates of monograms, 2l. 2s.

BUNYAN'S PILGRIM'S PROGRESS, STOTHARD'S Illustrated Edition. 8vo, with 17 exquisitely beautiful illustrations after this delightful Artist, executed on Steel by GOODALL and others, also numerous woodcuts, cloth gilt (pub. at 1l. 1s.), 12s.
——— the same, INDIA PROOFS, cloth gilt (pub. at 2l. 2s.), 1l. 1s.

BURNETT'S ILLUSTRATED EDITION OF SIR JOSHUA REYNOLDS ON PAINTING, 4to, 12 fine plates, cloth (pub at 2l. 2s.), 1l. 1s. 1842
——— the same, large paper, royal 4to, proof impressions of Plates, cloth (pub. at 4l. 4s.), 2l. 2s.

BYRON'S TALES AND POEMS, FINDEN'S Illustrated Edition, with 46 Engravings on Steel, 8vo, cloth extra, gilt edges (pub. at 1l. 1s.), 10s. 6d.

CANOVA'S WORKS, engraved in outline by Moses, with Descriptions and a Biographical Memoir by Cicognara. 3 vols., imp. 8vo, 155 plates, and fine portrait by Worthington, half-bound morocco (pub. at 6l. 12s.), 2l. 5s.

CARTER'S ANCIENT ARCHITECTURE OF ENGLAND. Illustrated by 103 Copper-plate Engravings, comprising upwards of Two thousand specimens. Edited by JOHN BRITTON, Esq. Royal folio (pub. at 12l. 12s.), half-bound morocco, 4l. 4s. 1837

CARTER'S ANCIENT SCULPTURE AND PAINTING NOW REMAINING IN ENGLAND, from the Earliest Period to the Reign of Henry VIII. With Historical and Critical Illustrations, by DOUCE, GOUGH, MEYRICK, DAWSON, TURNER, and BRITTON. Royal folio, with 120 large Engravings, many of which are beautifully coloured and several illuminated with gold (pub. at 15l. 15s.), half-bound morocco, 5l. 5s. 1838

CARTER'S GOTHIC ARCHITECTURE, and Ancient Buildings in England, with 120 Views, etched by himself. 4 vols, square 12mo (pub. at 2l. 2s.), half morocco, 18s. 1824

CATLIN'S NORTH-AMERICAN INDIANS. 2 vols. impl. 8vo. 360 Engravings (pub. at 2l. 12s. 6d.), cloth emblematically gilt, 1l. 10s.

CATTERMOLE'S EVENINGS AT HADDON HALL. 24 exquisite Engravings on Steel, from designs by himself. Post 8vo (originally pub. at 1l. 11s. 6d.), gilt cloth, gilt edges, 7s. 6d.

CATTERMOLE'S ILLUSTRATED HISTORY OF THE GREAT CIVIL WAR OF THE TIMES OF CHARLES I. AND CROMWELL, with 30 highly-finished Engravings on Steel, after CATTERMOLE, by ROLLS, WILLMORE, and other first rate Artists, imperial 8vo, cloth extra, gilt edges, 1l. 1s.

CHAMBERLAINE'S IMITATIONS OF DRAWINGS from the Great Masters in the Royal Collection, engraved by BARTOLOZZI and others, impl. fol., 70 Plates (pub. at 12l. 12s.), half bound morocco, gilt edges, 5l. 5s.

CLAUDE'S LIBER VERITATIS. A Collection of 300 Engravings in imitation of the original Drawings of CLAUDE, by EARLOM. 3 vols. folio (pub. at 31l. 10s.), half-bound morocco, gilt edges, 10l. 10s.

CLAUDE, BEAUTIES OF, 24 FINE ENGRAVINGS, containing some of his choicest Landscapes; beautifully Engraved on Steel, folio, with descriptive letter-press, and Portrait, in a portfolio (pub. at 3l. 12s.), 1l. 5s.

CONSTABLE'S GRAPHIC WORKS, many of them now first published, comprising forty large and highly-finished Mezzotinto Engravings on Steel, by DAVID LUCAS, with short descriptive letter-press, extracted from LESLIE'S Life of Constable, folio, half-bound morocco, gilt edges, 3l. 13s. 6d.

CONSTABLE, THE ARTIST, (Leslie's Memoirs of) including his Lectures, 2nd Edition with 2 beautiful Portraits, and the plate of "Spring," demy 4to, cloth (pub. at 1l. 1s.), 15s.

COESVELT'S PICTURE GALLERY. With an introduction by MRS. JAMESON. Royal 4to, 90 Plates beautifully engraved in outline. India Proofs (pub. at 5l. 5s.), half-bound morocco, extra, 3l. 3s.

COOKE'S SHIPPING AND CRAFT. A series of 65 brilliant Etchings, comprising picturesque, but at the same time extremely accurate Representations. Royal 4to (pub. at 3l. 13s. 6d.) gilt cloth, 1l. 11s. 6d.

COOKE'S PICTURESQUE SCENERY OF LONDON AND ITS VICINITY. 50 beautiful Etchings, after drawings by CALCOTT, STANFIELD, PROUT, ROBERTS, HARDING, STARK, and COTMAN. Royal 4to. Proofs (pub. at 5l.), gilt cloth, 2l. 2s.

CONEY'S FOREIGN CATHEDRALS, HOTELS DE VILLE, TOWN HALLS, AND OTHER REMARKABLE BUILDINGS IN FRANCE, HOLLAND, GERMANY, AND ITALY. 82 fine large Plates. Imperial folio (pub. at 10l. 10s.), half-morocco, gilt edges, 3l. 13s. 6d. 1842

CORONATION OF GEORGE THE FOURTH, by SIR GEORGE NAYLOR, in a Series of above 40 magnificent Paintings of the Procession, Ceremonial, and Banquet, comprehending faithful portraits of many of the distinguished Individuals who were present; with historical and descriptive letter-press, atlas folio (pub. at 52l. 10s.), half-bound morocco, gilt edges, 13l. 12s.

COSTUME AND HISTORY OF THE CLANS, by JOHN SOBIESKI STOLBERG STUART, and CHARLES EDWARD STUART, imperial folio, comprising 240 pages of letter-press and 36 finely executed Lithographs, crimson cloth boards (pub. at 6l. 6s.), 3l. 3s. *Edin.* 1845
——— the same, with the Plates most beautifully Coloured, half-bound morocco extra, gilt edges, 8l. 8s.

COTMAN'S SEPULCHRAL BRASSES IN NORFOLK AND SUFFOLK, tending to illustrate the Ecclesiastical, Military, and Civil Costume of former ages, with letter-press descriptions, etc., by DAWSON TURNER, SIR S. MEYRICK, etc. 173 Plates. The enamelled Brasses are splendidly illuminated, 2 vols. impl. 4to, half-bound morocco, gilt edges, 6l. 6s. 1836
——— the same, large paper, imperial folio, half morocco, gilt edges, 8l. 8s.

COTMAN'S ETCHINGS OF ARCHITECTURAL REMAINS in various counties in England, with Letter-press Descriptions by RICKMAN. 2 vols. imperial folio, containing 247 highly spirited Etchings (pub. at 24l.), half morocco, 8l. 8s. 1838

DANIELL'S ORIENTAL SCENERY AND ANTIQUITIES. The original magnificent edition, 150 splendid coloured Views, on the largest scale, of the Architecture, Antiquities, and Landscape Scenery of Hindoostan, 6 vols. in 3, elephant folio (pub. at 210l.), elegantly half-bound morocco, 63l. 10s.

DANIELL'S ORIENTAL SCENERY, 6 vols. in 3, small folio, 150 Plates (pub. at 15l. 15s.), half-bound morocco, 6l. 6d.
This is reduced from the preceding large work, and is uncoloured.

DANIELL'S ANIMATED NATURE, being Picturesque Delineations of the most interesting Subjects from all Branches of Natural History, 125 Engravings, with Letter press Descriptions, 2 vols. small folio (pub. at 15l. 15s.), half morocco (uniform with the Oriental Scenery) 3l. 3s.

DON QUIXOTE, PICTORIAL EDITION. Translated by JARVIS, carefully revised. With a copious original Memoir of Cervantes. Illustrated by upwards of 820 beautiful Wood Engravings after the celebrated Designs of TONY JOHANNOT, including 16 new and beautiful large Cuts, by ARMSTRONG, now first added. 2 vols. royal 8vo (pub. at 2l. 10s.), cloth gilt, 1l. 8s.

DULWICH GALLERY, a Series of 50 beautifully Coloured Plates, from the most celebrated Pictures in this Remarkable Collection, executed by R. COCKBURN (Custodian.) All mounted on Tinted Card-board in the manner of Drawings, imperial folio, including 4 very large additional Plates, published separately at from 3 to 4 guineas each and not before included in the Series. In a handsome portfolio, with morocco back (pub at 40l.), 10l. 10s.
"This is one of the most splendid and interesting of the British Picture Galleries, and has for some years been quite unattainable, even at the full price."

ECCLESTON'S INTRODUCTION TO ENGLISH ANTIQUITIES, thick 8vo, with numerous woodcuts, cloth (pub. at 1l. 1s.), 7s.

EGYPT—PERRING'S FIFTY-EIGHT LARGE VIEWS AND ILLUSTRATIONS OF THE PYRAMIDS OF GIZEH, ABOU ROASH, &c. Drawn from actual Survey and Admeasurement. With Notes and References to Col. Vyse's great Work, also to Denon, the great French Work on EGYPT, Rosellini, Belzoni, Burckhardt, Sir Gardner Wilkinson, Lane, and others. 3 Parts, elephant folio, the size of the great French "Egypte" (pub. at 16l. 15s.) in printed wrappers, 3l. 3s.; half bound morocco, 4l. 14s. 6d. 1842

ENGLEFIELD'S ANCIENT VASES, drawn and engraved by H. MOSES, imperial 8vo, 51 fine plates, 12 of which are now first published, cloth lettered (pub. at 1l. 16s.), 12s.

ENGLEFIELD'S ISLE OF WIGHT. 4to. 50 large Plates, engraved by COOKE, and a Geological Map (pub. 7l. 7s.), cloth, 2l. 5s. 1816

FLAXMAN'S HOMER. Seventy-five beautiful Compositions to the ILIAD and ODYSSEY, engraved under FLAXMAN'S inspection, by PIROLI, MOSES, and BLAKE. 2 vols. oblong folio (pub. at 4l. 4s.), boards 2l. 2s. 1805

FLAXMAN'S ÆSCHYLUS, Thirty-six beautiful Compositions from. Oblong folio (pub. at 2l. 12s. 6d.), boards 1l. 1s. 1835

B 2

FLAXMAN'S HESIOD. Thirty-seven beautiful Compositions from. Oblong folio (pub. at 2*l*. 12*s*. 6*d*.), boards 1*l*. 1*s*. 1827

"Flaxman's unequalled Compositions from Homer, Æschylus, and Hesiod, have long been the admiration of Europe; of their simplicity and beauty the pen is quite incapable of conveying an adequate impression."—*Sir Thomas Lawrence.*

FLAXMAN'S ACTS OF MERCY. A Series of Eight Compositions, in the manner of Ancient Sculpture, engraved in imitation of the original Drawings, by F. C. LEWIS. Oblong folio (pub. at 2*l*. 2*s*.), half-bound morocco, 15*s*. 1831

FROISSART. ILLUMINATED ILLUSTRATIONS OF. Seventy-four Plates, printed in Gold and Colours. 2 vols super-royal 8vo. half-bound, uncut (pub. at 6*l*. 10*s*.), 3*l*. 10*s*.

——— the same, large paper, 2 vols. royal 4to, half-bound, uncut (pub. at 10*l*. 10*s*.), 6*l*. 6*s*.

GALERIE DU PALAIS PITTI, in 100 livraisons, forming 4 thick vols. super-royal folio containing 500 fine Engravings, executed by the first Italian Artists, with descriptive letter-press in French (pub. at 50*l*.), 21*l*. *Florence*, 1837—45

——— the same, bound in 4 vols. half-morocco extra, gilt edges, 25*l*.

——— the same, LARGE PAPER, PROOF BEFORE THE LETTERS, 100 livraisons, imperial folio (pub. at 100*l*.), 30*l*.

——— the same, bound in 4 vols. half-morocco extra, gilt edges, 35*l*.

GELL AND GANDY'S POMPEIANA, or the Topography, Edifices, and Ornaments of Pompeii. Original Series, containing the Result of all the Excavations previous to 1819, new and elegant edition, in one vol. royal 8vo, with upwards of 100 beautiful Line Engravings by GOODALL, COOKE, HEATH, PYE, &c. cloth extra, 1*l*. 1*s*.

GEMS OF ART. 36 FINE ENGRAVINGS, after REMBRANDT, CUYP, REYNOLDS, POUSSIN, MURILLO, TENIERS, CORREGGIO, VANDERVELDE, folio, proof impressions, in portfolio (pub. at 8*l*. 8*s*.), 1*l*. 11*s*. 6*d*.

GILLRAY'S CARICATURES, printed from the Original Plates, all engraved by himself between 1779 and 1810, comprising the best Political and Humorous satires of the Reign of George the Third, in upwards of 600 highly-spirited Engravings. In 1 large vol. atlas folio (exactly uniform with the original Hogarth, as sold by the advertiser), half-bound red morocco extra, gilt edges, 8*l*. 8*s*.

GILPIN'S PRACTICAL HINTS UPON LANDSCAPE GARDENING, with some Remarks on Domestic Architecture. Royal 8vo, Plates, cloth (pub. at 1*l*.), 7*s*.

GOETHE'S FAUST, ILLUSTRATED BY RETZSCH in 26 beautiful Outlines, royal 4to (pub. at 1*l*. 1*s*.), gilt cloth, 10*s*. 6*d*.

This edition contains a translation of the original poem, with historical and descriptive notes.

GOODWIN'S DOMESTIC ARCHITECTURE. A Series of New Designs for Mansions, Villas, Rectory-Houses, Parsonage-Houses; Bailiff's, Gardener's, Gamekeeper's, and Park-Gate Lodges; Cottages and other Residences, in the Grecian, Italian, and Old English Style of Architecture; with Estimates. 2 vols. royal 4to, 96 Plates (pub. at 5*l*. 5*s*.), cloth, 2*l*. 12*s*. 6*d*.

GRINDLAY'S (CAPT.) VIEWS IN INDIA, SCENERY, COSTUME, AND ARCHITECTURE; chiefly on the Western Side of India. Atlas 4to. Consisting of 36 most beautifully coloured Plates, highly finished in imitation of Drawings; with descriptive Letter-press. (Pub. at 12*l*. 12*s*.), half-bound morocco, gilt edges, 3*l*. 8*s*. 1830

This is perhaps the most exquisitely-coloured volume of landscapes ever produced.

HAMILTON'S (LADY) ATTITUDES. 26 bold Outline Engravings, royal 4to, limp cloth, lettered (pub. at 1*l*. 11*s*. 6*d*.), 10*s*. 6*d*.

HANSARD'S ILLUSTRATED BOOK OF ARCHERY. Being the complete History and Practice of the Art; interspersed with numerous Anecdotes; forming a complete Manual for the Bowman 8vo. Illustrated by 38 beautiful Line Engravings, exquisitely finished, by ENGLEHEART, PORTBURY, etc. after Designs by STEPHANOFF (pub. at 1*l*. 11*s*. 6*d*.), gilt cloth, 10*s*. 6*d*.

HARRIS'S GAME AND WILD ANIMALS OF SOUTHERN AFRICA. Large imperial folio. 30 beautifully coloured Engravings, with 30 Vignettes of Heads, Skins, &c. (pub. at 10*l*. 10*s*.), half-morocco, 6*l*. 6*s*. 1814

HARRIS'S WILD SPORTS OF SOUTHERN AFRICA. Imperial 8vo. 26 beautifully coloured Engravings, and a Map (pub. at 2*l*. 2*s*.), gilt cloth, gilt edges, 1*l*. 1*s*. 1844

HEATH'S CARICATURE SCRAP BOOK, on 60 sheets, containing upwards of 1000 Comic Subjects, after SEYMOUR, CRUIKSHANK, PHIZ, and other eminent Caricaturists, oblong folio (pub. at 2*l*. 2*s*.), cloth gilt, 15*s*.

This clever and entertaining volume is now enlarged by ten additional sheets, each containing numerous subjects. It includes the whole of Heath's Omnium Gatherum, both Series: Illustrations of Demonology and Witchcraft; Old Ways and New Ways; Nautical Dictionary; Scenes in London; Sayings and Doings, etc.; a series of humorous Illustrations of Proverbs, etc. As a large and almost infinite storehouse of humour it stands alone. To the young artist it would be found a most valuable collection of studies; and to the family circle a constant source of unexceptionable amusement.

HERVEY'S (T. K.) ENGLISH HELICON; or POETS of the Nineteenth Century, 8vo, illustrated with 12 beautiful Steel Engravings, cloth, gilt edges, (pub. at 1l. 1s.), 9s.

HOGARTH'S WORKS ENGRAVED BY HIMSELF. 153 fine Plates, (including the two well-known "suppressed Plates,") with elaborate Letter-press Descriptions, by J. NICHOLS. Atlas folio (pub. at 50l.), half-bound morocco, gilt back and edges, with a secret pocket for suppressed plates, 7l. 7s.

HOLBEIN'S COURT OF HENRY THE EIGHTH. A Series of 90 exquisitely beautiful Portraits, engraved by BARTOLOZZI, COOPER, and others, in imitation of the original Drawings preserved in the Royal Collection at Windsor; with Historical and Biographical Letter-press by EDMUND LODGE, Esq. Published by JOHN CHAMBERLAINE. Imperial 4to, (pub. at 15l. 15s.), half-bound morocco, full gilt back and edges, 5l. 15s. 6d. 1812

HOFLAND'S BRITISH ANGLER'S MANUAL; Edited by EDWARD JESSE, Esq; or the Art of Angling in England, Scotland, Wales, and Ireland; including a Piscatorial Account of the principal Rivers, Lakes, and Trout Streams; with Instructions in Fly Fishing, Trolling, and Angling of every Description. With upwards of 80 exquisite Plates, many of which are highly-finished Landscapes engraved on Steel, the remainder beautifully engraved on Wood. 8vo, elegant in gilt cloth, 12s.

HOPE'S COSTUME OF THE ANCIENTS. Illustrated in upwards of 320 beautifully-engraved Plates, containing Representations of Egyptian, Greek, and Roman Habits and Dresses. 2 vols. royal 8vo, New Edition, with nearly 20 additional Plates, boards, reduced to 2l. 5s. 1841

HOWARD (FRANK) ON COLOUR, as a MEANS OF ART, being an Adaptation of the Experience of Professors to the practice of Amateurs, illustrated by 18 coloured Plates, post 8vo, cloth gilt, 8s.

In this able volume are shown the ground colours in which the most celebrated painters worked. It is very valuable to the connoisseur, as well as the student, in painting and water-colour drawing.

HOWARD'S (HENRY, R. A.) LECTURES ON PAINTING. Delivered at the Royal Academy, with a Memoir, by his Son, FRANK HOWARD, large post 8vo, cloth, 7s. 6d. 1848

HOWARD'S (FRANK) SPIRIT OF SHAKSPEARE. 483 fine Outline Plates, illustrative of all the principal Incidents in the Dramas of our national Bard, 5 vols, 8vo, (pub. at 14l. 8s.) cloth, 2l. 2s. 1827—33

⁎ The 483 Plates may be had without the letter-press, for illustrating all 8vo. editions of Shakspeare, for 1l. 11s. 6d.

HOWITT'S (MARY) LIVES OF THE BRITISH QUEENS; OR, ROYAL BOOK OF BEAUTY. Illustrated with 28 splendid Portraits of the Queens of England, by the first Artists, engraved on Steel under the direction of CHARLES HEATH. Imperial 8vo, very richly bound in crimson cloth, gilt edges, 1l. 11s. 6d.

HUNT'S (LEIGH) BOOK FOR A CORNER; illustrated with 80 extremely beautiful Wood Engravings from Designs by HULME and FRANKLIN. Post 8vo., cloth, 5s. 1851

HUNT'S EXAMPLES OF TUDOR ARCHITECTURE ADAPTED TO MODERN HABITATIONS. Royal 4to, 37 Plates (pub. at 2l. 2s.), half morocco, 1l. 4s.

HUNT'S DESIGNS FOR PARSONAGE-HOUSES, ALMS-HOUSES, ETC. Royal 4to, 21 Plates (pub. at 1l. 1s.), half morocco, 14s. 1841

HUNT'S DESIGNS FOR GATE LODGES, GAMEKEEPERS' COTTAGES, ETC. Royal 4to., 13 Plates, (pub. at 1l. 1s.), half morocco, 14s. 1841

HUNT'S ARCHITETTURA CAMPESTRE; OR, DESIGNS FOR LODGES, GARDENERS' HOUSES. ETC., IN THE ITALIAN STYLE. 12 Plates, royal 4to. (pub. at 1l. 1s.), half morocco, 14s. 1827

ILLUMINATED BOOK OF CHRISTMAS CAROLS. Square 8vo. 24 Borders illuminated in Gold and Colours, and 4 beautiful Miniatures, richly Ornamented Binding (pub. at 1l. 8s.), 15s. 1846

ILLUMINATED BOOK OF NEEDLEWORK. By Mrs. OWEN, with a History of Needle-work, by the COUNTESS of WILTON, Coloured Plates, post 8vo. (pub. at 16s.), gilt cloth, 5s. 1847

ITALIAN SCHOOL OF DESIGN. Consisting of 100 Plates, chiefly engraved by BARTOLOZZI, after the original Pictures and Drawings of GUERCINO, MICHAEL ANGELO, DOMENICHINO, ANNIBALE, LUDOVICO, and AGOSTINO CARACCI, PIETRO DA CORTONA, CARLO MARATTI, and others, in the Collection of Her Majesty. Imperial 4to. (pub. at 10l. 10s.), half morocco, gilt edges, 2l. 2s. 1812

JAMES' (G P. R.) BOOK OF THE PASSIONS, royal 8vo, illustrated with 16 splendid Line Engravings, after Drawings by EDWARD CORBOULD, STEPHANOFF, CHALON, KENNY MEADOWS, and JENKINS; engraved under the superintendence of CHARLES HEATH. New and improved edition (just published), elegant in gilt cloth, gilt edges (pub. at 1l. 11s. 6d.), 12s.

JAMESON'S (MRS.) BEAUTIES OF THE COURT OF CHARLES THE SECOND, with their Portraits after SIR PETER LELY and other eminent Painters; illustrating the Diaries of PEPYS, EVELYN, CLARENDON, &c. A new edition, considerably enlarged, with an Introductory Essay and additional Anecdotes. Imperial 8vo, illustrated by 21 beautiful Portraits comprising the whole of the celebrated suite of Paintings by LELY, preserved in the Windsor Gallery, and several from the Devonshire, Grosvenor, and Althorp Galleries, extra gilt cloth, 1*l*. 5*s*.

———— the same, imperial 8vo, *with India proof impressions*, extra gilt cloth, gilt edges, 2*l*. 2*s*.

JONES'S (OWEN) ILLUMINATED BOOKS OF THE MIDDLE AGES, with Historical and Descriptive letterpress by NOEL HUMPHREYS. Illustrated by 30 large Plates, splendidly printed in gold and colours, comprising some of the finest Examples of Illuminated Manuscripts of the Middle Ages, particularly Italian and French. Atlas folio, handsomely half-bound morocco, gilt edges (pub. at 16*l*. 16*s*.), 9*l*. 9*s*.

KINGSBOROUGH'S (LORD) ANTIQUITIES OF MEXICO, comprising Fac-similes of Ancient Mexican Paintings and Hieroglyphics, preserved in the Royal Libraries of Paris, Berlin, Dresden, Vienna; the Vatican and the Borgian Museum, at Rome; the Institute at Bologna; the Bodleian Library at Oxford; and various others; the greater part inedited. Also, the Monuments of New Spain, by M. DUPAIX, illustrated by upwards of 1000 elaborate and highly interesting Plates, accurately copied from the originals, by A. AGLIO, 9 vols. imperial folio, very neatly half bound morocco, gilt edges (pub. at 140*l*.), 35*l*.

———— the same, 9 vols. WITH THE PLATES BEAUTIFULLY COLOURED, half bound morocco, gilt edges, (pub. at 210*l*.), 63*l*.

———— the two Additional Volumes, now first published, and forming the 8th and 9th of the whole work, may be had separately, to complete the former seven, in red boards, as formerly done up, 12*l*. 12*s*.

KNIGHT'S (HENRY GALLY) ECCLESIASTICAL ARCHITECTURE OF ITALY, FROM THE TIME OF CONSTANTINE TO THE FIFTEENTH CENTURY. With an Introduction and Text. Imperial folio. First Series, containing 40 beautiful and highly interesting Views of Ecclesiastical Buildings in Italy, several of which are expensively illuminated in gold and colours, half-bound morocco, 5*l*. 5*s*. 1843

Second and Concluding Series, containing 41 beautiful and highly interesting Views of Ecclesiastical Buildings in Italy, arranged in Chronological Order; with Descriptive Letter-press. Imperial folio, half-bound morocco, 5*l*. 5*s*. 1844

KNIGHT'S PICTORIAL LONDON. 6 vols. bound in 3 thick handsome vols., imperial 8vo, illustrated by 650 Wood Engravings (pub. at 3*l*. 3*s*.), cloth gilt), 1*l*. 10*s*. 1841-44

LANDSEER'S (SIR EDWIN) ETCHINGS OF CARNIVOROUS ANIMALS, Comprising 38 subjects, chiefly early works o' this talented Artist, etched by his brother THOMAS or his Father, (some hitherto unpublished), with letter-press Descriptions, royal 4to., cloth, 1*l*. 1*s*. 1853

LONDON.—WILKINSON'S LONDINA ILLUSTRATA; OR, GRAPHIC AND HISTORICAL ILLUSTRATIONS of the most Interesting and Curious Architectural Monuments of the City and Suburbs of London and Westminster, *v. g.*, Monasteries, Churches, Charitable Foundations, Palaces, Halls, Courts, Processions, Places of early Amusements, Theatres, and Old Houses. 2 vols. imperial 4to, containing 207 Copperplate Engravings, with Historical and Descriptive Letter-press (pub. at 26*l*. 5*s*.), half-bound morocco, 5*l*. 5*s*. 1819.25

LOUDON'S EDITION OF REPTON ON LANDSCAPE GARDENING AND LANDSCAPE ARCHITECTURE. New Edition, 250 Wood Cuts, Portrait, thick 8vo, cloth lettered (pub. at 1*l*. 10*s*.), 15*s*.

MARCENY DE GHUY, ŒUVRES DE, contenant differens Morceaux d'Histoires, Portraits, Paysages, Batailles, etc., with above 50 remarkably fine Engravings, after Paintings by POUSSIN, VANDYCK, REMBRANDT, and others, including Portraits of Charles I.. the Maid of Orleans, &c. fine impressions. Imp. 4to, half bound morocco (pub. at 5*l*. 5*s*.), 1*l*. 16*s*. *Paris*, 1755

MARTIN'S CIVIL COSTUME OF ENGLAND, from the Conquest to the Present Period, from Tapestry, MSS., &c. Royal 4to, 61 Plates, beautifully Illuminated in Gold and Colours, cloth, gilt, 2*l*. 12*s*. 6*d*. 1842

MEYRICK'S PAINTED ILLUSTRATIONS OF ANCIENT ARMS AND ARMOUR, a Critical Inquiry into Ancient Armour as it existed in Europe, but particularly in England, from the Norman Conquest to the Reign of Charles II., with a Glossary, etc. by SIR SAMUEL RUSH MEYRICK, LL.D., F.S.A., etc., new and greatly improved Edition, corrected and enlarged throughout by the Author himself, with the assistance of Literary and Antiquarian Friends (ALBERT WAY, etc.) 3 vols. imperial 4to, illustrated by more than 100 Plates, splendidly illuminated, mostly in gold and silver, exhibiting some of the finest Specimens existing in England; also a new Plate of the Tournament of Locks and Keys (pub. at 21*l*.) half-bound morocco, gilt edges, 10*l*. 10*s*. 1844

SIR WALTER SCOTT justly describes this Collection as "THE INCOMPARABLE ARMOURY." *Edinburgh Review*.

MEYRICK'S ENGRAVED ILLUSTRATIONS OF ANCIENT ARMS & ARMOUR in the Collection of Goodrich Court, 150 Engravings by JOS. SKELTON, 2 vols. folio (pub. at 11*l*. 11*s*.), half morocco, top edges gilt, 4*l*. 14*s*. 6*d*.

MILLINGEN'S ANCIENT UNEDITED MONUMENTS; comprising Painted Greek Vases, Statues, Busts, Bas-Reliefs, and other Remains of Grecian Art. 62 large and beautiful Engravings, mostly coloured, with Letter-press Descriptions, imperial 4to. (pub. at 9l. 9s.) half morocco, 4l. 14s. 6d. 1832

MOSES'S ANTIQUE VASES, CANDELABRA, LAMPS, TRIPODS, PATERÆ, Tazzas, Tombs, Mausoleums, Sepulchral Chambers, Cinerary Urns, Sarcophagi, Cippi, and other Ornaments, 170 Plates, several of which are coloured, with Letter-press, by HOPE, small 8vo. (pub. at 3l. 3s.), cloth, 1l. 4s. 1814

MULLERS' ANCIENT ART AND ITS REMAINS, or a Manual of the Archæology of Art. By C. O. MULLER, author of "History and Antiquities of the Doric Race." New edition by WELCKER, translated by JOHN LEITCH. Thick 8vo. cloth lettered (pub. at 18s.), 12s.

MURPHY'S ARABIAN ANTIQUITIES OF SPAIN; representing, in 100 very highly finished line Engravings, by LE KEUX, FINDEN, LANDSEER, G. COOKE, &c., the most remarkable Remains of the Architecture, Sculpture, Paintings, and Mosaics of the Spanish Arabs now existing in the Peninsula, including the magnificent Palace of the Alhambra; the celebrated Mosque and Bridge at Cordova; the Royal Villa of Generalife; and the Casa de Carbon; accompanied by Letter-press Descriptions, in 1 vol. atlas folio, original and brilliant impressions of the Plates (pub. at 42l.), half morocco, 12l. 12s. 1813

MURPHY'S ANCIENT CHURCH OF BATALHA, IN PORTUGAL. Plans, Elevations, Sections, and Views of the; with its History and Description, and an Introductory Discourse on GOTHIC ARCHITECTURE, imperial folio, 27 fine Copper Plates, engraved by LOWRY (pub. at 6l. 6s.), half morocco, 2l. 2s. 1795

NAPOLEON GALLERY; or, Illustrations of the Life and Times of the Emperor, with 90 Etchings on Steel b REVEIL, and other eminent Artists, in one thick volume, post 8vo. (pub. at 1l. 1s.), gilt cloth, gilt edges, 10s. 6d.

NICOLAS'S (SIR HARRIS) HISTORY OF THE ORDERS OF KNIGHTHOOD OF THE BRITISH EMPIRE; with an Account of the Medals, Crosses, and Clasps which have been conferred for Naval and Military Services; together with a History of the Order of the Guelphs of Hanover. 4 vols. imperial 4to, splendidly printed and illustrated by numerous fine Woodcuts of Badges, Crosses, Collars, Stars, Medals, Ribbands, Clasps, &c., and many large Plates, illuminated in gold and colours, including full-length Portraits of Queen Victoria, Prince Albert, the King of Hanover, and the Dukes of Cambridge and Sussex. (Pub. at 14l. 14s.), cloth, with morocco backs, 5l. 15s. 6d. *Complete to* 1847

——— the same, with the Plates richly coloured, but not illuminated, and without the extra portraits, 4 vols. royal 4to, cloth, 3l. 13s. 6d.

"Sir Harris Nicolas has produced the first comprehensive History of the British Orders of Knighthood; and it is *one of the most elaborately prepared and splendidly printed works that ever issued from the press*. The Author appears to us to have neglected no sources of information, and to have exhausted them, as far as regards the general scope and purpose of the inquiry. The Graphical Illustrations are such as become a work of this character upon such a subject; at, of course, a lavish cost. The resources of the recently revived art of wood-engraving have been combined with the new art of printing in colours, so as to produce a rich effect, almost rivalling that of the monastic illuminations. *Such a book is sure of a place in every great library.* It contains matter calculated to interest extensive classes of readers, and we hope by our specimen to excite their curiosity."—*Quarterly Review.*

NICHOLSON'S ARCHITECTURE; ITS PRINCIPLES AND PRACTICE. 218 Plates by LOWRY, new edition, revised by JOS. GWILT, Esq., one volume, royal 8vo, 1l. 11s. 6d. 1848

For classical Architecture, the text book of the Profession, the most useful Guide to the Student, and the best Compendium for the Amateur. An eminent Architect has declared it to be "not only the most useful book of the kind ever published, but absolutely indispensable to the Student."

PICTORIAL HISTORY OF GERMANY DURING THE REIGN OF FREDERICK THE GREAT; including a complete History of the Seven Years' War. By FRANCIS KUGLER. Illustrated by ADOLPH MENZEL. Royal 8vo, with above 500 Woodcuts (pub. at 1l. 8s.), cloth gilt, 12s. 1845

PICTORIAL GALLERY OF RACE-HORSES. Containing Portraits of all the Winning Horses of the Derby, Oaks, and St. Leger Stakes, during the last Thirteen Years, and a History of the principal Operations of the Turf. By WILDRAKE (George Tattersall, Esq.). Royal 8vo, containing 95 beautiful Engravings of Horses, after Pictures by COOPER, HERRING, HANCOCK, ALKEN, &c. Also full-length characteristic Portraits of celebrated living Sportsmen ("Cracks of the Day"), by SEYMOUR (pub. at 2l. 2s.), scarlet cloth, gilt, 1l. 1s.

PICTORIAL HISTORY OF FRANCE AND ITS REVOLUTIONS, (comprising the period 1789 to 1848), by GEORGE LONG, with fine Portraits, and numerous large woodcuts, after Designs by HARVEY. Large imperial 8vo, cloth (pub. at 1l.), 12s.

PICTURESQUE TOUR OF THE RIVER THAMES, in its Western Course, including particular Descriptions of Richmond, Windsor, and Hampton Court. By JOHN FISHER MURRAY. Illustrated by upwards of 100 very highly-finished Wood Engravings by ORRIN SMITH, BRANSTON, LANDELLS, LINTON, and other eminent Artists. Royal 8vo. (pub. at 1l. 5s.), gilt cloth, 5s. 6d. 1845

The most beautiful volume of Topographical Lignographs ever produced.

PINELLI'S ETCHINGS OF ITALIAN MANNERS AND COSTUME, including his Carnival, Banditti, &c., 27 Plates, imperial 4to, half-bound morocco, 15s. *Rome*, 1840

PUGIN'S GLOSSARY OF ECCLESIASTICAL ORNAMENT AND COSTUME; setting forth the Origin, History, and Signification of the various Emblems, Devices, and Symbolical Colours, peculiar to Christian Designs of the Middle Ages. Illustrated by nearly 80 Plates, splendidly printed in gold and colours. Royal 4to, half morocco extra, top edges gilt, 6l. 6s.

PUGIN'S ORNAMENTAL TIMBER GABLES, selected from Ancient Examples in England and Normandy. Royal 4to, 30 Plates, cloth, 1l. 1s. 1839

PUGIN'S EXAMPLES OF GOTHIC ARCHITECTURE, selected from Ancient Edifices in England; consisting of Plans, Elevations, Sections, and Parts at large, with Historical and Descriptive letter-press, Illustrated by 225 Engravings by LE KEUX, 3 vols. 4to, (pub. at 12l. 12s.) cloth, 6l. 6s. 1836

PUGIN'S GOTHIC ORNAMENTS. 90 fine Plates, drawn on Stone by J. D. HARDING and others. Royal 4to, half morocco, 3l. 3s.

PUGIN'S NEW WORK ON FLORIATED ORNAMENT, with 30 Plates, splendidly printed in Gold and Colours, royal 4to, elegantly bound in cloth, with rich gold ornaments, (pub. at 3l. 3s.), 2l. 5s.

RADCLIFFE'S NOBLE SCIENCE OF FOX-HUNTING, for the use of Sportsmen, royal 8vo, nearly 40 beautiful Wood Cuts of Hunting, Hounds, &c. (pub. at 1l. 8s.), cloth gilt, 10s. 6d. 1839

RICAUTI'S SKETCHES FOR RUSTIC WORK, including Bridges, Park and Garden Buildings, Seats and Furniture, with Descriptions and Estimates of the Buildings. New Edition, royal 4to, 18 Plates, cloth lettered (pub. at 16s.), 12s.

RETZSCH'S OUTLINES TO SCHILLER'S "FIGHT WITH THE DRAGON." Royal 4to, containing 16 Plates, engraved by MOSES, stiff covers, 7s. 6d.

RETZSCH'S ILLUSTRATIONS TO SCHILLER'S "FRIDOLIN," Royal 4to, containing 8 Plates, engraved by MOSES, stiff covers, 4s. 6d.

REYNOLDS' (SIR JOSHUA) GRAPHIC WORKS. 300 beautiful Engravings (comprising nearly 400 subjects,) after this delightful painter, engraved on Steel by S. W. REYNOLDS. 3 vols. folio (pub. at 36l.), half bound morocco, gilt edges, 12l. 12s.

ROBINSON'S RURAL ARCHITECTURE; being a Series of Designs for Ornamental Cottages, in 96 Plates, with Estimates. Fourth, greatly improved, Edition. Royal 4to (pub. at 6l. 4s.), half morocco, 2l. 5s.

ROBINSON'S NEW SERIES OF ORNAMENTAL COTTAGES AND VILLAS. 56 Plates by HARDING and ALLOM. Royal 4to, half morocco, 2l. 2s.

ROBINSON'S ORNAMENTAL VILLAS. 96 Plates (pub. at 4l. 4s.) half morocco, 2l. 5s.

ROBINSON'S FARM BUILDINGS. 56 Plates (pub. at 2l. 2s.) half morocco, 1l. 11s. 6d.

ROBINSON'S LODGES AND PARK ENTRANCES. 48 Plates (pub at 2l. 2s.), half morocco, 1l 11s. 6d.

ROBINSON'S VILLAGE ARCHITECTURE. Fourth Edition, with additional Plate. 41 Plates (pub. at 1l. 16s.), half bound uniform, 1l. 4s.

ROBINSON'S NEW VITRUVIUS BRITANNICUS; or, Views, Plans and Elevations of English Mansions, viz., Woburn Abbey, Hatfield House, and Hardwicke Hall; also Cassiobury House, by JOHN BRITTON, imperial folio, 50 fine Engravings, by LE KEUX (pub. at 16l. 16s.), half morocco, gilt edges, 3l. 13s. 6d. 1847

ROYAL VICTORIA GALLERY, comprising 88 beautiful Engravings, after Pictures at BUCKINGHAM PALACE, particularly REMBRANDT, the O>TADES, TENIERS, GERARD DOUW, BOTH, CUYP, REYNOLDS, TITIAN, and RUBENS; engraved by GREATBACH, S. W. REYNOLDS, PRESBURY, BURNET, &c.; with letter-press by LINNELL, royal 4to. (pub. at 4l. 4s.), half morocco, 1l. 11s. 6d.

SCHOLA ITALICA ARTIS PICTORIÆ, or Engravings of the finest Pictures in the Galleries at Rome, imperial folio, consisting of 40 beautiful Engravings after MICHAEL ANGELO, RAPHAEL, TITIAN, CARACCI, GUIDO, PARMIGIANO, etc. by VOLPATO and others, fine impressions, half-bound morocco (pub. at 10l. 10s.), 2l. 12s. 6d. *Rome*, 1805

SHAW'S SPECIMENS OF ANCIENT FURNITURE. 75 Plates, drawn from existing authorities, with descriptions by SIR SAMUEL R. MEYRICK, K.H., medium 4to, plain (pub. at 2l. 2s.), 1l. 11s. 6d.

———— the same, with a portion of the plates coloured, medium 4to. (pub. at 4l. 4s.), 2l. 12s. 6d.).

———— the same, imperial 4to, large paper, with all the Plates finely coloured, (pub. at 8l. 8s.), 5l. 5s.

———— the same, imperial 4to, large paper, with the whole of the Plates extra finished in colours (pub. at 10l. 10s.), 6l. 6s.

SHAW'S ILLUMINATED ORNAMENTS OF THE MIDDLE AGES, from the 6th to the 17th Century, selected from manuscripts and early printed books, 59 Plates, carefully coloured from the originals, with descriptions by SIR FREDERICK MADDEN, K.H., in one vol. 4to (pub. at 5*l.* 5*s.*), 4*l.* 4*s.*

———— the same, large paper, highly-finished with opaque colours, and heightened with gold, imperial 4to (pub. at 10*l.* 10*s.*), 8*l.* 8*s.*

SHAW'S ALPHABETS, NUMERALS, AND DEVICES OF THE MIDDLE AGES, selected from the finest existing Specimens, 48 Plates (26 of them coloured) imperial 8vo. (pub. at 2*l.* 2*s.*), 1*l.* 11*s.* 6*d.*

———— the same, large paper, imperial 4to, with the coloured plates highly-finished, and heightened with gold (pub. at 4*l.* 4*s.*), 3*l.* 10*s.*

SHAW'S HAND-BOOK OF MEDIÆVAL ALPHABETS AND DEVICES, being a selection of 20 Plates of Alphabets, and 17 Plates of original specimens of Labels, Monograms, Heraldic Devices, &c. not heretofore figured, in all 37 Plates, printed in colours, imperial 8vo. in cloth boards (pub. at 1*l.* 16*s.*), 15*s.*

SHAW'S SPECIMENS OF THE DETAILS OF ELIZABETHAN ARCHITECTURE, with descriptions by T. MOULE, ESQ., 60 Plates, 4to, boards (pub. at 3*l.* 3*s.*). 1*l.* 11*s.* 6*d.*

———— the same, large paper, imperial 4to, proof plates on India paper, some coloured (pub. at 6*l.* 6*s.*), 2*l.* 3*s.*

SHAW'S ENCYCLOPÆDIA OF ORNAMENT, select examples from the purest and best specimens of all kinds and of all ages, 59 Plates, 4to, boards (pub. at 1*l.* 10*s.*), 1*l.* 5*s.*

———— the same, large paper, imperial 4to, all the Plates coloured, boards (pub. at 3*l.*), 2*l.* 12*s.* 6*d.*

SHAW'S SPECIMENS OF ORNAMENTAL METAL WORK, with 50 plates, 4to, boards (pub. at 2*l.* 2*s.*), 1*l.* 1*s.*

SHAW'S DECORATIVE ARTS OF THE MIDDLE AGES, exhibiting on 41 Plates, with numerous Woodcuts, beautiful specimens of the various kinds of Ancient Enamel, Metal Work, Wood Carvings, Paintings on Stained Glass, Initial Illuminations. Embroidery, Bookbinding, and other Ornamental Textures, also fine and elegant Initial letters to the various descriptions, imperial 8vo, boards (pub. at 2*l.* 2*s.*), 1*l.* 16*s.*

———— the same, large paper, imperial 4to, 41 Plates, some coloured, boards (pub. at 4*l.* 4*s.*) 3*l.* 10*s.*

———— the same, large paper, imperial 4to, with the whole of the plates coloured in the highest style, forming a very beautiful and interesting volume, boards (pub. at 8*l.* 8*s.*), 6*l.* 6*s.*

SHAW'S DRESSES AND DECORATIONS OF THE MIDDLE AGES, from the 7th to the 17th centuries, with an Historical Introduction and Descriptive Text to every Illustration, consisting of 85 Copper Plates of elaborate Woodcuts, a profusion of beautiful Initial Letters, and examples of curious and singular ornament enriching nearly every page of this highly decorated work, 2 vols., imperial 8vo, the plates carefully coloured, boards (pub. at 7*l.* 7*s.*), 5*l.* 15*s.* 6*d.*

———— the same, 2 vols large paper, imperial 4to, the plates highly coloured and picked-in with gold, boards (pub. at 18*l.*), 14*l.* 14*s.*

———— the same, large paper, imperial 4to, with the plates highly coloured and the whole of the Initial Letters and Illustrations picked in with gold (only 12 copies got up in this manner) (pub. at 30*l.*), 24*l.*

SHAW'S GLAZIER'S BOOK, or Draughts serving for Glaziers, but not impertinent for Plasterers, Gardeners, and others, consisting of elaborate designs for Casement Windows, Plasterer's work, garden walks, etc., 117 Plates, mostly taken from a work published in 1615, by WALTER GIDDE, with others from existing authorities added, demy 8vo, boards (pub. at 16*s.*), 10*s.* 6*d.*

SHAW AND BRIDGEN'S DESIGNS FOR FURNITURE, with Candelabra and interior Decoration, 60 Plates, royal 4to (pub. at 3*l.* 3*s.*), half-bound, uncut, 1*l.* 11*s.* 6*d.*   1838

———— the same, large paper, impl. 4to, the Plates coloured (pub. at 6*l.* 6*s.*), half-bd., uncut, 3*l.* 3*s.*

SHAW'S LUTON CHAPEL, its Architecture and Ornaments, illustrated in a series of 20 highly-finished Line Engravings, imperial folio (pub. at 3*l.* 3*s.*), half morocco, uncut, 1*l.* 16*s.*
1830

SILVESTRE'S UNIVERSAL PALEOGRAPHY, or Fac-similes of the writings of every age, taken from the most authentic Missals and other interesting Manuscripts existing in the Libraries of France, Italy, Germany, and England. By M. Silvestre, containing upwards of 300 large and most beautifully executed fac-similes, on Copper and Stone, most richly Illuminated in the finest style of art, 2 vols. atlas folio, half-morocco extra, gilt edges. 31*l.* 10*s.*

———— the Historical and Descriptive Letter-press by Champollion, Figeac, and Champollion, jun. With additions and corrections by Sir Frederick Madden. 2 vols. royal 8vo, cloth, 1*l.* 16*s.*
1850

———— the same, 2 vols. royal 8vo., hf. mor. gilt edges (uniform with the folio work), 2*l.* 8*s.*

SMITH'S (C. J.) HISTORICAL AND LITERARY CURIOSITIES. Consisting of Fac-similes of interesting Autographs, Scenes of remarkable Historical Events and interesting Localities, Engravings of Old Houses, Illuminated and Missal Ornaments, Antiquities, &c., containing 100 Plates, some illuminated, with occasional Letter-press. In 1 volume 4 to half morocco, uncut, reduced to 2*l.* 12*s.* 6*d.*

SMITH'S ANCIENT COSTUME OF GREAT BRITAIN AND IRELAND. From the 7th to the 16th Century, with Historical Illustrations, folio, with 62 coloured plates illuminated with Gold and Silver, and highly finished (pub. at 19l. 1s.), half bound morocco extra, gilt edges, 3l. 13s. 6d.

SPORTSMAN'S REPOSITORY: comprising a series of highly-finished Line Engravings, representing the Horse and the Dog, in all their varieties, by the celebrated engraver JOHN SCOTT, from original paintings by Reinagle, Gilpin, Stubbs, Cooper, and Landseer, accompanied by a comprehensive Description by the Author of the "British Field Sports," 4to, with 37 large Copper Plates, and numerous Woodcuts by Burnett and others (pub. at 2l. 12s. 6d.), cloth gilt. 1l. 1s.

STORER'S CATHEDRAL ANTIQUITIES OF ENGLAND AND WALES. 4 vols. 8vo, with 256 engravings (pub. at 7l. 16s.), half morocco, 2l. 12s. 6d.

STOTHARD'S MONUMENTAL EFFIGIES OF GREAT BRITAIN. 147 beautifully finished Etchings, all of which are more or less tinted, and some of them highly illuminated in gold and colours, with Historical Descriptions and Introduction, by KEMPE. Folio (pub. at 19l.), half morocco, 8l. 8s.

—————— or on large paper, Plates illuminated (pub. at 22l.), 13l. 13s.

STRUTT'S SYLVA BRITANNICA ET SCOTICA; or Portraits of Forest Trees, distinguished for their Antiquity, Magnitude, or Beauty, comprising 50 very large and highly finished painters' Etchings, imperial folio (pub. at 9l. 9s.), half morocco extra, gilt edges, 4l. 10s.
1825

STRUTT'S DRESSES AND HABITS OF THE PEOPLE OF ENGLAND, from the Establishment of the Saxons in Britain to the present time; with an historical and Critical Inquiry into every branch of Costume. New and greatly improved Edition, with Critical and Explanatory Notes, by J. R. PLANCHE, Esq., F.S.A. 2 vols. royal 4to, 153 Plates, cloth, 4l. 4s. The Plates coloured, 7l. 7s. The Plates splendidly Illuminated in gold, silver, and opaque colours, in the Missal style, 20l.
1843

STRUTT'S REGAL AND ECCLESIASTICAL ANTIQUITIES OF ENGLAND. Containing the most authentic Representations of all the English Monarchs from Edward the Confessor to Henry the Eighth; together with many of the Great Personages that were eminent under their several Reigns. New and greatly improved Edition, by J. R. PLANCHE', Esq., F.S.A. Royal 4to, 72 Plates, cloth, 2l. 2s. The Plates coloured, 4l. 4s. Splendidly illuminated, uniform with the Dresses, 12l. 12s.
1842

STUBBS' ANATOMY OF THE HORSE. 24 fine large Copper-plate Engravings, Imperial folio (pub. at 4l. 4s.), boards, leather back, 1l. 11s. 6d.
The original edition of this fine old work, which is indispensable to artists. It has long been considered rare.

TATTERSALL'S SPORTING ARCHITECTURE, comprising the Stud Farm, the Stall, the Stable, the Kennel, Race Studs, &c., with 43 beautiful Steel and Wood Illustrations, several after HANCOCK, cloth gilt (pub. at 1l. 11s. 6d.), 1l. 1s.
1850

TRENDALL'S DESIGNS FOR ROOFS OF IRON, STONE, AND WOOD, with Measurements, &c., for the use of Carpenters and Builders (an excellent practical work), 4to, limp cloth (pub. at 15s.), 7s. 6d.
1851

TURNER AND GIRTIN'S RIVER SCENERY; folio, 20 beautiful Engravings on Steel after the drawings of J. M. W. TURNER, brilliant impressions, in a portfolio, with morocco back (pub. at 5l. 5s.), reduced to 1l. 11s. 6d.

—————— the same, with thick glazed paper between the plates, half-bound morocco, gilt edges (pub. at 6l. 6s.), reduced to 2l. 2s.

TURNER'S LIBER FLUVIORUM, or River Scenery of France, 62 highly-finished Line Engravings on Steel by WILLMORE, GOODALL, MILLER, COUSENS, and other distinguished Artists, with descriptive Letter-press by LEITCH RITCHIE, and a Memoir of J. W. M. TURNER, R.A, by ALARIC A. WATTS, imperial 8vo, gilt cloth, 1l. 11s. 6d., or India Proofs, 3l. 3s.

WALKER'S ANALYSIS OF BEAUTY IN WOMAN. Preceded by a critical View of the general Hypothesis respecting Beauty, by LEONARDO DA VINCI, MENGS, WINCKELMANN, HUME, HOGARTH, BURKE, KNIGHT, ALISON, and others. New edition, royal 8vo, illustrated by 22 beautiful Plates, after drawings from life, by H. HOWARD, by GAUCI and LANE (pub. at 2l. 2s.), gilt cloth, 1l. 1s.

WALPOLE'S (HORACE) ANECDOTES OF PAINTING IN ENGLAND, with some Account of the Principal Artists, and Catalogue of Engravers, who have been born or resided in England, with Notes by DALLAWAY; New Edition, Revised and Enlarged, by RALPH WORNUM, Esq., complete in 3 vols. 8vo, with numerous beautiful portraits and plates, 2l. 2s.

WARRINGTON'S HISTORY OF STAINED GLASS, from the earliest period of the Art to the present time, illustrated by Coloured examples of Entire Windows, in the various styles, imperial folio, with 26 very large and beautifully coloured Plates (one of them nearly four feet in length) half bound morocco, gilt edges (pub at 8l. 8s.), 5l. 15s. 6d.

WATTS'S PSALMS AND HYMNS, ILLUSTRATED EDITION, complete, with indexes of "Subjects," "First Lines," and a Table of Scriptures, 8vo, printed in a very large and beautiful type, embellished with 24 beautiful Wood Cuts by MARTIN, WESTALL, and others (pub. at 1l. 1s.), gilt cloth, 7s. 6d.

PUBLISHED OR SOLD BY H. G. BOHN.   11

WESTWOOD'S PALEOGRAPHIA SACRA PICTORIA; being a series of Illustrations of the Ancient Versions of the Bible, copied from Illuminated Manuscripts, executed between the fourth and sixteenth centuries, royal 4to, 50 Plates beautifully illuminated in gold and colours, half-bound, uncut (pub. at 6l. 16s.), 3l. 16s.

WHISTON'S JOSEPHUS, ILLUSTRATED EDITION, complete; containing both the Antiquities and the Wars of the Jews. 2 vols. 8vo, handsomely printed, embellished with 52 beautiful Wood Engravings, by various Artists (pub. at 1l. 4s.), cloth boards, elegantly gilt, 14s.

WHITTOCK'S DECORATIVE PAINTER'S AND GLAZIER'S GUIDE, containing the most approved methods of imitating every kind of Fancy Wood and Marble, in Oil or Distemper Colour, Designs for Decorating Apartments, and the Art of Staining and Painting on Glass, &c., with Examples from Ancient Windows, with the Supplement, 4to, illustrated with 104 plates, of which 44 are coloured (pub. at 3l. 14s.), cloth, 1l. 16s.

WHITTOCK'S MINIATURE PAINTER'S MANUAL. Foolscap 8vo, 7 coloured plates, and numerous woodcuts (pub. at 5s.), cloth, 2s.

WIGHTWICK'S PALACE OF ARCHITECTURE, a Romance of Art and History. Imperial 8vo, with 211 Illustrations, Steel Plates and Woodcuts (pub. at 2l. 12s. 6d.), cloth, 1l. 1s.   1840

WILD'S ARCHITECTURAL GRANDEUR of Belgium, Germany, and France, 24 fine Plates by Le Keux, &c. Imperial 4to (pub at 1l. 18s.), half-morocco, 1l. 4s.   1837

WILD'S ENGLISH CATHEDRALS. Twelve select examples from the Cathedrals of England, of the Ecclesiastic Architecture of the Middle Ages, beautifully coloured, after the original drawings, by Charles Wild, imperial folio, mounted on tinted cardboard like drawings, in a handsome portfolio (pub. at 12l. 12s.), 5l. 5s.

WILD'S FOREIGN CATHEDRALS, 12 Plates, coloured and mounted like Drawings, in a handsome portfolio (pub. at 12l. 12s.), imperial folio, 5l. 5s.

WILLIAMS' VIEWS IN GREECE. 64 beautiful Line Engravings by Miller, Horsburgh, and others. 2 vols. imperial 8vo (pub. at 6l. 6s.), half-bound mor. extra, gilt edges, 3l. 12s. 6d.   1829

WINDSOR CASTLE AND ITS ENVIRONS, INCLUDING ETON, by Leitch Ritchie, new edition, edited by E. Jesse, Esq., illustrated with upwards of 60 beautiful Engravings on Steel and Wood, royal 8vo, gilt cloth, 15s.

WOOD'S ARCHITECTURAL ANTIQUITIES AND RUINS OF PALMYRA AND BAALBEC. 2 vols. in 1, imperial folio, containing 110 fine Copper-plate Engravings, some very large and folding (pub. at 7l. 7s.), half-morocco, uncut, 3l. 13s. 6d.   1827

Natural History, Agriculture, &c.

ANDREW'S FIGURES OF HEATHS. with Scientific Descriptions, 6 vols, royal 8vo, with 300 beautifully coloured Plates (pub. at 15l.), cloth gilt, 7l. 10s.   1845

BAUER AND HOOKER'S ILLUSTRATIONS OF THE GENERA OF FERNS, in which the characters of each Genus are displayed in the most elaborate manner in a series of magnified Dissections and Figures, highly-finished in Colours, imp. 8vo, Plates, 6l. 1838—42

BEECHEY.—BOTANY OF CAPTAIN BEECHEY'S VOYAGE, comprising an Account of the Plants collected by Messrs. Lay and Collie, and other Officers of the Expedition, during the voyage to the Pacific and Behring's Straits. By Sir William Jackson Hooker, and G. A. W. Arnott, Esq., illustrated by 100 Plates, beautifully engraved, complete in 10 parts, 4to (pub. at 7l. 10s.), 5l.   1831—41

BEECHEY.—ZOOLOGY OF CAPTAIN BEECHEY'S VOYAGE, compiled from the Collections and Notes of Captain Beechey, and the Scientific Gentlemen who accompanied the Expedition. The Mammalia by Dr. Richardson; Ornithology, by N. A. Vigors, Esq.; Fishes, by G. T. Lay, Esq., and E. T. Bennett, Esq.; Crustacea, by Richard Owen, Esq.; Reptiles, by John Edward Gray, Esq. Shells, by W. Sowerby, Esq.; and Geology, by the Rev. Dr. Buckland. 4to, illustrated by 47 Plates, containing many hundred Figures, beautifully coloured by Sowerby (pub. at 4l. 4s.), cloth, 3l. 13s. 6d.   1839

BOLTON'S NATURAL HISTORY OF BRITISH SONG BIRDS. Illustrated with Figures the size of Life, of the Birds, both Male and Female, in their most Natural Attitudes; their Nests and Eggs, Food, Favourite Plants, Shrubs, Trees, &c. &c. New Edition, revised and very considerably augmented, 2 vols. in 1, medium 4to, containing 80 beautifully coloured plates (pub. at 3l. 3s.), half-bound morocco, gilt backs, gilt edges, 2l. 2s.   1845

BROWN'S ILLUSTRATIONS OF THE LAND AND FRESH WATER SHELLS OF GREAT BRITAIN AND IRELAND; with Figures, Descriptions, and Localities of all the Species. Royal 8vo, containing on 27 large Plates, 330 Figures of all the known British Species, in their full size, accurately drawn from Nature (pub. at 15s.), cloth, 10s. 6d.   1845

CARPENTER'S ANIMAL PHYSIOLOGY; including a Comprehensive Sketch of the principal Forms of Animal Structure. New edition, carefully revised, with 267 capital Wood Illustrations, post 8vo, cloth, 5s.

CATLOW'S DROPS OF WATER; their marvellous Inhabitants displayed by the Microscope. Coloured plates, 12mo., cloth gilt, 5s.

CARPENTER'S VEGETABLE PHYSIOLOGY AND BOTANY, including the structures and organs of Plants, their characters, uses, geographical distribution, and classification, according to the Natural System of Botany. New and enlarged edition, with 225 capital illustrations on wood, post 8vo, cloth, *reprinting.*

CURTIS'S FLORA LONDINENSIS; Revised and Improved by GEORGE GRAVES, extended and continued by Sir W. JACKSON HOOKER; comprising the History of Plants indigenous to Great Britain, with Indexes; the Drawings made by SYDENHAM, EDWARDS, and LINDLEY. 5 vols. royal folio (or 109 parts), containing 647 Plates, exhibiting the full natural size of each Plant, with magnified Dissections of the Parts of Fructification, &c., all beautifully coloured (pub. at 57l. 4s. in parts), half-bound morocco, top edges gilt, 30l. 1835

DENNY—MONOGRAPHIA ANOPLURORUM BRITANNIÆ, OR BRITISH SPECIES OF PARASITE INSECTS (published under the patronage of the British Association) 8vo, numerous beautifully coloured plates of Lice, containing several hundred magnified figures, cloth, 1l. 11s. 6d. 1843

DE JUSSIEU'S ELEMENTS OF BOTANY, translated by J. H. WILSON, F.L.S., &c., thick post 8vo, with 750 capital Woodcuts, cloth (pub. at 12s. 6d.), 8s. 6d. *Van Voorst,* 1849

DON'S GENERAL SYSTEM OF GARDENING AND BOTANY, 4 vols. royal 4to, numerous Woodcuts (pub. at 11l. 8s.), cloth, 1l. 11s. 6d. 1831—1838

DON'S HORTUS CANTABRIGIENSIS; thirteenth Edition, 8vo (pub. at 1l. 4s.), cloth, 12s. 1845

DIXON'S GEOLOGY AND FOSSILS OF SUSSEX, edited by PROFESSOR OWEN; with 40 Plates, containing upwards of 1000 Figures, several coloured; royal 4to., (pub. at 3l. 3s.), cloth, 1l. 11s. 6d.

DONOVAN'S NATURAL HISTORY OF THE INSECTS OF CHINA. Enlarged by J. O. WESTWOOD, Esq., F.L.S., 4to, with 50 plates, containing upwards of 130 exquisitely coloured figures (pub. at 6l. 6s.), cloth gilt, 2l. 5s.

"Donovan's works on the Insects of India and China are splendidly illustrated, and extremely useful."—*Naturalist.*

"The entomological plates of our countryman Donovan are highly coloured, elegant, and useful, especially those contained in his quarto volumes (Insects of India and China), where a great number of species are delineated for the first time."—*Swainson.*

DONOVAN'S WORKS ON BRITISH NATURAL HISTORY. Viz; Insects, 16 vols.—Birds, 10 vols.—Shells, 5 vols.—Fishes, 5 vols.—Quadrupeda, 3 vols.—together 39 vols. 8vo, containing 1108 beautifully coloured plates (pub. at 66l. 9s.), boards, 22l. 17s. The same set of 39 vols. bound in 21 (pub. at 73l. 10s.), half green morocco extra, gilt edges, gilt backs, 30l. Any of the classes may be had separately.

DOYLE'S CYCLOPEDIA OF PRACTICAL HUSBANDRY, and Rural Affairs in General, New Edition, Enlarged, thick 8vo, with 70 wood engravings (pub. at 13s.), cloth, 8s. 6d. 1843

EPISODES OF INSECT LIFE, 3 vols. Crown 8vo, with 106 illustrations, tastefully drawn and engraved, elegantly bound in fancy cloth (pub. at 2l. 8s.), 1l. 7s.

——— the same, the plates beautifully coloured, bound in extra cloth, gilt back, sides, and edges (pub. at 3l. 3s.), 1l. 16s.

——— the second series, containing 36 illustrations, distinct and complete in itself, has lately been reprinted, and may now be had separately (pub. at 16s.), 9s.

——— or the second series, with coloured plates (pub. at 1l. 1s.), 16s.

DRURY'S ILLUSTRATIONS OF FOREIGN ENTOMOLOGY; wherein are exhibited upwards of 600 exotic Insects, of the East and West Indies, China, New Holland, North and South America, Germany, &c. By J. O. WESTWOOD, Esq., F.L.S. Secretary of the Entomological Society, &c. 3 vols. 4to, 150 Plates, most beautifully coloured, containing above 600 figures of Insects (originally pub. at 15l. 15s.), half-bound morocco, 6l. 16s. 6d. 1837

GOULD'S HUMMING BIRDS. A General History of the Trochilidæ, or Humming Birds, with especial reference to the Collection of J. GOULD, F.R.S., &c. (now exhibiting in the gardens of the Zoological Society of London), by W. C. L. MARTIN, late one of the Scientific Officers of the Zoological Society of London, fcap. 8vo, with 16 coloured Plates, cloth gilt, 5s.

——— the same, with the Plates BEAUTIFULLY COLOURED, heightened with gold, cloth gilt, 10s. 6d.

GREVILLE'S CRYPTOGAMIC FLORA, comprising the Principal Species found in Great Britain, inclusive of all the New Species recently discovered in Scotland. 6 vols. royal 8vo, 360 beautifully coloured Plates (pub. at 16l. 16s.), half-morocco, 8l. 8s. 1823—8

This, though a complete Work in itself, forms an almost indispensable Supplement to the thirty-six volumes of Sowerby's English Botany, which does not comprehend Cryptogamous Plants. It is one of the most scientific and best executed works on Indigenous Botany ever produced in this country.

HARDWICKE AND GRAY'S INDIAN ZOOLOGY. Twenty parts, forming two vols, royal folio, 202 coloured plates (pub. at 21*l*.), sewed, 12*l*. 12*s*., or half-morocco, gilt edges, 14*l*. 14*s*.

HARRIS'S AURELIAN; OR ENGLISH MOTHS AND BUTTERFLIES. Their Natural History, together with the Plants on which they feed; New and greatly improved Edition, by J. O. WESTWOOD, Esq., F.L.S., &c., in 1 vol. sm. folio, with 44 plates, containing above 100 figures of Moths, Butterflies, Caterpillars, &c., and the Plants on which they feed, exquisitely coloured after the original drawings, half-bound morocco, 4*l*. 4*s*. 1840

This is the extremely beautiful work is the only one which contains our English Moths and Butterflies of the full natural size, in all their changes of Caterpillar, Chrysalis, &c., with the plants on which they feed.

HOOKER AND GREVILLE, ICONES FILICUM; OR FIGURES OF FERNS. With DESCRIPTIONS, many of which have been altogether unnoticed by Botanists, or have not been correctly figured. 2 vols. folio, with 240 beautifully coloured Plates (pub. at 25*l*. 4*s*.), half-morocco, gilt edges, 12*l*. 12*s*. 1829—31

The grandest and most valuable of the many scientific Works produced by Sir William Hooker.

HOOKER'S EXOTIC FLORA, containing Figures and Descriptions of rare or otherwise interesting Exotic Plants, especially of such as are deserving of being cultivated in our Gardens. 3 vols. imperial 8vo, containing 232 large and beautifully coloured Plates (pub. at 15*l*.), cloth, 6*l*. 6*s*. 1823—1827

This is the most superb and attractive of all Dr. Hooker's valuable works.

"The 'Exotic Flora,' by Dr. Hooker, is like that of all the Botanical publications of the indefatigable author, excellent; and it assumes an appearance of finish and perfection to which neither the Botanical Magazine nor Register can externally lay claim."—*Loudon.*

HOOKER'S JOURNAL OF BOTANY, containing Figures and Descriptions of such Plants as recommend themselves by their novelty, rarity, or history, or by the uses to which they are applied in the Arts, in Medicine, and in Domestic Economy; together with occasional Botanical Notices and Information, and occasional Portraits and Memoirs of eminent Botanists. 4 vols. 8vo, numerous Plates, some coloured (pub. at 3*l*.), cloth, 1*l*. 1834—42

HOOKER'S BOTANICAL MISCELLANY, containing Figures and Descriptions of Plants which recommend themselves by their novelty, rarity, or history, or by the uses to which they are applied in the Arts, in Medicine, and in Domestic Economy, together with occasional Botanical Notices and Information, including many valuable Communications from distinguished Scientific Travellers. Complete in 3 thick vols. royal 8vo, with 153 plates, many finely coloured (pub. at 5*l*. 5*s*.), gilt cloth, 2*l*. 12*s*. 6*d*. 1830—33

HOOKER'S FLORA BOREALI-AMERICANA; OR THE BOTANY OF BRITISH NORTH AMERICA. Illustrated by 240 plates, complete in Twelve Parts, royal 4to (pub. at 12*l*. 12*s*.), 8*l*. The Twelve Parts complete, done up in 2 vols. royal 4to, extra cloth, 9*l*. 1829—40

HUISH ON BEES; THEIR NATURAL HISTORY AND GENERAL MANAGEMENT. New and greatly improved Edition, containing also the latest Discoveries and Improvements in every department of the Apiary, with a description of the most approved HIVES now in use, thick 12mo, Portrait and numerous Woodcuts (pub. at 10*s*. 6*d*.), cloth gilt, 6*s*. 6*d*. 1844

JARDINE'S NATURALIST'S LIBRARY, 40 vols, 1200 coloured Plates, extra red cloth, boards (pub. at 12*l*.), 7*l*.

——— or the volumes separately, according to the following arrangements, in red cloth, top edges gilt, 4*s*. 6*d*.

		Vol.			Vol.
1.	BIRDS.	1. British Birds, vol. 1	22.	ANIMALS.	8. Ruminating Animals, vol. 2 (Goats, Sheep, Oxen)
2.	,,	2. Ditto vol. 2			
3.	,,	3. Ditto vol. 3	23.	,,	9. Elephants, &c.
4.	,,	4. Ditto vol. 4	24.	,,	10. Marsupialia
5.	,,	5. Sun Birds	25.	,,	11. Seals, &c.
6.	,,	6. Humming Birds, vol. 1	26.	,,	12. Whales, &c.
7.	,,	7. Ditto vol. 2	27.	,,	13. Monkeys
8.	,,	8. Game Birds	28.	INSECTS.	1. Introduction to Entomology
9.	,,	9. Pigeons			
10.	,,	10. Parrots	29.	,,	2. British Butterflies
11.	,,	11. Birds of Western Africa vol. 1	30.	,,	3. British Moths, &c.
			31.	,,	4. Foreign Butterflies
12.	,,	12. Ditto vol. 2	32.	,,	5. Foreign Moths
13.	,,	13. Fly catchers	33.	,,	6. Beetles
14.	,,	14. Pheasants, Peacocks, &c.	34.	,,	7. Bees
15.	ANIMALS.	1. Introduction	35.	FISHES.	1. Introduction, and Foreign Fishes
16.	,,	2. Lions, Tigers			
17.	,,	3. British Quadrupeds	36.	,,	2. British Fishes, vol. 1
18.	,,	4. Dogs, vol. 1	37.	,,	3. Ditto vol. 2
19.	,,	5. Ditto, vol. 2	38.	,,	4. Perch, &c.
20.	,,	6. Horses	39.	,,	5. Fishes of Guiana, &c. vol. 1
21.	,,	7. Ruminating Animals, vol. 1 (Deer, Antelopes, &c.)	40.	,,	6. Ditto vol. 2

JOHNSON'S GARDENER, with numerous woodcuts, containing the Potato, one vol.—Cucumber and Gooseberry, 1 vol.—Grape Vine, 2 vols.—Auricula and Asparagus, one vol.—Pine Apple, two vols.—Strawberry, one vol.—Dahlia, one vol.—Peach, one vol.—together 10 vols., 12mo. Woodcuts (pub. at 1*l*. 5*s*.), cloth, 10*s*.
——— the same, bound in 3 vols. cloth, lettered, 9*s*.

JOHNSON'S FARMER'S ENCYCLOPÆDIA and Dictionary of Rural Affairs; embracing all the most recent discoveries in Agricultural Chemistry, adapted to the comprehension of unscientific readers, (by Cuthbert Johnson, Editor of the *Farmer's Almanac*) Illustrated by wood engravings, thick 8vo. cloth, NEW EDITION, (pub. at 2*l*. 10*s*.), 1*l*. 1*s*.

LEWIN'S NATURAL HISTORY OF THE BIRDS OF NEW SOUTH WALES.
Third Edition, with an Index of the Scientific Names and Synonymes, by Mr. GOULD and Mr. EYTON, folio, 27 plates, coloured (pub. at 4*l*. 4*s*.), half-bound morocco, 2*l*. 2*s*. 1838

LINDLEY'S BRITISH FRUITS; OR FIGURES AND DESCRIPTIONS OF THE MOST IMPORTANT VARIETIES OF FRUIT CULTIVATED IN GREAT BRITAIN. 3 vols. royal 8vo, containing 152 most beautifully coloured plates, chiefly by Mrs. WITHERS, Artist to the Horticultural Society (pub. at 10*l*. 10*s*.), half bound morocco extra, gilt edges, 5*l*. 5*s*. 1842

"This is an exquisitely beautiful work. Every plate is like a highly finished drawing, similar to those in the Horticultural Transactions."

LINDLEY'S DIGITALIUM MONOGRAPHIA. Folio, 28 plates of the Foxglove (pub. at 4*l*. 4*s*.), cloth, 1*l*. 11*s*. 6*d*.
——— the same, the plates beautifully coloured (pub. at 6*l*. 6*s*.), cloth, 2*l*. 12*s*. 6*d*.

LINDLEY'S LADIES' BOTANY; or, Familiar Introduction to the Natural System of Botany. Fifth edition, 2 vols. 8vo. with 100 coloured Plates, illustrating the Flower, Fruit, and Anatomy of every Tribe of Plants, (pub. at 2*l*. 10*s*.), cloth gilt, 1*l*. 5*s*.

LOUDON'S (MRS) ENTERTAINING NATURALIST, being Popular Descriptions, Tales, and Anecdotes of more than Five Hundred Animals, comprehending all the Quadrupeds, Birds, Fishes, Reptiles, Insects, &c., of which a knowledge is indispensable in polite education. With Indexes of Scientific and Popular Names, an Explanation of Terms, and an Appendix of Fabulous Animals. Illustrated by upwards of 500 beautiful woodcuts by BEWICK, HARVEY, WHIMPER, and others. New Edition, revised, enlarged, and corrected to the present state of Zoological Knowledge. In one thick vol. post 8vo, gilt cloth, 9*s*. 1850

LOUDON'S (J. C.) ARBORETUM ET FRUTICETUM BRITANNICUM, or the Trees and Shrubs of Britain, Native and Foreign, delineated and described; with their propagation, culture, management, and uses. Second improved Edition, 8 vols. 8vo, with above 400 plates of trees, and upwards of 2500 woodcuts of trees and shrubs (pub. at 10*l*.), 5*l*. 5*s*. 1844

LOUDON'S VILLA GARDENER, comprising the choice of a Suburban Villa Residence; the laying-out, planting, and culture of the garden and grounds; and every necessary information for the Amateur in collecting, placing, and rearing all the plants and trees usually cultivated in Great Britain; the management of the Villa Farm, Dairy, and Poultry Yard. Second edition, edited by Mrs. Loudon, 8vo, cloth extra, with upwards of 377 diagrams, &c. finely engraved on wood (pub. at 12*s*.), 8*s*. 6*d*.

LOW'S DOMESTIC ANIMALS OF GREAT BRITAIN, exemplified in fifty-six large and very beautifully coloured plates of the various breeds of the Horse, Ox, Sheep, and Hog, from drawings by Nicholson, R.S.A., after paintings by SHIELS, R.S.A., 2 vols. in 1, imp. 4to, half bound morocco, gilt edges (pub. at 16*l*. 16*s*.), 8*l*. 8*s*.

MANTELL'S (DR.) NEW GEOLOGICAL WORK. THE MEDALS OF CREATION or First Lessons in Geology, and in the Study of Organic Remains; including Geological Excursions to the Isle of Sheppey, Brighton, Lewes, Tilgate Forest, Charnwood Forest, Farringdon, Swindon, Caine, Bath, Bristol, Clifton, Matlock, Crich Hill, &c. By GIDEON ALGERNON MANTELL, Esq., LL.D., F.R.S., &c. Two thick vols, foolscap 8vo., with coloured Plates, and several hundred beautiful Woodcuts of Fossil Remains, cloth gilt, 1*l*. 1*s*. 1846

MANTELL'S (DR.) PICTORIAL ATLAS OF FOSSIL REMAINS, consisting of Coloured Illustrations selected from Parkinson's "Organic Remains of a Former World," and Artis's "Antediluvian Phytology," with descriptions, by Dr. Mantell, 4to, with 74 coloured plates, 2*l*. 5*s*. 1850

SCHLEIDEN'S PRINCIPLES OF SCIENTIFIC BOTANY; or Botany as an Inductive Science, translated by DR. EDWIN LANKESTER, 8vo, with nearly 400 Illustrations on wood and steel, cloth (pub. at 1l. 1s.), 10s. 6d. 1849

SELBY'S COMPLETE BRITISH ORNITHOLOGY. A most magnificent work of the Figures of British Birds, containing exact and faithful representations in their full natural size of all the known species found in Great Britain, 383 Figures in 228 beautifully coloured Plates. 2 vols. elephant folio, elegantly half-bound morocco (pub. at 105l.), gilt back and gilt edges, 31l. 10s. 1834

"The grandest work on Ornithology published in this country, the same for British Birds that Audubon's is for the Birds of America. Every figure, excepting in a very few instances of extremely large birds, is of the full natural size, beautifully and accurately drawn, with all the spirit of life."—*Ornithologist's Text Book.*

"What a treasure, during a rainy forenoon in the country, is such a gloriously illuminated work as this of Mr Selby! It is, without doubt, the most splendid of the kind ever published in Britain, and will stand a comparison, without any eclipse of its lustre, with the most magnificent ornithological illustrations of the French school. Mr. Selby has long and deservedly ranked high as a scientific naturalist."—*Blackwood's Magazine.*

SELBY'S ILLUSTRATIONS OF BRITISH ORNITHOLOGY. 2 vols. 8vo. Second Edition (pub. at 1l. 1s.), 12s. 1833

SIBTHORPE'S FLORA GRÆCA. The most costly and magnificent Botanical work ever published. 10 vols, folio, with 1000 beautifully coloured Plates, half-bound, morocco, publishing by subscription, and the number strictly limited to those subscribed for (pub. at 252l.), 63l.

Separate Prospectuses of this work are now ready for delivery. Only 40 copies of the original stock exist. No greater number of subscribers' names can therefore be received.

SIBTHORPE'S FLORÆ GRÆCÆ PRODROMUS; sive Plantarum omnium Enumeratio, quas in Provinciis aut Insulis Graeciae invenit JOH. SIBTHORPE: Characteres et Synonyma omnium cum Annotationibus JAC. EDV. SMITH. Four parts, in 2 thick vols. 8vo, (pub. at 2l. 2s.) 14s. *Londini, 1816*

SMITH'S (COLONEL HAMILTON) HISTORY OF THE HUMAN SPECIES, its Typical Forms, Primeval Distribution, Filiations and Migrations, with 34 coloured Plates (each containing two or more subjects), Portrait, and Vignette title-page, thick fcap. 8vo, full gilt cloth (pub. at 7s. 6d.), 5s.

This volume ranges with JARDINE'S NATURALIST'S LIBRARY.

SOWERBY'S MANUAL OF CONCHOLOGY. Containing a complete Introduction to the Science, illustrated by upwards of 650 Figures of Shells, etched on copper-plates, in which the most characteristic examples are given of all the Genera established up to the present time, arranged in Lamarckian Order, accompanied by copious Explanations; Observations respecting the Geographical or Geological distribution of each; Tabular Views of the Systems of Lamarck and De Blainville; a Glossary of Technical Terms, &c. New Edition, considerably enlarged and improved, with numerous Woodcuts in the text, now first added, 8vo, cloth, 18s.; or with the Plates coloured, cloth, 1l. 16s.

SOWERBY'S CONCHOLOGICAL ILLUSTRATIONS; OR, COLOURED FIGURES OF ALL THE HITHERTO UNFIGURED SHELLS, complete in 200 Parts, 8vo, comprising several thousand Figures, all beautifully coloured (pub. at 15l.), 7l. 10s. 1815

SPRY'S BRITISH COLEOPTERA DELINEATED; containing Figures and Descriptions of all the Genera of British Beetles, edited by SHUCKARD, 8vo, with 94 plates, comprising 686 figures of Beetles, beautifully and most accurately drawn (pub. at 2l. 2s.), cloth, 1l. 1s. 1840

"The most perfect work yet published in this department of British Entomology."

STEPHENS' BRITISH ENTOMOLOGY. 12 vols. 8vo, 100 coloured Plates (pub. at 31l.), half bound, 8l. 8s. 1828-46

—— Or separately, LEPIDOPTERA, 4 vols. 4l. 4s. COLEOPTERA, 5 vols. 4l. 4s. DERMAPTERA, ORTHOPTERA, NEUROPTERA, &c., 1 vol. 1l. 2s. HYMENOPTERA, 2 vols. 2l. 2s.

SWAINSON'S EXOTIC CONCHOLOGY; OR, FIGURES AND DESCRIPTIONS OF RARE, BEAUTIFUL, OR UNDESCRIBED SHELLS. Royal 4to, containing 94 large and beautifully coloured figures of Shells, half bound mor., gilt edges (pub. at 3l. 5s.), 2l. 12s. 6d

SWAINSON'S ZOOLOGICAL ILLUSTRATIONS; OR, ORIGINAL FIGURES AND DESCRIPTIONS OF NEW, RARE, OR INTERESTING ANIMALS, selected chiefly from the Classes of Ornithology, Entomology, and Conchology, 6 vols. royal 8vo, containing 318 finely coloured Plates (pub. at 16l. 16s.), half bound morocco, gilt edges, 9l. 9s.

SWEET'S FLORA AUSTRALASICA: OR, A SELECTION OF HANDSOME OR CURIOUS PLANTS, Natives of New Holland and the South Sea Islands. 10 Nos., forming 1 vol. royal 8vo, complete, with 56 beautifully coloured Plates (pub. at 3l. 15s.), cloth, 1l. 16s. 1827-28

SWEET'S CISTINEÆ: OR, NATURAL ORDER OF CISTUS, OR ROCK ROSE. 30 Nos., forming 1 vol.royal 8vo, complete, with 112 beautifully coloured Plates (pub. at 6l. 8s.), cloth, 2l. 12s. 6d. 1825

"One of the most interesting, and hitherto the scarcest, of Mr. Sweet's beautiful publications."

Miscellaneous English Literature,

INCLUDING

HISTORY, BIOGRAPHY, VOYAGES AND TRAVELS, POETRY AND THE DRAMA, MORALS, AND MISCELLANIES.

BARBAULD'S (MRS.) SELECTIONS from the SPECTATOR, TATLER, GUARDIAN, and FREEHOLDER, with a Preliminary Essay, new edition, complete in 2 vols, post 8vo. elegantly printed, with Portraits of Addison and Steele, cloth, (uniform with the *Standard Library*, (pub. at 10s.) 7s. *Moxon*, 1849

BLAKEY'S HISTORY OF THE PHILOSOPHY OF THE MIND; embracing the Opinions of all Writers on Mental Science from the earliest period to the present time, 4 vols. thick 8vo, very handsomely printed, cloth lettered, (pub. at 3l.), 1l. *Longmans*, 1850

BOSWELL'S LIFE OF DR. JOHNSON; BY THE RIGHT HON. J. C. CROKER. Incorporating his Tour to the Hebrides, and accompanied by the Commentaries of all preceding Editors, with numerous Additional Notes and Illustrative Anecdotes; to which are added Two Supplementary Volumes of Anecdotes by HAWKINS, PIOZZI, MURPHY, TYERS, REYNOLDS, STEVENS, and others. 10 vols. 12mo, illustrated by upwards of 50 Views, Portraits, and Sheets of Autographs, finely engraved on Steel, from Drawings by STANFIELD, HARDING, &c., cloth, reduced to 1l. 10s.

This new, improved, and greatly enlarged edition, beautifully printed in the popular form of Sir Walter Scott and Byron's Works, is just such an edition as Dr. Johnson himself loved and recommended. In one of the Ana recorded in the supplementary volumes of the present edition, he says: " Books that you may carry to the fire, and hold readily in your hand, are the most useful after all. Such books form the mass of general and easy reading."

BRITISH ESSAYISTS, viz., Spectator, Tatler, Guardian, Rambler, Adventurer, Idler, and Connoisseur. 3 thick vols. 8vo, Portraits (pub. at 2l. 5s.), cloth, 1l. 7s. Either volume may be had separate.

BRITISH POETS, CABINET EDITION, containing the complete Works of the principal English Poets from MILTON to KIRKE WHITE. 4 vols. post 8vo. (size of Standard Library), printed in a very small but beautiful type. 22 Medallion Portraits (pub. at 2l. 2s.), cloth, 15s.

BROUGHAM'S (LORD) POLITICAL PHILOSOPHY, and Essay on the British Constitution, 3 vols. 8vo. (pub. at 1l. 11s. 6d.), cloth, 1l. 1s. 1844-46
—— British Constitution (a portion of the preceding work), 8vo, cloth, 3s.

BURKE'S (EDMUND) WORKS With a Biographical and Critical Introduction by ROGERS. 2 vols. imperial 8vo, closely but handsomely printed (pub. at 2l. 2s.), cloth, 1l. 10s.

BURKE'S ENCYCLOPÆDIA OF HERALDRY; OR, GENERAL ARMOURY OF ENGLAND, SCOTLAND, AND IRELAND. Comprising a Registry of all Armorial Bearings, Crests, and Mottoes, from the Earliest Period to the Present Time, including the late Grants by the College of Arms. With an Introduction to Heraldry, and a Dictionary of Terms. Third Edition, with a Supplement. One very large vol. imperial 8vo, beautifully printed in small type, in double columns, by WHITTINGHAM, embellished with an elaborate Frontispiece, richly illuminated in gold and colours; also Woodcuts (pub. at 2l. 2s.), cloth gilt, 1l. 1s. 1844

The most elaborate and useful Work of the kind ever published. It contains upwards of 30,000 Armorial Bearings, and incorporates all that have hitherto been given by Guillim, Edmondson, Collins, Nisbet, Berry, Robson, and others; besides many thousand names which have never appeared in any previous Work. This volume, in fact, in a small compass, but without abridgment, contains more than four ordinary quartos.

BURNETT'S HISTORY OF HIS OWN TIMES, AND OF THE REFORMATION, with Historical and Biographical Notices. 3 vols. super royal 8vo. cloth, 1l. 11s. 6d.

BURNS' WORKS, WITH LIFE BY ALLAN CUNNINGHAM, AND NOTES BY SIR WALTER SCOTT, CAMPBELL, WORDSWORTH, LOCKHART, &c. Royal 8vo, fine Portrait and Plates (pub. at 18s.), cloth, uniform with Byron, 10s. 6d.

This is positively the only complete edition of Burns, in a single volume, 8vo. It contains not only every scrap which Burns ever wrote, whether prose or verse, but also a considerable number of Scotch national airs, collected and illustrated by him (not given elsewhere) and full and interesting accounts of the occasions and circumstances of his various writings. The very complete and interesting Life by Allan Cunningham alone occupies 164 pages, and the Indices and Glossary are very copious. The whole forms a thick elegantly printed volume, extending in all to 818 pages. The other editions, including one published in similar shape, with an abridgment of the Life by Allan Cunningham, comprised in only 47 pages, and the whole volume in only 504 pages, do not contain above two-thirds of the above.

CARY'S EARLY FRENCH POETS. A Series of Notices and Translations, with an Introductory Sketch of the History of French Poetry; Edited by his Son, the Rev. HENRY CARY, Foolscap 8vo, cloth, 5s. 1846

CARY'S LIVES OF ENGLISH POETS, supplementary to Dr. Johnson's "Lives." Edited by his Son. Foolscap 8vo, cloth, 7s. 1846

CHURTON'S RAILROAD BOOK OF ENGLAND; Historical, Topographical, and Picturesque; descriptive of all the Cities, Towns, Country Seats, and Subjects of local interest on the various Lines, imperial 8vo, cloth, with map and numerous cuts, (pub. at 1l. 1s.), reduced to 10s. 6d. 1851

CLASSIC TALES. Cabinet Edition, comprising the Vicar of Wakefield, Elizabeth, Paul and Virginia, Gulliver's Travels, Sterne's Sentimental Journey, Sorrows of Werter, Theodosius and Constantia, Castle of Otranto, and Rasselas, complete in 1 volume, 12mo; medallion Portraits (pub. at 10s. 6d.), cloth, 3s. 6d.

COPLEY'S (FORMERLY MRS. HEWLETT) HISTORY OF SLAVERY AND ITS ABOLITION. Second Edition, with an Appendix, thick small 8vo, fine Portrait of Clarkson (pub. at 6s.), cloth, 4s. 6d. 1839

COWPER'S POETICAL WORKS, including his Homer, edited by Cary. Illustrated edition, royal 8vo, with 18 beautiful Engravings on Steel, after Designs by Harvey, cloth, gilt edges, 15s.

CRAIK'S ROMANCE OF THE PEERAGE; or, CURIOSITIES OF FAMILY HISTORY. 4 vols. post 8vo, with fine Portraits on Steel of Walter Devereux Earl of Essex, Anne Duchess of Monmouth and Buccleuch, Mary Tudor, and Sir Robert Dudley, cloth (pub. at 2l. 2s.), 18s.

CRIMINAL TRIALS IN SCOTLAND, narrated by John Hill Burton. 2 vols. post 8vo, (pub. at 18s.), cloth, 9s. 1852

D'ARBLAY'S DIARY AND LETTERS; edited by her Niece, including the Period of her Residence at the Court of Queen Charlotte 7 vols, small 8vo. With Portraits, cloth extra, 14s.

DAVIS'S SKETCHES OF CHINA, During an Inland Journey of Four Months; with an Account of the War. 2 vols. post 8vo, with a new Map of China (pub. at 16s.), cloth 9s. 1841

DIBDIN'S (CHARLES) SONGS. Admiralty edition, complete, with a Memoir by T. Dibdin. Illustrated with 12 Characteristic Sketches, engraved on Steel by George Cruikshank. 12mo, cloth lettered, 5s. 1848

DOMESTIC COOKERY, by a Lady (Mrs. Rundell). New Edition, with numerous additional Receipts, by Mrs. Birch, 12mo, with 9 Plates (pub. at 6s.), cloth, 3s.

EGYPT AND NUBIA, illustrated from Burckhardt, Lindsay, and other leading Authorities, by J. A. St. John. 125 fine Wood Engravings. Demy 8vo, (pub. at 12s.), cloth, 5s.

EVELYN'S DIARY AND CORRESPONDENCE; with the Private Correspondence between Charles I. and Sir Edward Nicholas, Hyde Earl of Clarendon, Sir Richard Browne, &c. Portraits. New Edition, considerably enlarged, 4 vols, post 8vo. 1l.

FENN'S PASTON LETTERS, Original Letters of the Paston Family, written during the Reigns of Henry VI, Edward IV, and Richard III, by various persons of Rank and Consequence, chiefly on Historical Subjects. New Edition, with Notes and Corrections, complete. 2 vols. bound in 1, square 12mo (pub. at 10s.), cloth gilt, 5s. Quaintly bound in maroon morocco, carved boards. in the early style, gilt edges, 15s.

The original edition of this very curious and interesting series of historical Letters is a rare book, and sells for upwards of ten guineas. The present is not an abridgement, as might be supposed from its form, but gives the whole matter by omitting the duplicate version of the letters written in an obsolete language, and adopting only the more modern, readable version, published by Fenn.

'The Paston Letters are an important testimony to the progressive condition of society, and come in as a precious link in the chain of the moral history of England, which they alone in this period supply. They stand indeed singly in Europe.—*Hallam.*

FIELDING'S WORKS, EDITED BY ROSCOE, COMPLETE IN ONE VOLUME (Tom Jones, Amelia, Jonathan Wild, Joseph Andrews, Plays, Essays, and Miscellanies.) medium 8vo, with 20 capital plates by Cruikshank (pub. at 1l. 4s.), cloth gilt, 14s.

"Of all the works of imagination to which English genius has given origin, the writings of Henry Fielding are perhaps most decidedly and exclusively her own."—*Sir Walter Scott.*
"The prose Homer of human nature."—*Lord Byron.*

FOSTER'S ESSAYS ON DECISION OF CHARACTER; on a Man's Writing Memoirs of Himself; on the epithet Romantic; on the Aversion of Men of Taste to Evangelical Religion, &c. Fcap. 8vo, Eighteenth Edition (pub. at 6s.), cloth, 5s.

"I have read with the greatest admiration the Essays of Mr. Foster. He is one of the most profound and eloquent writers that England has produced."—*Sir James Mackintosh.*

FOSTER'S ESSAY ON THE EVILS OF POPULAR IGNORANCE. New Edition, elegantly printed, in fcap. 8vo, now first uniform with his Essays on Decision of Character, cloth, 5s.

"Mr. Foster always considered this his best work, and the one by which he wished his literary claims to be estimated."
"A work which, popular and admired, as it confessedly is, has never met with the thousandth part of the attention which it deserves."—*Dr. Pye Smith.*

FROISSART'S CHRONICLES OF ENGLAND, FRANCE, AND SPAIN, &c. Translated by COLONEL JOHNES, with 120 beautiful Woodcuts, 2 vols, super-royal 8vo, (pub. at 1l. 16s.), cloth lettered, 1l. 8s. 1848

FROISSART, ILLUMINATED ILLUSTRATIONS OF, 74 Plates, printed in gold and colours, 2 vols. super-royal 8vo, half bound, uncut (pub. at 4l. 10s.), 3l. 10s.
——— the same, large paper, 2 vols. royal 4to, half bound, uncut (pub. at 10l. 10s.), 6l. 6s.

FROISSART'S CHRONICLES, WITH THE 74 ILLUMINATED ILLUSTRATIONS, INSERTED, 2 vols. super-royal 8vo, elegantly half-bound red morocco, gilt edges, emblematically tooled (pub. at 6l. 6s.), 5l. 10s. 1849

GAZETTEER.—NEW EDINBURGH UNIVERSAL GAZETTEER, AND GEOGRAPHICAL DICTIONARY, more complete than any hitherto published. New Edition, revised and completed to the present time, by JOHN THOMSON (Editor of the *Universal Atlas*, &c.), very thick 8vo (1040 pages) Maps (pub. at 18s.), cloth, 12s.
This comprehensive volume is the latest, and by far the best Universal Gazetteer of its size. It includes a full account of Afghanistan, New Zealand, &c. &c.

GELL'S (SIR WILLIAM) TOPOGRAPHY OF ROME AND ITS VICINITY. An improved Edition, complete in one vol. 8vo, with several Plates, cloth, 12s. With a very large Map of Rome and its Environs (from a most careful trigonometrical survey), mounted on cloth and folded in a case so as to form a volume. Together 2 vols. 8vo, cloth, 1l. 1s. 1846
"These volumes are so replete with what is valuable, that were we to employ our entire journal, we could after all afford but a meagre indication of their interest and worth. It is, indeed, a lasting memorial of eminent literary exertion, devoted to a subject of great importance, and one dear, not only to every scholar, but to every reader of intelligence to whom the truth of history is an object of consideration."

GLEIG'S MEMOIRS OF WARREN HASTINGS, first Governor-General of Bengal. 3 vols. 8vo, fine Portrait (pub. at 2l. 5s.), cloth, 1l. 1s. 1841

GIL BLAS, translated from the French of LE SAGE. With 24 fine line Engravings after SMIRKE, 4 vols. in 2, fcap. 8vo. extra cloth, gilt edges, (pub. at 1l. 16s.), 10s. 1822

GOLDSMITH'S WORKS, with a Life and Notes, 4 vols. fcap. 8vo, with engraved Titles and Plates by STOTHARD and CRUIKSHANK. New and elegant Edition (pub. at 1l.), extra cloth, 12s.
"Can any author—can even Sir Walter Scott, be compared with Goldsmith for the variety, beauty, and power of his compositions! You may take 'him and 'cut him out in little stars,' so many lights does he present to the imagination."—*Athenæum*.
"The volumes of Goldsmith will ever constitute one of the most precious 'wells of English undefiled.'"—*Quarterly Review*.

GOOD'S (DR. JOHN MASON) BOOK OF NATURE; 3 vols., foolscap 8vo, cloth, (pub. at 1l. 4s.), 10s. 6d.

GORDON'S HISTORY OF THE GREEK REVOLUTION, and of the Wars and Campaigns arising from the Struggles of the Greek Patriots in emancipating their country from the Turkish yoke. By the late THOMAS GORDON, General of a Division of the Greek Army. Second Edition, 2 vols. 8vo, Maps and Plans (pub. at 1l. 16s.), cloth, 10s. 6d. 1842

GORTON'S BIOGRAPHICAL DICTIONARY. A new and enlarged Edition, with a Supplement, completing the Work to the present time, 4 vols. 8vo, cloth lettered, 1l. 11s. 6d.

HEEREN'S (PROFESSOR) HISTORICAL WORKS, translated from the German viz.—ASIA, New Edition, complete in 2 vols.—AFRICA, 1 vol.— EUROPE AND ITS COLONIES, 1 vol.—ANCIENT GREECE, and HISTORICAL TREATISES, 1 vol.—MANUAL OF ANCIENT HISTORY, 1 vol.—together 6 vols. 8vo (formerly pub. at 7l.), cloth lettered, uniform, 2l. 5s.
New and Complete Editions, with General Indexes.
"Professor Heeren's Historical Researches stand in the very highest rank among those with which modern Germany has enriched the Literature of Europe."—*Quarterly Review*.

HEEREN'S HISTORICAL RESEARCHES INTO THE POLITICS, INTERCOURSE, AND TRADES OF THE ANCIENT NATIONS OF AFRICA; including the Carthaginians, Ethiopians, and Egyptians. New edition, corrected throughout, with an Index, Life of the Author, new Appendixes, and other Additions. Complete in 1 vol. 8vo, cloth, 14s.

HEEREN'S HISTORICAL RESEARCHES INTO THE POLITICS, INTERCOURSE, AND TRADES OF THE ANCIENT NATIONS OF ASIA: including the Persians, Phœnicians, Babylonians, Scythians, and Indians. New and improved Edition, complete in 2 vols. 8vo, elegantly printed (pub. originally at 2l. 5s.), cloth, 1l. 4s.
"One of the most valuable acquisitions made to our historical stories since the days of Gibbon."—*Athenæum*.

HEEREN'S ANCIENT GREECE, translated by BANCROFT; and HISTORICAL TREATISES; viz.—I. The Political consequences of the Reformation. II. The Rise, Progress, and Practical Influence of Political Theories. III. The Rise and Growth of the Continental Interests of Great Britain. In 1 vol 8vo. with Index, cloth, 13s.

HEEREN'S MANUAL OF THE HISTORY OF THE POLITICAL SYSTEM OF EUROPE AND ITS COLONIES, from its formation at the close of the Fifteenth Century, to its re-establishment upon the Fall of Napoleon; translated from the Fifth German Edition, New Edition, complete in 1 vol. 8vo. cloth. 14s.

"The best History of Modern Europe that has yet appeared, and it is likely long to remain, without a rival."—*Athenæum.*
"A work of sterling value, which will diffuse useful knowledge for generations, after all the shallow pretenders to that distinction are fortunately forgotten."—*Literary Gazette.*

HEEREN'S MANUAL OF ANCIENT HISTORY, particularly with regard to the Constitutions, the Commerce, and the Colonies of the States of Antiquity. Third Edition, corrected and improved. 8vo (pub. at 18s.), cloth 12s. 1847
*** *New Edition, with Index.*

"We never remember to have seen a Work in which so much useful knowledge was condensed into so small a compass. A careful examination convinces us that this book will be useful for our English higher schools or colleges, and will contribute to direct attention to the better and more instructive parts of history. The translation is executed with great fidelity."
—*Quarterly Journal of Education.*

HEEREN'S MANUAL OF ANCIENT GEOGRAPHY, For the use of Schools and Private Tuition. Compiled from the Works of A. H. L. HEEREN, 12mo (pub. at 2s. 6d.), cloth, 2s. *Oxford, Talboys,* 1830

HOBBES' COMPLETE WORKS, English and Latin, edited by SIR W. MOLESWORTH. Portrait and plates. 16 vols, 8vo, (pub.at 8l. 8s.), cloth, 5l. 5s.
The Latin Works form 5 vols, the English Works 11 vols, each with a General Index. As fewer were printed of the Latin than of the English, the former are not sold separately, but the English 11 vols. may be had for 1l. 16s.

HUME AND SMOLLET'S HISTORY OF ENGLAND, complete in 1 large vol., with a Memoir of Hume, impl. 8vo, fine portraits of the authors, extra cloth (pub. at 1l. 5s.), 1l. 1s.

JAMES'S WILLIAM THE THIRD, comprising the History of his Reign, illustrated in a series of unpublished letters, addressed to the Duke of Shrewsbury, by JAMES VERNON, Secretary of State; with Introduction and Notes, by G. P. R. JAMES, Esq., 3 vols. 8vo, Portraits (pub. at 2l. 2s.), cloth, 18s. 1841

JAENISCH'S CHESS PRECEPTOR; a new Analysis of the openings of Games; translated, with Notes, by WALKER, 8vo, cloth, lettered (pub. at 15s.), 9s. 6d. 1847

JOHNSON'S (DR.) ENGLISH DICTIONARY, printed verbatim from the Author's last Folio Edition. With all the Examples in full. To which are prefixed a History of the Language, and an English Grammar. 1 large vol. imperial 8vo (pub. at 2l. 2s.), cloth, 18s.

JOHNSON'S (DR.) LIFE AND WORKS, by MURPHY. New and improved Edition, complete in 2 thick vols. 8vo, Portrait, cloth lettered (pub. at 1l. 11s. 6d.), 15s. 1830

JOHNSONIANA; a Collection of Miscellaneous Anecdotes and Sayings, gathered from nearly a hundred different Publications, and not contained in BOSWELL'S Life of Johnson. Edited by J. W. CROKER, M.P. thick fcap. 8vo, portrait and frontispiece (pub. at 10s.), cloth, 4s. 6d.

JOHNSTON'S TRAVELS IN SOUTHERN ABYSSINIA, through the Country of Adel, to the Kingdom of Shoa. 2 vols. 8vo, Map and Plates (pub. at 1l. 8s.) cloth, 10s. 6d. 1844

KNIGHT'S JOURNEY-BOOKS OF ENGLAND. BERKSHIRE, including a full Description of Windsor. With 22 Engravings on Wood, and a large illuminated Map. Reduced to 1s. 6d.

HAMPSHIRE, including the Isle of Wight. With 32 Engravings on Wood, and a large illuminated Map. Reduced to 2s.

DERBYSHIRE, including the Peak, &c. With 25 Engravings on Wood, and a large illuminated Map. Reduced to 1s. 6d.

KENT, with 54 Engravings on Wood, and a large illuminated Map. Reduced to 2s. 6d.

KNIGHT'S OLD ENGLAND'S WORTHIES: a PORTRAIT GALLERY of the most eminent Statesmen, Lawyers, Warriors, Artists, Men of Letters and Science, &c., of Great Britain, accompanied by full and original Biographies (written by LORD BROUGHAM, CRAIK, DE MORGAN, and others), imperial 4to, with 76 fine Portraits on steel, 12 large coloured Plates of remarkable buildings, and upwards of 250 historical and decorative Vignettes on wood, cloth gilt (pub. at 1l. 2s. 6d.), 15s.

KNOWLES'S IMPROVED WALKER'S PRONOUNCING DICTIONARY, containing above 50,000 additional Words; to which is added an Accentuated Vocabulary of Classical and Scripture Proper Names, new edition, in 1 thick handsome volume, large 8vo, with Portrait, cloth lettered (pub. at 1l. 4s.), 7s. 6d.

LACONICS; OR, THE BEST WORDS OF THE BEST AUTHORS. Seventh Edition. 3 vols. 18mo, with elegant Frontispieces, containing 30 Portraits (pub. at 15s.). cloth gilt. 7s. 6d.

This pleasant collection of pithy and sententious readings, from the best English authors of all ages, has long enjoyed great and deserved popularity.

LOW'S DOMESTICATED ANIMALS OF GREAT BRITAIN; comprehending the Natural and Economical History of Species and Varieties; with Observations on the principles and practice of Breeding. Thick 8vo, (pub. at 1l. 8s.), cloth, 5s.

LAING'S KINGS OF NORWAY; THE HEIMSKRINGLA, or CHRONICLE of the KINGS OF NORWAY, translated from the Icelandic of Snorro Sturleson, with a preliminary Dissertation and Notes by SAMUEL LAING, Esq.; 3 vols., 8vo.; cloth, (pub. at 1l. 16s.), 18s.

LAMB'S (CHARLES) WORKS, complete; containing his Letters, Essays of Elia, Poems, Plays, &c., with Life of the Author, including the additional Memorials, by SIR T. N. TALFOURD, in 1 stout volume royal 8vo, handsomely printed, with Portrait and Vignette Title, (pub. at 16s.), cloth, 12s.

LEAKES (COL.) TRAVELS IN THE MOREA. 3 vols. 8vo. With a very large Map of the Morea. and upwards of 30 various Maps, Plans, Plates of ancient Greek Inscriptions, &c. (pub. at 2l. 5s.), cloth, 1l. 8s. 1830

LEWIS'S (MONK) LIFE AND CORRESPONDENCE, with many Pieces in Prose and Verse, never before published. 2 vols. 8vo, Portrait (pub. at 1l. 8s.), cloth, 12s. 1839

LEIGH HUNT'S STORIES FROM THE ITALIAN POETS, (Dante, Ariosto, Boiardo, Tasso, Pulci), with Lives of the Writers. 2 vols, post 8vo, (pub. at 1l. 4s.), cloth, 10s.
*** This elegant work is for the Italian Poets what Lamb's Tales are for Shakespeare.

LODGE'S (EDMUND) ILLUSTRATIONS OF BRITISH HISTORY, BIOGRAPHY, AND MANNERS. In the Reigns of Henry VIII., Edward VI., Mary, Elizabeth, and James I. Second Edition, with above 80 Autographs of the principal Characters of the period. Three vols. 8vo. (pub. at 1l. 16s.), cloth, 1l. 1838

MACGREGOR'S COMMERCIAL STATISTICS OF ALL NATIONS. A Digest of the Resources, Legislation, Tariffs, Dues, Shipping, Imports, Exports, Weights and Measures, &c., &c. of All Nations, including all the British Commercial Treaties, 5 large vols, super-royal 8vo. cloth, (pub. at 7l. 10s.), 2l. 12s. 6d.

MALCOLM'S MEMOIR OF CENTRAL INDIA. Two vols. 8vo, third edition, with large Map (pub. at 1l. 8s.), cloth, 18s. 1839

MALTE-BRUN AND BALBI'S UNIVERSAL GEOGRAPHY; comprising, 1. The History of Geographical Discovery; 2. Principles of Physical Geography; 3. Complete Description, from the most recent sources, of all the Countries of the World. New and enlarged Edition, revised and corrected throughout, with an Alphabetical Index of 13,500 Names. Thick 8vo, cloth (pub. at 1l. 10s.), reduced to 15s. 1851

MARRYAT'S BORNEO AND THE INDIAN ARCHIPELAGO. Imperial 8vo, richly illustrated with numerous beautiful Lithographs, tinted like Drawings, and Engravings on wood (pub. at 1l. 11s. 6d.), cloth gilt, 12s. 1848

MARTIN'S (MONTGOMERY) BRITISH COLONIAL LIBRARY; forming a popular and Authentic Description of all the Colonies of the British Empire and embracing the History—Physical Geography—Geology—Climate—Animal, Vegetable, and Mineral Kingdoms—Government—Finance—Military Defence—Commerce—Shipping—Monetary System—Religion—Population, White and Coloured—Education and the Press—Emigration—Social State, &c., of each Settlement. Founded on Official and Public Documents, furnished by Government, the Hon. East India Company, &c. Illustrated by Original Maps and Plates. 8 volumes, fcap. 8vo. cloth, 1l. 1s.
Each volume of the above series is complete in itself, and sold separately, as follows, at 3s. 6d.:—

THE CANADAS, UPPER AND LOWER.
NEW SOUTH WALES, VAN DIEMEN'S LAND, SWAN RIVER, and SOUTH AUSTRALIA.
THE WEST INDIES. Vol. I.—Jamaica, Honduras, Trinidad, Tobago, Granada, the Bahamas, and the Virgin Isles.
THE WEST INDIES. Vol. II.—British Guiana, Barbadoes, St. Lucia, St. Vincent, Demerara, Essequibo, Berbice, Anguilla, Tortola, St. Kitt's, Barbuda, Antigua, Montserrat, Dominika, and Nevis.
NOVA SCOTIA, NEW BRUNSWICK, CAPE BRETON, PRINCE EDWARD'S ISLE, THE BARMUDAS, NEWFOUNDLAND, and HUDSON'S BAY.
THE EAST INDIES. Vol. I. containing Bengal, Madras, Bombay, Agra, &c.
THE EAST INDIES. Vol. II.
BRITISH POSSESSIONS IN THE INDIAN AND ATLANTIC OCEANS, viz.—Ceylon, Penang, Malacca, Singapore, Sierra Leone, the Gambia, Cape Coast Castle, Accra, the Falkland Islands, St. Helena, and Ascension.

MARTIN'S (MONTGOMERY) CHINA, Political, Commercial, and Social. Two vols. 8vo, 6 Maps, Statistical Tables, &c, (pub. at 1l. 4s.), cloth, 14s. 1847

MAXWELL'S LIFE OF THE DUKE OF WELLINGTON. Three handsome vols. 8vo. Embellished with numerous highly-finished Line-Engravings by COOPER and other eminent Artists, consisting of Battle-Pieces, Portraits, Military Plans and Maps; besides a great number of fine Wood Engravings; (pub. at 3l. 7s.), elegant in gilt cloth, 1l. 16s. Large paper, India proofs (pub. at 5l.), gilt cloth, 2l. 12s. 6d.

"Mr. Maxwell's 'Life of the Duke of Wellington, in our opinion, has no rival among similar publications of the day. . . . . We pronounce it free from flattery and bombast, succinct and masterly. . . . . The type and mechanical execution are admirable; the plans of battles and sieges numerous, ample, and useful; the portraits of the Duke and his warrior Contemporaries many and faithful; the battle pictures animated and brilliant; and the vignettes of costumes and manners worthy of the military genius of Horace Vernet himself."—*Times.*

MAXWELL'S HISTORY OF THE IRISH REBELLION OF 1798, with Memoirs of the Union, and of Emmett's Insurrection in 1803, cloth, 8vo. with Portraits and numerous Illustrations on steel by GEORGE CRUIKSHANK, new edition, gilt cloth, (pub. at 16s.), 9s.

PUBLISHED OR SOLD BY H. G. BOHN. 21

MINIATURE LIBRARY (BOHN'S.)
All foolscap 12mo., printed on the finest paper, *and very elegantly boarded in the new style of morocco cloth.*

BARBAULD AND AIKIN'S EVENINGS AT HOME; comprising a great variety of amusing Instruction for Young Persons, complete, elegantly printed, frontispieces, cloth gilt (pub. at 6s.), 3s.; or with gilt edges, 3s. 6d.

BOURRIENNE'S MEMOIRS OF NAPOLEON. One stout, closely but elegantly printed volume, fcap. 12mo. with fine equestrian portrait of Napoleon, and frontispiece, cloth gilt, (pub. at 5s.), 3s. 6d.; or with gilt edges, 4s.

BUNYAN'S PILGRIM'S PROGRESS. Quite complete, including the Third Part with a Life and numerous explanatory Notes by the REV. T. SCOTT. Elegantly printed on fine wove paper, and embellished with 25 fine full-sized Woodcuts by HARVEY, containing all in Southey's edition, also a fine frontispiece and vignette, cloth gilt, 3s. 6d.; or with gilt edges, 4s.

BYRON'S POETICAL WORKS, including several Suppressed Poems not published in other editions, in 1 thick vol., with a beautiful Frontispiece, cloth gilt, 3s. 6d.; or with gilt edges, 4s.

BYRON'S DON JUAN. complete, elegantly printed, frontispieces, cloth gilt, (pub. at :s.), 2s. 6d.; or with gilt edges, 3s.

CHEEVER'S LECTURES ON BUNYAN'S PILGRIM'S PROGRESS, and the Life and Times of Bunyan, frontispieces, cloth gilt, 2s. 6d.

COLERIDGE'S SELECT POETICAL WORKS, cloth gilt, 2s.; or gilt edges, 2s. 6d.

COWPER'S POETICAL WORKS, with a short Life by SOUTHEY, including (for the first time in a small size), all the COPYRIGHT POEMS, complete in one handsome volume, fcap. 24mo, (700 pages), very elegantly printed, with two extremely beautiful Frontispieces after HARVEY, engraved on Steel by GOODALL, cloth gilt, 3s. 6d.; or with gilt edges, 4s.

DRYDEN'S POETICAL WORKS, complete in 1 vol. with a Portrait, Frontispiece and Vignette Title, cloth gilt, 3s. 6d.; or with gilt edges, 4s.

ENCYCLOPÆDIA OF MANNERS AND ETIQUETTE; comprising an improved edition of Chesterfield's Advice to his Son on Men and Manners; and THE YOUNG MAN'S OWN BOOK; a Manual of Politeness, Intellectual Improvement, and Moral Deportment, calculated to form the Character on a solid Basis, and to insure Respectability and Success in Life, one elegantly printed volume, frontispiece, cloth gilt, 2s.; or with gilt edges, 2s. 6d.

HEBER'S (BISHOP) AND MRS. HEMAN'S POETICAL WORKS. Three vols. in one, cloth gilt, 2s. 6d.; or with gilt edges, 3s.

HERRICK'S POETICAL WORKS, complete in one thick volume, elegantly printed, fine frontispiece by CATTERMOLE, cloth gilt, 3s.; or with gilt edges, 3s. 6d.

JOE MILLER'S JEST BOOK; being a Collection of the most excellent Bon Mots, Brilliant Jests, and Striking Anecdotes in the English Language, complete in one thick and closely but elegantly printed volume, frontispiece, cloth gilt (pub. at 4s.), 3s.; or with gilt edges, 3s. 6d.

NEW JOE MILLER. A Selection of Modern Jests, Witticisms, Droll Tales, &c. cloth gilt, 2s. 6d.; or with gilt edges, 3s.

LONGFELLOW'S POETICAL WORKS, viz., Voices of the Night—Evangeline—Seaside and Fireside—Spanish Students—Poetical Translations, 2 vols. in 1, portrait and frontispieces, cloth gilt, 2s. 6d.; or with gilt edges, 3s.

LONGFELLOW'S PROSE WORKS, viz., Outre-Mer—Hyperion—Kavanagh, 3 vols. in 1, cloth gilt 2s. 6d.; or with gilt edges, 3s.

MILTON'S POETICAL WORKS, with Life and Notes by DR. STEBBING; to which is prefixed DR. CHANNING'S Essay on Milton. Frontispiece, cloth gilt, (pub. at 6s.), 3s. 6d.; or with gilt edges, 4s.

OSSIAN'S POEMS, translated by MACPHERSON; with Dissertations concerning the Era and Poems of OSSIAN; and DR. BLAIR'S Critical Dissertation.— Complete in 1 neatly printed volume, frontispiece, new Edition, cloth gilt (pub. at 4s.), 3s.; or with gilt edges, 3s. 6d.

POPE'S HOMER'S ILIAD, complete, with Explanatory Notes and Index, and an Essay on the Life, Writings, and Genius of Homer, elegantly printed, frontispieces, cloth gilt (pub. at 6s.), 3s.; or with gilt edges, 3s. 6d.
This is the only pocket edition with notes.

SCOTT'S (SIR WALTER) POETICAL WORKS; containing Lay of the Last Minstrel, Marmion, Lady of the Lake, Don Roderick, Rokeby, Ballads, Lyrics, and Songs, with Notes, and a Life of the Author, complete in 1 elegantly printed volume, portrait and frontispiece, cloth gilt (pub. at 5s.), 3s. 6d.; or with gilt edges, 4s.

STURM'S REFLECTIONS ON THE WORKS OF GOD, and of his Providence throughout all Nature, translated from the German, complete in 1 elegantly printed vol., frontispiece, cloth gilt (pub. at 5s), 3s. ; or with gilt edges, 3s. 6d.

THOMSON'S SEASONS, with his Castle of Indolence; 4 beautiful woodcuts, cloth gilt, 2s.; or with gilt edges, 2s 6d.

VATHEK AND THE AMBER WITCH. Two vols. in one, cloth gilt, 2s. 6d.; or with gilt edges, 3s.

MONSTRELET'S CHRONICLES OF ENGLAND AND FRANCE, by COLONEL JOHNES, with Notes, and upwards of 100 Woodcuts (uniform with Froissart), 2 vols. super-royal 8vo, cloth lettered (pub. at 1l. 16s.), 1l. 4s.

NELSON'S LETTERS AND DISPATCHES, by SIR HARRIS NICOLAS, 7 vols, 8vo. (pub. at 8l. 10s.), cloth, 2l. 10s. 1845—46

NUGENT'S MEMORIALS OF HAMPDEN, his Party and Times. Third Edition. With a Memoir of the Writer. Portraits. Post 8vo, (pub. at 12s.), 6s.

PEPY'S DIARY AND CORRESPONDENCE, edited by LORD BRAYBROOKE. New and improved Edition, with important Additions, including upwards of Two Hundred Letters. 4 vols, crown 8vo, cloth extra, 1l. 1854

PERCY'S RELIQUES OF ANCIENT ENGLISH POETRY, consisting of Old Heroic Ballads, Songs, and other Pieces of our Earlier Poets, together with some few of later date, and a copious Glossary, complete in 1 vol. medium 8vo. New and elegant Edition, with beautifully engraved Title and Frontispiece, by STEPHANOFF (pub. at 15s.), cloth gilt, 7s. 6d.

POPE'S POETICAL WORKS, complete in 1 thick volume, foolscap 8vo., frontispiece and vignette, cloth gilt, (pub. at 5s.), 3s. 6d, 1843

RAFFLES' HISTORY OF JAVA, with an Account of Bencoolen, and Details of the Commerce and Resources of the Indian Archipelago. Edited by LADY RAFFLES. Together 2 vols. 8vo, and a splendid quarto Atlas, containing upwards of 100 Plates by DANIELL, many finely coloured (pub. at 3l. 10s.), cloth, 1l. 7s.

ROBINSON CRUSOE. Cabinet Pictorial Edition, including his further Adventures, with Life of DEFOE, &c , upwards of 60 fine Woodcuts, from Designs by HARVEY, post 8vo. New and improved Edition, with additional cuts, cloth gilt, 4s. 6d.

The only small edition which is quite complete.

"Perhaps there exists no work, either of instruction or entertainment, in the English language, which has been more generally read or more deservedly admired, than the Life and Adventures of Robinson Crusoe."—*Sir Walter Scott.*

ROBIN HOOD; a Collection of all the Poems, Songs, and Ballads relating to this celebrated Yeoman; to which is prefixed, his History from inedited Documents, and a Memoir of RITSON, by J. M. GUTCH, F.S.A. Two vols. elegantly printed in crown 8vo, with Portrait of Ritson, and upwards of 120 tasteful wood engravings by FAIRHOLT, extra cloth (pub. at 1l. 10s.), reduced to 15s.

ROLLIN'S ANCIENT HISTORY. A New and complete Edition, with engraved Frontispieces and 7 Maps. 2 vols. bound in 1 stout handsome vol. royal 8vo, (pub. at 1l. 4s.), cloth, 12s.

The only complete edition in a compact form; it is uniform in size and appearance with Moxon's Series of Dramatists, &c. The previous editions of Rollin in a single volume are greatly abridged, and contain scarcely half the work.

ROSCOE'S LIFE AND PONTIFICATE OF LEO THE TENTH. New and much improved Edition, edited by his Son, THOMAS ROSCOE. Complete in 1 stout vol. 8vo, closely but very handsomely printed, illustrated by 3 fine Portraits, and numerous illustrative Engravings, as head and tail-pieces, cloth, 1l. 4s. 1845

ROSCOE'S LIFE OF LORENZO DE MEDICI, CALLED "THE MAGNIFICENT." New and much improved Edition, edited by his Son, THOMAS ROSCOE. Complete in 1 stout vol. 8vo, closely but very handsomely printed, illustrated by numerous Engravings, introduced as head and tail-pieces, cloth, 12s. 1845

"I have not terms sufficient to express my admiration of Mr. Roscoe's genius and erudition, or my gratitude for the amusement and information I have received. I recommend his labours to our country as works of unquestionable genius and uncommon merit. They add the name of Roscoe to the very first rank of English Classical Historians."—*Matthias, Pursuits of Literature.*

"Roscoe is, I think, by far the best of our Historians, both for beauty of style and for deep reflections; and his translations of poetry are equal to the originals."—*Walpole, Earl of Orford*

ROSCOE'S ILLUSTRATIONS, HISTORICAL AND CRITICAL, of the Life of Lorenzo de Medici, with an Appendix of Original Documents. 8vo, Portrait of Lorenzo, and Plates (pub. at 14s.), boards, 7s., or in 4to, printed to match the original edition. Portrait and Plates (pub. at 1l. 11s. 6d.), boards, 10s.

*** This volume is supplementary to all editions of the work.

ROXBURGHE BALLADS, edited by JOHN PAYNE COLLIER, post 4to, beautifully printed by WHITTINGHAM, and embellished with 50 curious Woodcuts, half bound morocco, in the Roxburghe style (pub. at 1l. 4s.), 12s. 1847

SHAKESPEARE'S PLAYS AND POEMS. VALPY'S Cabinet Pictorial Edition, with Life, Glossarial Notes, and Historical Digests of each Play, &c. 15 vols. foap. 8vo, with 171 Plates engraved on steel after Designs of the most distinguished British Artists; also Facsimiles of all the known Autographs of Shakespeare (pub. at 3l. 15s.), cloth, rich gilt, 2l. 5s. 1843

SHAKSPEARE'S PLAYS AND POEMS. 1 vol. 8vo, with Explanatory Notes, and a Memoir by DR. JOHNSON, Portrait (pub. at 15s.), cloth, 7s. 6d.

SHAKSPEARE'S PLAYS AND POEMS. Pocket Edition, with a Life by ALEXANDER CHALMERS, complete in 1 thick vol. 12mo. printed in a Diamond type, with 40 steel Engravings (pub. at 10s. 6d.), cloth, 5s. 1845

SHAKSPERE'S PLAYS AND POEMS, with Explanatory Notes, and a Sketch of his Life and Writings, edited by CHARLES KNIGHT. Illustrated by 40 large Designs on wood by W. HARVEY. Sixth Edition, thick 8vo. cloth, 10s. 6d.

SCHLOSSER'S HISTORY OF THE XVIIIth CENTURY, AND OF THE XIXth till the Overthrow of the French Empire; with particular reference to Mental Cultivation and Progress. Translated from the German by DAVISON, with copious Index. 8 thick vols, 8vo, (pub. at 4l. 16s.), cloth extra, 1l. 2s.

SHIPWRECKS AND DISASTERS AT SEA. Narratives of the most remarkable Wrecks, Conflagrations, Mutinies, &c. comprising the "Loss of the Wager," "Mutiny of the Bounty," &c. 12mo, Frontispiece and Vignette (pub. at 6s.), cloth, 3s.

SMOLLETT'S WORKS. Edited by ROSCOE. Complete in 1 vol. (Roderick Random, Humphrey Clinker, Peregrine Pickle, Launcelot Greaves, Count Fathom, Adventures of an Atom, Travels, Plays, &c.) Medium 8vo, with 21 capital Plates, by CRUIKSHANK (pub. at 1l. 4s.), cloth gilt, 14s.

"Perhaps no book ever written excited such peals of inextinguishable laughter as Smollett's."—*Sir Walter Scott.*

STERNE'S WORKS. Complete in 1 vol. 8vo, Portrait and Vignette (pub. at 18s.) cloth, 10s. 6d.

ST. PIERRE'S WORKS. including the "Studies of Nature," "Paul and Virginia," and the "Indian Cottage," with a Memoir of the Author, and Notes, by the REV. E. CLARKE complete in 2 thick vols. fcap. 8vo, Portrait and Frontispieces (pub. at 16s.), cloth, 7s. 1846

SWIFT'S WORKS. Edited by ROSCOE. Complete in 2 vols, medium 8vo, Portrait, (pub. at 1l. 12s.), cloth gilt, 1l. 4s.

"Whoever in the three kingdoms has any books at all has Swift."—*Lord Chesterfield.*

SYRIA AND THE HOLY LAND, their Scenery and their People; being Incidents of History and Travel, from BURCKHARDT, LINDSAY, ROBINSON and other leading Authorities, by W. K. KELLY. With 180 fine Wood Engravings. Demy 8vo, (pub. at 12s.), cloth, 5s.

TAAFE'S HISTORY OF THE KNIGHTS OF MALTA, &c., 4 vols. in 2, 8vo. cloth gilt, (pub. at 2l. 10s.), 10s. 6d. 1852

TAYLOR'S (W. B. S.) HISTORY OF THE UNIVERSITY OF DUBLIN. Numerous Wood Engravings of its Buildings and Academic Costumes (pub. at 1l.), cloth, 7s. 6d. 1845

THIERS' HISTORY OF THE FRENCH REVOLUTION, the 10 parts in 1 thick vol· royal 8vo, handsomely printed, cloth lettered (pub. at 1l. 5s.), 10s.

THIERS' HISTORY OF THE CONSULATE AND EMPIRE OF NAPOLEON, the 10 parts in 1 thick vol., royal 8vo, handsomely printed, cloth lettered (pub. at 1l. 5s.), 10s.

TUCKER'S LIGHT OF NATURE PURSUED. Complete in 2 vols. 8vo. (pub. at 1l. 10s.), cloth, 15s.

"The 'Light of Nature' is a work which, after much consideration, I think myself authorized to call the most original and profound that has ever appeared on moral philosophy.—*Sir James Mackintosh.*

TYTLER'S ELEMENTS OF GENERAL HISTORY. New Edition, thick 12mo, (526 closely printed pages), steel Frontispiece (pub. at 5s.), cloth, 3s. 6d.

WADE'S BRITISH HISTORY, CHRONOLOGICALLY ARRANGED. Comprehending a classified Analysis of Events and Occurrences in Church and State, and of the Constitutional, Political, Commercial, Intellectual, and Social Progress of the United Kingdom, from the first Invasion by the Romans to the Accession of Queen Victoria, with very copious Index and Supplement. New Edition. 1 large remarkably thick vol. royal 8vo, (1300 pages), cloth, 18s.

WALPOLE. MEMOIRS OF HORACE WALPOLE & HIS CONTEMPORARIES. By ELIOT WARBURTON, including Original Letters, chiefly from Strawberry Hill, 2 vols., 8vo., with Portraits of Walpole and Miss Berry, (pub. at 1l. 8s.), 9s.

WATERSTON'S CYCLOPÆDIA OF COMMERCE, MERCANTILE LAW, FINANCE, COMMERCIAL GEOGRAPHY AND NAVIGATION. *New Edition in the press.*

WELSFORD ON THE ORIGIN AND RAMIFICATIONS OF THE ENGLISH LANGUAGE, preceded by an Enquiry into the Primitive Seats, Early Migrations, and Final Settlements of the principal European Nations, 8vo. cloth lettered, (pub. at 14s.), 5s.

WELSFORD'S MITHRIDATES MINOR: or an Essay on Language; 8vo., cloth, lettered, (pub. at 10s. 6d.), 5s. 1848

WEBSTER'S AND WORCESTER'S NEW CRITICAL AND PRONOUNCING DICTIONARY OF THE ENGLISH LANGUAGE, Including Scientific Terms: to which are added WALKER'S Key to the Pronunciation of Classical and Scriptural Proper Names, much enlarged: and a Pronouncing Vocabulary of Modern Geographical Names. New Edition, enlarged and entirely revised by WORCESTER. In 1 thick vol. royal 8vo (pub. at 1l. 8s.), cloth, 12s. 1851

WHITE'S FARRIERY, improved by ROSSER, 8vo, with Plates engraved on steel (pub. at 14s.), cloth, 7s. 1847

WHYTE'S HISTORY OF THE BRITISH TURF, FROM THE EARLIEST PERIOD TO THE PRESENT DAY. 2 vols. 8vo, Plates (pub. at 1l. 8s.), cloth, 12s. 1840

WILLIS'S PENCILLINGS BY THE WAY. A new and beautiful Edition, with additions, fcap. 8vo, fine Portrait and Plates (pub. at 6s.), extra red Turkey cloth, richly gilt back, 3s. 6d.

WRIGHT'S COURT HAND RESTORED, or the Student assisted in reading old Charters, Deeds, &c. small 4to. 23 plates (pub. at 1l. 6s.), cloth, 15s. 846

Theology, Morals, Ecclesiastical History, &c.

BARRETT'S SYNOPSIS OF CRITICISMS upon those Passages of the OLD TESTAMENT in which Commentators have differed from the Authorized Version; together with an explanation of difficulties in the Hebrew and English Texts, 5 vols, royal 8vo, (pub. at 3l. 10s.), cloth, 1l. 1s.

BAXTER'S (RICHARD) WORKS, with Sketch of the Life, and Essay on the Genius of the Author, 4 vols. imperial 8vo, (pub. at 4l. 4s.), 2l. 12s. 6d.

BINGHAM'S ANTIQUITIES OF THE CHRISTIAN CHURCH. New and improved Edition, carefully revised, with an enlarged Index. 2 vols. impl. 8vo, cloth, 1l. 11s. 6d. 1850
"Bingham is a writer who does equal honour to the English clergy and to the English nation, and whose learning is only to be equalled by his moderation and impartiality."—*Quarterly Rev.*

CALMET'S DICTIONARY OF THE BIBLE, WITH THE BIBLICAL FRAGMENTS, by the late CHARLES TAYLOR. 5 vols. 4to. Illustrated by 202 Copper-plate Engravings. Eighth greatly enlarged Edition, beautifully printed on fine wove paper (pub. at 10l. 10s.), gilt cloth, 4l. 14s. 6d.
"Mr. Taylor's improved edition of Calmet's Dictionary is indispensably necessary to every Biblical Student. The additions made under the title of 'Fragments' are extracted from the most rare and authentic Voyages and Travels into Judea and other Oriental countries; and comprehend an assemblage of curious and illustrative descriptions, explanatory of Scripture incidents, customs, and manners, which could not possibly be explained by any other medium. The numerous engravings throw great light on Oriental customs."—*Horne.*

CALMET'S DICTIONARY OF THE HOLY BIBLE, abridged, 1 large vol. imp. 8vo, Woodcuts and Maps (pub. at 1l. 4s.), cloth, 15s.

CARY'S TESTIMONIES OF THE FATHERS OF THE FIRST FOUR CENTURIES TO THE CONSTITUTION AND DOCTRINES OF THE CHURCH OF ENGLAND, as set forth in the XXXIX Articles, 8vo, (pub. at 12s.), cloth, 7s. 6d. *Oxford, Talboys.*
"This work may be classed with those of Pearson and Bishop Bull; and such a classification is no mean honour."—*Church of England Quarterly.*

CHARNOCK'S DISCOURSES UPON THE EXISTENCE AND ATTRIBUTES OF GOD. Complete in 1 thick closely printed vol. 8vo, with Portrait (pub. at 14s.), cloth, 6s. 6d.
"Perspicuity and depth, metaphysical sublimity and evangelical simplicity, immense learning but irrefragable reasoning, conspire to render this performance one of the most inestimable productions that ever did honour to the sanctified judgment and genius of a human being."—*Toplady.*

CHRISTIAN EVIDENCES. Containing the following esteemed Treatises, with Prefatory Memoirs by the Rev. J. S. MEMES, LL.D., viz.:—Watson's Apology for Christianity; Watson's Apology for the Bible; Paley's Evidences of Christianity; Paley's Horæ Paulinæ; Jenyns' Internal Evidence of the Christian Religion; Leslie's Truth of Christianity Demonstrated; Leslie's Short and Easy Method with the Deists; Leslie's Short and Easy Method with the Jews; Chandler's Plain Reasons for being a Christian: Lyttleton on the Conversion of St. Paul; Campbell's Dissertation on Miracles; Sherlock's Trial of the Witnesses, with Sequel; West on the Resurrection. In 1 vol. royal 8vo (pub. at 14s.), cloth, 10s.

CHRISTIAN TREASURY. Consisting of the following Expositions and Treatises, Edited by MEMES, viz.:—Magee's Discourses and Dissertations on the Scriptural Doctrines of Atonement and Sacrifice; Witherspoon's Practical Treatise on Regeneration; Boston's Crook in the Lot; Guild's Moses Unveiled; Guild's Harmony of all the Prophets; Less's Authenticity, Uncorrupted Preservation, and Credibility of the New Testament; Stuart's Letters on the Divinity of Christ. In 1 vol. royal 8vo (pub. at 12s.), cloth, 8s.

CRUDEN'S CONCORDANCE TO THE OLD AND NEW TESTAMENT, revised and condensed by G. H. HANNAY, thick 18mo, beautifully printed (pub. at 6s.), cloth, 3s. 6d.
"An extremely pretty and very cheap edition. It contains all that is useful in the original work, omitting only prepositions, conjunctions, &c., which can never be made available for purposes of reference. Indeed it is all that the Scripture student can desire."—*Guardian.*

EVELYN'S RATIONAL ACCOUNT OF THE TRUE RELIGION, now first published from the original MS. in the Library at Wootton, edited, with Notes, by the Rev. R. M. EVANSON, B.A., 2 vols. post 8vo. (uniform with his Diary), cloth, (pub. at 1l. 1s.), 7s. 6d.

FOX'S BOOK OF MARTYRS; the Acts and Monuments of the Church, edited by DR. CUMMING, 3 vols. imp. 8vo' with upwards of 1000 wood illustrations, imperial 8vo, extra cloth (pub. at 3l. 13s. 6d.), 2l. 12s. 6d.

FULLER'S (REV. ANDREW) COMPLETE WORKS; with a Memoir of his Life, by his Son, 1 large vol. imperial 8vo, New Edition, Portrait (pub. at 1l. 10s.), cloth, 15s.

GRAVES'S (DEAN) LECTURES ON THE PENTATEUCH. 8vo, New Edition (pub. at 13s.), cloth, 9s. 1846

HALL'S (THE REV. ROBERT) COMPLETE WORKS, with a Memoir of his Life, by Dr. OLINTHUS GREGORY, and Observations on his Character as a Preacher, by JOHN FOSTER, Author of Essays on Popular Ignorance, &c.; 6 vols. 8vo, handsomely printed, with beautiful Portrait (pub. at 3l. 15s.), cloth, contents lettered, 1l. 11s. 6d.
The same, printed in a smaller size, 6 vols. fcap. 8vo, 1l. 1s., cloth lettered.
"Whoever wishes to see the English language in its perfection must read the writings of that great Divine, Robert Hall. He combines the beauties of JOHNSON, ADDISON, and BURKE, without their imperfections."—*Dugald Stewart.*
"I cannot do better than refer the academic reader to the immortal works of Robert Hall. For moral grandeur, for Christian truth, and for sublimity, we may doubt whether they have their match in the sacred oratory of any age or country."—*Professor Sedgwick.*
"The name of Robert Hall will be placed by posterity among the best writers of the age, as well as the most vigorous defenders of religious truth, and the brightest examples of Christian charity."—*Sir J. Mackintosh.*

HENRY'S (MATTHEW) COMMENTARY ON THE PSALMS. Complete in one thick closely printed volume, post 8vo. with 26 illustrations on wood, cloth, (*uniform with the Standard Library*), 4s. 6d. 1852

HILL'S (REV. ROWLAND) MEMOIRS, by his Friend, the Rev. W. JONES. Edited, with a Preface, by the Rev. JAMES SHERMAN (ROWLAND HILL'S Successor as Minister of Surrey Chapel). Second Edition, carefully revised, thick post 8vo, fine steel Portrait (pub. at 10s.), cloth, 5s.

HOPKINS'S (BISHOP) WHOLE WORKS, with a Memoir of the Author, and a very extensive general Index of Texts and Subjects, 2 vols, royal 8vo (pub. at 1l. 4s.), cloth, 15s.
"Bishop Hopkins's works form of themselves a sound body of divinity. He is clear, vehement, and persuasive."—*Bickersteth.*

HORNE ON THE PSALMS, a Commentary on the Book of Psalms, in which their literal sense and metaphorical application is pointed out. New and elegant edition, complete in one volume, 8vo, cloth (pub. at 2s.), 6s. 6d.

HUNTINGDON'S (COUNTESS OF) LIFE AND TIMES. By a Member of the Houses of Shirley and Hastings. Sixth Thousand, with a copious Index. 2 large vols. 8vo, Portraits of the Countess, Whitfield, and Wesley (pub. at 1l. 4s.), cloth, 14s.

LEIGHTON'S (ARCHBISHOP) WHOLE WORKS; to which is prefixed a Life of the Author, by the Rev. N. T. PEARSON. New Edition, 2 thick vols. 8vo, Portrait (pub. at 1l. 4s.) extra cloth, 16s. The only complete Edition.

LEIGHTON'S COMMENTARY ON PETER; with Life by PEARSON, complete in 1 thick handsomely printed vol. 8vo, Portrait (pub. at 12s.), cloth, 9s.

LIVES OF THE ENGLISH SAINTS. By the Rev. J. H. NEWMAN and others. 8 thick vols., 12mo, cloth, lettered, 10s. 6d.

M'CRIE'S LIFE OF JOHN KNOX, with illustrations of the History of the Reformation in Scotland. New Edition with numerous Additions, and a Memoir, &c. by ANDREW CRICHTON, Fcap. 8vo (pub. at 5s.), cloth, 3s. 6d. 1847

MAGEE'S (ARCHBISHOP) WORKS, comprising Discourses and Dissertations on the Scriptural Doctrines of Atonement and Sacrifice; Sermons, and Visitation Charges. With a Memoir of his Life, by the Rev. A. H. KENNY, D.D. 2 vols. 8vo (pub. at 1l. 6s.), cloth, 18s.
"Discovers such deep research, yields so much valuable information, and affords so many helps to the refutation of error, as to constitute the most valuable treasure of biblical learning of which a Christian scholar can be possessed."—*Christian Observer.*

MORE'S (HANNAH) LIFE, by the Rev. HENRY THOMPSON, post 8vo, printed uniformly with her works, Portrait, and Wood Engravings (pub. at 12s.), extra cloth, 6s. Cadell, 1838
"This may be called the official edition of Hannah More's Life. It brings so much new and interesting matter into the field respecting her, that it will receive a hearty welcome from the public. Among the rest, the particulars of most of her publications will reward the curiosity of literary readers."—*Literary Gazette.*

MORE'S (HANNAH) WORKS, complete in 11 vols. fcap. 8vo, with portrait and vignette titles, cloth, 1l. 12s. 6d.
1855

MORE'S (HANNAH) SPIRIT OF PRAYER, fcap. 8vo, Portrait (pub. at 6s.), cloth, 4s.
Cadell, 1842

MORE'S (HANNAH) ESSAY ON THE CHARACTER AND PRACTICAL WRITINGS OF ST. PAUL, post 8vo (pub. at 10s. 6d.), cloth, 5s.

MORE'S (HANNAH) PRACTICAL PIETY; Or the Influence of the Religion of the Heart on the Conduct of the Life, 32mo, Portrait, cloth, 2s. 6d.
The only complete small edition. It was revised just before her death, and contains much improvement, which is copyright.

MORE'S (HANNAH) SACRED DRAMAS chiefly intended for Young People, to which is added "Sensibility," an Epistle, 32mo (pub. at 2s. 6d.), gilt cloth, gilt edges, 2s.
This is the last genuine edition, and contains some copyright additions, which are not in any other.

MORE'S (HANNAH) SEARCH AFTER HAPPINESS; with Ballads, Tales, Hymns, and Epitaphs, 32mo (pub. at 2s. 6d.), gilt cloth, gilt edges, 1s. 6d.

NEFF (FELIX) LIFE AND LETTERS OF, translated from the French of M. Bost, by M. A. Wyatt, fcap. 8vo, Portrait (pub. at 6s.), cloth, 2s. 6d.
1843

NEWTON'S (REV. JOHN) WORKS, with a Life of the Author, by the Rev. Richard Cecil, and an introduction by the Rev. T. Cunningham, M.A. imperial 8vo, with Portrait (pub. at 1l. 5s.), 15s.

PALEY'S WORKS, in 1 vol. consisting of his Natural Theology, Moral and Political Philosophy, Evidences of Christianity, Horæ Paulinæ, Clergyman's Companion in visiting the Sick, &c. 8vo, handsomely printed in double columns (pub. at 10s. 6d.), cloth, 5s.

RIDDLE'S ECCLESIASTICAL CHRONOLOGY; or Annals of the Christian Church from its Foundation to the Present Time; containing a View of General Church History (including Controversies, Sects, and Parties, Ecclesiastical Writers, &c.) 8vo, cloth (pub. at 15s.), reduced to 7s. 6d.

ROBINSON'S SCRIPTURE CHARACTERS; or, a Practical Improvement of the Principal Histories of the Old and New Testament, 2 thick vols., 8vo, handsomely printed, with Portrait and Life of the Author, cloth lettered, (pub. at 1l. 1s.), 10s. 6d.

SCOTT'S (REV. THOMAS) COMMENTARY ON THE BIBLE, with the Author's last Corrections and Improvements, and 84 beautiful Woodcut Illustrations and Maps. 3 vols. imperial 8vo (pub. at 4l. 4s.), cloth, 1l. 16s.
1850

SIMEON'S WORKS, including his Skeletons of Sermons and Horæ Homileticæ, or Discourses digested into one continued Series, and forming a Commentary upon every Book of the Old and New Testament; to which are annexed an improved edition of Claude's Essay on the Composition of a Sermon, and very comprehensive Indexes, edited by Rev. Thomas Hartwell Horne, 21 vols. 8vo (pub. at 10l. 10s.), cloth, 7l. 7s.

The following miniature editions of Simeon's popular works are uniformly printed in 32mo, and bound in cloth:

THE CHRISTIAN'S ARMOUR, 9d.
THE EXCELLENCY OF THE LITURGY, 9d.
THE OFFICES OF THE HOLY SPIRIT, 9d.
HUMILIATION OF THE SON OF GOD; TWELVE SERMONS, 9d.
APPEAL TO MEN OF WISDOM AND CANDOUR, 9d.
DISCOURSES ON BEHALF OF THE JEWS, 1s. 6d.

"The works of Simeon, containing 2536 discourses on the principal passages of the Old and New Testament will be found peculiarly adapted to assist the studies of the younger clergy in their preparation for the pulpit; they will likewise serve as a Body of Divinity; and are by many recommended as a Biblical Commentary, well adapted to be read in families."—*Lowndes*.

SMYTH'S (REV. DR.) EXPOSITION OF VARIOUS PASSAGES OF HOLY SCRIPTURE, adapted to the Use of Families, for every Day throughout the Year, 2 vols. 8vo (pub. at 1l. 11s. 6d.), cloth, 9s.
1842

SORTAIN'S (REV. JOSEPH) SERMONS, on some of the most important topics of Morality, Doctrine, and Religious Opinion, preached at Brighton, 8vo, cloth, (pub. at 12s.), 6s.

SOUTH'S (DR. ROBERT) SERMONS: to which are annexed the chief heads of the Sermons, a Biographical Memoir, and General Index, 2 vols. royal 8vo (pub. at 1l. 4s.), cloth, 15s.

STEBBING'S HISTORY OF THE CHURCH OF CHRIST, from the Diet of Augsburg, 1530, to the present Century, 3 vols. 8vo (pub. at 1l. 16s.), cloth, 12s.
1849

SPOTTISWOODE'S HISTORY OF THE CHURCH OF SCOTLAND. Edited by the Right Rev. Dr. Russell. 3 vols, 8vo, (pub. at 1l. 10s.), cloth extra, 12s.

TAYLOR'S (JEREMY) COMPLETE WORKS, with an Essay, Biographical and Critical; 3 large vols. imperial 8vo, Portrait (pub. at 3l. 15s.), cloth, 2l. 2s.

TAYLOR'S (ISAAC OF ONGAR) NATURAL HISTORY OF ENTHUSIASM, Tenth Edition, fcap. 8vo, cloth, 5s.
"It is refreshing to us to meet with a work bearing, as this unquestionably does, the impress of bold, powerful, and original thought. Its most strikingly original views, however, never transgress the bounds of pure Protestant orthodoxy, or violate the spirit of truth and soberness; and yet it discusses topics constituting the very root and basis of those furious polemics which have shaken repeatedly the whole intellectual and moral world."—*Athenæum.*

TAYLOR'S (ISAAC) FANATICISM. Third Edition, carefully revised. Fcap. 8vo cloth, 6s.
"It is the reader's fault if he does not rise from the perusal of such a volume as the present a wiser and a better man.—*Eclectic Review.*

TAYLOR'S (ISAAC) SATURDAY EVENING, Seventh Edition. Fcap. 8vo, cloth, 5s.
"'Saturday Evening,' and 'Natural History of Enthusiasm,' are two noble productions."—*Blackwood's Magazine.*

TAYLOR'S (ISAAC) ELEMENTS OF THOUGHT, or concise Explanations, alphabetically arranged, of the principal Terms employed in the usual Branches of Intellectual Philosophy. Ninth Edition. 12mo, cloth, 4s.

SIMPSON'S KEY TO THE BIBLE, containing a Summary of Biblical Knowledge, and a Dictionary of all the principal Words in the Old and New Testament, illustrated by three maps, and 124 beautiful woodcuts, 8vo, cloth lettered, (pub. at 14s.), 7s. 1853

TOMLINE'S (BISHOP) ELEMENTS OF CHRISTIAN THEOLOGY, Fourteenth Edition, with additional Notes and Summary, by STEBBING. 2 vols. 8vo, cloth, lettered (pub. at 1l. 1s.), 16s. 6d.

TOMLINE'S (BISHOP) INTRODUCTION TO THE STUDY OF THE BIBLE, OR ELEMENTS OF CHRISTIAN THEOLOGY. Containing Proofs of the Authenticity and Inspiration of the Holy Scriptures; a Summary of the History of the Jews; an Account of the Jewish Sects; and a brief Statement of the Contents of the several Books of the Old and New Testaments. Nineteenth Edition, elegantly printed on fine paper, 12mo (pub. at 5s. 6d.), cloth, 3s. 6d.
"Well adapted as a manual for students in divinity, and may be read with advantage by the most experienced divine."—*Marsh's Lectures.*

WHEELER'S (REV. N.) SERMONS; preached in the Parish Churches of Old and New Shoreham, (in the vicinity of Brighton), Sussex, large type, 8vo, cloth, (pub. at 10s. 6d.), 5s.

WILBERFORCE'S PRACTICAL VIEW OF CHRISTIANITY, With a comprehensive Memoir of the Author, by the Rev. T. PRICE, 18mo, printed in a large handsome type (pub. at 6s.), gilt cloth, 3s. 6d. 1845

Foreign Languages and Literature.
INCLUDING
CLASSICS AND TRANSLATIONS, CLASSICAL CRITICISM, DICTIONARIES, GRAMMARS, COLLEGE AND SCHOOL BOOKS, ATLASES, &c.

ATLASES.—A NEW GENERAL ATLAS, engraved by SIDNEY HALL, demy folio, 53 large Maps, with the Divisions and Boundaries carefully coloured, and a complete General Index. New Edition, corrected to the present time, half morocco, 3l. 12s. 6d.

WILKINSON'S CLASSICAL AND SCRIPTURAL ATLAS, with Historical and Chronological Tables, imperial 4to. New and improved Edition, 33 maps, coloured (pub. at 2l. 4s.), half bound morocco, 1l. 11s. 6d. 1843

WILKINSON'S GENERAL ATLAS. New and improved Edition, with all the Railroads inserted. Population according to the last Census, Parliamentary Returns, &c., imperial 4to. 46 Maps, coloured (pub. at 1l. 16s.), half bound morocco, 1l. 5s.

AINSWORTH'S LATIN DICTIONARY, by Dr. JAMIESON, an enlarged Edition, containing all the words of the Quarto Dictionary. Thick 8vo, neatly bound (pub. at 14s.) 9s. 1847

BIBLIA HEBRAICA, EX EDITIONE VANDER HOOGHT. Recognovit J. D. ALLEMAND. Very thick 8vo, handsomely printed (pub. at 1l. 5s.), cloth, 10s. 6d. *Lond. Duncan,* 1850

BOURNE'S (VINCENT) POETICAL WORKS, Latin and English, 18mo (pub. at 3s. 6d.), cl th, 2s. 6d. 1838

——— the same, large paper, an elegant volume, 12mo (pub. at 5s.), cloth, 3s. 6d. 1838

CICERO'S LIFE, FAMILIAR LETTERS, AND LETTERS TO ATTICUS, by MIDDLETON, MELMOTH, and HEBERDEN, complete in one thick vol. royal 8vo, portrait, (pub. at 1l. 4s.), cloth, 12s. 1848

CORPUS POETARUM LATINORUM. Edidit G. S. WALKER. Complete in 1 very thick vol. royal 8vo (pub. at 2l. 2s.), cloth, 18s.
This comprehensive volume contains a library of the poetical Latin classics, correctly printed from the best texts, viz:—

Catullus,	Virgil,	Lucan,	Sulpicia,	Calpurnius Siculus
Tibullus,	Ovid,	Persius,	Statius,	Ausonius,
Propertius,	Horace,	Juvenal,	Silius Italicus,	Claudian.
Lucretius,	Phædrus,	Martial,	Valerius Flaccus,	

DAMMII LEXICON GRÆCUM, HOMERICUM ET PINDARICUM. Curâ DUNCAN, royal 4to, New Edition, printed on fine paper (pub. at 3l. 5s.), cloth, 1l. 1s. 1842
"An excellent work, the merits of which have been universally acknowledged by literary characters."—*Dr. Dibdin.*

DEMOSTHENES, translated by LELAND, the two vols. 8vo, complete in 1 vol. 12mo handsomely printed in double columns, in pearl type, portrait (pub. at 4s.), cloth, 3s.

DONNEGAN'S GREEK AND ENGLISH LEXICON, enlarged; with examples, literally translated, selected from the classical authors. Fourth Edition, considerably enlarged, carefully revised, and materially improved throughout; thick 8vo (1752 pages) (pub. at 2l. 2s.), cloth, 15s.

GRAGLIA'S ITALIAN-ENGLISH AND ENGLISH-ITALIAN DICTIONARY, with a compendious Italian Grammar and Supplementary Dictionary of Naval Terms, 18mo, roan (pub. at 8s.), 4s. 6d.

HERMANN'S MANUAL OF THE POLITICAL ANTIQUITIES OF GREECE, Historically considered, translated from the German, 8vo (pub. at 18s.), cloth, 10s. 6d.
Oxford, Talboys, 1836
"Hermann's Manual of Greek Antiquities is most important."—*Thirlwall's Hist. of Greece,* vol. 1, p. 443.

HERODOTUS, CAREY'S (REV. H.) GREEK AND ENGLISH LEXICON TO HERODOTUS, adapted to the Text of Gaisford and Baehr, and all other Editions, 8vo, cloth (pub. at 12s.), 8s.

LEMPRIERE'S CLASSICAL DICTIONARY. Miniature Edition, containing a full Account of all the Proper names mentioned in Ancient Authors, and much useful information respecting the uses and habits of the Greeks and Romans. New and complete Edition, elegantly printed in pearl type, in 1 very thick vol. 18mo (pub. at 7s. 6d.), cloth, 4s. 6d.

LIVII HISTORIA, EX RECENSIONE DRAKENBORCHII ET KREYSSIG; Et Annotationes CREVIERII, STROTHII, RUPERTI, et aliorum; Animadversiones NIEBUHRII, WACHSMUTHII, et suas addidit TRAVERS TWISS, J. C. B. Coll. Univ. Oxon. Socius et Tutor. Cum Indice amplissimo, 4 vols. 8vo (pub. at 1l. 18s.), cloth, 1l. 1s. *Oxford,* 1841
This is the best and most useful edition of Livy ever published in octavo, and it is preferred in all our universities and classical schools.

LIVY. Edited by PRENDEVILLE. Livii Historiæ libri quinque priores, with English Notes, by PRENDEVILLE. New Edition, 12mo, neatly bound in roan, 5s.
————— the same, Books I to III, separately; cloth, 3s. 6d.
————— the same, Books IV and V, cloth, 3s. 6d.

NEWMAN'S PRACTICAL SYSTEM OF RHETORIC; or, the Principles and Rules of Style, with Examples. Sixth Edition, 12mo (pub. at 5s. 6d.), cloth 3s. 6d.

OXFORD CHRONOLOGICAL TABLES OF UNIVERSAL HISTORY, from the earliest Period to the present Time: in which all the great Events, Civil, Religious, Scientific, and Literary, of the various Nations of the World are placed, at one view, under the eye of the Reader in a Series of parallel columns, so as to exhibit the state of the whole Civilized World at any epoch, and at the same time form a continuous chain of History, with Genealogical Tables of all the principal Dynasties. Complete in 3 Sections; viz.:—I. Ancient History, II. Middle Ages. III. Modern History. With a most complete Index to the entire work, folio (pub. at 1l. 16s.), half-bound morocco, 1l. 1s.
The above is also sold separately, as follows:—
THE MIDDLE AGES AND MODERN HISTORY, 2 parts in 1, folio (pub. at 1l. 2s. 6d.), sewed, 13s.
MODERN HISTORY, folio (pub. at 12s.), sewed, 8s.

PLUTARCH'S LIVES, by the LANGHORNES. Complete in 2 vols. 8vo. (pub. at 1l. 1s.), cloth, 10s. 6d.

RAMSHORN'S DICTIONARY OF LATIN SYNONYMES, for the Use of Schools and Private Students. Translated and edited by DR. LIEBER. Post 8vo. (pub. at 7s.), cloth, 4s. 6d.
1841

SCHOMANN'S HISTORY OF THE ASSEMBLIES OF THE ATHENIANS, translated from the Latin, with a complete Index, 8vo. (pub. at 10s. 6d.), cloth, 5s. *Camb.* 1838
A book of the same school and character as the works of HEEREN, BOECKH, SCHLEGEL, &c.

ELLENDT'S GREEK AND ENGLISH LEXICON TO SOPHOCLES, translated by CARY. 8vo, (pub. at 12s.), cloth, 6s. 6d. *Oxford, Talboys,* 1841

STUART'S HEBREW CHRESTOMATHY, designed as an Introduction to a Course of Hebrew Study. Third Edition, 8vo, (pub. at 14s.), cloth, 9s. *Oxford, Talboys,* 1834
This work, which was designed by its learned author to facilitate the study of Hebrew, has had a very extensive sale in America. It forms a desirable adjunct to all Hebrew Grammars, and is sufficient to complete the system of instruction in that language.

TAYLOR'S (ISAAC, OF ONGAR) HOME EDUCATION; a new and enlarged edition, revised by the Author, fcap. 8vo, cloth, 5s.

TROLLOPE'S (REV. WM.) ANALECTA THEOLOGICA, sive SYNOPSIS CRITICORUM; a Critical, Philological, and Exegetical Commentary on the New Testament; adapted to the Greek Text, compiled and digested from the most approved sources, British and Foreign; and so arranged as to exhibit at one view the comparative weight of different opinions on disputed texts, 2 very thick vols., 8vo, cloth lettered, (pub. at 1l. 12s.), 12s.

TACITUS, (the Latin Text), complete, from the Text of BROTIER, with his Explanatory Notes in English, edited, for the use of Schools and Colleges, by A. J. VALPY, M.A. 2 vols. post 8vo, (pub. at 1l. 4s.), cloth, 10s. 6d.

TERENTIUS, CUM NOTIS VARIORUM, CURA ZEUNII, cura GILES; acced. Index copiosissimus. Complete in 1 thick vol. 8vo, (pub. at 10s.), cloth, 8s. 1837

VIRGIL EDWARDS'S SCHOOL EDITION. Virgilii Æneis, cura EDWARDS, ct Questiones Virgilianæ, or Notes and Questions, adapted to the middle Forms in Schools, 2 vols in 1, 12mo, bound in cloth (pub. at 6s. 6d.), 3s.
*** Either the Text or Questions may be had separately (pub. at 3s. 6d.), 2s. 6d.

WILSON'S (JAMES PROFESSOR OF FRENCH IN ST. GREGORY'S COLLEGE) FRENCH-ENGLISH AND ENGLISH-FRENCH DICTIONARY, containing full Explanations, Definitions, Synonyms, Idioms, Proverbs, Terms of Art and Science, and Rules of Pronunciation in ea h Language. Compiled from the Dictionaries of the Academy, BOWYER, CHAMBAUD, GARNER, LAVEAUX, DES CARRIERES and FAIN, JOHNSON and WALKER. 1 large closely printed vol. imperial 8vo, (pub. at 2l. 2s.), cloth, 18s.

XENOPHONTIS OPERA, GR. ET LAT. SCHNEIDERI ET ZEUNII, Accedit Index (PORSON and ELMSLEY's Edition), 10 vols. 12mo, handsomely printed in a large type, done up in 5 vols. (pub. at 4l. 10s.), cloth, 18s. 1841

────── the same, large paper, 10 vols. crown 8vo, done up in 5 vols. cloth, 1l. 5s.

XENOPHON'S WHOLE WORKS, translated by SPELMAN and others. The only complete Edition, 1 thick vol. 8vo, portrait, (pub. at 15s.), cloth, 10s.

Novels, Works of Fiction, Light Reading.

CRUIKSHANK "AT HOME;" a New Family Album of Endless Entertainment, consisting of a Series of Tales and Sketches by the most popular Authors, with numerous clever and humorous Illustrations on Wood, by CRUIKSHANK and SEYMOUR. Also, CRUIKSHANK'S ODD VOLUME, OR BOOK OF VARIETY. Illustrated by Two Odd Fellows—SEYMOUR and CRUIKSHANK. Together 4 vols. in 2, fcap. 8vo, (pub. at 2l. 12s.), cloth, gilt, 10s. 6d. 1845

HOWITT'S (WILLIAM) GERMAN EXPERIENCES. Addressed to the English, both Goers Abroad and Stayers at Home. 1 vol. fcap. 8vo, (pub. at 6s.), cloth, 3s. 6d. 1844

MARRYAT'S (CAPT.) POOR JACK. Illustrated by 46 large and exquisitely beautiful Engravings on Wood, after the masterly Designs of CLARKSON STANFIELD, R.A. 1 handsome vol. royal 8vo, (pub. at 14s.), gilt cloth, 9s.

MARRYAT'S PIRATE AND THE THREE CUTTERS. 8vo, with 20 most splendid line Engravings, after STANFIELD, engraved on Steel by CHARLES HEATH (originally pub. at 1l. 4s.) gilt cloth, 10s. 6d.

MARRYAT'S (CAPT.) PRIVATEER'S MAN OF ONE HUNDRED YEARS AGO. new edition, illustrated with 8 highly finished line Engravings on steel, in the manner of Stothard, fcap. 8vo. gilt cloth, 5s.

MARRYAT'S (CAPT.) MASTERMAN READY, or the Wreck of the Pacific (written for Young People). New edition, complete in 1 vol. fcap. 8vo. with 92 beautiful engravings on wood, cloth extra, gilt, 6s. 1856

MARRYAT'S MISSION, OR SCENES IN AFRICA. (Written for Young People). New edition, fcap. 8vo, with 8 Illustrations on wood by GILBERT & DALZIEL, cloth, ex. gilt, 5s.

MARRYAT'S SETTLERS IN CANADA (Written for Young People). New edition, fcap. 8vo., with 10 Illustrations on wood by GILBERT and DALZIEL, cloth, extra gilt, 5s.

MAYHEW'S IMAGE OF HIS FATHER; or, One Boy is More Trouble than a Dozen Girls; a Tale, with 12 capital Engravings by PHIZ. New Edition, in 1 vol. post 8vo. cloth gilt, (pub. at 7s.), reduced to 3s. 6d.

MILLER'S GODFREY MALVERN, OR THE LIFE OF AN AUTHOR. By the Author of "Gideon Giles," "Royston Gower," "Day in the Woods," &c. &c. 2 vols. in 1, 8vo, with 24 clever Illustrations by PHIZ (pub. at 13s.), cloth, 6s. 6d. 1842
"This work has a tone and an individuality which distinguishes it from all others, and cannot be read without pleasure. Mr. Miller has the forms and colours of rustic life more completely under his control than any of his predecessors."—*Athenæum.*

MITFORD'S (MISS) OUR VILLAGE; complete in 2 vols. post 8vo, a Series of Rural Tales and Sketches. New Edition, beautiful Woodcuts, gilt cloth, 10s.

SKETCHES FROM FLEMISH LIFE. By HENDRIK CONSCIENCE. Square 12mo, 12 Wood Engravings (pub. at 6s.), cloth, 4s. 6d.

Juvenile and Elementary Books, Gymnastics, &c.

ALPHABET OF QUADRUPEDS. Illustrated by Figures selected from the works of the Old Masters, square 12mo, with 24 spirited Engravings after BERGHEM, REMBRANDT, CUYP, PAUL POTTER, &c. and with initial letters by MR. SHAW, cloth, gilt edges (pub. at 4s. 6d.), 3s. 1850

——— the same, the Plates coloured, gilt cloth, gilt edges (pub. at 7s. 6d.), 5s.

CRABB'S (REV. G.) NEW PANTHEON, or Mythology of all Nations; especially for the Use of Schools and Young Persons; with Questions for Examination on the Plan of PINNOCK. 18mo, with 30 pleasing Lithographs (pub. at 3s.), cloth, 2s. 1847

DRAPER'S JUVENILE NATURALIST, or Country Walks in Spring, Summer, Autumn, and Winter. Square 12mo, with 80 beautifully executed Woodcuts (pub. at 7s. 6d.), cloth, gilt edges, 3s. 6d. 1842

EVANS'S TALES OF CHIVALRY; or, Evenings with the Chroniclers, square 16mo. 16 woodcuts, cloth lettered, (pub. at 4s. 6d.), 3s. 6d.

EVANS'S TRUE TALES OF THE OLDEN TIME, selected from FROISSART. Third Edition, handsomely printed, 16 fine woodcuts, square 16mo, gilt cloth, (pub. at 4s. 6d.), 3s. 6d

GAMMER GRETHEL'S FAIRY TALES AND POPULAR STORIES, translated from the German of GRIMM (containing 42 Fairy Tales), post 8vo, numerous Woodcuts by GEORGE CRUIKSHANK (pub. at 7s. 6d.), cloth gilt, 5s. 1849

GOOD-NATURED BEAR. A Story for Children of all Ages, by R. H. HORNE. Square 8vo, Plates (pub. at 5s.), cloth, 3s., or with the Plates coloured, 4s. 1850

GRIMM'S TALES FROM EASTERN LANDS. Square 12mo, Plates (pub. at 5s.), cloth, 3s. 6d., or Plates coloured, 4s. 6d. 2067

HOWITT'S (MARY) CHILD'S PICTURE AND VERSE BOOK, commonly called "Otto Speckter's Fable Book;" translated into English Verse, with French and German Verses opposite, forming a Triglott, square 12mo, with 100 large Wood Engravings (pub. at 10s. 6d.), extra Turkey cloth, gilt edges, 5s. 1848
This is one of the most elegant juvenile books ever produced, and has the novelty of being in three languages.

ILLUSTRATED DITTIES OF THE OLDEN TIME; a Series of 29 exquisitely graceful Designs, illustrative of popular Nursery Rhymes, small 4to, elegantly bound in cloth, 5s.

LAMB'S TALES FROM SHAKSPEARE, designed principally for the use of Young Persons (written by Miss and CHARLES LAMB), Sixth Edition, embellished with 20 large and beautiful Woodcut Engravings, from Designs by HARVEY, fcap. 8vo., (pub. at 7s. 6d.), cloth gilt, 3s. 6d.

L. E. L. TRAITS AND TRIALS OF EARLY LIFE. A Series of Tales addressed to Young People. By L. E. L. (MISS LANDON). Fourth Edition, fcap. 8vo, with a beautiful Portrait engraved on Steel (pub. at 5s.), gilt cloth, 3s. 1845

LOUDON'S (MRS.) ENTERTAINING NATURALIST; being popular Descriptions, Tales and Anecdotes of more than 500 Animals, comprehending all the Quadrupeds, Birds, Fishes, Reptiles, Insects, &c., of which a knowledge is indispensable in Polite Education. Illustrated by upwards of 500 beautiful Woodcuts, by BEWICK, HARVEY, WHIMPER, and others, post 8vo, gilt cloth, 6s.

MARTIN AND WESTALL'S PICTORIAL HISTORY OF THE BIBLE; the letterpress by the REV. HOBART CAUNTER, 8vo, 144 extremely beautiful Wood Engravings by the first Artists (including reduced copies of MARTIN'S celebrated Pictures, Belshazzar's Feast, The Deluge, Fall of Nineveh, &c.), cloth gilt, gilt edges, reduced to 12s.
A most elegant present to young people.

MARRYAT'S MASTERMAN READY, PRIVATEER'S MAN, MISSION, and SETTLERS. see previous page.

MERRY TALES FOR LITTLE FOLK; illustrated with upwards of Two Hundred and Fifty Wood Engravings; new and improved edition, elegantly printed, extra cloth gilt, 3s. 6d.
*** This highly popular volume contains 40 different Stories of the olden time.

PERCY TALES OF THE KINGS OF ENGLAND; Stories of Camps and Battle-fields, Wars, and Victories (modernized from HOLINSHED, FROISSART, and the other Chroniclers), 2 vols. in 1, square 12mo. (Parley size.) Fourth Edition, considerably improved, completed to the present time, embellished with 16 exceedingly beautiful Wood Engravings (pub. at 8s.), cloth gilt, gilt edges, 5s.
This beautiful volume has enjoyed a large share of success, and deservedly.

ROBIN HOOD AND HIS MERRY FORESTERS. By STEPHEN PERCY. Square 12mo, 8 Illustrations by GILBERT (pub. at 4s.), cloth, 3s. 6d., or with coloured Plates, 5s. 1850

SHERWOOD'S (MRS.) ROBERT AND FREDERICK; a Tale for Youth, fcap. 8vo, with 20 highly finished wood Engravings, cloth, gilt edges, (pub. at 9s. 6d.), reduced to 4s. 6d.

PUBLISHED OR SOLD BY H. G. BOHN. 81

REYNARD THE FOX, THE MOST DELECTABLE HISTORY OF. Square 12mo, with 24 Etchings by EVERDINGEN, extra gilt cloth, (pub. at 6s.), 4s.; or, with the plates coloured, extra cloth, gilt edges, (pub. at 8s.), 6s.

SPENSER'S FAERIE QUEEN (TALES FROM). Square 16mo, plates, extra cloth, (pub. at 3s. 6d.), 2s. 6d.; or, coloured plates, extra cloth, gilt edges, (pub. at 6s. 6d.), 3s. 6d.

STRICKLAND'S (MISS JANE) EDWARD EVELYN. A Tale of the Rebellion of 1745; to which is added, "The Peasant's Tale," by JEFFERYS TAYLOR, fcap. 8vo; 2 fine Plates (pub. at 5s.), cloth gilt, 2s. 6d. 1849

TALES OF THE GENII; or the delightful Lessons of Horam, the Son of Asmar, by SIR CHARLES MORRELL. New Edition, collated and edited by Philojuvenis, post 8vo. with numerous woodcuts and 5 steel engravings in the manner of Stothard, cloth extra *just ready*, 8s.

TOMKIN'S BEAUTIES OF ENGLISH POETRY, selected for the use of Youth, and designed to inculcate the Practice of Virtue. Twentieth Edition, with considerable additions, royal 18mo. very elegantly printed, with a beautiful Frontispiece after HARVEY, elegant, gilt edges, 3s. 6d.

YOUTH'S (THE) HAND-BOOK OF ENTERTAINING KNOWLEDGE, in a Series of Familiar Conversations on the most interesting Productions of Nature and Art, and on other Instructive Topics of Polite Education. By a Lady (MRS. PALLISER, the Sister of CAPTAIN MARRYAT. 2 vols. in 1, fcap. 8vo. Woodcuts, (pub. at 15s.), cloth gilt, 3s. 6d. 1846

This is a very clever and instructive book, adapted to the capacities of young people, on the plan of the Conversations on Chemistry, Mineralogy, Botany, &c.

Music and Musical Works.

THE MUSICAL LIBRARY. A Selection of the best Vocal and Instrumental Music, both English and Foreign. Edited by W. AYRTON, Esq., of the Opera House. 8 vols. folio, comprehending more than 400 pieces of Music, beautifully printed with metallic types (pub. at 4l. 4s.), sewed, 1l. 11s. 6d.

The Vocal and Instrumental may be had separately, each in 4 vols. 16s.

MUSICAL CABINET AND HARMONIST. A Collection of Classical and Popular Vocal and Instrumental Music; comprising Selections from the best productions of all the Great Masters; English, Scotch, and Irish Melodies; with many of the National Airs of other Countries, embracing Overtures, Marches, Rondos, Quadrilles, Waltzes, and Gallopades; also Madrigals, Duets, and Glees; the whole adapted either for the Voice, the Piano-forte, the Harp or the Organ; with Pieces occasionally for the Flute and Guitar, under the superintendence of an eminent Professor. 4 vols. small folio, comprehending more than 300 pieces of Music, beautifully printed with metallic types (pub. at 2l. 2s.), sewed, 16s.

The contents of the work are quite different from the Musical Library, and the intrinsic merit of the selection is equal.

MUSICAL GEM; a Collection of 300 Modern Songs, Duets, Glees, &c. by the most celebrated Composers of the present day, adapted for the Voice, Flute, or Violin (edited by JOHN PARRY). 3 vols. in 1, 8vo, with a beautifully engraved Title, and a very richly illuminated Frontispiece (pub. at 1l. 1s.), cloth gilt, 10s. 6d. 1841

The above capital collection contains a great number of the best copyright pieces, including some of the most popular songs of Braham, Bishop, &c. It forms a most attractive volume.

Medicine, Surgery, Anatomy, Chemistry, Physiology, &c.

BATEMAN AND WILLAN'S DELINEATIONS OF CUTANEOUS DISEASES, 4to. containing 72 Plates, beautifully and very accurately coloured under the superintendence of an eminent Professional Gentleman (DR. CARSWELL), (pub. at 12l. 12s.), half bound mor. 5l. 5s. 1840

"Dr. Bateman's valuable work has done more to extend the knowledge of cutaneous diseases than any other that has ever appeared."—*Dr. A. T. Thompson.*

BEHR'S HAND-BOOK OF ANATOMY, by BIRKETT (Demonstrator at Guy's Hospital), thick 12mo, closely printed, cloth lettered (pub. at 10s. 6d.), 3s. 6d. 1846

BOSTOCK'S (DR.) SYSTEM OF PHYSIOLOGY, comprising a Complete View of the present state of the Science. Fourth Edition, revised and corrected throughout, 8vo, (900 pages), (pub. at 1l.), cloth, 8s. 1834

BURN'S PRINCIPLES OF MIDWIFERY. Tenth and best Edition, thick 8vo, cloth lettered, (pub. at 16s.), 5s.

CELSUS DE MEDICINA. Edited by E. Milligan, M.D. cum Indice copiosissimo ex edit. Targæ. Thick 8vo, Frontispiece, (pub. at 16s.), cloth, 9s. 1831
   This is the very best edition of Celsus. It contains critical and medical notes, applicable to the practice of this country; a parallel Table of ancient and modern Medical terms, synonymes, weights, measures, &c. and. Indeed, everything which can be useful to the Medical Student; together with a singularly extensive Index.

ELLIOTSON'S (DR.) HUMAN PHYSIOLOGY, illustrated with numerous woodcuts, fifth edition, thick 8vo. cloth, (pub. at 2l. 2s.), 10s. 6d.

LAWRENCE'S LECTURES ON COMPARATIVE ANATOMY, PHYSIOLOGY, ZOOLOGY, AND THE NATURAL HISTORY OF MAN. New Edition, post 8vo, with a Frontispiece of Portraits, engraved on Steel, and 12 Plates, cloth, 5s.

LAWRENCE (W.) ON THE DISEASES OF THE EYE. Third Edition, revised and enlarged. 8vo, (830 closely printed pages), (pub. at 1l. 4s.), cloth, 10s. 6d. 1844

LEY'S (DR.) ESSAY ON THE CROUP. 8vo, 5 Plates (pub. at 15s.), cloth, 3s. 6d. 1836

NEW LONDON SURGICAL POCKET BOOK. Thick royal 18mo. (pub. at 12s.), half bound, 5s. 1844

PARIS' (DR.) TREATISE ON DIET AND THE DIGESTIVE FUNCTIONS, Fifth Edition (pub. at 12s.), cloth, 5s.

PLUMBE'S PRACTICAL TREATISE ON THE DISEASES OF THE SKIN, Fourth Edition, Plates, thick 8vo (pub. at 1l. 4s.), cloth, 6s. 6d.

SINCLAIR'S (SIR JOHN) CODE OF HEALTH AND LONGEVITY. Sixth Edition complete in 1 thick vol. 8vo, Portrait (pub. at 1l.), cloth, 6s.

SOUTH'S DESCRIPTION OF THE BONES; together with their several Connexions with each other, and with the Muscles, specially adapted for Students in Anatomy, numerous Woodcuts, third edition, 12mo, cloth lettered (pub. at 7s.), 3s. 6d. 1837

STEPHENSON'S MEDICAL ZOOLOGY AND MINERALOGY; including also an Account of the Animal and Mineral Poisons. 45 coloured Plates, royal 8vo, (pub. at 2l. 2s.), cloth, 1l. 1s. 1838

WOODVILLE'S MEDICAL BOTANY. Third Edition, enlarged by Sir W. Jackson Hooker. 5 vols. 4to, with 310 Plates, engraved by Sowerby, most carefully coloured (pub. at 10l. 10s.), half-bound morocco, 5l. 5s. The Fifth, or Supplementary Volume, entirely by Sir W. J. Hooker, to complete the old Editions. 4to, 36 coloured Plates (pub. at 2l. 12s. 6d.), boards, 1l. 11s. 6d. 1832

Mathematics.

BRADLEY'S GEOMETRY, PERSPECTIVE, AND PROJECTION, for the use of Artists. 8 Plates and numerous Woodcuts (pub. at 7s.), cloth, 5s. 1846

EUCLID'S SIX ELEMENTARY BOOKS, by Dr. Lardner, with an Explanatory Commentary, Geometrical Exercises, and a Treatise on Solid Geometry. 8vo, Ninth Edition, cloth, 6s.

JAMIESON'S MECHANICS FOR PRACTICAL MEN; including Treatises on the Composition and Resolution of Forces; the Centre of Gravity; and the Mechanical Powers; illustrated by Examples and Designs. Fourth Edition, greatly improved, 8vo, (pub. at 15s.), cloth, 7s. 6d. 1850

"A great mechanical treasure."—*Dr. Birkbeck.*

BOOKS PRINTED UNIFORM WITH THE STANDARD LIBRARY.

CHILLINGWORTH'S RELIGION OF PROTESTANTS. 500 pp. 3s. 6d.

CARY'S TRANSLATION OF DANTE. (Upwards of 600 pages), extra blue cloth with a richly gilt back, 7s. 6d. 1847

LAMARTINE'S THREE MONTHS IN POWER; a History of his Political Career. Post 8vo, sewed, 2s.

MACLISE'S COMPARATIVE OSTEOLOGY; demonstrating the Archetype Skeleton of Vertebrated Animals. Folio, 54 plates, cloth, 1l. 5s.

STANDARD LIBRARY CYCLOPÆDIA OF POLITICAL, CONSTITUTIONAL, Statistical, and Forensic Knowledge. 4 vols, 3s. 6d. each.
   The Compiler, Mr. George Long, is one of the most competent Scholars of the day.

MICHELET'S HISTORY OF THE FRENCH REVOLUTION, translated by C. Cocks, 3 vols. in 1, 4s.

STARLING'S (MISS) NOBLE DEEDS OF WOMAN, or Examples of Female Courage, Fortitude, and Virtue. Third Edition, enlarged and improved, with two very beautiful Frontispieces, elegant in cloth, 5s.

PRINTED BY HARRISON AND SONS, ST. MARTIN'S LANE.

BOHN'S CLASSICAL LIBRARY.

A SERIES OF LITERAL PROSE TRANSLATIONS OF THE GREEK AND LATIN CLASSICS. WITH NOTES AND INDEXES.

Uniform with the STANDARD LIBRARY, *5s. each (except Thucydides, Æschylus, Virgil, Horace, Cicero's Offices, Demosthenes, Appendix to Æschylus, Aristotle's Organon, all of which are 3s. 6d. each volume).*

1. **HERODOTUS.** By the REV. HENRY CARY, M.A. *Frontispiece.*
2 & 3. **THUCYDIDES.** By the REV. H. DALE. In 2 Vols. (3s. 6d. each). *Frontispiece.*
4. **PLATO.** Vol. I. By CARY. [The Apology of Socrates, Crito, Phædo, Gorgias, Protagoras, Phædrus, Theætetus, Euthyphron, Lysis.] *Frontis.*
5. **LIVY'S HISTORY OF ROME**, literally translated. Vol. I., Books 1 to 8.
6. **PLATO.** Vol. II. By DAVIS. [The Republic, Timæus, and Critias.]
7. **LIVY'S HISTORY OF ROME.** Vol. II., Books 9 to 26.
8. **SOPHOCLES.** The Oxford Translation, revised.
9. **ÆSCHYLUS**, literally translated. By an OXONIAN. (Price 3s. 6d.)
9* ———— Appendix to, containing the new readings given in Hermann's posthumous edition of Æschylus, translated and edited by G. BURGES, M.A. (3s. 6d.)
10. **ARISTOTLE'S RHETORIC AND POETIC.** With Examination Questions.
11. **LIVY'S HISTORY OF ROME.** Vol. III., Books 27 to 36.
12 & 14. **EURIPIDES**, literally translated. From the Text of Dindorf. In 2 Vols.
13. **VIRGIL.** By DAVIDSON. New Edition, Revised. (Price 3s. 6d.) *Frontispiece.*
15. **HORACE.** By SMART. New Edition, Revised. (Price 3s. 6d.) *Frontispiece.*
16. **ARISTOTLE'S ETHICS.** By PROF. R. W. BROWNE, of King's College.
17. **CICERO'S OFFICES.** [Old Age, Friendship, Scipio's Dream, Paradoxes, &c.]
18. **PLATO.** Vol. III. By G. BURGES, M.A. [Euthydemus, Symposium, Sophistes, Politicus, Laches, Parmenides, Cratylus, and Meno]
19. **LIVY'S HISTORY OF ROME.** Vol. IV. (which completes the work).
20. **CÆSAR AND HIRTIUS.** With Index.
21. **HOMER'S ILIAD**, in prose, literally translated. *Frontispiece.*
22. **HOMER'S ODYSSEY, HYMNS, EPIGRAMS, AND BATTLE OF THE FROGS AND MICE.**
23. **PLATO.** Vol. IV. By G. BURGES, M.A. [Philebus, Charmides, Laches, The Two Alcibiades, and Ten other Dialogues.]
24, 25, & 32. **OVID.** By H. T. RILEY, B.A. Complete in 3 Vols. *Frontispieces.*
26. **LUCRETIUS.** By the REV. J. S. WATSON. With the Metrical Version of J. M. GOOD.
27, 30, 31, & 34. **CICERO'S ORATIONS.** By C. D. YONGE. Complete in 4 Vols. (Vol. 4 contains also the Rhetorical Pieces.)
28. **PINDAR.** By Dawson W. TURNER. With the Metrical Version of MOORE. *Front.*
29. **PLATO.** Vol. V. By G. BURGES, M.A. [The Laws.]
33 & 36. **THE COMEDIES OF PLAUTUS**, By H. T. RILEY, B.A. In 2 Vols.
35. **JUVENAL, PERSIUS, &c.** By the REV. L. EVANS, M.A. With the Metrical Version of GIFFORD. *Frontispiece.*
37. **THE GREEK ANTHOLOGY**, translated chiefly by G. BURGES, A.M., with Metrical Versions by various Authors.
38. **DEMOSTHENES.** The Olynthiac, Philippic, and other Public Orations, with Notes, Appendices, &c., by C. RANN KENNEDY. (3s. 6d.)

BOHN'S CLASSICAL LIBRARY.

39. **SALLUST, FLORUS,** and **VELLEIUS PATERCULUS**, with copious Notes, Biographical Notices, and Index, by the Rev. J. S. WATSON, M.A.

40. **LUCAN'S PHARSALIA,** with copious Notes, by H. T. RILEY, B.A.

41. **THEOCRITUS, BION, MOSCHUS** and **TYRTÆUS,** by the Rev. J. BANKS, M.A. With the Metrical Versions of CHAPMAN. *Frontispiece.*

42. **CICERO'S ACADEMICS, DE FINIBUS** and **TUSCULAN QUESTIONS,** by C. D. YONGE, B.A. With Sketch of the Greek Philosophy.

43. **ARISTOTLE'S POLITICS AND ECONOMICS,** by E. WALFORD, M.A., with Notes, Analyses, Life, Introduction, and Index.

44. **DIOGENES LAERTIUS LIVES AND OPINIONS OF THE ANCIENT PHILOSOPHERS,** with Notes by C. D. YONGE, B.A.

45. **TERENCE** and **PHÆDRUS,** by H. T. RILEY. To which is added SMART'S Metrical Version of Phædrus. *Frontispiece.*

46 & 47. **ARISTOTLE'S ORGANON,** or, Logical Treatises, and the Introduction of Porphyry, with Notes, Analysis, Introduction and Index, by the Rev. O. F. OWEN, M.A. 2 Vols., 3s. 6d. per Vol.

48 & 49. **ARISTOPHANES,** with Notes and Extracts from the best Metrical Versions, by W. J. HICKIE, in 2 Vols. *Frontispiece*

50. **CICERO ON THE NATURE OF THE GODS, DIVINATION, FATE, LAWS, REPUBLIC,** &c., translated by C. D. YONGE, B.A.

51. **APULEIUS.** [The Golden Ass, Death of Socrates, Florida, and Defence or Discourse on Magic]. To which is added a Metrical Version of Cupid and Psyche; and Mrs. Tighe's Psyche. *Frontispiece.*

52. **JUSTIN, CORNELIUS NEPOS** and **EUTROPIUS,** with Notes and a General Index, by the Rev. J. S. WATSON, M.A.

53 & 58. **TACITUS.** Vol 1. The Annals. Vol. II. The History, Germania, Agricola, &c. With Index.

54. **PLATO** Vol VI., completing the work, and containing Epinomis, Axiochus, Eryxias, on Virtue, on Justice, Sisyphus, Demodocus, and Definitions; the Treatise of Timæus Locrus on the Soul of the World and Nature; the Lives of Plato by Diogenes Laertius, Hesychius, and Olympiodorus; and the Introductions to his Doctrines by Alcinous and Albinus; Apuleius on the Doctrines of Plato, and Remarks on Plato's Writings by the Poet Gray. Edited, with Notes, by G. BURGES, M.A., Trin. Coll., Camb. With general Index to the 6 Volumes.

55, 56, 57 **ATHENÆUS.** The Deipnosophists, or the Banquet of the Learned, translated by C. D. YONGE, B.A., with an Appendix of Poetical Fragments rendered into English verse by various Authors, and a general Index. Complete in 3 Vols.

59. **CATULLUS, TIBULLUS,** and the **VIGIL OF VENUS.** A literal prose translation. To which are added Metrical Versions by LAMB, GRAINGER, and others. *Frontispiece.*

60. **PROPERTIUS, PETRONIUS ARBITER,** and **JOHANNES SECUNDUS,** literally translated, and accompanied by Poetical Versions, from various sources; to which are added the Love Epistles of ARISTÆNETUS. Edited by W. K. KELLY.

61, 74, & 82 **THE GEOGRAPHY OF STRABO** translated, with copious Notes, by W. FALCONER, M.A., and H. C HAMILTON, Esq. In 3 vols., and Index.

62. **XENOPHON'S ANABASIS,** or Expedition of Cyrus, and **MEMORABILIA,** or Memoirs of Socrates, translated by the Rev. J. S. WATSON, with a Geographical Commentary by W. F. AINSWORTH. *Frontispiece.*

63. ——————— CYROPÆDIA and HELLENICS, by the Rev. H. DALE, and the Rev. J. S. WATSON.

2 e

BOHN'S CLASSICAL LIBRARY.

64, 67, 69, 72, 78, & 81. **PLINY'S NATURAL HISTORY**, with copious Notes, by Dr. BOSTOCK and T. H. RILEY. In 6 volumes. Vols. I., II., III., IV., V. and VI.

65. **SUETONIUS.** Lives of the Cæsars, and other Works. THOMSON'S Translation revised by T. FORESTER.

66. **DEMOSTHENES ON THE CROWN, AND EMBASSY.** by C. RANN KENNEDY.

68. **CICERO ON ORATORY AND ORATORS**, by the Rev. J. S. WATSON, M.A.
*** This volume completes the Classical Library edition of Cicero.

70. **GREEK ROMANCES.** Heliodorus, Longus, and Achilles Tatius.

71 & 76. **QUINTILIAN'S INSTITUTES OF ORATORY.** By the Rev J. S. WATSON, M.A. Complete, with Notes, Index, and Biographical Notice. 2 volumes.

73. **HESIOD, CALLIMACHUS, AND THEOGNIS**, in Prose, by BANKS, with the Metrical Versions of ELTON, TYTLER, and FRERE.

75. **DICTIONARY OF LATIN QUOTATIONS**, with the Quantities marked and English Translations; including Proverbs, Maxims, Mottoes, Law Terms and Phrases; with a Collection of above 500 GREEK QUOTATIONS.

77. **DEMOSTHENES AGAINST LEPTINES, MIDIAS, ANDROTION, AND ARISTOCRATES.** By CHARLES RANN KENNEDY.

79. **XENOPHON'S MINOR WORKS**; translated by the Rev. J. S. WATSON.

80. **ARISTOTLE'S METAPHYSICS**, literally translated, with Notes, Analysis, Examination Questions and Index, by the Rev. JOHN H. M'MAHON, M.A.

BOHN'S ANTIQUARIAN LIBRARY.

Uniform with the STANDARD LIBRARY, price 5s.,

1. **BEDE'S ECCLESIASTICAL HISTORY, & THE ANGLO-SAXON CHRONICLE**
2. **MALLET'S NORTHERN ANTIQUITIES.** 1 f BISHOP PERCY. With Abstrac of the Erbyggia Saga, by SIR WALTER SCOTT. Edited by J. A. BLACKWELL.
3. **WILLIAM OF MALMESBURY'S CHRONICLE OF THE KINGS OF ENGLAND.**
4. **SIX OLD ENGLISH CHRONICLES**: viz., Ass r's Life of Alfred; the Chronicles of Ethelwerd, Gildas, Nennius, Geoffry of Monmouth, and Richard of Cirencester.
5. **ELLIS'S EARLY ENGLISH METRICAL ROMANCES.** Revised by J. ORCHARD HALLIWELL. Complete in one vol., *Illuminated Frontispiece.*
6. **CHRONICLES OF THE CRUSADERS:** Richard of Devizes. Geoffrey de Vinsauf. Lord de Joinville. Complete in 1 volume. *Frontispiece.*
7. **EARLY TRAVELS IN PALESTINE.** Willibald, Sæwulf, Benjamin of Tudela, Mandeville, La Brocquiere, and Maundrell. In one volume. *With Map.*
8, 10, & 12. **BRAND'S POPULAR ANTIQUITIES OF GREAT BRITAIN.** By SIR HENRY ELLIS. In 3 Vols.
9 & 11. **ROGER OF WENDOVER'S FLOWERS OF HISTORY** (formerly ascribed to Matthew Paris.) In 2 Vols.
13. **KEIGHTLEY'S FAIRY MYTHOLOGY.** Enlarged. *Frontispiece* by CRUIKSHANK.
14, 15, & 16. **SIR THOMAS BROWNE'S WORKS.** Edited by SIMON WILKIN *Portrait.* In 3 Vols. With Index.
17. 19, & 31 **MATTHEW PARIS'S CHRONICLE**, containing the History of England from 1235, with Index to the whole, including the portion published under the name of ROGER OF WENDOVER, in 3 Vols. (See 9 and 11). *Portrait.*
18. **YULE-TIDE STORIES.** A collection of Scandinavian Tales and Traditions, edited by B. THORPE, Esq.
20 & 23. **ROGER DE HOVEDEN'S ANNALS OF ENGLISH HISTORY**, from A.D. 732 to A.D. 1201. Translated by H. T. RILEY, Esq., B.A. In 2 Vols.
21. **HENRY OF HUNTINGDON'S HISTORY OF THE ENGLISH**, from the Roman Invasion to Henry II.; with The Acts of King Stephen, &c.

3 e

BOHN'S ANTIQUARIAN LIBRARY.

22. **PAULI'S LIFE OF ALFRED THE GREAT.** To which is appended ALFRED'S ANGLO-SAXON VERSION OF OROSIUS, with a literal translation. Notes, and an Anglo-Saxon Grammar and Glossary, by B. THORPE, Esq.

24 & 25. **MATTHEW OF WESTMINSTER'S FLOWERS OF HISTORY,** especially such as relate to the affairs of Britain, from the beginning of the world to A.D. 1307. Translated by C. D. YONGE, B.A. In 2 Vols.

26. **LEPSIUS'S LETTERS FROM EGYPT, ETHIOPIA, and the PENINSULA OF SINAI.** Revised by the Author. Translated by LEONORA and JOANNA B. HORNER. With Maps and Coloured View of Mount Barkal.

27, 28, 30 & 36. **ORDERICUS VITALIS** His Ecclesiastical History of England and Normandy, translated, with Notes, the Introduction of Guizot, Critical Notice by M. Deuille, and very copious Index, by T. FORESTER, M.A. In 4 Vols.

29. **INGULPH'S CHRONICLE OF THE ABBEY OF CROYLAND,** with the Continuations by Peter of Blois and other Writers. Translated, with Notes and an Index, by H. T. RILEY, B.A.

32. **LAMB'S SPECIMENS OF ENGLISH DRAMATIC POETS** of the time of Elizabeth; including his Selections from the Garrick Plays.

33. **MARCO POLO'S TRAVELS,** the translation of Marsden, edited, with Notes and Introduction, by T. WRIGHT, M.A., F S.A., &c.

34. **FLORENCE OF WORCESTER'S CHRONICLE,** with the Two Continuations; comprising Annals of English History, from the Departure of the Romans to the Reign of Edward I. Translated, with Notes, by T. FORESTER, Esq.

35. **HAND-BOOK OF PROVERBS,** comprising the whole of Ray's Collection, and a complete alphabetical Index, in which are introduced large Additions collected by HENRY G. BOHN.

37. **CHRONICLES OF THE TOMBS:** a select Collection of Epitaphs; with Essay on Monumental Inscriptions, &c., by T. J. PETTIGREW, F R.S., F S.A.

38. **A POLYGLOT OF FOREIGN PROVERBS;** comprising French, Italian, German, Dutch, Spanish, Portuguese & Danish. With English Translations, & General Index.

BOHN'S HISTORICAL LIBRARY,
Uniform with the STANDARD LIBRARY, *price 5s. per Volume.*

1, 2 & 3 **JESSE'S MEMOIRS OF THE COURT OF ENGLAND DURING THE REIGN OF THE STUARTS,** including the PROTECTORATE. In 3 vols., with General Index, and upwards of 40 Portraits engraved on steel.

BOHN'S PHILOLOGICO-PHILOSOPHICAL LIBRARY.
Uniform with the STANDARD LIBRARY, *price 5s. per Volume.*

1. **TENNEMANN'S MANUAL** of the **HISTORY of PHILOSOPHY,** revised and continued by J. R. MORELL.

2. **ANALYSIS and SUMMARY of HERODOTUS,** with synchronistical Table of Events, Tables of Weights, Money, &c.

3. **TURNER'S (DAWSON W.) NOTES TO HERODOTUS,** for the use of Students. With Map, Appendices, and Index.

4. **LOGIC, or the SCIENCE OF INFERENCE,** a popular Manual, by J. DEVEY.

5. **KANT'S CRITIQUE OF PURE REASON,** translated by MEIKLEJOHN.

6. **ANALYSIS AND SUMMARY OF THUCYDIDES,** by T. WHEELER. New Edition, with the addition of a complete Index.

7 & 8. **WRIGHT'S PROVINCIAL DICTIONARY.** A Dictionary of Obsolete and Provincial English. Compiled by THOMAS WRIGHT, Esq., M.A., F.S.A., H.M.R.S.L., &c., (1048 pages). In 2 vols. post 8vo. 10s.—or bound in one thick volume, half morocco, marbled edges, 12s. 6d.

Lightning Source UK Ltd.
Milton Keynes UK
UKHW021140271118
333021UK00007B/162/P